PRINCIPLES OF FLIGHT

Dr. Stuart E. Smith

STUDY GUIDE SERIES for PART-FCL examinations

British Library Cataloguing in Publication Data.
A catalogue record for this book is pending from the British Library.

First published in the United Kingdom by Cranfield Aviation Training School Limited. 2002

Further volumes in this series are:
Aircraft General Knowledge: Airframes / Systems / Powerplant / Electrics / Emergency Equipment
Aviation Law & ATC Procedures
Flight Planning & Monitoring
General Navigation
Human Performance & Limitations
Instrumentation
Meteorology
Operational Procedures
Performance
Principles of Flight
Radio Navigation
VFR & IFR Communications

Series editor: Dr. Stuart E. Smith

CRANFIELD AVIATION TRAINING SCHOOL LTD. PART-FCL GBR.ATO-0136
CATS INNOVATION CENTRE, LUTON, Bedfordshire LU2 8DL U.K.

www.catsaviation.com

CRANFIELD AVIATION TRAINING SCHOOL LTD. PART-FCL GBR.ATO-0136
CATS INNOVATION CENTRE, LUTON, Bedfordshire LU2 8DL U.K.   www.catsaviation.com

Principles of Flight

CRANFIELD AVIATION TRAINING SCHOOL LTD. PART-FCL GBR.ATO-0136
CATS INNOVATION CENTRE, LUTON, Bedfordshire LU2 8DL U.K.
www.catsaviation.com

Principles of Flight

CRANFIELD AVIATION TRAINING SCHOOL LTD. PART-FCL GBR.ATO-0136
CATS INNOVATION CENTRE, LUTON, Bedfordshire LU2 8DL U.K.   www.catsaviation.com

Principles of Flight

CRANFIELD AVIATION TRAINING SCHOOL LTD. PART-FCL GBR.ATO-0136
CATS INNOVATION CENTRE, LUTON, Bedfordshire LU2 8DL U.K.   www.catsaviation.com

Principles of Flight

CRANFIELD AVIATION TRAINING SCHOOL LTD. PART-FCL GBR.ATO-0136
CATS INNOVATION CENTRE, LUTON, Bedfordshire LU2 8DL U.K.   www.catsaviation.com

Principles of Flight

CRANFIELD AVIATION TRAINING SCHOOL LTD. PART-FCL GBR.ATO-0136
CATS INNOVATION CENTRE, LUTON, Bedfordshire LU2 8DL U.K.   www.catsaviation.com

Principles of Flight

CRANFIELD AVIATION TRAINING SCHOOL LTD. PART-FCL GBR.ATO-0136
CATS INNOVATION CENTRE, LUTON, Bedfordshire LU2 8DL U.K.   www.catsaviation.com

Principles of Flight

CRANFIELD AVIATION TRAINING SCHOOL LTD. PART-FCL GBR.ATO-0136
CATS INNOVATION CENTRE, LUTON, Bedfordshire LU2 8DL U.K.

www.catsaviation.com

Principles of Flight

CRANFIELD AVIATION TRAINING SCHOOL LTD. PART-FCL GBR.ATO-0136
CATS INNOVATION CENTRE, LUTON, Bedfordshire LU2 8DL U.K.   www.catsaviation.com

Principles of Flight

CHAPTER 1

Basics, Laws and Definitions

AIRLINE TRANSPORT PILOTS LICENCE

(080 00 00 00 – PRINCIPLES OF FLIGHT)

081 01 01 00 Basics, Laws and Definitions

081 01 01 01 Laws and definitions
- List the SI-units for mass, acceleration, velocity, density, temperature, pressure, force, wing loading and power
- Describe Newton´s Laws
- Describe Newton´s first law of continuity
- Describe Newton's second law (law of motion)
- Describe the equation of momentum (impulse), Newton's third law
- Explain air density
- List the atmospheric properties that effect air density
- Explain how temperature and pressure changes affect density
- Define static pressure
- Define dynamic pressure
- Define the formula for dynamic pressure
- Apply the formula for a given altitude and speed
- Define Bernoulli´s theorem
- Define total pressure
- Apply the theorem for a given speed and altitude
- Apply the theorem to a venturi
- Describe how the IAS is acquired from the pitot-static system
- Describe the Ideal Gas Law
- Describe the Equation of Continuity
- Describe viscosity
- Define the speed of sound and its symbol
- Describe how atmospheric properties affect the speed of sound
- Define IAS, CAS, EAS, TAS and Mach number

081 01 01 02 Basics about airflow
- Describe stationary and not stationary airflow
- Explain the concept of a streamline
- Describe and explain airflow through a stream tube
- Explain the difference between two and three dimensional airflow

081 01 01 03 Aerodynamic forces and moments on the surfaces
- Describe the force resulting from the pressure distribution around an aerofoil
- Resolve the resultant force into the components 'lift' and 'drag'
- Describe the direction of lift and drag
- Define the aerodynamic moment
- List the factors that affect the aerodynamic moment
- Describe the aerodynamic moment for a symmetrical aerofoil.
- Describe the aerodynamic moment for a positively cambered aerofoil.
- Forces and equilibrium of forces Refer 081 08 00 00
- Define angle of attack

081 01 01 04 Shape of an aerofoil
- Describe the following parameters of an aerofoil:
- Leading edge
- Trailing edge
- Chordline
- Thickness to chord ratio
- Location of maximum thickness
- Camberline
- Camber
- Nose radius
- Angle of attack

CRANFIELD AVIATION TRAINING SCHOOL LTD. PART-FCL GBR.ATO-0136
CATS INNOVATION CENTRE, LUTON, Bedfordshire LU2 8DL U.K.
www.catsaviation.com

- Angle of incidence
- Describe a symmetrical and an asymmetrical aerofoil

081 01 01 05 The wing shape
- Describe the following parameters of a wing:
- Span
- Root chord
- Tip chord
- Taper ratio
- Wing area
- Mean aerodynamic chord MAC
- Aspect ratio
- Dihedral angle

081 01 02 00 The Two-dimensional Airflow about an aerofoil
081 01 02 01 Streamline pattern
- Describe the streamline pattern over an aerofoil
- Describe converging and diverging streamlines and their effect on static pressure and velocity
- Describe up-wash and down-wash

081 01 02 02 Stagnation point
- Describe the stagnation point
- Explain the effect on the stagnation point relative to angle of attack changes
- Explain local pressure changes

081 01 02 03 Pressure distribution
- Describe an approximate pressure distribution over an aerofoil
- Describe where the minimum local static pressure is typically situated on an aerofoil

081 01 02 04 Centre of pressure and aerodynamic centre
- Define the centre of pressure and aerodynamic centre.
- Explain centre of pressure movement with angle of attack.

081 01 02 05 Lift and downwash
- Explain the association between lift and downwash

081 01 02 06 Drag and wake
- List two physical phenomena that cause drag
- Describe skin friction drag
- Describe pressure (form) drag
- Explain why drag and wake cause a loss of energy (momentum)

081 01 02 07 Influence of angle of attack
- Explain the influence of angle of attack on lift

081 01 02 08 Flow separation at high angles of attack
- Refer to 081 01 08 01

081 01 02 09 The Lift - a graph
- Describe the lift and angle of attack graph
- Explain the significant points on the graph.
- Describe lift against a graph for a symmetrical profile

081 01 03 00 The Coefficients
- Explain why coefficients are used in general

081 01 03 01 The lift coefficient CL
- Describe the lift formula
- List factors that influence lift
- Describe which factors are dominating in the lift formula
- Describe the CL - a graph (symmetrical and positively cambered profile
- Describe the typical difference in CL - a graph for fast and slow profile design
- Define the CLmax and astall on the graph
- State the approximate stall angle of attack

081 01 03 02 The drag coefficient CD
- Describe the drag formula
- List the factors that influence drag
- Indicate which factor is dominating in the drag formula
- State that drag increases as a function of the square of the speed
- State that drag is proportional to the density of the airflow
- Describe the CL - CD graph
- Indicate minimum drag on the graph
- Explain why the CL - CD ratio is important as a measure of performance
- State the normal values of CL - CD

081 01 04 00 The Three-dimensional Airflow about an Aeroplane
- Explain the difference between the angle of attack and the attitude of an aeroplane

081 01 04 01 Streamline pattern
- Describe the general streamline pattern around the wing, tail section and fuselage
- Explain and describe the causes of spanwise flow over top and bottom surfaces
- Describe tip vortices and local a
- Explain how tip vortices vary with angle of attack
- Explain up-wash and down-wash due to tip vortices
- Describe span-wise lift distribution
- Describe the causes, distribution and duration of the wake turbulence behind an aeroplane
- Describe the influence of flap deflection on the tip vortex
- List the parameters that influence the wake turbulence

081 01 04 02 The Induced Drag
- Explain what causes the induced drag
- Describe the approximate formula for the induced drag coefficient
- State the factors that affect induced drag
- Describe the relationship between induced drag and total drag in the cruise
- Describe the effect of weight on induced drag at a given IAS
- Describe the design means to decrease induced drag
- Winglets
- Tip tanks
- Wing span loading
- Influence of wing twist
- Influence of camber change
- Describe the influence of tip vortices on the angle of attack.
- Explain induced local angle of attack.
- Explain the influence of the induced angle of attack on the direction of the lift vector
- Explain the relationship between induced drag and
- Speed
- Aspect ratio
- Wing planform
- Explain the induced drag coefficient.
- Explain the relationship between the induced drag coefficient and the angle of attack or lift coefficient.
- Explain the influence of induced drag on
- CL - angle of attack graph, show effect on graph when comparing high and low aspect ratio wings
- CL - CD (aeroplane polar), show effect on graph when comparing high and low aspect ratio wings.
- Parabolic aeroplane polar in a graph and as a formula ($CD = CDp + KCL2$)

081 01 05 00 The Total Drag
- Explain how lift affects drag

081 01 05 01 The parasite drag
- List the types of drag that are included in the parasite drag
- Describe profile drag.
- Describe interference drag.
- Describe friction drag

081 01 05 02 The parasite drag and speed
- Describe the relationship between parasite drag and speed.

081 01 05 03 The induced drag and speed
- Refer to 081 01 04 02

081 01 05 04 The total drag
081 01 05 05 The total drag and speed
- Describe total drag - IAS graph

081 01 05 06 Minimum drag
- Indicate the IAS for the minimum drag from the graph

081 01 05 07 The drag - speed graph
- Describe the effect of aeroplane gross weight on the graph
- Describe the effect of pressure altitude on:
- Drag - IAS graph
- Drag - TAS graph
- Describe speed stability from the graph
- Describe non-stable, neutral and stable IAS regions
- Explain what happens to the IAS and drag on the non-stable region if speed suddenly decreases

081 01 06 00 The Ground Effect
- Explain what happens to the tip vortices, down-wash, airflow pattern and lift vector close to the ground.

081 01 06 01 Effect on CDI
- Describe the influence of the ground effect on CDI
- Explain the effects on entering and leaving the ground effect

081 01 06 02 Effect on a stall
- Describe the influence of the ground effect on astall

081 01 06 03 Effect on CL
- Describe the influence of the ground effect on CL

081 01 06 04 Effect on take-off and landing characteristics of an aircraft
- Describe the influence of the ground effect on take-off and landing characteristics of an aeroplane
- Describe the difference between
- High and low wing characteristics
- High and low tail characteristics
- Explain the effects on static pressure measurements at the static ports when entering and leaving ground effect.

081 01 07 00 The relation between the lift coefficient and the speed for constant lift
- Describe the relationship between lift coefficient and speed for constant lift as a formula

081 01 07 01 As a formula
- Explain the effect on CL during speed increase/decrease in level flight.

081 01 07 02 In a graph
- Explain using a graph, the effect on speed at various angles of attack and CL, at a given weight.
- Calculate the change of CL as a function of IAS

081 01 08 00 The Stall
081 01 08 01 Flow separation at increasing angles of attack
- Define the boundary layer
- Describe the thickness of a typical boundary layer
- List the factors that effect the thickness
- Describe the laminar layer
- Describe the turbulent layer
- Define the transition
- List the differences between laminar and turbulent boundary layers
- Explain why the laminar boundary layer separates easier than the turbulent one
- List the factors that slow down the airflow over the aft part of an aerofoil, as angle of attack is increased
- Define the separation point
- Define the critical or stalling angle of attack
- Describe the influence of increasing the angle of attack on
- The forward stagnation point

- The pressure distribution
- Location of the centre of pressure
- CL and L
- CD and D
- The pitching moment (straight and swept back wing)
- The down-wash at horizontal stabiliser
- Explain what causes the possible natural buffet on the controls in a pre-stall condition
- Describe the effectiveness of the flight controls in a pre-stall condition
- Describe and explain the normal post-stall behaviour of a wing / aeroplane
- Describe the dangers of using the controls close to the stall

081 01 08 02 The stall speed
- Solve the 1g stall speed from the lift formula
- Define the FAA stall speed
- Describe and explain the Influence of the following parameters on the stall speed:
- Centre of gravity
- Power setting
- Wing loading (W/S) or gross mass
- Wing contamination
- Angle of sweep
- Define the load factor n
- Describe the general idea why the load factor increases in turns
- Describe and explain the Influence of the load factor (n) on the stall speed
- Calculate the increase of stall speed as a function of the load factor
- Calculate the increase of stall speed in a horizontal coordinated turn as a function of bank angle
- Calculate the change of stall speed as a function of the gross weight

081 01 08 03 The initial stall in span-wise direction
- Explain the initial stall sequence on the following planforms
- Elliptical
- Rectangular
- Moderate and high taper
- Sweepback or delta
- Explain the influence of aerodynamic twist (wash out) and geometric twist
- Explain the influence of deflected ailerons
- Explain the influence of fences, vortilons, saw teeth, vortex generators.

081 01 08 04 Stall warning
- Explain why stall warning is necessary
- Explain when aerodynamic and artificial stall warnings are used
- Explain why JAR and FAR require a margin to stall speed.
- Describe:
- Buffet
- Stall strip
- Flapper switch (leading edge stall warning vane)
- Angle of Attack vane
- Angle of Attack probe
- Stick shaker
- Describe warnings of:
- high speed buffet
- Describe the recovery after:
- stall warning
- stall
- stick pusher actuation

081 01 08 05 Special phenomena of stall
- Describe the basic stall requirements for JAR/ FAR transport category aeroplanes
- Explain the difference between the power-off and power-on stalls and recovery
- Describe the stall and recovery in a climbing and descending turn
- Describe stalling and recovery characteristics on:
- Swept back wings
- T-tailed aeroplane
- Canards
- Describe super- or deep-stall

- Describe the philosophy behind the stick pusher system
- Explain the effect of ice, frost or snow on the stagnation point
- Explain the absence of stall warning
- Explain the abnormal behaviour of the stall
- Describe and explain the stabiliser stall
- Describe when to expect in-flight-icing
- Explain how the effect is changed when retracting/extending lift augmentation devices
- Describe how to recover from a stall after a configuration change caused by in-flight-icing
- Explain the effect of a contaminated wing
- Explain what "on-ground" icing is.
- Describe the aerodynamic effects of de/anti-ice fluid after the hold/overtime has been reached
- Describe the aerodynamic effects of heavy tropical rain on stall speed and drag
- Explain how to avoid spins
- List the factors that cause a spin to develop
- Describe spin development, recognition and recovery
- Describe the differences in recovery techniques for aeroplanes that have different mass distributions between the wing and the fuselage

081 01 09 00 CLMAX Augmentation
081 01 09 01 Trailing edge flaps and the reasons for use in take-off and landing
- Describe trailing edge flaps and the reasons for their use during take-off and landing
- Identify the differing types of trailing edge flaps given a relevant diagram
- Split flaps
- Plain flaps
- Slotted flaps
- Fowler flaps
- Describe their effect on wing geometry
- Describe how the wing's effective camber increases
- Describe how the effective chordline differs from the normal chordline
- Describe their effect on the stalling speed
- Describe their effect on aeroplane pitching moments.
- Compare their influence on the CL - a graph
- Indicate the variation in CL at any given angle of attack
- Indicate the variation in CD at any given angle of attack
- Indicate their effect on CLMAX
- Indicate their effect on the stalling angle of attack
- Indicate their effect on angle of attack at a given CL
- Compare their influence on the CL - CD graph
- Indicate how the (CL/CD)MAX differs from that of a clean wing
- Explain the influence of trailing edge deflection on glide angle
- Describe flap asymmetry
- Explain the effect on aeroplane controllability
- Describe trailing edge flap effect on take-off and landing
- Explain the advantages of lower nose attitudes
- Explain why take-off and landing speeds/distances are reduced

081 01 09 02 Leading edge devices and the reasons for use in take-off and landing
- Describe leading edge high lift devices
- Identify the differing types of leading edge high lift devices given a relevant diagram
- Krueger flaps
- Variable camber flaps
- Slats
- State their effect on wing geometry
- Describe the function of the slot
- Describe how the wing's effective camber increases
- Describe how the effective chordline differs from the normal chordline
- State their effect on the stalling speed
- Compare their influence on the CL - a graph, compared trailing edge flaps and clean wing.
- Indicate the effect of leading edge devices on CLMAX
- Explain how the CL curve differs from that of a clean wing
- Indicate the effect of leading edge devices on the stall angle of attack
- Compare their influence on the CL - CD graph
- Describe slat asymmetry
- Describe the effect on aeroplane controllability

- Describe automatic slat operation
- Explain the reasons for using leading edge high lift devices on take-off and landing
- Explain the disadvantage of increased nose up attitudes
- Explain why take-off and landing speeds/distances are reduced

081 01 09 03 Vortex generators
- Explain the purpose of vortex generators
- Describe their basic operating principle
- State their advantages and disadvantages

080 01 10 00 Means to Decrease the CL - CD Ratio, increasing drag
081 01 10 01 Spoilers and the reasons for use in the different phases of flight
- Describe spoilers and the reasons for use in the different phases of flight
- Roll spoilers
- Flight spoilers (speed brakes)
- Ground spoilers (Lift dumpers)
- Describe the operation of ground spoilers (lift dumpers)
- Describe the purpose of a spoiler-mixer unit
- Describe the effect of spoilers on the CL - a graph
- Describe the influence of spoilers on the CL - CD graph and lift/drag ratio

081 01 10 02 Speedbrakes as a means of increasing drag and the reasons for use in the different phases of flight
- Describe speed brakes and the reasons for use in the different phases of flight
- State their influence on the CL - CD graph and lift/drag ratio
- Explain how speed brakes increase parasite drag
- Describe how speed brakes affect the minimum drag speed
- Describe their effect on rate of descent

081 01 11 00 Boundary Layer
081 01 11 01 Different types
- Refer to 081 01 08 01

081 01 11 02 Advantages and disadvantages of different types of boundary layer on pressure drag and friction drag
081 01 12 00 Special Circumstances
081 01 12 01 Ice and other contamination
- Explain the effect of ice and other contamination on aeroplane performance
- Describe the effects of ice accumulations at the stagnation point
- Describe the effects on ice, frost, snow on the surface condition
- Describe how it affects the boundary layer
- Describe how rain and other liquids affect the surface condition
- Describe its effect on aeroplane weight
- Explain its effect on lift and drag
- Describe the effect of contamination of the leading edge
- Explain the effect on aeroplane controllability
- List the causes of leading edge contamination
- Describe the effects of contamination on the stall
- Describe the effect on the boundary layer condition
- Describe the effect on the stalling angle of attack
- Describe the effect on the stalling speed
- Describe how contamination leads to loss of controllability
- State the effect of tail icing
- Describe the effects on control surface moment (stick forces)
- Describe the influence of contamination on high lift devices during take-off, landing and low speeds
- Explain why contamination degrades high lift devices efficiency
- Explain why contamination increases the take-off and landing distances/speeds
- Describe how contamination reduces the coefficient of lift
- Explain the effect of contamination on the lift/drag ratio
081 01 12 02 Deformation and modification of airframe, ageing aircraft
- Describe the effect of airframe deformation and modification of an ageing aeroplane on aeroplane performance
- Explain the effect on boundary layer condition of an ageing aeroplane
081 02 00 00 TRANSONIC AERODYNAMICS
081 02 01 00 The Mach number definition

081 02 01 01 Speed of sound
- Define the speed of sound
- Define the Mach number as a function of TAS and speed of sound

081 02 01 02 Influence of temperature and altitude
- Describe the influence of temperature on the speed of sound
- Explain the variation of the speed of sound with altitude
- Explain the absence of change of Mach number with varying temperature at constant flight level and Calibrated Airspeed
- Explain the change of TAS as a function of altitude at a given Mach number
- Explain the change of Mach number at varying altitude in the standard atmosphere (troposphere and stratosphere) with constant Calibrated Airspeed and with constant True Airspeed.

081 02 01 03 Compressibility
- State that compressibility means that density can change along a streamline
- State that Mach number is a measure of compressibility

081 02 02 00 Normal shockwaves
- List the subdivision of aerodynamic flow:
- Subsonic flow
- Low-subsonic, non-compressible flow
- High subsonic, compressible flow
- Transonic flow, mixture of local speeds above and below the speed of sound
- Supersonic flow, all speeds higher than the speed of sound

081 02 02 01 Mcrit and exceeding Mcrit
- Describe how the streamline pattern changes due to compressibility.
- Describe Mcrit
- Describe a normal shock wave in a transonic flow with respect to:
- temperature, pressure, velocity and density changes
- location in a supersonic area of the stream pattern
- length of the shockwave and orientation relative to the wing surface

081 02 02 02 Influence of
- Explain the influence of increasing Mach on a normal shock wave, at positive lift with respect to:
- Strength
- Position relative to the wing
- second shock wave at the lower surface
- Explain the influence of control surface deflection with respect to
- the effect of Mcrit
- loss of control effectiveness
- Explain how increase of the angle of attack influences normal shock wave and Mcrit
- Explain the effect of aerofoil thickness on Mcrit
- Explain the influence of the angle of sweep with respect to
- the increase of Mcrit
- effective thickness/chord change.
- velocity component perpendicular to the leading edge.
- Describe the influence of the angle of sweep at subsonic speed with respect to
- CLMAX
- efficiency of high lift devices.
- pitch-up stall behaviour.
- Explain area ruling in aeroplane design

081 02 02 03 Influence on
- Describe the consequences of exceeding Mcrit with respect to
- gradient of the CL-a graph
- CLMAX (stall speed)
- Explain the behaviour of CD versus M at constant angle of attack
- Explain effect of Mach number on the CL-CD graph

081 02 02 04 Aerodynamic heating
- State that aerodynamic heating is caused by compression and friction.

081 02 02 05 Shock stall/Mach buffet
- Explain shock stall and describe its relationship with Mach buffet.

081 02 02 06 Influence on
- Describe the influence on:
- Wave drag
- Explain the influence of shock stall on the location of the centre of pressure with respect to
- loss of lift at the wing root
- reduction of downwash at the wing root
- List the aerodynamic and mechanical counter measures for the Mach tuck-under effect

CRANFIELD AVIATION TRAINING SCHOOL LTD. PART-FCL GBR.ATO-0136
CATS INNOVATION CENTRE, LUTON, Bedfordshire LU2 8DL U.K.   www.catsaviation.com

1-8   Principles of Flight

081 02 02 07 Buffet margin, aerodynamic ceiling
- Describe the influence on the buffet margin of
- angle of attack
- Mach number
- pressure altitude
- mass
- load factor
- Describe the 1.3 g altitude with respect to the buffet margin
- Describe what can be obtained from the buffet boundary chart
- Find:
- Buffet restricted speed limits at a given pressure altitude
- Aerodynamic ceiling at a given mass.
- Load factor and bank angle at which buffet occurs at a given mass, Mach number and pressure altitude
- Illustrate the behaviour of the buffet margin when an aeroplane is descending or ascending at a given indicated airspeed, or Mach number.

081 02 02 08 Meaning of the expression 'coffin corner'
- Identify the VMO and MMO values
- Identify the stall speed
- Identify the "coffin corner"
- Describe:
- the allowable speed range in the coffin corner
- the influence of mass on the coffin corner boundaries
- the consequences of exceeding VMO
- the consequences of exceeding MMO
- Describe the influence of:
- buffet on the flight envelope
- mass on the values of VMO and MMO
- temperature on the pressure altitude at which the VMO limit intersects the MMO limit

081 02 03 00 Means to avoid the effects of exceeding Mcrit

081 02 03 01 Vortex generators
- Explain the use of vortex generators as a means to avoid or restrict flow separation

081 02 03 02 Supercritical profile
- Identify the following shape characteristics of a supercritical aerofoil shape:
- Blunt nose
- Large thickness
- S-shaped camber line
- Flat upper surface
- Thick trailing edge
- Explain with respect to a supercritical aerofoil:
- the increased number of smaller and weakened shockwaves compared those of a classic profile
- the absence of a strong influence on Mcrit
- aft loading
- Explain the following advantages of a supercritical aerofoil:
- allows use of less sweep angle
- may be built lighter, due to greater thickness
- allows storage of more fuel
- allows use of a higher aspect ratio
- Explain the following disadvantages of a supercritical aerofoil:
- Negative camber at the aerofoil front side
- Buffet may cause severe oscillations

081 03 00 00 SUPERSONIC AERODYNAMICS

081 03 01 00 Oblique Shockwaves

081 03 01 01 Mach cone
- Define Mach Cone
- Explain that the Mach cone top angle decreases with increasing Mach number
- Define the bow wave
- Identify the Mach cone area of influence of a pressure disturbance due to the presence of the aeroplane

081 03 01 02 Influence of aircraft weight
- Describe influence of weight (wing loading)

081 03 01 03 Expansion waves
- Describe shock waves and expansion waves with respect to the streamline pattern and variation of pressure, temperature, density and velocity along a streamline
- Describe the velocity behind a normal and an oblique shockwave

081 03 01 04 Centre of pressure
- Describe the movement of the centre of pressure with increasing Mach number
- Describe the pressure distribution in chord direction in supersonic flight

081 03 01 05 Wave drag
- Describe wave drag
- Describe effect on control surface hinge moment
- Describe effect on control surface efficiency
- Explain that an oblique shockwave moves with aeroplane ground speed over the earth surface

081 04 00 00 STABILITY

081 04 01 00 Condition of equilibrium in stable horizontal flight

081 04 01 01 Precondition for static stability
- Explain an equilibrium of forces and moments as the condition for the concept of static stability
- Identify
- Longitudinal static stability
- Directional static stability
- Lateral static stability

081 04 01 02 Sum of moments
- Identify the moments considered in the equilibrium of moments: moments about all three axes

081 04 01 03 Sum of forces
- Identify the forces considered in the equilibrium of forces

081 04 02 00 Methods of achieving balance

081 04 02 01 Wing and empennage (tail and canard)
- Explain the stabiliser and the canard as the means to satisfy the condition of nullifying the total sum of the moments about the lateral axis
- Explain the influence of the location of the wing centre of pressure relative to the centre of gravity on the magnitude and direction of the balancing force on stabiliser and canard
- Explain the influence of the indicated airspeed on the magnitude and direction of the balancing force on stabiliser and canard
- Explain the influence of the balancing force on the magnitude of the wing/fuselage lift

081 04 02 02 Control surfaces
- Explain the use of the elevator deflection or stabiliser angle for the generation of the balancing force
- Explain the elevator deflection required to balance thrust changes

081 04 02 03 Ballast or weight trim
- Explain the most advantageous location of the centre of gravity
- Explain the control of the location of the centre of gravity by means of fuel distribution and loading

081 04 03 00 Longitudinal Stability

081 04 03 01 Basics and definitions
- Define static stability
- Identify a statically stable, neutral and unstable equilibrium
- Define dynamic stability
- Identify a dynamically stable, neutral and unstable motion
- Explain what combinations of static and dynamic stability will return an aeroplane to the equilibrium state after a disturbance
- Describe the phugoid and short period motion in terms of period and damping
- Explain that during the phugoid motion the angle of attack remains approximately constant
- Explain that during the short period motion the aeroplane speed remains approximately constant
- Explain why short period motion is more important for flying qualities than the phugoid
- Define and describe pilot induced oscillations
- Explain the effect of high altitude on dynamic stability

081 04 03 02 Static stability
- Explain why static stability is the opposite of manoeuvrability

081 04 03 03 Neutral point/location of neutral point
- Neutral point / location of neutral point
- Define neutral point
- Explain why the location of the neutral point is only dependent on the aerodynamic design of the aeroplane

081 04 03 04 Contribution of
- Indicate the location of the neutral point relative to the locations of the aerodynamic centre of the wing and tail/canard
- Explain the influence of the downwash variations with angle of attack variation on the location of the neutral point

081 04 03 05 Location of centre of gravity
- Explain the influence of the location of the centre of gravity on static and dynamic stability of the aeroplane
- Explain the approved forward and aft limits of the centre of gravity with respect to the criteria of control forces, elevator effectiveness and stability
- Define the minimum stability margin

081 04 03 06 The Cm-a graph

- Define the aerodynamic pitching moment coefficient (Cm)
- Describe the Cm-a graph with respect to
- positive and negative sign
- linear relationship
- angle of attack for equilibrium state
- relationship of slope and static stability

081 04 03 07 Contribution of
- Explain
- the effect on the Cm-a graph with a shift of CG in the forward and aft direction.
- the effect on the Cm-a graph when the elevator is moved up or down.
- the effect on the Cm-a graph when the trim is moved.
- the wing contribution and the effect of the location of the cg with respect to the aerodynamic centre on the wing contribution
- the contribution of the fuselage and the effect of the location of the centre of gravity on the fuselage contribution
- the contribution of the tail
- the contribution of the configuration (gear and flaps)
- the contribution of aerofoil camber

081 04 03 08 The elevator position - speed graph (IAS)
- Describe the elevator position speed graph
- Explain:
- the gradient of the elevator position speed graph
- the influence of the airspeed on the stick position stability

081 04 03 09 Contribution of
- Explain the contribution on the elevator position - speed graph of:
- Location of centre of gravity
- Trim (trim tab and stabiliser trim)
- high lift devices

081 04 03 10 The stick force speed graph (IAS)
- Define the stick force speed graph
- Describe the minimum gradient for stick force versus speed that is required for certification according to JAR 23 and JAR 25
- Explain the importance of the stick force gradient for good flying qualities of an aeroplane
- Identify the trim speed in the stick force speed graph

081 04 03 11 Contribution of
- Explain the contribution of:
- Location of the centre of gravity
- Trim (trim tab and stabiliser trim)
- Mach number and the effect of Mach tuck-under and the Mach trim system
- Downspring
- bob weight
- friction
- State that:
- In transonic flow due to the Mach tuck under effect the stick force gradient may be too small or unstable
- the Mach trim system restores stick force gradient

081 04 03 12 The manoeuvring/stick force per g
- Define the stick force per g
- Explain why:
- the stick force per g has a prescribed minimum and maximum value
- the stick force per g decreases with pressure altitude at the same Indicated Airspeeds

081 04 03 14 Contribution of
- Explain that the stick force per g is:
- dependent on location of centre of gravity
- independent of the trim setting
- independent of a down spring in the control system
- greater with the application of a bob weight in the control system

081 04 03 15 Stick force per g and the limit load factor
- Explain why the prescribed minimum and maximum values of the stick force per g are dependent on the limit load factor
- Calculate the stick force to achieve a certain load factor at a given manoeuvre stability

081 04 03 16 Refer to 081 05 02 03

081 04 04 00 Static directional stability

081 04 04 01 Slip angle b
- Define slip angle
- Identify b as the symbol used for the slip angle

081 04 04 02 Yaw moment coefficient CN

CRANFIELD AVIATION TRAINING SCHOOL LTD. PART-FCL GBR.ATO-0136
CATS INNOVATION CENTRE, LUTON, Bedfordshire LU2 8DL U.K.   www.catsaviation.com

CATS

1-11   Principles of Flight

- Define the yawing moment coefficient CN
- Define the relationship between CN and b for an aeroplane with static directional stability

081 04 04 03 CN - b graph
- Explain why
- CN depends on the angle of slip
- CN equals zero for that angle of slip that provides static equilibrium about the aeroplane's normal axis
- If no asymmetric engine thrust, flight control or loading condition prevails, the equilibrium angle of slip equals zero
- Identify how the slope of the CN-b graph is a measure for static directional stability

081 04 04 04 Contribution of
- Describe how the following aeroplane components contribute to static directional stability:
- Wing
- Fin
- Dorsal fin
- Ventral fin
- Angle of sweep of the wing
- Angle of sweep of the fin
- location of centre of gravity
- fuselage at high angles of attack
- strakes
- Explain why both the fuselage and the fin contribution reduce static directional stability after an aft shift of the centre of gravity

081 04 05 00 Static lateral stability
081 04 05 01 Bank angle Ø
- Define bank angle Ø

081 04 05 02 The roll moment coefficient Cl
- Define the rolling moment coefficient Cl

081 04 05 03 Contribution of angle of slip b
- Explain how without co-ordination, the bank angle creates slip angle

081 04 05 04 The Cl-b graph
- Describe Cl-b graph
- Identify the slope of the Cl-b graph as a measure for static lateral stability

081 04 05 05 Contribution of
- Explain the contribution to the static lateral stability of:
- dihedral, anhedral
- high wing, low wing
- sweep angle of the wing
- ventral fin
- vertical tail
- Mach number

081 04 05 06 Effective lateral stability
- Define effective dihedral
- Explain the negative effects of high static lateral stability in
- Strong crosswind landings
- Asymmetric thrust situations at high power setting and low speed (go-around, take off)

081 04 06 00 Dynamic lateral/directional stability
081 04 06 01 Effects of asymmetric propeller slipstream
081 04 06 02 Tendency to spiral dive
- Explain how lateral and directional stability are coupled
- Explain how high static stability and a low static lateral stability may cause spiral divergence (unstable spiral dive) and under which conditions the spiral dive mode is neutral or stable
- Describe an unstable spiral dive mode with respect to deviations in speed, roll attitude, nose low pitch attitude and decreasing altitude

081 04 06 03 Dutch roll
- Describe Dutch roll
- Explain:
- why Dutch roll occurs when the dihedral effect is large compared to static directional stability.
- the condition for a stable Dutch roll motion and those for marginally stable, neutral or unstable Dutch roll motion
- the function of the yaw damper

081 04 06 04 Effects of altitude on dynamic stability
- Explain that increased pressure altitude reduces dynamic lateral/directional stability

081 05 00 00 CONTROL
081 05 01 00 General
081 05 01 01 Basics, the Three Planes and Three Axis
- Define

- Lateral axis
- Longitudinal axis
- Normal axis
- Describe the motion about the three axes
- Name and describe the devices that control these motions

081 05 01 02 Camber change
- Explain how camber is changed by movement of a control surface

081 05 01 03 Angle of Attack change
- Explain the influence of local angle of attack change by movement of a control surface

081 05 02 00 Pitch Control

081 05 02 01 Elevator/all flying tail
- Explain the working principle of the horizontal tailplane (stabilizer)
- Explain the working principle of the elevator and describe its function.
- State graphically the effect of elevator deflection on the moment curve.
- Explain why the moment curve is independent of angle of attack.
- Describe the loads on the tailplane in normal flight, lower than normal flight speeds, and higher than normal speed.

081 05 02 02 Downwash effects
- Explain the effect of downwash on the tailplane angle of attack.
- Explain in this context the use of a T-tail or stabilizer trim.

081 05 02 03 Ice on tail
- Explain how ice can change the aerodynamic characteristics of the tailplane.
- Explain how this can affect the tail's proper function

081 05 02 04 Location of centre of gravity
- Explain the relationship between pitching moment coefficient and lift coefficient
- Explain the relationship between elevator deflection and location of c.g. in straight flight and in a g manoeuvre

081 05 03 00 Yaw control
- Explain the working principle of the rudder and describe its function.
- State the relationship between rudder deflection and the moment about the normal axis
- Describe the effect of sideslip on the moment about the normal axis

081 05 03 01 Pedal/Rudder ratio changer
- Describe the purpose of the rudder ratio changer.

081 05 03 02 Moments due to engine thrust
- Describe the effect of engine thrust on pitching moments
- Explain fin stall due to rudder displacement

081 05 03 03 Engine failure (n - 1)
- Refer to 081 08 02 00

081 05 04 00 Roll control

081 05 04 01 Ailerons
- Describe the purpose of the ailerons
- Describe the adverse effects of ailerons.
- Explain in this context the use of inboard and outboard ailerons
- Explain outboard aileron lockout and conditions under which this feature is used
- Describe the use of aileron deflection in normal flight, flight with side slip, cross wind landings, horizontal turns, flight with one engine out.
- Define roll rate
- List the factors that effect roll rate
- Flaperons, aileron droop

081 05 04 03 Spoilers
- Explain how spoilers affect lift
- Explain how spoilers can be used to control the rolling movement in combination with or instead of the ailerons

081 05 04 04 Adverse yaw
- Explain how the use of ailerons induce adverse yaw

081 05 04 05 Means to avoid adverse yaw
- Explain how the following reduce adverse yaw
- Frise ailerons
- Differential ailerons deflection
- Coupling aileron deflection
- Roll spoilers
- effects of asymmetric propeller slipstream

081 05 05 00 Interaction in different planes (yaw/roll)
- Describe the coupling effect of roll and yaw
- Explain the secondary effect of ailerons

CRANFIELD AVIATION TRAINING SCHOOL LTD. PART-FCL GBR.ATO-0136
CATS INNOVATION CENTRE, LUTON, Bedfordshire LU2 8DL U.K.   www.catsaviation.com

CATS

1-13   Principles of Flight

- Explain the secondary effect of rudder
081 05 05 01 Limitations of asymmetric power
- Refer to 081 08 02 06
081 05 06 00 Means to reduce control forces
081 05 06 01 Aerodynamic balance
- Describe the working principle of the nose and horn balancing (positioning of the hinge line in elevator, aileron and rudder)
- Describe the working principle of internal balance
- Describe the working principle of
- Balance tab
- Anti-balance tab
- Spring tab
- Servo tab
081 05 06 02 Artificial means
- List the examples of artificial means of assisting aerodynamic force
- Describe fully powered controls
- Describe power assisted controls
- Explain why artificial feel is required
- Explain how artificial feel is produced (inputs)
- Dynamic pressure
- Stabilizer setting
081 05 07 00 Mass Balance
- Refer 081 06 01 00
081 05 08 00 Trimming
081 05 08 01 Reasons for trimming
- State the reasons for trimming devices.
081 05 08 02 Trim tabs
- Describe the working principle of a trim tab
081 05 08 03 Stabiliser trim/Trim rate versus IAS
- Describe stabilizer trim/trim rate verses IAS
- Explain the advantages of a stabiliser trim versus a trim tab
- Explain elevator deflection when aeroplane is trimmed for fully powered and power assisted pitch controls
- Explain the cg position influence on the stabiliser setting
- In-flight
- Take-off
- Explain the influence of take-off stabiliser trim setting on stick force during rotation at varying c.g. positions within the allowable c.g. range
081 06 00 00 Limitations
081 06 01 00 Operating Limitations
- Describe the phenomenon of flutter, and list the factors:
- Elasticity
- Backlash
- Aero-elastic coupling
- Mass distribution
- List the flutter modes of an aeroplane
- Wing
- Tailplane
- Fin
- Control surfaces including tabs
- Describe the use of mass balance to alleviate the flutter problem by adjusting the mass distribution
- Wing mounted pylons
- Control surface mass balance
- List the possible actions in the case of flutter in flight
- Describe the phenomenon of aileron reversal
- At low speeds - aileron deflection/stalling angle relationship
- At high speeds - aileron deflection causing the wing to twist
- Describe the aileron reversal speed in relationship to VNE and VNO
- Describe the reason for flap/landing gear limitations
- VLO
- VLE
- Explain why there is a difference between VLO and VLE in the case of some aeroplane types
- Define VFE
- Describe flap design features to prevent overload

080 06 01 01 VMO, VNO, VNE
- Define VMO and VNE
- Describe the difference between VMO and VNE
- Describe the relationship between VMO and VC
- Define VNO
- Explain that VMO can be exceeded during a descent at constant Mach number

081 06 01 02 MMO
- Define MMO and state its limiting factors
- Explain that MMO can be exceeded during a climb at constant IAS

081 06 02 00 Manoeuvring Envelope

081 06 02 01 Manoeuvring load diagram
- Describe the manoeuvring load diagram
- Identify the varying features on the diagram
- Load factor 'n'
- Speed scale, equivalent airspeed, EAS
- CLmax boundary
- VA design manoeuvring speed
- VC design cruising speed
- VD design dive speed, a speed set sufficient above VC to allow for the effects of a defined 'upset'
- State the load factor limits for JAR 23 and 25 aeroplanes in a typical cruise condition and with flaps extended

081 06 02 02 Contribution of mass, altitude and Mach number
- State the relationship of mass to
- Load factor limits
- Accelerated stall speed limit
- VA, VB and VC
- Explain the relationship between VA and aeroplane mass
- Explain the relationship between VA and VS in a formula
- Calculate the change of VA with changing weight
- Describe the effect of altitude on Mach number, in respect to limitations

081 06 03 00 Gust Envelope

081 06 03 01 Gust Load Diagram
- Recognise a typical gust load diagram
- Identify the various features shown on the diagram
- Load factor 'n'
- Calculate n as a result of increasing angle of attack.
- Speed scale, equivalent airspeed, EAS
- CL MAX boundary
- Vertical gust velocities
- Relationship of VB to VC and VD
- Gust limit load factor
- Define VRA

081 06 03 02 Contribution of mass, altitude, speed, Mach number, aspect ratio and wing sweep
- Explain the relationship between mass, altitude, speed, Mach number, aspect ratio and wing sweep on gust loads

081 07 00 00 Propellers

081 07 01 00 Conversion of engine torque to thrust
- Describe thrust and torque load

081 07 01 01 Meaning of pitch
- Describe the geometry of a typical propeller blade element at a representative span location
- Blade chord line
- Propeller rotational velocity vector
- True airspeed vector
- Blade angle of attack
- Pitch or blade angle
- Advance or helix angle

081 07 01 02 Blade twist
- Explain why blade twist is necessary

081 07 01 03 Fixed pitch and variable pitch/constant speed
- List the different types of propeller
- Fixed pitch
- Adjustable pitch or variable pitch (non-governing)
- Variable pitch (governing)/constant speed
- Explain the relationship between blade angle, blade angle of attack and speed for constant speed propeller and a fixed pitch propeller

081 07 01 04 Propeller efficiency versus speed

- Define propeller efficiency
- Explain the relationship between propeller efficiency and speed (TAS)
- Plot propeller efficiency against speed for the types of propellers listed in 081 07 01 03 above
- Explain the relationship between blade angle and thrust

081 07 01 05 Effects of ice on a propeller
- Describe the effects of ice on a propeller

081 07 02 00 Engine Failure or Engine Stop
- Engine Failure or Engine Stop (shut-down)

081 07 02 01 Windmilling drag
- List the effects of an inoperative engine on the performance and controllability of an aeroplane
- Thrust loss/drag increase
- Influence on yaw moment during asymmetric power

081 07 02 02 Feathering
- Explain the reasons for feathering and the effect on performance and controllability
- influence on yaw moment during asymmetric power

081 07 03 00 Design features for power absorption
- Describe the factors concerning propeller design which increase power absorption.

081 07 03 01 Aspect ratio of blade
- Define blade aspect ratio

081 07 03 02 Diameter of Propeller
- Explain the reasons for restricting propeller diameter

081 07 03 03 Number of blades
- Define "solidity".
- Describe the advantages and disadvantages of increasing the number of blades

081 07 03 04 Propeller noise
- Explain how propeller noise can be minimized

081 07 04 00 Moments and couples due to propeller operation

081 07 04 01 Torque reaction
- Describe the following methods for counteracting engine torque
- Counter-rotating propellers
- Contra-rotating propellers

081 07 04 02 Gyroscopic precession
- Describe the effect on the aeroplane due to the gyroscopic effect

081 07 04 03 Asymmetric slipstream effect
- Describe the possible asymmetric effects of the rotating propeller slipstream

081 07 04 04 Asymmetric blade effect
- Describe the asymmetric blade effect

081 08 00 00 FLIGHT MECHANICS

081 08 01 00 Forces Acting on an Aeroplane

081 08 01 01 Straight horizontal steady flight
- Describe the forces acting on an aeroplane in straight horizontal steady flight
- List the four forces and state where they act
- Explain how the four forces are balanced
- Describe the function of the tailplane

081 08 01 02 Straight steady climb
- Describe the forces acting on an aeroplane in a straight steady climb
- Name the forces parallel and perpendicular to the direction of flight
- Apply the formula relating to the parallel forces ($T = D + W \sin q$)
- Apply the formula relating to the perpendicular forces ($L = W \cos q$)
- Explain why thrust is greater than drag
- Explain why lift is less than mass

081 08 01 03 Straight steady descent
- Describe the forces acting on an aeroplane in a straight steady descent
- Name the forces parallel and perpendicular to the direction of flight
- Apply the formula parallel to the direction of flight ($T = D - W \sin q$)
- Apply the formula relating to the perpendicular forces ($L = W \cos q$)
- Explain why lift is less than mass
- Explain why thrust is less than drag

081 08 01 04 Straight steady glide
- Describe the forces acting on an aeroplane in a straight steady glide
- Name the forces parallel and perpendicular to the direction of flight
- Apply the formula for forces parallel to the direction of flight ($D = W \sin q$)
- Apply the formula for forces perpendicular to the direction of flight ($L = W \cos q$)
- Describe the relationship between the glide angle and the lift/drag ratio

- Describe the relationship between angle of attack and the best lift/drag ratio
- Explain the effect on glide angle with a wind component
- Explain the effect on glide angle with mass change

081 08 01 05 Steady co-ordinated turn
- Describe the forces acting on an aeroplane in a steady co-ordinated turn
- Resolve the forces acting horizontally and vertically during a co-ordinated turn (tan$f$ = Vgr2)
- Explain how to correct an unco-ordinated turn
- Explain why the angle of bank is independent of weight and only depends on TAS and radius of turn
- Resolve the forces to show that for a given angle of bank the radius of turn is determined solely by airspeed (tan$f$ = Vgr2)
- Calculate the turn radius at a given angle of bank and TAS
- Explain why the load factor is greater than one in a co-ordinated turn.
- Explain why lift is less than mass
- Explain why thrust is less than drag

081 08 01 04 Straight steady glide
- Describe the forces acting on an aeroplane in a straight steady glide
- Name the forces parallel and perpendicular to the direction of flight
- Apply the formula for forces parallel to the direction of flight (D = W sin q)
- Apply the formula for forces perpendicular to the direction of flight (L = W cos q)
- Describe the relationship between the glide angle and the lift/drag ratio
- Describe the relationship between angle of attack and the best lift/drag ratio
- Explain the effect on glide angle with a wind component
- Explain the effect on glide angle with mass change

081 08 01 05 Steady co-ordinated turn
- Describe the forces acting on an aeroplane in a steady co-ordinated turn
- Resolve the forces acting horizontally and vertically during a co-ordinated turn (tan$f$ = Vgr2)
- Explain how to correct an unco-ordinated turn
- Explain why the angle of bank is independent of weight and only depends on TAS and radius of turn
- Resolve the forces to show that for a given angle of bank the radius of turn is determined solely by airspeed (tan$f$ = Vgr2)
- Calculate the turn radius at a given angle of bank and TAS
- Explain why the load factor is greater than one in a co-ordinated turn.
- Calculate the lift increase as a function of the bank angle
- Define angular velocity.
- Define rate of turn and rate one turn.
- Explain the influence of TAS on rate of turn at a given bank angle

081 08 02 00 Asymmetric thrust
- Describe the effects on the aeroplane during flight with asymmetric thrust
- Define critical engine

081 08 02 01 Moments about the vertical axis
- Describe the moments about the normal axis
- Explain the yawing moments about the cg
- Describe the change to yawing moment caused by power changes
- Describe the changes to yawing moment caused by engine distance from cg
- Describe the methods to achieve balance

081 08 02 02 Forces on vertical fin
- Describe the forces acting on the fin
- Describe the side force on the fin which counteracts the aeroplane yawing moment about the cg
- Resolve the aeroplane yawing moment and fin side force by simple calculation

081 08 02 03 Influence of bank angle
- Describe the influence of bank angle on yawing moment
- Explain the effect on fin side force when the aeroplane is banked towards the live engine
- Explain why the bank angle must be limited
- Explain the effect on fin angle of attack due to side-slip

081 08 02 04 Influence of aircraft weight
- Describe the effect of weight increase
- Describe how weight increase will increase the yawing moment
- Describe the effect on side-slip with weight increase
- Describe the effect on rudder effectiveness

081 08 02 05 Influence of use of ailerons
- Describe the influence of ailerons
- Explain why aileron effectiveness is reduced

081 08 02 06 Influence of special propeller effects on roll moments
- Describe the effect on roll moment created by propeller effect

- Explain the influence of torque reaction
- Explain the influence of flaps on roll moment
081 08 02 07 Influence of slip angle on roll moments
- Describe the influence of slip angle on roll moments
- Explain how slip angle changes the CL of the left and right wings
081 08 02 08 VMCA
- Define VMCA
- Describe how VMCA is obtained
081 08 02 09 VMCL
- Define VMCL
- Describe how VMCL is obtained
081 08 02 10 VMCG
- Define VMCG
- Describe how VMCG is obtained.
081 08 02 11 Influence of altitude
- Describe the influence of altitude
- Explain why VMCA and VMCG reduces with an increase in altitude
- Explain the significance of power/thrust available and power/thrust required
- Derive the effect on rate of climb and angle of climb
081 08 03 00 Emergency descent
- Describe low and high speed emergency descent
- Explain the advantages and disadvantages of low and high speed emergency descent
081 08 03 01 Influence of configuration
- Describe the influence of configuration on emergency descent
- Describe the methods to increase drag
081 08 03 02 Influence of chosen Mach number and IAS
- Explain why MMO is the limiting speed at altitude
- Explain why indicated airspeed is the limiting speed at low level
- Describe the dangers when recovering from emergency descent
081 08 03 03 Typical points on polar curve
- Identify the typical points on a polar curve
081 08 03 04 Windshear
- Effect on take-off and landing
- Describe the influence of increasing and decreasing windspeed
- Describe a typical recovery from windshear

1.1   Laws and Definitions

Aerodynamics is the study of the interaction between air and solid bodies moving through it. Physical laws have been formulated which may be applied to describe the behaviour of airflow and define the various aerodynamic forces and moments acting on a surface. These laws provide the basis for the understanding of the principles of flight.

1.1.1   Definitions

Inertia: a property of matter by which it continues in its existing state of rest or uniform motion in a straight line.

Mass: the quantity of matter a body contains (units being in kg).

Acceleration: m per s per s (m / s^2).

Velocity: the measure of the rate of movement of an object in a given direction.

Momentum: the quantity of motion of a moving body, measured as a product of its mass and velocity.

Force: an influence tending to change the motion of a body or produce motion or stress in a stationary body.

1.1.2   Newton's Laws

There is a natural tendency for things to continue doing what they are already doing. A body that is at rest tends to remain at rest. A body that is moving tends to continue moving, at the same speed and in the same direction. This is the first principle of mechanics, called Newton's First Law of Motion.

> Newton's First Law of Motion states that a body at rest will remain at rest and a moving body will continue to move at the same speed in the same direction

Stationary objects and objects moving steadily are in equilibrium and have a property called inertia. Inertia may be measured in terms of mass. There are two quantities that decide the difficulty of starting or stopping a body, its mass and its velocity. The combined quantity, mass multiplied by velocity, is called momentum. The International System (SI) unit for velocity is metres per second (m / s), so momentum is measured in kilogram(s) multiplied by metres per second (kg m / s).

Forces try to alter things; to change the momentum of objects. However, they do not always succeed. If the forces acting on a body are in equilibrium (exactly balanced) there is no change of momentum. If you push down on a book at rest on a table, the table will resist the force with an equal and opposite force of reaction, so the forces are in equilibrium. If you press too hard, the table might break, in which case the forces will no longer be in equilibrium and a sudden and unwanted acceleration will occur. The SI unit for force is the Newton (N).

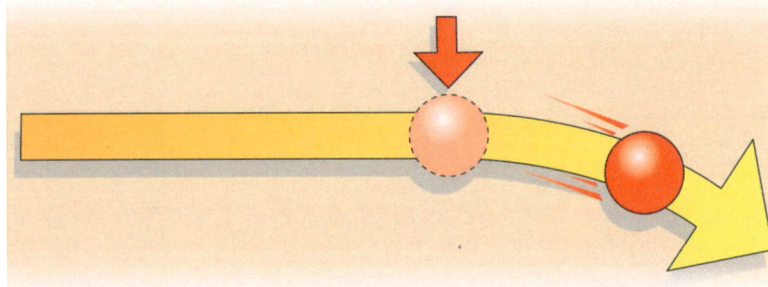

Figure 1.1 The effect of force on a moving body

If the forces are not in balance, then the acceleration will be proportional to force and inversely proportional to the mass of the object, which is described by Newton's Second Law.

> Newton's Second Law of Motion of a body states that in order to change the state of a body at rest or moving in a straight line at a constant speed, a force must be exerted on it:
>
> $$F = m \times a$$
>
> Where F is the force, m is the mass of the body and a is acceleration

> Weight is the force with which an object is attracted toward the centre of the earth. It is expressed as:
>
> $$F = m \times g$$
>
> Where m is the mass of the object and g is the gravity constant. It has the value 9.81 m / s^2 in the SI system.

All objects near the surface of the Earth experience the force of gravity (weight). If there is no opposing force, then they will start to move (i.e. accelerate). The rate at which they accelerate is independent of their mass. In the vacuum of space, a feather and a lump of lead would fall at the same rate. In the atmosphere, however, the feather would be subjected to a much larger aerodynamic resistance force in relation to the accelerating gravity force (the weight), and therefore, the feather would fall more slowly. The mass of a body depends on the amount of matter in it, and it will not vary with its position on the Earth, nor will it be any

CRANFIELD AVIATION TRAINING SCHOOL LTD. PART-FCL GBR.ATO-0136
CATS INNOVATION CENTRE, LUTON, Bedfordshire LU2 8DL U.K.   www.catsaviation.com

1-19   Principles of Flight

different if were on the moon. The weight (the force due to gravity) will change, however, because the gravity constant will be different on the moon, and varies slightly between different points on the Earth.

A force is said to do work on a body when it moves the body in the direction in which it is acting. The amount of work done is measured by the product of the force and the distance moved in the direction of the force.

Work done = force x distance moved

The unit of work is the Newton metre (Nm) and is also called a joule (J)

Power is the rate of doing work:

$$Power = \frac{Work\ done}{Time}$$

The unit of power is joules per second (J / s) or watt (W)

A body is said to have energy if it has the ability to do work, the amount of energy is measured by the amount of work that it can do. The units of energy are the same as those of work. Consider two objects colliding. The total momentum after the collision is the same as the total momentum before; the momentum lost by one ball is exactly the same as the momentum gained by the other. This is the principle of the conservation of momentum. The law applies whether the objects rebound, or whether they stick together. The total mechanical energy after the collision is not the same as before. Energy is dissipated into the air in the form of heat and sound. Newton's Third Law of Motion states that for every action there is an equal and opposite reaction. If an object influences a second object with a certain force, the second object will influence the first with exactly the same force. An action force causes a reaction force in the opposite direction.

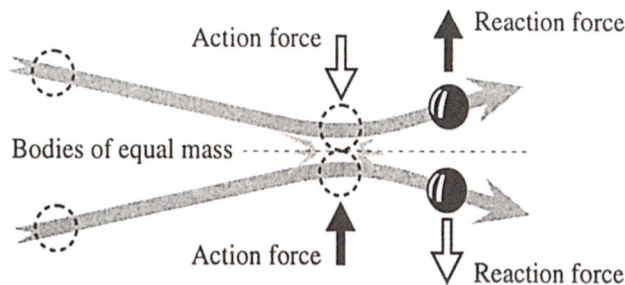

Figure 1.2 Action and Reaction Forces

Newton's Third Law of Motion states that for every action there is an equal and opposite reaction

If the bodies have different mass, the body with the smallest mass will change its motion path the most.

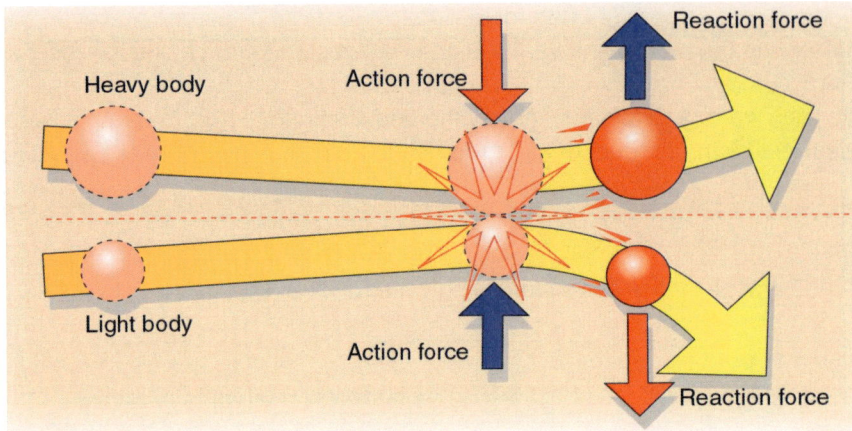

Figure 1.3 Action and Reaction Forces with unequal masses

An aircraft wing influences its surrounding mass of air with action and reaction forces. If the air is pushed downwards (action force) a corresponding reaction force upwards is exerted by the wing.

1.1.3   *Units*

The metric system known as the Systeme International (SI) is now in general use.

> The basic units of this system are the kilogram (kg) for mass, the metre (m) for distance, and the second (s) for time

Temperatures are measured in degrees Celsius (^{o}C), or Kelvin (K) when measured relative to absolute zero; 0° C is equivalent to 273 K. A temperature change of one degree Celsius is the same as a change of one degree Kelvin, it is just the starting or zero point which is different. The degree symbol (^{o}) is not used when temperatures are displayed in degrees Kelvin.

Forces and hence weights are measured in Newtons (N). To convert masses in kilograms to Newtons, multiply by the gravity constant 9.81.

1.1.4   *Properties of the Atmosphere*

The aerodynamic forces and moments acting on a surface are due to the properties of the air mass in which the surface is present. The composition of the Earth's atmosphere by volume is approximately 78% nitrogen, 21% oxygen, and 1% water vapour, argon, carbon dioxide, and other trace gases. For the majority of all aerodynamic considerations air is considered as a uniform mixture of these gases. The usual quantities used to define the properties of an air mass are pressure, temperature, density and viscosity.

The static pressure of the air at any altitude results from the mass of air supported above that level. Due to its mass, the very tall ($\approx$100 km) column of air above us creates a very high pressure in all directions on everything beneath it.

CRANFIELD AVIATION TRAINING SCHOOL LTD. PART-FCL GBR.ATO-0136
CATS INNOVATION CENTRE, LUTON, Bedfordshire LU2 8DL U.K.   www.catsaviation.com
1-21   Principles of Flight

The atmosphere

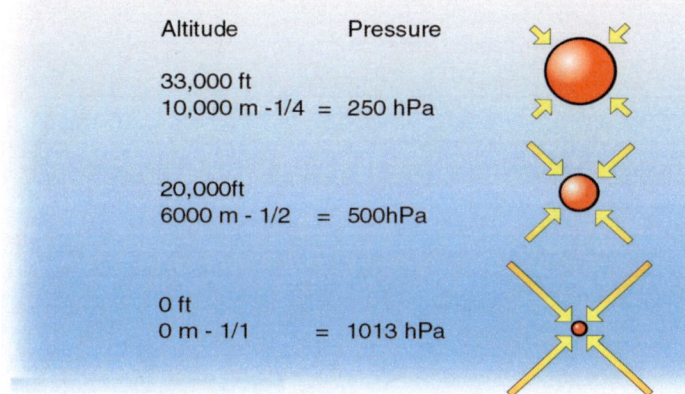

Altitude	Pressure
33,000 ft	
10,000 m -1/4 =	250 hPa
20,000ft	
6000 m - 1/2 =	500hPa
0 ft	
0 m - 1/1 =	1013 hPa

Figure 1.4 Pressure in the atmosphere

The pressure at sea level normally ranges from 990 to 1030 hecto-Pascals (hPa) with a mean value of 1013 hPa. The pressure reduces with altitude rapidly. At 20000' (6000 m) the pressure is only half of that at sea level. At sea level, the force due to the pressure of the column of air above is approximately 100000 N/m^2 and only a slight relative difference in pressure (1%) around the aircraft wings is needed to lift a very heavy aircraft. A pressure difference of only 1% gives a pressure difference of 1000 N/m^2. The loading on aircraft wings normally ranges from 500 to 5000 N/m^2.

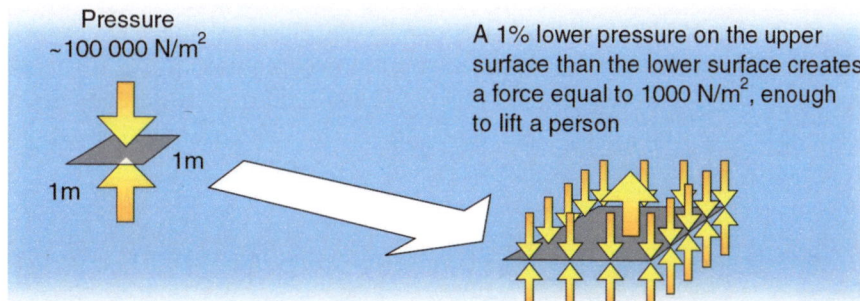

Pressure
~100 000 N/m^2

1m

1m

A 1% lower pressure on the upper surface than the lower surface creates a force equal to 1000 N/m^2, enough to lift a person

Figure 1.5 Pressure differential and lift

The reduction of pressure caused by increased altitude causes a reduced force at a given pressure difference over a surface. A 1% difference at 20000' produces a pressure difference of 500 N / m^2 instead of the 1000 N / m^2 at ground level. So, the possibility to fly by using wings becomes limited at extremely high altitudes. When air flows around a moving body it produces a force called drag, which increases rapidly with speed and limits the maximum speed. The density of the air causes friction between the body and the air that will put a limit to the maximum speed. The friction causes heating of the body and the surrounding air. At low speeds the generation of heat due to friction is negligible, but at very high speeds the friction produces such heat that the airframe could be weakened and lose its required strength. The flight envelope in which an aircraft can fly is limited by altitude and speed. Aircraft can use only a small part of this envelope.

CRANFIELD AVIATION TRAINING SCHOOL LTD. PART-FCL GBR.ATO-0136
CATS INNOVATION CENTRE, LUTON, Bedfordshire LU2 8DL U.K.   www.catsaviation.com

1-22   Principles of Flight

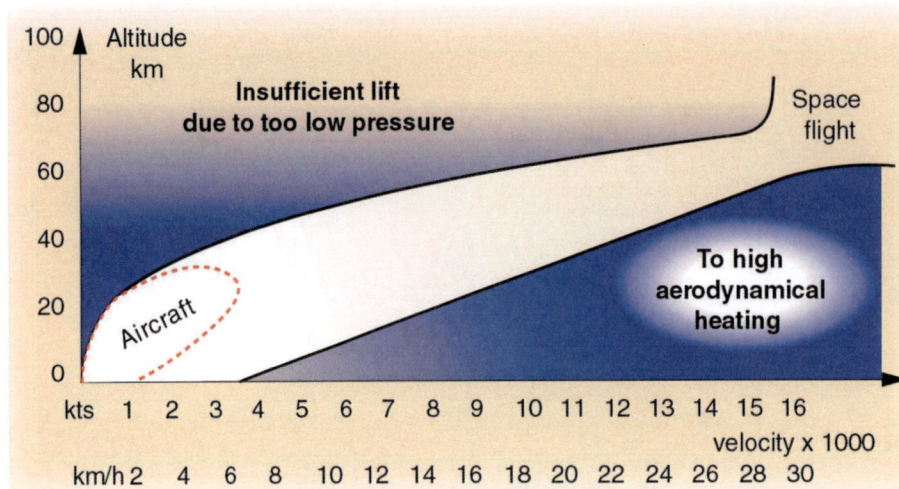

Figure 1.6 Aircraft flight envelope

Only experimental aircraft can fly to the altitudes and speeds on the edges of the envelope. The normal figures for today's aircraft, e.g. a jet fighter aircraft, are limited to an altitude of 60000' (18 km) and to a speed of 1100 KT (2000 kph).

1.1.5   *Air as a fluid*

A fluid is a substance that possesses the property of flowing freely and does not have a definite shape but tends to conform to the outline of its container. Fluids can be classified as liquids or gases. Liquids occupy a definite volume independent of the volume in which they are contained; gases expand to fill the entire volume of the container in which they are placed. Fluids behave differently when they are flowing. Heavy oil takes a longer time to flow and fill a vessel than water does. The different behaviour of fluids is due to the different internal friction created between the layers of the fluid when it is in motion. This is called viscosity.

> The viscosity of air is a measure of the resistance of one layer of air to movement over the neighbouring layer

1.1.6   *Pressure, Temperature, Density*

A certain mass of fluid is made up of millions of molecules. Molecules are in rapid and random motion even when the fluid is not in motion, colliding with each other and any surface placed in or surrounding the fluid. For a small body immersed in a fluid at rest, the same pressure acts in all directions.

> In a fluid at rest the pressure at each point acts in all directions at the same time. This is known as Pascal's Law

Molecules exert a force on surfaces they are in contact with. The ratio between applied force perpendicular to the surface and the surface area is called pressure.

> $$\text{Pressure} = \frac{\text{Force}}{\text{Area}}$$
>
> It is measured in Newtons per square metre (N/m^2)

> The temperature of a fluid is a measure of its molecular motion

The temperature of a fluid is a measure of its molecular motion. The greater the molecular motion, the higher the temperature. The temperature at which no molecular motion occurs is known as absolute zero or 0 K (equal to –273 $^{\circ}$C). The absolute temperature scale is the temperature measured starting from absolute zero = 0 Kelvin (-273° C).

Density, designated by the Greek letter ρ (rho) is the ratio between the mass of a fluid and its volume.

$$\text{Density} = \frac{\text{Mass}}{\text{Volume}}$$

The SI unit for density is kilograms per cubic metre (kg / m^3)

1.1.6.1 *Relationship between pressure, temperature and density*

Air density is an important factor since it affects both the force acting on the aircraft and engine performance. The density of a mass of air can be changed by varying the volume the air occupies, or by varying the pressure and the temperature of the air. If pressure is increased, the air is compressed into a smaller volume and the density increases. If pressure is decreased, air expands, filling a greater volume, and the density decreases. If the temperature is increased and the pressure kept constant, the air expands to fill a greater volume and density decreases.

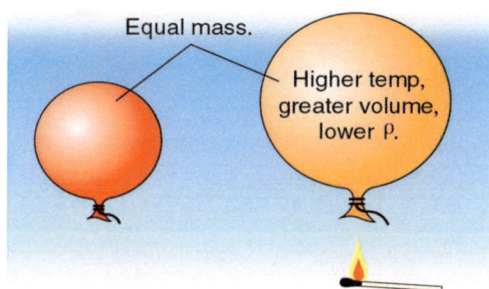

Figure 1.7 Increasing temperature reduces density

If the temperature is decreased, the air will occupy a smaller volume and the density will increase. Density (ρ) is directly proportional to pressure and in inversely proportional to temperature:

$$\rho \propto \frac{P}{T}$$

This relationship may be expressed as a formula known as the equation of state.

The Equation of State: P = ρRT

where P = pressure, ρ = density, T = absolute temperature, R is the gas constant

In the atmosphere both temperature and pressure decrease with increasing altitude; thus density also changes with altitude. As a result of a greater rate of decrease in pressure than in temperature, the overall effect is that density decreases with an increase in altitude.

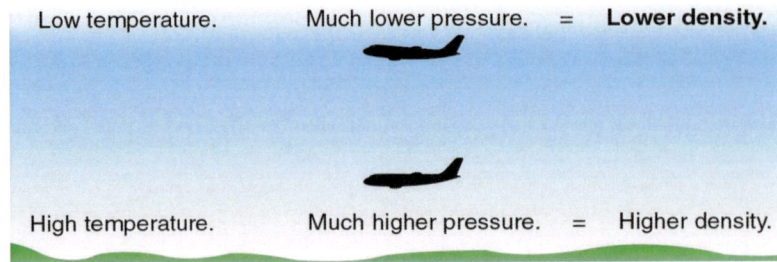

Figure 1.8 Density decreases with altitude

Aircraft and engine performance are affected by altitude since density decreases with an increase in altitude.

1.1.7 Fluid compressibility

When external pressure is exerted on a mass of fluid the volume of fluid decreases. When the same mass is contained in a smaller volume, the mass per unit volume (the density) increases. The amount by which the density changes depends on the kind of fluid and on the pressure applied. If the fluid is a liquid, the change in volume is minimal in spite of high pressure. Thus, liquids are virtually incompressible and consequently their density is nearly constant. If the fluid is a gas, or a mixture of gases like air, the change in volume can be large and the density is therefore variable. Gases are compressible.

> Liquids are virtually incompressible and have nearly constant density
> Gases are compressible and their density is variable

However, at speeds well below the speed of sound air may be considered to be virtually incompressible. The effect of air compressibility becomes important when airspeed is high (>300 KT), as the air begins to behave like a compressible fluid.

The local speed of sound (LSS) is the speed at which small pressure disturbances are propagated through the air. The propagation speed is solely a function of air temperature and may be calculated using the following formula:

$$LSS \ (KT) = 38.94 \sqrt{Temp \, K}$$

Example:

What is the speed of sound if the outside air temperature is +5°C?

Solution:

To get the temperature in Kelvin add 273 to the temperature in degrees Celsius.
Temp K = +5 + 273 = 278 °C

$$LSS = 38.94 \sqrt{278} = \underline{649.3 \ KT}$$

1.1.8 Static Pressure

For a mass of air at rest, the pressure of the air is exerted in all directions on a surface. This pressure is called the static pressure of the atmosphere.

> The static pressure of the atmosphere is caused by the weight of the air acting on a surface acting equally in all directions

1.1.9 Dynamic Pressure

When air in motion strikes a surface it exerts a force on that surface which is proportional to the dynamic pressure. Dynamic pressure depends on the speed that the surface moves at relative to the air and also the density of the air. If the relative speed between the air and the surface is increased, the dynamic pressure is also increased. This is due to the greater number of molecules per s that strike the surface. If the air becomes denser at constant relative speed, dynamic pressure increases, as the denser air contains a greater number of molecules per unit volume; consequently, the number of molecules per s that strikes the surface is greater. Dynamic pressure may also be referred to as "q".

> Dynamic pressure is expressed as: $\frac{1}{2}\rho V^2$
>
> where ρ = air density and V = the relative speed

1.1.10 Bernoulli's Theorem

Daniel Bernoulli, 1700 -1782, was a scientist who studied the behaviour of fluids. He drew conclusions about the relation between pressure and kinetic energy. He deduced that "the sum of energies is a constant". The two energies he was referring to are the kinetic energy, i.e. energy of movement, and the pressure energy, i.e. potential energy. The potential energy / volume unit corresponds to the static pressure. In other words: you cannot get something for nothing. If velocity (the kinetic energy) is increased, the pressure (in this case perpendicular to a surface parallel to the airflow) must decrease. Since kinetic energy is a function of the mass and the velocity, the connection between pressure and velocity may be found. That is: a decrease in pressure causes an increase in velocity. Bernoulli's Theorem is interpreted as the total pressure remaining constant in a steady streamline flow. So, the sum of static and dynamic pressure is called the total pressure, which is constant:

Total pressure (P_{tot}) = Static pressure (p) + dynamic pressure (q)

> Static pressure + Dynamic pressure = constant

The conclusion of Bernoulli's Theorem is that an increase in speed (dynamic pressure) at a point along a streamline causes a decrease in the static pressure at that point, while a decrease in dynamic pressure causes an increase in the static pressure at that point.

> At zero speed the total pressure is equal to the static pressure

> In a steady streamline flow increased flow velocity parallel to a surface means decreased static pressure perpendicular to that surface

1.1.11 Equation of Continuity

> The principle of mass conservation states that mass is constant and can be neither created nor destroyed

Consider a tube with different cross-sectional areas. Applying the principle of mass conservation means that the mass flowing through each cross section of the tube during a certain time (mass flow) must be constant.

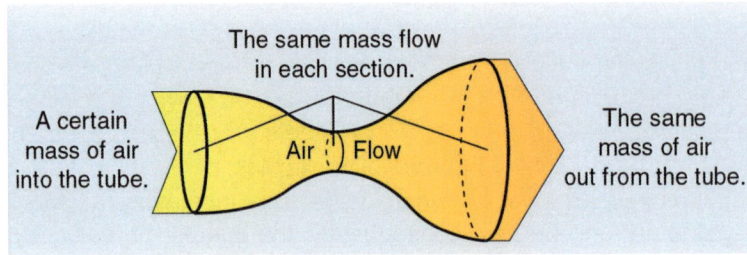

Figure 1.9 Mass flow in tube

Mass flow is obtained by multiplying the density (ρ) by the cross-sectional area (A) by the velocity (V):

Mass flow = ρ x A x V

The equation of continuity is the mathematical expression of the principle of mass conservation applied to a defined fluid flow and is:

ρ x A x V = constant.

Equation of continuity: ρ A V = constant

For airflow at low speed, air can be assumed to be incompressible and the density is therefore constant; in this case the equation of continuity can be simplified:

A x V = constant

Example:

Air flows into section A1 (area = 2 m^2) of a tube at a speed V1 = 100 m/s. What will the speed of the air be at section A2 (area = 4 m^2)?

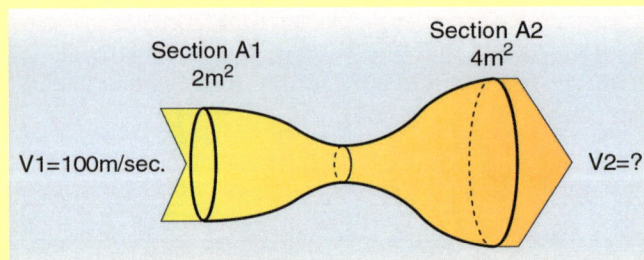

Figure 1.10 Mass flow in a tube example

Solution:

$$A1 \; V1 = A2 \; V2$$

$$V2 = \frac{A1}{A2} V1 = \frac{2}{4} \times 100 = 50 \text{ m/s}$$

Therefore the speed at section A2 = <u>50 m/s</u>

1.1.12   *The Venturi tube*

The venturi tube provides one of the most interesting examples of Bernoulli's Theorem. The tube gradually narrows and then expands gradually to the exit. Its effectiveness as a means of causing a decrease of pressure below that of the atmosphere depends very much on the exact shape. As the flow approaches the constriction the velocity increases to maintain the same mass flow. As the velocity increases the dynamic pressure goes up and in accordance with Bernoulli's Theorem, static pressure decreases.

Static pressure reaches a minimum value where the speed and the dynamic pressure are at their maximum

After that, the speed decreases gradually and consequently the static pressure increases again. The venturi effect is thought to occur around a wing and results in the generation of lift.

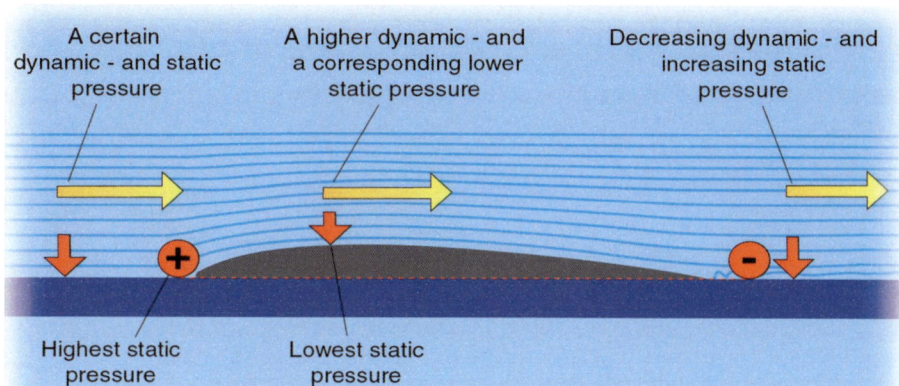

Figure 1.11 Venture effect around a wing

1.1.13 *Airspeed measurement*

If a tube is pointed directly into the flow of air, and the other end connected to a pressure-measuring device, then that device will read the stagnation pressure. The tube is full of air and its exit is blocked, so that no air can flow down the tube; the oncoming air is brought to rest as it meets the open end of the tube. This type of tube is called a pitot tube and provides a means of measuring stagnation (total) pressure. If a non-forward facing small hole is made in the fuselage of the aircraft which is connected to a pressure-measuring device. The hole does not impede the flow of air, so the pressure measured is the local static pressure. A hole used for this purpose is called a static vent. Since static pressure plus dynamic pressure equals stagnation pressure, it follows that: Stagnation pressure - Static pressure = Dynamic pressure. If instead of connecting the static pressure vent and the pitot tube to two separate pressure-measuring devices, they are connected to one device, which measures the difference in pressure then, a measurement of the dynamic pressure can be made. This dynamic pressure is proportional to indicated airspeed. The pressure difference-measuring device used on aircraft consists of either a diaphragm or a capsule. The stagnation pressure is applied to one side, and the static pressure is applied to the other. The resulting deflection of the diaphragm can then either be amplified through a series of levers to cause a dial pointer to move or can be used to produce a proportional electrical output to be fed into an appropriate electronic circuit. This instrument gives a reading that is proportional to dynamic pressure. The pressure gauge is then calibrated to indicate flight speed in the standard sea level air mass. There are many conditions of flight where the airspeed indicator does not truly reflect the actual velocity through the air mass. These various speeds are defined by the Joint Aviation Requirements as follows:

Airspeed	Definition
Indicated Airspeed (IAS)	the actual instrument indication for some given flight condition
Calibrated Airspeed (CAS)	IAS corrected for **P**osition and **I**nstrument error
Equivalent Airspeed (EAS)	CAS corrected for **C**ompressibility error (at airspeeds above 300 KT, gives the airspeed indication an erroneous magnification)
True Airspeed (TAS)	EAS corrected for **D**ensity error

Compressibility effects depend upon the relationship of airspeed to the speed of sound. The term used to describe this relationship is the Mach number, MN, and this term is the ratio of the true airspeed (TAS) to the speed of sound (LSS).

$$MN = \frac{TAS}{LSS}$$

1.2 Basics about airflow

Due to the presence of an aerofoil, molecules of air change their directions of motion and speed. If successive molecules of air follow the same steady path, the flow makes steady stream lines. The streamline nearest to the aerofoil most closely follows the contour of the surface.

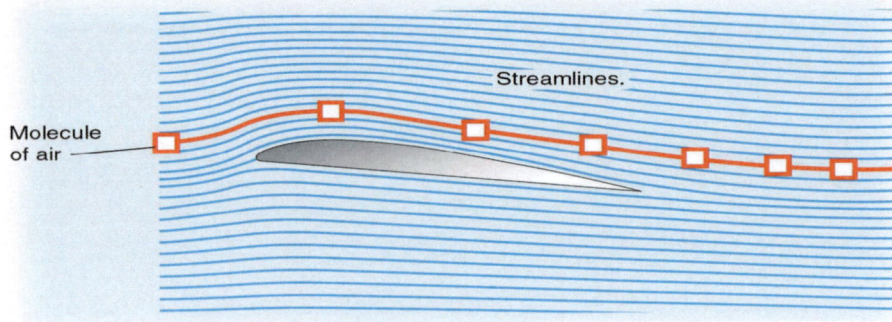

Figure 1.12 Streamlines

Streamline flow is a flow where the successive molecules of air follow the same steady path, called a streamline. Steady streamlines means steady flow

In streamline flow the velocity may change from one point to another along the streamline, but at each fixed point the velocity will be the same for all successive molecules as time goes on. Consider an imaginary circle in a flow. If all the streamlines passing through the outer edge of the circle are drawn, they generate a tubular surface, which is called a stream tube. Since the velocity vector is always tangential to the surface of such a tube, there is no flow into or out of the tube through its imaginary walls, but only along the tube.

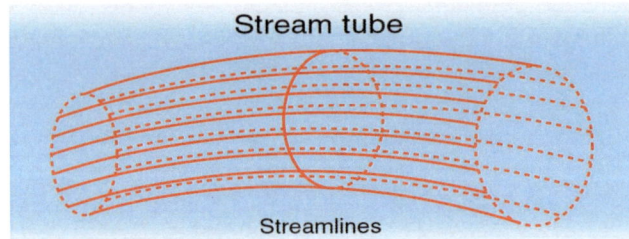

Figure 1.13 Stream tube

Airflow cannot be streamlined around all bodies. Upstream of a cylinder streamlines follow the contour of the surface, but due to friction and pressure distribution, they become chaotic when leaving the contour.

Figure 1.14 Turbulent flow downstream of a cylinder

Behind the cylinder, the molecules of air do not follow a steady path, and successive molecules travel along a path that is very different from that of the preceding molecules.

The type of flow where the molecules of air do not follow a steady path is called turbulent flow

For a certain point in turbulent flow, the fluid molecules flowing through that point will have different velocities and directions as time goes on.

1.2.1 *Two-dimensional flow and circulation*

When a wing is moving through the air, the air adapts itself to the changed situation. If an aerofoil is moved from a stationary position, the particles in the air change their position during the motion of the aerofoil.

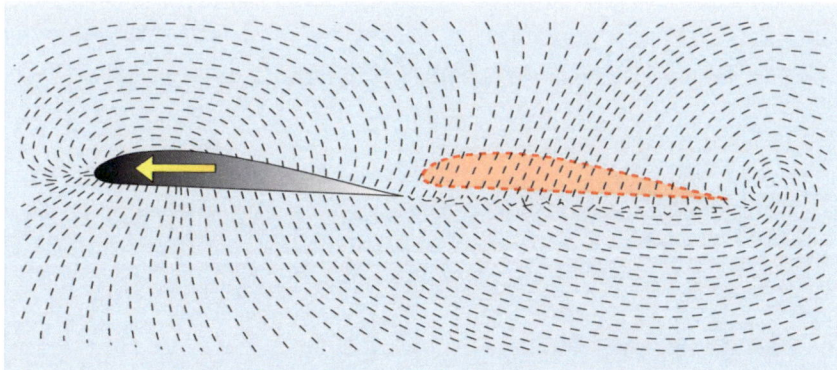

Figure 1.15 Particles in the air change their position during the forward movement of an aerofoil

The particles near the upper surface are moved upwards, rearwards and downwards, and those at the lower part move mainly downwards. A vortex generated behind the starting point is known as a "starting vortex" which causes the motion below the surface to be more rearwards, and the motion above the surface to be more steeply downwards compared to a situation where the aerofoil is in continuous motion. As soon as the wing starts to move forwards, the lower surface of the wing pushes the air downwards and slightly forwards. Thus, a slightly higher pressure is developed below the wing surface. The air near the leading edge tries to avoid the high pressure below and flows upwards towards the lower pressure area / region, making these particles of air flow first slightly forwards, then upwards and rearwards at a relatively high speed. The air near the upper surface, however, has to fill the low pressure region where the upper surface of the wing was just positioned, causing the particles of air to flow rearwards and downwards. A particle of air positioned slightly in front of and below an arriving aerofoil, travels around the aerofoil and make a circular path as shown:

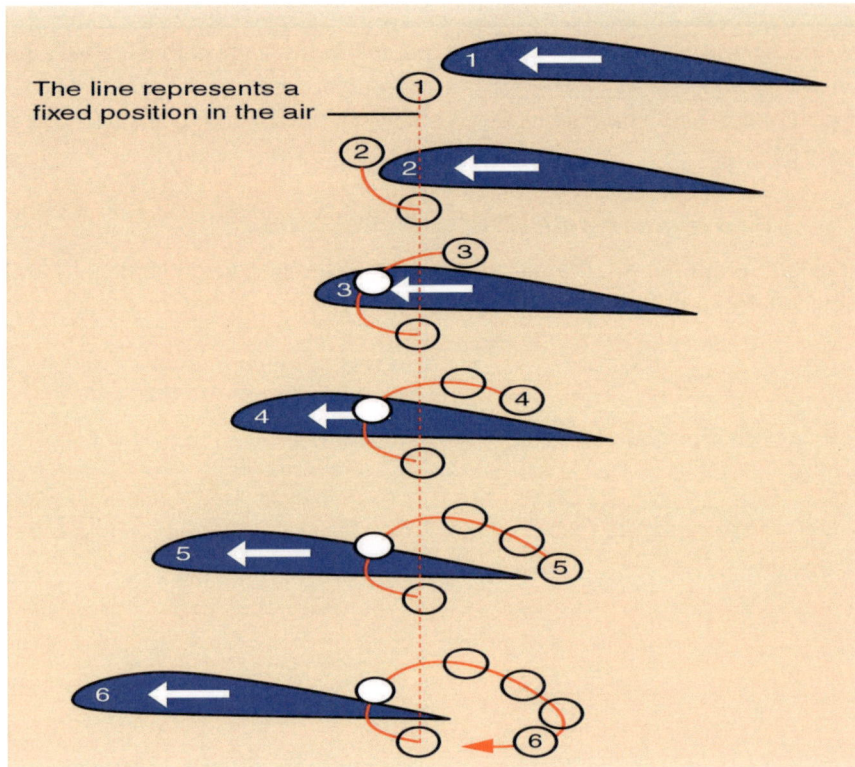

Figure 1.16 Circular flow around an aerofoil

Relative to the surrounding air, the particles of air have moved forwards below, upwards at the leading edge, rearwards-downwards above and downwards behind the aerofoil. A circulation relative to the aerofoil is thus created. However, it should not be seen as if a particle near the lower surface has been moved forward in relation to the surface circulating all the way around the aerofoil. The particles have internal velocity vectors parallel to the aerofoil surface.

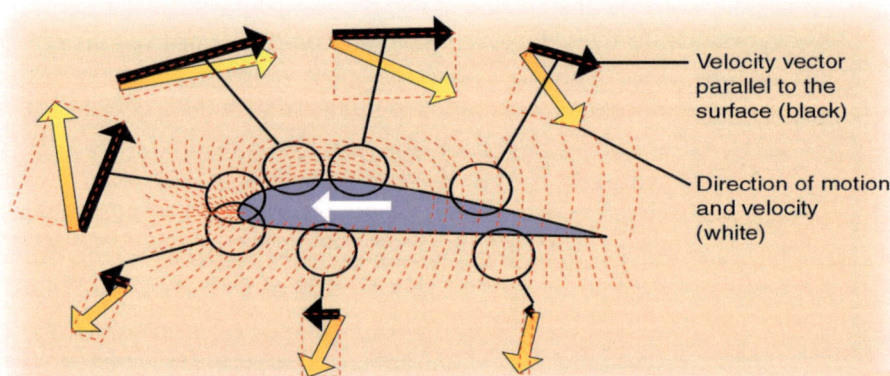

Figure 1.17 Internal velocity vectors

The velocity of the air, is greatest where it flows from the highest to the lowest pressure, i.e. at the forward part of the upper surface of the wing.

The highest flow velocity parallel to the surface is developed at the forward part of the upper surface of the wing where the pressure gradient along the aerofoil is highest

The lowest relative velocity is where the aerofoil pushes the air slightly forwards, i.e. at the lower surface near the leading edge.

1.2.2   *Three dimensional airflow*

When an aircraft moves through the air its influence on the air is to divert the mass of air downwards. The reaction force from the mass of air causes an upward lift force on the wings.

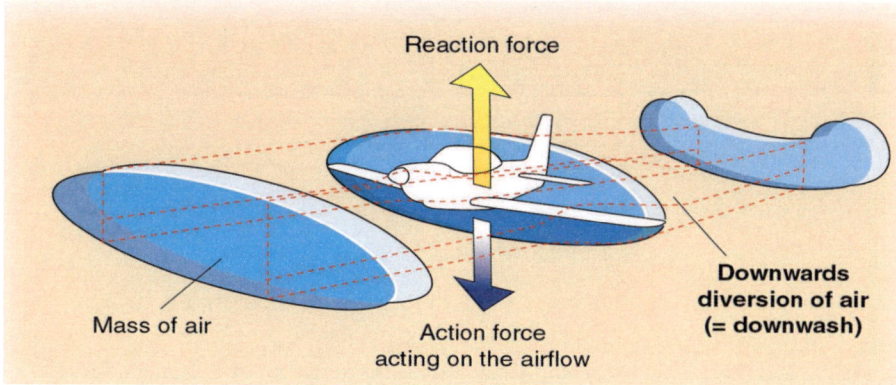

Figure 1.18 Downwash

In order to achieve equilibrium between the accelerating force and the lift force at different speeds, the angle of the downwash has to be greater at low speeds than at high speeds or the accelerated mass of air has to be greater.

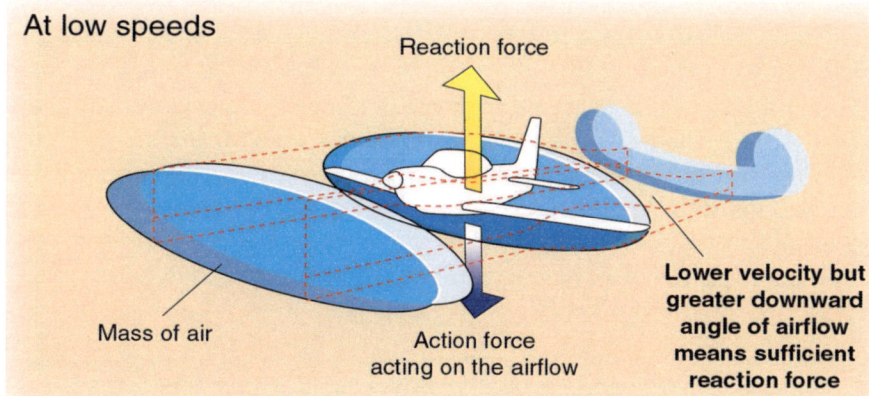

Figure 1.19 Greater angle of downwash is required at low speeds

The lift force is exactly the same force as the force required to accelerate the effected mass of air downwards during flight

There is also an upwash in front of the aerofoil due to the pressure differences around the aerofoil, but the net effect is a downwash of the air when lift is produced. The upwash and downwash angles vary with the distance from the wing. Far ahead and behind the wing, the upwash and downwash is zero.

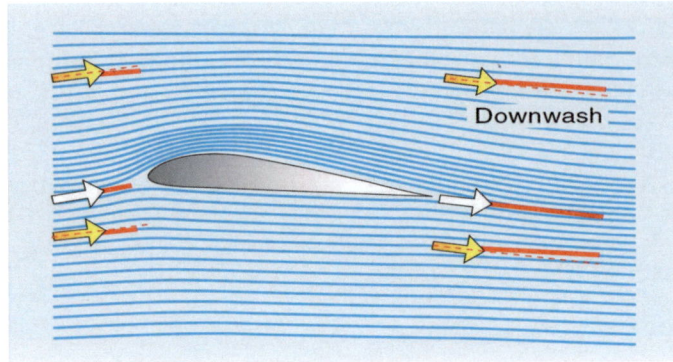

Figure 1.20 Downwash in streamline flow

The pressure differences are not dominated by the high pressure below the wings, but are due to the diversion of the air. The pressure difference is dominated by a lower pressure above the wings compared to the surrounding static pressure and the slight, if any, higher pressure below the wing. The pressure difference that acts on the surfaces creates a force that when multiplied by the corresponding area, is equal to and opposite to the gravitational action, i.e. the weight.

Lower pressure above the wing than below the wing causes a pressure that acts as a lift force

1.3 Aerodynamics forces and moments on surfaces

The flow pattern around a body is the same no matter if the body is moving through the air or if the air is flowing past the body. Close to the body, the local flow velocities will vary and be different from the velocity of the undisturbed flow well away from the body. In order to measure this difference, the free stream velocity between the aerofoil and the air at a certain distance from the aerofoil where the streamlines are not yet influenced by the presence of the aerofoil must be compared, otherwise the relative speed will be incorrect. Free stream velocity is usually given other names, such as relative velocity or relative wind.

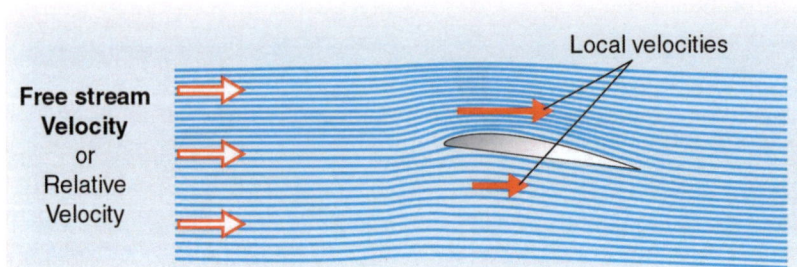

Figure 1.21 Relative velocity

The free stream velocity or relative velocity is measured in front of the body where the streamlines are not yet influenced by the presence of the body.

1.3.1 Pressure distribution

In order to make it easier to see what happens to flow and pressure distribution, a fixed aerofoil in an airflow will be considered. Imagine a very thin flat plate in a flow. If the plate is parallel to the free stream direction, the flow is undisturbed.

Figure 1.22 Flat plate in airflow

The angle between the plate and the flow direction is known as the Angle of attack (A of A or α). Changing the angle of attack alters the pressure situation and the flow pattern around the plate. Raising the plate increases the angle of attack and the air accelerates downwards giving a slightly higher pressure below the surface and a slightly lower pressure above the surface. To avoid the higher pressure on the lower side the air is forced upwards towards the lower pressure on the upper side. A slight upwash is therefore created in front of the plate.

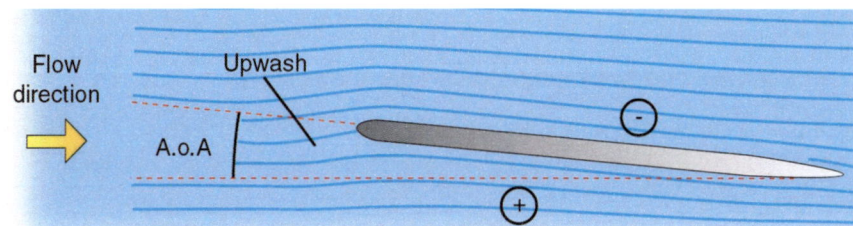

Figure 1.23 The higher pressure below and the lower pressure above the plate cause an upwash of the air in front of the plate

The air that flows near the leading edge upper surface speeds up as it flows from the higher to a lower pressure. This increase in speed along the aerofoil causes a local small decrease in the static pressure. In addition to that, the acceleration of the mass of air in the curved path around the leading edge of the plate leads to an additional decrease in the static pressure on the surface.

When the flow has passed the leading edge, the speed of the flow decreases again as it approaches the trailing edge where there is a comparatively higher pressure.
Lower flow velocity along the lower surface of the aerofoil causes a slightly higher static pressure.

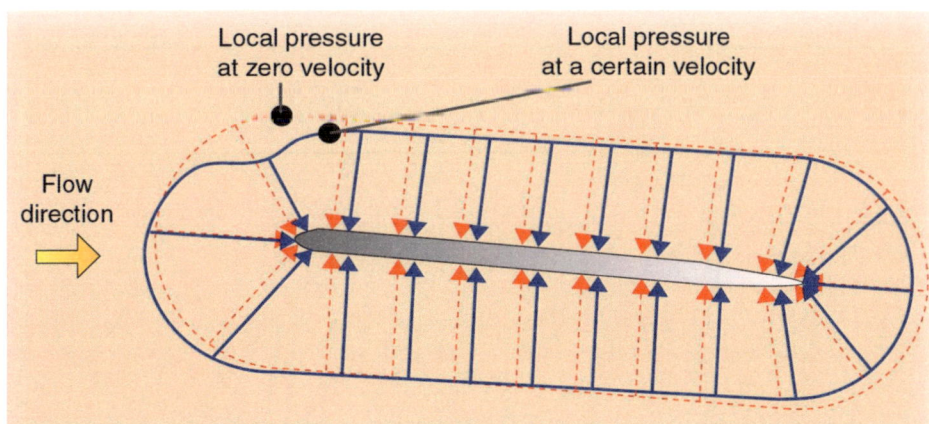

Figure 1.24 Static pressure around a plate at rest (dotted arrows), and in a motion relative to the air (solid arrows)

In reality there is only a small percentage of change in pressure difference, and the distribution may vary much in detail depending on the shape of the aerofoil section and the angle of attack.

CRANFIELD AVIATION TRAINING SCHOOL LTD. PART-FCL GBR.ATO-0136
CATS INNOVATION CENTRE, LUTON, Bedfordshire LU2 8DL U.K.

www.catsaviation.com

1-34

Principles of Flight

1.3.2 Total aerodynamic force of a plate

The pressure difference on the surfaces of the plate produces a total aerodynamic force that is directed principally upwards.

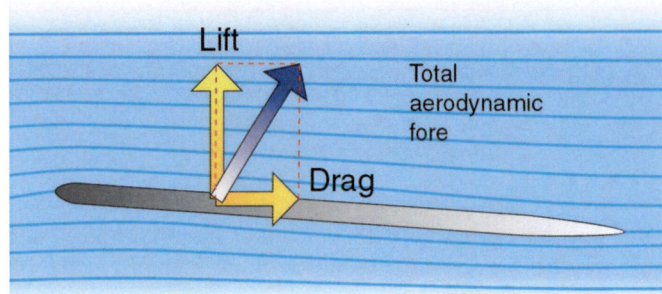

Figure 1.25 Total aerodynamic force is a product of lift and drag

> LIFT is the component of the Total Aerodynamic Force acting perpendicular to the flight direction
> DRAG is the component of the Total Aerodynamic Force acting parallel to the flight direction

1.3.3 Symmetrically curved aerofoil sections

If, instead of a flat plate, a symmetrical cambered aerofoil section is placed in an airflow a different flow pattern emerges. At zero angle of attack there will be some pressure differences between the leading edge and the trailing edge that changes the flow velocity near the surface.

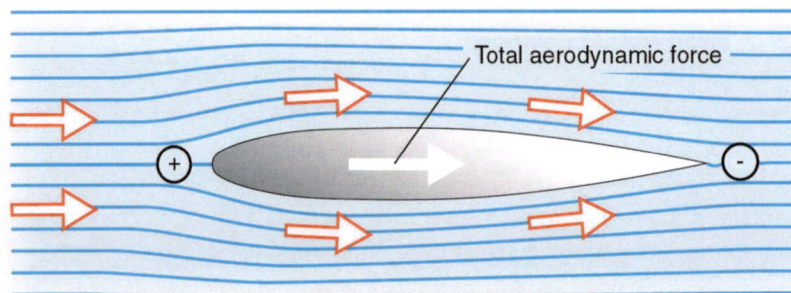

Figure 1.26 A symmetrical cambered plate in an airflow

The change in velocity causes a decrease in the static pressure normal to the surface except at the leading edge where it increases.

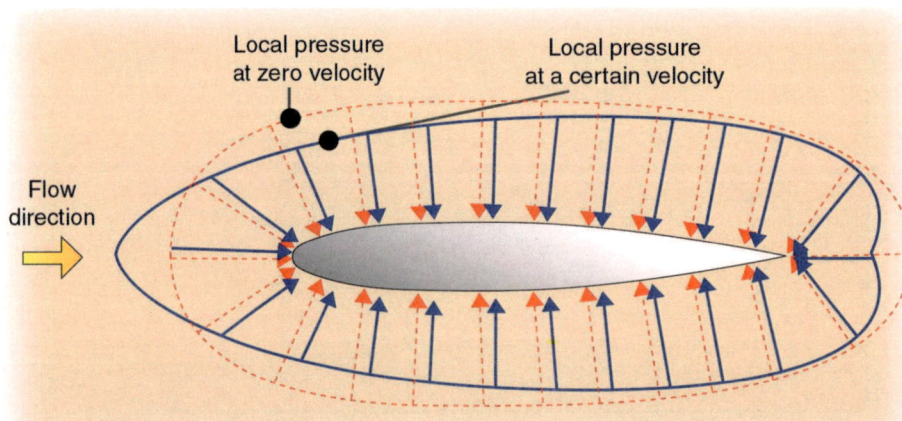

Figure 1.27 Pressure patterns around a symmetrical cambered plate in an airflow

A symmetrical aerofoil section at zero angle of attack does not create any pressure difference between the upper and the lower surface. But at a given angle of attack the flow is different and hence the pressure and the forces change.

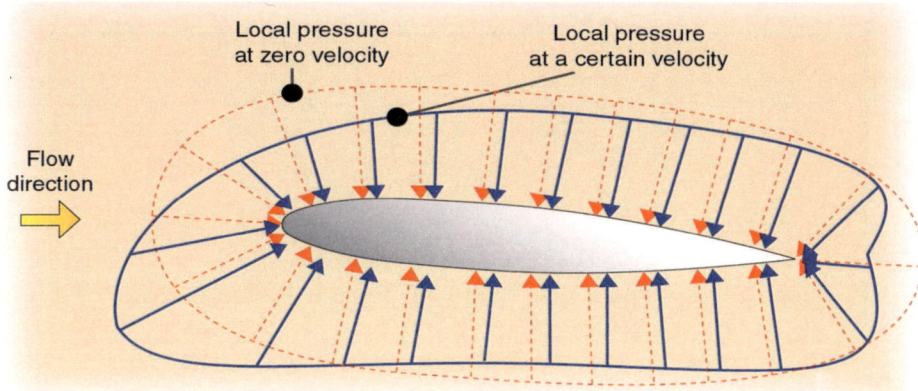

Figure 1.28 Pressure patterns around a symmetrical cambered plate with increased angle of attack in an airflow

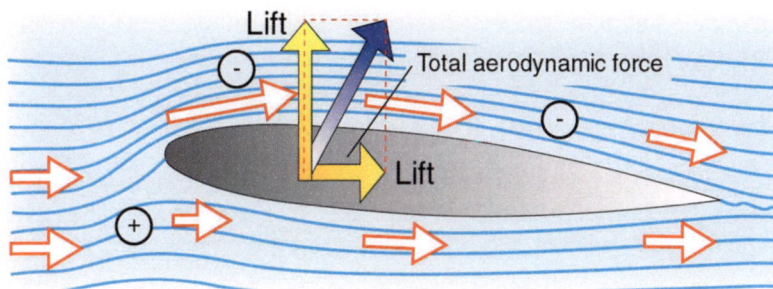

Figure 1.29 Total aerodynamic force for a symmetrical cambered plate with increased angle of attack in an airflow

A symmetrically curved aerofoil creates greater pressure differences than a flat plate at the same angle of attack

1.3.4 Asymmetric aerofoil sections

An asymmetrically curved aerofoil can be used to even higher pressure differences at a given angle of attack. The pressure distribution is changed in comparison with the symmetrical section.

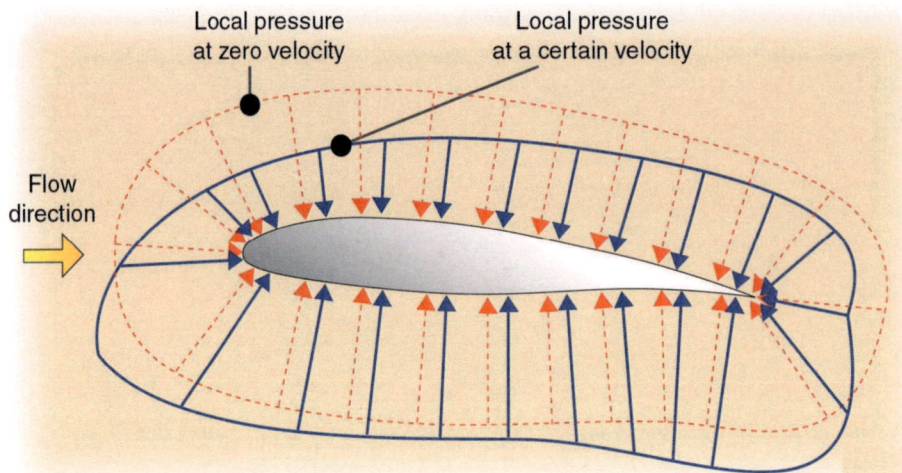

Figure 1.30 Pressure patterns around an asymmetrical cambered plate with increased angle of attack in an airflow

Suction over the leading edge contributes to a more upright total aerodynamic force with the effect of less drag from the aerofoil.

If lift and drag generated by a flat plate and by an aerofoil section at the same angles of attack is compared, the aerofoil section gives a greater lift and less drag.

1.4   *Shape of an airfoil*

The mean camber line is a line drawn halfway between the upper and lower surfaces of an aerofoil. It shows the average curvature of the aerofoil section. It is unlikely to be a straight line. The shape of the mean camber line is important when determining the aerodynamic characteristics of the aerofoil section.

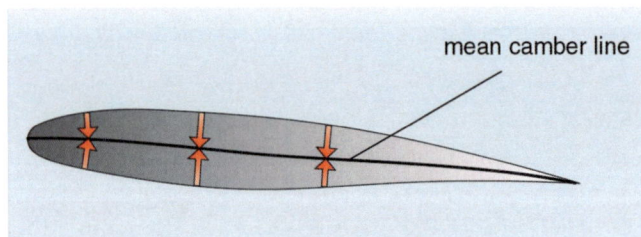

Figure 1.31 Mean camber line

> The mean camber line is the line drawn halfway between the upper and lower surfaces of the aerofoil. It depicts the average curvature of the aerofoil

> The leading edge is the point where the mean camber line intersects the front part of the aerofoil section. The trailing edge is the point where the mean camber line intersects the rear part

The chord line is a straight line joining the leading edge and the trailing edge. The length of the chord line is known as the chord.

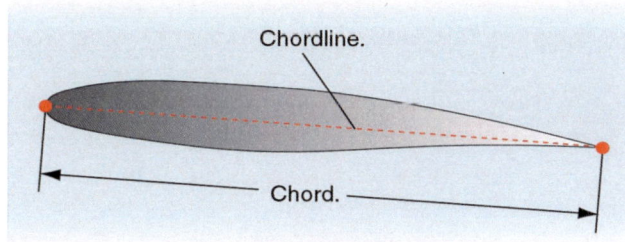

Figure 1.32 Chord line

The chord of a wing may vary greatly from its root near the fuselage to the wingtip. The root chord is greater than the tip chord.

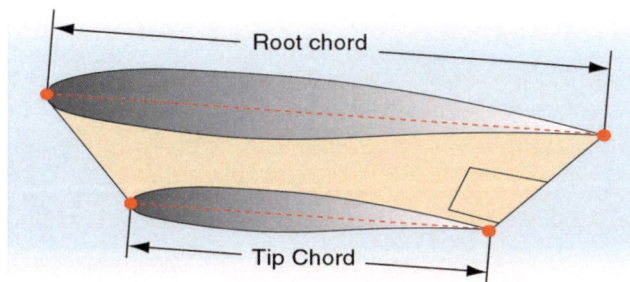

Figure 1.33 Chord line at the wing root and wing tip

> The chord line is a straight line joining the leading edge and the trailing edge
> Chord is the length of the chord line

The distance between the mean camber line and the chord line is called camber.
The point where the distance between the mean camber line and the chord line is the greatest is called the maximum camber. A symmetrical aerofoil has zero camber.

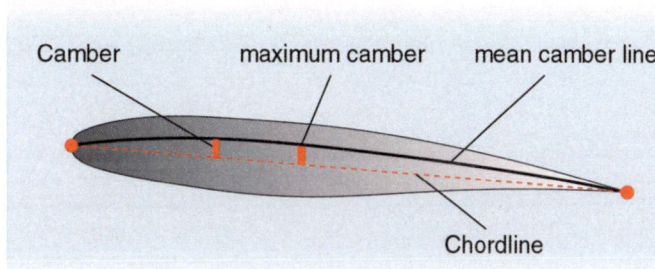

Figure 1.34 Camber

> The distance between the mean camber line and the chord line is called the camber. The point where this distance is greatest is called the maximum camber

The maximum thickness of an aerofoil is measured where the distance is the greatest between the upper and the lower surfaces.

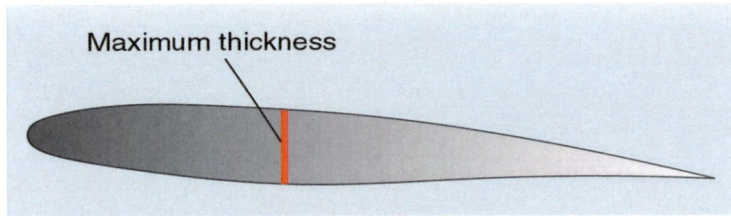

Figure 1.35 Thickness

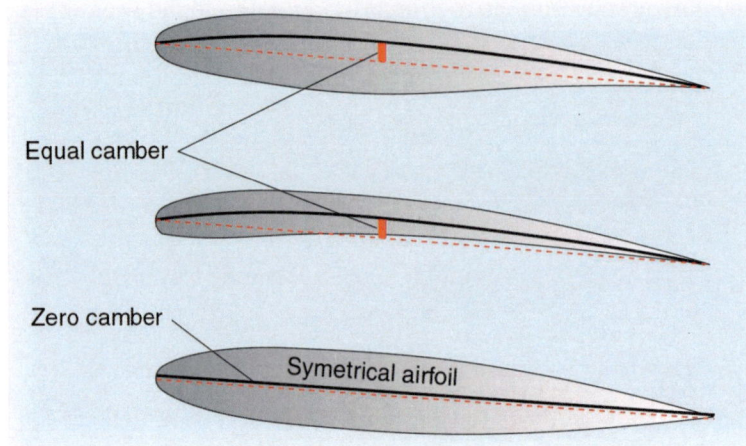

Figure 1.36 A highly cambered wing may be thick or thin.

The radius of the leading edge of the aerofoil has a great impact on the behaviour of the flow around the aerofoil. A relatively large leading edge radius makes it easier for the airflow to follow the aerofoil upper surface at high angles of attack. A very small leading edge radius may cause the flow separation to start at the leading edge instead of the trailing edge.

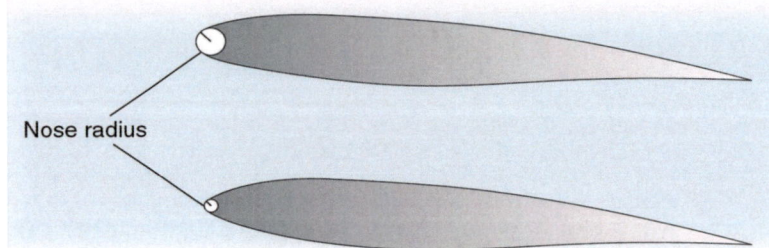

Figure 1.37 Nose radius

The angle of attack is the angle between the chord line of the aerofoil and the free stream V. It is abbreviated as A.of.A or by the character α. The angle of attack is always based on the relative airflow free from the influence of the aerofoil.

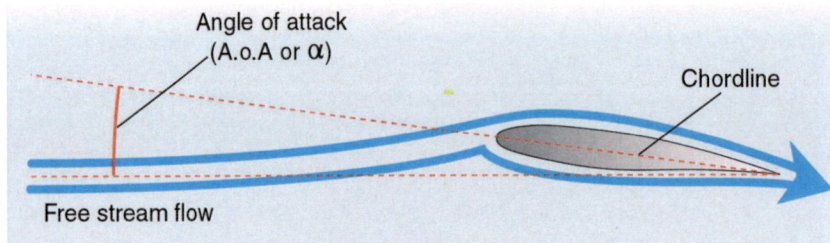

Figure 1.38 Angle of attack

The local angle of attack is the angle between the chord line of the aerofoil and the relative airflow. It is abbreviated as A.o.A or by the character α

The A.of.A is usually given as a value relative to the aircraft symmetrical axis. It is important not to confuse the angle of attack with the pitch angle or the attitude of the aircraft, which is relative to the horizon.
The figure below shows a climb situation, where the pitch angle from the horizon to the aircraft axis is large, but the angle of attack from the air flow to the aircraft axis is actually quite small.

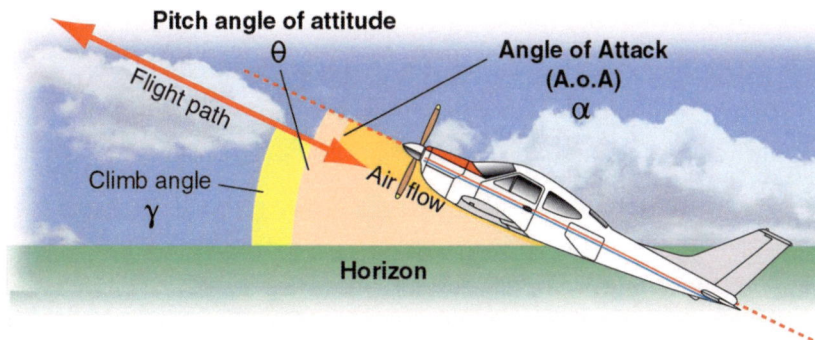

Figure 1.39 Large pitch angle but small angle of attack

1.4.1   *Distribution of local velocity and pressure on the aerofoil section*

Due to the pressure distribution around a lifting surface there will always be an upwash of the airflow in front of the aerofoil and a downwash behind it.
The airflow close to and ahead of the aerofoil is pushed forwards, giving a gradual decrease in speed relative to the aerofoil. The airflow that meets the aerofoil surface at a perpendicular angle stops when it reaches the surface. That point is called the stagnation point.

Figure 1.40 Stagnation point

Near a lifting surface there is an upwash of the airflow in front of the aerofoil and a downwash behind it.

The stagnation point is near the leading edge of the aerofoil where the airflow stops and the surrounding flow splits to follow either the upper or the lower surface

The air following the upper surface accelerates towards the area with lower pressure, reaching the maximum speed where the pressure gradient is at maximum at approximately the thickest part of the aerofoil section, and then decelerates gradually as it deviates from the area with lowest pressure.
The air that flows under the aerofoil is moved upwards ahead of the aerofoil in order to avoid the higher pressure below the surface and decelerate as it flows towards the higher pressure. The air then progressively accelerates as it approaches the trailing edge.

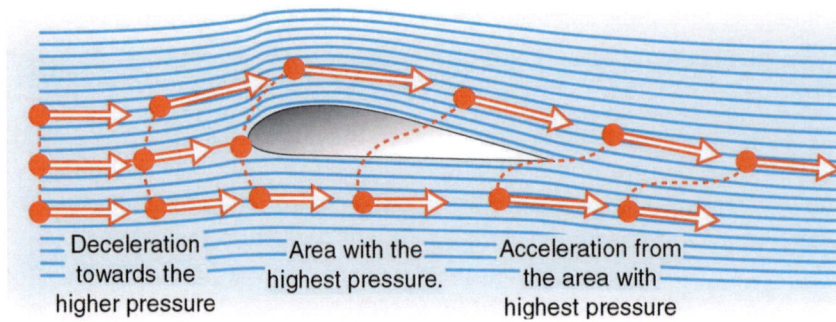

Deceleration towards the higher pressure — Area with the highest pressure. — Acceleration from the area with highest pressure

Figure 1.41 Acceleration of air towards the trailing edge

Consequently the velocity of the airflow varies chord wise and is different on the upper and the lower surface. When the airflow reaches the trailing edge, there are equal velocities of the air from both surfaces, but the air elements that were divided at the leading edge have different positions due to the circulation of the air around the aerofoil.

At the trailing edge, the air above and below the aerofoil has the same velocity, but the elements of air from the upper surface are further back than the elements of the lower surface.

An increase in local speed causes a decrease in static pressure over the surface. A decrease in local speed causes an increase in static pressure over the surface. On most parts of the lower surface of the aerofoil there is therefore a slightly higher static pressure than the free stream static pressure.

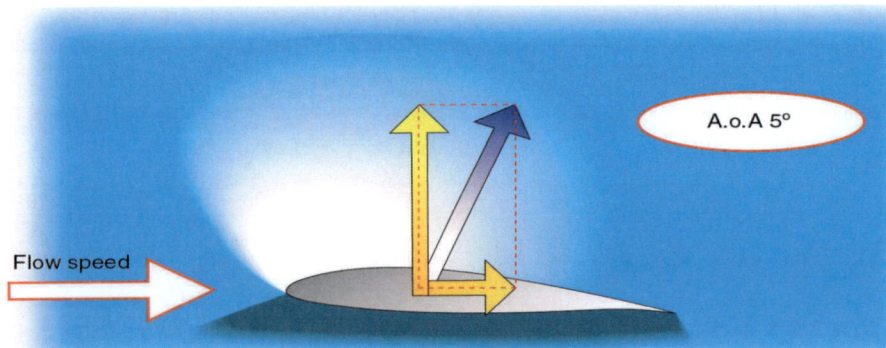

Flow speed

A.o.A 5°

Figure 1.42 Pressure distribution patterns (lighter areas represent a lower pressure than the free stream static pressure, and darker areas represent a higher static pressure)

At a higher angle of attack there is a higher pressure below and lower pressure above the aerofoil, which increases the flow velocity at the upper surface near the leading edge. This increases the total pressure difference, creating a higher lift at the same flow velocity.

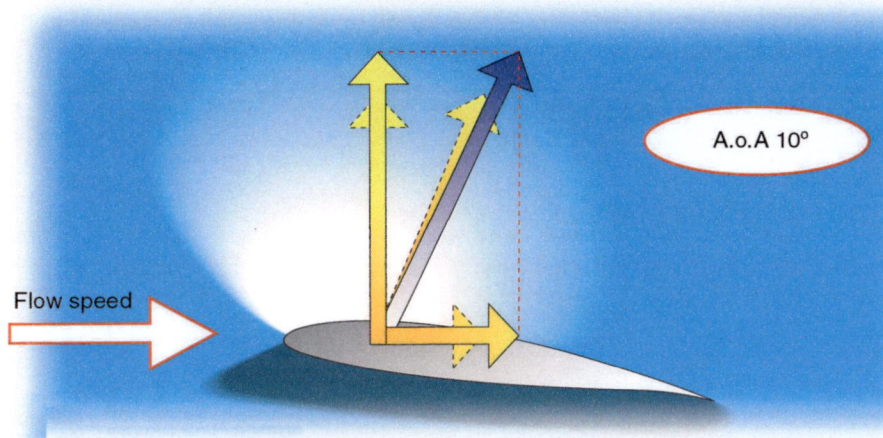

Figure 1.43 More lift at higher angle of attack for the same flow velocity

On a cambered aerofoil section with a very low angle of attack, both upper and lower surface pressure can be lower than the free stream static pressure. As long as lift is produced, there will be a pressure difference between the surfaces.

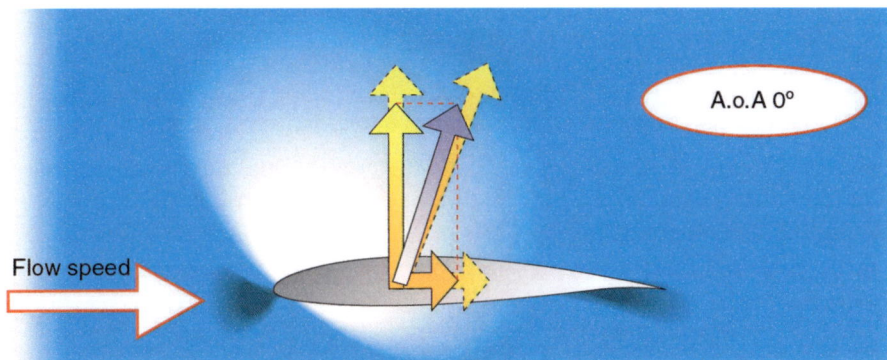

Figure 1.44 Cambered aerofoil

To simplify the drawings of pressure distribution, arrows pointing away from the aerofoil to indicate a pressure less than the free airstream static pressure may be employed. Arrows pointing towards the surface indicate a pressure greater than the free airstream static pressure. A minus sign indicates lower pressure and a plus sign to indicates a relatively higher pressure than the free airstream pressure.

Figure 1.45 Pressure patterns

1.4.2   *Centre of pressure*

The difference in pressure between the upper and lower surfaces of the aerofoil is the origin of the total aerodynamic force exerted on the aerofoil. The total aerodynamic force acts along a line whose intersection with the chord line is called the centre of pressure, abbreviated C.P. The total aerodynamic force has two

CRANFIELD AVIATION TRAINING SCHOOL LTD. PART-FCL GBR.ATO-0136
CATS INNOVATION CENTRE, LUTON, Bedfordshire LU2 8DL U.K.   www.catsaviation.com
1-42   Principles of Flight

components, one perpendicular to the relative airflow called lift and the other parallel to the relative airflow called drag.

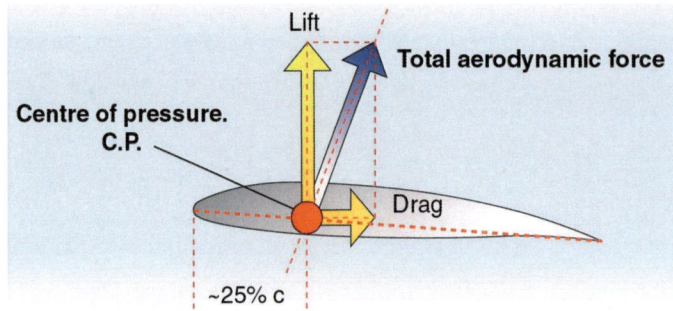

Figure 1.46 Centre of pressure

The total aerodynamic force acts at the centre of pressure (CP)

The location of the C.P. varies with the angle of attack but in general it is located within the forward half of the chord at approximately 25 % of the chord.

1.5 Behaviour when changing the angle of attack

1.5.1 Critical angle of attack and stall

When the angle of attack is low, a streamline flow around the aerofoil may be observed. The streamlines follow the upper surface of the wing all the way to the trailing edge. The air flows first towards decreasing pressure, then towards increasing pressure.

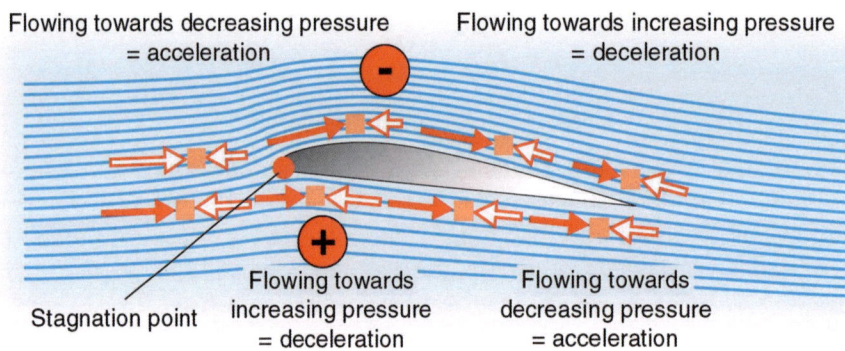

Figure 1.47 Streamline flow

When the angle of attack is increased, the stagnation point is moved further down on the lower surface, the circulation will increase and the differences of the local velocities around the aerofoil will be greater.

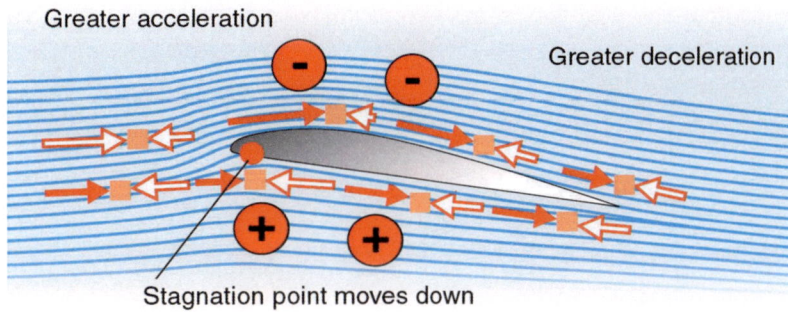

Figure 1.48 With increasing angle of attack the stagnation point is moved further down on the lower surface, the circulation increases and the differences of the local velocities around the aerofoil are greater

If the angle of attack is increased to a certain degree, the pressure difference between the area with maximum velocity and the trailing edge may become too great, slowing down the flow velocity near the trailing edge. This prevents the air from following the surface and causes the airflow to break away and separate from the rear surface.

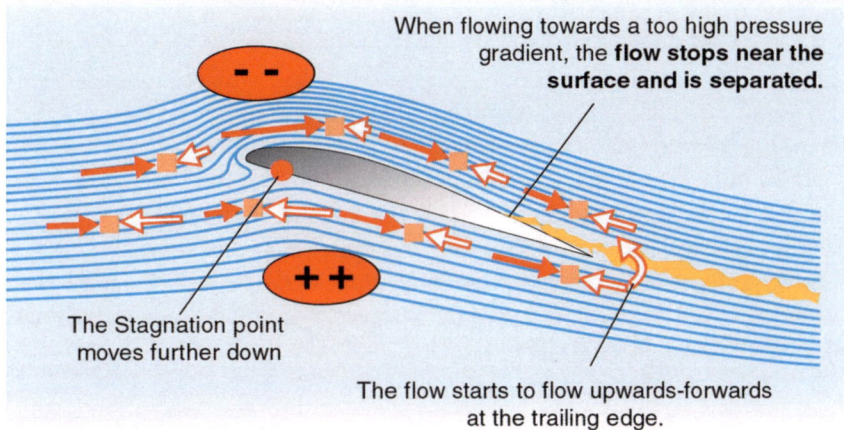

Figure 1.49 Flow separation with high angle of attack

When the angle of attack is increased, the area of separation becomes greater and very turbulent. The point where the separation starts, called the separation point, moves forward to the area with the lowest pressure.

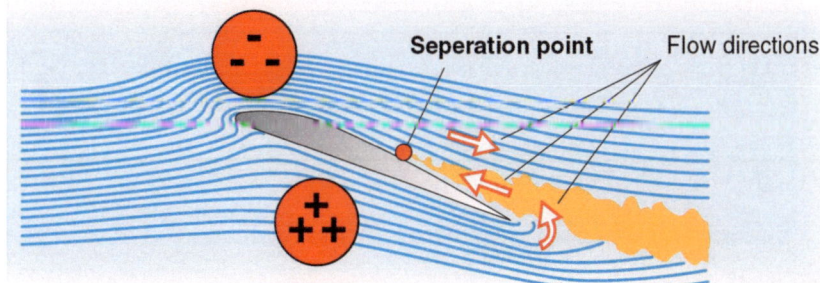

Figure 1.50 Separation point

The airflow breaks away and separates from the surface at the separation point and becomes very turbulent.

If the angle of attack is increased further, the separation point moves gradually towards the leading edge

If a certain value of the angle of attack, called the critical angle of attack, α_{crit}, or stall angle of attack, is exceeded the airflow becomes separated over a very large portion of the upper surface of the aerofoil. The separation of airflow makes the static pressure in this area of the upper surface increase which means less

CRANFIELD AVIATION TRAINING SCHOOL LTD. PART-FCL GBR.ATO-0136
CATS INNOVATION CENTRE, LUTON, Bedfordshire LU2 8DL U.K.   www.catsaviation.com

1-44   Principles of Flight

pressure difference in comparison with the pressure on the lower surface. Lift can increase no further. This condition is defined as aerofoil stall.

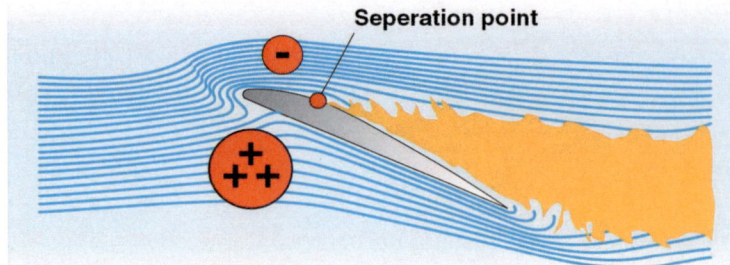

Figure 1.51 The stall

If the critical angle of attack or stall angle of attack is exceeded, the airflow is separated on a very large portion of the upper surface of the aerofoil causing less pressure differences. This condition is defined as aerofoil stall

The expansion of the zone of lower static pressure on the upper surface of the aerofoil and the movement of its maximum value towards the leading edge continue until the angle of attack reaches the stall angle of attack. Once the stall angle of attack is exceeded, the airflow breaks away completely from the upper surface of the aerofoil and the aerofoil is stalled. The streamline flow over the upper surface of the aerofoil is reduced and as a consequence, the zone of lower static pressure on the upper surface of the aerofoil is also much reduced. When the airflow over the wing is separated from the surface, the downward acceleration of the air mass is greatly reduced. This stalled condition is also known as loss of impulse.

The shape of the trailing edge is very important in this matter. A very sharp trailing edge permits the upper airflow to maintain a higher speed at a higher angle of attack. If the trailing edge is rounded, the high pressure from the lower side will easily flow upwards / forwards and slow down the flow velocity from the upper surface, giving a rather low critical angle of attack.

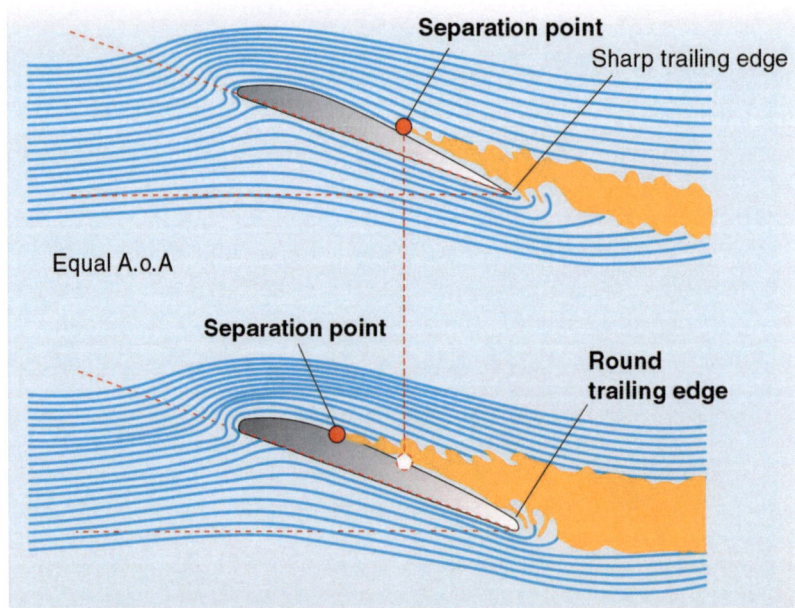

Figure 1.52 Sharp trailing edges increase stalling angle of attack. Rounded trailing edges decrease stalling angle of attack

A rounded trailing edge gives a lower stall angle of attack

1.5.2 Total aerodynamic force and centre of pressure at a changed angle of attack

The change in the distribution of pressure around the aerofoil, which is a result of the increase in the angle of attack, causes a similar change in the total aerodynamic force. With an increase in the angle of attack at a constant speed, the value of the total aerodynamic force increases at the same time as the centre of pressure moves towards the leading edge. Once the critical angle has been reached, the total aerodynamic force reaches its maximum value, and the centre of pressure will be located in its most forward position.

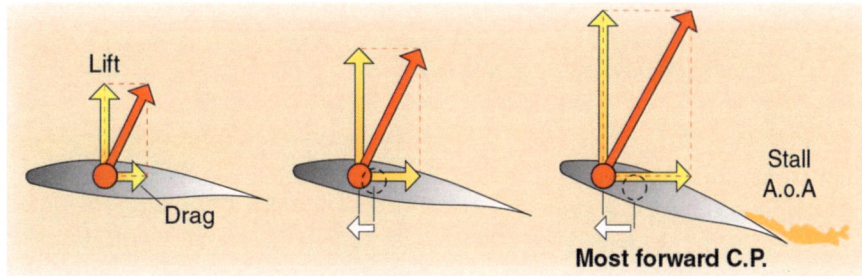

Figure 1.53 Once the critical angle has been reached, the total aerodynamic force reaches its maximum value, and the centre of pressure will be located in its most forward position

Once the critical angle of attack is exceeded and the aerofoil is stalled, the total aerodynamic force is directed more rearwards. The lift decreases dramatically, and the centre of pressure moves rearwards.

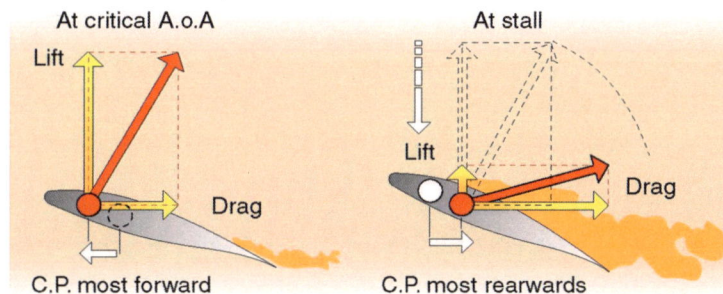

Figure 1.54 Once the critical angle of attack is exceeded and the aerofoil is stalled, the total aerodynamic force is directed more rearwards. The lift decreases dramatically, and the centre of pressure moves rearwards.

Lift increases with an increase in the angle of attack up to the point where it reaches its maximum value. The maximum value of lift is obtained when the angle of attack is equal to the stall angle of attack. An angle of attack higher than the stall angle of attack will only reduce the lift.

> The maximum value of lift is obtained when the angle of attack is equal to the stall angle of attack

Drag, however, continues to increase with a further increase in the angle of attack. While lift generated by a stalled aerofoil decreases dramatically, drag is still increasing considerably.

> The lift generated by a stalled aerofoil is still present but decreases dramatically while the drag still increases considerably

CHAPTER 2

Lift

2.1   *Lift Formula*

2.1.1   *Presentation of the lift formula*

Lift is created by the difference in pressure between the upper and lower surfaces of the aerofoil. It is a component of the total aerodynamic force perpendicular to the free stream.

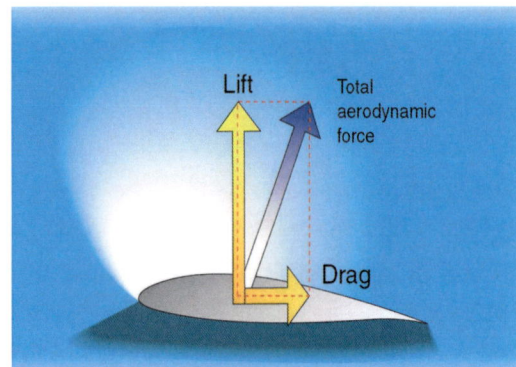

Figure 2.1

> Lift is always perpendicular to the flight path (or the free stream)

Lift can be defined by using the formula below, which comprises most factors that affect lift in various ways.

> Lift = Dynamic pressure x Coefficient of Lift x Wing Surface
>
> or:
>
> $$L = q \, C_L \, S$$

2.1.2   *Dynamic Pressure*

Dynamic pressure varies with speed. The higher the speed, the higher the dynamic pressure and consequently, the lift.

> DYNAMIC PRESSURE = $\frac{1}{2} \rho V^2$

> V represents TAS and since the term is squared a doubling of TAS will mean that dynamic pressure is quadrupled

Dynamic pressure also varies with density and, in this case too, the higher the density the higher the dynamic pressure and consequently, the lift. As you will remember, if the speed remains constant and density increases, we will have a greater number of molecules per second that impact the wing, therefore dynamic pressure is proportional to density ρ.

2.1.3   *Physical explanation of Coefficient of Lift: C_L*

If a thin flat plate and an aerofoil section is placed in a fluid in relative motion, the two bodies create two different pressure distributions and the difference in pressure between upper and lower surfaces creates two different values of total aerodynamic force.

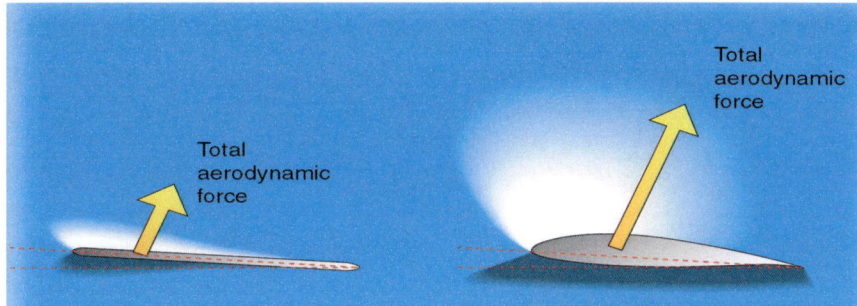

Figure 2.2 Different aerofoil shapes create different values of aerodynamic force

Increasing the angle of attack of a given aerofoil increases the circulation and results in a greater pressure difference between the surfaces and a higher lift.

Figure 2.3 Increasing angle of attack increases the value aerodynamic force

The ability of the aerofoil to create lift is therefore related to the angle of attack and the shape of the aerofoil section. This is represented by a non-dimensional coefficient called the coefficient of lift, abbreviated C_L.

The greater the coefficient of lift, the greater the ability to produce lift

In order to find out the coefficient of lift for a certain aerofoil at different A.o.A., the lift for every A.o.A is divided by the given dynamic pressure, $\frac{1}{2}\rho V^2$, and the wing (or reference) area, S.

$$C_L = \frac{L}{\frac{1}{2}\rho V^2 S}$$

For a two-dimensional wing, the wing area, S, per unit length is the chord (c) multiplied by unity.

The ability of the aerofoil to create lift is related to the angle of attack and the shape of the aerofoil section. For a given aerofoil shape and A.o.A there is a certain coefficient of lift

2.1.4   *Wing area*

Lift is a force and is affected by wing area. A force is the result of the action of pressure on a surface. Force = Pressure x Surface Area, therefore the larger the area, the greater the force. With a constant dynamic pressure and coefficient of lift, the greater the wing area, the greater the lift. If the wing area is doubled, the lift will also approximately doubled.

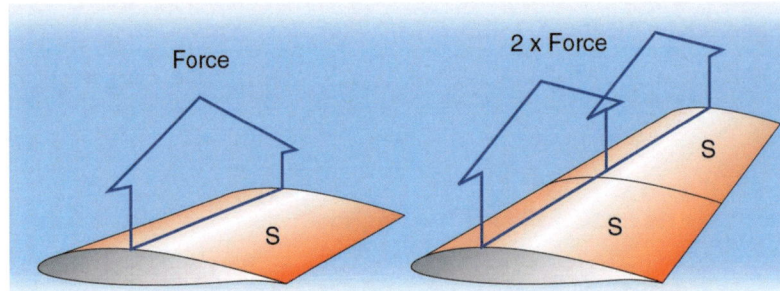

Figure 2.4 Increasing wing area increases lift

2.1.5   *Wing loading*

During flight, lift is necessary to counteract the weight. The ratio between aircraft weight and wing area is called wing loading. For example an aircraft with 20 m² of wing area and a weight of 1000 kg will have to carry 50 kg for every m² of wing surface and has a wing loading of 50 kg / m².

$$\text{Wing Loading} = \frac{\text{Aircraft Weight}}{\text{Wing Area}}$$

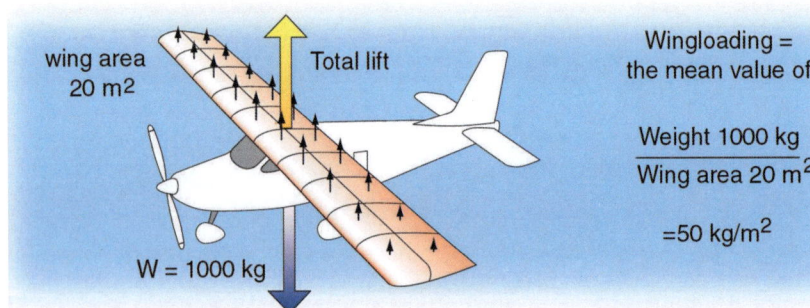

Figure 2.5 The ratio between weight and area is called wing loading

2.1.6   *Small pressure differences to produce lift*

Even though the pressure differences around the wings may be very small, the lifting force will be great, as shown in the following example: The static pressure at sea level is approx. 10 N / cm² equal to 100 000 N / m². If this pressure decreases by only 2% at the upper surface and increases by 1 % at the lower surface, i.e. a total difference of 3%, the pressure difference will be 3000 N / m². This force will lift approximately 300 kg / m². A quite normal wing loading may range from about 50 kg / m² for a light aircraft to 500 kg / m² for a jet fighter.

2.2   *Effect of angle of attack on lift*

2.2.1   *C_L versus A.of.A*

The coefficient of lift is directly affected by the shape of the aerofoil section and by the angle of attack. We will now analyse the effects on lift when we change the angle of attack for a certain aerofoil section.

Let us place a wing with a known symmetrical profile and a certain surface area in a wind tunnel. Using a fan, we can create an airflow with a certain speed V and a certain density ρ which will be constant during the entire experiment. Using a dynamometer we can measure the lift at every angle of attack and, dividing it by the dynamic pressure and the wing surface area, obtain the Coefficient of Lift. If we use a symmetrical aerofoil, at zero angle of attack we have zero lift.

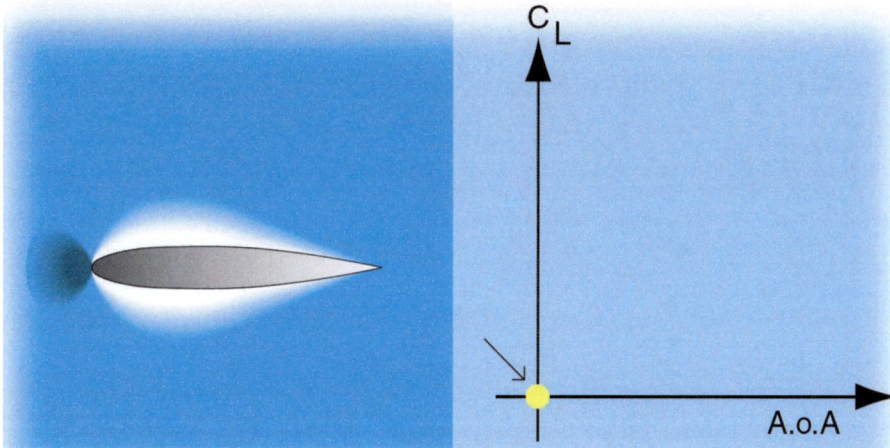

Figure 2.6

If we draw a curve representing the coefficient of lift as a function of the angle of attack as shown above, called a C_L/α curve, the first point will correspond to zero angle of attack and zero coefficient of lift.

Let us now change the angle of attack. With a small value, we can see that the coefficient of lift increases proportionally so that we get a new dot on the graph.

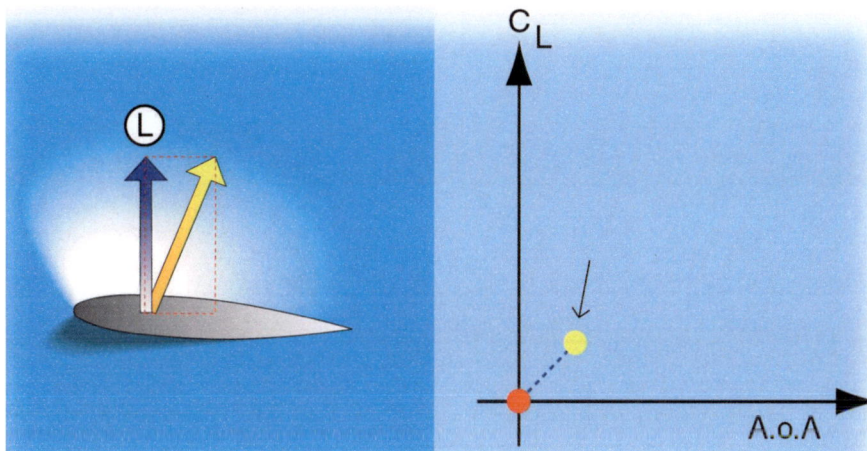

Figure 2.7

When we increase the angle of attack, the coefficient of lift also increases, giving another dot on the graph. This is achieved at a medium angle of attack like the one shown here.

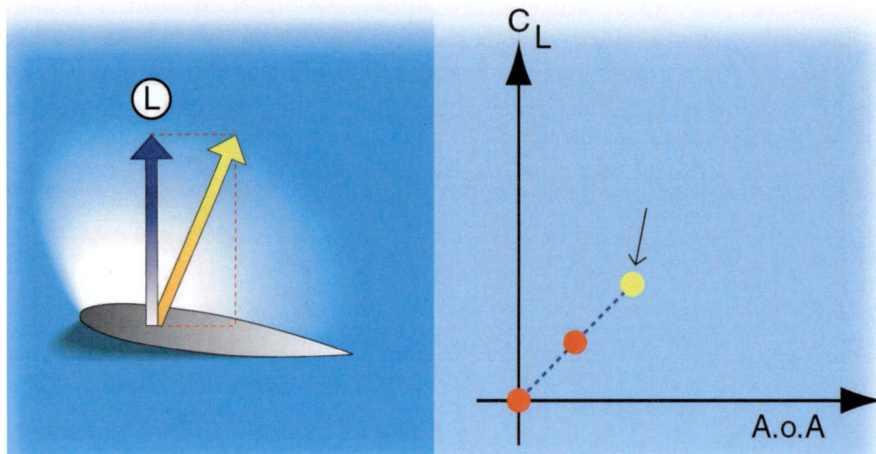

Figure 2.8

2.2.2　　　　C_{Lmax}

It has already been stated that at the stall angle of attack we have the maximum value of lift, corresponding to the maximum coefficient of lift.

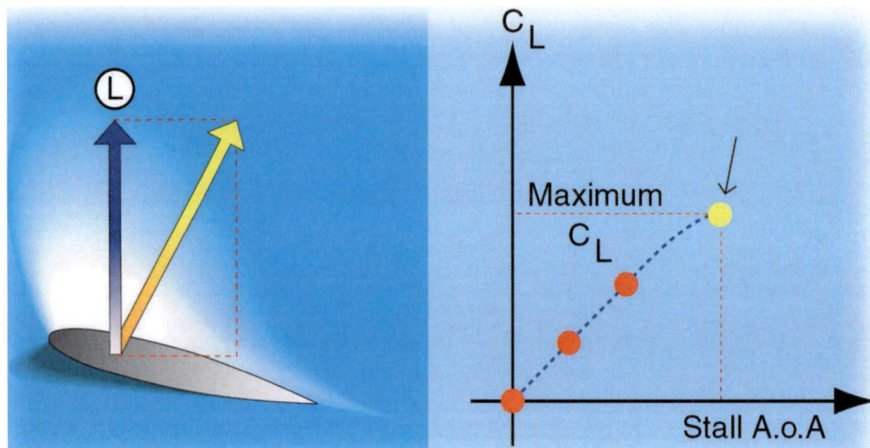

Figure 2.9

C_L increases until it reaches C_L max, which corresponds to the stall A.o.A

2.2.3　　　　*Stall angle of attack*

If we exceed the stall or "critical" angle of attack we note that the coefficient of lift, and thus lift, decreases dramatically. This, as you know, is the stall of the aerofoil.

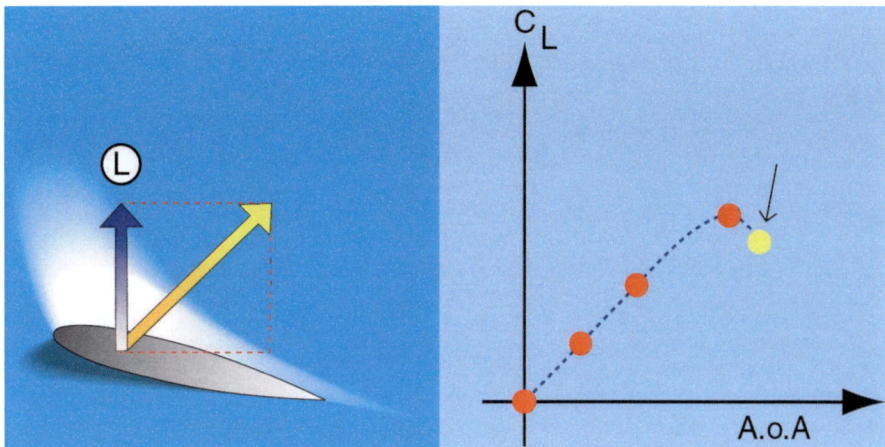

Figure 2.10

Here you find a typical curve of the coefficient of lift / angle of attack. It refers to a asymmetrical aerofoil. At an angle of attack of about 20° (the critical angle) we have the maximum coefficient of lift, about 1.6. By increasing the angle of attack, we reach aerofoil stall and the coefficient of lift therefore decreases rapidly.

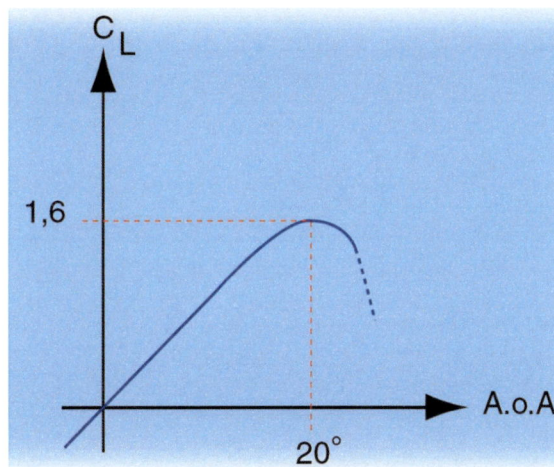

Figure 2.11

C_L increases correspondingly with the angle of attack. Above the stall A.of.A. C_L decreases rapidly.

2.3   *Effect of the aerofoil section on the C_L curve*

This section deals with the effect of aerofoil section on coefficient Lift curve.

2.3.1   *Symmetrical aerofoils and asymmetrical aerofoils*

Below, we have both a symmetrical aerofoil and an asymmetrical aerofoil. As we have learnt, the symmetrical aerofoil has zero camber and the asymmetrical one has a certain camber.

If we place a symmetrical aerofoil in an airflow, it will change the fluid speed around its surfaces. When the speed increases, the static pressure decreases; so in this case, we obtain the same suction above as below the aerofoil. As a result of the equal and opposite pressure distribution, the symmetrical aerofoil creates zero lift at zero angle of attack.

An asymmetrical aerofoil also changes the fluid speed around its surfaces. However, as you already know, the flow above the upper surface will in this case create a lower static pressure. As a result, we will obtain an asymmetrical pressure distribution. The fluid accelerates around both the upper and the lower surfaces but in different ways. We will have a greater suction above than below, thus obtaining a positive lift already at zero angle of attack.

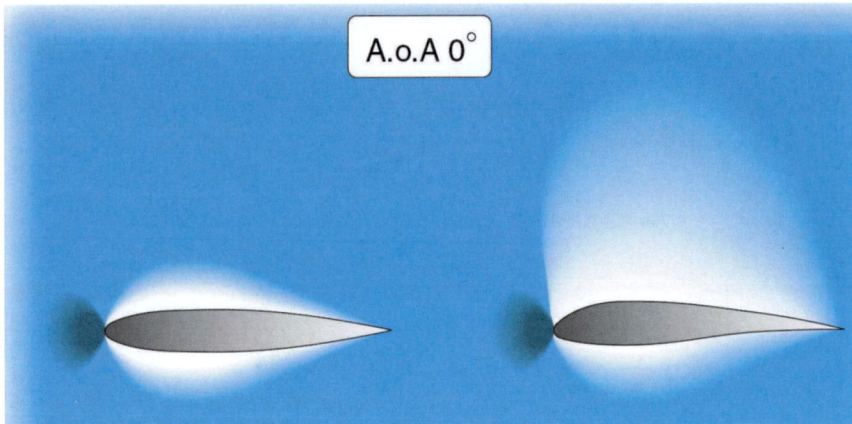

Figure 2.12

At zero A.of.A. an asymmetrical aerofoil gives a small lift

For an asymmetrical aerofoil the curve of the coefficient of lift /angle of attack does not start from the axis origin because at zero angle of attack we already have a certain amount of lift.

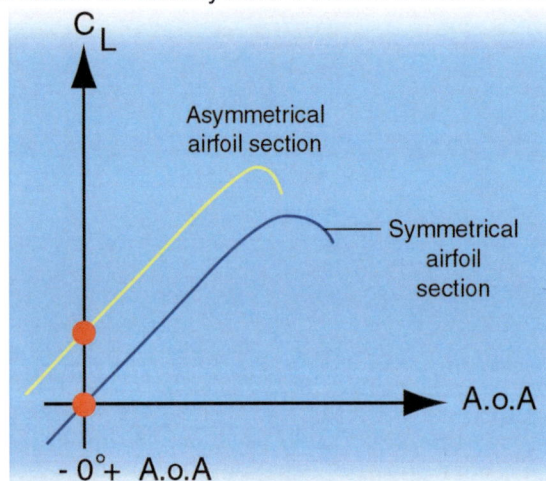

Figure 2.13

When the fluid flows parallel to the chord line direction of an asymmetrical aerofoil, it does not give zero lift. To obtain zero lift from an asymmetrical aerofoil, it must be at a negative angle of attack. In this position, the fluid will flow around the aerofoil along a particular direction called the "zero lift line".

CRANFIELD AVIATION TRAINING SCHOOL LTD. PART-FCL GBR.ATO-0136
CATS INNOVATION CENTRE, LUTON, Bedfordshire LU2 8DL U.K.

www.catsaviation.com

2-7

Principles of Flight

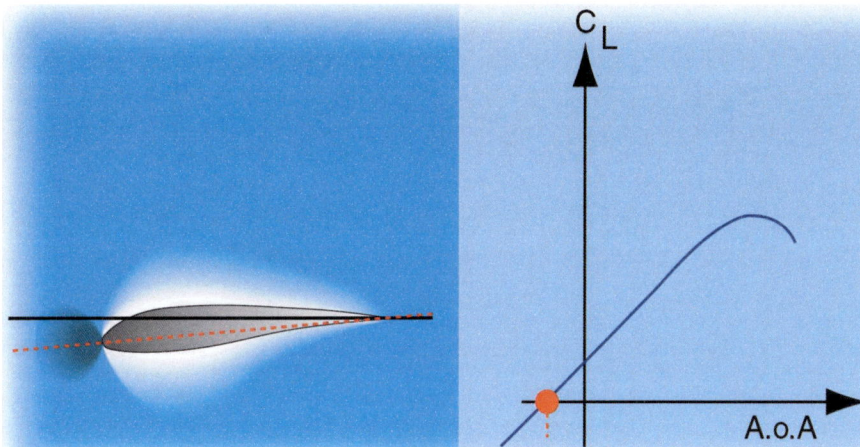

Figure 2.14

On an asymmetrical aerofoil section, the "zero lift line" will not coincide with the chord line.

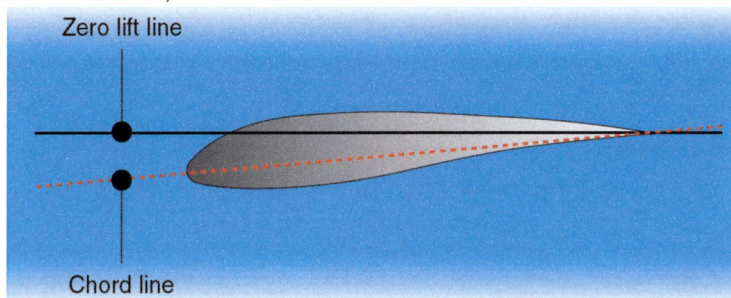

Figure 2.15

The angle between the chord line and the free stream is the geometrical A.of.A.

The angle between the zero lift line and the free stream is the aerodynamic A.of.A.

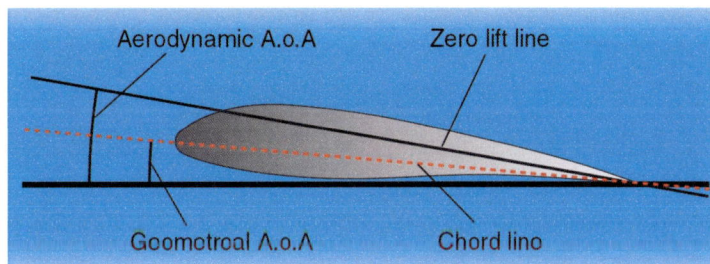

Figure 2.16

For a symmetrical aerofoil, the zero lift line coincides with the chord line so that the aerodynamic angle of attack coincides with the geometrical angle of attack. The C_L/α curve is normally based on the geometrical A.o.A.

2.3.2 *Effect of changing the camber and thickness of the aerofoil*

We have seen that at the same angle of attack, we obtain different coefficients of lift using different aerofoil section shapes.

The main geometrical characteristics of the aerofoil that affect the coefficient of lift are the thickness and the camber.

If we use aerofoils with the same camber but different thickness, we will note that by increasing thickness we obtain a higher coefficient of lift for a certain Angle of Attack but the slope of the C_L/a curves is equal.

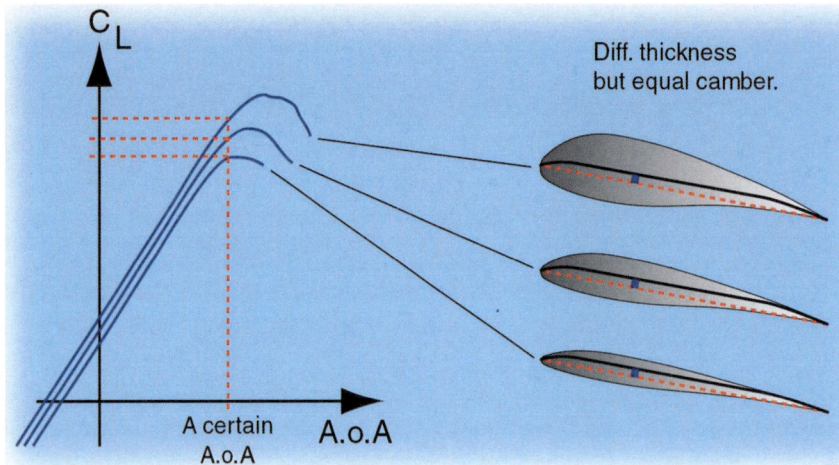

Figure 2.17

Changing the camber together with the thickness has a great influence on the curve of the coefficient of lift versus the angle of attack and on the maximum coefficient of lift.

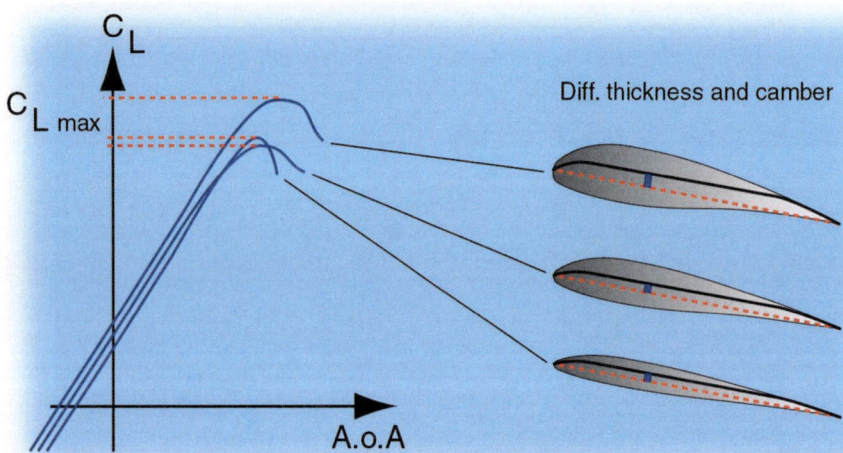

Figure 2.18

Camber in combination with thickness and nose radius have a great impact on the aerofoil stall characteristics. You can see that different geometrical characteristics of the aerofoil can cause different and sometimes more abrupt stall phenomena.

CRANFIELD AVIATION TRAINING SCHOOL LTD. PART-FCL GBR.ATO-0136
CATS INNOVATION CENTRE, LUTON, Bedfordshire LU2 8DL U.K.   www.catsaviation.com

2-9   Principles of Flight

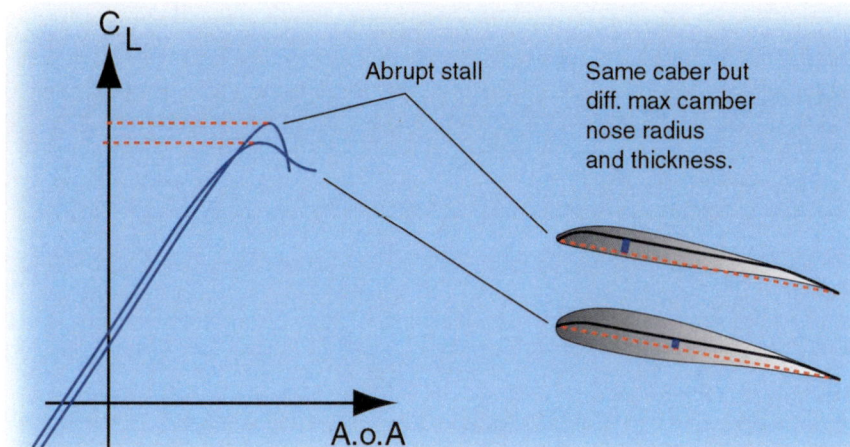

Figure 2.19

Camber, in combination with thickness and nose radius, has a great influence on the aerofoil stall characteristics

2.3.3   *Inverted flight and aerofoil section*

Despite of having a positively cambered aerofoil section, an aircraft is able to fly upside-down, but not at the same angle of attack as in normal flight at the same speed.

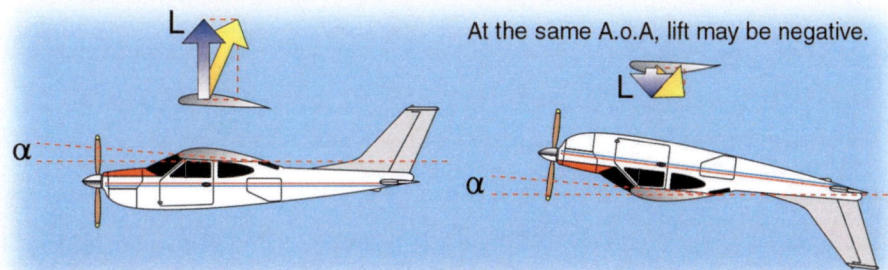

Figure 2.20

In order to sustain flight upside-down at equal speed, the A.of.A has to be much greater.

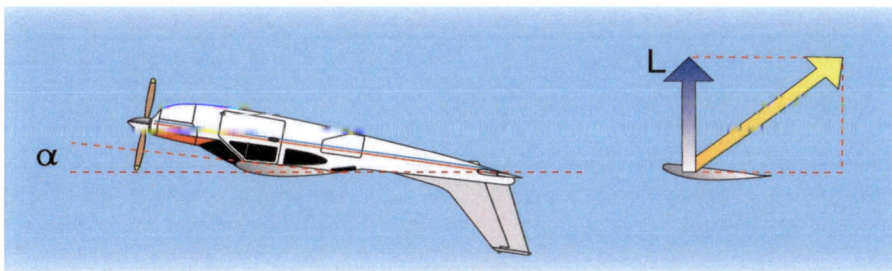

Figure 2.21

In order to understand the difference, let us look at a C_L/α graph for a certain wing with a positively cambered aerofoil section. In normal cruise conditions only a very low A.of.A is necessary in order to achieve the required lift.

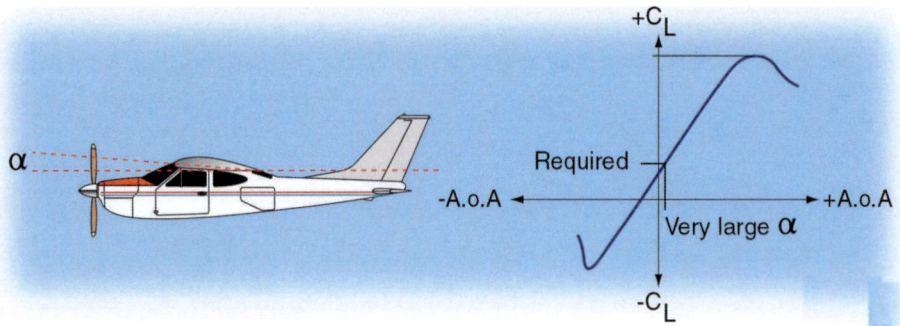

Figure 2.22

If we invert the curve of the C_L/A.of.A graph for the aerofoil section, we will see that in order to attain the same lift upside-down in equal conditions, the A.of.A has to be much higher in order to get the corresponding C_L value.

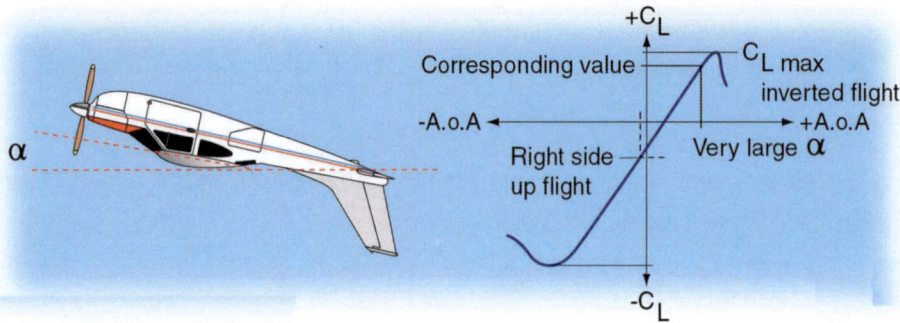

Figure 2.23

Notice the smaller margin to the maximum C_L, the stall A.of.A, and also the steeper drop of the curve after the critical A.of.A, which will cause an abrupt stall phenomenon.

The next figure illustrates how the pressure distribution may look for an aerofoil section in right side up and inverted flight respectively, having the same coefficient of lift.

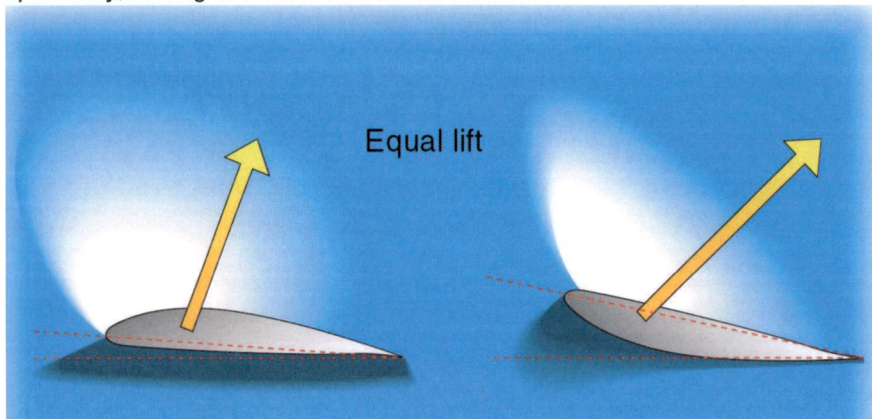

Figure 2.24

It is possible to fly upside-down with a positively cambered aerofoil wing, but at the cost of much deteriorated lift/drag and stall characteristics. When making inverted flight with a positively cambered wing, the A.o.A must be greater at equal speed and the stall characteristic is more violent than in erected flight. Since most aircraft have the wings at a certain angle of incidence to the aircraft longitudinal axis, the pitch angle has to be very high in order to maintain the altitude.

CRANFIELD AVIATION TRAINING SCHOOL LTD. PART-FCL GBR.ATO-0136
CATS INNOVATION CENTRE, LUTON, Bedfordshire LU2 8DL U.K.   www.catsaviation.com

2-11   Principles of Flight

2.4 Effect of dynamic pressure

This section describes the effects of speed and density on Lift, and the relationship between the Angle of Attack and speed.

2.4.1 Different speeds

Before continuing with the effect of dynamic pressure, you should be aware of the different ways speed can be expressed in aviation. What you see on the speed indicator is your indicated air speed (IAS), and for high speed aircraft, also the speed relative to the speed of sound or Mach number (Mach or M). But IAS is not the true speed relative to the air. It has to be corrected because of the errors due to the position of the tubes that feed the indicator with air for the static and dynamic pressure. Correction for position error gives the calibrated air speed (CAS). In addition, you have to make corrections for the outside air temperature (OAT), the pressure at that altitude, and, at high speeds, also for the compressibility effects that gives the Equivalent Air Speed (EAS). Finally, in order to know the speed relative to the ground you also have to take into account the component of wind speed in the flight direction.

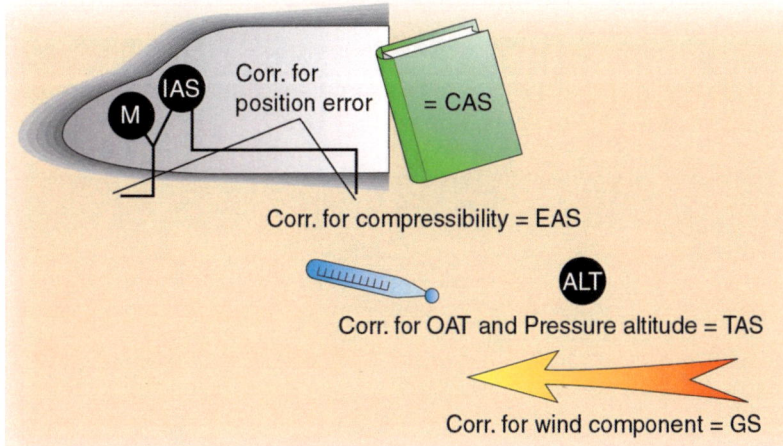

Figure 2.25

CAS and EAS are rather good approximations of the dynamic pressure. Note! If the speed in the different diagrams is only designated V, it is the true air speed TAS that is accounted for. You will find more information about speed in Mach numbers in the chapter 19.

2.4.2 Effects of speed and density

Lift is affected by the dynamic pressure. We can modify the dynamic pressure by acting on speed and/or density. Therefore we can change lift itself by modifying speed and/or density. An aerofoil section moving through the air at a speed V and at a certain angle of attack creates a certain amount of lift, which depends upon the air density. If the same aerofoil moves through a less dense mass of air, at the same speed and angle of attack, it will create less lift.

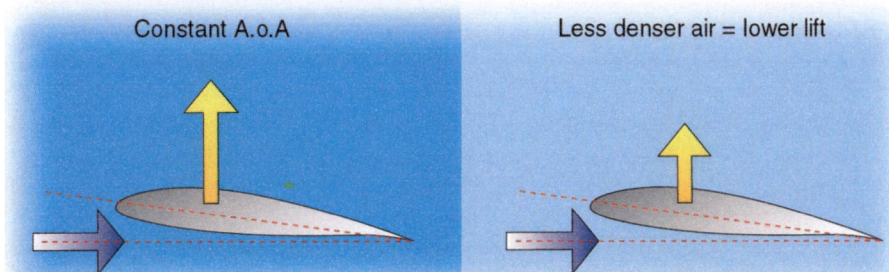

Figure 2.26

Lift depends upon ρ and V^2. If density decreases, lift also decreases.

We must change the speed in order to maintain the same value of dynamic pressure. For example, in order to create a certain amount of lift in less dense air at a constant angle of attack, the relative speed needs to be 100 KT instead of 80 KT in order to create the same lift.

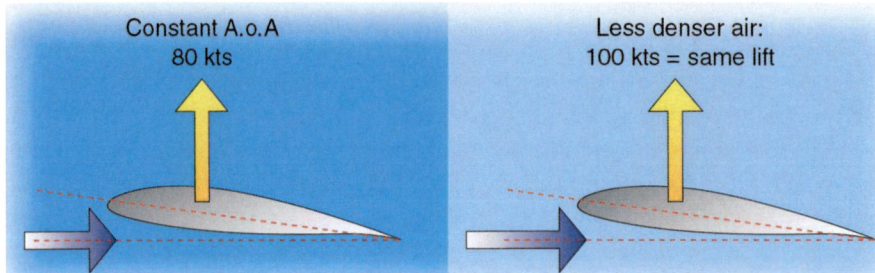

Figure 2.27

If density decreases, an increase in speed is necessary in order to maintain the same lift at constant A.of.A.

If we want to maintain the same TAS but still create the same amount of lift at a different air density, we must change the angle of attack, as the next example shows.

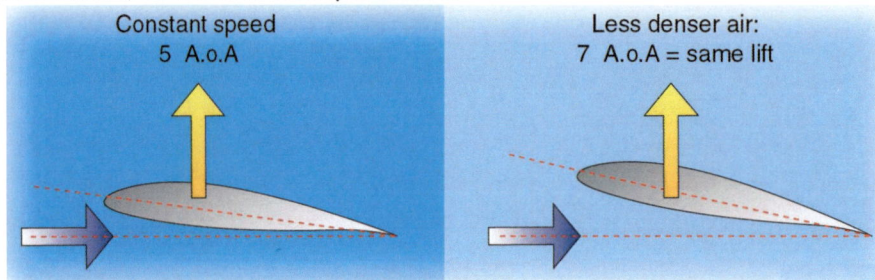

Figure 2.28

2.4.3   *Relationship between A.of.A. and airspeed*

In horizontal and level flight it is necessary to counteract the weight of the aircraft with lift. If the weight does not change, the lift must always be the same. Since the dynamic pressure varies with V^2, a reduction of the speed to half the value decreases the dynamic pressure to only a 1/4 of the previous value. In order to maintain constant lift when reducing speed, the lift coefficient has to increase. In this example, where the airspeed is 122 KT, we need an angle of attack of 1° only. This angle gives a coefficient of lift, C_L 0.2, sufficient to produce a lift equal to the weight of the aircraft. When the aircraft decelerates to 77 KT, we must increase the angle of attack to 5°, C_L 0.5, in order to obtain the same amount of lift.

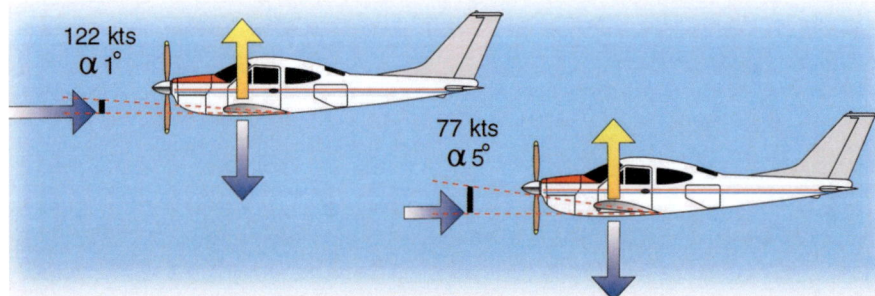

Figure 2.29

With constant density and wing loading, the A.o.A. and speed are closely related to each other

In order to further reduce the aircraft speed and remain at the same altitude, we must increase the angle of attack until reaching the critical one. The corresponding critical speed will be the lowest possible at that weight. We cannot maintain level flight below this speed without stalling. In fact, we can see that in this example, the wings must have an angle of attack equal to 15°, the stall A.of.A for that aircraft, in order to fly at 50 KT, thus obtaining the maximum C_L of 1.2.

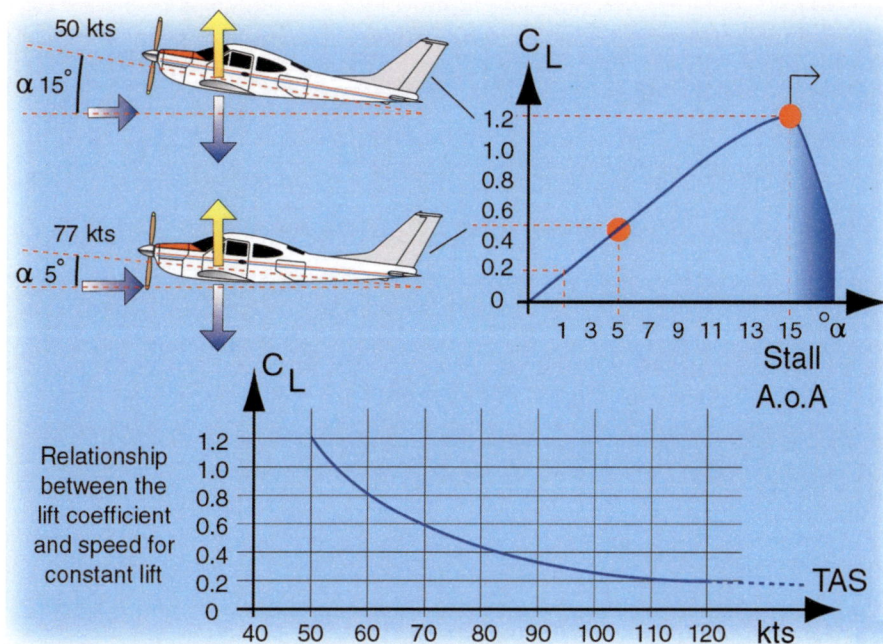

Figure 2.30

At constant lift but half the TAS, the lift coefficient C_L needs to be 4 times higher. Constant IAS gives constant A.o.A and C_L at incompressible flow speeds

It is very important that pilots know the relationship between airspeed and angle of attack, because in light aircraft there is generally nothing on board indicating the angle of attack, only an airspeed indicator.

The stall A.o.A. gives the maximum C_L and the minimum speed allowed for that weight. The stall is due to the angle of attack being too high and not directly to the speed being too low

When the stall angle of attack is exceeded, we experience stall phenomena. The corresponding speed which will be a little lower than the stall A.o.A, is called the stalling speed for straight and level flight and is designed V_S. However, it is important to remember that the stall is due to the angle of attack being too high and not directly to the speed being too low. You may also stall at a very high speed if, for example, you are making a very steep turn or a rapid pull-up.

2.5   The lift formula

In order to understand why there are limitations for flying in some conditions, you have to understand and remember the factors that influence the creation of lift:

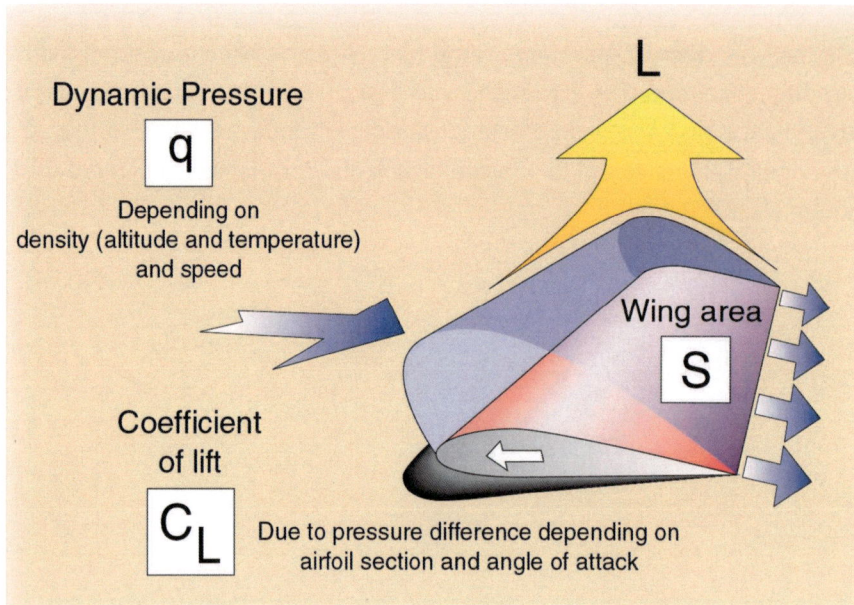

Figure 2.31

Lift = Dynamic pressure x Coefficient of Lift x Wing area

$$L = q\, C_L\, S$$

CRANFIELD AVIATION TRAINING SCHOOL LTD. PART-FCL GBR.ATO-0136
CATS INNOVATION CENTRE, LUTON, Bedfordshire LU2 8DL U.K.

www.catsaviation.com

2-15

Principles of Flight

CHAPTER 3

Drag

3.1   Introduction to drag

Drag is the aeronautical term for the resistance experienced by all bodies moving through the air. Drag is one of the components of the total aerodynamic force. It is the component that is parallel to the relative motion and counteracts the motion of the body forward into the free stream direction, i.e. drag is always parallel to the free stream and is opposite to the flight path.

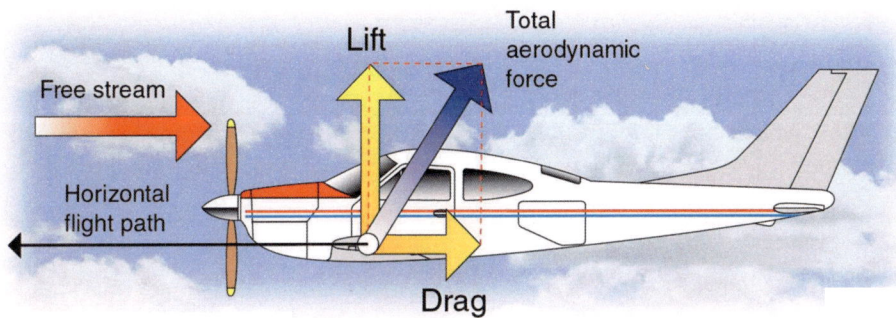

Figure 3.1

> Drag is the component of the total aerodynamic force which resists the motion of the body forward into the wind direction

3.1.1   Drag is always parallel to the relative wind.

The force that we use to counteract drag in level flight is the powerplant-produced thrust. It is therefore easy to imagine the advantages of low drag. To obtain the same performance with less drag, smaller engines are required. In that way fuel consumption will be lower, a greater payload can be carried and the operating costs will be lower.

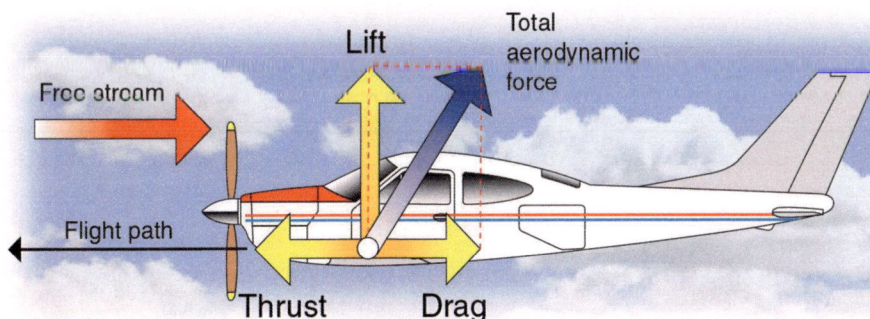

Figure 3.2

The total drag is the sum of the various drag forces acting on the aeroplane. A part of total drag is called parasite drag, or more correctly: zero lift drag.

3.1.2 *Streamline and turbulent flows*

In order to have a good understanding of the mechanisms of drag creation we need to review some basic concepts concerning the flow around a body. Streamline flow is a flow where the successive molecules of air follow the same steady path. A streamline indicates the direction of flow at all points along it: there will be no air crossing the streamline. In a streamline flow, all successive molecules passing through a specific point will do that with the same velocity and direction.

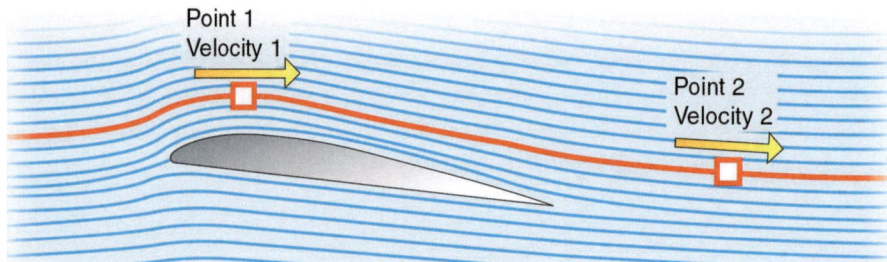

Figure 3.3

Turbulent flow is a flow where the elements of air do not follow a steady path. In turbulent flow, the fluid elements passing through a fixed point will change both the magnitude and the direction of their velocity V in the course of time.

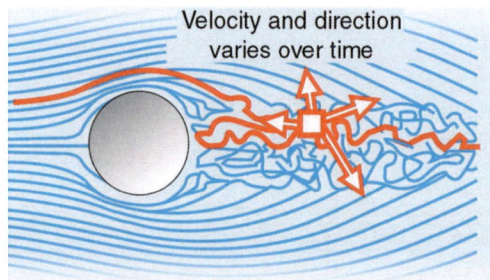

Figure 3.4

Let us consider the surface of a body in contact with an airflow at a certain airspeed V. As we approach the surface of the body, the local speed decreases; the closer we come to the surface of the body, the lower the speed will be. When we reach the surface of the body, the local speed is zero.

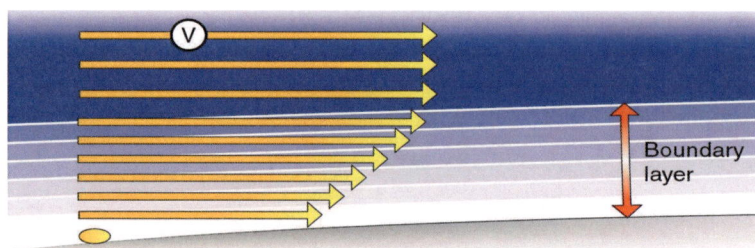

Figure 3.5

The region between the surface of the body, where the local speed is zero, and the first point, where the local speed is equal to the speed of the airflow, is called the boundary layer

The change in speed is due to the fact that the influence of the fluid viscosity starts to make itself felt at a certain distance from the surface. Normally the boundary layer is a very thin layer. In the section shown, for example, its actual thickness is only about 2 to 10 mm. However, on the aft body of e.g. a long fuselage, it may be ~100 mm. Due to the viscosity effect, there is friction between the body surface and the air.

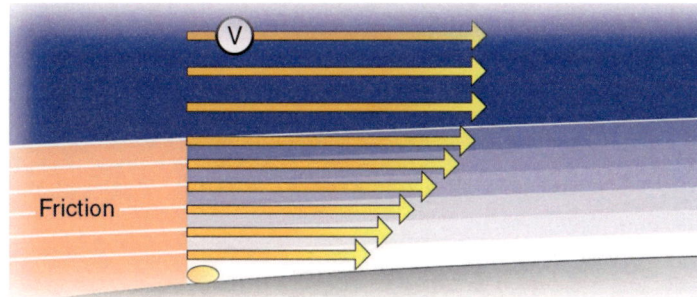

Figure 3.6

3.1.3 *Laminar boundary layer, Transition point, Turbulent boundary layer*

If the surface of the body is very smooth, the flow in the boundary layer will initially be very orderly and parallel. Consequently, above this smooth surface we have the so-called "laminar boundary layer".

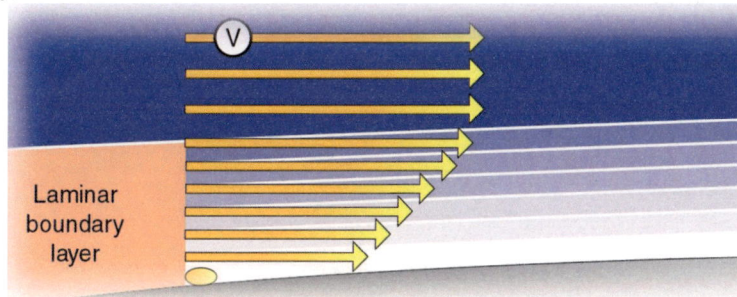

Figure 3.7

The first part of the boundary layer above a smooth surface is the LAMINAR layer

The laminar boundary layer is, however, very unstable and small disturbances such as rivets or even scratches on the surface will trigger a tumbling motion resulting in a transition to a turbulent boundary layer.

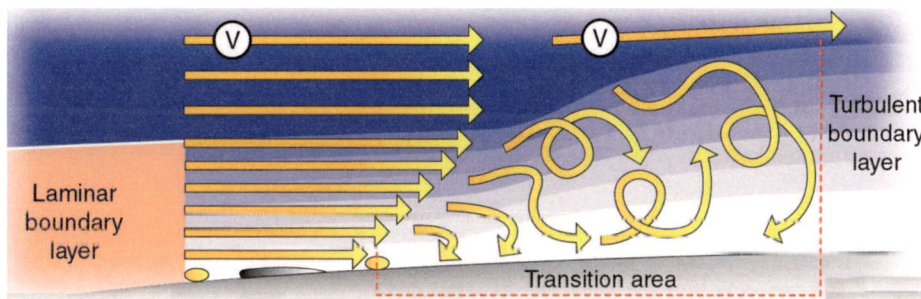

Figure 3.8

Slight disturbances may cause a TURBULENT BOUNDARY LAYER.

Notice that the turbulent boundary layer will be thicker than the laminar one. A rough surface is not the only factor that may cause a turbulent boundary layer. An increase in pressure that causes dramatic changes in the layer's speed may also lead to a turbulent boundary layer. In fact, the laminar boundary layer suddenly becomes turbulent, at least beyond the maximum thickness of the profile, due to the increase in pressure. The position on the surface (where this transition occurs) is called the transition point, which is followed by a transition area.

CRANFIELD AVIATION TRAINING SCHOOL LTD. PART-FCL GBR.ATO-0136
CATS INNOVATION CENTRE, LUTON, Bedfordshire LU2 8DL U.K.   www.catsaviation.com

3-3   Principles of Flight

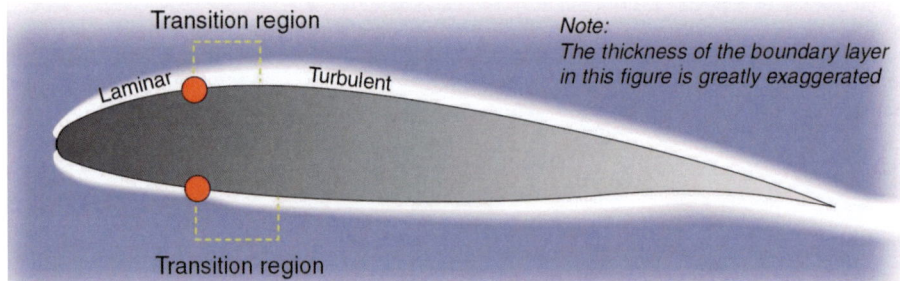

Figure 3.9

> The boundary layer changes from laminar to a thicker turbulent layer at the TRANSITION POINT. As already mentioned, the turbulent boundary layer is thicker than the laminar one and creates more friction

In the turbulent boundary layer, the speed, and thus the energy, close to the surface is higher than that of the laminar flow. The reason for this is turbulent mixing. Due to turbulent mixing, the low-speed air particles close to the surface are brought out into the high-speed flow where they increase their speed due to the collision with particles at higher speed and vice versa.

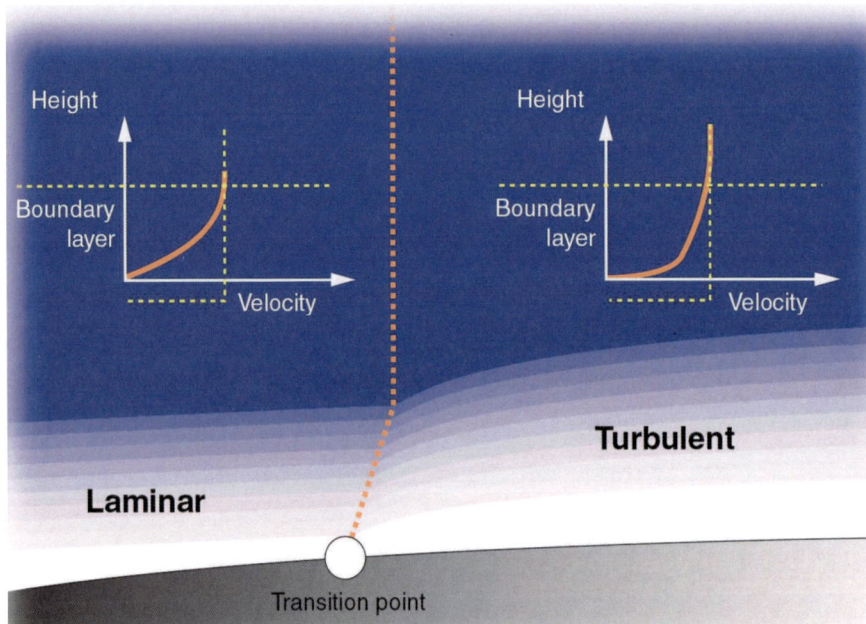

Figure 3.10

However, there is an advantage of the high drag turbulent boundary layer over the laminar boundary layer. The higher energy in the turbulent boundary layer makes it more resistant to flow separation, i.e. flow separation occurs at a higher angle of attack than that of the laminar boundary layer.

> The turbulent boundary layer is more resistant to flow separation than the laminar one

On most aircraft wings, the transition point is located near the leading edge, but on some glider aircraft with so-called laminar wing sections and with extreme smooth surfaces, the transition point may be located at 50% of the chord. The location of the transition point is not constant. It will change with a change in pressure distribution, with the degree of friction from the surface and the most important parameter: Reynolds number.

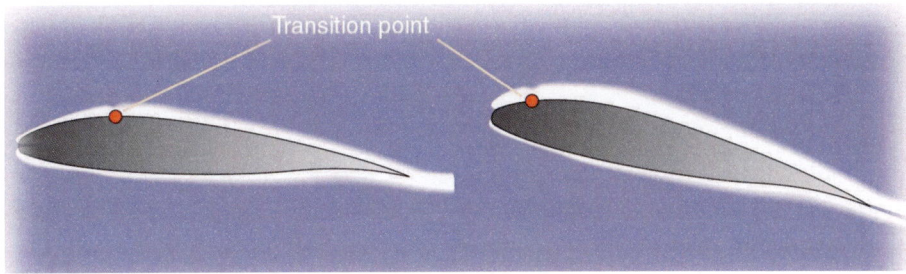

Figure 3.11

The laminar boundary layer is normally quite short, while the turbulent boundary layer covers most of the chord

3.1.4 *Reynolds number*

We have already mentioned that, due to the compressibility effects (called Mach effects), the flow and hence the pressure distribution is changed at high speeds. This will cause a critical high-speed value. However, there is also a critical low speed value due to the viscosity of the air.

At very low speeds the energy from the mass of air flowing over a surface is too low compared to the friction of the surface and this will affect the boundary layer. The factors that determine the flow characteristics around a wing are the velocity V (cm/s), the wing chord c (cm) and the kinematic viscosity of air (at sea level at 15°C it is $^1/_{0.14}$ or ~7). The product of these is called Reynolds number (Re or R) after the discoverer of this relationship. It is a non-dimensional parameter of great importance. The number tells the ratio between the force of the mass flow and force of the friction. The formula by which we get the Re number, is at sea level Re = V x c x 7.

As can be seen from the formula, the chord is also of importance. For example, the airflow around a very small model aircraft wing (made to exact scale of a real aircraft wing) will not be the same, in comparison with the real aircraft wing. It will have other lift and drag coefficients, especially below a certain Re number.

Consequently, a model aircraft which has a wing chord of 20 cm and which flies at 5 m/s will have the same Re number as another wing with a chord of 10 cm at 10 m/s. (Re = 500 cm/s x 20 cm x 7 = 1000 x 10 x 7 = 70000).

When performing the wind tunnel test on an exact model of a "real" aircraft the Re number of the test must be as high as possible to come close to the Re number of the "real" aircraft in corresponding conditions. One way to increase the Re number in wind tunnel tests is to change the flow viscosity by using a gas other than air and/or to increase the pressure.

A given wing section has a certain critical Re-number, Re_{crit}. Below that critical Re, the lift coefficient will drop significantly and the drag coefficient will increase.

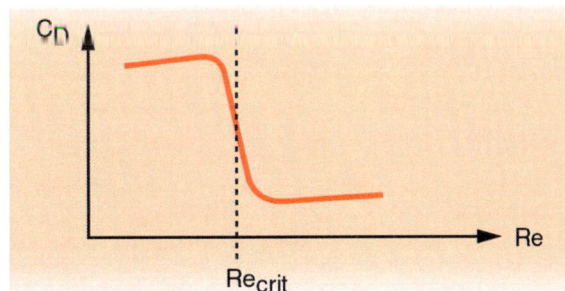

Figure 3.12

This is an important factor when designing aircraft. A very small lifting surface, e.g. a canard, will have a significantly different boundary layer and lift and drag compared to the main plane, especially at low speeds. At high speeds and with the correct shape of the canard section, the canard will have less reduced performance.

The force of the mass flow and the force of the friction have great impact on the boundary layer. The behaviour of the boundary layer is very much dependant on the Reynolds number.

3.1.5 Separation point

When the pressure difference along an aerofoil is too great, the flow velocity will be so low that the flow in the turbulent boundary layer will start to separate from the aerofoil at a point called the separation point. Let us take a look at an aerofoil in relative motion. We can see that from point A to point B, the air accelerates due to the decreasing static pressure. Crossing section B, the air starts to decelerate due to the increasing static pressure and continues decelerating until point C is reached.

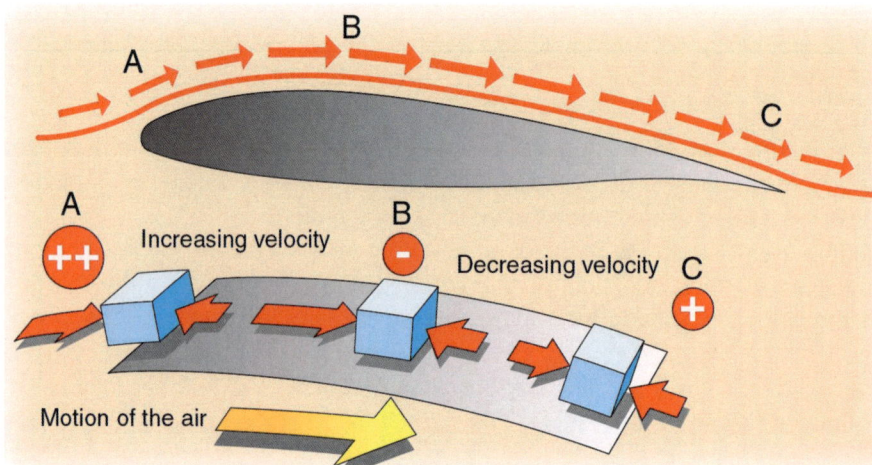

Figure 3.13

As we move from section B to C, pressure increases and speed decreases. When the pressure difference is such that the speed in the boundary layer is so low that it can no longer flow against the increasing pressure, we reach the flow separation. The point where the separation will start, is called the "separation point".

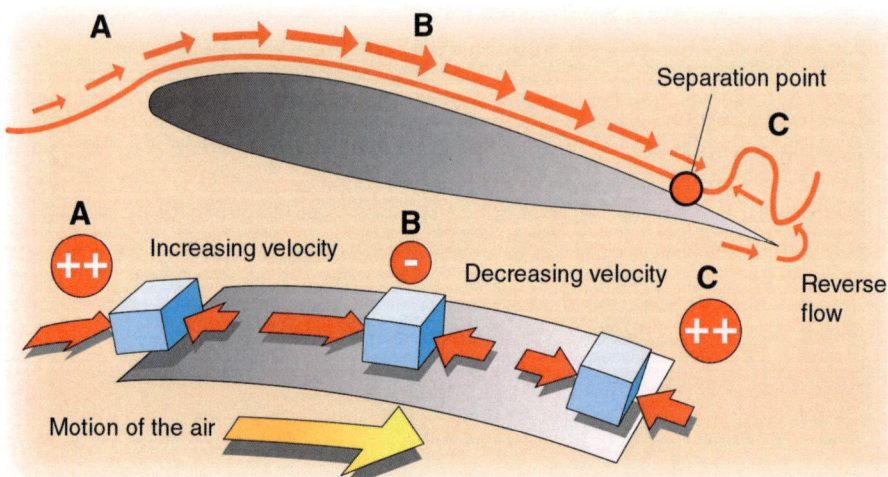

Figure 3.14

When the speed is so low that it can no longer flow against the increasing pressure, we reach the FLOW SEPARATION point

In the region preceding the separation point, the layer of air at zero speed that is closest to the body will rapidly increase in thickness, and due to the increase in pressure from B to C, this surface layer may start to flow against the main flow, causing flow separation.

At the separation point, the layer of air at zero speed that is closest to the body starts to flow against the main flow. The flow separation causes a turbulent wake behind the body moving through the air as we can see in the picture below. The earlier the flow separation, the greater the turbulent wake.

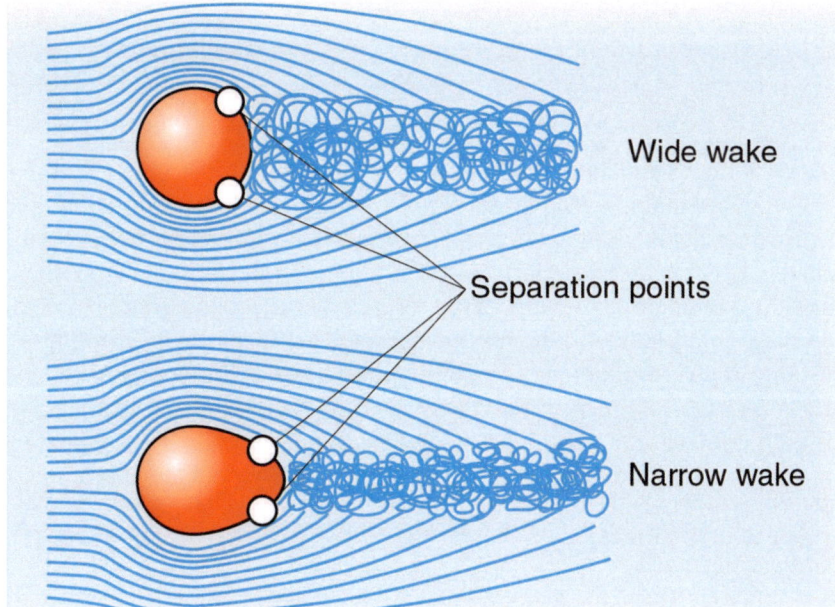

Figure 3.15

The earlier the flow separation, the greater the turbulent wake

The shape of the flow separation depends on the shape of the aerofoil and the conditions in the boundary layer. Thick profiles have early separation and large wakes, while thin profiles have separation points very close to the trailing edge and thus small wakes.

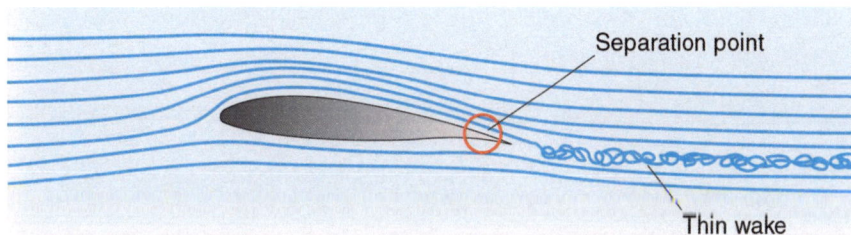

Figure 3.16

Thin profiles have separation points close to the trailing edge and small wakes

For conventional aircraft that have wing-profiles with turbulent boundary layers, the flow separation point is usually very close to the trailing edge at low angles of attack but moves forward as the angle of attack increases.

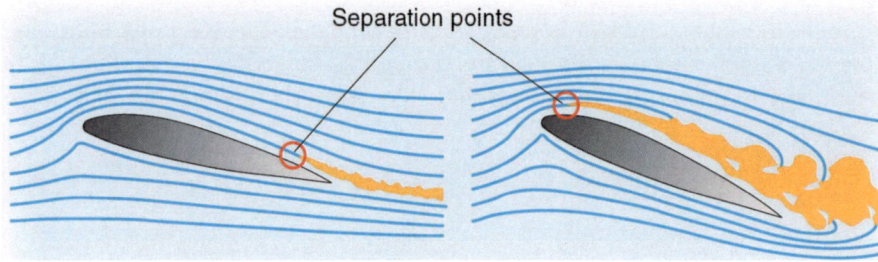

Figure 3.17

When a certain angle of attack is reached, the flow separation point on the upper surface of the profile has moved so much further forward that the wing stalls.

However, the actual Re number also has an effect on the flow separation, hence also the drag. This is illustrated by the example of a circular cylinder. The upper figure in the next illustration shows the case of a flow at low Re number. The boundary layer is laminar, and early separation takes place, giving a large dead air region and a high drag coefficient. At a higher Re number, transition takes place at a point upstream of the separation point. As a result, the turbulent boundary layer remains attached to the surface until a point much further round is reached. The size of the dead air region is much reduced, as shown in the lower figure, and so is the drag coefficient. Consequently, at a higher speed the Re number is higher resulting in the transition point moving forward reducing the dead air region and hence also the drag coefficient.

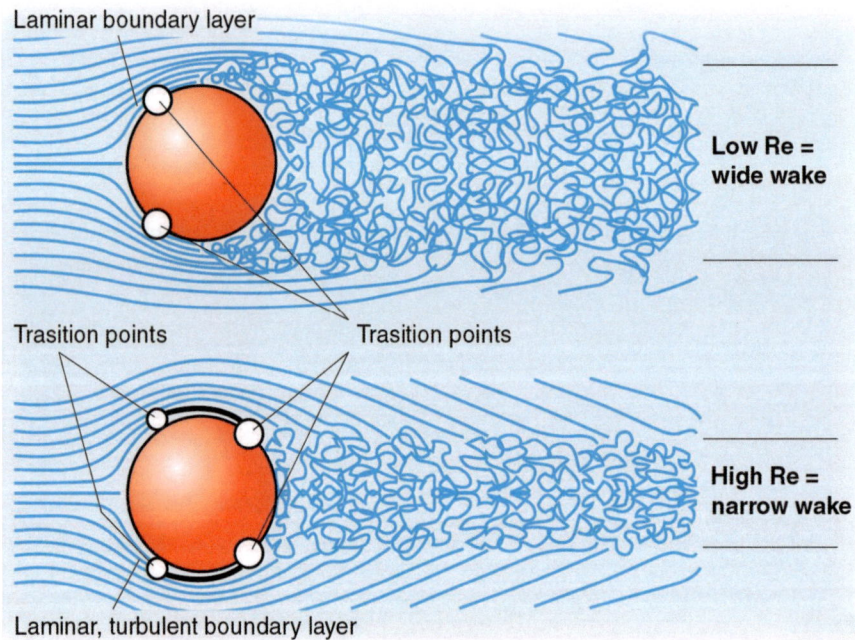

Figure 3.18

The transition point moves forward with increasing speed

Notice the difference between the transition point and the separation point.

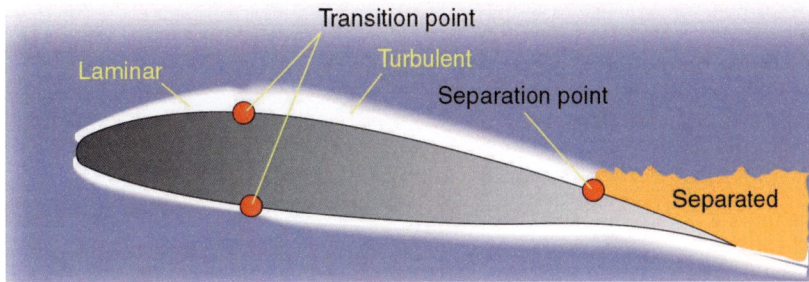

Figure 3.19

3.2   *Profile Drag*

This section deals with form drag dependent upon airflow separation, and how to reduce form drag.

Form drag depends upon airflow separation.

Parasite drag or zero lift drag, consists of three components:
    Profile drag,
    Skin friction drag and
    Interference drag

In addition to the types of drag mentioned, there is another type at high speeds near the speed of sound that is called wave drag. However, we will not deal with that until chapter 19.

We will now analyse each of these components, starting with form drag. In order to understand how form drag is generated, let us first consider an ideal situation. Let us imagine a cylinder moving in a fluid without viscosity. In this ideal situation there will be no separation and the fluid will follow the shape of the cylinder.

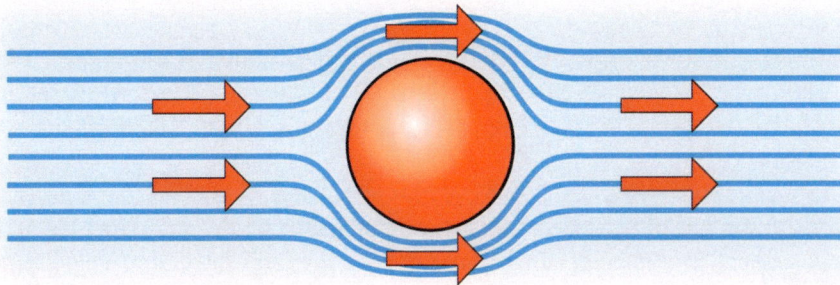

Figure 3.20 In a fluid without viscosity there will be no flow separation

Remember that a fluid without viscosity is only an ideal situation: the velocity of the airflow varies from the free stream velocity at the front of the cylinder to the maximum value on its upper and lower surfaces. After that, the velocity of the airflow decreases until reaching the free stream velocity again at the back of the cylinder.

Let us now consider what happens in the case of a real fluid. A cylinder moving in a real fluid, in other words a fluid with a certain degree of viscosity, behaves very differently. The fluid will follow the shape of the cylinder only until separation occurs, then it breaks away.

In practice, the flow varies from the free stream velocity at the front of the cylinder to the maximum value around the upper and lower surfaces of it. Then the flow breaks away and, as a consequence, the velocity of this flow does not reach that of the free stream flow behind the cylinder.

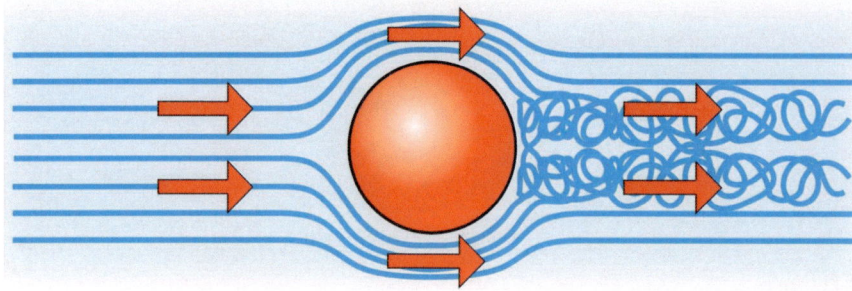

Figure 3.21

In a real fluid, flow separation occurs. As a consequence, the velocity of this flow does not reach that of the free stream flow behind the cylinder. As we already know, the variation in velocity around the body causes a variation in the pressure. If we measured the pressure around the body moving in an ideal fluid without viscosity, the result would be the pressure distribution shown below. The pressure at the front and at the back of the cylinder has the same value because the velocity also has the same value at the front and at the back.

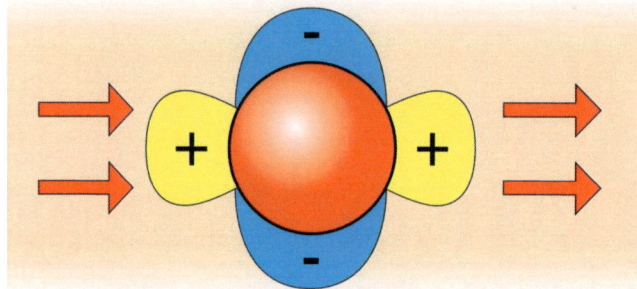

Figure 3.22

In an ideal fluid, the pressure in the area in front of the body is equal to the pressure behind the body.

The pressure distribution is equivalent to the resultant force. If we consider the resultant force in the relative wind direction, in other words the drag, we find that it is null because the forward and aft pressures are equivalent to two equal and opposite forces. The cylinder moving in an ideal fluid will therefore have no drag.

Let us now consider a situation where the same cylinder is moving through a real fluid. We can see that the pressure distribution on the aft part of the cylinder is different from the pressure distribution on the front, because, as we have seen, the velocity of this flow does not reach the same velocity as the free stream behind the body.

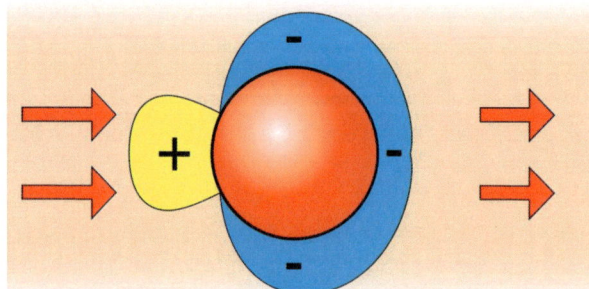

Figure 3.23

In a real fluid there is a certain difference in pressure between the front part of the body and the aft.

This means that the force acting on the aft part of the cylinder is no longer balanced by the force acting on the front part. As a consequence, there is a resultant force in the direction of the relative wind. This force is a type of drag and is called FORM DRAG.

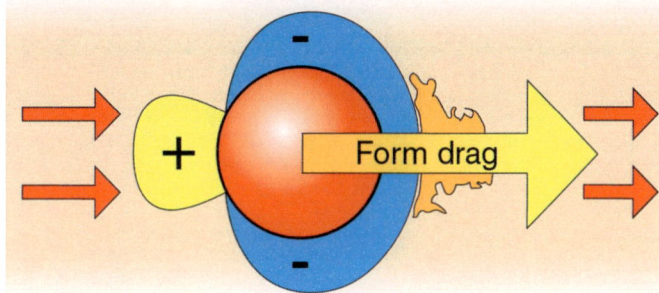

Figure 3.24

The drag resulting from the difference in pressure between the front and the aft part of the body is called the FORM DRAG

If we only have one half of the cylinder, the separation point moves forwards and the turbulent wake becomes greater. In this case the form drag increases due to the increased difference in pressure between the front and aft parts of the body.

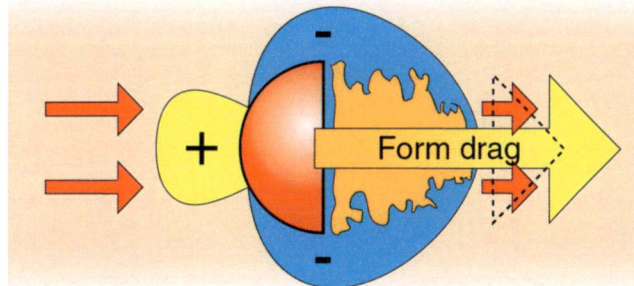

Figure 3.25

If the separation point moves forwards, the form drag increases

The shape of the body determines the amount of form drag. The shape of the forward surface of the body determines the velocity and, as a consequence, the pressure distribution on the front part of the body. The shape of the body also determines the position of the separation point, the dimensions of the turbulent wake and, as a consequence, the pressure distribution on the aft surface of the body.

If we consider a blunt body, such as a flat plate perpendicular to the relative wind, we can see a sudden and great variation in fluid velocity in front of the plate and a large turbulent wake behind it. Thus there is a great difference in pressure between the front and back surfaces of the plate. As a result the flat plate experiences high form drag.

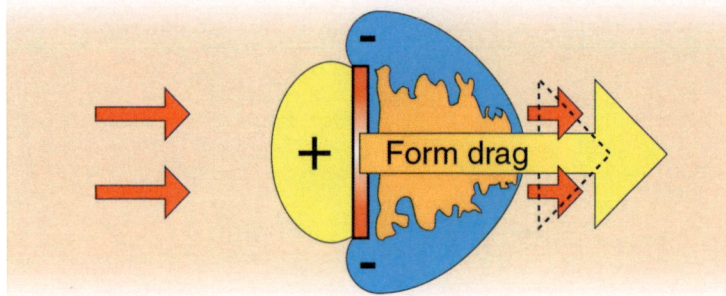

Figure 3.26

A flat plate perpendicular to the relative wind creates a high variation in fluid velocity and a large wake and thus produces great form drag.

Let us now consider a body with the same front area but with a pointed fore-body. There will be a smoother speed transition from the front of the body to the thickest part, but it creates a turbulent wake of almost the same dimension.

Because of the pointed fore-body, there is a smaller difference in pressure between the fore and aft surfaces. As a result, this body experiences less form drag than a flat plate.

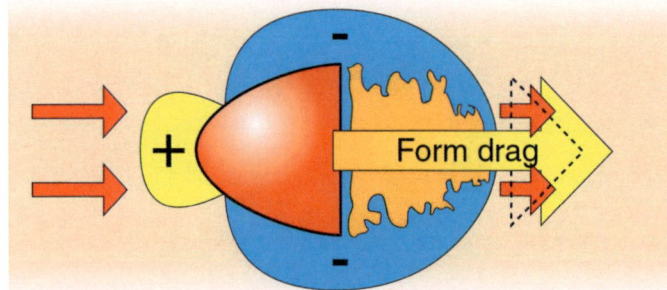

Figure 3.27

A body with a pointed fore-body has a smoother transition in fluid velocity than a flat plate and consequently it produces less form drag

If we now consider a body with the same front area and fore-body but with a fairing at the aft part, we can see that we have a smooth transition of fluid velocity from the front to the back of the body and therefore also a smaller wake. This is the shape of an aerofoil. The aerofoil experiences the smallest difference in pressure between the fore and aft surfaces and, as a consequence, it produces the lowest value of form drag.

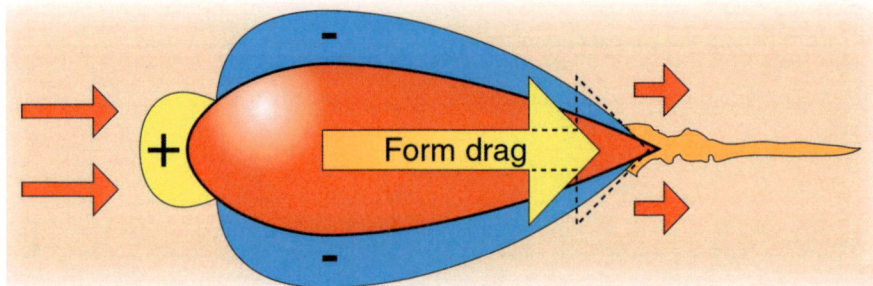

Figure 3.28

CRANFIELD AVIATION TRAINING SCHOOL LTD. PART-FCL GBR.ATO-0136

CATS CATS INNOVATION CENTRE, LUTON, Bedfordshire LU2 8DL U.K.

www.catsaviation.com

3-12

Principles of Flight

If we consider two different aerofoils with different thickness, we can see that the thicker aerofoil has an early point of separation and a large wake, thus experiencing a certain degree of form drag. When the thickness of the aerofoil is reduced, the separation point moves backwards and the form drag is reduced.

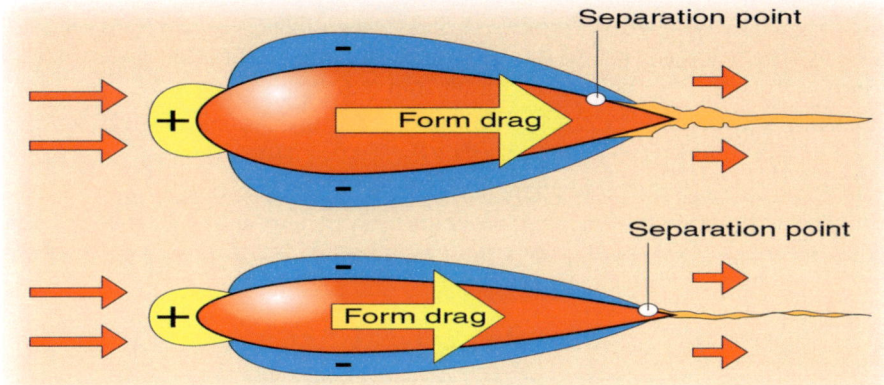

Figure 3.29

The further back the separation point, the smaller the turbulent wake and form drag

You have seen that a given aerofoil at a low angle of attack experiences a given form drag due to the shape of its front and aft parts. You have also seen that with an increase in the angle of attack, the separation point moves forwards. As a consequence, the thickness of the turbulent wake increases and so does the difference in pressure between the front and aft parts of the aerofoil. The form drag therefore increases.

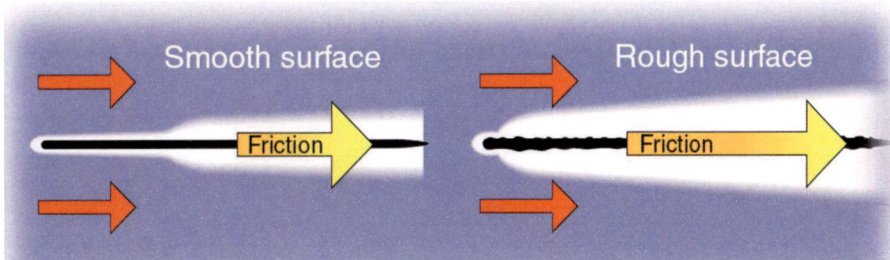

Figure 3.30

When the A.of.A. increases, form drag increases

3.2.1   *Reducing form drag*

When an aircraft is designed, its shape must be such as to reduce the form drag as much as possible. You never see an aircraft with a blunt fore body or a blunt aft body, like some motorcars. Likewise, if we cannot avoid the presence of some protrusions on the aircraft body, e.g. antennas, landing gear etc., the only way to reduce the form drag is to streamline the protrusions, thus obtaining a smaller difference in pressure between the front and the aft. Circular protrusions create high drag, so landing gear fairings and spinner fairings are examples of what can be done with shape in order to reduce the form drag of an aircraft.

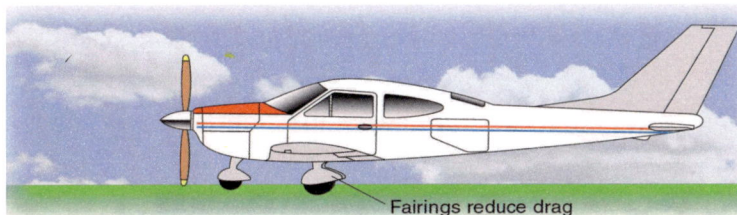

Figure 3.31

CRANFIELD AVIATION TRAINING SCHOOL LTD. PART-FCL GBR.ATO-0136
CATS INNOVATION CENTRE, LUTON, Bedfordshire LU2 8DL U.K.   www.catsaviation.com

3-13   Principles of Flight

3.3 Skin Friction Drag

3.3.1 Skin friction drag due to friction

Let us now analyse another component of parasite drag, i.e. skin friction drag. When the air moves around a body, the layers of air close to the surface of the body gradually decelerate because of the air viscosity. The viscosity creates friction between the body and the air and this friction acts within the boundary layer. The friction between the body and the air disturbs the flow of the air near the surface, i.e. the body draws the air in the same direction as the body. This is called SKIN FRICTION DRAG. Using a very thin flat plate parallel to the relative motion we can assume that there is no flow separation due to the form of the body. The resistance experienced by the body in this situation is the skin friction drag only. Skin friction drag depends upon surface roughness. The rougher the surface, the greater the skin friction drag.

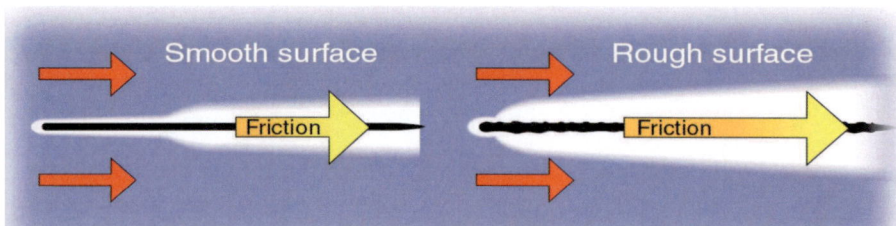

Figure 3.32

A rough surface causes higher skin friction drag because the boundary layer becomes almost immediately turbulent. As you know, the turbulent boundary layer creates more friction and is thicker than the laminar one. Skin friction drag also depends upon the size of the body surface. However, a larger surface gives a higher Reynolds number. Generally, the higher the Reynolds number the greater the tendency to resist separation, giving a corresponding lower skin friction coefficient C_f. In addition, increased speed gives a higher Re-number, decreasing the C_D. A larger surface area, and/or a higher speed, increases the Re-number, giving a lower C_D. Consequently, skin friction drag = skin friction coefficient C_f x dynamic pressure q x wetted area (total curved area).

3.3.2 Reducing skin friction drag

If we want to reduce skin friction drag, for a given surface, we must use smooth surfaces. The smoother the surface, the lower the skin friction drag. However, a reduction in the area and the speed of the surface will also reduce the friction drag.

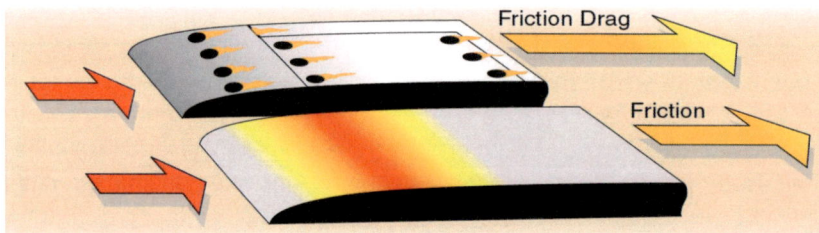

Figure 3.33

3.4 Interference Drag

3.4.1 Interference of vortices

We have now reached the last component of parasite drag namely, interference drag. When we put together two bodies with different shapes, for example a fuselage and a wing, the difference in local airflow speed between the two surfaces causes differences in pressure, which create vortices. These vortices create drag, which is called interference drag.

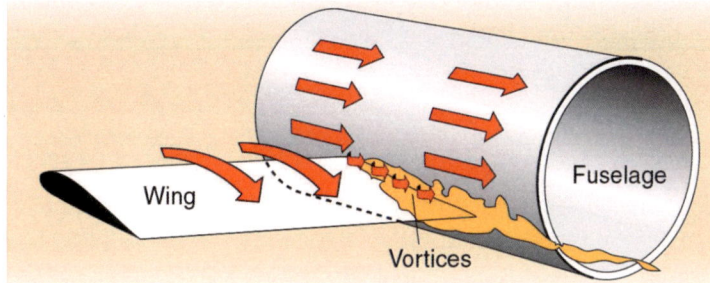

Figure 3.34

3.4.2 *Reducing interference drag.*

The most common way of reducing interference drag is to put a fairing, also called fillet, at the junction of the two surfaces. This fillet changes the airflow in the junction, and reduces the vortices.

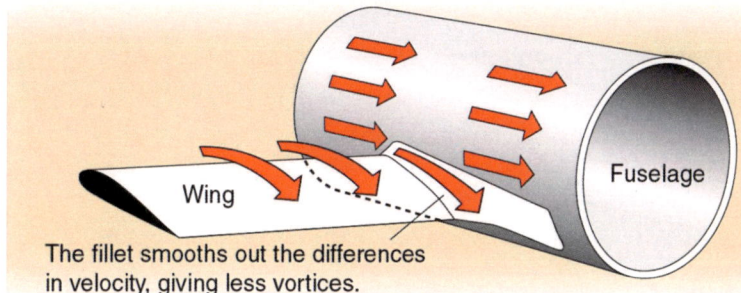

Figure 3.35

Difference in local airflow speed between surfaces causes vortices

3.5 *Parasite Drag as the sum of drags*

3.5.1 *Sum of drags*

We have now analysed all the components of parasite drag: form drag, skin friction drag and interference drag. Parasite drag, or zero lift drag, is the sum of all of these.

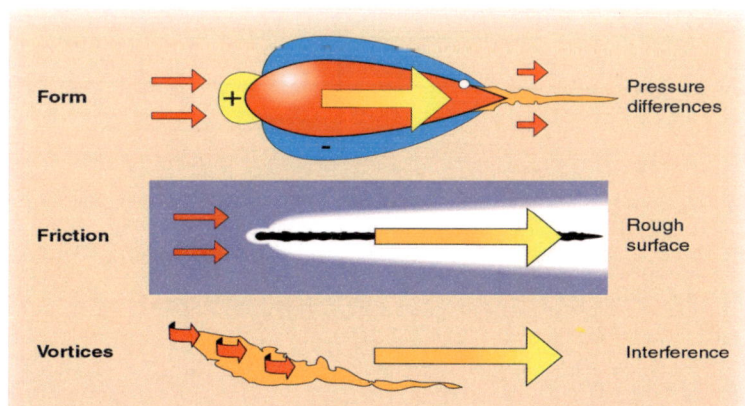

Figure 3.36

3.5.2   *Parasite drag formula*

Parasite drag is abbreviated D_0 , 0 for "zero lift", and is affected by the same factors that affect lift, but instead of lift it expresses the capacity of the body to create drag due to form, friction and interference. The next factor is the dynamic pressure, and finally the reference area of the body. Thus, parasite drag (zero lift drag) is expressed by the formula:

$$D_0 = C_{D0} \text{ (coefficient)} \times q \text{ (dynamic pressure)} \times S \text{ (reference area)}$$

The coefficient of parasite drag CD_0 expresses the capacity of the body to create form drag, skin friction drag and interference drag. It is therefore the sum of these drag coefficients. This coefficient is almost independent of velocity and completely independent of the creation of lift (C_D = D/q x S). However, to be precise, due to effects of Re-number, it decreases somewhat if speed increases, and increases somewhat if altitude is increased. Parasite drag is proportional to dynamic pressure V^2. If dynamic pressure increases, parasite drag also increases. As you can see from the formula, parasite drag is directly proportional to the velocity squared. The parasite drag value is of course ZERO if the speed is zero, because if a body does not move it does not experience any parasite drag. Parasite drag is also proportional to the reference area S, the projecting area of a body seen in the direction of flow. If we increase the reference area of the aircraft, parasite drag will also increase.

3.5.3   *Parasite drag versus airspeed.*

If we draw a curve representing the variation in parasite drag as a function of airspeed, we see that, at zero airspeed, parasite drag is zero. By increasing the airspeed to a given value V, we obtain a given parasite drag D_0.

Since D_0 is determined by the square of speed, D_0 will be four times greater if we double the speed

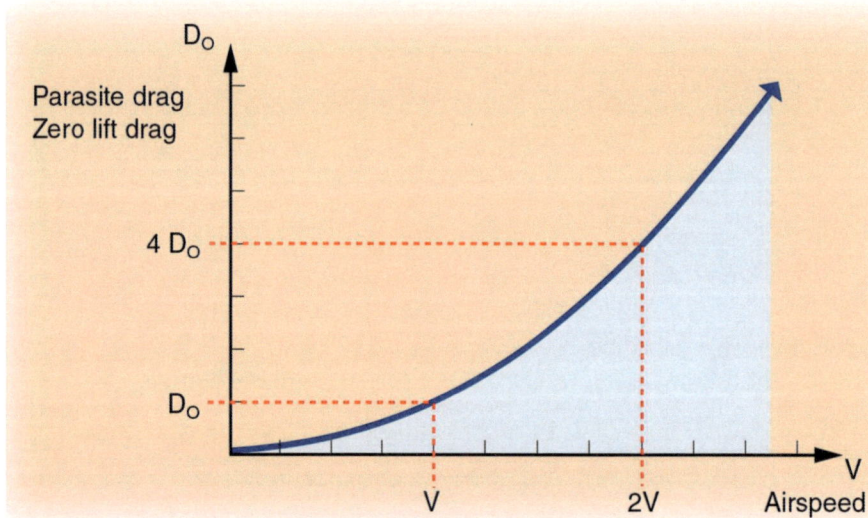

Figure 3.37 Zero Lift Drag

CRANFIELD AVIATION TRAINING SCHOOL LTD. PART-FCL GBR.ATO-0136
CATS INNOVATION CENTRE, LUTON, Bedfordshire LU2 8DL U.K.   www.catsaviation.com
3-16   Principles of Flight

CHAPTER 4

INDUCED DRAG and TOTAL DRAG

4.1 Induced Drag

4.1.1 Induced drag caused by the production of lift.

All bodies (aircraft, car, elephant, a man riding a bike etc.) moving through the air, creates a certain parasite drag also called ZERO Lift Drag. For an aircraft that is able to produce lift using wings, an ADDITIONAL type of drag is created. This additional drag is 'lift induced' drag, usually simply called induced drag. We will now see how it works. When lift is produced, air is accelerated downwards, the pressure on the upper wing surface being less than that on the lower wing surface. As the air flows rearwards, some air will flow around the wing tip from the high pressure area under the wing to the low pressure area above the wing, and the surrounding air outside the aircraft will fill the low pressure in the area above stretching behind the wing. These factors will produce large vortices behind each wing tip.

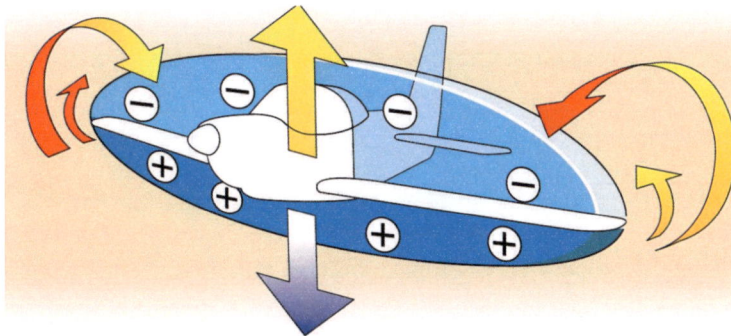

Figure 4.1 Three-dimensional flow

The airflow under the wing surface tries to avoid the higher pressure in this area, resulting in a spanwise flow component of air outwards from the fuselage. On the upper surface, however, the airflow tries to fill the lower pressure, resulting in a spanwise component towards the fuselage.

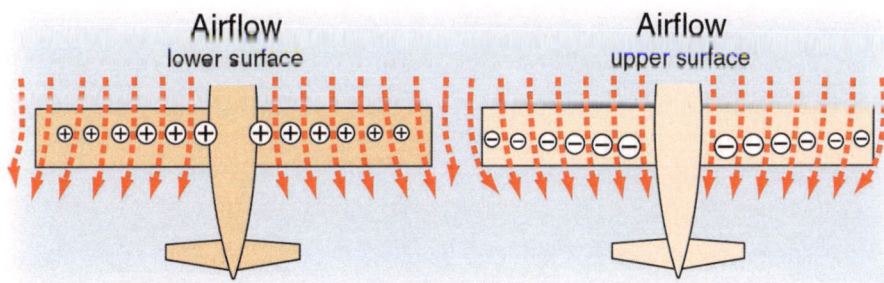

Figure 4.2

These different components of flow will together spill around the wing tips forming a twisting vortex core behind each wing tip.

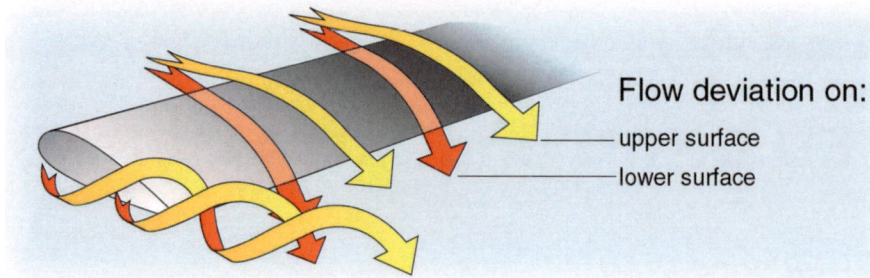

Figure 4.3

The upward flow in the vortex is outside the span of the wing, but the downward flow is behind the trailing edge of the wing, within the span of the wing. The net *effect is a downwash behind the wing, which influences the airflow around the wing.*

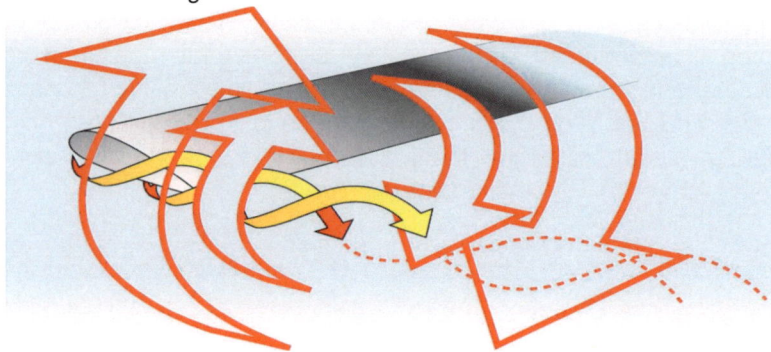

Figure 4.4

In a 3-d flow, there is an overall downwash of air behind the trailing edge within the span of the wing

This three-dimensional flow will cause a very complicated flow pattern behind the wing which also influences the wing itself.

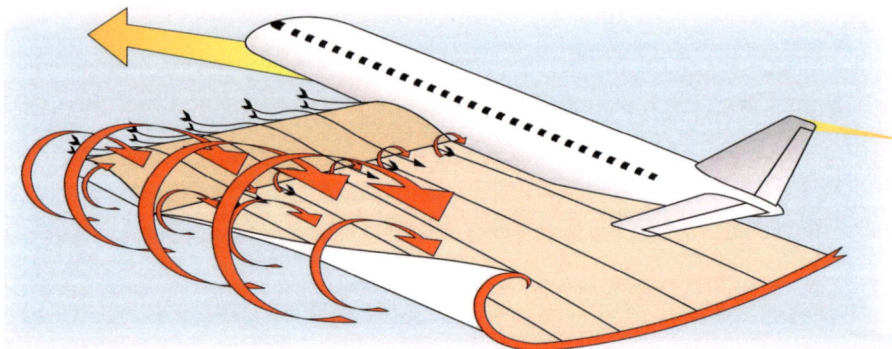

Figure 4.5

The wings are, so to speak, flying in a self-induced downwash. The presence of the downwash causes a local airflow that is different from the airflow well ahead of the wing. This influences the wing itself. The direction of the local airflow lies between the direction of the free stream airflow, well ahead of the wing, and the direction of the downwash behind it. So the lift force generated perpendicular to this local relative wind will be tilted somewhat backwards.

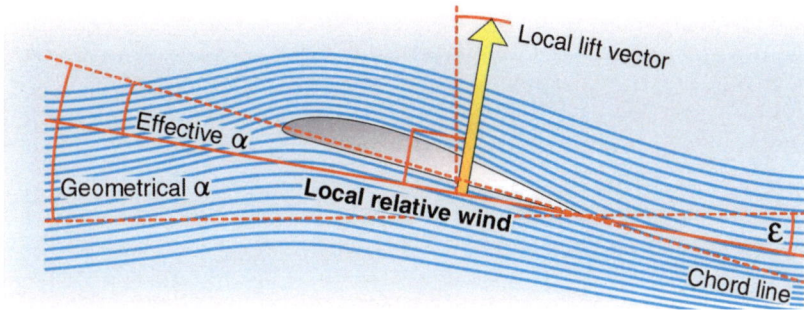

Figure 4.6

If we did not have the downwash, e.g. an infinite span wing, the local airflow experienced by the aerofoil would be parallel to the free stream giving a highly effective angle of attack. We would then obtain a certain total aerodynamic force with a given lift and a given drag known as the parasite or zero lift drag D_0.

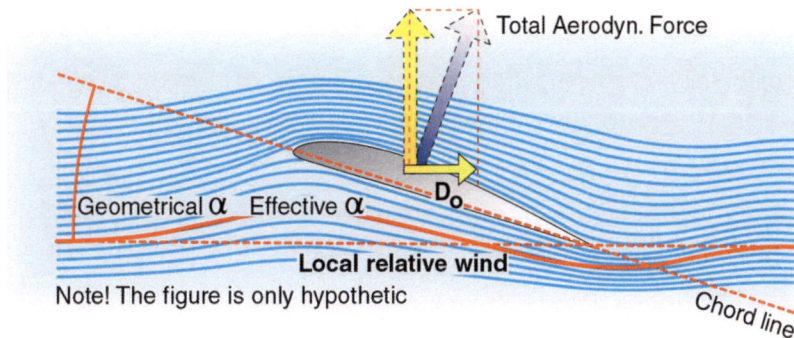

Figure 4.7

Because of the downwash, the local airflow experienced by the wing is inclined downwards to a certain degree ε (epsilon). As a consequence, the total aerodynamic force produced by the wing is inclined backwards to the same degree ε. Since the aerodynamic force is inclined backwards, the lift is decreased and the drag is increased. This increase in drag, which is due to the presence of the downwash, is an induced by-product of the production of lift and is called INDUCED DRAG, abbreviated Di.

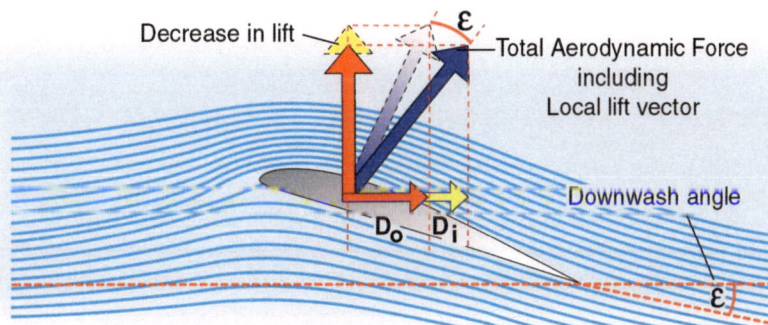

Figure 4.8

In order to simplify the picture, we will take a look at the local lift vector again. With an increase in the A.of.A, the downwash angle will increase, the effective A.of.A will be less than the geometrical A.of.A and the local lift vector will be tilted more backwards giving higher induced drag.

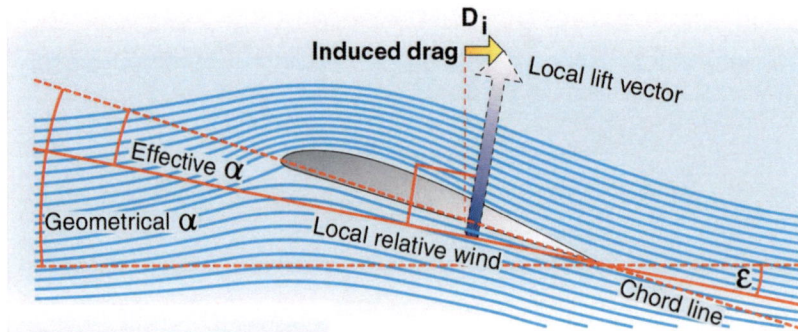

Figure 4.9

When the angle of attack increases, C_L increases. This produces not only a greater difference in pressure between the upper and lower wing surfaces but also a greater downwash behind the wing. The induced drag increases.

Due to the presence of the downwash, the drag increases by a certain amount called INDUCED DRAG, D_i. When the angle of attack increases, induced drag increases

At zero aerodynamic A.of.A. we have zero C_L and consequently, there is no difference in pressure between the upper and lower wing surfaces and no downwash. The induced drag is therefore zero.

Figure 4.10

Note: A twisted wing may produce low induced drag even if the total wing C_L = 0.

4.1.2 Factors influencing induced drag

The ratio between the aircraft weight and the wing span (b), is called the span loading. It indicates how many Newton the wing can carry for every meter of wing span.

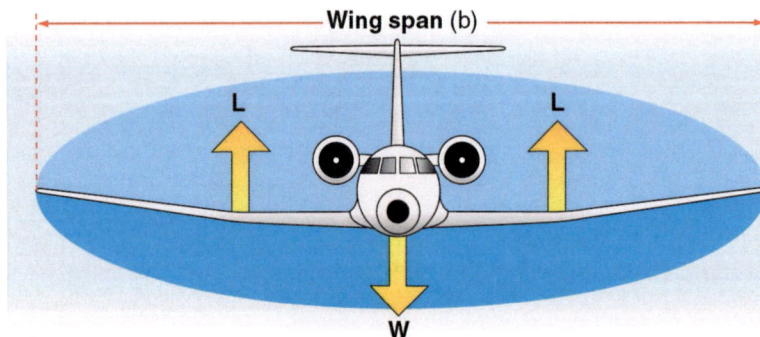

Figure 4.11

The ratio between the aircraft weight and the wing span is called the SPAN LOADING

If we consider two aircraft with the same wing span but with different weight, we see that the light one has lower span loading and the heavy one has higher span loading. The heavy aircraft has to carry more load for every meter of wing span.

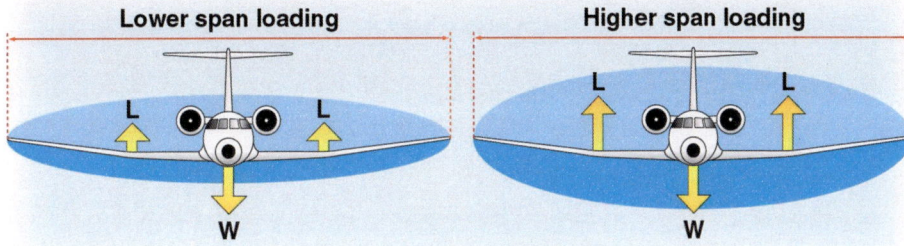

Figure 4.12

Note: In every day language, the term for span loading is kg/m and for wing loading kg/m^2 but, in physics language, it is a force that should be expressed in Newton's.

> When weight increases, for the same wingspan, the span loading increases

Induced drag is strictly related to span loading. If we have low span loading we only need a low downwash and a minor difference in pressure between the upper and lower surfaces of the wing. This creates low intensity wing tip vortices and low induced drag.

LOW SPAN LOADING means:
- A low angle of downwash
- A minor loss of lift due to a more upright local lift vector
- A slight difference in pressure between the upper and lower surfaces of the wing
- Low intensity wing tip vortices
- Low induced drag.

If we increase the span loading using a shorter wing with the same aircraft weight, we have to obtain a greater difference in pressure and higher downwash, which creates stronger vortices and gives higher induced drag.

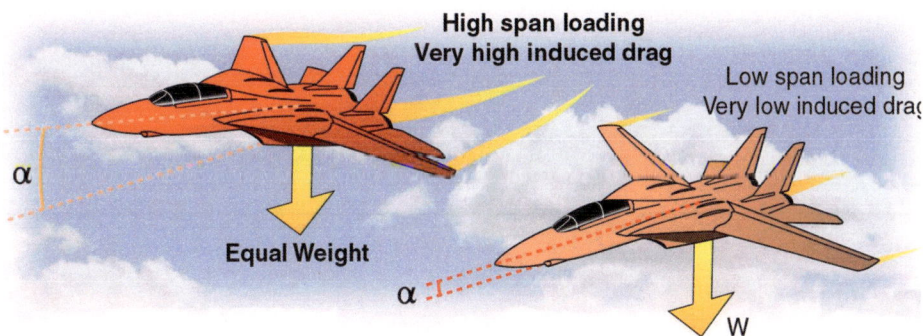

Figure 4.13

> When span loading increases induced drag increases

4.1.3   *Relationship between induced drag and airspeed.*

In straight and level flight with a given weight, the lift must remain constant in order to balance the weight when speed is changed.

When airspeed is reduced, you have to increase the A.of.A. (and the coefficient of lift) to achieve the same lift. Thus, as you will remember, high angles of attack are associated with low airspeeds and vice versa. The example below illustrates some A.of.A in combination with speed.

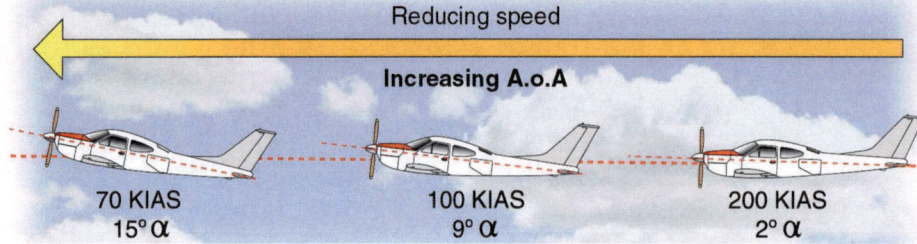

Figure 4.14

In straight and level flight for a given weight, high angles of attack are associated with low airspeeds and vice versa

When the A.of.A. is increased, C_L is increased due to the greater difference in pressure between the upper and lower surfaces of the wing. This causes the spanwise flow that spills around the wing tip to form a stronger vortex and a higher downwash, which means higher induced drag.

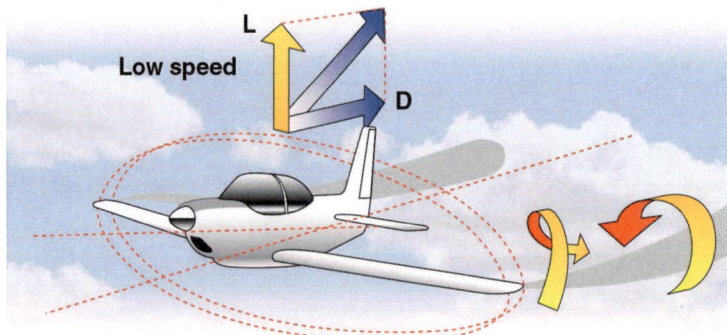

Figure 4.15

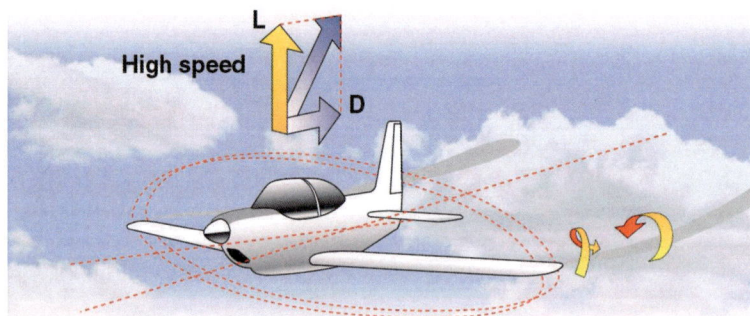

Figure 4.16

When the A.of.A. is increased, C_L is increased giving higher induced drag.

o, induced drag varies with airspeed. Low airspeeds are associated with high induced drag while high airspeeds are associated with low induced drag. We can see on the graph that, close to stalling speed, the induced drag tends to be infinite, while at high airspeeds the induced drag tends to be equal to zero. When flying at half of this speed the induced drag is four times higher.

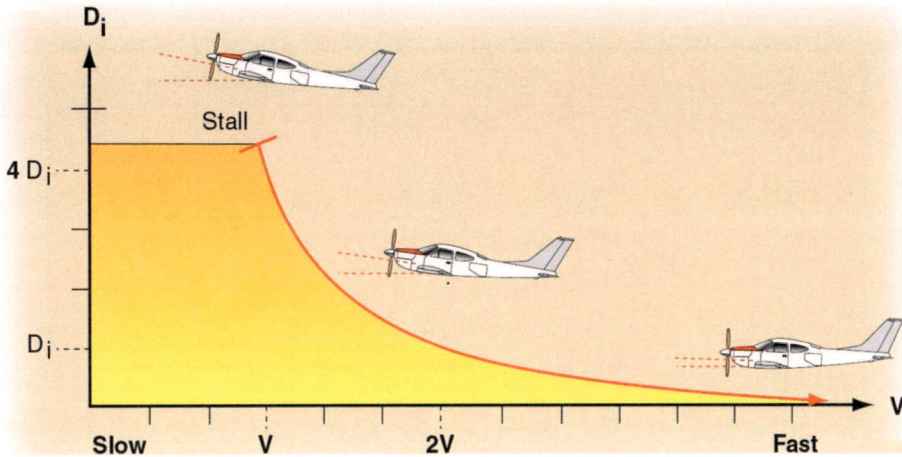

Figure 4.17

LOW AIRSPEEDS equal HIGH INDUCED DRAG while HIGH AIRSPEEDS equal LOW INDUCED DRAG

Flying at high altitudes is like flying at low speeds. In order to compensate the low dynamic pressure due to low density at high altitudes, increasing the A.of.A must increase CL. This will create a higher induced drag than that at low altitudes at the same true airspeed.

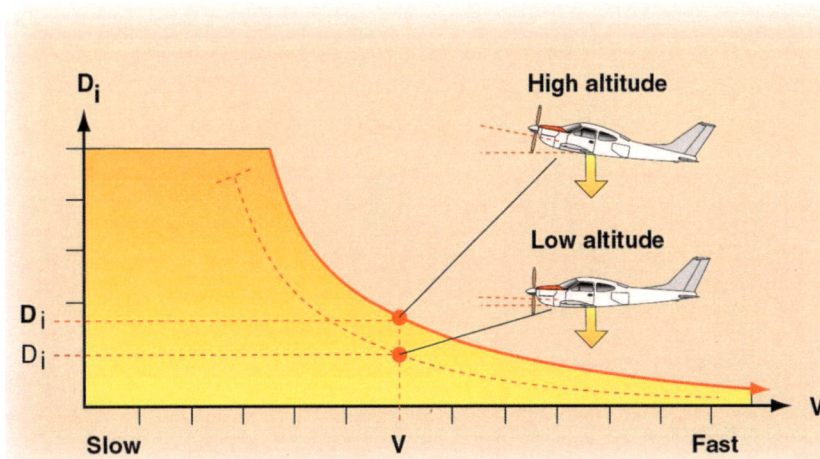

Figure 4.18

Flying at HIGH ALTITUDES equals HIGHER INDUCED DRAG at the SAME TRUE AIRSPEED

However, this relationship is valid at constant weight only; in fact, if we increase the aircraft weight by loading it we increase the span loading and we must produce more lift. At the same speed we will consequently create more induced drag than with a lighter aircraft.

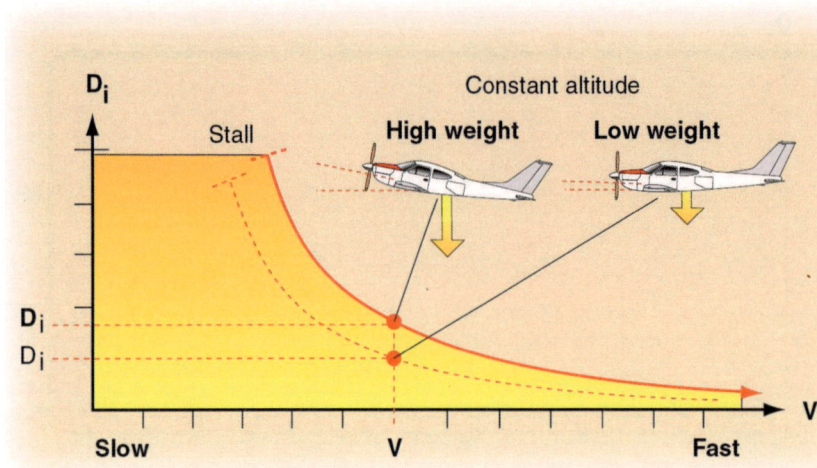

Figure 4.19

More weight means more induced drag at the same speed. An increase in weight by 10% increases D_i by 20%. We have seen that the induced drag created by a certain wing is related mainly to C_L. The induced drag is the resultant from the square of the C_L. The capacity of the wing to create induced drag is expressed by the induced drag coefficient called CD_i. Like induced drag it is proportional to the square of the C_L (see the complete formula below).

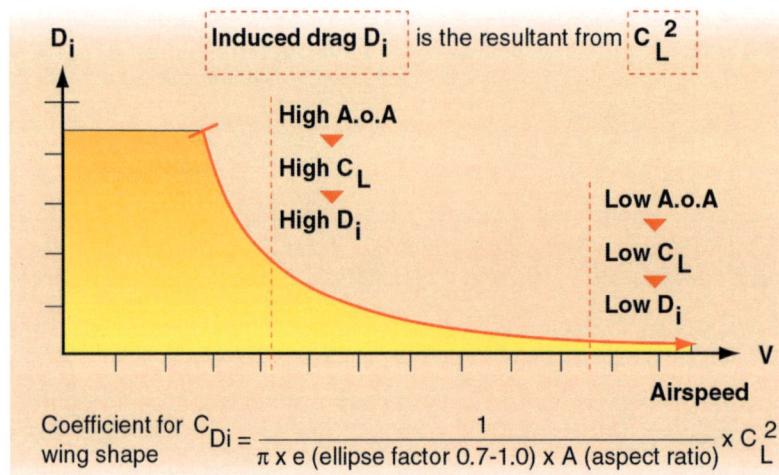

$$C_{Di} = \frac{1}{\pi \times e \text{ (ellipse factor 0.7-1.0)} \times A \text{ (aspect ratio)}} \times C_L^2$$

Figure 4.20

The induced drag is expressed by the induced drag coefficient called C_{Di}, which is proportional to C_L^2.

The picture below shows the elliptical area with low pressure on the upper surface of the wing. It is visible because the aircraft is flying in rather humid air and the produced low pressure decreases the temperature below the actual dew point. The vortex core from the aircraft right wing is also visible for the same reason.

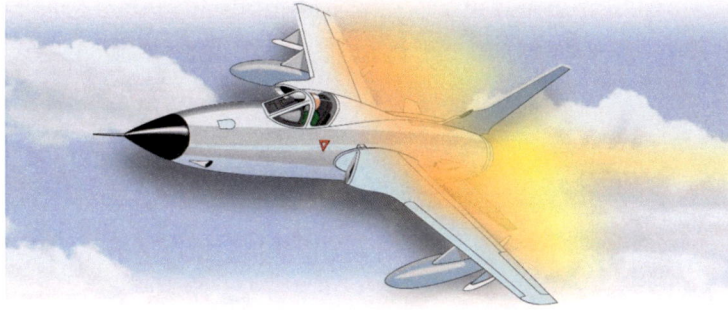

Figure 4.21

4.2   *Reducing Induced Drag*

This section describes how we can reduce the INDUCED DRAG by changing ASPECT RATIO, GEOMETRIC WASHOUT, AERODYNAMIC WASHOUT, WING PLANFORM and WING TIP MODIFICATION.

4.2.1   *Aspect ratio*

The main cause of induced drag is the downwash caused by the wing and the wing tip vortex. The part of the wing that is near the tip produces the greatest share of the induced drag. With a long wing a smaller fraction of the wing is affected by the downwash which results in a better ratio between lift and drag. Thus, if we want to reduce the induced drag we must reduce the intensity of the wing tip vortex.

The wing aspect ratio "A" is the first factor that can affect induced drag. It is the ratio between the span of the wing "b" and the geometric mean chord "c". Thus $A = b/c = b^2/bc = b^2/S$. The latter, span^2/area, is the most commonly used. Wings with the same area can be designed with different aspect ratios.

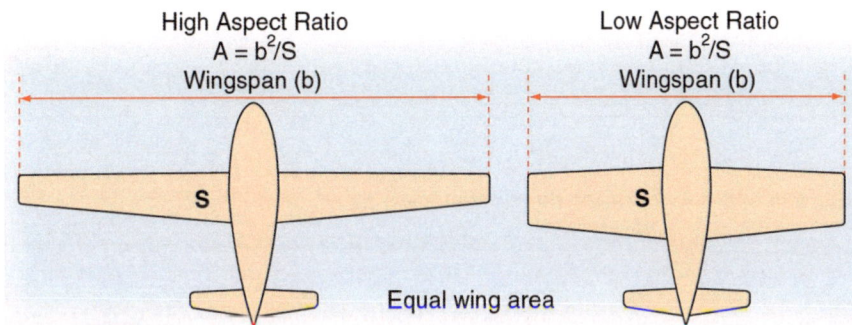

Figure 4.22

$$\text{Aspect ratio} = \frac{\text{wing span squared}}{\text{wing area}}$$

Let us consider two different wings with the same area but with different aspect ratios. If we compare the span loading of two aircraft of the same weight, with the same wing area, but with different aspect ratios, the span loading of the wing with a lower aspect ratio is higher than the other one.

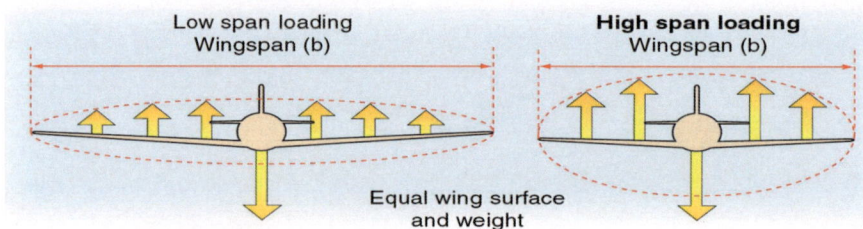

Figure 4.23

This higher span loading has to be compensated for by increasing the A.o.A.. In other words, a wing with a low aspect ratio must have a greater A.o.A. to create a certain C_L at the same speed as a wing with a high aspect ratio.

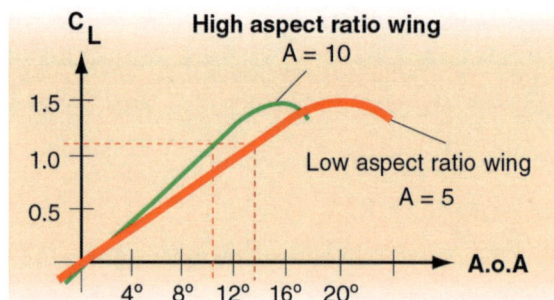

Figure 4.24

In order to create the same C_L at the same speed, wings with a low aspect ratio need a higher A.o.A. than wings with a high aspect ratio

As we already know, a higher A.of.A. increases the downwash near the wing and the intensity of the wing tip vortex. Therefore it also enhances the induced drag.

At the same speed, a wing with a low aspect ratio gives a higher induced drag than one with a higher aspect ratio

This effect explains why a glider, which of course must create very low induced drag, has such a great wingspan. This is done in order to increase the aspect ratio as much as possible.

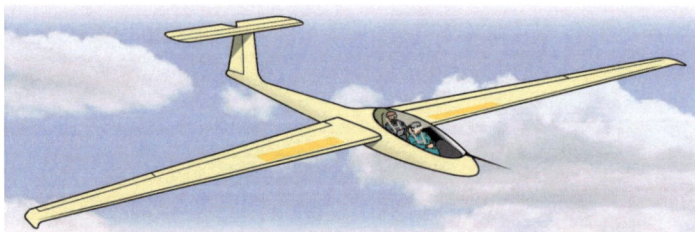

Figure 4.25

4.2.2   *Geometric washout and aerodynamic washout*

Another way of reducing induced drag is to create a so-called geometric twist or washout. If the wing is built with a twist, the angle of attack at the wing tip is lower than the angle of attack at the wing root near the fuselage. The smaller difference in pressure between the upper and lower surfaces of the wing near the wing tip reduces the airflow that spills around the wing tip. This causes a reduced formation of wing tip vortices and lower induced drag.

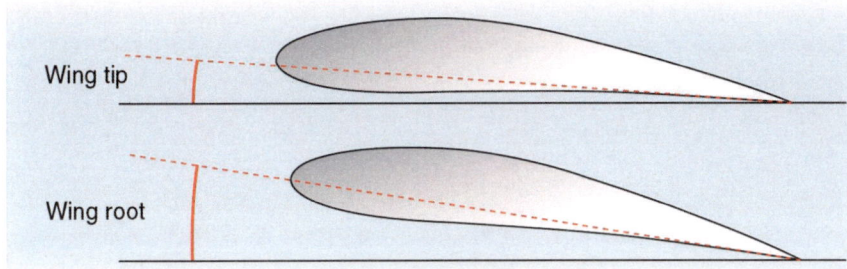

Figure 4.26

On a GEOMETRIC TWIST, the smaller difference in pressure near the tip causes lower induced drag

Another way to achieve the same result is to use the so-called aerodynamic washout. In order to decrease C_L from the wing root to the wing tip, different profiles are used. In this case, successively thinner and less cambered profiles are used from the root to the tip.

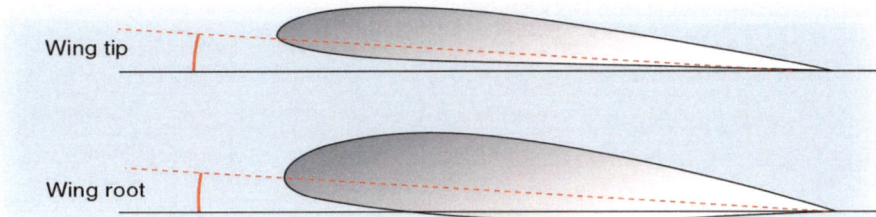

Figure 4.27

AERODYNAMIC WASHOUT (TWIST) consists in changing the shape of the wing section from the wing root to the wing tip

A wing can have both geometric and aerodynamic twist in order to obtain low induced drag and good stall characteristics.

4.2.3   *Wing plan form*

The wing plan form also has a considerable influence on induced drag. The lowest induced drag for a given wingspan is attained when the downwash angle is constant across the span. This is true for an elliptical wing, or more precisely, a wing with elliptical loading. Thus, the load distribution is a function of the plan form of the wing. An untwisted elliptical wing of constant section has elliptic loading and this is the optimum shape as far as induced drag is concerned.

Figure 4.28

However, an elliptical wing is complicated and difficult to produce with different sections and curvature all over the wing. A straight tapered wing of taper ratio 2:1 (twice the wing root chord to wing tip chord) behaves very much as an elliptical wing. This is one of the reasons why most wing plan forms are moderately tapered. For all other wings, which do not have elliptic loading, the value of induced drag is usually about 1.1 to 1.3 times higher.

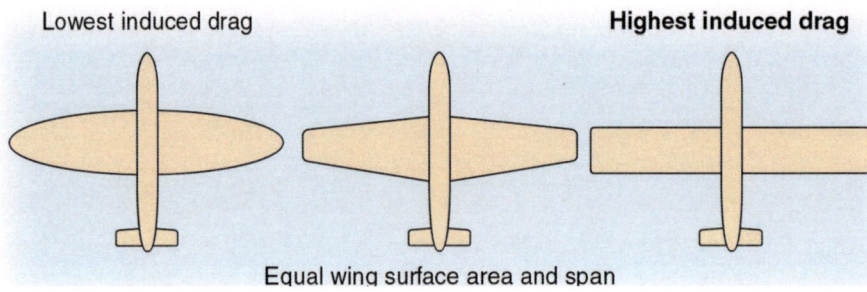

Figure 4.29

4.2.4   *Wing tip modification.*

The wing tip can be modified in order to reduce induced drag. By making it more difficult for the airflow to spill around the wing tip, a better pressure distribution around the wing can be produced demanding a lower A.o.A for a given lift. A lower A.of.A will create a weaker wing tip vortex.

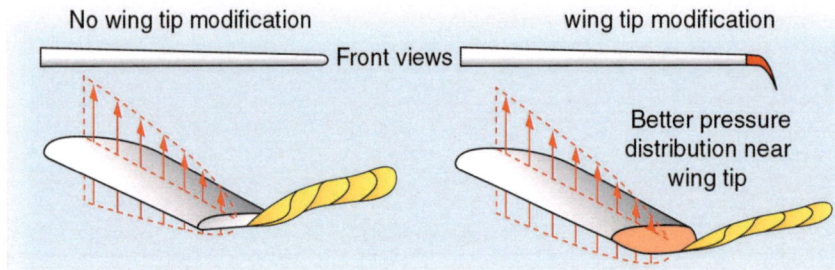

Figure 4.30

For the same reason the winglet reduces induced drag. But in addition to this, the low pressure area on the upper surface is stretched out to the wing tip since the pressure spill over the wingtip is avoided by the winglet surface.

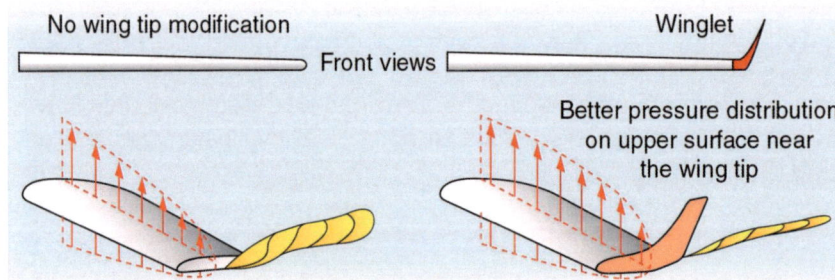

Figure 4.31

A wing tip tank also makes it more difficult for the airflow to spill around the wing tip and thus less induced drag is produced.

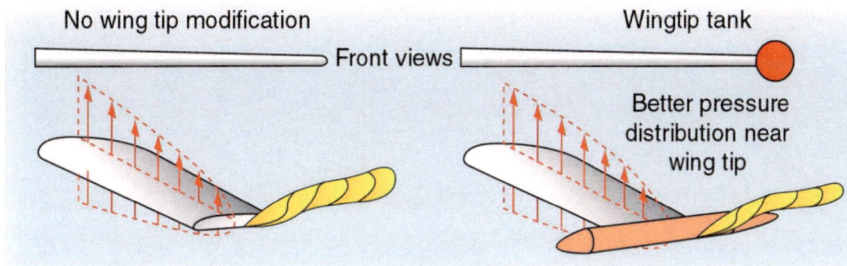

Figure 4.32

However, these wing tip modifications increase parasite drag and must therefore be introduced only when the total effect is positive.

Normally, these types of wing tip modifications, i.e. winglets, are used on long range aircraft flying at high altitudes where the low static pressure gives less dynamic pressure demanding a relative high angle of attack to produce the required lift.

Figure 4.33

Wing tip modifications decrease induced drag but increase parasite drag and must therefore be introduced only when the total effect is positive

All creation of lift will simultaneously cause undesirable drag. In order to make an aircraft able to fly with a reasonable use of power, the wing aerofoil section has to be designed to create a high lift compared to the drag. A high lift/drag ratio is obtained by letting a low pressure on the upper surface be the dominating factor of pressure difference. This can be obtained by using an aerofoil section that needs only a low A.of.A to create a certain lift.

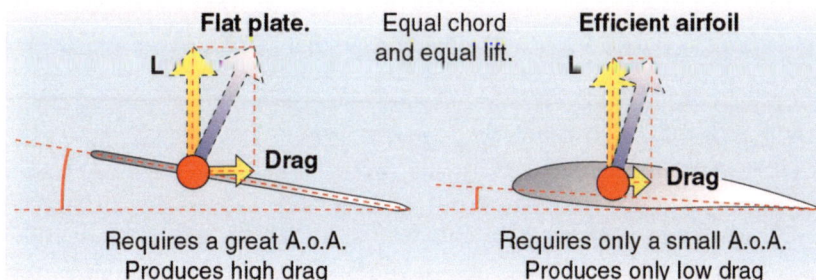

Figure 4.34

4.3 TOTAL DRAG

4.3.1 Total drag as the sum of $D_0 + D_i$.

Zero Lift Drag or Parasite Drag is the sum of:
* form drag,
* skin friction drag
* Interference drag.

We always experience parasite drag when we move through the air.

Figure 4.35

As opposed to parasite drag, induced drag only occurs when we produce lift.

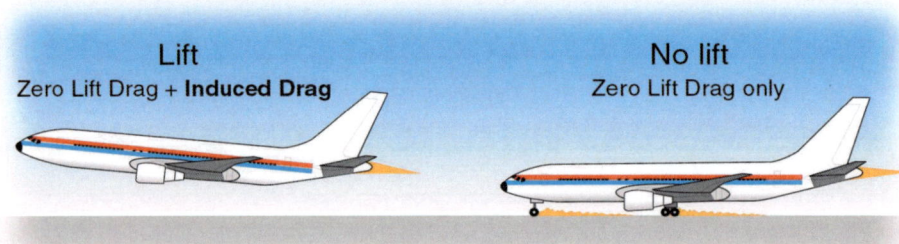

Figure 4.36

Induced drag is a by-product of the creation of lift. The sum of parasite drag and induced drag is called total drag. It is the total of the resistance experienced by an aircraft when flying in the air.

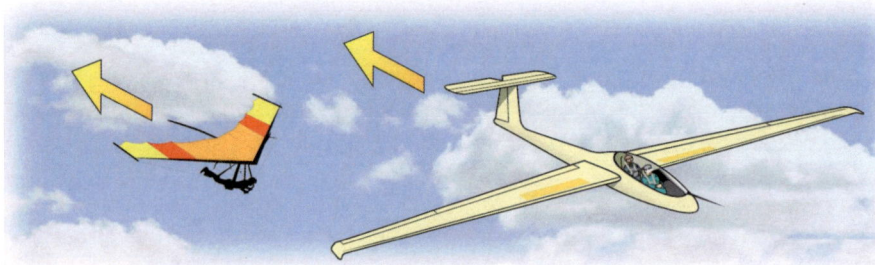

Figure 4.37

When flying at high speeds close to the speed of sound we encounter still another type of drag, Shock Drag or Wave Drag, due to the effects of air compressibility. We will deal with this later in the chapter: Aerodynamics of High Speed Aircraft.

Shockwaves

Figure 4.38

WAVE DRAG or SHOCK DRAG is created only at high speeds

4.3.2   *Total drag versus airspeed.*

We know that parasite drag is directly proportional to V^2. This means that parasite drag is zero at zero speed and increases with the square of the airspeed.

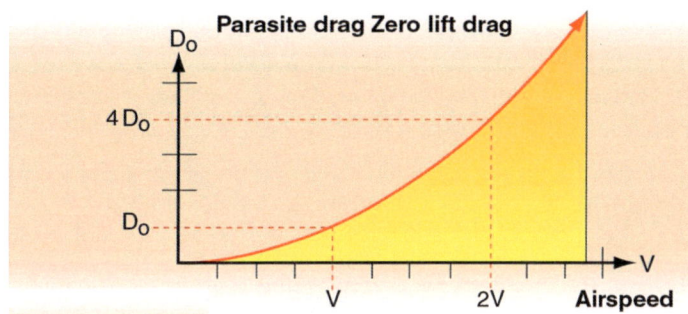

Figure 4.39

Contrary to parasite drag, induced drag is inversely proportional to V^2. This means that induced drag tends to be very high at zero speed, decreasing as the speed increases.

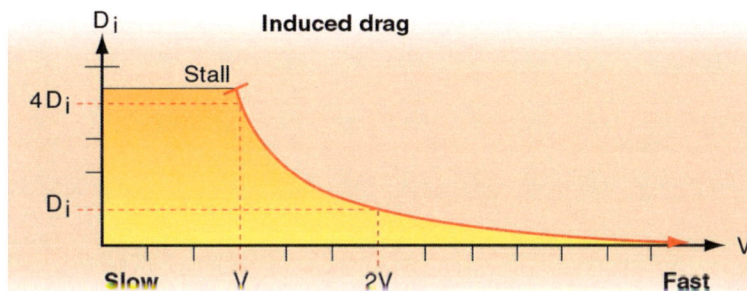

Figure 4.40

To calculate the variation in total drag with speed, we must add induced drag to parasite drag for each speed, $D_i + D_0 = D_{tot}$.

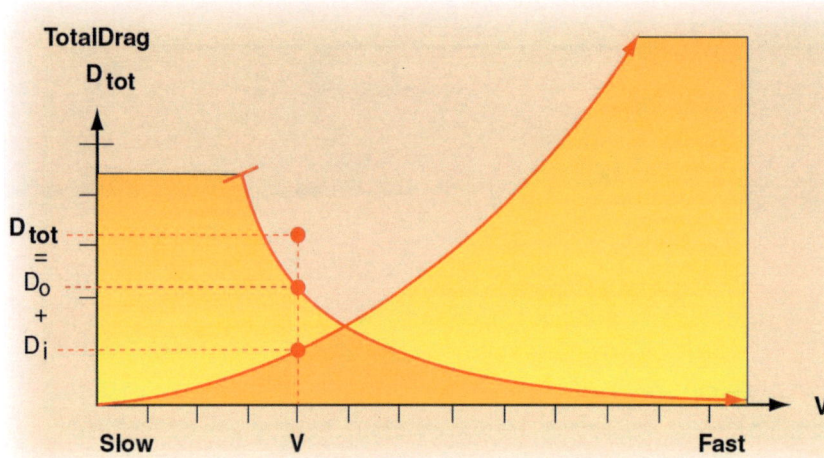

Figure 4.41

You can see that at low speeds, induced drag is predominant while the parasite drag component of the total drag is very small. If we increase the speed to an intermediate value where $D_i = D_0$ (1/1), we can see that, by adding the parasite drag to induced drag, we obtain a minimum value of total drag. This airspeed value is very important. It is called the most efficient airspeed, designated V_{imd}.

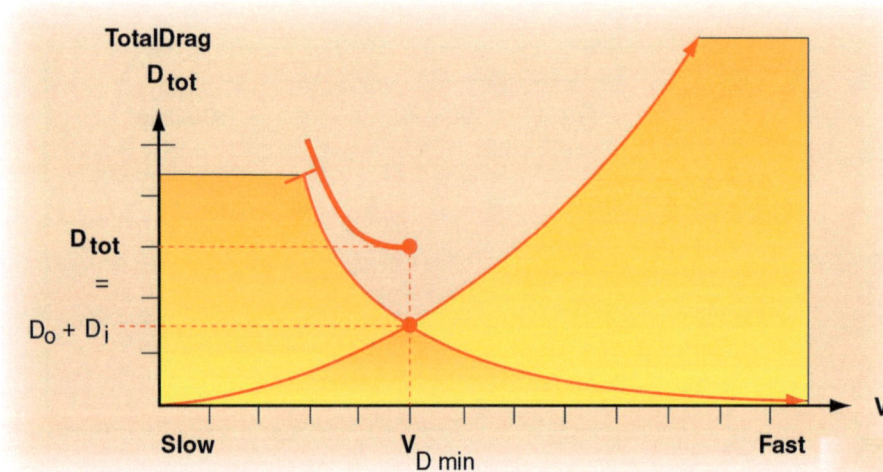

Figure 4.42

At an intermediate airspeed V_{imd} where $D_i = D_0$, we have minimum total drag

At high speed, parasite drag is predominant while there is a very small component of induced drag in the total drag.

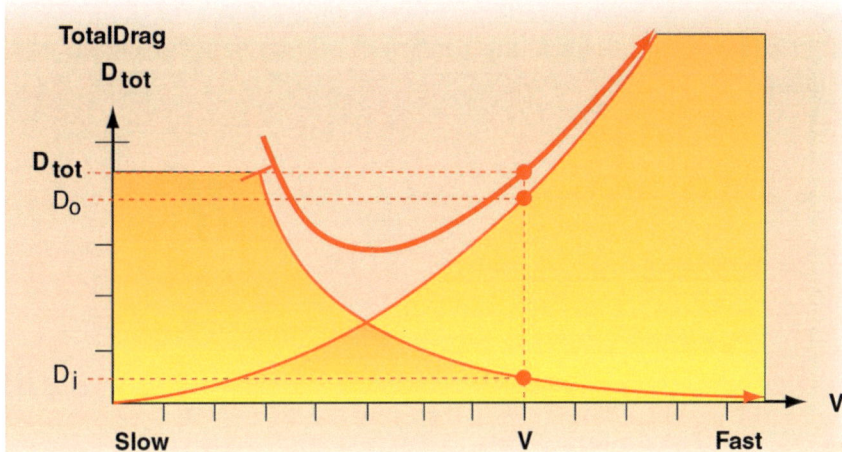

Figure 4.43

Total drag does not have the lowest value at the lowest flying speed

4.3.3 *Coefficient of total drag*

Total drag, like all aerodynamic forces, is expressed as a dynamic pressure factor multiplied by the area. We see that total drag is directly proportional to dynamic pressure "q" and to the reference area "S". This reference area is usually the wing area. We also have the coefficient C_D which, as we have seen before, represents the factors of the aircraft that create total drag. This, in turn, is the sum of the coefficient of parasite drag and the coefficient of induced drag.

Total Drag		Dynamic pressure		Reference area		Coefficient of drag
D_{tot}	=	q $\frac{1}{2} \rho V^2$	x	S	x	C_D $C_{Do} + C_{Di}$

Figure 4.44

The coefficient of drag C_D takes into account the shape of the aircraft e.g. wing aspect ratio "A", wing plan form, and the angle of attack. We can draw curves representing the variation of C_D with the angle of attack for different aspect ratios.

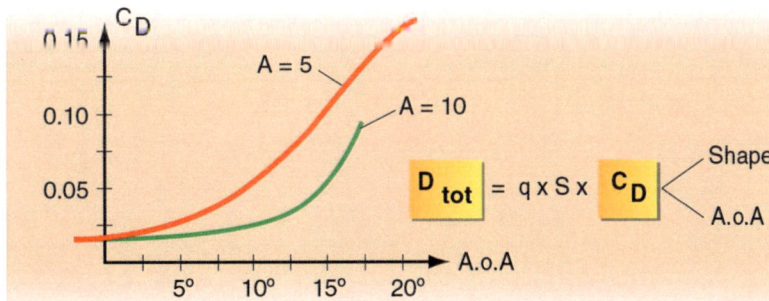

Figure 4.45

The C_D takes into account the shape of the aircraft and the A.of.A

Since the aspect ratio of an aircraft does not change, we will have a look at what happens at different angles of attack. Note that at high angles of attack, the coefficient of drag is high close to the stalling angle and plays a major role in the formula.

Figure 4.46

At high angles of attack there are high values of C_D

At low angles of attack near cruising speed, the coefficient of drag is low, but the airspeed "V" is higher. This has a major effect on the total drag.

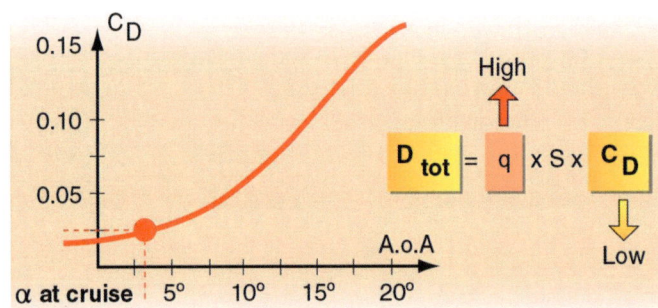

Figure 4.47

At low angles of attack C_D is low but we have high speeds giving high total drag

This explains why the drag force D is high at an extreme angle of attack as well as at high airspeeds. Drag reaches its minimum value at the most efficient airspeed abbreviated V_{imd}.
The total drag depends upon the dynamic pressure and is thus affected by speed and also by air density. If the air density decreases, the total drag decreases proportionally.

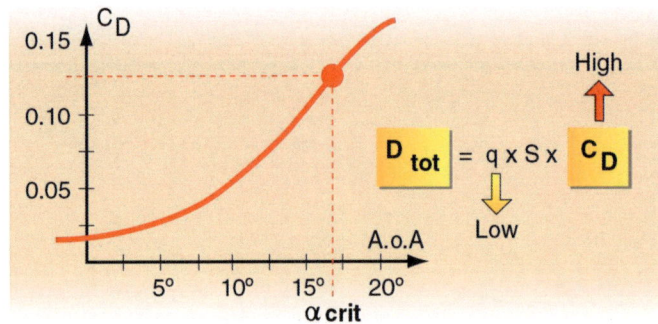

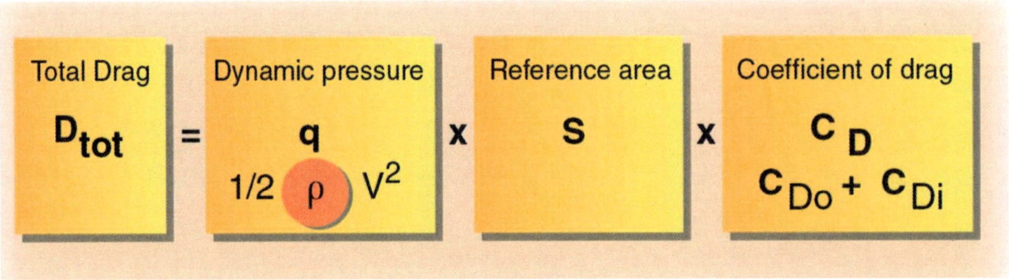

Figure 4.48

If air density decreases, the total drag decreases proportionally

Coming back to the total drag versus airspeed curve, we must mention that it is drawn for a given aircraft weight and a given aircraft configuration. If the weight of the aircraft increases, we must produce more lift thus causing increased induced drag. We can see that as the speed increases, we have higher total drag, even with the same weight, e.g. 1500 kg.. At 2000 kg the total drag increases further.

Figure 4.49

With an increase in weight, the total drag is increased

We can also see that when the weight of the aircraft increases, the most efficient airspeed increases.

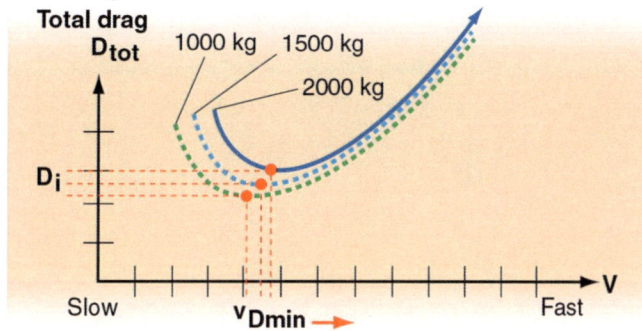

Figure 4.50

As weight increases, the airspeed with minimum drag increases

All these considerations are valid if the aircraft is in level flight. When we make a steep turn, for example, or a pull-up, an excess of lift over weight is required to balance the centrifugal force, and more drag is created.

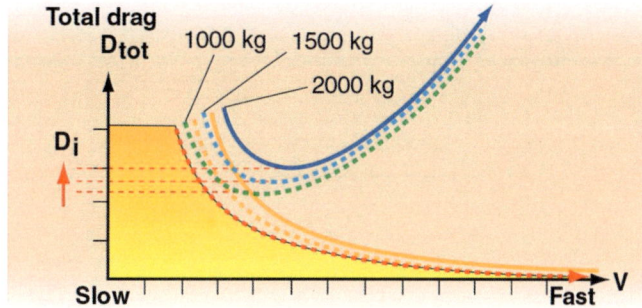

Total Drag		Dynamic pressure		Reference area		Coefficient of drag
D_{tot}	$=$	q $\frac{1}{2}\rho V^2$	$\times$	S	$\times$	C_D $C_{Du} + C_{Di}$

Figure 4.51

Manoeuvring requires an excess of lift, which creates more drag

When the configuration of the aircraft changes, the total drag changes. When the landing gear is extended, the total drag increases.

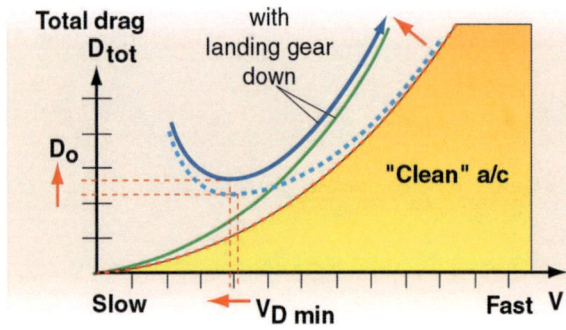

Figure 4.52

By extending the LANDING GEAR, we increase the drag

Using high lift devices such as flaps, drag increases significantly. We see the effect of a partial extension of the flaps on the curve of total drag versus airspeed. When the deflection of the flaps increases further, the drag increases even more.

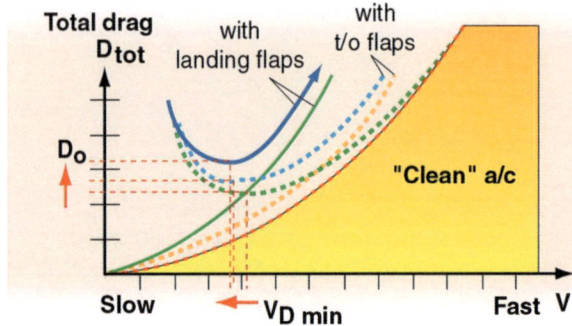

Figure 4.53

As the FLAP DEFLECTION ANGLE increases, the total drag increases

4.3.4 *Different curves of total drag with different aspect ratios*

The wing aspect ratio has a major influence, especially on induced drag. Here we see two different curves of total drag versus airspeed for two aircraft with the same wing area but with different aspect ratios.

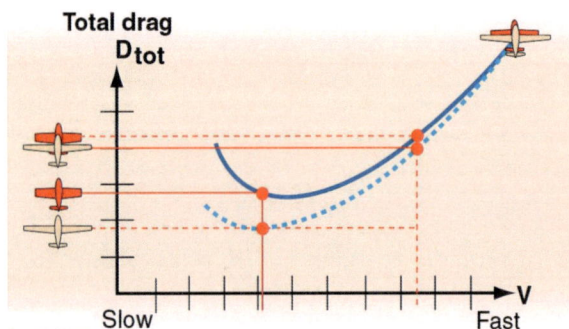

- Figure 4.54

At low speed the wing with a high aspect ratio has lower total drag because of the lower induced drag

Aircraft designed to fly at speeds near the speed of sound mostly have short wings with a low aspect ratio. The reason for this is that the wing section must be very thin in order to reduce the wave drag at transonic or supersonic speeds. The combination of a thin and long wing will be very heavy in order to have the required strength, consequently a thin wing must be short to reduce weight. This is the reason why high-speed jet fighters operating at high speeds at all altitudes, usually have wings of low aspect ratio. On the contrary, aircraft, which fly slowly or quite fast jet aircraft at high altitudes, have wings with high aspect ratio.

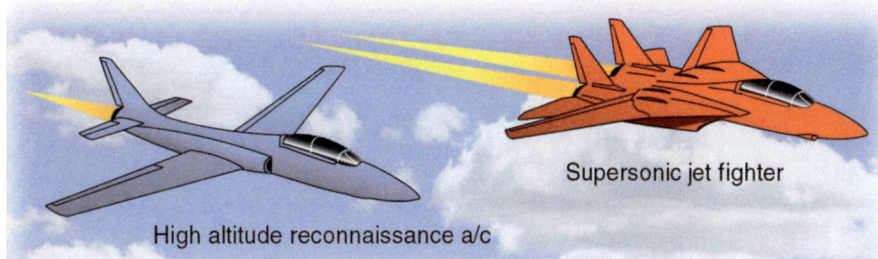

Figure 4.55

Transport aircraft, which are designed to carry high loads long distances, have wings with high aspect ratios and tapered wings, sometimes equipped with "winglets".

Figure 4.56

Sophisticated gliders with long slender wings have less total drag than hang gliders, despite the lower total weight of the latter.

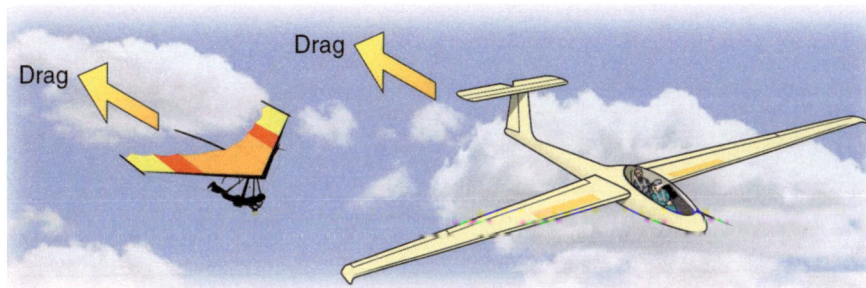

Figure 4.57

Self Assessment Test 01

1   The wing span is the distance:
A)   From the leading edge to trailing edge
B)   From wing tip to wing tip
C)   From wing tip to fuselage center line
D)   Between top and bottom of the wing at the thickest point

2   The angle of attack is the angle between the:
A)   Chord line and the longitudinal axis
B)   Wing and the lateral axis
C)   The chord line and the direction of the airflow
D)   The direction of the airflow and the fuselage for aft datum

3   The taper ratio is:
A)   The ratio of root incidence to tip incidence
B)   The ratio of the wing root thickness to tip thickness
C)   The ratio of wing chord to tailplane chord
D)   The ratio of tip chord to root chord

4   A stagnation point is a point where:
A)   The static pressure is exactly equal to ambient atmospheric pressure
B)   The airspeed is reduced to zero and pressure is less than ambient atmospheric pressure
C)   The airflow becomes laminar
D)   The airspeed is reduced to zero and pressure is higher than ambient atmospheric pressure

5   Wash out is:
A)   A decrease in chord from root to tip
B)   An increase in incidence from root to tip
C)   A decrease in incidence from root to tip
D)   A decrease in aspect ratio from root to tip

6   The chord line is:
A)   A line tangential to the wing surface at the leading edge
B)   A line perpendicular to the longitudinal axis
C)   A line equidistant from upper and lower surface
D)   A straight line from leading edge to trailing edge

7   The aspect ratio is:
A)   The ratio between the span and the mean chord
B)   The ratio between the square of the span and the mean chord
C)   The ratio between the span and the wing area
D)   The ratio of root chord to tip chord

8   The airflow over a wing causes:
A)   A decrease in speed and an increase in pressure over both the upper and lower surfaces
B)   A decrease in speed and a decrease in pressure over the upper surface, and an increase in speed and a decrease in pressure over the lower surface
C)   An increase in speed and a decrease in pressure over the upper surface, and an increase in pressure and a decrease in speed over the lower surface
D)   A decrease in speed and an increase in pressure over the upper surface and a decrease in pressure and an increase in speed over the lower surface

9   The boundary layer of a body in a moving airstream is:
A)   A thin layer of air over the surface where the air is stationary
B)   A layer of separated flow where the air is turbulent
C)   A layer of air over the surface where the airspeed is changing from free stream to zero speed
D)   A layer of air which is moving at free stream speed

10   Minimum total drag of an aircraft occurs:
A)   When induced drag is least
B)   At the stalling speed
C)   When profile drag equals induced drag
D)   At the best rate of climb speed

11   The induced drag of an aircraft:
A)   Increases with increasing speed
B)   Is unaffected by speed
C)   Increases as aspect ratio is increased
D)   Decreases with increasing speed

12   The stalling angle of attack of a typical aerofoil is approximately:
A) -5°
B) 15°
C) 5°
D) 60°

13   The optimum angle of attack of an aerofoil is the angle at which:
A)   The highest lift/drag ratio is produced
B)   The aerofoil produces zero lift
C)   The aerofoil produces maximum lift
D)   The aerofoil produces minimum drag

14   The optimum angle of attack for a aerofoil is about ....$^{\circ}$ with the wing at an angle close to ....
A)   4   a stall
B)   16   a stall
C)   4   the cruise
D)   16   the cruise

15   If the angle of attack is increased the centre of pressure will:
A)   Move rearward
B)   Be dissipated
C)   Remain stationary
D)   Move forward

16   Near to a stall, when increasing power, the vertical component of thrust produced:
A)   Immediately induces a stall
B)   Will oppose the weight thus giving a slightly lower stalling speed
C)   Will oppose lift giving a smaller stalling angle
D)   Will give a higher rate of sink

17   If you are flying at 100 KT and you increase your speed to 200 KT, profile drag:
A)   Doubles
B)   Quadruples
C)   Increases by a factor of $\sqrt{2}$
D)   Remains the same

18 The centre of pressure of an aerofoil is:-
A) The point where the pressure on the under surface of the wing is highest
B) The point on the leading edge of the wing where the airflow can be considered stagnated
C) The point where the pressure on the upper surface of the wing is lowest
D) The point on the chord line where the lift force acts

19 If the density of the air is increased with a fixed angle of attack and TAS, the lift:-
A) May increase or decrease depending on the pressure
B) Increases
C) Decreases
D) Remains the same

20 A high aspect ratio wing:-
A) Increases induced drag
B) Decreases induced drag
C) Decreases skin friction drag
D) Has no effect on induced drag

21 Zero lift (i.e. parasite) drag consists of:-
A) Form drag and induced drag
B) Form drag, skin friction drag and interference drag
C) Form drag, skin friction drag, induced drag and interference drag
D) Form drag and skin friction drag only

22 Total drag is made up of:
A) Parasite drag and induced drag
B) Zero lift drag and parasite drag
C) Form drag and induced drag
D) Zero lift drag, form drag and drag caused as a result of the production of lift

23 As flaps are lowered on the approach land the:
A) Form drag increases as the camber of the wing increases
B) Induced drag decreases
C) Skin friction drag increases
D) Form drag increases as the camber of the wing decreases

24 After cruising at minimum drag speed on a 3 h flight, towards the end of the flight you would have to:
A) Cruise at a higher speed as the minimum drag speed increases as fuel is burned
B) Cruise at a lower speed as minimum drag speed decreases as weight decreases
C) Cruise at the same speed as the minimum drag speed is independent of weight
D) None of the above are correct

25 At the speed for minimum drag:
A) Parasite drag = total drag
B) Induced drag = total drag
C) Total drag = weight
D) Parasite drag = induced drag

Self Assessment Test 01 Answers

1	B
2	C
3	D
4	D
5	C
6	D
7	A
8	C
9	C
10	C
11	D
12	B
13	A
14	C
15	D
16	B
17	B
18	D
19	B
20	B
21	B
22	A
23	A
24	B
25	D

CHAPTER 5

Force and moment equilibrium

5.1 Weight

5.1.1 Basics

The weight vector is always vertical and directed towards the centre of the Earth.

Figure 5.1

Weight is generally incorrectly expressed in kilograms or pounds. Since it is a force, it should be expressed in Newton's. This force is given by the mass, in kg or lbs., of the body multiplied by the gravity acceleration equal to 9.81 m/s^2.

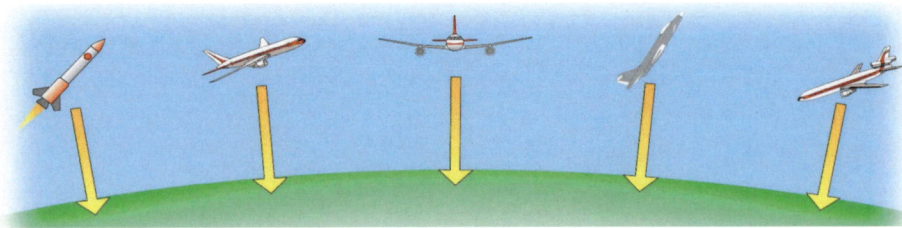

Figure 5.2

Some aircraft manufacturers express the aircraft weight in their manuals using kilograms. Others use pounds. It is very important to know how to convert from one unit to the other. 1 kg is equal to 2.20 lbs. and 1 lb. is equal to 0.45 kg. An aircraft weighing 1000 kg has a weight of 2200 lbs. In general it is easy to remember that 1 kilogram is slightly more than 2 lbs.

5.1.2 Centre of gravity

The point at which the weight seemingly acts is called the "Centre of gravity", C.G. and is usually represented by a little circle.

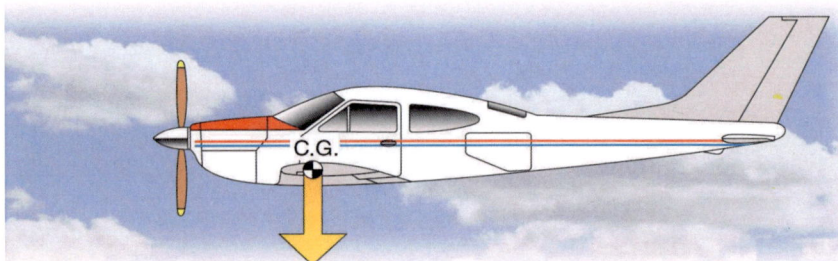

Figure 5.3

The weight of an aircraft is generally calculated by adding to the BASIC EMPTY WEIGHT, which is specified in the aircraft manual, all the additional loads: PERSONS on board, BAGGAGE and FUEL.
The weight of the aircraft determined in this way is called the ACTUAL TAKE-OFF WEIGHT or, when in the air, ACTUAL GROSS WEIGHT.

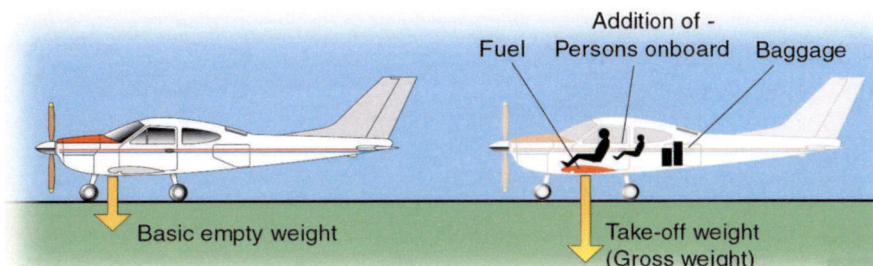

Figure 5.4

Actual Take-Off Weight = Basic Empty Weight + Persons + Baggage + Fuel

For several structural and aerodynamic reasons the ACTUAL TAKEOFF WEIGHT must not exceed a given weight called the MAXIMUM TAKE-OFF WEIGHT, which is specified in the aircraft manual.

For heavy aircraft flying long distances, the difference between the TAKE-OFF WEIGHT and the successive LANDING WEIGHT can be considerable, due to the large quantity of fuel used during the flight.

In the same way that we can affect the aircraft weight by loading it in different ways, we can also affect the position of the centre of gravity. The empty aircraft is characterised by a specific position of the centre of gravity and a given empty weight. If we increase the weight in the rear zone, for example by putting heavy loads in the baggage compartment, the aircraft weight increases and the centre of gravity moves backwards.

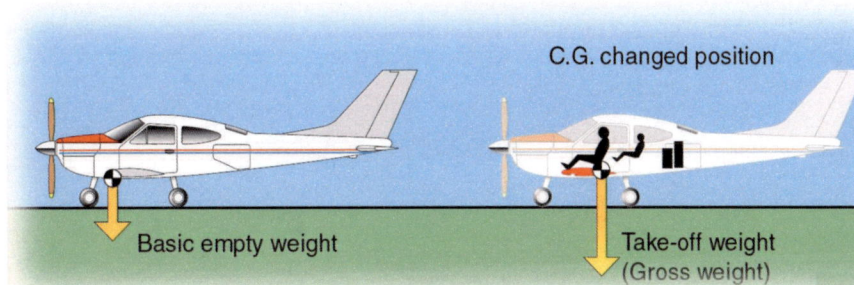

Figure 5.5

The position and amount of loading affect WEIGHT and CENTRE OF GRAVITY

5.1.3 Acceleration forces

Another important factor that must be well considered is the acceleration forces to which the aircraft is subject when performing certain manoeuvres like turns, pull-ups or acrobatics.

During a turn, a force is required to create the angular acceleration and therefore, in fact, the angle of bank ϕ (phi) has the purpose of generating that component of lift that accelerates the aircraft into the turn. The aircraft will then be subjected to another force created by the inertia of the mass called centrifugal force (FCF). It is dragged along the radius and tends to move away from the centre of rotation. In this situation, the centrifugal force, combined with the aircraft weight, generates a resultant force sometimes called the apparent weight which the wings have to compensate for by creating equal lift, i.e. lift greater than that necessary to counteract the weight only.

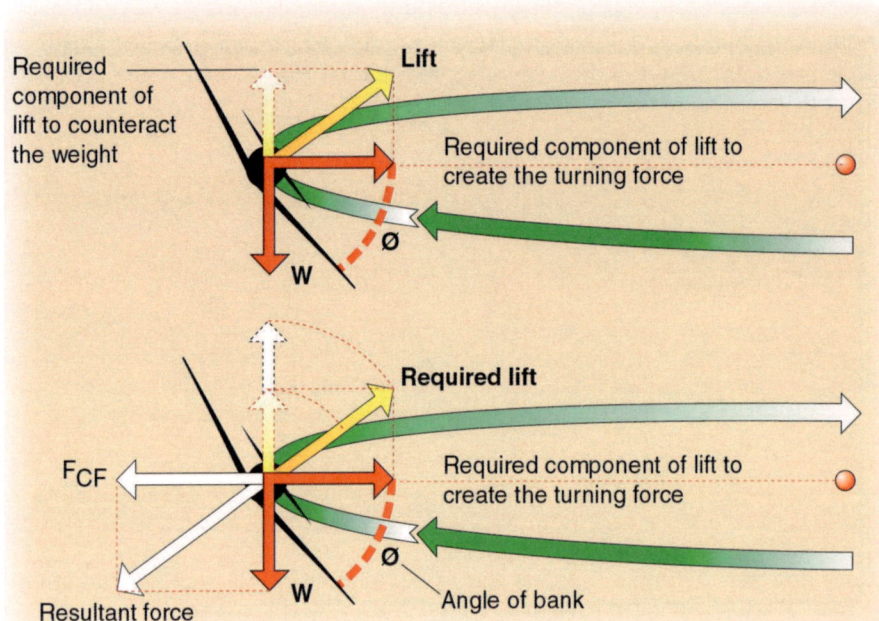

Figure 5.6

In the same way, during a pull-up, there is a centrifugal force that, added to the aircraft weight, requires of the wings a lift greater than the weight of the aircraft. If the centrifugal force is equal to the force of gravity, the lift required must be two times the weight. In this case we say that the load factor, abbreviated to n, is 2. If the aircraft is equipped with an accelerometer, or "g-meter", it will show 2 g.

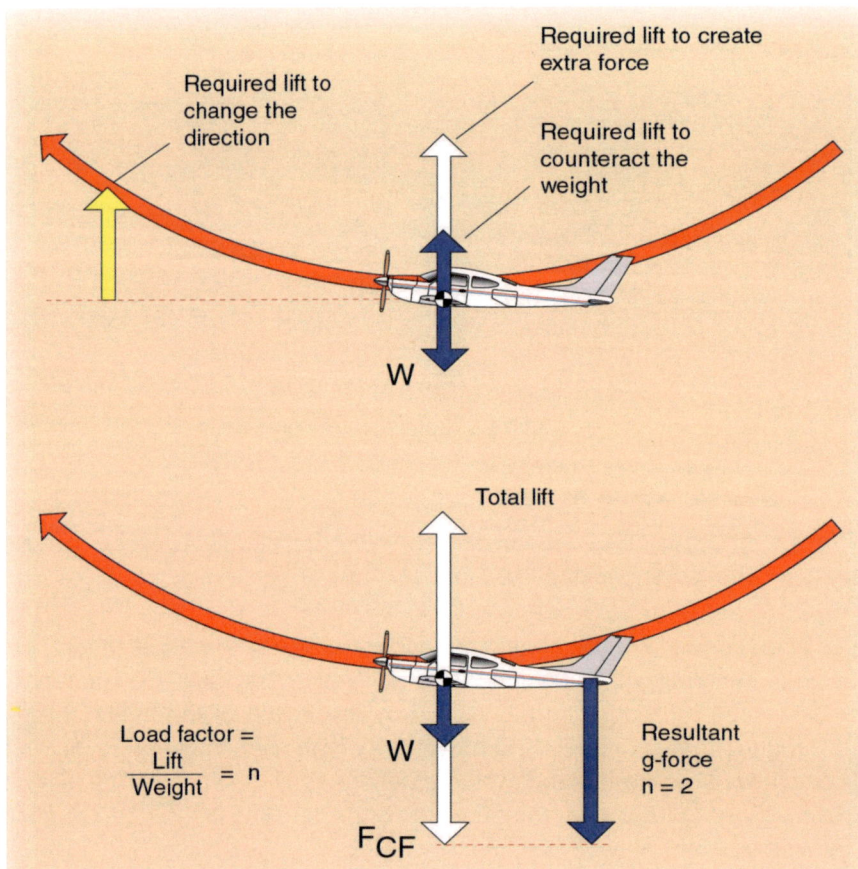

Figure 5.7

If you were sitting on a spring balance during a 2g pull-up, it would show a weight twice as high as your weight on the ground. The steeper the pull-up or the turn, the greater the centrifugal force and thus the load factor. If the load factor is equal to 3, the lift is three times the weight and you experience 3 g.

During straight and level flight, the load factor is equal to one because lift is equal to weight. In inverted flight, the load factor (on the wings) is equal to minus one.

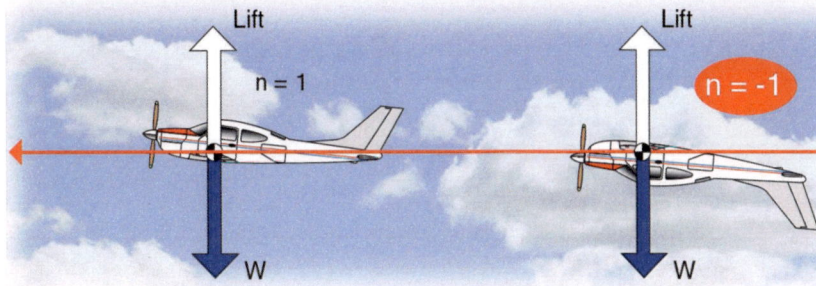

Figure 5.8

5.2 Equilibrium

5.2.1 Basics

We have earlier analysed all the main forces acting on the aircraft i.e. LIFT, DRAG, THRUST and WEIGHT. The purpose of this section is to show their relationship in different phases of flight. In order to facilitate comprehension, we will consider the centre of gravity of the aircraft as the point at which all four forces act.

In straight and level flight, lift is equal to weight and thus the LOAD FACTOR is equal to one. The aircraft produces drag that must be balanced by equal and opposite thrust in order not to change the airspeed.

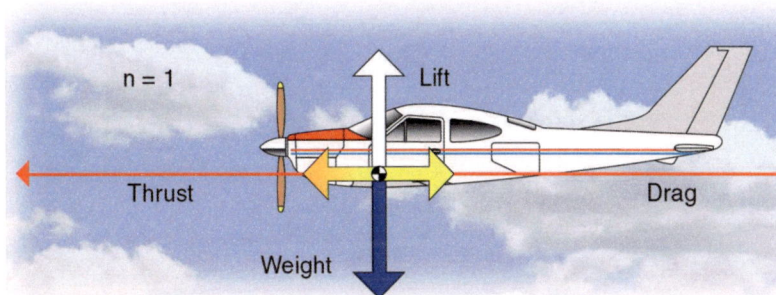

Figure 5.9

When the aircraft is climbing at a given airspeed with a given angle of climb γ (gamma), the weight of the aircraft is the same but directed towards the centre of the earth instead of perpendicular to the flight path. We already know that, opposed to this, lift is perpendicular to the flight path, and in this case the lift must balance not the whole weight but only its component along the lift direction.

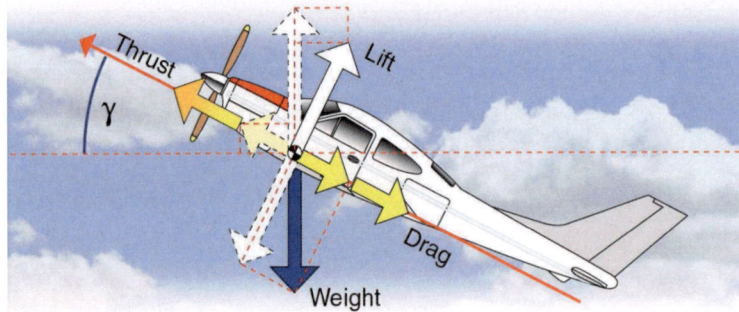

Figure 5.10

During climb the lift must balance only the component of weight along the lift direction

The other component of weight is in the same direction as DRAG. If we want to maintain the same speed while climbing, we must use more engine power because we must balance the DRAG plus the component of weight in the DRAG direction.

In climb, thrust must balance the drag plus a component of the weight

In the same way, when the aircraft descends at a given airspeed with a given angle of descent -γ, the weight of the aircraft is the same and it is always directed towards the centre of the earth.

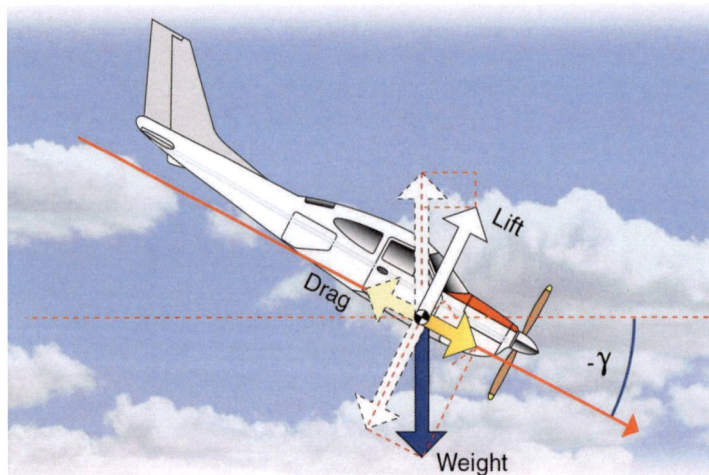

Figure 5.11

Lift is always perpendicular to the flight path and, in this case too, it must balance not the whole weight but only its component along the lift direction.

During descent the lift must balance only the component of weight along the lift direction

The other component of weight is in the same direction as the THRUST. If we want to maintain the same airspeed while descending, we must reduce engine power because we must balance the DRAG minus the component of weight in the THRUST direction.

In descent, the component of weight in the flight direction may balance the corresponding amount of drag

Now let us look at the aircraft from behind, when it is making a right turn with a certain bank angle. The weight of the aircraft is always directed towards the centre of the earth. As the circular motion starts, the

CRANFIELD AVIATION TRAINING SCHOOL LTD. PART-FCL GBR.ATO-0136
CATS INNOVATION CENTRE, LUTON, Bedfordshire LU2 8DL U.K.   www.catsaviation.com

5-5   Principles of Flight

centrifugal force is created. The centrifugal force (FCF) tends to move the aircraft away from the centre of rotation.

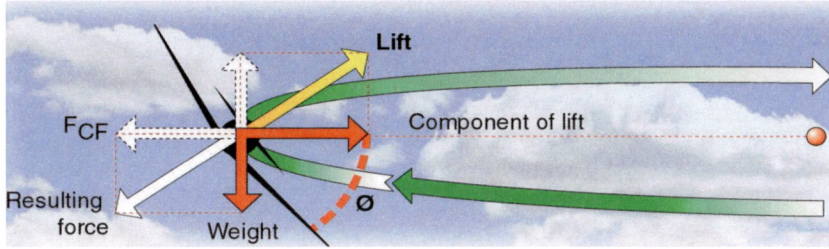

Figure 5.12

In order to maintain the correct circular path, the component of lift generated by the lateral inclination must balance the centrifugal force

You can see that the lift must be much greater than the aircraft weight because it has to balance the force originating from the composition of weight and centrifugal force i.e. the resulting force. The greater the bank angle, the steeper the turn and the greater the resulting force, which results in more lift required.

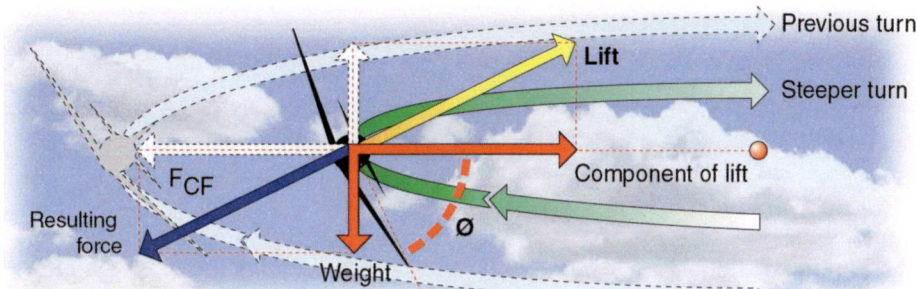

Figure 5.13

The greater the bank angle, the greater the need of lift

The same situation viewed from somewhat above shows that, in order to counteract the apparent weight, the lift must be greater. As you already know; an increase in lift causes an increase in induced drag. So, in order to continue a turn at a given airspeed, the THRUST must be increased in order to be equal to the DRAG.

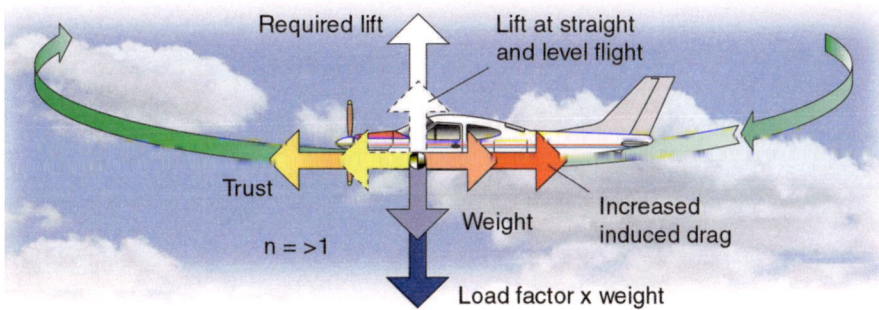

Figure 5.14

5.3   *Equilibrium of moment*

A turning moment round, for example a centre of gravity, is the product of the forces given by the distance between C.G. and the point of application of forces. For example, if there is a lifting force at a given distance in front of the C.G., there must be a counteracting force giving the same turning moment in the other direction to achieve equilibrium of moment. Different forces at different arms from the C.G can provide this counteracting moment.

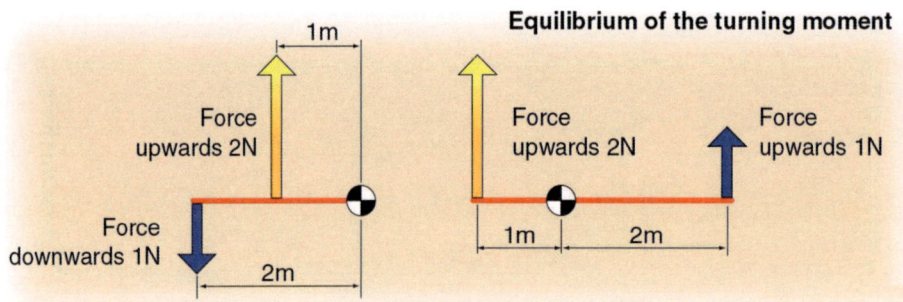

Figure 5.15

In order to achieve equilibrium of moment, the total of all moments must be zero. On a flying aircraft there are forces from wings, tail, weight, drag and thrust etc. but in order to achieve a balanced flight all these forces should result in equilibrium of moment.

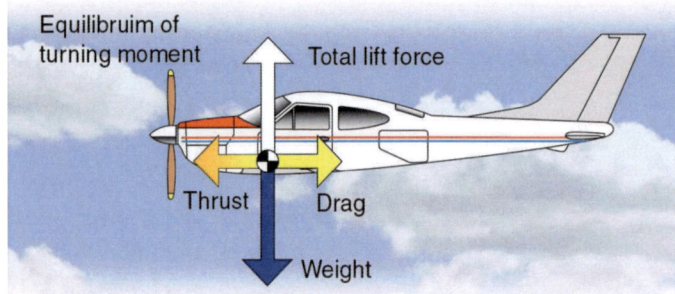

Figure 5.16

But when the aircraft enters a gust directed upwards, a momentary unbalance between the wing and tail is created by the lift, giving a total lifting force acting behind the C.G. that will turn the aircraft nose down.

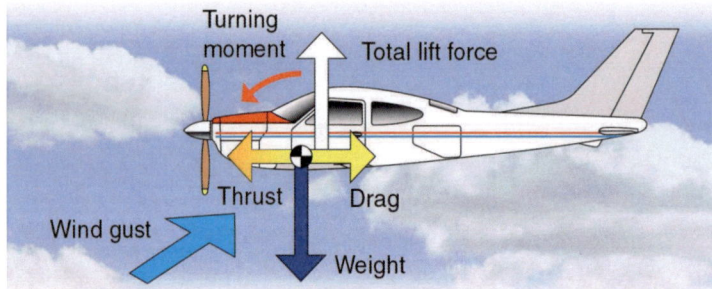

Figure 5.17

This turning motion will change the lift distribution in the way that a new equilibrium is obtained.

Equilibrium of moment is reached when the resultant of all moments is zero

CHAPTER 6

Flight Controls

6.1   General Introduction and Control Effectiveness

6.2   Introduction

All aircraft have flight control systems that allow you to manoeuvre and trim the aircraft round each of the three axes. The control surfaces are usually hinged near the extremities of the aerofoil so that they can have a long moment arm from the centre of gravity and the greatest leverage possible. Changing the airflow around the aerofoil can generate the required moments. This is done by means of changed camber or changed A.of.A. The flight control surfaces, if manually deflected, are connected to the controls by cables and/or pushrods. Large and/or fast aircraft require servos to handle the large control forces, in most cases hydraulically operated with mechanical or electrical signals. In all aircraft the direction of control inputs are the same. The ailerons for lateral control (i.e. in roll) and the elevators for longitudinal control (i.e. in pitch) may be moved by a control wheel, also known as a Deperdussin control, or by a stick, depending on the type of aircraft.

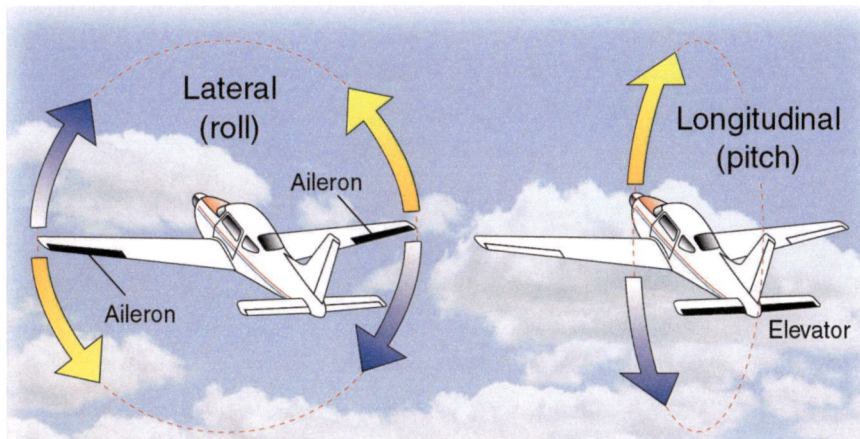

Figure 6.1

The stick is usually installed in aircraft designed for rapid manoeuvres like military and acrobatic planes.

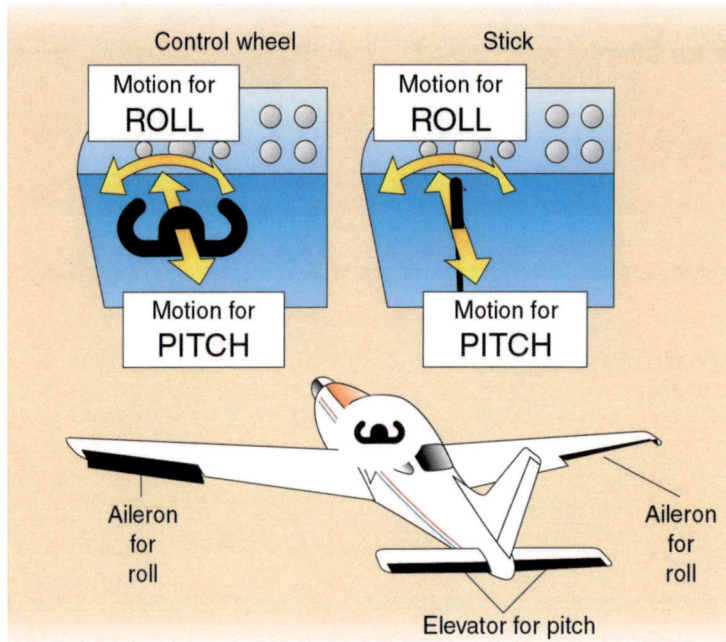

Figure 6.2

If you want to raise the nose, you pull the control wheel or the stick towards you in the same natural way as if the controls where fixed to the aircraft and vice versa. When making a rolling movement to the right, you rotate the control wheel in the same direction, or if there is a stick, by moving it to the right. This means that a manoeuvre upward to the right can be performed by moving the stick slightly to the right/backwards.

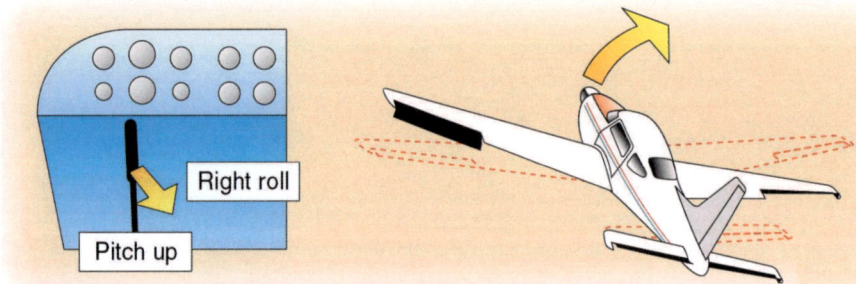

Figure 6.3

For directional control (yaw) a rudder is located on the fin and is moved by the use of pedals. By pushing the right pedal forward, the nose yaws to the right and vice versa.

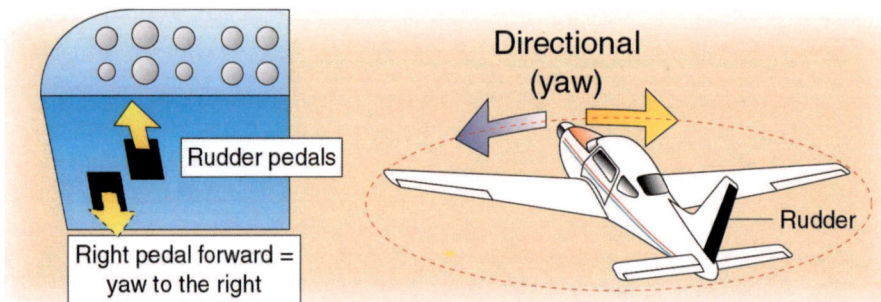

Figure 6.4

Notice that the rudder pedals are used in the opposite way that steering is made on a bicycle and in a boat with tiller.

CRANFIELD AVIATION TRAINING SCHOOL LTD. PART-FCL GBR.ATO-0136
CATS INNOVATION CENTRE, LUTON, Bedfordshire LU2 8DL U.K.   www.catsaviation.com

6-2   Principles of Flight

Each control provides movement or control around a specific axis. Roll, or lateral, control is effected around the roll axis. The roll axis is the aeroplane's longitudinal (X) axis. Pitch (or longitudinal) control is effected around the pitch axis. This is the aeroplane's lateral (Y) axis.

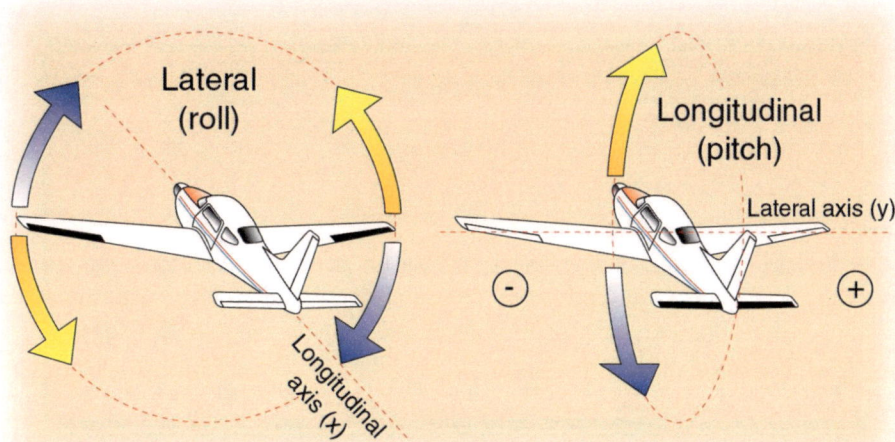

Figure 6.5

Finally, directional control is active around the directional or yaw axis. This is the aeroplane's vertical (z) axis.

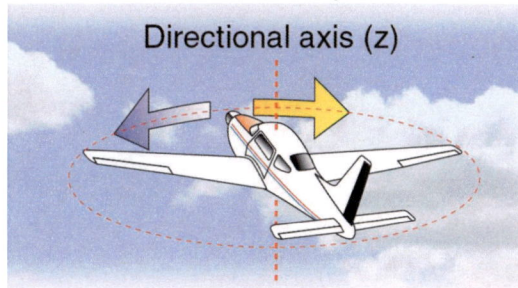

Figure 6.6

The elevator is the primary flight control for pitching around the lateral axis. It is operated by forward and backward movements of the control column or the stick.

The ailerons for lateral control in roll around the longitudinal axis are operated by the rotation of the control wheel or by the lateral movement of the stick.

The rudder, for directional control in yaw, is operated by pushing forward one of the two interconnected rudder pedals. Right pedal forward causes a right yaw.

6.3   *Control effectiveness*

The effectiveness when moving the control surfaces is called the manoeuvrability of the aircraft and differs considerably between aircraft.

By the stability of an aircraft we mean the aircraft's ability to return to its original flight path after a disturbance. An aircraft with too high stability has poor manoeuvrability. The aircraft designer must achieve a reasonable balance between stability and manoeuvrability, bearing in mind the qualities that are the most desirable for the intended use of the aircraft.

Figure 6.7

The deflection of the control surface, changes the circulation, and thus changes the pressure distribution over the entire aerofoil chord and not just over the control surface itself no matter if it is a control surface at the trailing edge changing the camber, or a control surface changing the A.o.A. The effect is to change the lift produced by the total aerofoil/control combination.

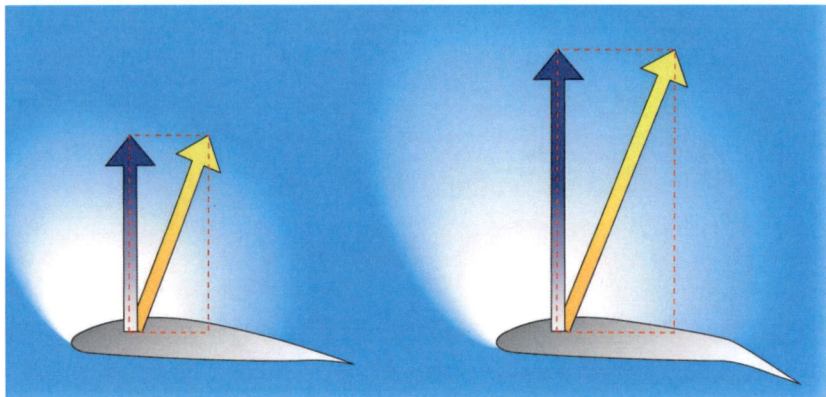

Figure 6.8

There are many factors that can influence the effectiveness of the control surface. The size, the shape and the distance from the centre of gravity can be considered constant while the airspeed and the angle of deflection of the control surface are considered variable.

If, for example, an aileron is deflected downwards, the angle of attack and the camber of the wing increases, thereby increasing the produced lift. The greater the control surface deflection the greater the change in lift. In order to get the aircraft rolling around its centre of gravity, the other aileron is deflected upwards, reducing the angle of attack and the camber of the wing, and thereby reducing the lift produced by that wing.

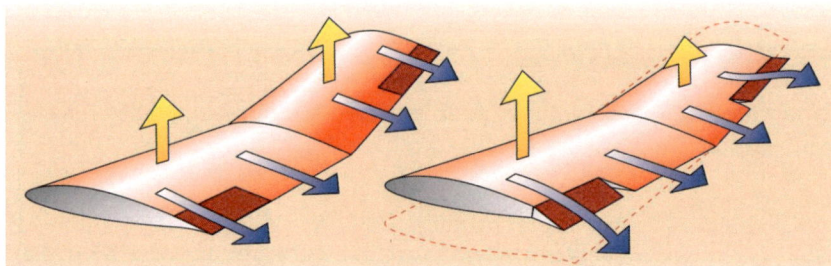

Figure 6.9

The change in rolling moment is the change in lift multiplied by the distance between the point of application and the centre of gravity.

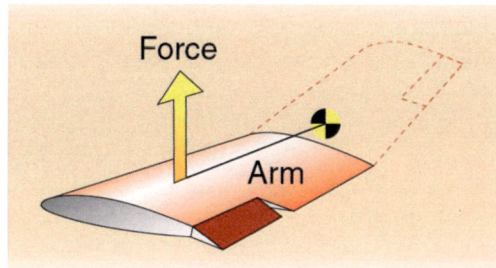

Figure 6.10

The aerodynamic force varies with dynamic pressure; thus, doubling the airspeed quadruples the effect of the same control surface deflection. Basically, the change in A.of.A is proportional to the change in elevator angle, regardless of speed. But the change in load factor varies with the speed for a given elevator angle. Consequently in a mechanical control system, the required stick force for a given change in load factor is roughly constant regardless of speed, but the elevator angle for a given change in load factor varies with speed.

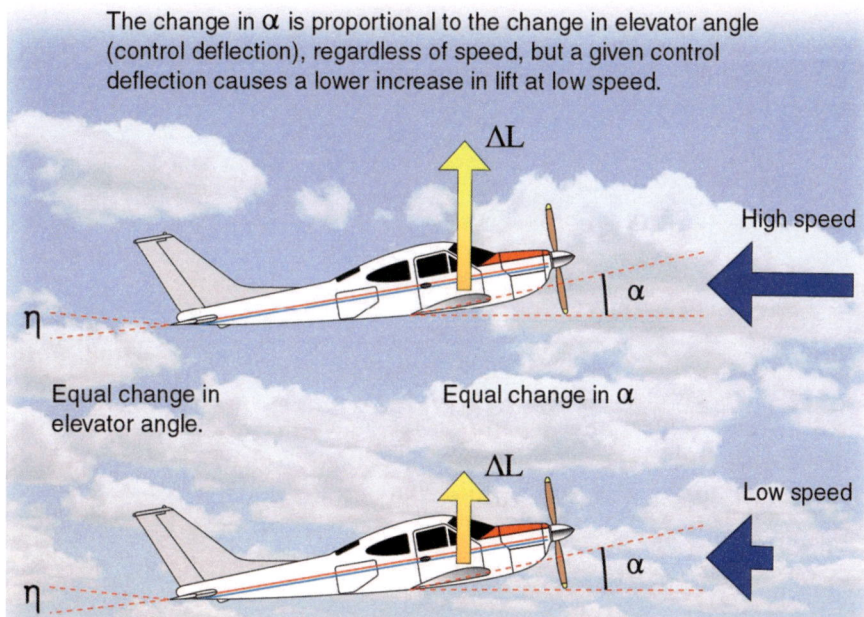

The change in α is proportional to the change in elevator angle (control deflection), regardless of speed, but a given control deflection causes a lower increase in lift at low speed.

Figure 6.11

> The required stick force for a given change in load factor is roughly constant regardless of speed, but the elevator angle for a given change in load factor varies with speed

At low airspeeds, but with high power set, the slipstream generated by the propeller may flow faster over the tail section, making the elevator and rudder more effective than it would be at the same speed with no power on. The ailerons are not affected by the slipstream and will therefore remain comparatively ineffective.

> At low airspeeds, but with high power set, the propeller slipstream may flow faster over the tail section, making the elevator and rudder more effective

As the propeller slipstream flows at higher velocity and in a direction slightly outwards radially, a low pressure zone is created at the slipstream centre. This creates a force on the airflow elements towards the centre. That force will therefore curve the path of the flow elements. The rotational direction of the curved slipstream is determined by the propeller blade rotation. As the slipstream corkscrews around the fuselage, it strikes one side of the fin at a different angle than the other. When viewed from the cockpit, most propellers rotate clockwise, so the slipstream strikes the fin on the left side and pushes the tail to the right. While the aerofoil section of the fin and the rudder is usually symmetrical, the fin may be constructed slightly offset on some propeller driven aircraft in order to balance the effect of the slipstream in cruise condition.

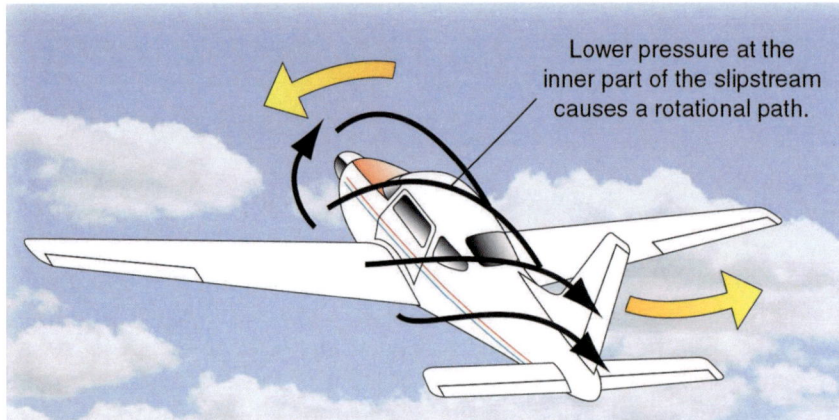

Figure 6.12

If the slipstream over the fin and rudder changes, the rudder deflection must be changed to balance it. Applying power at low speed causes the nose to yaw left; especially during take-off. You must therefore push the right rudder pedal to balance the slipstream effect.

6.3.1   *Stick force*

When a control surface is deflected, the aerodynamic force struggles against the deflection. This causes a force/moment that acts on the control surfaces in an attempt to return the surface to its original position. You feel this as a stick force.

The stick force is due to the moment around the hinge line of the control surface

The aircraft becomes "nose light" (commonly speaking "tail heavy") and is less stable when the C.G. moves backward, and its controls are more sensitive. This means that, for a given elevator angle, the increase in C_L will increase more than if the C.G. is positioned towards the forward limit.

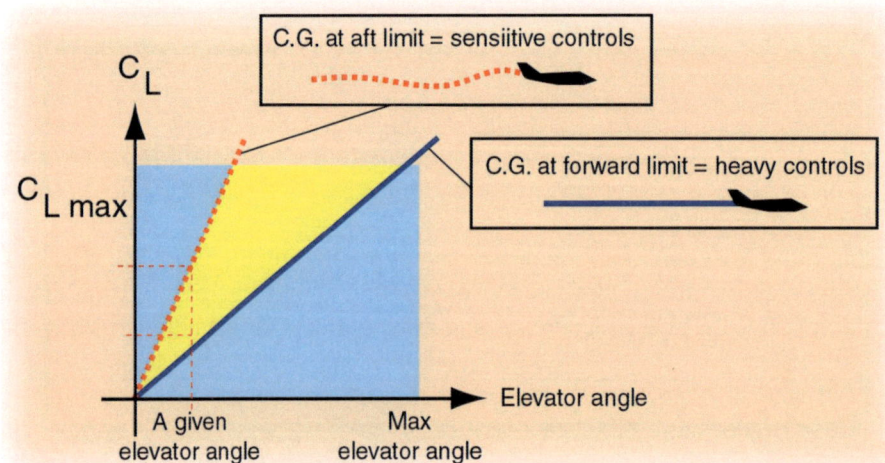

Figure 6.13

When the centre of gravity moves backward, the aircraft becomes less stable and its controls more sensitive

At the same time, the stick force required to achieve the desired change in pitch is low. The aircraft will be more manoeuvrable, but it may also be more sensitive.

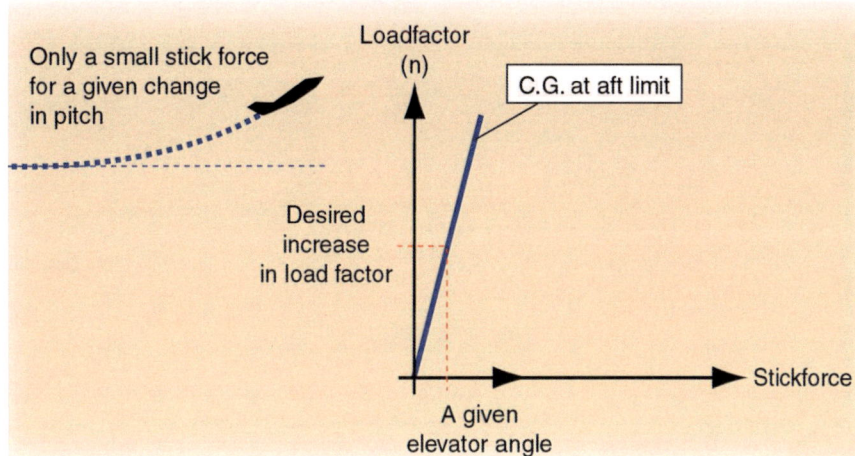

Figure 6.14

Obviously, if the centre of gravity moves forward, the stick force required to achieve a given change in load factor will be higher.

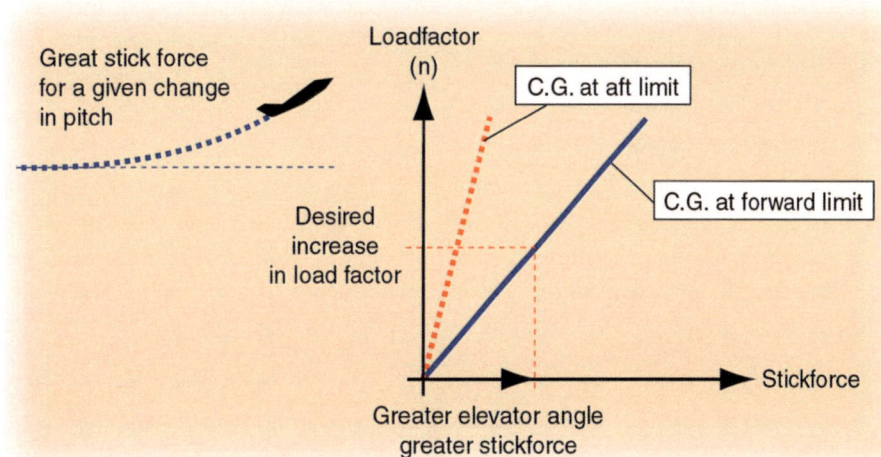

Figure 6.15

When the centre of gravity moves backward, the stick force required to achieve the desired change in pitch will be low, and vice versa

Both lateral and directional stability are only slightly affected by the longitudinal position of the centre of gravity. Therefore the aileron and rudder force usually do not change much with the position of the centre of gravity. If the flight control is hinged at its leading edge, the stick forces required are very high, especially regarding heavy or fast aeroplanes. The designer can reduce your work by means of aerodynamic balance.

6.4   *Aerodynamic Balance*

Aerodynamic balance is normally achieved by an inset in the hinge line back from the leading edge into the control surfaces or by a horn balance. The surface in front of the hinge-line will produce a force acting opposite to the control force, reducing the moment while still maintaining control effectiveness. This aerodynamic balance is usually used on aircraft with mechanically activated control surfaces.

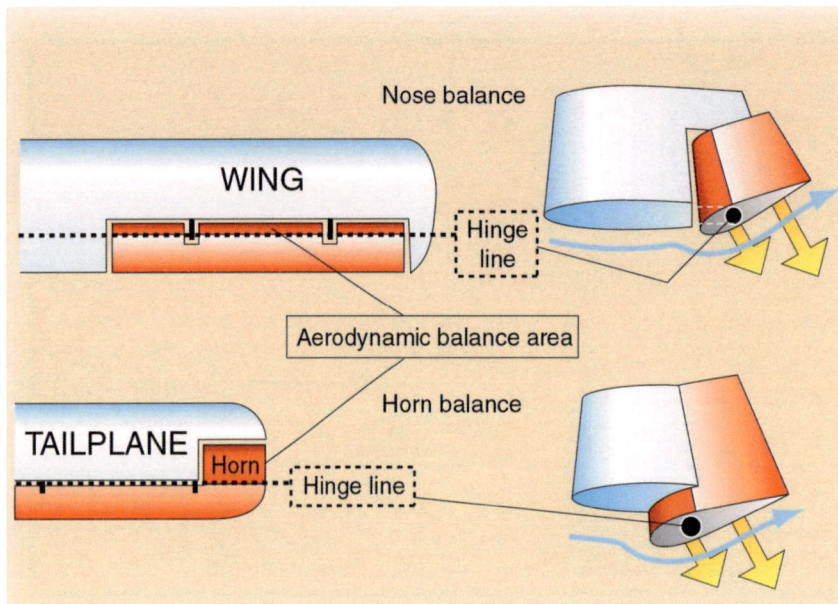

Figure 6.16

> The surface in front of the hinge line will produce a force acting opposite to the control force, reducing the moment but still maintaining control effectiveness

6.5 Balance Tab

On conventional tail planes it is quite common to have a balance tab incorporated in the elevator. It is mechanically linked to the elevator by a linkage that causes it to move in the opposite direction. When you exert forward pressure on the control column, the elevator goes down and the balance tab is raised. The balance tab of the elevator generates a small downward aerodynamic force that holds the elevator down, reducing the control load required by you. The balance tab may also function as a trim tab. The linkage between the main surface and the balance tab is then variable in length when using the trim.

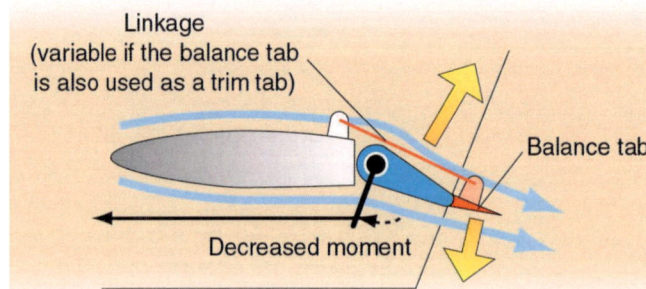

Figure 6.17

> A balance tab is incorporated in the elevator. It is mechanically linked to the elevator by a linkage that causes it to deflect in the opposite direction

Another way of making a control surface aerodynamically balanced is by using a spring tab, a servo tab or internal balance (sealed nose balance). The purpose is the same, to reduce the control force from a deflected control surface. The spring tab is connected directly to the control stick, but the main surface is connected to the stick via a spring to the free turning control horn. A spring tab distributes the stick force between the tab and the main control in varying ratios.

The principle of a servo tab is that when the pilot moves the control stick, this controls the tab directly. The deflected tab then creates a hinge moment which deflects the main control surface. However, this kind of control surface can only be find on old big aircraft. Its disadvantages are that the surface has to be bigger than for a conventional control surface, the control effectiveness decreases with increased deflection angle, the pilot does not know the deflection angle of the surface during taxi and it can be damaged when taxiing with a tailwind.

On the internal balance, or sealed nose balance, there is a plate or "tongue" which is projected forward from the nose of the control surface. This plate is joined to the main part of the wing, tail plane or fin by a loose fold of some fabric, which constitutes a seal between the two sides of the control surface. When, for example, an elevator is deflected downwards, a pressure difference is created on the two sides, creating an upward force forward of the hinge.

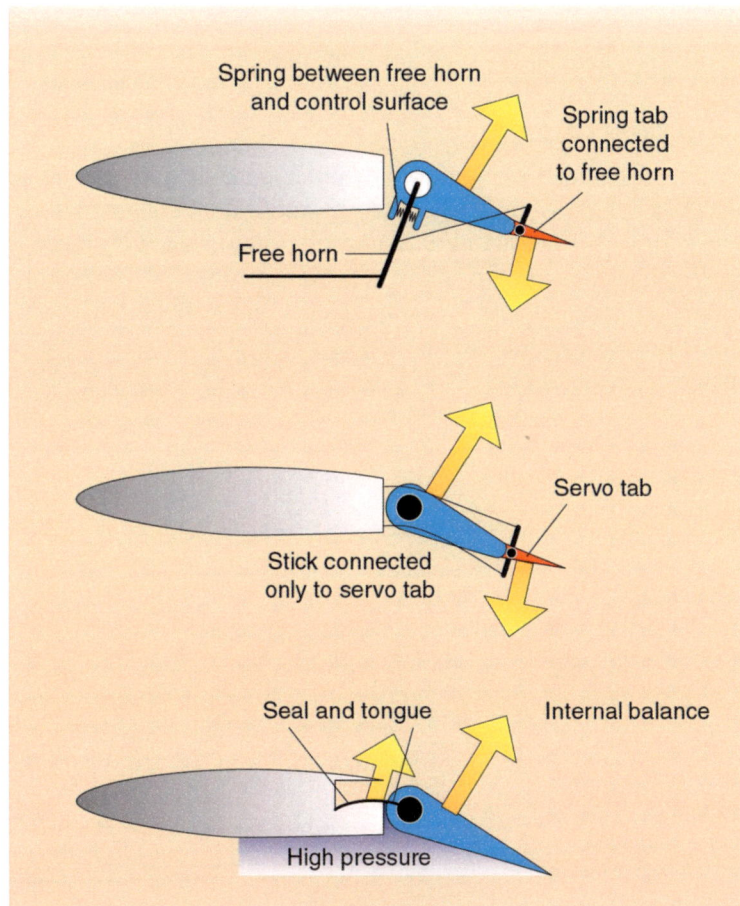

Figure 6.18

6.6 Stabilator And Anti Balance Tab

A stabilator is a movable surface acting like a combined stabiliser/elevator surface. Because of its combined functions, the stabilator has a much larger moving area than the elevator and thus produces a more powerful response to the control input. To prevent you from moving the stabilator too far and from getting too much control, it often embodies an anti balance tab that increases the control forces at high angles.

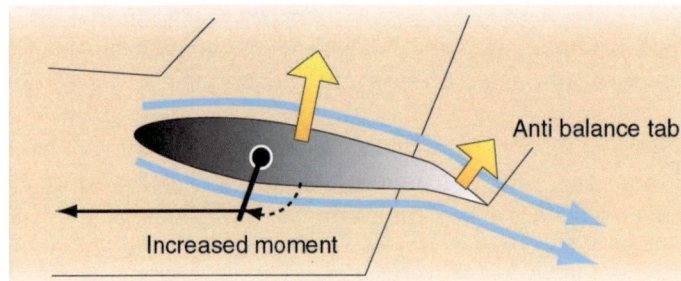

Figure 6.19

An anti balance tab moves in the same direction as the trailing edge of the stabilator and generates an aerodynamic force which makes it heavier to move the stabilator further

6.6.1 Artificial balance

Regarding many large and/or high speed aircraft, aerodynamic balancing is not sufficient to reduce the stick force to an acceptable level. It is then necessary to use powered controls, i.e. the deflection of a control is made by means of hydraulic pressure creating the necessary force. However, there is still an advantage of using aerodynamic balancing to reduce the loads on the powered control. The controls may be fully powered to 100%, or be power-assisted controls that to some extent ease the manual control forces. With fully powered controls the pilot does not feel the control forces in the normal way, which makes it necessary to add artificial feel to the control column. Inputs, which vary the control forces in relation to the flight condition, are; the dynamic pressure, load factor or Mach number.

6.6.2 Trim tab

An aircraft is in trim in pitch, roll or yaw when it maintains a constant flight path, and the sum of all moments will be 0. This is done by means of the control surfaces. In order to fly the aircraft without your exerting any steady pressure on a particular control surface, an aircraft has trim tabs. The function of the trim tab is to reduce the moment at the hinge line of the control surface to zero. It works in the same way as a balance tab but is operated by a separate trimwheel or electrically operated trim motor. The aircraft will stay in trim until the power, the airspeed or the centre of gravity changes. Aircraft with a stabilator usually have the elevator trim incorporated so that trimming moves the entire stabilator. For high-speed aircraft with electrical motors that change the trim tab, the rate of change in trim tab may vary with indicated air speed. This allows you as a pilot to choose a comfortable trim setting at all speeds.

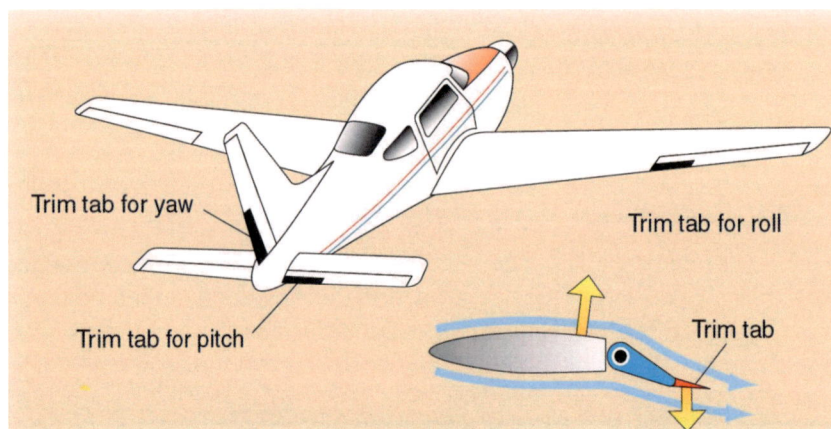

Figure 6.20

The function of a trim tab is to reduce the moment at the hinge line of the control surface to zero

6.7 Trim/stabiliser setting for take-off

During flight, you will trim to reduce control forces when conditions change. Before take-off, you cannot feel the control forces that you feel when airborne. It is therefore very important to set the trim according to the actual centre of gravity and flap setting. This trim setting must be determined by reference to the Pilot Operating Handbook. An aircraft that is wrongly trimmed can become uncontrollable once it is airborne.

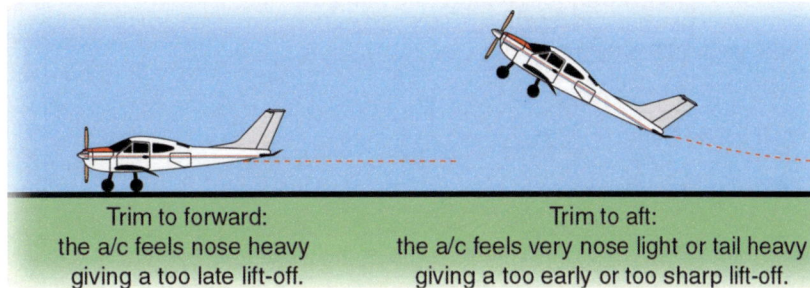

Trim to forward:
the a/c feels nose heavy
giving a too late lift-off.

Trim to aft:
the a/c feels very nose light or tail heavy
giving a too early or too sharp lift-off.

Figure 6.21

Control surfaces trim the aircraft to the equilibrium of moment. The trim tab trims the stick forces to zero

6.8 Control surface flutter and mass balance

At high speeds some control surfaces have a tendency to flutter. This flutter is a vibration, which is caused on the one hand by the combined effects of changes in pressure distribution over the surface as the angle of attack is altered, and on the other the elastic forces set up by the distortion of the structure itself. These oscillations can quickly reach dangerous proportions.

To eliminate the tendency to flutter, the aircraft designer needs to alter the mass distribution of the surface, not in order to maintain the control level but to avoid flutter or vibration.

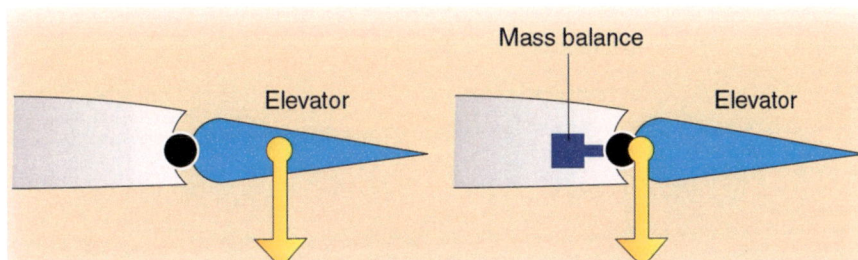

Figure 6.22

To prevent flutter the mass balance is placed forward of the hinge line in order to bring the centre of gravity of the control surface up to the hinge line or somewhat in front of it. It can also be prevented by making the structure rigid. On the inset hinge or horn balance, this mass can be incorporated in the area ahead of the hinge line, but elsewhere the mass must be placed on an arm that extends forward of the hinge line.

The mass balance is added to all control surfaces to avoid flutter

6.9 Flight Controls About The Three Axes

6.9.1 Primary and second effects

In this section we describe the flight controls by distinguishing them according to the plane in which they operate: the pitching, rolling or yawing plane. We also define the V_{MC} (Minimum control airspeed).

6.9.2 *Flight controls in the pitching plane.*

The primary control in the pitching plane is the elevator. When the control column is pulled, the elevator moves upward, changing the camber of the tailplane so that a downward force acts on the tailplane and the aeroplane rotates, nose up. When the control column is pushed forwards, the elevator moves downwards, changing the camber of the tailplane elevator section. This produces an upward lift force on the tail and a moment around the centre of gravity that moves the nose downwards.

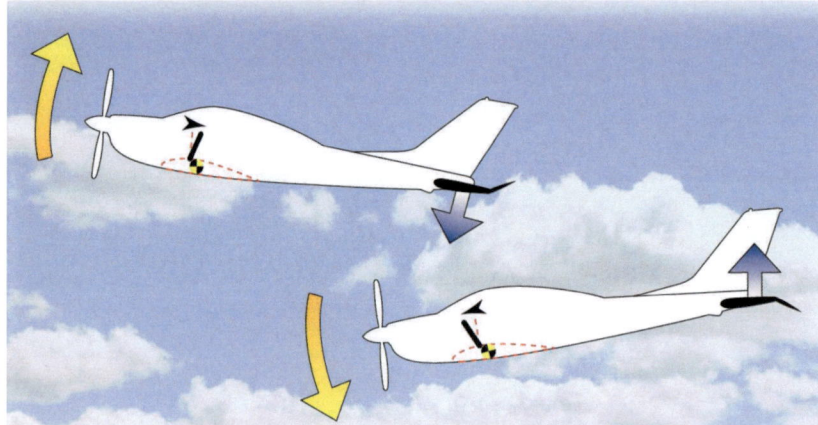

Figure 6.23

The tail moment depends upon the lift produced and on the distance between the tail and the centre of gravity. If the centre of gravity is too far in front of the point where the wing lift is acting, called the wing centre of pressure (C.P.), the aircraft will be difficult to trim.

Even if the control column is pulled completely back with the C.G. forward of the forward C.G. position, the elevator displacement will not be sufficient to provide enough tail force downwards to take the aircraft to the high angle of attack required at low speeds.

The allowed forward limit of the centre of gravity may be one of the factors determined by the amount of pitch control available from the elevator

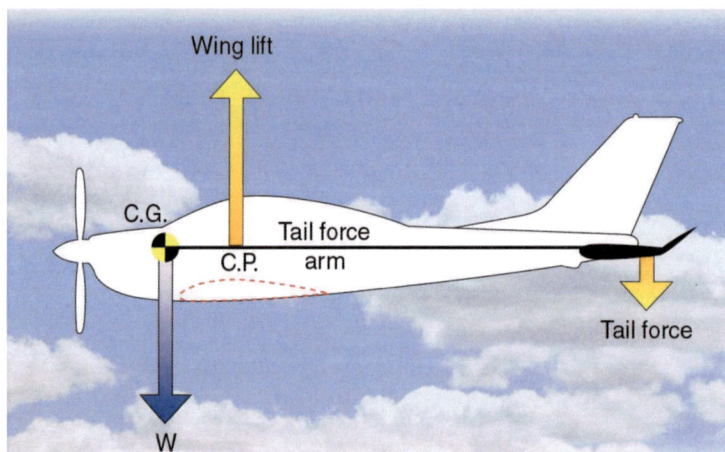

Figure 6.24

However, the longitudinal stability and/or the stick force requirements determine the aft limit of the centre of gravity.

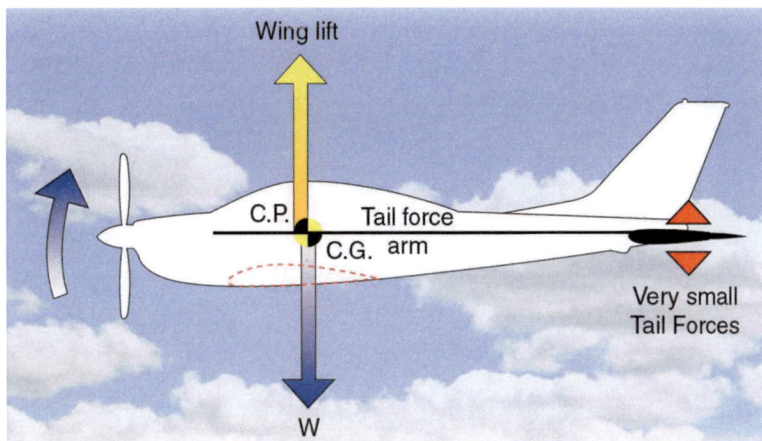

Figure 6.25

The allowed forward limit of C.G. may be determined by the amount of pitch control available from the elevator. The aft limit of C.G. is determined by the longitudinal stability or stickforce requirements

6.9.3   *Flight controls in the rolling plane.*

The primary controls in the rolling plane are the ailerons. They are moved by rotating the control wheel or by the lateral displacement of the stick. The ailerons act in opposite directions: while one aileron goes up, decreasing the lift generated by that wing, the other aileron goes down, increasing the lift generated by the opposite wing. The aileron movement changes the camber of the wing. An increased camber raises the wing while decreased camber will lower the wing.

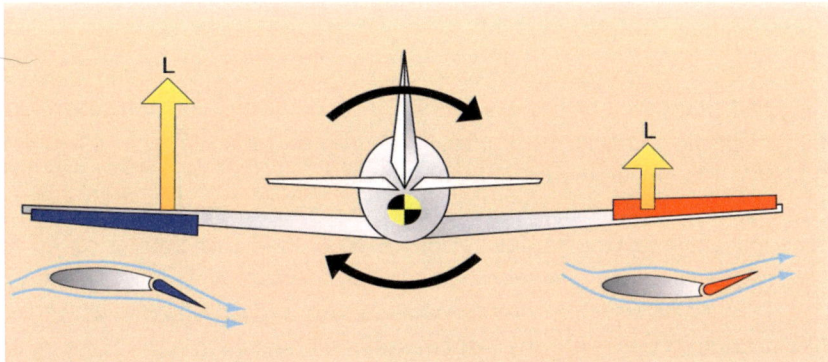

Figure 6.26

A resultant rolling moment is exerted on the aircraft, its amplitude depending on the magnitude of the different lift forces and on the moment arm. For this reason the ailerons are outboard, giving a long moment arm to the centre of gravity. A change in camber also involves a change in drag. When camber increases, both lift and drag will increase. When camber decreases, both lift and drag will decrease.

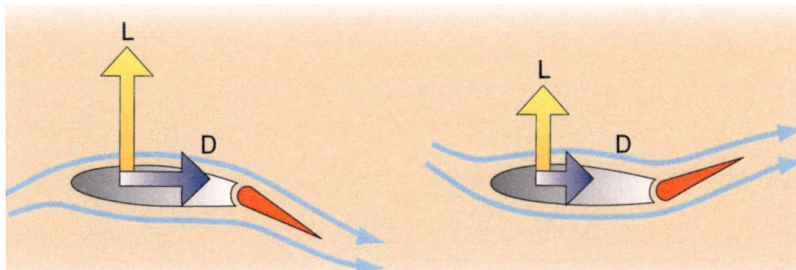

Figure 6.27

6.9.4   *Adverse aileron yaw*

The different lift forces cause the aeroplane to bank in one direction while the different aileron drag causes it to yaw in the other. This undesired effect occurs especially at low airspeeds due to the need for large aileron deflections.

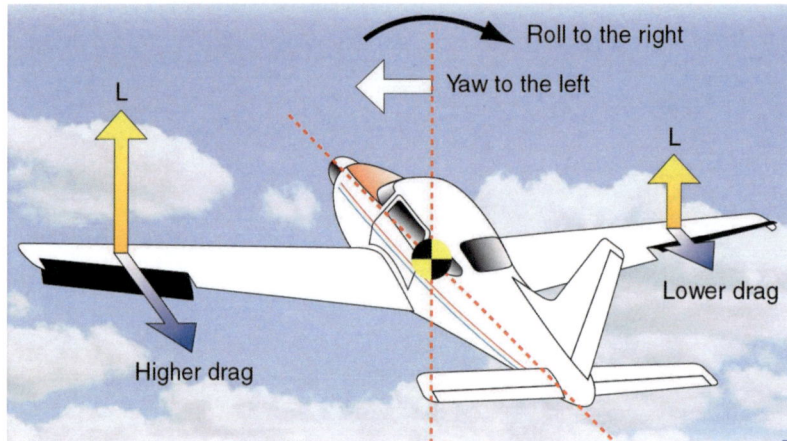

Figure 6.28

This effect is called aileron drag or adverse aileron yaw and can be reduced by the designer, incorporating differential aileron movement, or coupling aileron and rudder.

> Adverse aileron yaw is the tendency of the aeroplane to yaw in the opposite direction from the roll because of the different aileron drag

6.10   *Differential ailerons and Frise ailerons*

Differential aileron movement is designed to increase the drag on the descending wing. In other words, the upward aileron is deflected through a higher angle than the one going down. The greater deflection of the aileron upward on the descending wing causes increased drag and the tendency to yaw the aircraft into the same direction as the bank. The adverse yaw is thus reduced.

Another way to reduce the adverse yaw somewhat on older aircraft is to use so called Frise ailerons. This kind of aileron has a shape that, when it moves downwards, the complete top surface of the wing and the aileron will have a smooth, uninterrupted contour causing very little drag. But when moved upwards the leading edge of the aileron will jut out below the bottom surface of the wing and cause increased drag.

The leading edge of a Frise aileron also acts as an aerodynamic balancing device. The leading edge of the up going control surface causes a nose-down hinge moment, and so reduces the restoring nose-up moment. The danger of this type of balance is that if the control deflection is large, the result will most likely be overbalance. The reasons why modern aircraft do not have Frise ailerons is the requirements that an aileron should not be deflected if being over-balanced should the connection between the ailerons be broken.

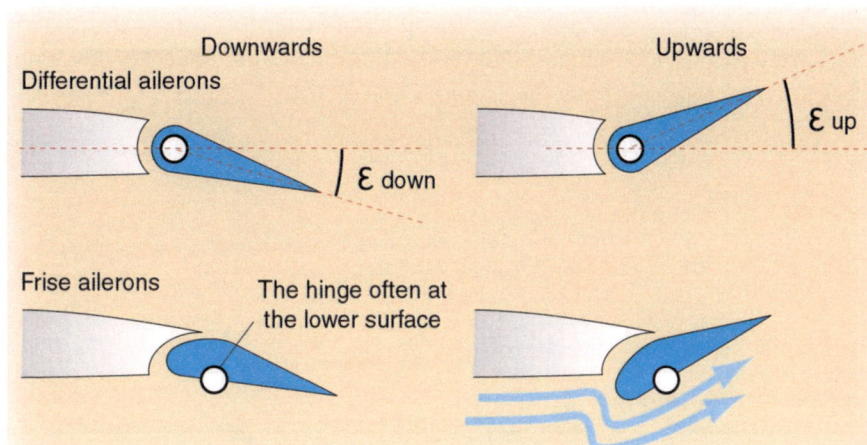

Figure 6.29

Notice that the adverse yaw cannot be completely reduced at all speeds. Normally you will always have adverse yaw at low speeds, despite having differential or Frise ailerons.

Differential ailerons or Frise aileron movement causes increased drag on the descending wing. The adverse yaw is thus reduced at all speeds but to a lesser degree at low speeds

6.11   *Inboard ailerons and flaperons*

Transport aircraft may have both outbound and inbound ailerons. The inbound ailerons can be used alone, i.e. during cruising or high speed, where only small aileron deflection and a short moment arm is necessary to achieve the required rolling moment. At low speeds the inbound ailerons may be a supplement to the outer ailerons in order to increase the rolling rate. This mixed use of the outer and inner ailerons is automatic. Another reason for not using the outer ailerons at high speeds is the tendency to reversed control response due to the wing twisting tendency when using the outer ailerons.

The trailing edge may have a combination of trailing edge flaps and ailerons, called flaperons. When the flaps are lowered, the outer part, or sometimes the whole flaps, can also be used as ailerons. This combination increases the max C_L considerable.

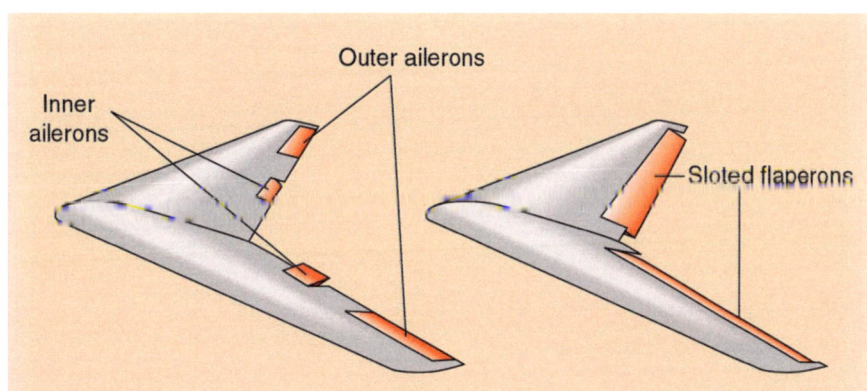

Figure 6.30

6.12   *Rudder coupled ailerons*

In order to get good balance between the rudder forces and the control in yaw, some aircraft are equipped with a pedal/rudder ratio changer.

On some aircraft, the rudder is coupled with the aileron system so that when the aircraft is banked, the rudder deflects automatically to yaw the aircraft into the turn, reducing the adverse yaw.

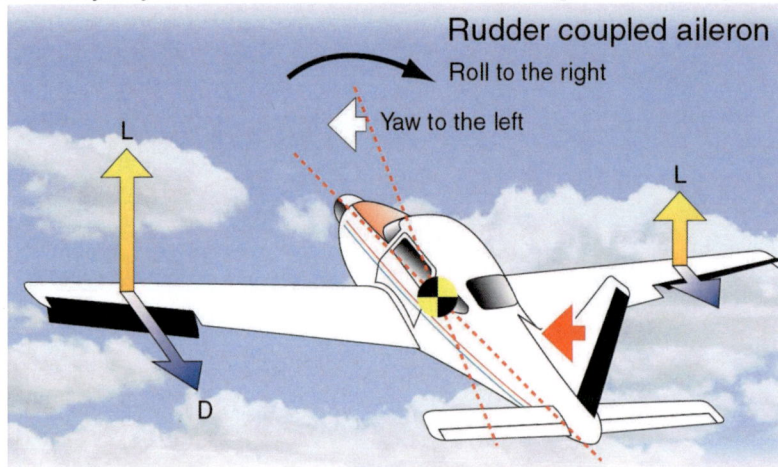

Figure 6.31

The rudder-aileron coupling reduces the adverse yaw when you give aileron input

6.13   Spoilers

Instead of using ailerons, spoilers on the wing can be used for lateral control. A spoiler has the advantage that it reduces lift and increases the drag of the down going wing, causing no adverse yaw. The disadvantage is that the aircraft is not moving laterally around its longitudinal axis since the other wing is not simultaneously raised.

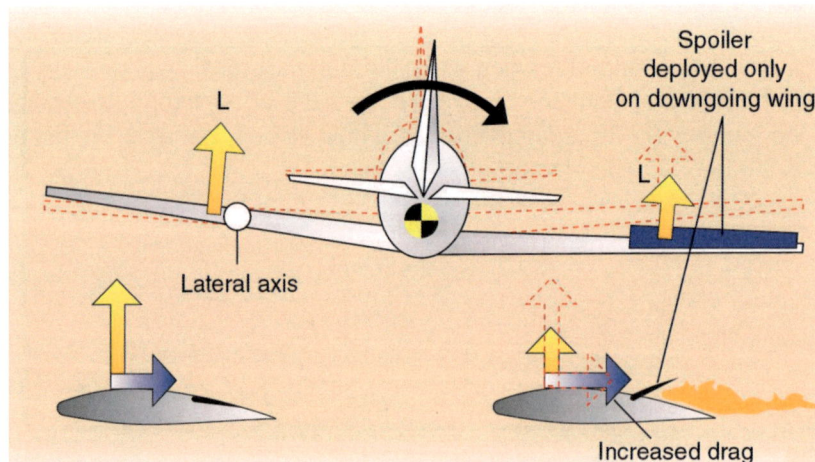

Figure 6.32

Spoilers used as ailerons cause no adverse yaw.

6.14   Secondary effects of aileron deflections

While the ailerons are deflected, there is a certain amount of adverse aileron yaw opposite to the bank direction. But once established in the bank with the ailerons in neutral position, the lift becomes tilted, causing an unbalanced horizontal lift component that causes the aircraft to slip to the same direction as the bank.

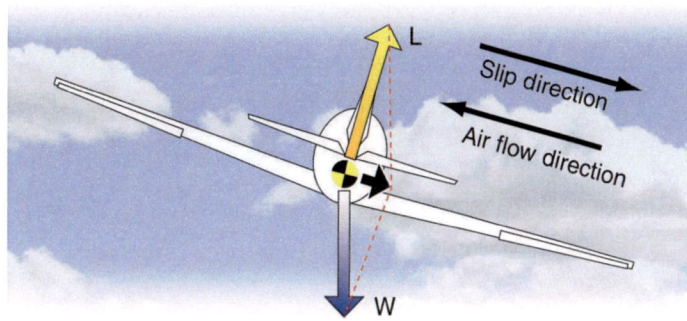

Figure 6.33

The aeroplane will yaw gradually towards the lower wing. If this effect is not corrected, the result will be a descending spiral.

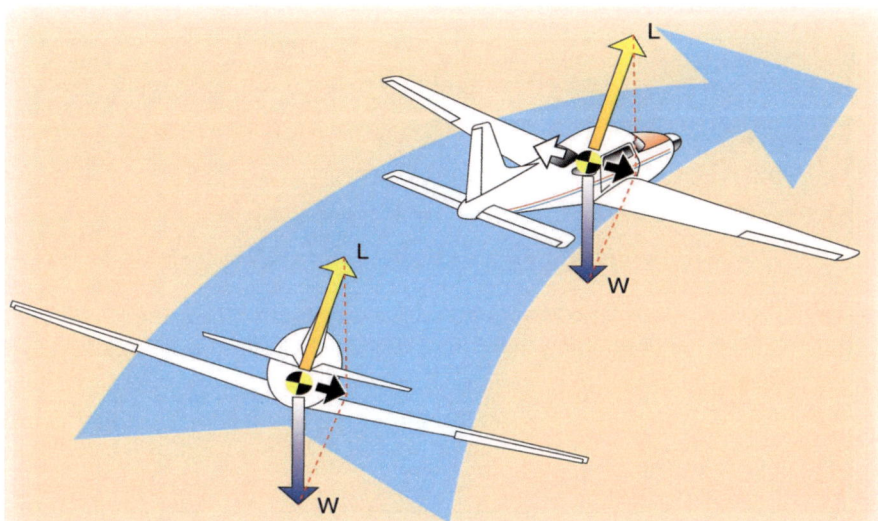

Figure 6.34

If you only bank the aircraft, it will begin to slip sideways and yaw.

6.15   *Asymmetric slipstream effect on lateral control*

In a situation when a twin-engined propeller driven aircraft has engine failure, the slipstream from the live engine will add to the lift on that wing. This causes a roll towards the dead engine side, which has to be counteracted by means of the ailerons. When trailing edge flaps are deflected, the differences in lift on the wing will be further increased.

CRANFIELD AVIATION TRAINING SCHOOL LTD. PART-FCL GBR.ATO-0136
CATS INNOVATION CENTRE, LUTON, Bedfordshire LU2 8DL U.K.
6-17

www.catsaviation.com
Principles of Flight

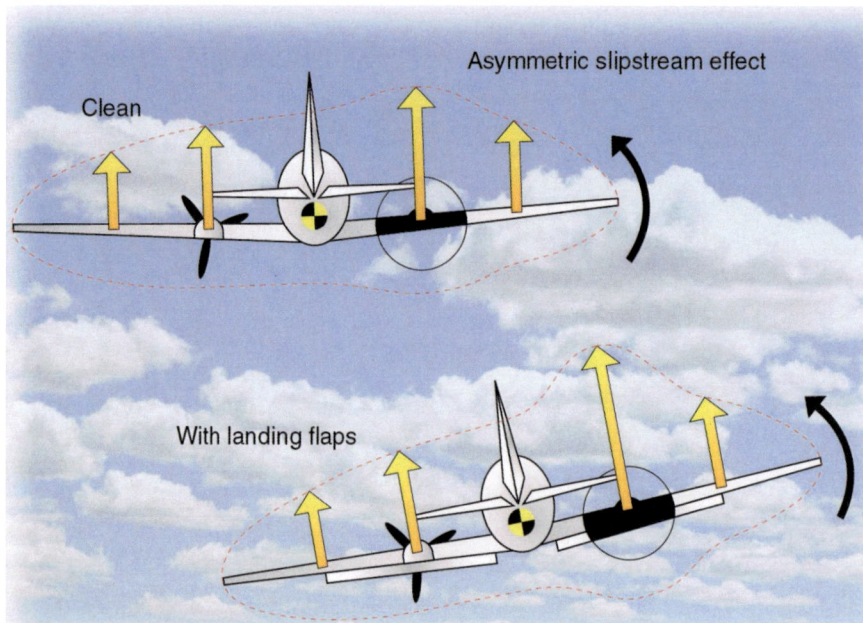

Figure 6.35

6.16   *Flight controls in the yawing plane*

The rudder is hinged on the rear of the fin and is moved by the rudder pedals. When we push the right pedal for example, the rudder moves right, changing the airflow in the whole fin-rudder system; a force sideways is generated and the aircraft yaws to the right.

The primary effect of rudder deflection is to yaw the aircraft. This causes the outer wing to momentarily speed up, generating a secondary effect of more lift, and after a brief period of inertia, the aircraft starts to roll in the direction of the turn.

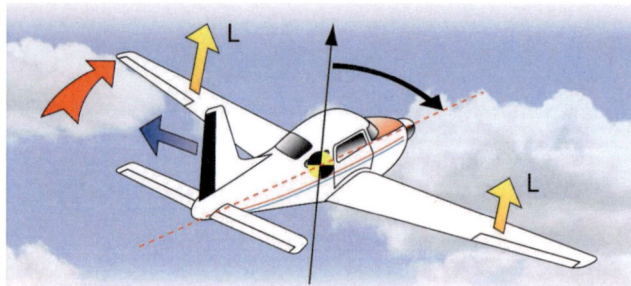

Figure 6.36

Yaw-roll coupling means a yaw causes a roll in the same direction

All aircraft have, more or less, a yaw-roll coupling. But especially the effect of dihedral wings and swept wings are considerable on yaw-roll when sideslipping.

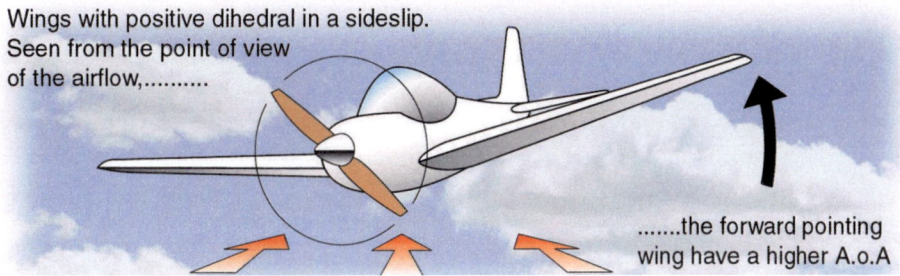

Wings with positive dihedral in a sideslip. Seen from the point of view of the airflow,..........

.......the forward pointing wing have a higher A.o.A

Figure 6.37

On an aircraft with swept wings, the yaw-roll coupling is very obvious. The forward pointing wing will have a greater span towards the meeting airflow than the aft pointing one and so gets a higher CL for a certain A.o.A

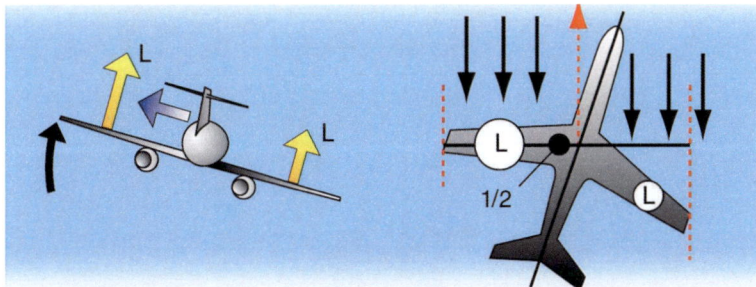

Figure 6.38

All aircraft have, more or less, a yaw-roll coupling.

The moment in the directional plane will be modified due to the change in engine thrust directly caused by the non symmetrical application of thrust line, and it will be induced due to the secondary effects of the propeller slipstream rotation.

The descending blade provides more thrust than the ascending one, especially at low speeds and high A.of.A. and in thrust situations, i.e. during climb. This causes an asymmetrical thrust application on the propeller rotational plane, called p-factor.

In order to maintain the heading in such situations, the yaw caused by the P-factor and the slipstream effect must be compensated for by using the rudder.

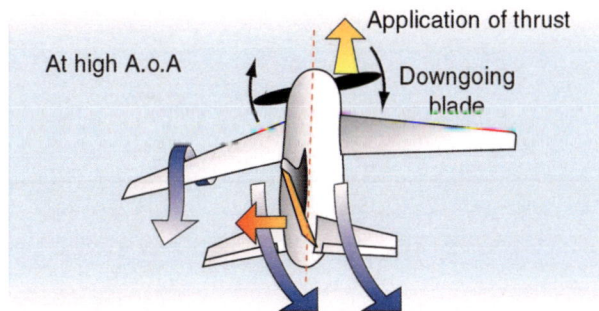

At high A.o.A

Application of thrust

Downgoing blade

Figure 6.39

6.17   *Minimum Control Speed*

Both the engines of light twins usually rotate clockwise. This does not cause any problems during normal operations, but in case of engine failure, the live engine which has its down going propeller blade at its outer side will produce a greater turning moment because of its longer arm than if the other engine was the only thrust producer.

> The critical engine is the engine that, if it fails, generates the most critical situation

The larger moment caused by the engine that is still running must be balanced by the combined action of rudder and ailerons. This means that if the left engine is dead and that situation generates a greater turning moment than if the right engine was stopped, the left engine will be the critical one. On aircraft equipped with engines that rotate clockwise, the critical engine is the left one. Where both engines rotate counter clockwise, which is unusual, the critical engine is of course the right one.

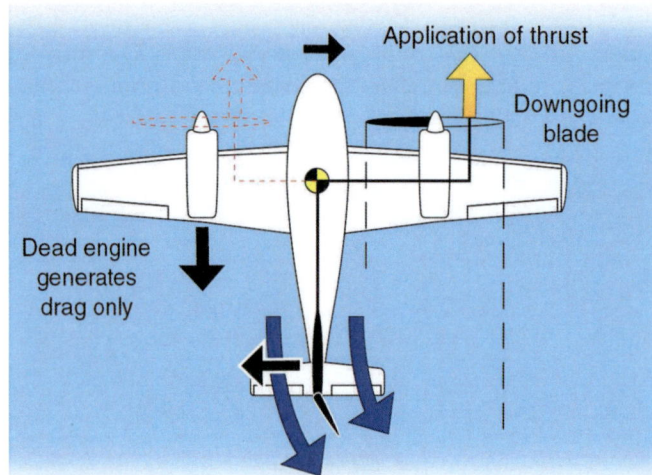

Figure 6.40

On an aircraft equipped with propellers that rotate clockwise seen from the rear, the critical engine is the left one.

Since the control of the aircraft in yaw depends on the aerodynamic force that the rudder and fin can produce, there will be a minimum speed at which the aircraft can be controlled around its yaw axis. This minimum control speed is determined with the critical engine dead and its propeller windmilling, and the other engine, or engines, at take-off power. This speed is called the minimum control airspeed, abbreviated as V_{MC}.

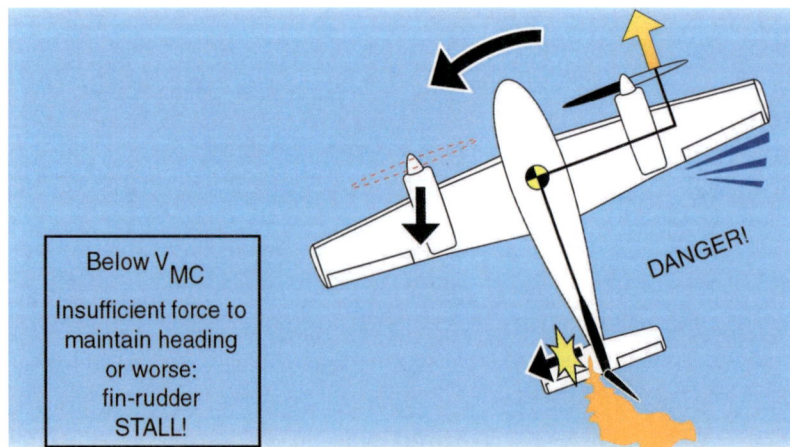

Figure 6.41

> If you allow flight speed to fall below the V_{MC} with full power on in the live engine condition, the fin-rudder is unable to give enough counteracting force, or worse, it may stall, causing an uncontrolled snaproll which may lead to an unrecoverable spin or else an extremely dangerous situation.

CRANFIELD AVIATION TRAINING SCHOOL LTD. PART-FCL GBR.ATO-0136
CATS INNOVATION CENTRE, LUTON, Bedfordshire LU2 8DL U.K.   www.catsaviation.com

6-20

Principles of Flight

The Pilot Operating Manuals of all multi-engine aircraft indicate the value of the minimum control speed in the chapter on limitations or performance. The V_{MC} is also normally marked on the airspeed indicator by a red line.

Transport aircraft have in fact three minimum control speeds. One, abbreviated V_{MCG}, when being on the ground during take-off acceleration after engine failure, another one abbreviated V_{MCA}, when being airborne, and finally one at approach configuration for landing V_{MCL}.

V_{MCG} is defined as the minimum speed at which directional control on the ground can be recovered and maintained under the following conditions:
- sudden engine failure of the most critical engine;
- take-off thrust of the remaining engines;
- flaps in take-off position;
- control maintained by rudder only (no reliance on the use of either nose wheel steering when e.g. slippery runway, or wheel brakes).

Figure 6.42

V_{MCA} is defined as the minimum speed at which directional control can be recovered and maintained in flight under these conditions:
- sudden engine failure of the most critical engine (causing the highest turning moment from the running engine(s);
- take-off thrust of the remaining engines;
- flaps in take-off position;
- landing gear up;
- zero yaw or an angle of bank not over 5° towards live engine.
-

Figure 6.43

V_{MCL} is defined as the minimum speed at which directional control during landing approach with all engines operating can be recovered and maintained under the following conditions:
- with sudden engine failure of the most critical engine;
- when the aircraft is in the most critical configuration for approach;
- with the most unfavourable C.G;
- when the aircraft is trimmed for approach with all engines operating;
- with the maximum landing weight at sea level;
- when the available take-off power or thrust of the operating engines are at their maximum.

Factors which decrease the available power or thrust will automatically lower the min. control speeds. Thus, the min. control speeds will decrease with increasing airport elevation and/or outer air temperature (OAT).

Transport aircraft have the following minimum control speeds:

V_{MCG} = minimum control speed on the ground roll, take-off

V_{MCA} = minimum control speed airborne, for take-off

V_{MCL} = minimum control speed, for landing approach

6.18   *Reverse control*

A wing will always be more or less elastic because a rigid wing would be to heavy. On a long, slim and swept wing, the turning moment created by, for example, a deflected aileron, may twist the wing in the opposite direction to the aileron. The down going aileron creates a greater lift in the aft part of the outer wing section which may lead to lower total A.of.A of the outer part of the wing than predicted, giving a reduced aileron effect.

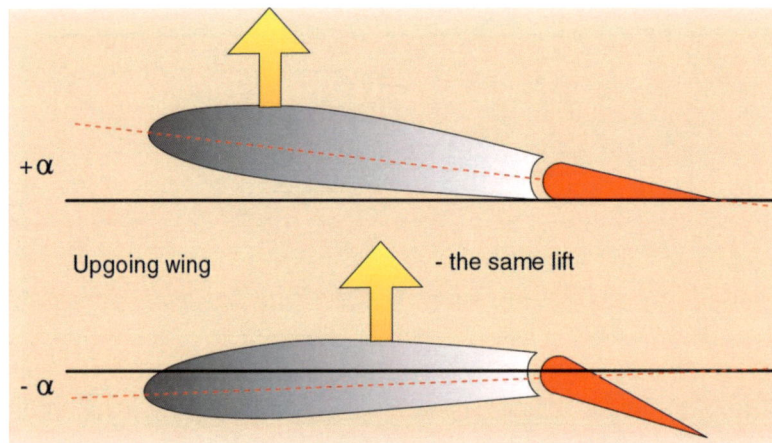

Figure 6.44

In order to reduce this undesired effect, the aileron may be located nearer the wing root or the wings may have additional inner ailerons where the wing is more stiff. Another way is to make use of spoilers or a combination of both. From the aero elasticity point of view, the spoiler will cause a lower twisting moment on the wing. One way to reduce the risk for a control reverse, is to locate the ailerons nearer the wing root or to make use of a spoiler or both.

6.19   *Special Combinations of Control Surfaces*

Many aircraft designed for high speed have no horizontal tail surface but a so called "delta wing" with control surfaces for pitch and roll on the trailing edge of the wing. Here we explain how these and other combinations of control surfaces work.

6.19.1   *Combined elevators/ailerons (elevons)*

The control surfaces need to have a certain distance from the C.G. in order to get sufficient moment arm. But the ailerons do not need to be positioned perpendicular to the longitudinal axis from the C.G.

A "Delta wing" is a wing with a planform like the Greek letter Δ (delta), which means that the aerofoil chord is very long for a given wing area. The relative long moment arm from the C.G. to the trailing edge allows the position of the elevator surfaces to be located there. The control surfaces at the trailing edge are often designed to be a combination of pitch and lateral control. This combination is called elevons.

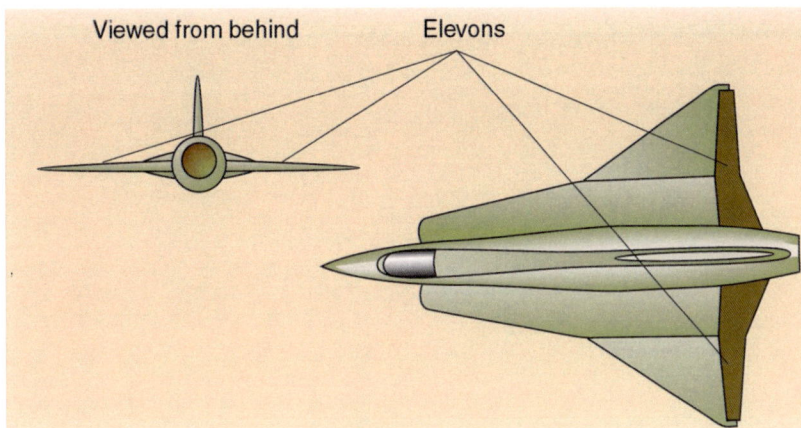

Figure 6.45

In the next figure you see how different control inputs will change the setting of the elevons.

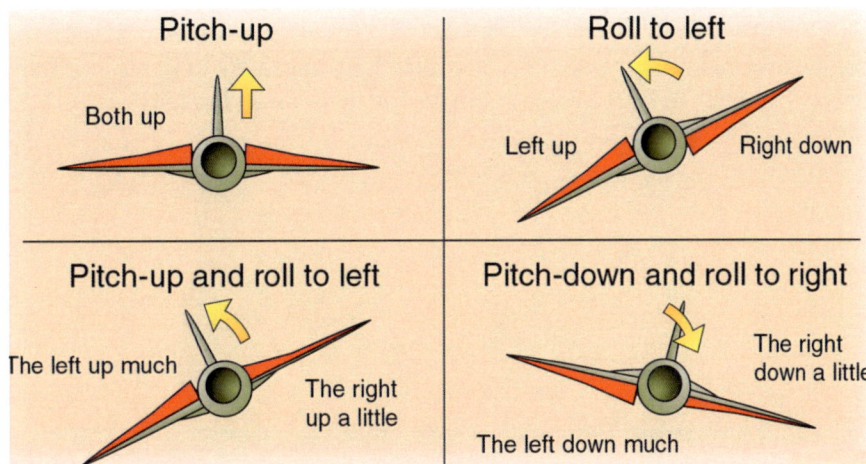

Figure 6.46

Elevons are a combination of elevators and ailerons

There might be some disadvantages of this kind of control surfaces. When having a maximum elevator-up, the roll rate will be limited because the roll is only made by use of the "down going" elevons. Another disadvantage may be the relative short moment arm from the C.G. to the elevons, which demands a rather large force downwards on the tail to trim the aircraft in pitch at low speed. The tail down force reduces the total lift from the aircraft. This means that a greater lift on the wing is required, which increases the induced drag.

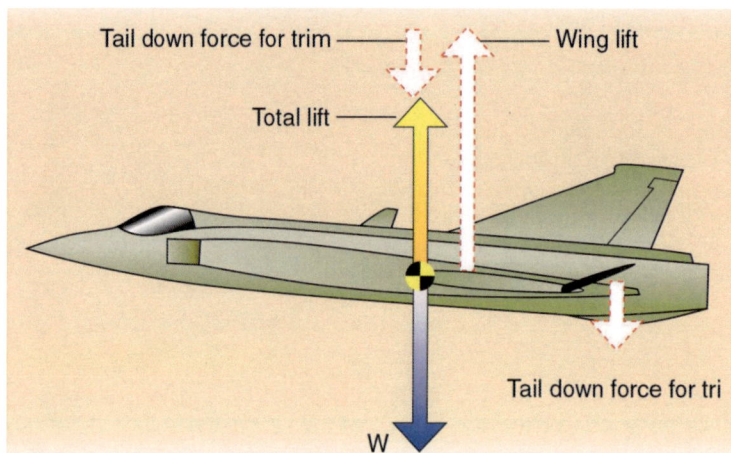

Figure 6.47

6.19.2 *Pitch control of canard aircraft*

In order to avoid this additional trim drag, some modern jet fighters are equipped with a lifting surface in front of the C.G., a so-called "canard", to lift the nose instead of pushing down the tail.

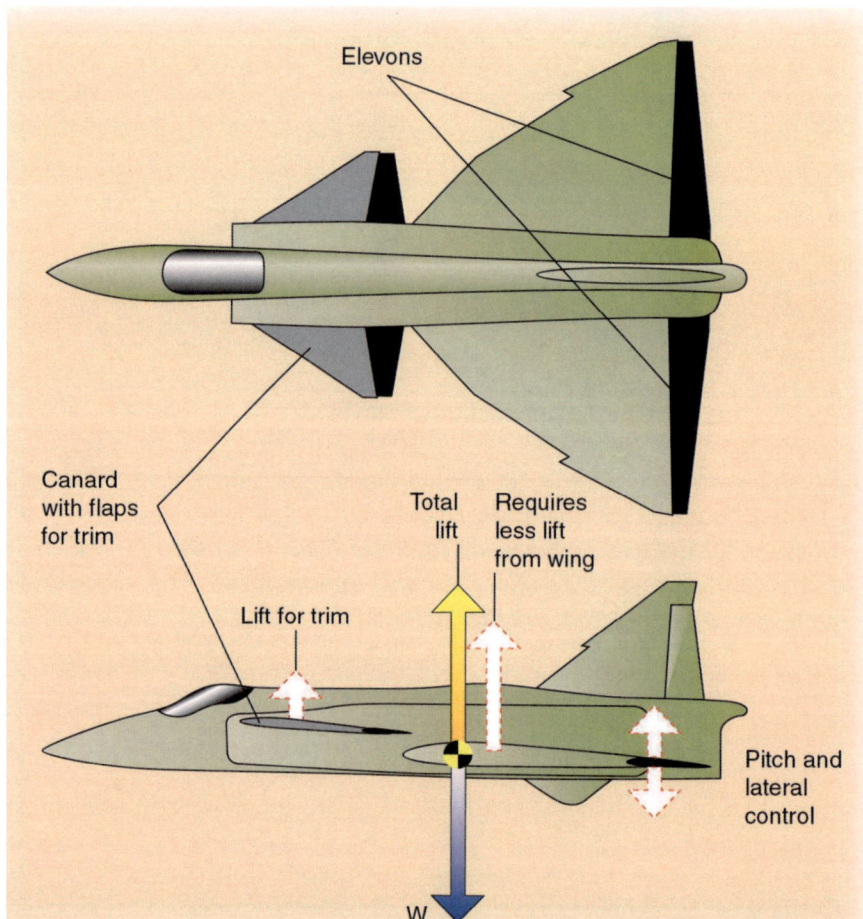

Figure 6.48

However, the canard is often only a trim device, not a main control surface. The pitch and lateral control is attained by means of elevons at the trailing edge of the main wing.

6.19.3   *Separate tail surfaces as ailerons*

In order to reduce take-off and landing speed for a high speed aircraft, it may be necessary to use the whole length of the wing trailing edge as high lift devices, i.e. advanced flaps. For lateral control, separate tail surfaces may be used as a elevons together with spoilers, giving additional lateral output in combination with pitch control.

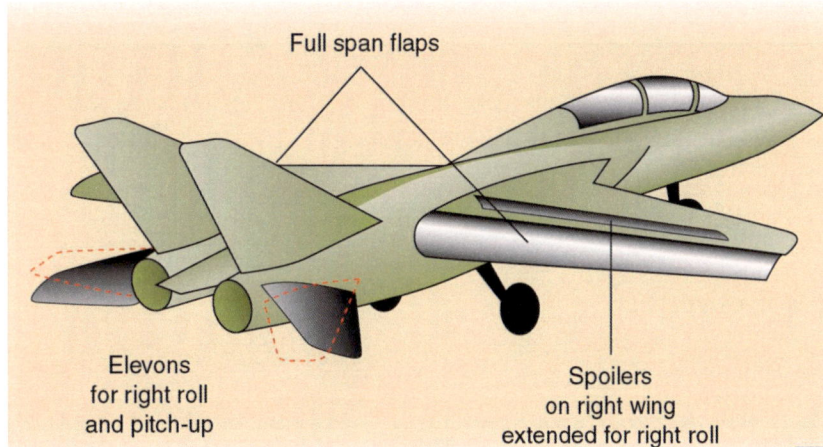

Figure 6.49

6.19.4   *Use of all surfaces for control*

Most modern fighters use all movable surfaces for control; fully movable canards, elevons on the wings that can also be used as flaps, high lift devices at the leading edge, all to control the aircraft around all axes.

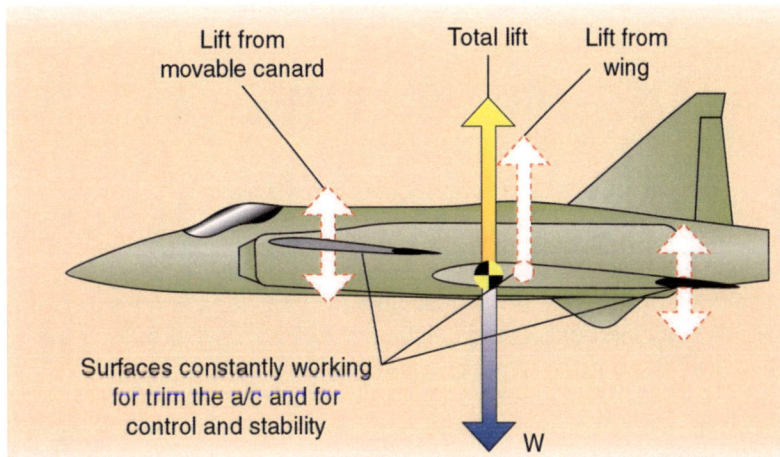

Figure 6.50

6.20   *Fly By Wire*

Many modern aircraft, especially those with reduced static stability, have a so-called fly by wire system. This means that the control inputs from the pilot consist of electrical signals via one or more computers to the hydraulic servo actuators connected to the control surfaces. The computers then combine the inputs from the control stick with other inputs from, for example, sensors used for dynamic stability and sensors limiting the A.of.A. The fly by wire system has many advantages, such as making the aircraft less sensitive to variation in the position of C.G. But it has also some disadvantages, e.g. there is no feedback from the deflection angle of the control surfaces. This will results in the pilot being unable to feel the control forces.

Self Assessment Test 02

1   Control surface vibration at high airspeed is known as:-
A)   Vibration
B)   Snatch
C)   Reversal
D)   Flutter

2   A device designed to assist the pilot in moving the controls against the force of the air flow is known as:
A)   A mass balance
B)   An aerodynamic balance
C)   A trimming tab
D)   A free control

3   A horn balance is an example of:
A)   A mass balance
B)   An aerodynamic balance
C)   A trimming tab
D)   A free control

4   If the elevator jammed in the neutral position whilst an aircraft is airborne, moving the elevator trim tab in the opposite direction to that normally required to correct a nose heavy tendency would cause:-
A)   An increase in nose heaviness
B)   No effect on the trim
C)   A reduction in the nose heaviness
D)   The aeroplane to maintain its altitude

5   Flutter is eliminated from a control surface by a:-
A)   Mass balance
B)   Powered flying control
C)   Aerodynamic balance
D)   Firm grip

6   If an aircraft fitted with a variable incidence tailplane flew "tail heavy", in order to correct the tail heaviness the tailplane incidence would be:-
A)   Increased by raising the leading edge of the tailplane
B)   Decreased by rising the leading edge of the tailplane
C)   Increased by raising the trailing edge of the tailplane
D)   Decreased by raising the trailing edge of the tailplane

7   A servo tab is a form of:-
A)   Servo powered flying control
B)   Trimming tab
C)   Aerodynamic balance
D)   Mass balance

8   An anti-balance tab:
A)   Increases the likelihood of vibration
B)   Improves the feel of the controls
C)   Protects against control reversal
D)   Is a form of mass balance for use at very low airspeeds such as when taxying on the ground in strong winds

9   A fixed trimming tab can:
A)   Never be adjusted
B)   Should only be adjusted if the aeroplane is re-rigged
C)   Be adjusted on the ground only
D)   Can be adjusted in the air but is usually locked for cruising speed

10   A spring balance tab:
A)   Is only effective at low airspeed
B)   Is only effective at high airspeed
C)   Is always effective
D)   Relies on spring pressure rather than a moving tab

11   A control surface is mass balanced by:
A)   The attachment of weights acting forward of the centre line
B)   Fitting a balance tab
C)   The attachment of weights acting on the hinge line
D)   The attachment of weights acting aft of the hinge line

12   The purpose of mass balancing is to:
A)   Provide equal control forces on all aeroplane controls
B)   Relieve stick forces
C)   Aerodynamically assist the pilot in moving the controls
D)   Eliminate control flutter

13   On an aircraft which is fitted with spoilers for lateral control, a roll to the left is caused by:
A)   Left spoiler extending and the right spoiler remaining retracted
B)   Right spoiler extending and the left spoiler remaining retracted
C)   Both spoilers extending
D)   None of the above

14   Which of the following best defines a horn balance?
A)   A projection of the outer edge of the control surface forward of the hinge line
B)   A rod projecting forward of the control surface with a weight on the end
C)   A rod projecting upward from the main control surface to which the control cables are attached
D)   A free control

15   A "Frise" aileron is designed to:
A)   Move further up than down
B)   Incorporate a mass balance
C)   Correct for adverse aileron yaw
D)   Reduce control loads to zero

16　A spring tab provides:
A)　A constant spring tension to trim a tab system
B)　Feel feed-back in a control system
C)　A reduction in the effort needed to move controls against high air loads
D)　An increased load on the stick when trying to move the flight controls

17　If an aircraft keeps yawing to the left, it may be trimmed by:
A)　Moving the fixed trimming tab on the rudder to the left
B)　Moving the adjustable trim tab on the rudder to the right
C)　Keeping the left rudder pedal forward
D)　Both (a) and (b) are correct

18　On take-off an aircraft is tail heavy and it is subsequently discovered that the elevator control locks have not been removed. In an attempt to correct the pilot moves the elevator trim tab wheel forwards. This will cause:
A)　A decrease in tail heaviness
B)　An increase in tail heaviness
C)　No effect
D)　None of the above are correct

19　If the pilot's control column is moved forward on an aeroplane with a servo tab operated elevator system the:
A)　Servo tabs will move down
B)　Servo tabs will not move until the elevator moves
C)　Servo tabs will move up
D)　Servo tabs will move up causing the elevator to move up

20　Anti-balance tabs are used to:
A)　Relieve stick loads
B)　Trim the aircraft
C)　Prevent control surface flutter
D)　Give more feel to the control column

CRANFIELD AVIATION TRAINING SCHOOL LTD. PART-FCL GBR.ATO-0136
CATS INNOVATION CENTRE, LUTON, Bedfordshire LU2 8DL U.K.　　www.catsaviation.com

CATS

6-28　　　　　　　　　　　　　　　　　　　　　　　　Principles of Flight

Self Assessment Test 02 Answers

1	D
2	B
3	B
4	C
5	A
6	A
7	C
8	B
9	C
10	B
11	A
12	D
13	A
14	A
15	C
16	C
17	A
18	B
19	C
20	D

CRANFIELD AVIATION TRAINING SCHOOL LTD. PART-FCL GBR.ATO-0136
CATS INNOVATION CENTRE, LUTON, Bedfordshire LU2 8DL U.K.

www.catsaviation.com

6-29

Principles of Flight

CHAPTER 7

Stalling

7.1 Total aerodynamic reaction and centre of pressure

When flying in straight and level flight at a certain altitude and at cruising speed, in order to maintain the altitude while reducing speed from cruising speed, the nose of the aircraft must be raised gradually to increase the A.of.A.

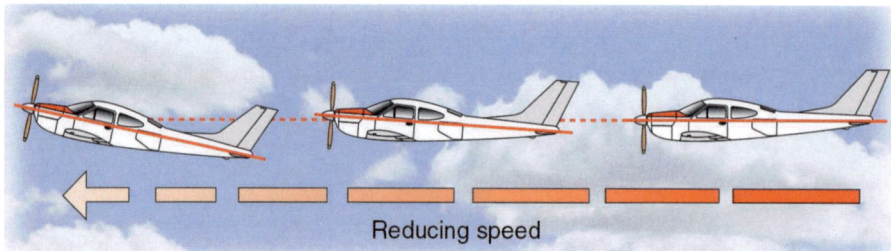

Figure 7.1 Increasing angle of attack whilst reducing airspeed enables level flight to be maintained

As speed is decreased still further, in a well-designed aircraft, the airframe and controls begin to vibrate, in a condition known as buffet.

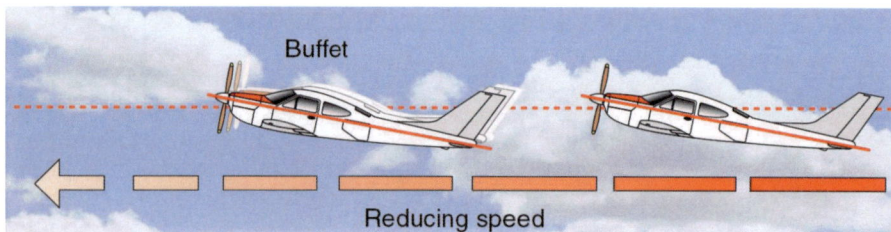

Figure 7.2 Buffet before the stall

If speed is reduced still further, the vibrations become excessive and it is no longer possible to maintain altitude and the aeroplane sinks and pitches down. The aircraft has stalled and controlled flight at altitude and speed under this condition is no longer possible.

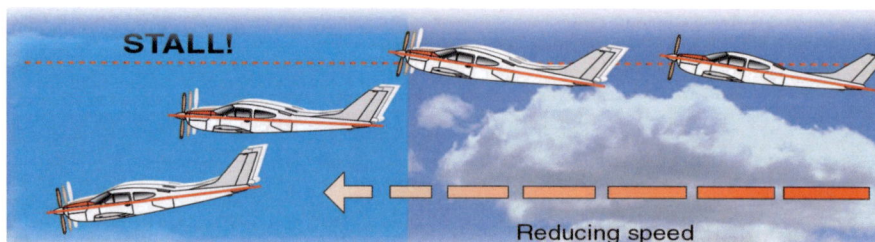

Figure 7.3 The stall

This is a stall due to low speed in level flight, but a stall can appear at high speed at high load factor, and some aircraft may have very abrupt stall characteristic without preceding buffeting. A special kind of stall appears at very high speeds due to the compressibility effect of the air.

When the aeroplane is in straight and level flight, the lift generated by the airflow on the wing balances the weight

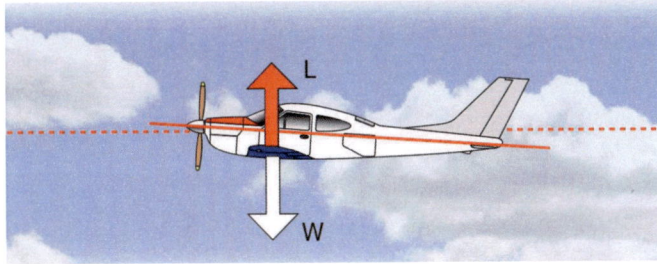

Figure 7.4

7.1.1   *Pressure distribution*

Acceleration of the air downwards and the change of fluid speed around the aerofoil cause a different distribution of pressure on the upper and lower surfaces of the aerofoil. Measurements of the local static pressure on the upper surface of the aerofoil show a maximum value of negative pressure scale corresponding to the maximum value of speed reached on that surface. Moving towards the trailing edge, there is an increase in static pressure resulting from the decrease in fluid speed.

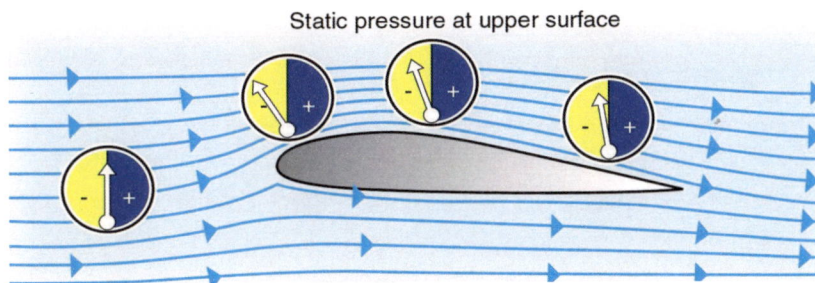

Figure 7.5

The local static pressure on the upper surface of the aerofoil has a minimum value of static pressure corresponding to the maximum value of speed reached on that surface. Measurements of the local static pressure on the lower surface of the aerofoil show a positive but a gradually decreasing value of static pressure. The decrease in local static pressure near the trailing edge is caused by the slow increase in fluid speed on the lower surface of the aerofoil.

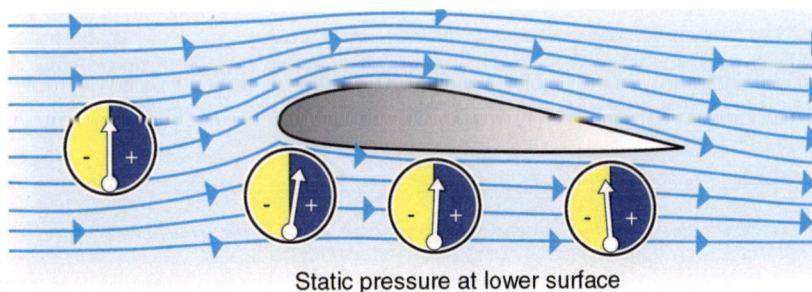

Figure 7.6

The local static pressure on the lower surface of the aerofoil shows a positive and decreasing value of static pressure. With an increased A.of.A. the pressure differences increase and the upper low pressure zone is moved further forward.

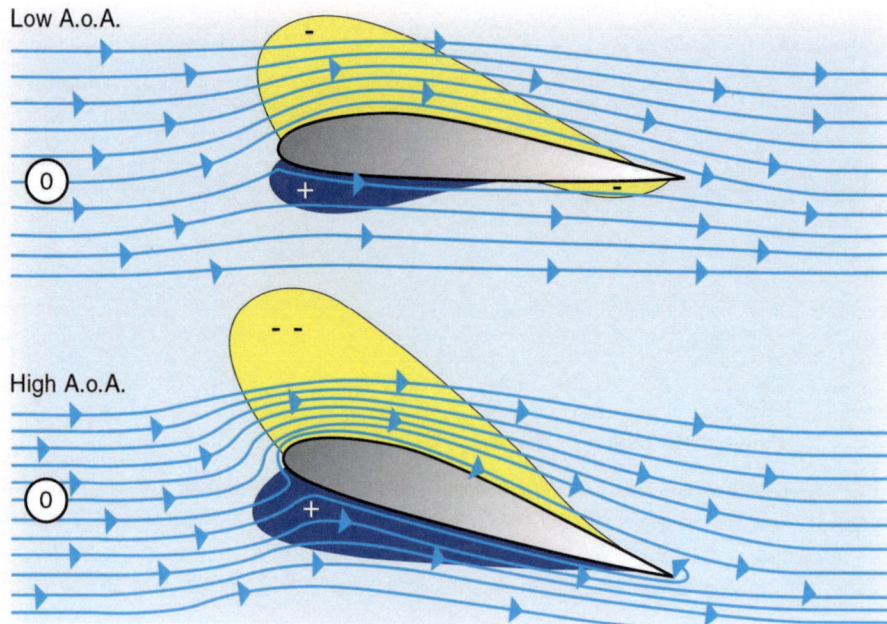

Low A.o.A.

High A.o.A.

Figure 7.7

7.1.2   *Stall angle of attack and stall*

When the pressure difference between the upper front surface and the lower aft surface is too great, the airstream can no longer flow attached to the upper surface. Instead the air at the lower surface near the trailing edge starts to counteract the low energy flow from the upper surface.

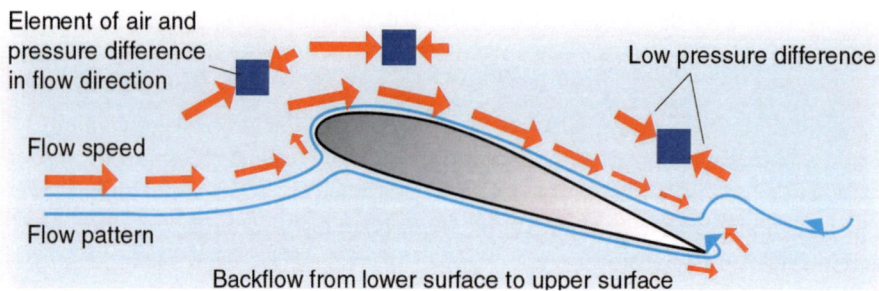

Element of air and pressure difference in flow direction

Low pressure difference

Flow speed

Flow pattern

Backflow from lower surface to upper surface

Figure 7.8

If you increase the angle of attack further, the "backflow" and consequently the separation point, gradually moves towards the leading edge until you reach the stall (critical) angle of attack.

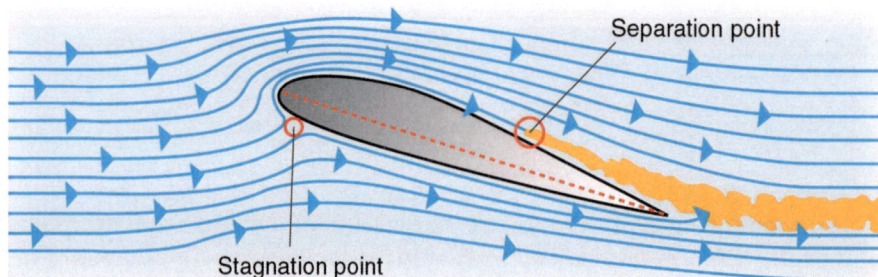

Separation point

Stagnation point

Figure 7.9

When we increase the angle of attack up to the stall angle, the separation point gradually moves towards the leading edge.

CRANFIELD AVIATION TRAINING SCHOOL LTD. PART-FCL GBR.ATO-0136
CATS INNOVATION CENTRE, LUTON, Bedfordshire LU2 8DL U.K.   www.catsaviation.com

CATS

7-3   Principles of Flight

When exceeding the stall angle of attack, the movement of the separation point towards the leading edge is sudden. The airflow, now separated, turbulent and at low velocity (low energy), affects a large portion of the upper surface reducing the pressure differences around the aerofoil. This condition is defined as aerofoil stall.

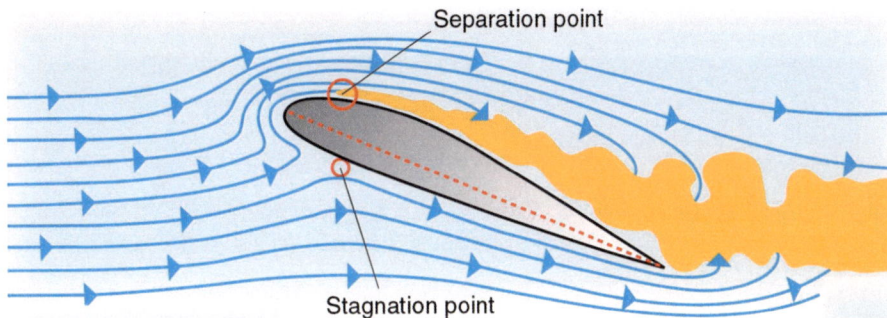

Figure 7.10

Exceeding the stall angle of attack causes stall. The flow breaks away from the upper surface of the aerofoil, which leads to a drastic reduction of the pressure differences at upper and lower aerofoil surfaces

7.1.3 *Aerofoil behaviour and stall effects*

When the angle of attack increases, the area of the zone of lower pressure on the upper surface of the aerofoil will be larger, moving towards the leading edge. With the increase of the angle of attack, the value of the total aerodynamic reaction increases as well, and the centre of pressure moves towards the leading edge. Once the stall angle has been reached, the total aerodynamic reaction reaches its maximum value and the centre of pressure is at its most forward position.

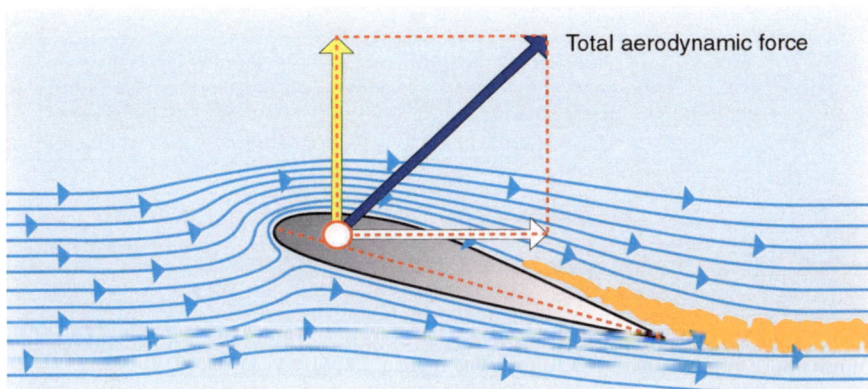

Figure 7.11

This behaviour continues only until the stall angle of attack is exceeded. When the airflow breaks away from the upper surface of the aerofoil and the aerofoil has stalled, there is a drastic reduction of the zone of lower static pressure on the upper surface of the aerofoil.

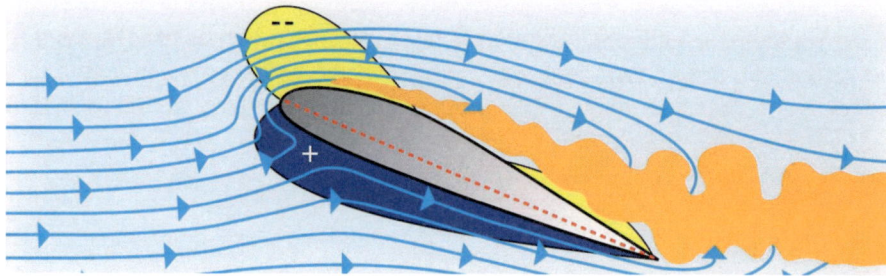

Figure 7.12

When the stall angle of attack is exceeded and the aerofoil has stalled, the separation wake covers most of the upper surface and the lift component of the total aerodynamic reaction dramatically decreases and the centre of pressure moves towards the trailing edge.

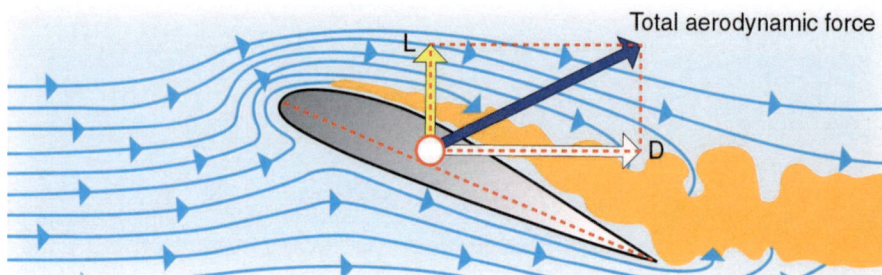

Figure 7.13

When the stall angle is exceeded the drag continues to increase, The rearward movement of the centre of pressure, with respect to the centre of gravity, generates a moment which tends to lower the nose of the aircraft. However, depending on the location of the horizontal stabiliser, some aircraft may pitch-up instead of pitch-down.

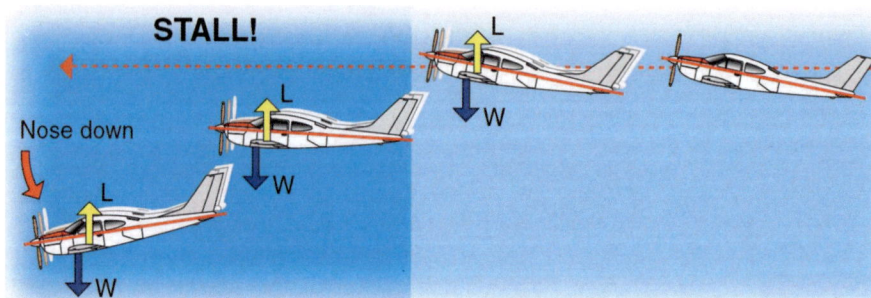

Figure 7.14

When in the stall, the drag increases and the rearward movement of the centre of pressure with respect to the centre of gravity generates a moment, which tends to lower the nose of the aircraft. Depending on the location of the horizontal stabiliser, some aircraft may pitch-up instead of pitch-down

7.1.4 *Behaviour of the boundary layer*

To understand the behaviour of the fluid when the angle of attack is increased, it is necessary to consider the effects of fluid viscosity. The viscosity of the fluid causes the separation of the airflow from the aerofoil. If the fluid were not viscous, it would slip along the surface of the aerofoil without adhering to it. However, the viscosity of the fluid causes it to adhere to the surface of the aerofoil. The effect of fluid viscosity takes place mainly in the thin boundary layer around the aerofoil.

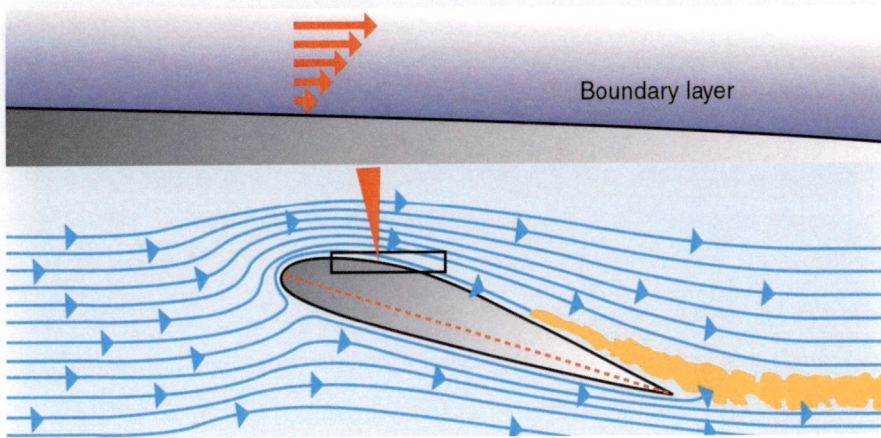

Figure 7.15

The effect of fluid viscosity takes place mainly in the boundary layer

Owing to the viscosity of fluids, the speed of the fluid within the boundary layer is gradually reduced. The speed gradually decreases until it is zero on the surface of the aerofoil.

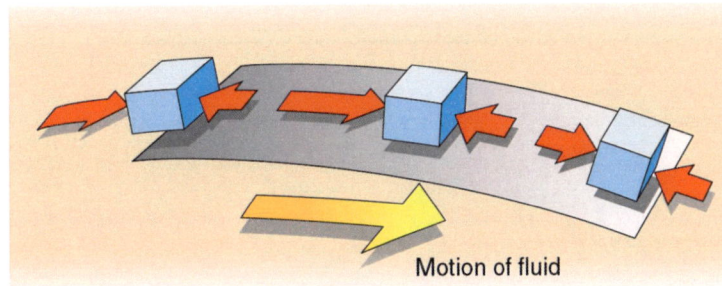

Figure 7.16

Between the leading edge and the maximum thickness, the pressure distribution around the aerofoil generates a total reaction which facilitates the movement of the fluid element of the boundary layer. But between the approximate position of maximum thickness and the trailing edge, the pressure distribution generates a total reaction on the elements in the boundary layer which slows down its rearward movement.

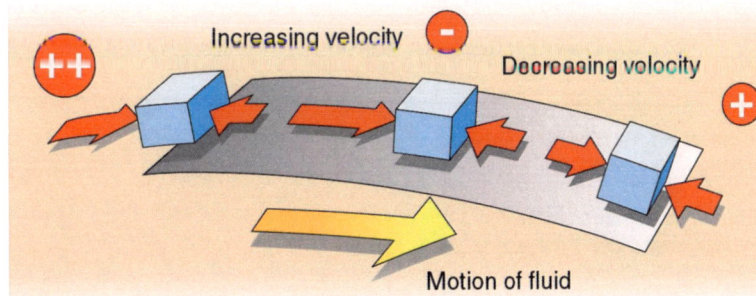

Figure 7.17

Forces resulting from the different pressures around the aerofoil generate a total reaction on the boundary layer element, the movement of which first is increased, and later decreased. The speed of the fluid in the boundary layer nearest the surface is further reduced. At the separation point the fluid reverses its direction, the boundary layer separates and a thicker wake is generated.

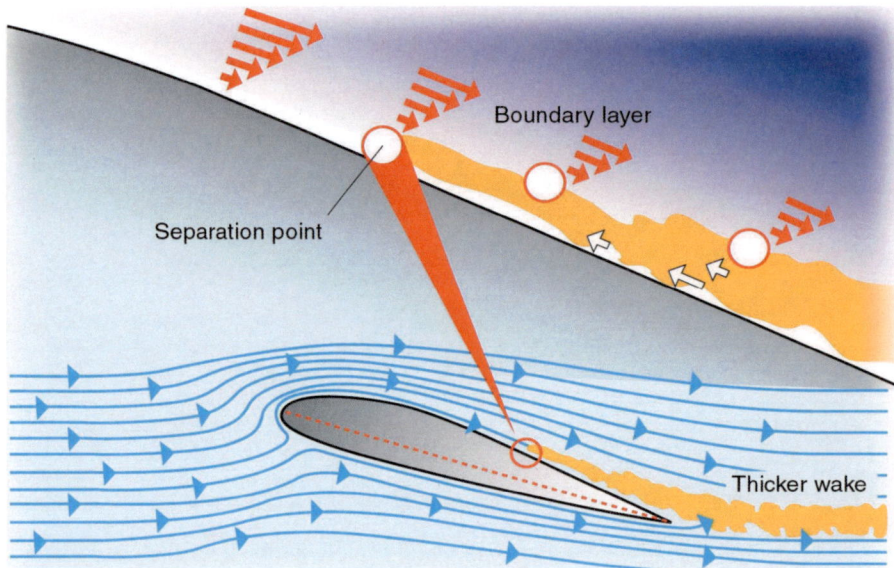

Figure 7.18

If the angle of attack is increased, the maximum value of the lower pressure on the upper surface moves towards the leading edge and the shape of the pressure distribution will be a steeper slope which causes the separation point to move closer to the leading edge.

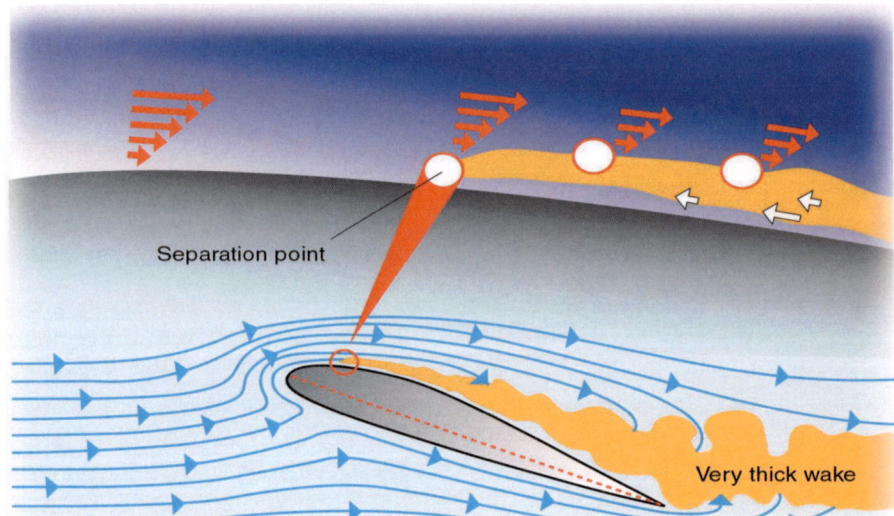

Figure 7.19

At the stall, the separation point is close to the leading edge, thus a large portion of the airflow on the upper surface of the aerofoil is separated and turbulent.

7.1.5 *Impact on the coefficient of lift*

When the angle of attack is altered, the fluid behaviour is reflected in the behaviour of the lift coefficient. The lift coefficient increases in a nearly linear fashion until flow separation starts. When the angle of attack has reached the stall value (α critical.), the flow separation is so great that a further increase of A.of.A will only reduce the lift coefficient, C_L.

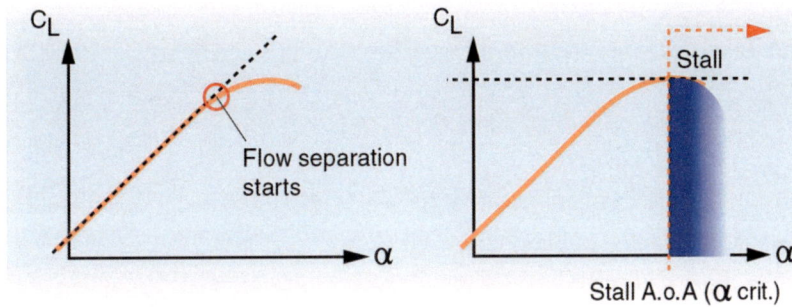

Figure 7.20 C_L increases with angle of attack up to α_{crit}

When the stall angle of attack is reached, the lift coefficient assumes its maximum value. Once the critical angle of attack has been exceeded, the lift coefficient dramatically decreases because the aerofoil is stalled.

C_L reaches its maximum value, C_L max, at the stall angle of attack (α_{crit})

7.1.6 Effect of different aerofoil sections on $C_{L\,max}$ and α_{crit}

Depending on the shape of the aerofoil section, the value of C_L max and α critical. varies a lot. Also the behaviour near the stalling A.of.A varies a lot.

An aerofoil with high thickness to chord ratio or an aerofoil with an aft location of the max camber and/or max thickness, will have flow separation at the trailing edge at relatively low A.of.A. due to the distribution of the pressure differences along the chord. In addition, a rounded trailing edge will facilitate the flow of high pressure at the lower surface near the trailing edge, to creep around the trailing edge and hinder the upper surface boundary layer, thus starting an early flow separation. Below you find the typical curves of CL/a for some aerofoil sections:

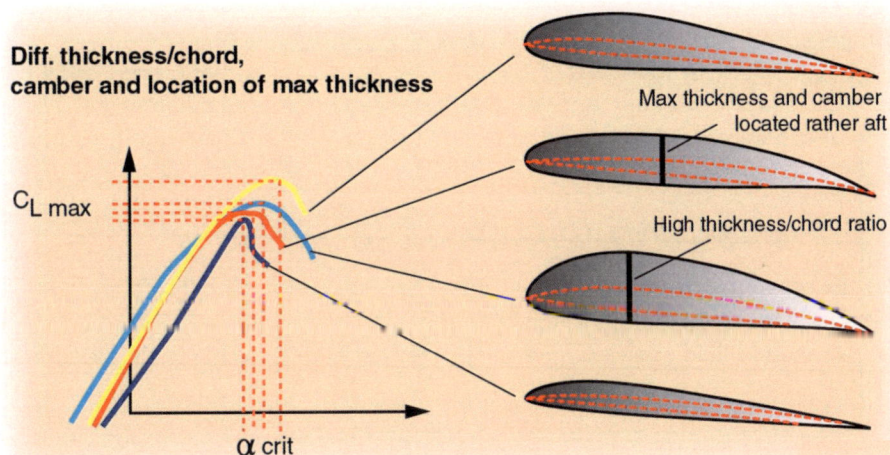

Figure 7.21

Note that a very thin section or a section with high thickness to chord ratio, has a lower α_{crit} than a medium section.

The form of the leading edge has very great influence on the α critical. A very sharp leading edge will cause flow separation at the leading edge already at low A.of.A. This type of leading edge stall will not be preceded by buffeting and the stall characteristic is often more violent than with flow separation started at the trailing edge. On the contrary, a downwards pointing rounded leading edge facilitates the flow from the stagnation point around the leading edge and therefore will allow high A.of.A. before flow separation begins.

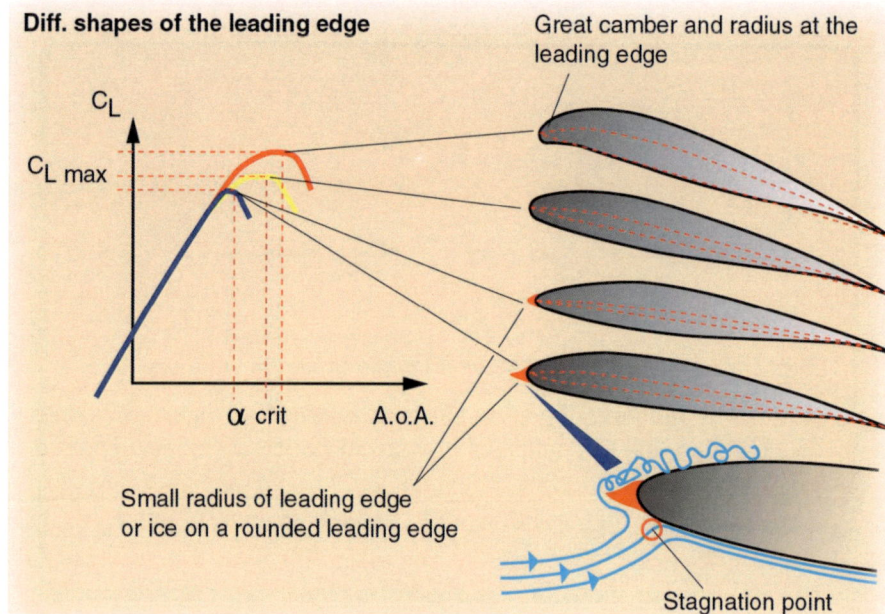

Figure 7.22

The highest possible C_L and α_{crit} depends very much on:

- Thickness/chord ratio.
- Camber, and particularly the degree of camber near the leading edge.
- Radius of leading edge, clean leading edge.
- Chord wise location of the points of maximum thickness and maximum camber.
- Sharpness of the trailing edge.

7.1.7   *Effect of Re number on maximum lift*

For aerofoils with moderate thickness ratio, there is a significant increase in C_{Lmax} with increasing Re number. On the other hand, for a thin aerofoil section, the effect of Re number is relatively insignificant. In general, the effects of the Re number are less for cambered than for symmetrical sections. At low Re numbers, the effect of camber is more significant. The opposite is true of Re numbers greater than 6×10^6, where camber loses some of its effect.

7.1.8   *Effects of flap extension on aerofoil stall*

One way to further increase the lift generated by the aerofoil section, is to change the camber of the aerofoil section by extending a trailing edge flap. Visualising the airflow around the aerofoil with the flap extended, you will notice an increase in fluid speed on the upper surface and a considerable steeper downwash of the fluid.

CRANFIELD AVIATION TRAINING SCHOOL LTD. PART-FCL GBR.ATO-0136
CATS INNOVATION CENTRE, LUTON, Bedfordshire LU2 8DL U.K.   www.catsaviation.com
7-9   Principles of Flight

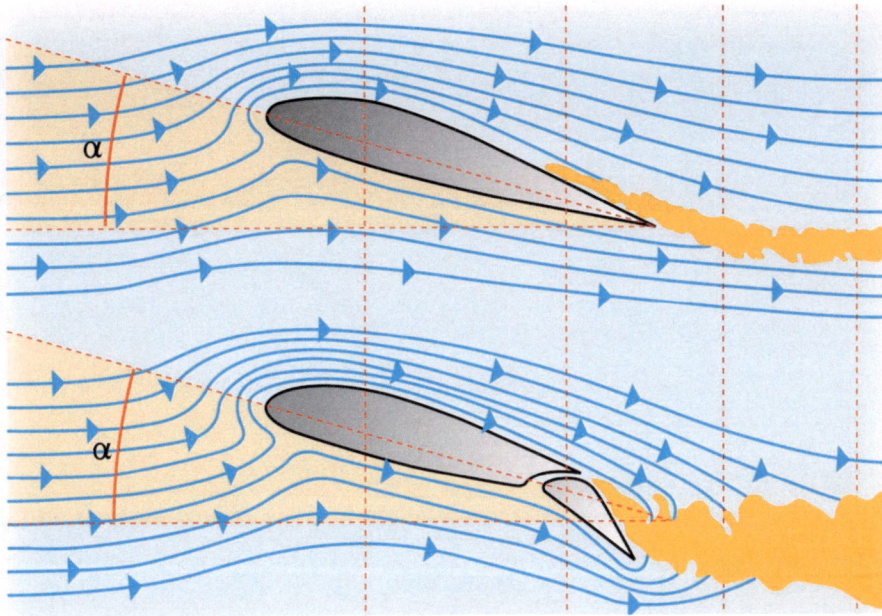

Figure 7.23

Notwithstanding the same geometrical A.of.A, the increased acceleration of air mass downwards gives a different speed distribution on the aerofoil with the flap extended, causing a change in the pressure distribution on the aerofoil along the whole chord.

These pressure modifications increase the lift and drag for a given angle of attack and the centre of pressure on the wing moves rearward.

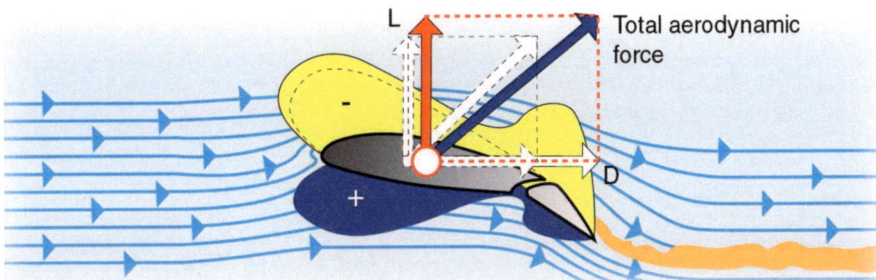

Figure 7.24

However, the greater pressure differences generated when extending the flap will cause the flow separation to start at a lower value of stall angle of attack than the value attainable with the flap retracted.

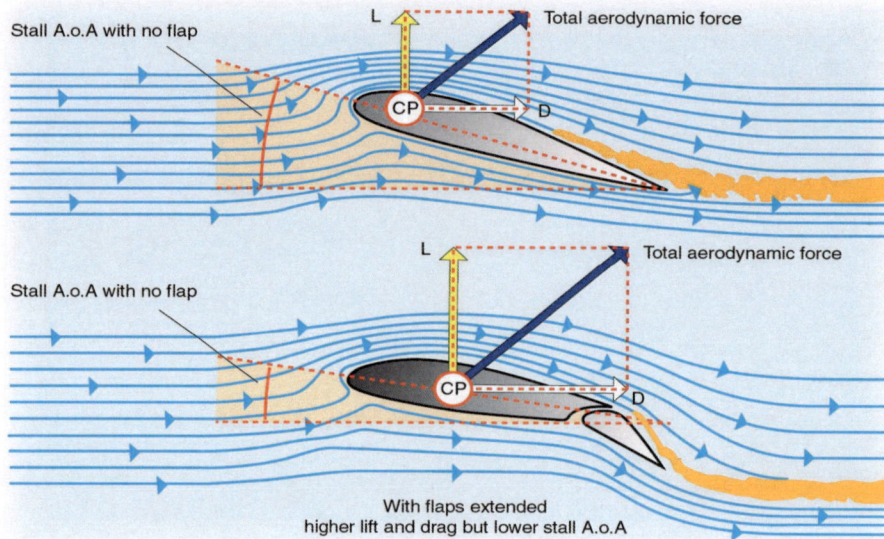

Figure 7.25

The behaviour of the aerofoil, both with the flap extended and with the flap retracted, is clearly shown on the diagram of the lift coefficient. With the flap extended the aerofoil reaches a higher value of maximum lift coefficient at a lower stall angle of attack.

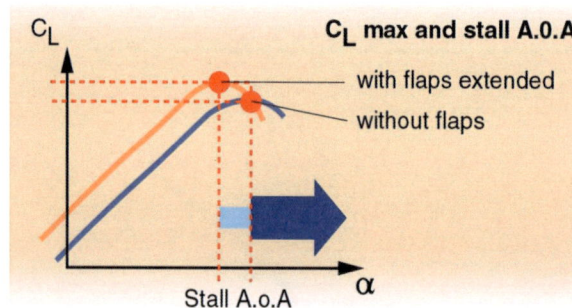

Figure 7.26

Flap extension causes:

- an increase in aerofoil lift and drag at constant aerofoil A.of.A
- a decrease of the stall angle of attack.

7.1.9   *Definitions of stalling speed*

FAA defines stalling speed as follows (FAR 23):

V_S is the calibrated stalling speed, or the minimum steady flight speed, in KT, at which the aircraft is controllable with:

1.   Zero thrust at stalling speed, or, if the resultant thrust has no appreciable effect on the stalling speed with engines idling and throttles closed;

2.   Propeller pitch controls in the positions required in item 1 above.

3.   The weight as a factor which corresponds with the required performance standard;

4.   The most unfavourable C.G. allowable.

Stalling speed V_S is the minimum speed obtained as follows:-

Trim the aircraft for straight flight at any speed not lower than 1.2 V_S or higher than 1.4 V_S. At a speed sufficiently above the stalling speed to ensure a steady condition, apply the elevator control at a rate so that the reduction in aircraft speed does not exceed 1 Kt/sec.

The stalling speed V_S found in the Pilot Operating Handbook is based on a slow reduction in speed in straight and level flight.

7.2 Wing Stall

This section describes the behaviour of the stalled wing, the effects of wing geometry and of propeller slipstream on stall. It also describes the behaviour of the aircraft in and out of ground effect.

7.2.1 Rectangular wing stall

Now that we have described aerofoil stall, we shall examine the behaviour of the stalled wing. The airflow around the wing is influenced by the acceleration of air mass downward, and the pressure distribution around the wing. These factors generate a span wise flow i.e. an induced flow on the wing, which will create an intense vortex behind each wing tip.

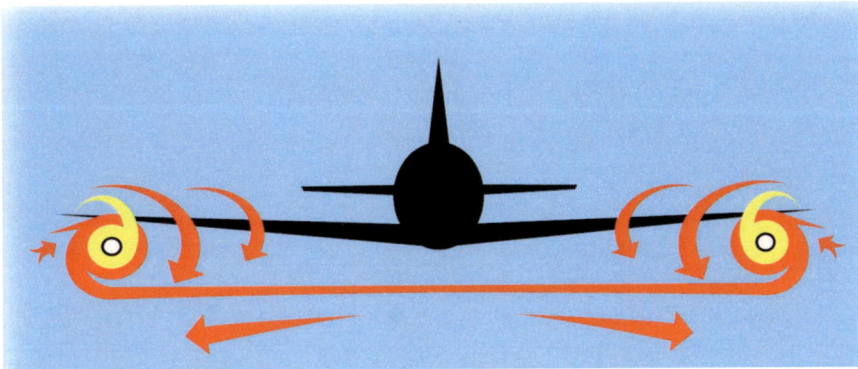

Figure 7.27

Induced spanwise flow due to the pressure distribution around the wing generates vortices behind the wing tips

Let us consider a rectangular wing with constant aerofoil section and no twist. You will notice the distribution of the lower pressure on the upper surface and the induced speed along the wing span. Induced flow is not constant but results in a maximum value towards each wing tip and a minimum value at the wing-root.

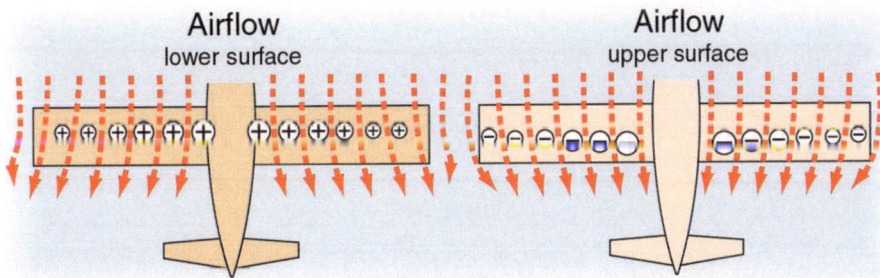

Figure 7.28

Around a rectangular wing the induced flow varies along the wing span.
The lower pressure at the upper surface near the wing root and the corresponding higher pressure at the lower surface change the relative speed and the actual angle of attack along the wing span.
The actual angle of attack at which the relative speed meets a wing section is determined by the pressure distribution around the wing, i.e. the lift distribution. As you already know, most of the lift is created at the inner part of the wing. The free stream meets the aerofoils of the wing at an angle of attack that gradually decreases from the wing root to the wing tip. (This is known as 'washout').

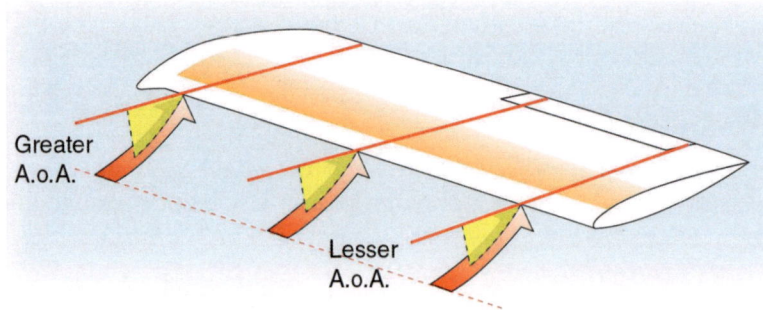

Figure 7.29

The free stream meets the aerofoils of the wing at an angle of attack that gradually decreases from the wing root to the wing tip. When the angle of attack of the wing increases, the aerofoil at each wing root is the first to reach the stall angle of attack and then stall.

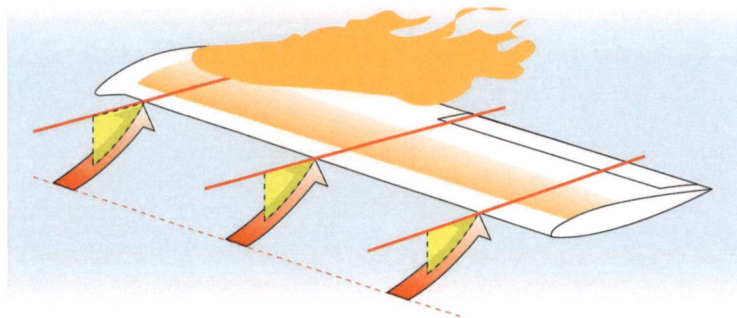

Figure 7.30

The aerofoils at the wing roots are the first to reach the stall angle of attack

As the angle of attack increases further, the stall also reaches the wing tip.

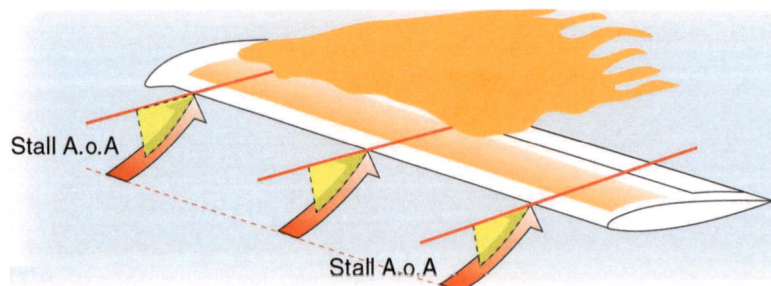

Figure 7.31

The ailerons therefore maintain their effectiveness even at high angles of attack because they are located towards the wing tip which is the last part to stall

You are warned of an impending stall by onset of buffet from the flow separation on the wing upper surface, on the fuselage and, often, the tailplane. This buffet is generated by the separated airflow which, on a well designed aircraft, breaks away first at the wing root.

Flow separation is felt as buffeting on the aircraft wing, fuselage and on the tail if located within the wing wake.

Figure 7.32

The location of the horizontal tail plane has a great influence on how well you will notice the stall warning from buffeting. A tail located within the wing wake will warn you by vibrations in the control column from the turbulent wing wake and the elevator effectiveness will be somewhat reduced. However, if the tail is located well below or above, e.g. as in a so-called T-tail configuration, the buffet will only be felt through the separation on the wing, and the elevator will still have full authority.

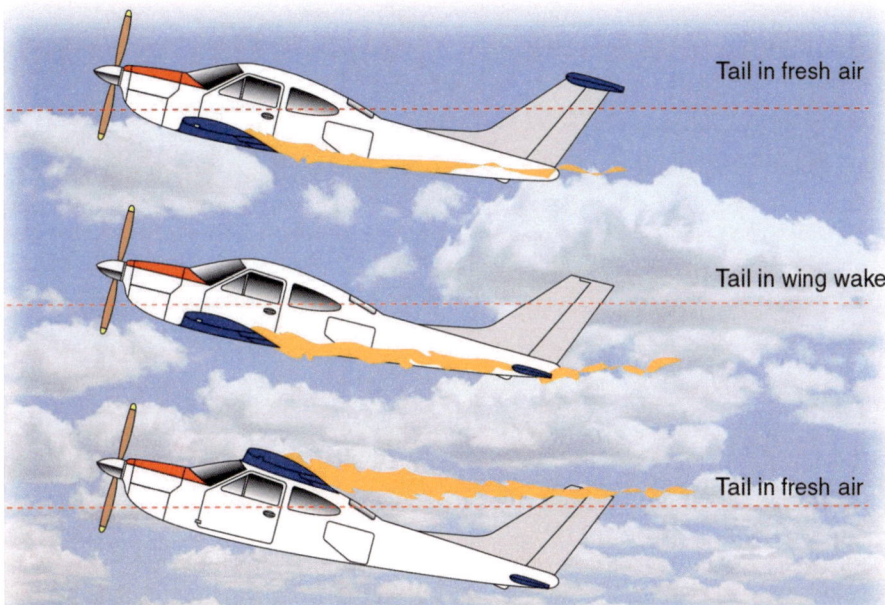

Tail in fresh air

Tail in wing wake

Tail in fresh air

Figure 7.33

Depending on the tail location, the stall warning buffeting and elevator response vary a lot on different aircraft

7.2.2   *Effects of wing planform on stall*

The behaviour of the wing at stall is affected by its geometry, by the effect of the propeller slipstream and by the proximity to the ground. We shall first of all describe the effect of wing geometry. In particular, we shall examine the effect of the wing planform, the wing sweepback and the formation of ice on the wing. On the moderately tapered wing, the stall angle of attack is reached first at the central area of the wing because of the induced speed distribution along the wing span. If the angle of attack is increased, the stalled area expands towards the wing root as well as towards the wing tip.

CRANFIELD AVIATION TRAINING SCHOOL LTD. PART-FCL GBR.ATO-0136
CATS INNOVATION CENTRE, LUTON, Bedfordshire LU2 8DL U.K.   www.catsaviation.com
7-14   Principles of Flight

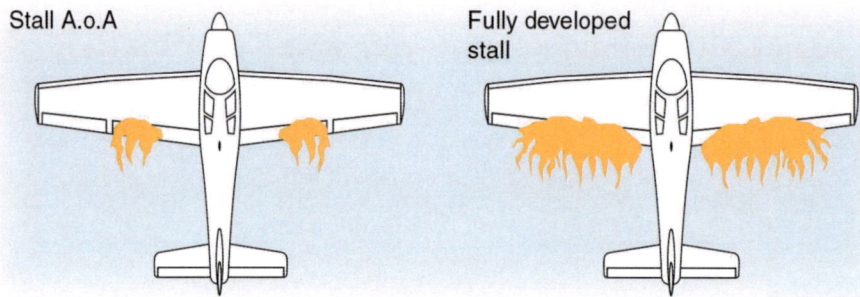

Figure 7.34

On a moderately tapered wing, the critical angle of attack is reached first in the central area of the wing. If the angle of attack is increased, the stalled area extends towards the wing root and the wing tip.

7.2.3 Wing tip stall

On a highly tapered wing without washout, the stall angle of attack is reached first of all by the aerofoil of the wing tip. If the angle of attack is increased, the stalled area gradually expands towards the wing root.

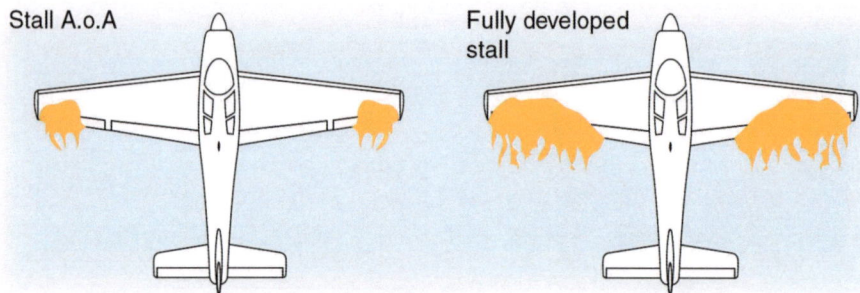

Figure 7.35

Wing tip stall causes some major problems. The ailerons lose their effectiveness long before the complete wing stall. There is little or no buffet to warn of an impending stall because the turbulent separated airflow area is rather small and does not meet either the fuselage or the empennage. In addition, since stall rarely involves both wings at the exactly same time, there is an asymmetrical lift situation that causes a rolling moment.

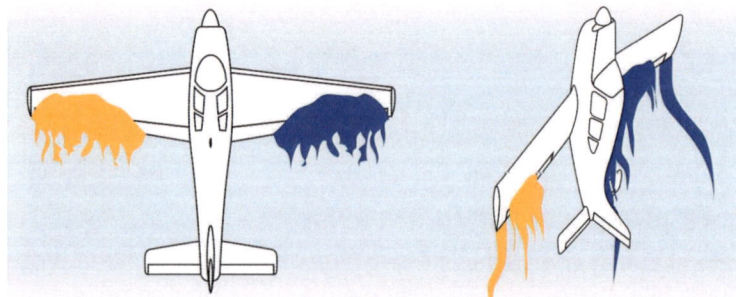

Figure 7.36

Wing tip stall causes: little or no buffeting, an early loss of effectiveness of the ailerons, and rolling disturbances of the aircraft.

7.2.4 Modifications to avoid wing tip stall

To avoid having the stall begin at the wing tips, modifications to the geometry of the wing, such as geometrical or aerodynamically washout, can be introduced.

The geometrical wing washout reduces the aerofoil angle of attack along the wing. The aerodynamic washout allows the outer parts of the wing to have a greater stall angle of attack than the wing root. The aerofoils at the wing root will then be the first to reach the stall angle of attack and will therefore stall first.

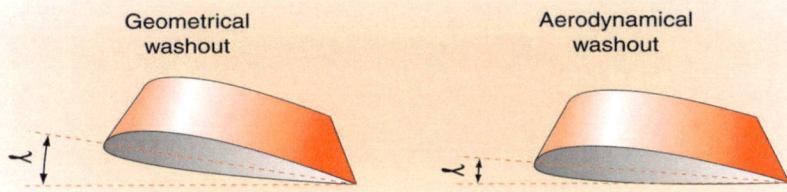

Figure 7.37

The wing washout delays the stall of the wing tips

If this kind of wing design is not satisfactory, vortex generators can be added at certain positions in order to revitalise the turbulent boundary layer, thus delaying the stall in this area.

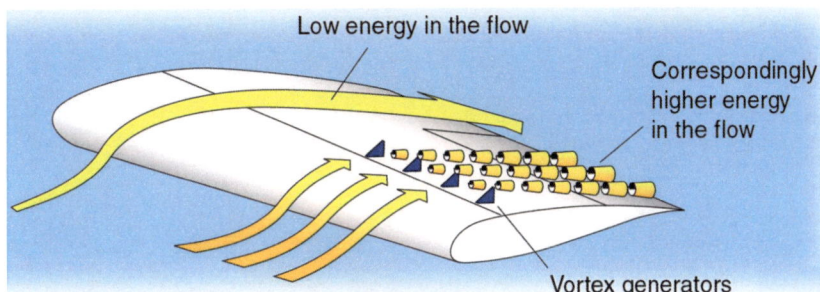

Figure 7.37

Another way of ensuring better stall performance of the tapered wing is to force the stall to begin at the wing root. For this purpose the aerofoils at the wing roots are equipped with strips called stalling strips. These modify the leading edge shape, causing an earlier separation of the boundary layer.

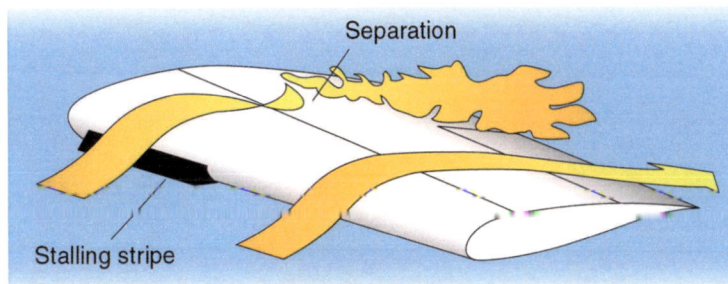

Figure 7.38

Stalling strips cause the desired separation of the boundary layer at the wing-root at a lower angle of attack in comparison with a "clean" wing. In this way we get a natural stall warning by buffet

7.2.5 Effects of swept wings on stall

Sweepback influences the behaviour of the wing at stall. If you observe the flow along the upper surface of the wing, you will notice that the flow deviates towards the low-pressure area further aft and out at the wing tip.

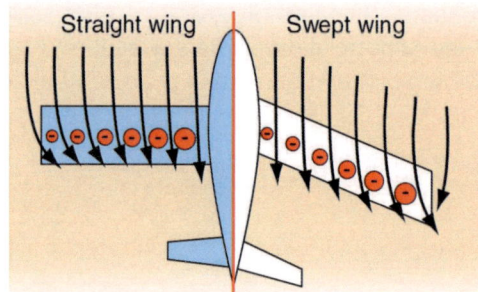

Figure 7.39

The airflow along the upper surface of a swept wing deviates towards the wing tip

If the angle of attack is increased, this deviation of the boundary layer becomes greater and the flow slows down. The slowest boundary layer is near the wing tip. The separation therefore begins to take place at the wing tip and then gradually extends towards the wing-root.

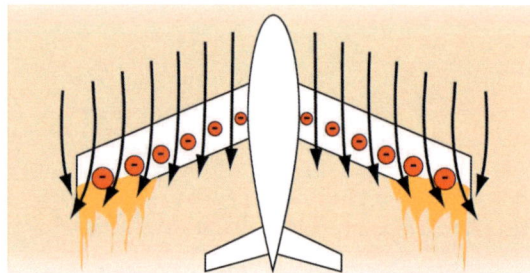

Figure 7.40

On a swept wing; when the angle of attack is increased the separation of the boundary layer begins at the wing tips

This kind of stall may lead to an undesired rapid pitch-up and lateral disturbances due to lift being lost aft of C.G. In order to delay the wing tip stall of a swept wing, the deviation of the boundary layer towards the wing tip can be prevented by installing "wing fences" on the upper surface of the wing.

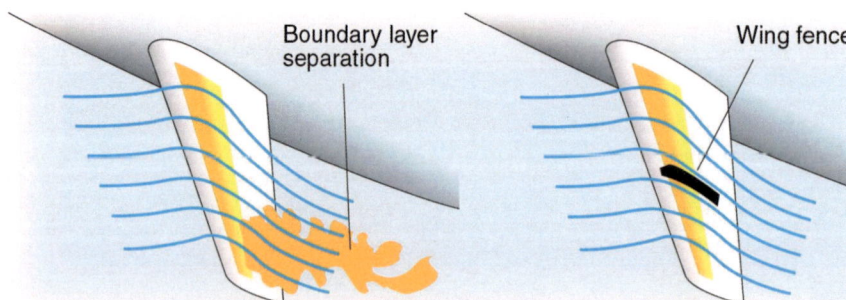

Figure 7.41

Another way to prevent span wise flow from giving wing tip stall, is to install small "vortilons" on the lower surface of the wing near the leading edge, or the leading edge may have a "sawteeth". At high angles of attack, the "vortilons" or "sawtooth" produce a vortex that flows over the wing. This reduces the sensitivity of the airflow to the lower pressure further out and back, and so reduces the risk of stall at the outer wing section.

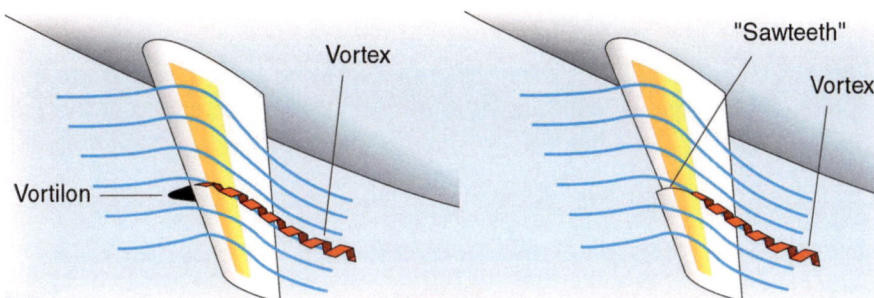

Figure 7.42

The wing fences delay the wing tip stall of a swept wing and the vortilon or "sawtooth" produce a vortex that prevents premature stalling of the outer wing section

7.2.6 Stalling of a canard aircraft

A canard aircraft has its main plane rear of the canard. If the wing stalls first the canard will lift the nose further, causing a dangerous deep stall. In order to get acceptable stall characteristics, i.e. the nose goes down and reduces the A.of.A. when stalling, the canard has to be designed to stall earlier than the main plane.

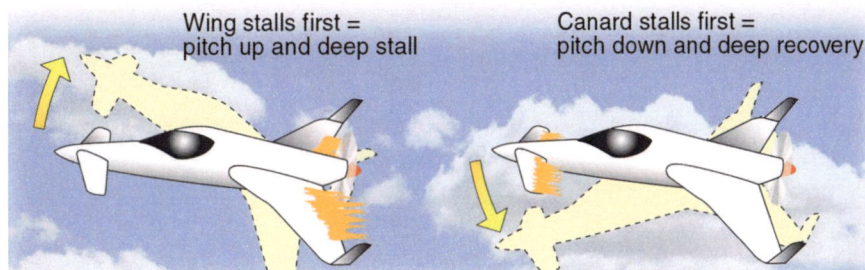

Figure 7.43

7.2.7 Effects of ice formation on stall

Ice formation on the wing alters the shape of the aerofoil and the skin friction, causing a change in pressure distribution and therefore also a boundary layer separation at a relative low angle of attack. The stall in the presence of ice is therefore often not expected, which may cause very dangerous situations.

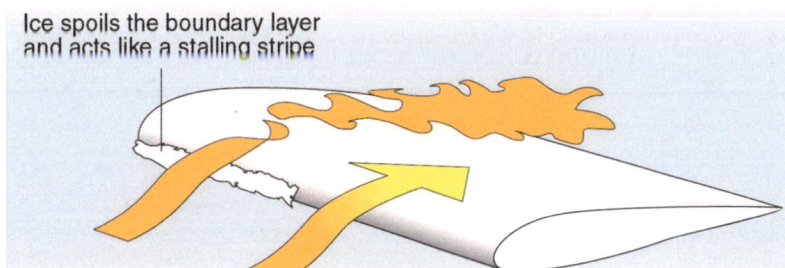

Figure 7.44

Ice formation on the wing alters the shape of the aerofoil and the skin friction, causing stall at a lower angle of attack than anticipated

CRANFIELD AVIATION TRAINING SCHOOL LTD. PART-FCL GBR.ATO-0136
CATS INNOVATION CENTRE, LUTON, Bedfordshire LU2 8DL U.K.

CATS

www.catsaviation.com

7-18

Principles of Flight

7.2.8 Effects of propeller slipstream on stall

Let us now consider the effects of the propeller slipstream on wing stall. To generate thrust, the propeller accelerates a certain quantity of air. At high angles of attack, the greater speed of the propeller slipstream and its direction parallel to the incidence of the wing delays the boundary layer separation in the area of the wing affected by it.

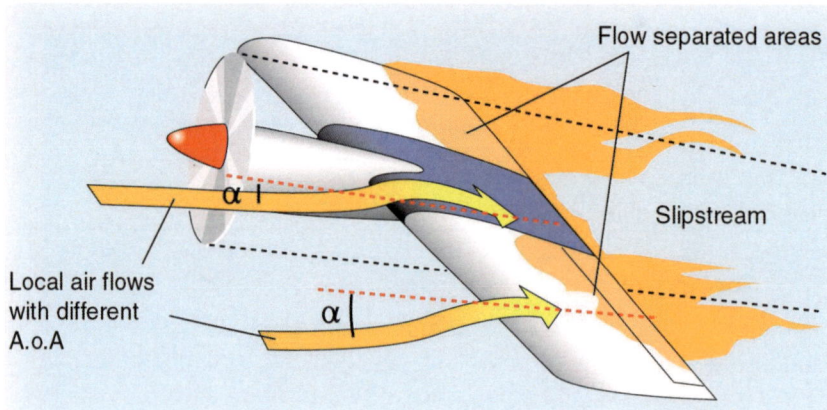

Figure 7.45

> The boundary layer separation is delayed in the area of the wing affected by the propeller slipstream

The increased propeller slipstream over the wings, in a high power situation at low speed, will create more lift than at idle power, giving a lower stalling speed. However, as the outer parts of the wings are not within the slipstream the stall may begin at the wing tips in a high power/low speed situation.

In a situation with low speed and a high power propeller slipstream, the stall may begin at the wing tips.

7.2.9 Effects of the ground effect on stall

When the aircraft flies at an altitude above the ground which is less than its wing span, the airflow around the wing is modified. This phenomenon, which takes place close to the ground, is called the "ground effect".

When in ground effect there is a greater upwash of the airflow in front of the wing at a given A.of.A. giving an increased suction at the fore part of the wings. This generates a higher lift coefficient at the same angle of attack than what would have been the case out of the ground effect.

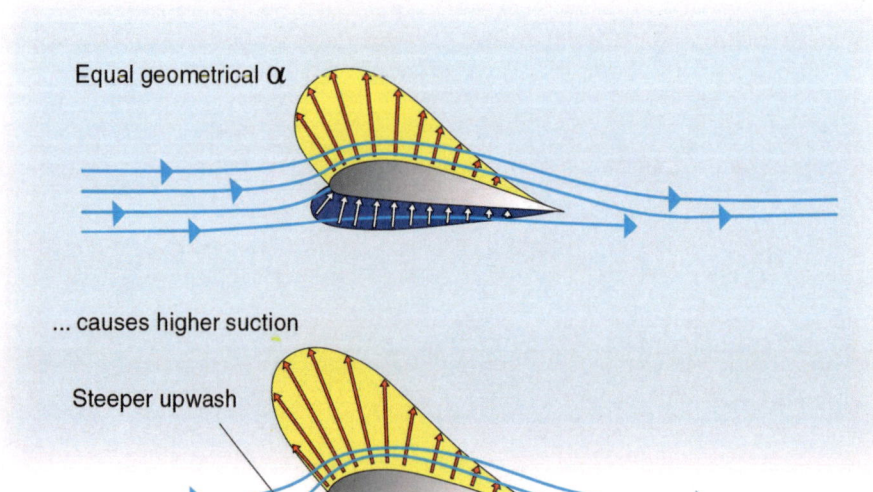

Figure 7.46

In the area of ground effect, the aerodynamic angle of attack increases. The wing affected by the ground effect generates a lift coefficient which is greater than that generated out of the ground effect at the same geometrical angle of attack.

However, the ground effect does not influence the value of the maximum lift coefficient generated by the wing, because the increased upwash in front of the wing also reduces the critical angle of attack.

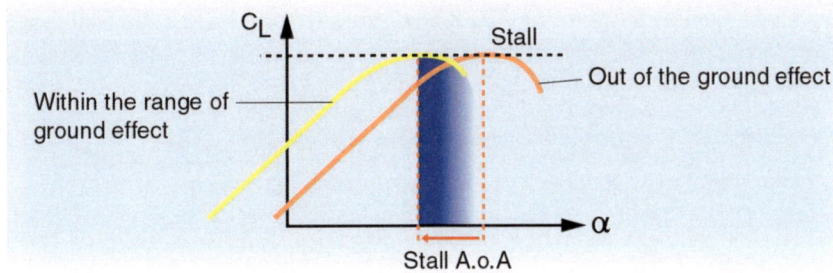

Figure 7.47

The wing affected by the ground effect generates the same maximum lift coefficient at a lower critical angle of attack

This causes stall at lower pitch attitude than that which is normal when reaching stall out of the ground effect.

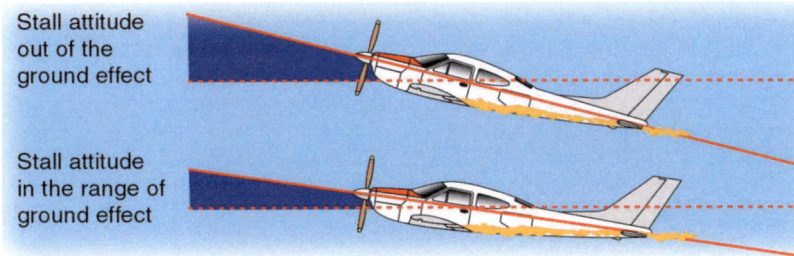

Figure 7.48

7.3   *Stalling Speed*

7.3.1   *Stalling speed and stall angle of attack*

A knowledge of the factors that influence stalling speed is very important to you as a pilot. Below the actual stalling speed; the lift decreases and the drag increases. There is no longer balance between the lift and the weight of the aeroplane, which causes it to rapidly deviate from its intended flight path.

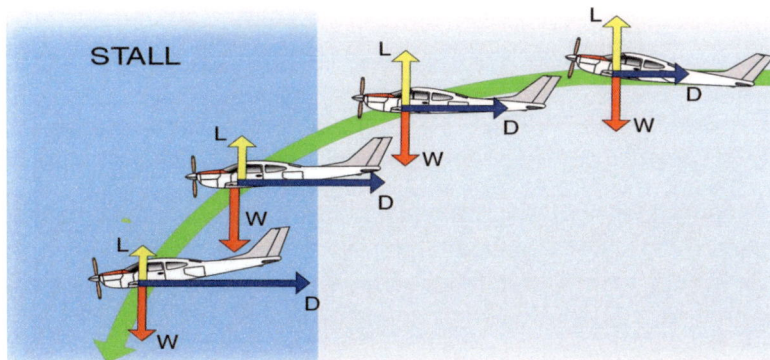

Figure 7.49

Stall takes place when the angle of attack is greater than the stall angle. This condition can exist at ANY speed (high speed at high load factor) and at ANY attitude of the aeroplane

You can stall when flying straight and level at a speed of 50 KT, with a nose up attitude, if you exceed the stall angle of attack. You can stall when descending at a speed of 50 KT with a nose down attitude, if you exceed the stall angle of attack. It is also possible to stall when making a pull-out from a dive too quickly or when making a very steep turn at a speed of 200 KT or more if you exceed the stall angle of attack without considering the maximum permissible load factor.

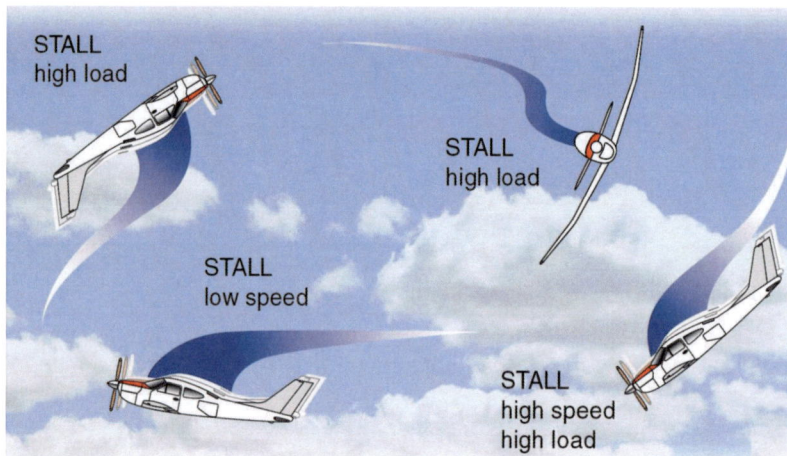

Figure 7.50

Stall takes place whenever the ANGLE OF ATTACK is greater than the stall angle, irrespective of the speed or attitude of the aircraft

7.3.2 *Relationship between lift and speed*

The lift L depends upon several factors. One of these factors is the lift coefficient C_L of the wing section, which, as you know, reaches its maximum value at the stall angle of attack.

$$L = \boxed{C_L \text{ max}} \times \tfrac{1}{2}\rho V^2 \times S$$

Figure 7.51

Another factor is the wing area S.

$$L = C_L \text{ max} \times \tfrac{1}{2}\rho V^2 \times \boxed{S}$$

Figure 7.52

The third factor is the dynamic pressure, which is equal to half the product of air density at the flight altitude $\tfrac{1}{2}\rho$ and the speed squared V^2 of the aeroplane with respect to the air. The speed V is the true air speed (TAS). The dynamic pressure, however, is roughly proportional to the speed shown at the air speed indicator. This speed is normally called indicated air speed (IAS).

$$L = C_L \text{ max} \times \boxed{1/2\ \rho V^2} \times S$$

Figure 7.53

To further increase the lift when flying at the critical angle of attack (giving the maximum lift coefficient) with a wing of a certain area S, the dynamic pressure has to be increased. This is the problem when flying at high altitudes. So, when flying at high altitude, you must obtain the same dynamic pressure as that at lower altitudes to have the same lift. The indicated air speed is nearly proportional to the dynamic pressure. The indicated stalling air speed, IAS, therefore remains nearly constant in relation to altitude. With an increase in altitude, the air density ρ decreases and the true stalling air speed, TAS, must increase to maintain the same dynamic pressure. Therefore, at high altitudes, the aeroplane stalls at nearly the same indicated air speed as that at low altitude but at a higher true air airspeed.

At high altitudes

$$L = C_L \text{ max} \times 1/2\ \underset{\text{low}}{\rho}\ \underset{\text{high}}{V^2} \times S$$

At low altitudes

$$L = C_L \text{ max} \times 1/2\ \underset{\text{high}}{\rho}\ \underset{\text{low}}{V^2} \times S$$

Figure 7.54

The stall IAS remains roughly constant in relation to altitude. The stall TAS instead, increases with altitude

But air density ρ also decreases as temperature increases. A take-off from an airport at high elevation, and in addition to that on a very hot day, demands a very high true air speed for lift-off and a long take-off run, in order to produce the required dynamic pressure needed to avoid stall IAS.

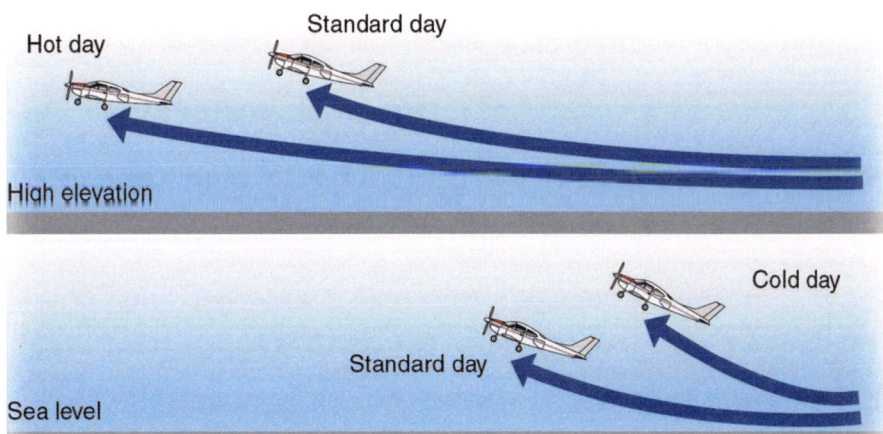

Figure 7.55

High altitudes and high temperatures require very high TAS to reach the required minimum IAS in order to avoid stall.

7.3.3   *Indicated Air Speed (IAS)*

The importance of the indicated airspeed regarding stall is obvious if we compare the obtained lift at different indicated speeds at a constant angle of attack, ρ and wing surface.

At an indicated airspeed of 100 KT the lift will be four times what it was at 50 KT. Another example; if your calculated speed of approach is 100 KT indicated airspeed, an inadvertent reduction to 90 KT will sacrifice 19% of lift. If you lose another 6 KT from a wind shear, the lift will fall to 70% unless you are able to increase the lift coefficient.

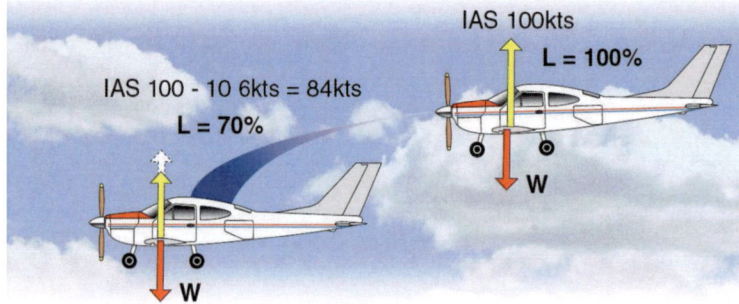

Figure 7.56

At 50 KIAS the lift is only 25% of what it would be at 100 KIAS at a given A.of.A. and wing area.

7.3.4   *Factors affecting stalling speed*

However, it is not only the dynamic pressure that affects the stalling speed. Any factor affects the stalling speed which determines a greater or lesser capacity of the wing to generate lift, such as Mach effects (increased Mach number decreases V_s) and high altitude (change the Reynolds number and increases V_s). Another factor is a change in the lift required by the wings.

The stalling speed is affected by the wing loading, which depends on a lot of things such as;

- the weight of the aeroplane,
- load factors due to manoeuvres or turbulence,
- changes in the position of the centre of gravity,
- use of power (propeller slip stream or vertical component of thrust).
- the lift coefficient, which may be changed by the use of high lift devices and ice formation.
-

FACTORS AFFECTING THE STALLING SPEED		
	Increasing Vs	Decreasing Vs

WING LOADING	**Higher weight**
	Higher load factor:
	    manoevres
	    turbelence
		Lower weight
		Lower load factor

Position of C.G.	**Forward**	Aft
COEFFICIENT OF LIFT	**Ice and contamination**	High lift devices
	Effect of altitude	

Figure 7.57

CRANFIELD AVIATION TRAINING SCHOOL LTD. PART-FCL GBR.ATO-0136
CATS INNOVATION CENTRE, LUTON, Bedfordshire LU2 8DL U.K.   www.catsaviation.com
7-23   Principles of Flight

7.3.5   *Wing loading (W/S)*

We will first look at the influence of the wing loading. If the weight of the aeroplane increases, the wing loading will be higher. The lift must increase proportionally in order to maintain the aircraft in straight and level flight. As the maximum lift coefficient C_L and the wing surface area are fixed values, the dynamic pressure has to increase, which means that the stalling speed also increases with higher weight.

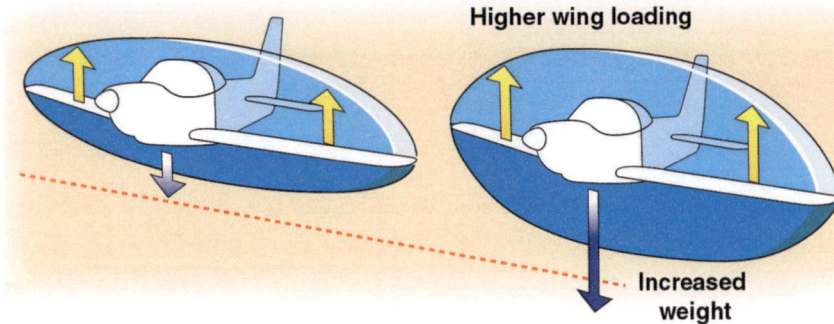

Figure 7.58

> When the weight of the aeroplane increases, the wing loading will be higher, causing the stalling speed to increase

On the contrary, if the weight of the aeroplane decreases, the wing loading will be lower and the lift must decrease proportionally in order to maintain straight and level flight. So, if the weight of the aeroplane decreases, the stalling speed also decreases. In the same way as the wing loading increases with an increase in weight, it is increased by a higher load factor. The ratio between the lift L generated by the wing, and the weight of the aeroplane W, is, as you know, the load factor, "n". When the aeroplane is pulled out of a dive or making a turn, the lift therefore increases proportionally to the load factor at which the manoeuvre is carried out. The stalling speed during a manoeuvre therefore increases in proportion to the square root of the load factor.

> The stalling speed increases in proportion to the square root of the load factor

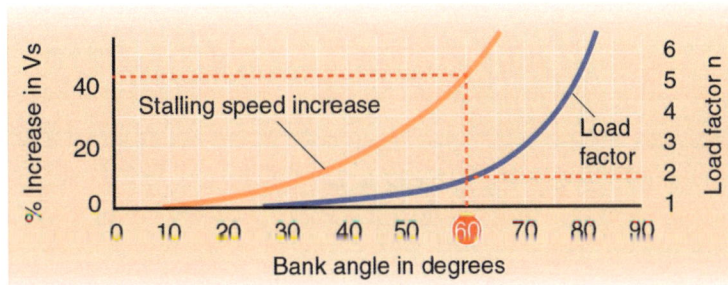

Figure 7.59

> An increase in the load factor will influence the wing loading in the same way as an increase in weight

The relationship between the load factor and the percentage of increase in stalling speed can be visualised in a diagram. Since the load factor during a turn is proportional to the lateral bank angle of the aeroplane, the diagram also indicates this.

CRANFIELD AVIATION TRAINING SCHOOL LTD. PART-FCL GBR.ATO-0136
CATS INNOVATION CENTRE, LUTON, Bedfordshire LU2 8DL U.K.   www.catsaviation.com

7-24   Principles of Flight

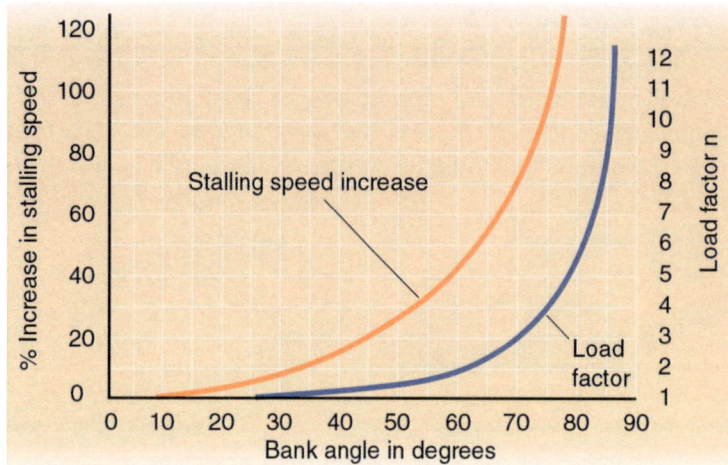

Figure 7.60

Using the diagram, you can find out the increase in stalling speed corresponding to a certain load factor. For example, if the load factor is equal to 2, the percentage of increase in stalling speed is approx. 40%.

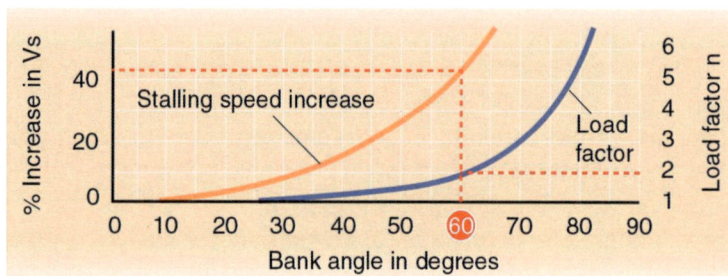

Figure 7.61

The greater the lateral bank angle during a turn, the greater the load factor and, as a result, the higher the stalling speed.

In a level turn at:
45° lateral bank = load factor ~1.4, increases V_s by ~20%
60° lateral bank = load factor ~2.0, increases V_s by ~40%
70° lateral bank = load factor ~3.0, increases V_s by ~70%
80° lateral bank = load factor ~6.0, increases V_s by ~140%

7.3.6 *Wind gusts*

In turbulent air, there are wind gusts that may cause a sudden increase in the angle of attack. The inertia of the aeroplane may cause it to exceed the critical angle of attack and stall at a higher speed.

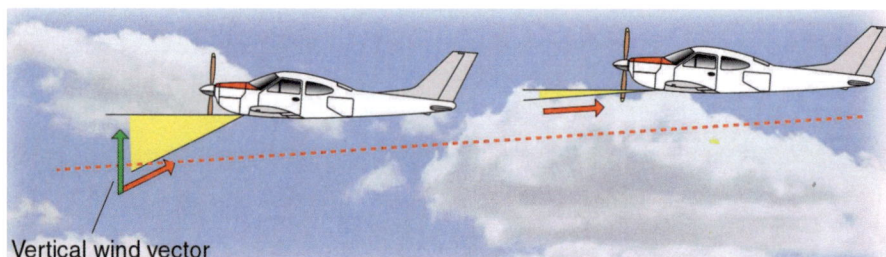

Vertical wind vector

Figure 7.62

7.3.7   *Position of the centre of gravity*

The point of application of the wing lift and the centre of gravity are not normally in the same position. Thus, a pitching moment is generated, and that pitching moment is balanced by the moment due to the tailplane force. When the centre of gravity is located in a normal forward position with respect to the centre of pressure, a nose down pitching moment is generated. The further forward the position of the centre of gravity, the greater the nose down moment, and so a greater downward force must be generated by the tailplane to maintain the attitude of flight. The wing lift must therefore balance the weight of the aircraft plus the force downward generated by the tailplane.

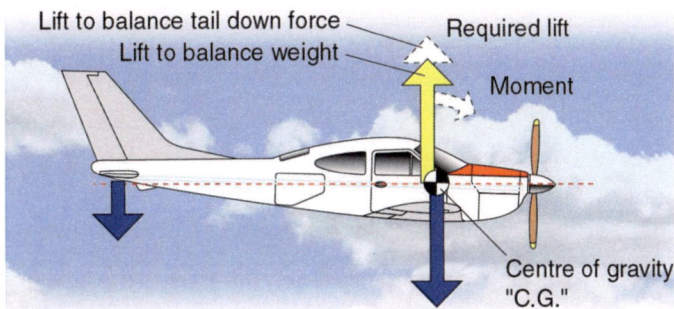

Figure 7.63

The required lift generated by the wing increases with a forward centre of gravity and as a result, so does the stalling speed.

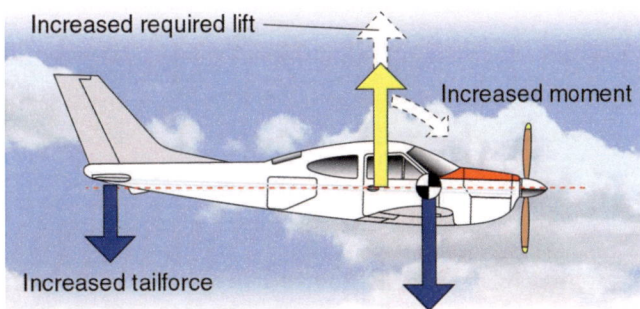

Figure 7.64

The further forward the position of the centre of gravity, the greater the downward force acting on the tailplane, which causes an increase in stalling speed

7.3.8   *High lift devices and their impact on C_L*

Extension of high lift devices, like slats and flaps, modifies the aerofoil and increases the maximum lift coefficient that can be obtained by the wing. Some kinds of flaps also increase the wing surface area. As a result, the same value of lift can be obtained at a lower stalling speed. It is not uncommon for transport aircraft to have a 25%, or greater reduction of stalling speed when the flaps are set for take-off.

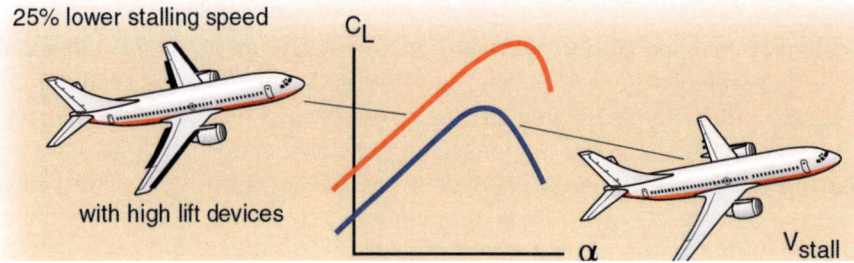

25% lower stalling speed

C_L

with high lift devices

α

V_{stall}

Figure 7.65

The use of take-off flaps on transport aircraft usually reduces the stalling speed by about 25%. Neglecting to set the take-off flaps while performing the lift-off at a speed determined for the use of flaps, will result in a stall

7.3.9   Use of power

The presence of power has an effect on the stalling speed. On propeller driven aeroplanes, some parts of the wings are affected by the propeller slipstream. The propeller accelerates the fluid in the slipstream, and, as a result, it produces greater dynamic pressure, and more air is accelerated downwards. The lift generated by the wing increases and as a result, the stalling speed decreases.

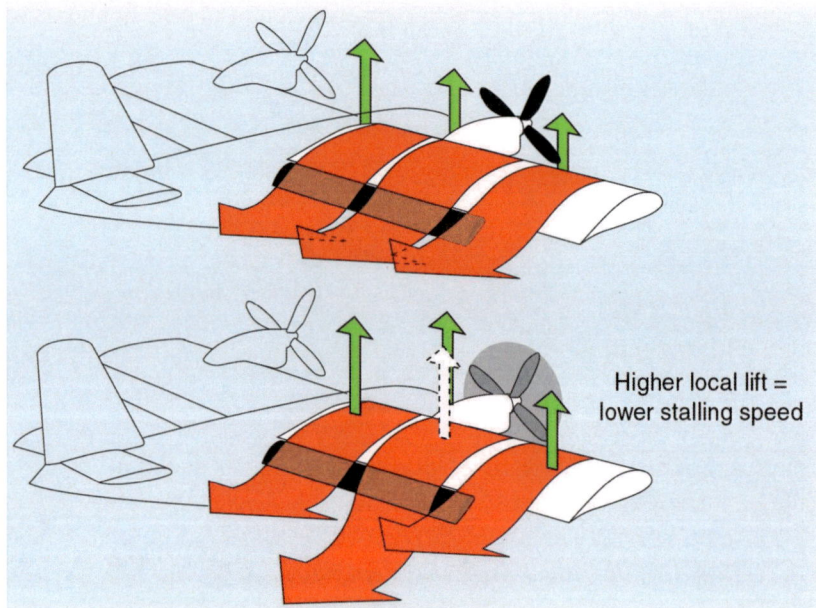

Higher local lift = lower stalling speed

Figure 7.66

The presence of the propeller slipstream over the wings has the result of increasing the lift generated by the wing giving a decreased stalling speed at high power

When the aeroplane is at a high nose up attitude, the thrust T, of the propeller has a vertical component Tv in the lift direction. This component of the thrust is added to the lift. The required lift, which the wing must generate, decreases and, as a result, so does the stalling speed.

Regarding jet aircraft, there is no propeller slipstream effect. The decrease in the stalling speed is due only to the thrust component T_v. The decrease in stalling speed is therefore less than that obtained with a propeller aircraft.

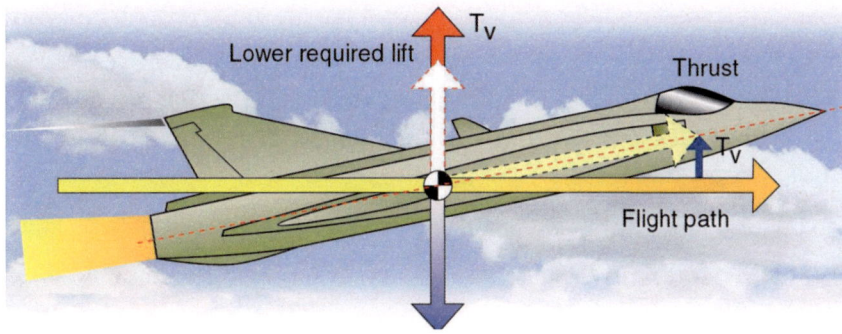

Figure 7.67

In a jet aircraft the presence of power decreases the stalling speed only at high nose up attitude.

7.3.10   *Stalling speed and ground effect*

The stalling speed does not usually vary when the aeroplane is close to the ground. As you will find in the lesson Lift/Drag and Ground effect, the maximum lift coefficient generated by the wing does not change and, as a result, neither does the stalling speed.

7.3.11   *Effect of wing contamination on stalling speed*

Ice formation on the wing leading edge or on its upper surface decreases the stall angle of attack, and therefore also the max lift coefficient, giving a significantly higher stalling speed. In addition, the ice makes the aircraft heavier causing a further increase in stalling speed.

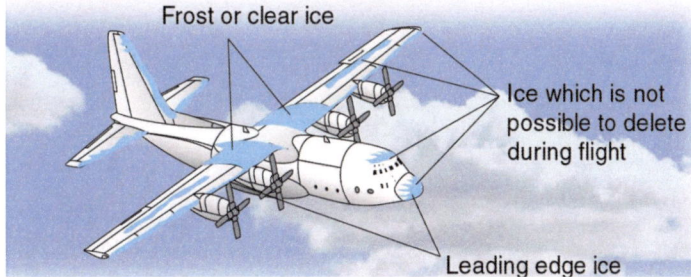

Figure 7.68

Any contamination (ice, dirt, bugs etc) has a very great influence on the stalling speed. In addition to that; the more sophisticated the wings are, the more sensitive they are to contamination.
The next figure shows how bad it can be.

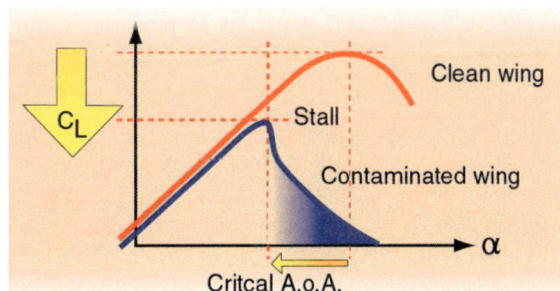

Figure 7.69

The more sophisticated the wings are, the more sensitive they are to contamination.
Ice formation also changes the stall characteristics of the aircraft, often giving an unpredicted violent stall.

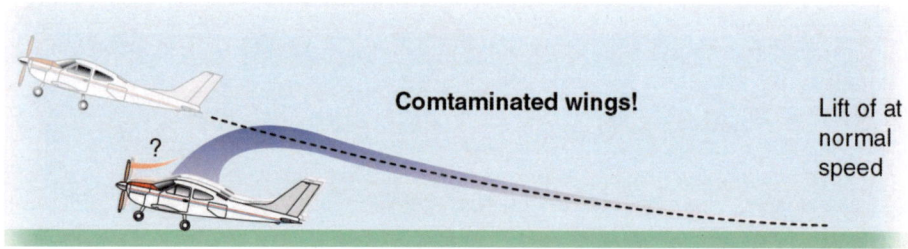

Figure 7.70

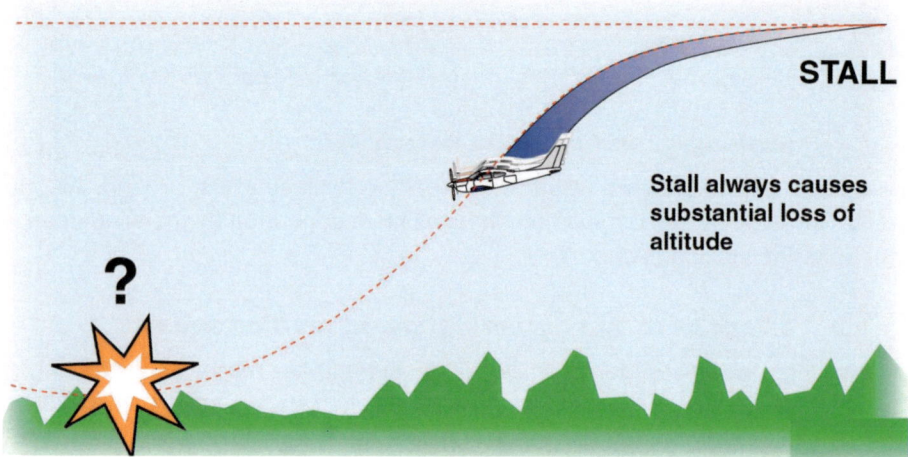

Figure 7.71

Ice formation on the wing increases the stalling speed significantly and changes the characteristics of the stall to be more abrupt

7.4   *Stall Recognition and Recovery*

7.4.1   *Symptoms of approaching stall*

High 'nose up' attitude and low speed are not the only symptoms of approaching stall. The aeroplane can stall at any speed and in any attitude whenever the critical angle of attack is exceeded. You must be able to recognise the warnings of approaching stall and recover from stall with the minimum loss of height.

Figure 7.72

Low-speed stall is preceded by some typical NATURAL stall warnings:

*   the controls feel less firm and less effective;
*   the onset of buffet is felt in the airframe and often through the control column. The natural stall warning is called buffeting.

However, stall at high speed due to a high load factor will not lead to reduced control effectiveness, only the buffeting and/or the stall warning devices will give the warning.

Figure 7.73

High-speed stall has less natural stall warning.

7.4.2   *Stall warning devices*

Natural stall warning caused by buffeting from flow separation on selected parts of the wing can be created by means of stalling stripes. If this is not satisfactory, artificial stall warning devices have to be added.

Most aircraft are fitted with a kind of artificial stall warning device such as a flashing red light, a buzzer or a stickshaker to give an additional warning of impending stall, especially if the natural stall warning is weak. Normally they are set to warn 5 to 10 KT before stall. These stall-warning devices are activated by sensors that detect the angle of attack. Most light aircraft are equipped with a sensor, called a flapper switch. This consists of a small movable plate below the leading edge of the wing. Normally, the stagnation point is in front of the plate but when the angle of attack is too great, the stagnation point moves behind it and the plate is turned forward, activating a switch which activates a red light and/or a horn or a buzzer.

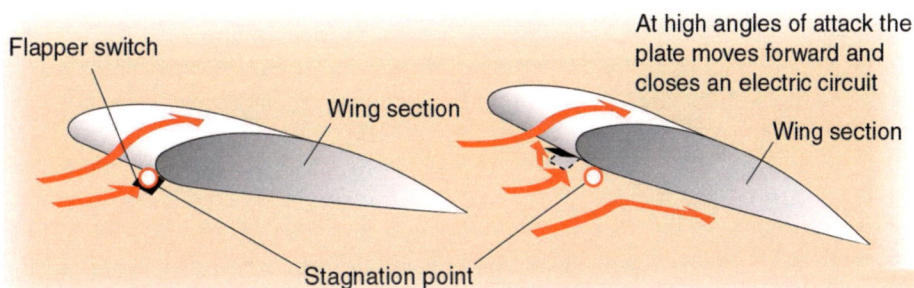

Figure 7.74 Flapper switch

Another more sophisticated device is the A.of.A vane, a sensor. This makes use of a small vane that turns in the direction of the relative wind. When the angle of the vane is close to the critical angle of attack, a signal activates the stall warning devices in the cockpit and/or gives indication to an angle of attack indicator.

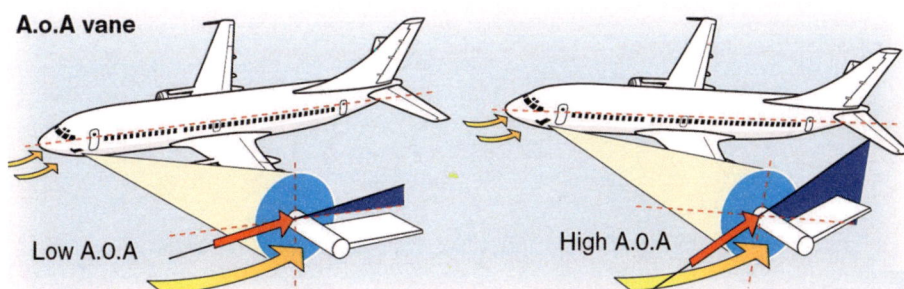

Figure 7.75 Angle of attack vane

Another kind of sensor is the A.of.A probe that measures the angle of attack. It is a fixed cone with pressure holes distributed on its surface so that there will be differences in pressure when changing the angle of attack.

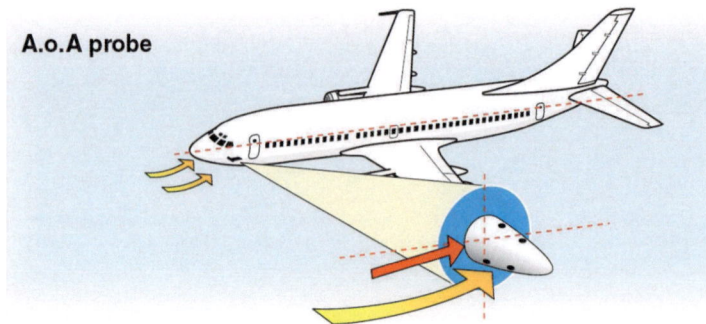

Figure 7.76

Artificial stall-warning devices warn the pilot of impending stall with a flashing red light, a buzzer or a stick shaker. The stick shaker is set to vibrate the control column at speed greater than V_S. Since most kinds of stall warning have to be adjusted to a fixed value of A.of.A. they will not give adequate warnings when the wings are contaminated. A contaminated wing will stall at a lower A.of.A than clean wings. Aircraft that may very quickly get into a deep stall may have a stick shaker or stick pusher to prevent the A.of.A from exceeding a certain value.

7.4.3   *Stall recovery*

As the aeroplane approaches the stall condition, you will feel the natural stall warning by the onset of buffeting in the airframe, and often through the control column. The shaking is more intense as the aeroplane comes even closer to stall. If you continue to increase the angle of attack, maintaining a back pressure on the stick, the stall angle of attack is exceeded and the aeroplane stalls, losing altitude quickly and normally dropping its nose. If you keep holding back the stick, once the aeroplane has lowered its nose and started to regain speed, it tends to pitch its nose up, and stalls again. If you do not recover from stall by lowering the nose and relaxing the back pressure, the aeroplane continues to stall and rapidly lose altitude, often oscillating in pitch.

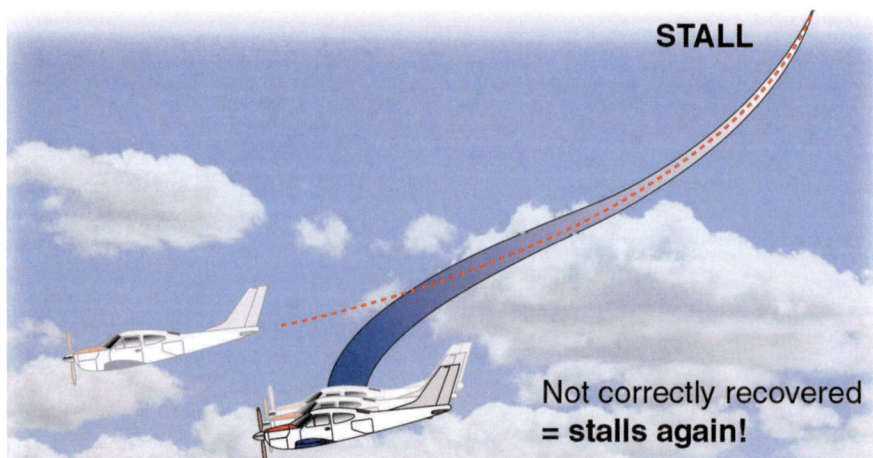

Figure 7.77

You recover from stall by letting the stick go forward, which lowers the nose of the aeroplane and, in doing so, decreases the angle of attack below the stall angle. In order to avoid asymmetrical stall, centre the stick and rudder pedals.

If the stall is due to low speed, you should simultaneously give full power to ensure a rapid gain in speed. When the aeroplane has regained flying speed, further altitude loss can be avoided by gently raising the nose to the horizon to avoid a secondary stall. Recovery from stall ALWAYS INVOLVES A LOSS OF ALTITUDE, and in most cases, a great loss of altitude. When practising stall, which must be done at safe high altitude, the loss of altitude will not be so obvious. But stalling at low altitudes, for instance when traffic patterns are followed, is extremely dangerous. In order to regain flying speed as quickly as possible, apply FULL power during stall recovery. By doing so the aeroplane will regain speed more rapidly and can be eased out of the descent back into normal flight with less loss of altitude.

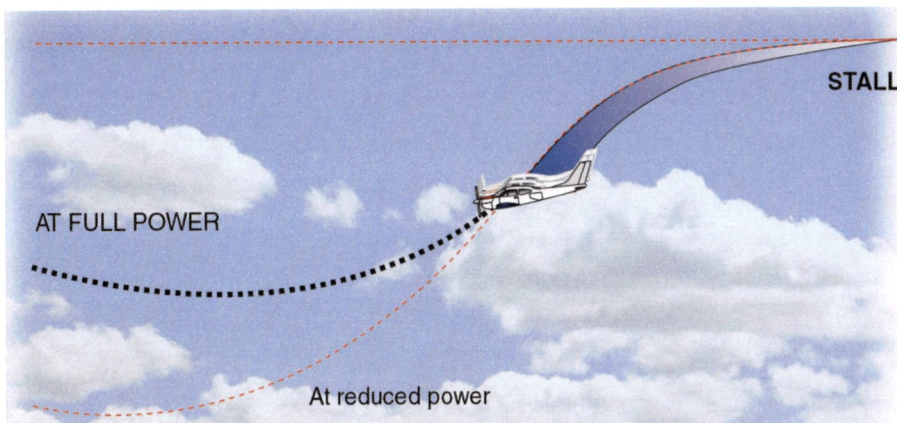

Figure 7.78

Loss of altitude during stall can be minimised if full power is applied during stall recovery

7.4.4 Incipient stall recovery

Once you have become aware of the stall warnings, you are in a condition known as "incipient" stall. The wing has begun to stall in some areas but has not yet stalled completely. A complete stall can be avoided by immediately letting the stick go forward, thus decreasing the angle of attack and by applying full power (if power is still available) to regain speed. If the aeroplane is recovered during incipient stall, there will only be a small loss of altitude.

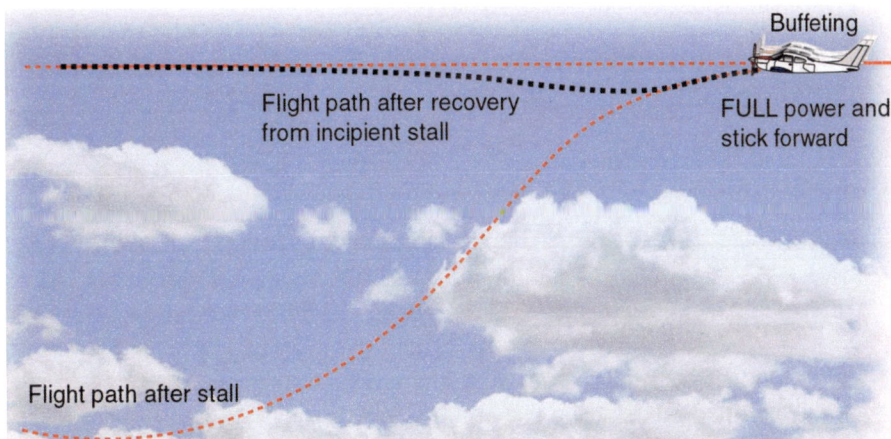

Figure 7.79

Recovery from incipient stall is carried out by immediately letting the stick go forward and applying full power. This gives the minimum loss of altitude

7.4.5 *Pilot mistakes in conditions near to the stall*

When the aeroplane is near the stall or in stall recovery, it is easy to make errors that can cause a further stall or a spin. For this reason the aeroplane must immediately be recovered in the correct way and be eased up gently. If you pull up into level flight too soon or too suddenly when you have regained sufficient speed, the stall angle of attack will again be exceeded and the aeroplane will stall again. This second stall is known as secondary stall. By moving the stick sideways to pick up a dropping wing, the aileron on the dropping wing is deflected downwards increasing the angle of attack further. The aileron deflection may therefore cause earlier stall of the dropping wing, the lift of the wing decreases, and the wing drops further rather than raising. The aeroplane accentuates its roll and can enter a spin. Instead, when close to the stall, fly with co-ordinated controls with the ball centred. A descending wing should be corrected for using the rudder pedals rather than the stick, e.g. when the left wing descends, use right rudder. In this way the momentarily increased forward speed of the descending wing may help it to avoid stall. However, a wing-drop when being in stall, should not been corrected, instead centre all controls. Then, during the acceleration, roll the wings level.

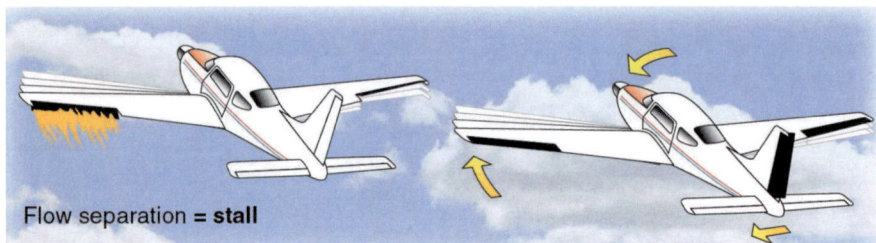

Flow separation = **stall**

Figure 7.80 On light aircraft correct for a descending wing with opposite rudder

The behaviour of the aeroplane is different in the stall depending on the flight configuration and condition. Three main types of stall are examined: low-speed stall in clean or in landing configuration; stall in manoeuvre, also known as g-stall and finally; high-speed stall near the speed of sound.

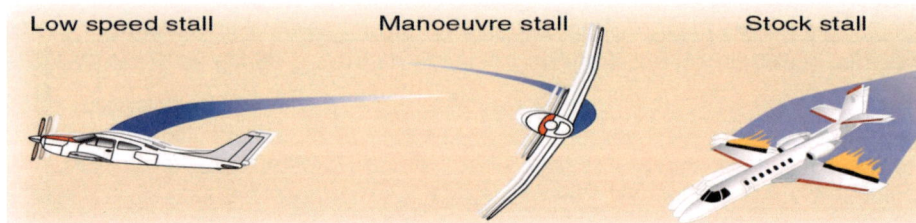

Low speed stall   Manoeuvre stall   Stock stall

Figure 7.81

7.4.6 *Stall in clean configuration*

Clean configuration means that the aircraft has flaps and landing gear up if applicable. To practise the stall, you must reduce power and maintain altitude by exerting (backward) pressure on the stick. As the speed decreases raise the nose more and more to maintain level flight. When approaching the stall the control effectiveness decreases and the stick becomes sloppy. Further increase of the angle of attack causes the operation of artificial stall warning followed by the natural stall warning caused by airflow separation on the wing and the onset of buffeting in airframe and controls. Maintaining the backward pressure on the stick, the stall angle of attack is exceeded and the aeroplane stalls. The lift decreases dramatically and the aeroplane loses altitude. A well designed aircraft will pitch nose down. To recover from the stall, ease the stick forward and apply full power. The aeroplane will dive slightly and start to regain speed. Once it has regained some speed, the aeroplane must be eased out of the dive back into normal flight.

7.4.7   *Stall in landing configuration*

In landing configuration, the aeroplane has its flaps and landing gear down. The flap deflection increases the lift and changes the lift distribution on the wing giving a decreased stall angle of attack and stalling speed. The decreased stalling speed in landing configuration causes an even more sloppy sensation of the controls. The lower stall angle of attack causes a lower pitch angle at stall. The use of flap deflection and landing gear also increases the drag considerably.

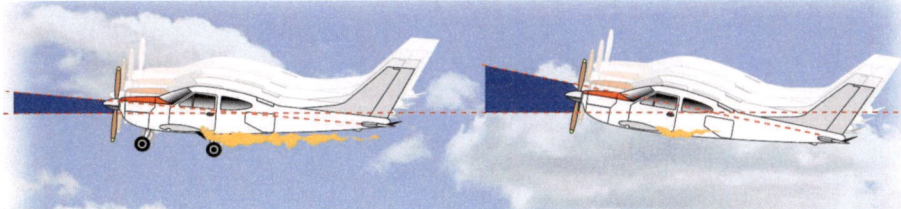

Figure 7.82 Stall in the landing configuration is at a lower angle of attack but occurs a lower speed

Stall in landing configuration occurs at a lower speed and at a lower stall angle of attack and a lower pitch angle in comparison with that of the clean configuration. The increased drag from the flaps and landing gear reduces the increase in speed

Stall recovery is normally carried out by easing the stick forward to place the nose slightly below the horizon and applying full power at the same time. Depending on aircraft type and position of the centre of gravity, the stick may have to go fully forward to lower the nose, and the deflection of the flaps reduced in order to gain sufficient speed. Once the aeroplane regains sufficient speed, it should be eased out of the dive back into level or climbing flight.

7.4.8   *Manoeuvre stall or g-stall*

The stall in manoeuvre takes place when the load factor is so high that the stall angle of attack is exceeded. G-stall can occur at any speed. In a turn, the load factor increases with the lateral bank angle and the stalling speed therefore increases with lateral bank angle as well.

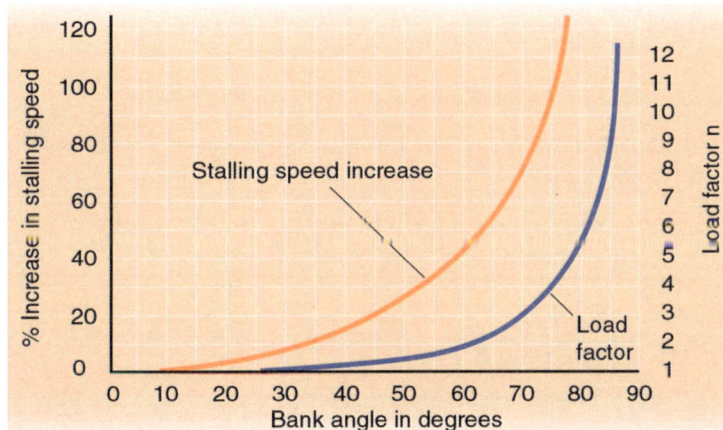

Figure 7.83

If, during a turn, you continue to increase the pull on the stick increasing the load factor, the required lift will soon demand such a high angle of attack that the stall angle will be exceeded and the aeroplane will stall. During a balanced turn, the behaviour of stall is similar to that during a stall in clean configuration, but the controls will not feel sloppy due to the higher speed.

The stall in manoeuvre, also known as G-STALL, takes place when the load factor during the manoeuvre is so high that the stall angle of attack is exceeded regardless of actual speed.

The required higher lift during a turn also creates higher induced drag lowering the speed

Depending on the actual speed at recovery from g-stall, the actions to be taken differ. If the speed is still high, you only need to ease your back pressure on the stick. If the speed is low you have to centre the controls and give full power and then bring the aircraft back to normal level flight.

7.4.9 Power on/power off stall

When flying in a low-speed and high power condition, e.g. a steep climb, the stalling speed will be lower than that of a power off stall at 1g. In this situation the component of thrust in the vertical plane, relieves the loading on the wings, allowing significantly lower airspeed before stalling. This means that the control response will be low, which can be hazardous in gusty wind conditions since it reduces the controllability of the aircraft.

Another difficult situation is when the power is reduced in a high power/low-speed condition. The wing loading increases when power is reduced and stall may occur without any warning. For this reason, stall can also begin without sufficient warning when making a low angle/high power approach to maintain speed and the throttle is closed rapidly when over the runway threshold.

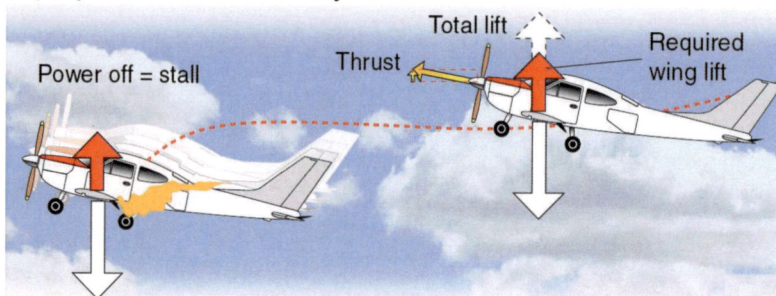

Figure 7.84

7.4.10 Stall in slipping turns

The behaviour of the aeroplane during stall in a turn is different depending on whether the aeroplane is flying in a "ball centred" turn, in a slipping turn or in a skidding turn. If the aeroplane is slipping into the turn, the lift distribution is asymmetrical, causing the outer wing to stall first, and the aeroplane rolls outwards in the turn. Stall recovery is carried out by first centring the controls, then by bringing the aeroplane back into straight and level flight.

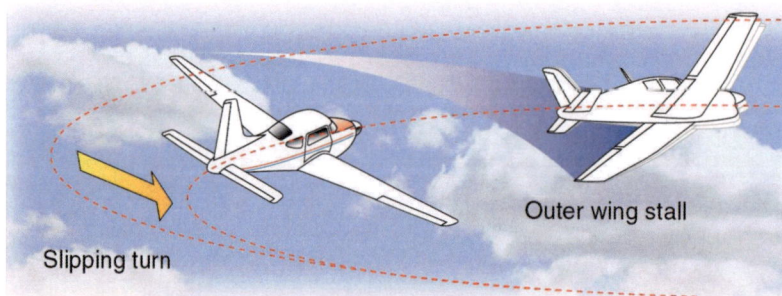

Figure 7.85

If the aeroplane is slipping into the turn, the outer wing stalls first and the aeroplane rolls outwards in the turn

7.4.11 Stall in skidding turns

If the aeroplane is skidding out of the turn, the lift distribution is also asymmetrical, causing the inner wing to stall first, and the aeroplane rolls inwards in the turn. Stall recovery must be carried out promptly in order to

CRANFIELD AVIATION TRAINING SCHOOL LTD. PART-FCL GBR.ATO-0136

CATS CATS INNOVATION CENTRE, LUTON, Bedfordshire LU2 8DL U.K.

www.catsaviation.com

7-35

Principles of Flight

avoid entering a spin. Stall recovery is carried out in the same way as in a slipping turn first by centring the control then by returning to straight and level flight.

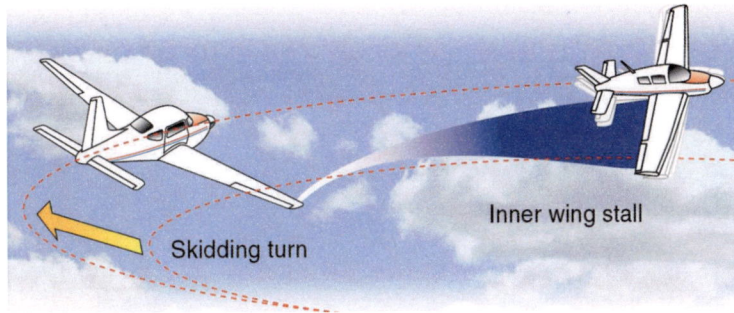

Figure 7.86

If the aeroplane is skidding out of the turn, the inner wing stalls first and the aeroplane rolls inwards in the turn and, if not corrected, tends to enter a spin

When stall occurs with wing drop, always first centre the stick both laterally and longitudinally. A stall in slipping or skidding turns may use more altitude in the recovery due to the asymmetric stall, which may cause a snaproll to a low nose, inverted flight. During non-aerobatic flight, always fly ball centred.

7.4.12   *Stall during climbing or descending turns*

When you make a climbing turn, the outer wing will have a higher A.of.A than the inner wing. Since the stall is caused by too high A.of.A, the outer wing will stall earlier than the inner wing.

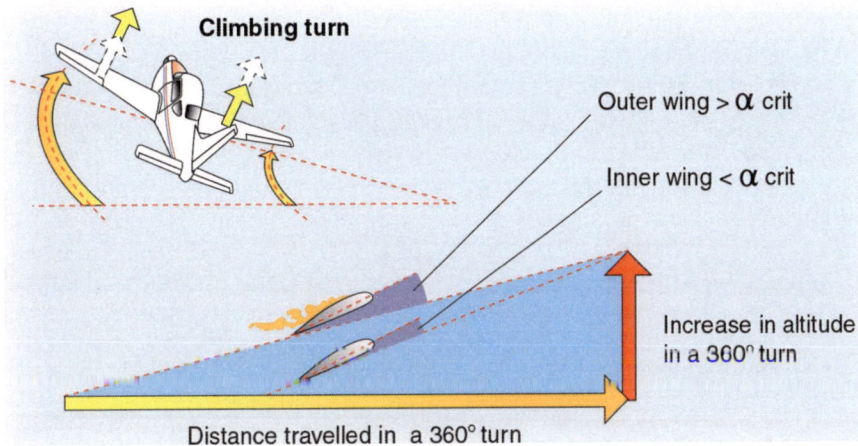

Figure 7.87

However, since the higher lift on the outer wing causes a roll in the direction of the turn, opposite aileron is given to maintain a constant angle of bank. This downward aileron on the inner wing may stall first depending on the aerodynamic configuration of the aileron.

In a descending turn, the inner wing will instead have a higher A.o.A than the outer wing, which normally makes the inner wing stall first.

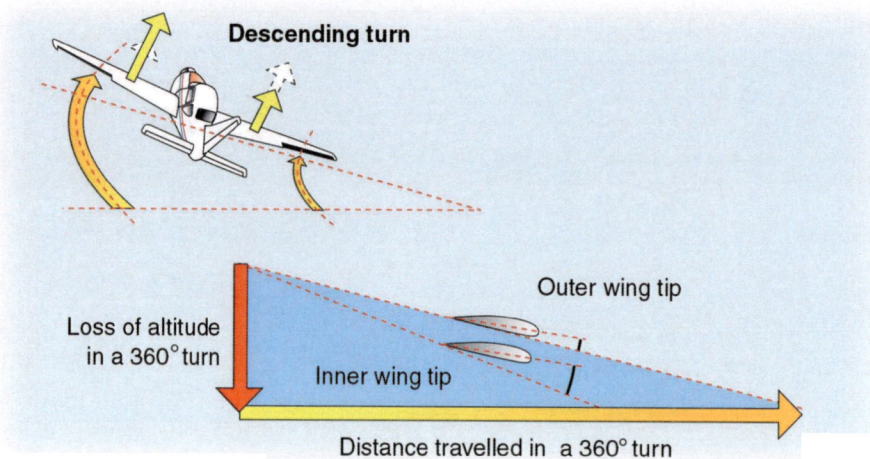

Figure 7.88

Asymmetrical stall is always more altitude consuming than symmetrical stall since you have to roll the wings level before pulling up in order to reach level flight to the smallest loss of altitude. Therefore, a descending turn near the ground, e.g. in the landing traffic pattern, always has to be carefully performed with enough speed and the ball centred.

7.4.13 *Dynamic stall*

Dynamic stall may occur at a higher critical angle of attack than the "normal" one. The flow separation that provokes stall, starts when the A.of.A is too great, and if the A.of.A is further increased lift is reduced. However, if the increase in the angle of attack is very rapid e.g. due to a very sharp vertical gust, the flow separation may be delayed for a second and a higher A.o.A is reached before the flow separation and stall begin. In this way a higher load factor than that planned may be reached at a given speed. If you encounter a vertical gust of a certain vertical velocity your load factor will increase. If your speed is low you may stall, due to the fact that the critical A.o.A is reached. However, the influence of a vertical gust on the load factor increases proportionally with the speed. Consequently, higher speed means a greater increase in load factor. This means that at high speeds the increase in load factor may be so great that you will get a very high load factor before stall.

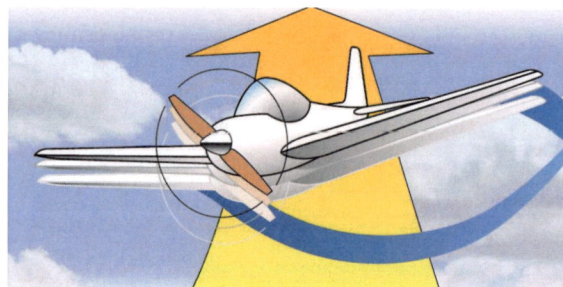

Figure 7.89

In a very sharp vertical wind gust, a dangerously high load factor can be reached before the stall.
Aircraft are designed to withstand a certain load factor called Safe Load Factor. (E.g. for a light general purpose aircraft 3,8 g.) In addition to that there is a safety factor of 1,5 giving an Ultimate Load Factor of 5,7 g, above which the aircraft may break apart or other structural damage may occur. When flying in turbulent weather, the speed should be high enough that stall is avoided, but at the same time the speed should be low enough not to break the wings.

In your Pilot Operation Handbook for the aircraft you will find Recommended Rough Air Penetrating Speeds, or if not applicable, use the speed V_A. These are the speeds that will minimise the risk of getting far too high a load factor. But, as can be seen in the next figure, there is no guarantee that the designed load factors are not exceeded! The diagram below shows the possible and permitted load factor of a light aircraft.

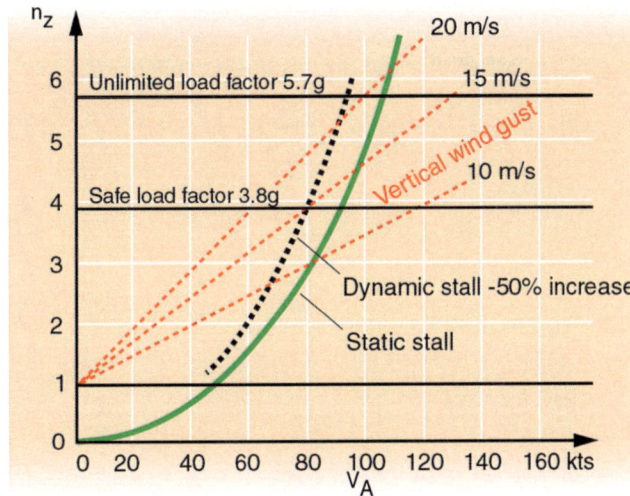

Figure 7.90

At low speeds, the load factors reached are limited by stall, and in this example at ~90 KT the aircraft stalls at 3.8 g at a sharp gust of ~13 m/s. That is the designed Safe Load Factor the aircraft should withstand without any damages. But still, at 90 KT, due to the delayed "dynamic stall", there is a risk that the load-factor may increase to the Ultimate Load Factor if you encounter a very sharp vertical gust of above 20 m/s
If a vertical gust of low intensity is encountered at a high speed, the aeroplane may still be damaged. If the speed is 130 KT while encountering a sharp gust of only above 15 m/s, the Ultimate Load Factor is exceeded. There is another risk of getting far too high a load factor when making a pull-up from a dive at high speed in only moderate turbulence. The intentional load factor of the pull-up may be near the Safe Load Factor but the combination of high speed and wind gusts may instantly create a dangerously high load factor. When flying at speeds within the yellow range of the ASI you should be in smooth air. When flying in turbulent weather, especially below CU and CB clouds, or near (or in) a CB-cloud, there is no guarantee that the vertical wind gusts may not exceed the value the aircraft is designed for. Never fly intentionally in a cumulonimbus cloud.

Self Assessment Test 03

1   With the CG on the forward limit, the stalling speed would be:
A)   Independent of the CG position
B)   Higher than with the CG on the aft limit
C)   Lower than with the CG on the aft limit
D)   The same as with the CG on the aft limit

2   What effect does an increased load factor have on an aircraft?
A)   The aircraft will have a tendency to spin
B)   The aircraft will suffer immediate structural failure
C)   The aircraft will have a tendency to roll and yaw
D)   The aircraft will stall at a higher speed

3   As the CG is changed, recovery from a stall becomes progressively:
A)   More difficult as the CG moves aft
B)   More difficult as the CG moves forward
C)   Less difficult as the CG moves aft
D)   Is unaffected by the CG position, only by all up weight

4   A wing stalling angle is:
A)   Increased in a high rate of turn
B)   Decreased by a high rate of turn
C)   Decreased in any turn
D)   Unaffected by a turn

5   In a level banked turn, the stalling speed will:
A)   Decrease
B)   Increase
C)   Remain the same
D)   Vary inversely with wing loading

6   A low wing loading (e.g. aircraft weight has been reduced):
A)   Increases take-off run, stalling speed and landing speed
B)   Decreases stalling speed, landing speed and landing run
C)   Increases stalling speed
D)   Does not affect any of the above

7   With increasing angle of attack the CP will reach its most forward point:
A)   At the stalling angle
B)   Just above the stalling angle
C)   Just below the stalling angle
D)   At various points dependent on aircraft weight

8   The critical angle of attack at which a given aircraft stalls is dependent on:
A)   Gross weight
B)   Attitude and airspeed
C)   Design of the wing
D)   Altitude

CRANFIELD AVIATION TRAINING SCHOOL LTD. PART-FCL GBR.ATO-0136
CATS CATS INNOVATION CENTRE, LUTON, Bedfordshire LU2 8DL U.K.   www.catsaviation.com
7-39   Principles of Flight

9   Which action will result in a stall:
A)   Exceeding the critical angle of attack
B)   Flying at too low an airspeed
C)   Raising the aircraft's nose too high
D)   Lowering the aircraft's nose too low

10   An aircraft is said to stall when:
A)   The lift force from the wings is greater than the weight
B)   The airflow over the top surface of the wing separates which results in a large increase of drag and a large loss of lift
C)   The angle of attack of the wings is greater than 10 degrees
D)   It flies too slowly at low altitude

11   At the stalling angle of attack the lift/drag ratio will be:
A)   Higher than at the optimum angle of attack
B)   Lower than at the optimum angle of attack
C)   The same as at the optimum angle of attack
D)   The angle of attack does not affect the lift/drag ratio

Self Assessment Test 03 Answers

1	B
2	D
3	A
4	D
5	B
6	B
7	C
8	C
9	A
10	B
11	B

CRANFIELD AVIATION TRAINING SCHOOL LTD. PART-FCL GBR.ATO-0136
CATS INNOVATION CENTRE, LUTON, Bedfordshire LU2 8DL U.K.

www.catsaviation.com

7-41

Principles of Flight

CHAPTER 8

Lift Augmentation /Modification

Devices that modify the coefficient of lift and/or drag of an aerofoil are often fitted on the wings. This may be in order to reduce the stalling speed and the length of the runway necessary for take off and landing, but also to increase drag to get a steeper approach path.

8.1   *Lift Augmentation/Modification*

8.1.1   *Introduction*

A modern aircraft should be designed to fly fast with the use of a reasonable amount of power, but it should also be able to fly slowly enough to use relatively short runways for take-off and landing. However, the use of large wings for low speed produces high drag at high speed; this is obviously a conflicting situation for the designer. A solution can be to use so-called high lift devices.

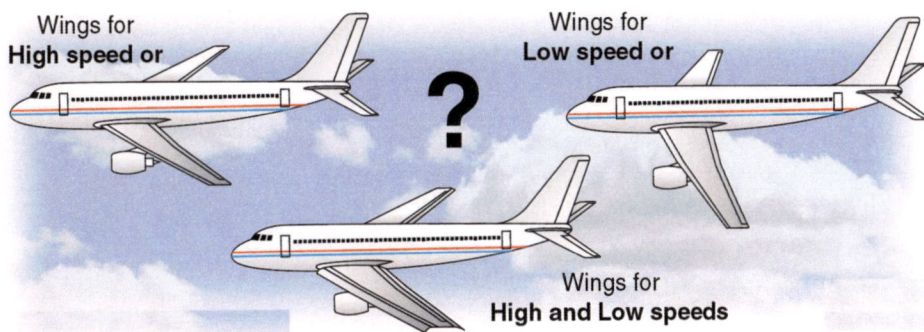

Figure 8.1

Let us start with a short review of lift. As already seen in the lesson on lift, the total quantity of lift is the result of many factors: the dynamic pressure, the lift coefficient and the wing surface area.

Lift (L) = Dynamic pressure (q) x Coefficient of Lift (C_L) x Wing Area (S).

If we consider the density of air as constant, the total lift can be changed by changing the dynamic pressure with the speed, the lift coefficient or the wing surface area.

CRANFIELD AVIATION TRAINING SCHOOL LTD. PART-FCL GBR.ATO-0136
CATS CATS INNOVATION CENTRE, LUTON, Bedfordshire LU2 8DL U.K.   www.catsaviation.com

8-1   Principles of Flight

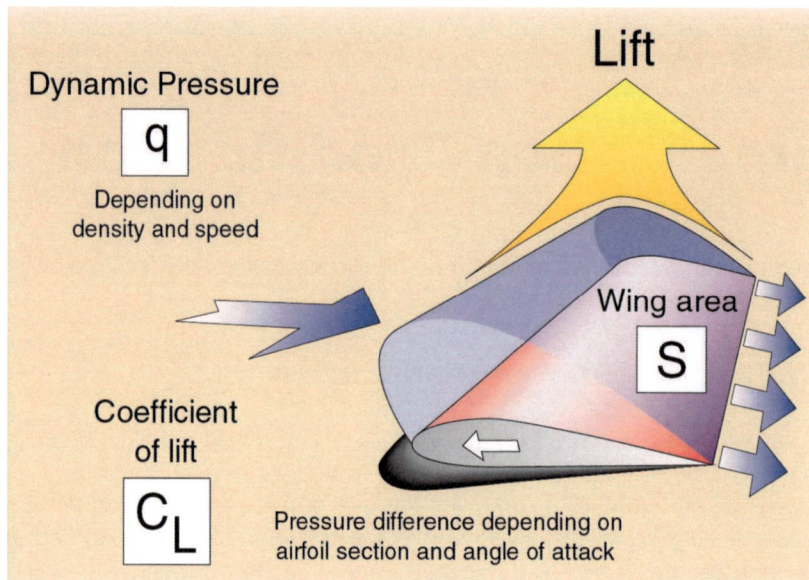

Figure 8.2

Generally, lift can be increased at low speeds by the use of devices which give one or often a combination of the following: increased camber of the wing section (C_L), improved boundary layer (C_L) and increased wing area (S).

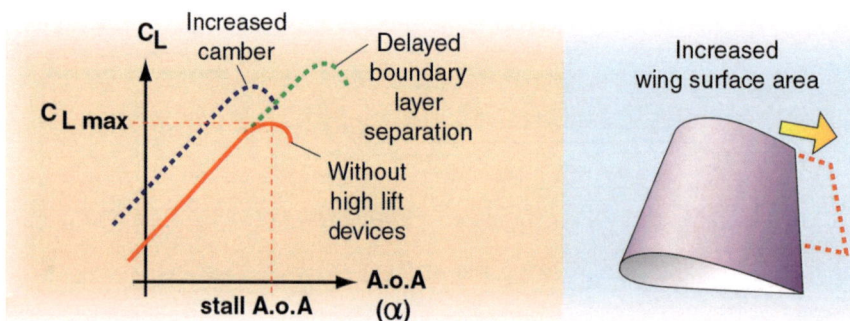

Figure 8.3

These high lift devices can be mounted both on the trailing edge and on the leading edge, and even if they have different aerodynamic influence, they are able to increase the maximum lift of the wing.

At a given speed, lift depends on the C_L and the wing area S

However, sometimes it is necessary to reduce the lift and increase the drag. These lift-reducing devices are called spoilers.

8.1.2 *Trailing edge high lift devices*

There are many different types of trailing edge high lift devices. The most important thing to remember is that they all work in the same way. The high lift devices of the trailing edge, called flaps, produce the required increase in lift at a lower angle of attack than with a clean wing. Flap deflection results in increased lift and drag at a given angle of attack. The maximum lift also increases but the stalling angle of attack normally decreases.

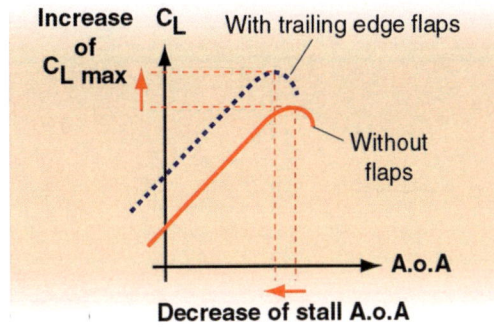

Figure 8.4

The flaps of the trailing edge produce the required increase in lift at a lower angle of attack than with a clean wing

Wings with deflected flaps usually stall at a lower A.of.A than wings without flaps. This is due to the fact that the pressure gradients at the C_L max for both cases are roughly equal.

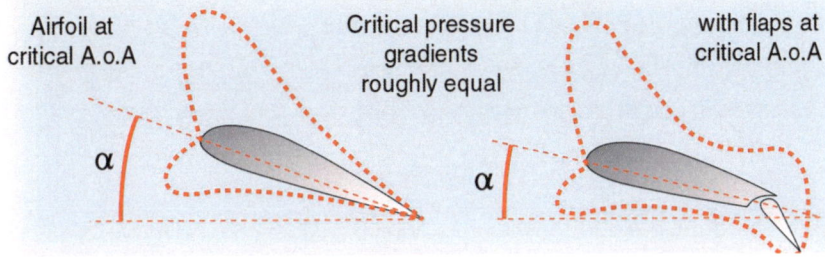

Figure 8.5

Flaps are designed to increase the wing camber which will increase the downwash and in that way increase the circulation around the aerofoil, which increases the pressure difference between the upper and lower surfaces. It will also move the C.P. rearwards creating a nose-down moment and an increase in drag.

Deflection of trailing edge flaps increases the circulation, and so increases the pressure differences. It will also move the C.P. rearwards and increase the drag

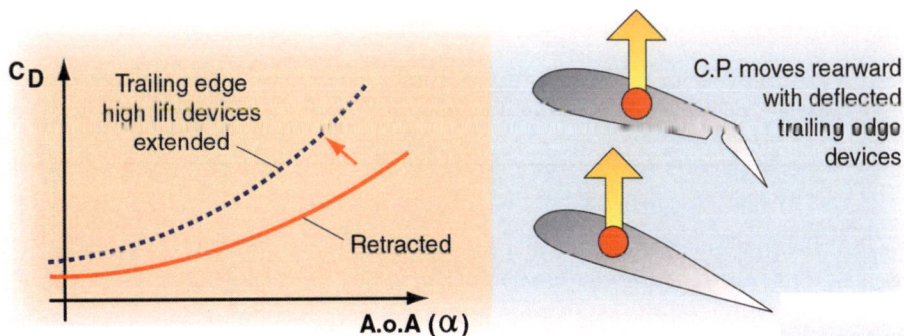

Figure 8.6

Here are a few examples of some main types of flaps and their approximate increases in C_L.

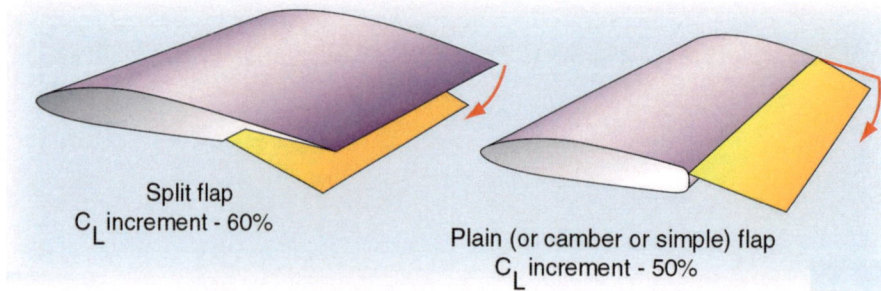

Figure 8.7

To improve the efficiency of the flaps, air can be accelerated through the slot between the wing and the flaps which makes the boundary layer above the flap more effective.

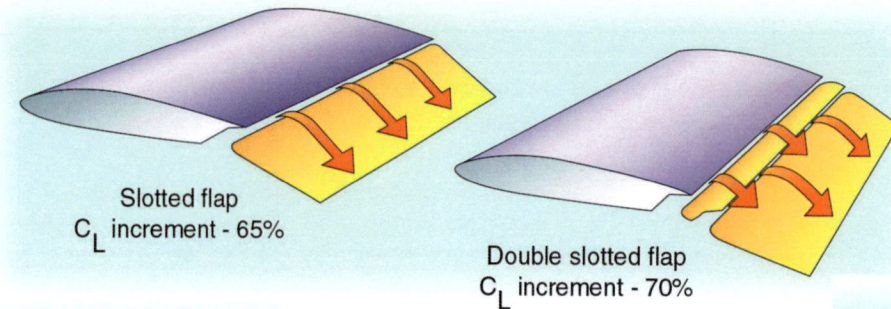

Figure 8.8

Another type of flap is the double-slotted fowler flap, which is designed to move backwards to increase the total wing area. When being moved backwards it also moves downwards to increase the camber, and finally it is slotted to increase the efficiency of the boundary layer.

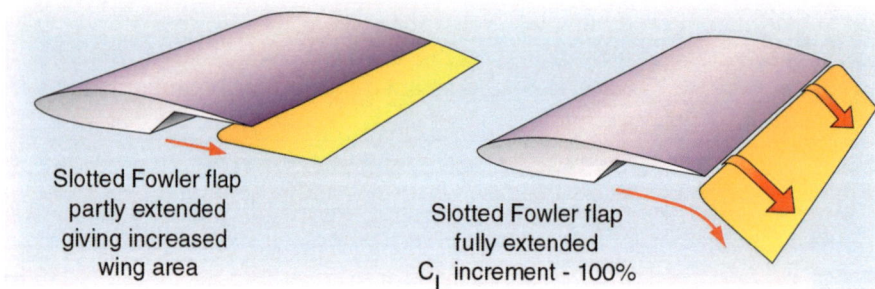

Figure 8.9

Slotted fowler flaps are first extended rearwards then deflected downwards, which increases both the wing surface and the CL

The lift/drag ratio can be changed very effectively by means of the flaps. Small flap deflections increase the margin to the stall with only a moderate increase in drag. This small flap deflection is therefore often used during take-off and during approaches for landing. In addition, flap deflection also increases the ground effect. Small flap deflections are often used to increase the margin to stall with only a minor increment in drag. By extending the flaps fully, normally approximately 30-45°, the increment in drag is greater than the increment in lift. This full deflection of flaps is therefore normally used from final approach down to landing to allow a rather steep descent while maintaining low speed.

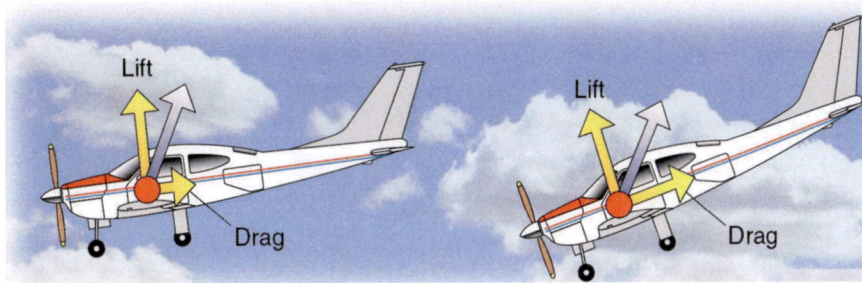

Figure 8.10

Full flap deflection is normally used to increase the drag while maintaining the margin to the stall

With the trailing edge flaps extended, the required nose attitude is lower at a given airspeed. This permits a steeper descent path for approach and landing, and makes it easier to see the runway and the surrounding obstacles.

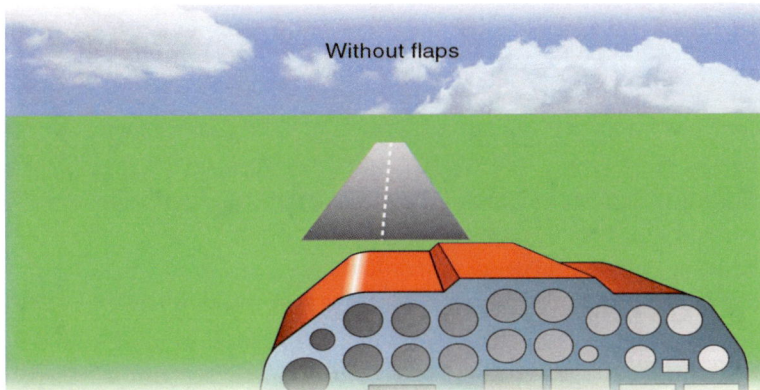

Figure 8.11

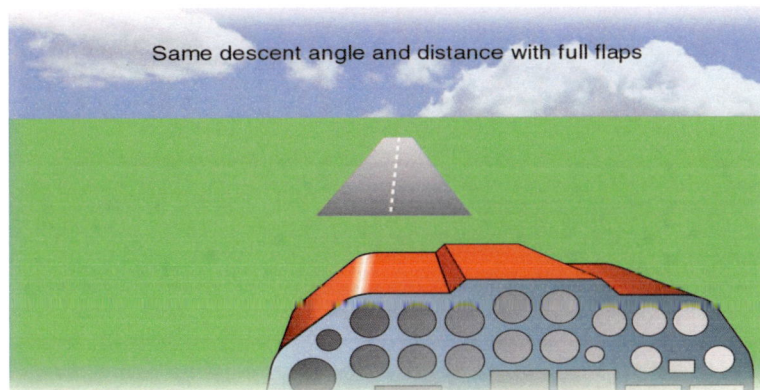

Figure 8.12

The maximum certified flap deflection is almost always used to decrease the approach speed and allow a steeper descent path.

The trailing edge flap decreases the stalling speed, it increases drag and permits a steeper descent path for landing

CRANFIELD AVIATION TRAINING SCHOOL LTD. PART-FCL GBR.ATO-0136
CATS INNOVATION CENTRE, LUTON, Bedfordshire LU2 8DL U.K.   www.catsaviation.com

8-5   Principles of Flight

8.2   *Lift Modification Devices*

8.2.1   *Leading edge devices*

As you already know, the C_L increases with increased A.of.A. up to a maximum value. Increasing the A.of.A. beyond this critical stall value only reduces the C_L.

However, there are some high lift devices which can improve the boundary layer, energise it, which results in a higher stall A.of.A.

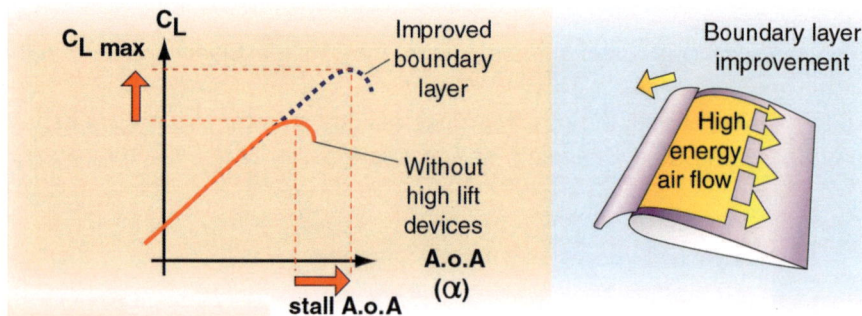

Figure 8.13

The high lift devices of the leading edge increase the maximum angle of attack and the maximum C_L and consequently they decrease the stalling speed. This gives considerably better low-speed qualities and shortens the required runway length for take-off and landing.

When extending the leading edge high lift devices, there will be an increase in lift and an increase in drag. Zero lift drag increases due to the changed aerofoil section and induced drag increases due to increased pressure differences. It will also give a small pitch-up moment.

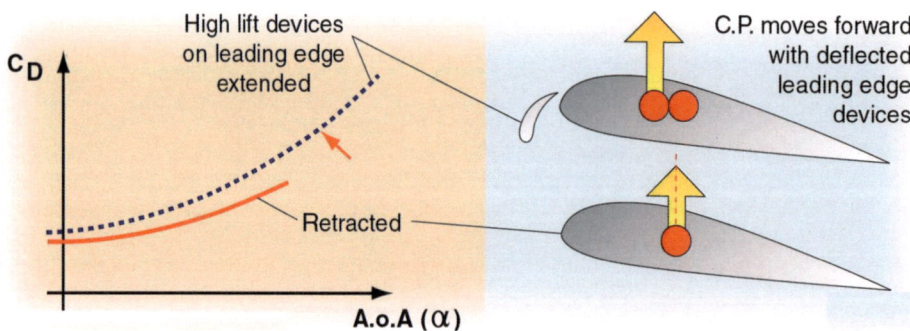

Figure 8.14

> The use of high lift devices at the leading edge also may cause a small increase in drag and trim change

There are many types of leading edge high lift devices. It is also possible to design a wing equipped with different types. The most common ones are: slots, slats, movable slats and leading edge flaps.

8.2.1.1   *Slots and fixed slats*

Slots and fixed slats are fixed openings in the leading edge of the wing designed in such a way that the high pressure flow from the lower surface of the wing is accelerated through the convergent slot to the fast airflow at the upper surface of the wing.

CRANFIELD AVIATION TRAINING SCHOOL LTD. PART-FCL GBR.ATO-0136
CATS INNOVATION CENTRE, LUTON, Bedfordshire LU2 8DL U.K.   www.catsaviation.com
8-6   Principles of Flight

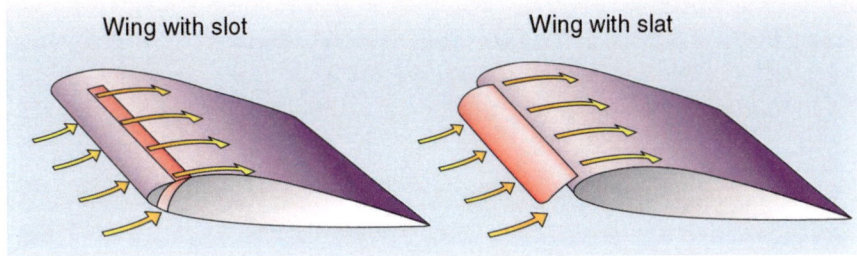

Figure 8.15

The attached flow is thus maintained for a longer distance, allowing higher angles of attack before flow separation.

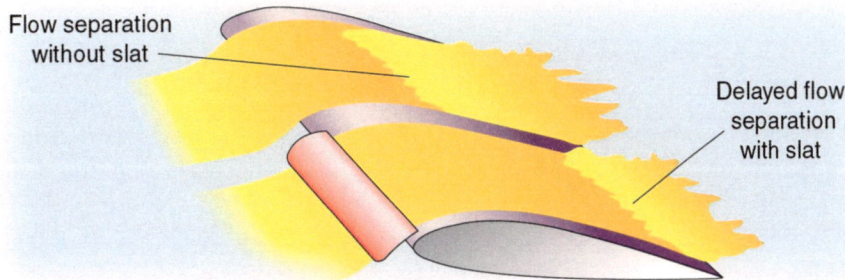

Figure 8.16

Slots and slats allow air from the high pressure area from under the wing to be accelerated through the slot to the faster airflow at the upper surface

8.2.1.2   *Movable Slats*

Slots or fixed slats create undesirable drag at high speeds. On modern aircraft designed for high speeds, the slats are designed to be used only above a certain A.of.A. by making them movable. Movable slats open automatically or manually only when flying above a certain A.of.A. to ensure a sufficient stall margin.

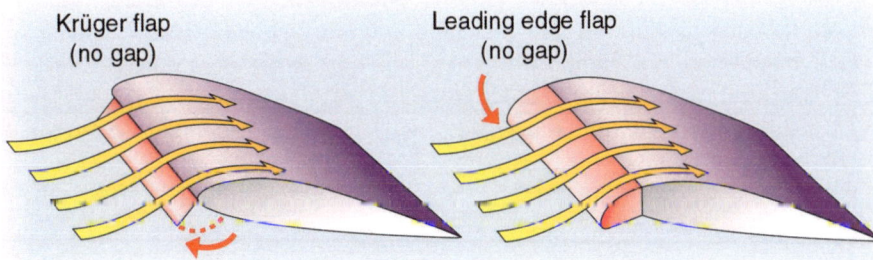

Figure 8.17

8.2.1.3   *Leading edge flaps*

Another way to produce more efficient airflow at a high A.of.A. is to give the wing section a dropped nose, which helps the airflow to remain streamlined over the wing for a greater distance. Leading edge flaps give the wing section a dropped nose, resulting in a higher CL at high A.of.A. Of the two kinds of leading edge flaps: the most simple design is called the Krüger flap (to the left).

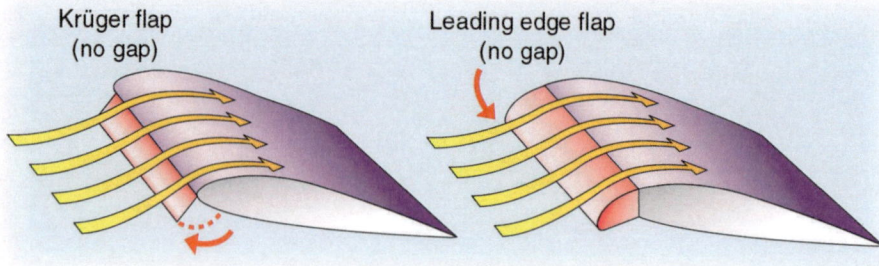

Figure 8.18

> The leading edge flaps give increased camber at the leading edge allowing a greater angle of attack

8.2.1.4   *Combined leading edge flaps and slats*

Many modern aircraft use a combination of leading edge flaps and slats. At moderate speeds and A.of.A, the slat is lowered a bit without any open slot. When flying at very low speeds and high A.of.A, the slat is deflected further and the slot between the slat and wing is opened allowing fresh air to energise the boundary layer.

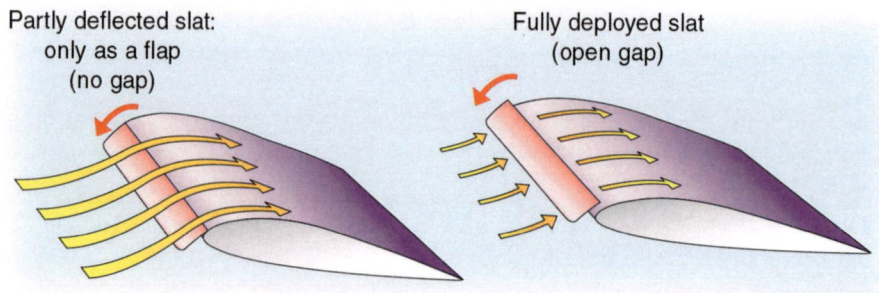

Figure 8.19

All these high lift devices increase the stalling A.of.A. and the maximum lift, making it possible to fly at a higher A.of.A. It is very important to bear this in mind because, on most modern jets, the leading edge devices are the first to be extended during the approach and the last to be raised after take-off. This allows the same speed to be maintained at a higher angle of attack and at a higher power setting than with a clean wing. These high lift devices may lower the stalling speed by 30% compared to the stalling speed with clean wings. This means that the required length of the runway during take-off and landing is considerably shorter.

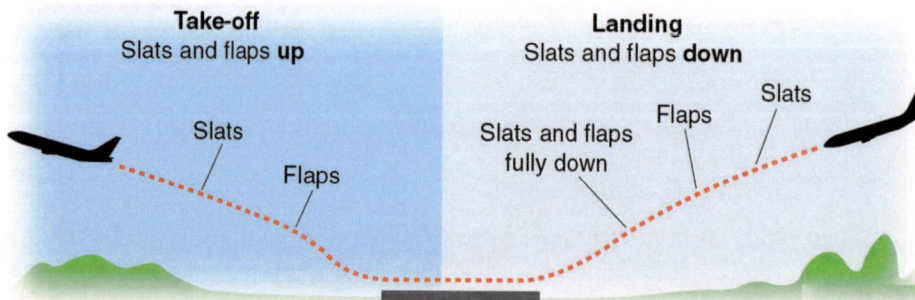

Figure 8.20

> High lift devices allow lower flying speed, requiring a shorter runway for take-off and landing

CRANFIELD AVIATION TRAINING SCHOOL LTD. PART-FCL GBR.ATO-0136
CATS INNOVATION CENTRE, LUTON, Bedfordshire LU2 8DL U.K.   www.catsaviation.com
8-8   Principles of Flight

8.2.1.5   *Automatic operation of leading edge slats*

Some aircraft are equipped with automatic slats. These are hinged in such a way that the pressure distribution at high A. o A. pushes the slat forwards/downwards at high A. o A.

This kind of automatic slat has to be very well balanced and glide easily to have the desired effect. A slightly damaged automatic slat may open at a higher A.of.A. than the normal operating one. This will cause asymmetrical lift and unacceptable roll disturbances at high A.o A.

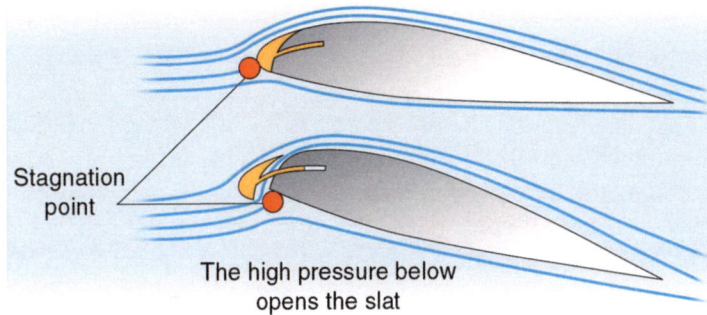

Figure 8.21

When carrying out the walk-around check on an aircraft with automatic slats, make sure they glide easily out and in on both wings.

8.2.2   *Spoilers*

In some flight conditions it is necessary to reduce lift for control or to increase drag. This is especially important for high-speed jet aircraft. An effective way to reduce lift is to create a disturbance in the airflow on the upper surface of the wing causing turbulence and eddies. Of course, this will also increase the drag.

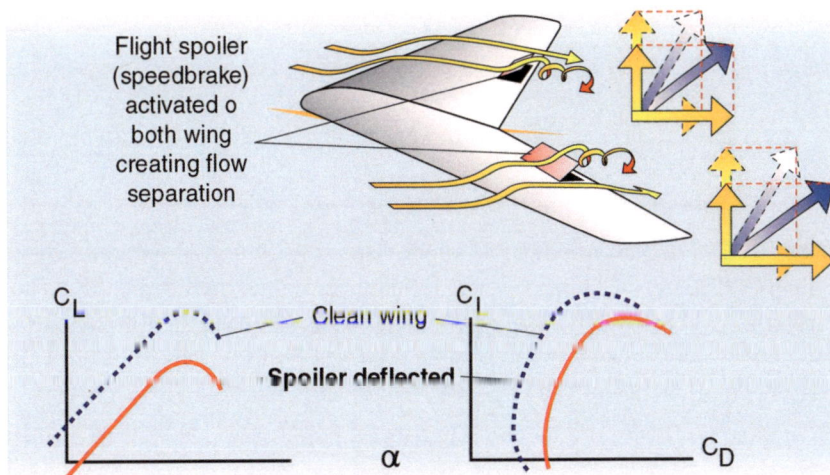

Figure 8.22

On many aircraft, spoilers have three functions. The first is to increase the drag in order to manage a steeper gradient of descent. In this case the spoilers are also called speedbrakes. The second function is to reduce lift after landing. This is usually done through full extension of the spoilers or speedbrakes and additional surfaces, which in this position are called liftdumpers.

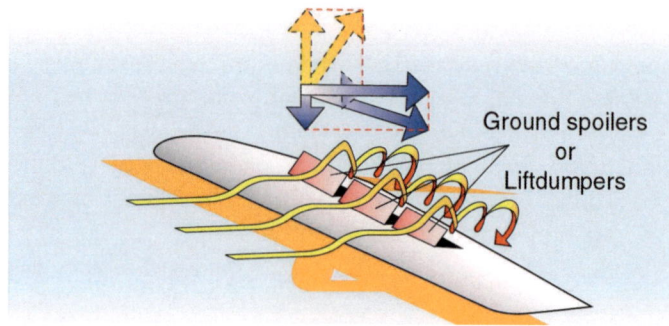

Figure 8.23

The third function is to help the ailerons in roll control. They will extend on the descending wing only, decreasing the lift, while the spoiler on the rising wing is not used. On many modern jets, the ailerons are locked during high cruising speed to avoid control reverse due to wing aero elasticity, and the lateral control is performed by using inner aileron and spoilers. A mix of the different spoiler functions can be used, e.g. simultaneously as speed brake and roll spoiler.

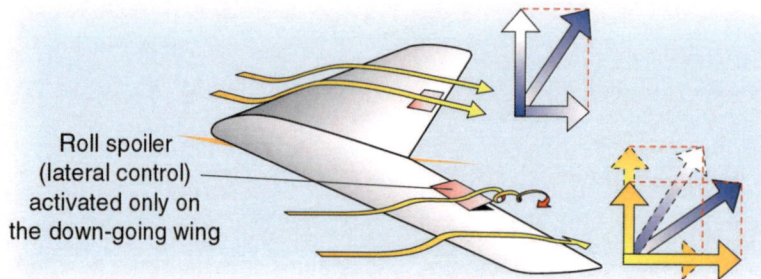

Figure 8.24

At low speeds the ailerons work normally and the spoilers will extend to increase the roll rate only if a certain stick or control wheel angle is exceeded. You will find more information in the Chapter 6 on Flight Controls.

Spoilers may be used in different ways, but they always decrease lift and increases drag.

8.2.3 Total effect of a typical wing

The big jet wing is designed to give the best performance at cruising speed, which may be four times faster than the normally accepted speed for take-off and landing. For this reason lift modification devices have become very important on most transport aircraft; consequently, knowledge of their aerodynamic behaviour is important for you as a pilot. The figure below shows a typical modern aircraft wing with all the devices for lift augmentation extended.

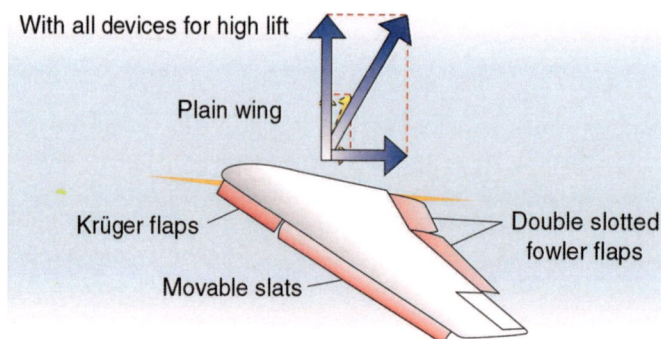

Figure 8.25

The devices for lift augmentation located on both the leading and the trailing edge are able to reduce the stalling speed by approximately 60%. Obviously the take-off and landing rolls are considerably shortened by the use of lift augmentation devices. Basically, from an aerodynamic point of view, the lift-off speed decreases when the angle of flaps for take-off increases, but the drag increases as well, causing the climb gradient to be lower than with a small angle of flap setting. It is obvious that choice of flap angle has to be a compromise between the requirements for take-off roll length and climb.

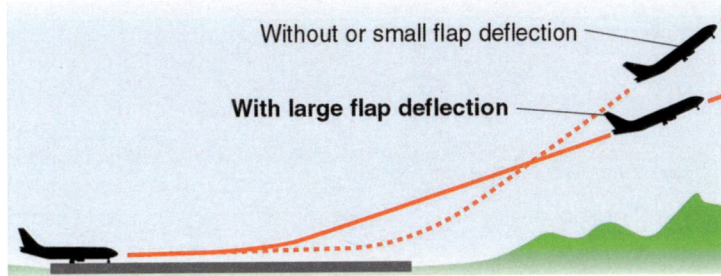

Figure 8.26

If the angle of the flaps for take-off is increased, the lift-off speed decreases but the climb gradient becomes lower than with a low flap angle

In many cases, aircraft are certified to take off and land with a certain flap angle. The very high drag caused by the flaps in landing position can usually become a negative factor in the case of a go-around with an engine failure. The drag may be so high that a go-around will not be possible without reducing the flap setting.

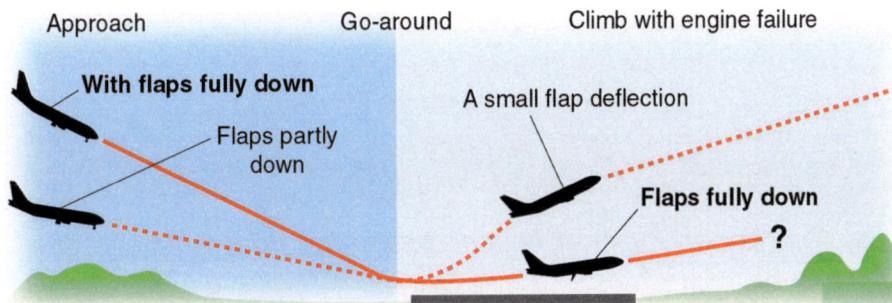

Figure 8.27

The position of the flaps for take-off and landing on a marginal runway and with high terrain in the climb direction must be carefully determined. It is important for a pilot to realise that the use of high lift devices increases drag. However, near stalling speed, the drag of an aircraft with extended high lift devices may be less than the drag of a clean aircraft, and definitely less than that of a stalled clean aircraft.

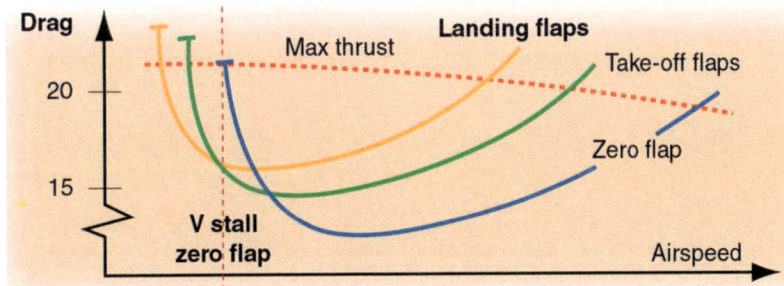

Figure 8.28

This means that flap retraction too early may lead to stall or to a semi-stalled high drag condition.

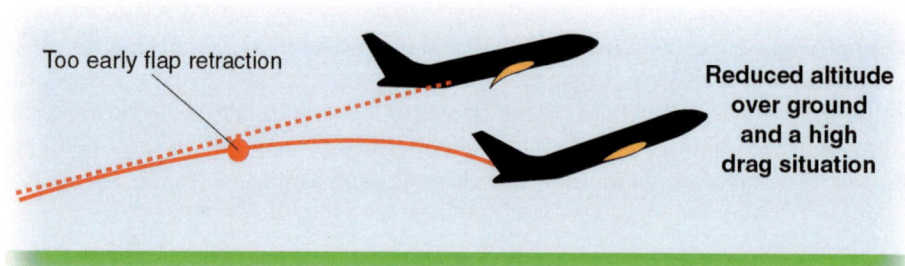

Figure 8.29

8.2.4 *Flap or slat asymmetry*

The effect of asymmetrical deflection of flaps or slats is highly dangerous. Roll control can be reduced to such a degree that you are unable to maintain wings level. If an asymmetrical condition occurs, use the aircraft emergency checklist to take appropriate actions. If roll control cannot be maintained with ailerons only, do not forget your rudder. The yaw/roll coupling helps you, for example, to raise the left wing by using right rudder input, especially on an aircraft with swept wings.

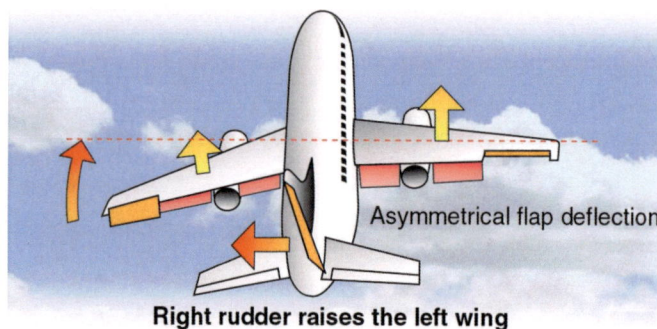

Right rudder raises the left wing

Figure 8.30

8.2.5 *Different kinds of trailing edge high lift devices*

The design of high lift devices can differ a lot and so can their effect. In the next figures you see tables with different types of high lift devices.

Note: since the effects of the devices depend upon the shape of the basic aerofoil, and the exact design of the devices themselves, the values given can only be considered as approximations. To simplify the diagram the aerofoils and the flaps have only small angles, and not the angles giving maximum lift. The given nose-up or nose-down moment is only valid for the isolated wing, not for the whole aircraft, which depends on the aircraft configuration.

High-lift devices	Incr. of max. lift	α crit	Remarks
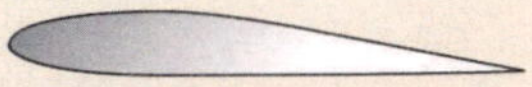 Basic airfoil	-	15°	Effects of all high-lift devices depend on the shape of basic airfoil.
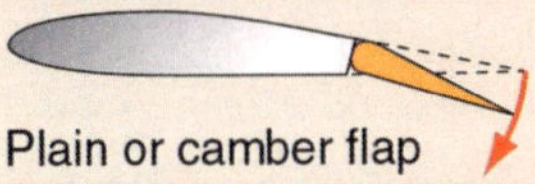 Plain or camber flap	50%	12°	Increased camber. Much drag when fully lowered. Nose down pitching moment.
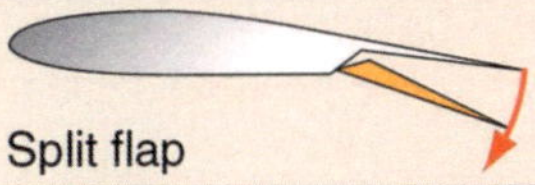 Split flap	60%	14°	Increased camber. Even more drag than plain flap. Nose down pitching moment.
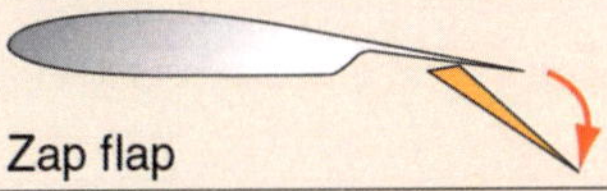 Zap flap	90%	13°	Increased camber. and wing area. Much drag. Nose down pitching moment.
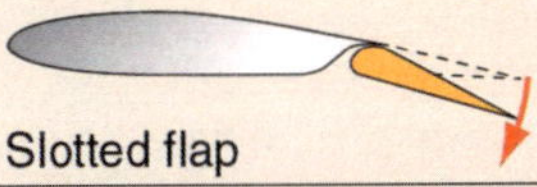 Slotted flap	65%	16°	Control of boundary layer. Increased camber. Stalling delayed. Not so much drag.
 Double slotted flap	70%	18°	Same as single-slotted flap. Only to a greater degree. Triple slots sometimes used.
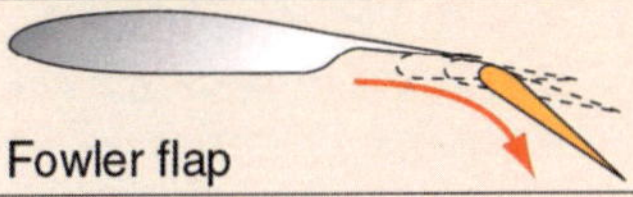 Fowler flap	90%	15°	Increased camber and wing area. Best flaps for lift. Complicated mech-anism. Nose down pitching moment.
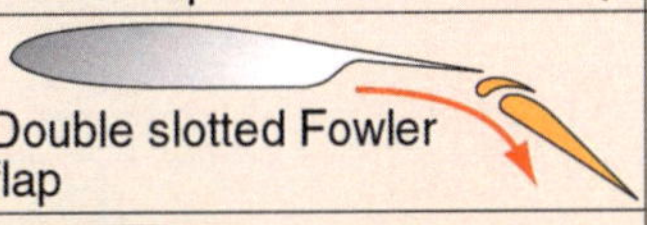 Double slotted Fowler flap	100%	20°	Same as for Fowler flap, only to a greater degree. Triple slots sometimes used.
 Douglas flap	-	-	Increased camber and wing area. Rather simple mechanism. Nose pitching moment.
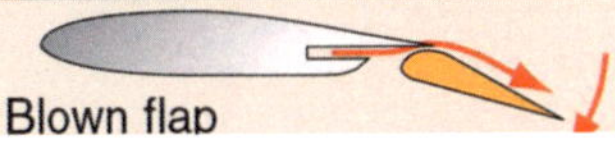 Blown flap	80%	16°	Effects depend very much on details of arrangement.

Figure 8.31

8.2.6   *Different kinds of leading edge high lift devices*

High-lift devices	Incr. of max. lift	α crit	Remarks
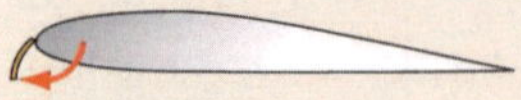 Krüger flap	50%	25°	Nose-flap attached to leading edge. Greater A.o.A. Reduces lift at small deflections. Nose up pitching moment.
 Leading edge flap	40%	20°	Nose-flap Increased camber. Greater A.o.A. Nose-up pitching moment. Slight extra drag at high speed
 Slotted wing	40%	20°	Control of boundary layer. Greater A.o.A. Slight Extra drag at high speed.
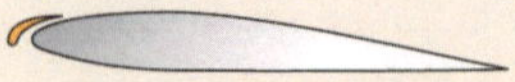 Fixed slat	50%	20°	Control of boundary layer. Greater A.o.A. Extra drag at high speed. Nose up pitching moment.
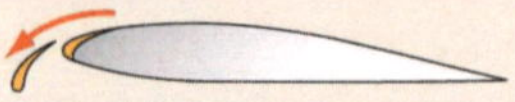 Movable slat	60%	22°	Control of boundary layer. Increased camber and area. Greater A.o.A. Nose up pitching moment

Figure 8.32

8.2.7   *Combinations of high lift devices on leading and trailing edge*

High-lift devices	Incr. of max. lift	α crit	Remarks
 Slat and slotted flap	75%	25°	More control of boundary layer. Increased camber and area. Greater A.o.A. Pitching moment can be neutralized
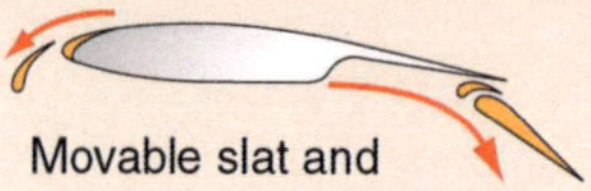 Movable slat and double-slotted Fowler flap	120%	28°	Complicated Mechanism. The best combination for lift; treble slots may be used. Greater A.o.A. Pitching moment can be neutralized.

Figure 8.33

8.3   *Controlled Vortices*

8.3.1   *Airflow at very high angles of attack*

As you know, the airflow around a wing consists of a very short laminar boundary layer near the leading edge of the wing and a long turbulent boundary layer covering the remaining part of the aerofoil chord.

When a wing has too great an A.of.A the pressure distribution around the wing will hinder the airflow over the wing, leading to a turbulent boundary layer with very low energy. When the A.of.A is too high, the turbulent boundary layer starts to separate from the upper wing surface producing a lift reducing reversed flow over the rear part of the wing chord.

CRANFIELD AVIATION TRAINING SCHOOL LTD. PART-FCL GBR.ATO-0136
CATS INNOVATION CENTRE, LUTON, Bedfordshire LU2 8DL U.K.

www.catsaviation.com

8-14

Principles of Flight

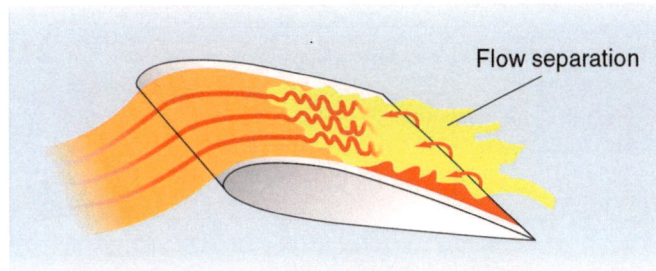

Figure 8.34

A highly swept wing can reach a higher A.of.A without stalling than a straight wing. This high A.of.A can be reached due to the fact that vortices are generated by the leading edge because of the longitudinal pressure distribution.

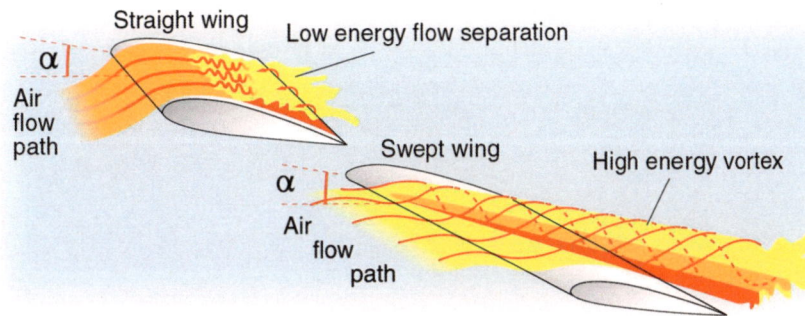

Figure 8.35

At high A.of.A, the air in the vortices circulates around a core with very high internal velocity, causing a low pressure in its core due to its radial motion. The surrounding air outside the vortices will also be energised allowing a total flow pattern rearwards without lift reducing separation.

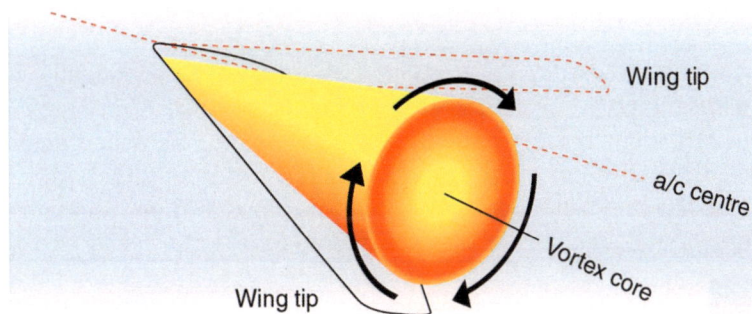

Figure 8.36

Controlled vortices supply energy to the airflow on the upper side of the wing, allowing higher A.of.A. before flow separation

In a C_L versus A.of.A diagram you see that the critical A.of.A may be very high, but also that a higher A.of.A is required to get a certain C_L attained by a highly swept wing or delta wing.

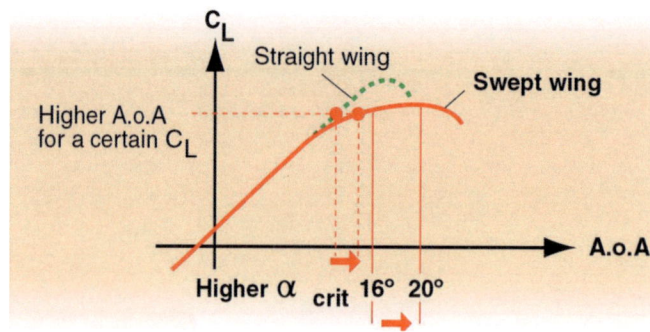

Figure 8.37

These high intensity vortices require a lot of energy which cause a lot of drag. In the drag versus speed diagram below you can see the difference in drag produced in the low speed region for a straight winged aircraft and a swept winged aircraft respectively (conditions otherwise equal).

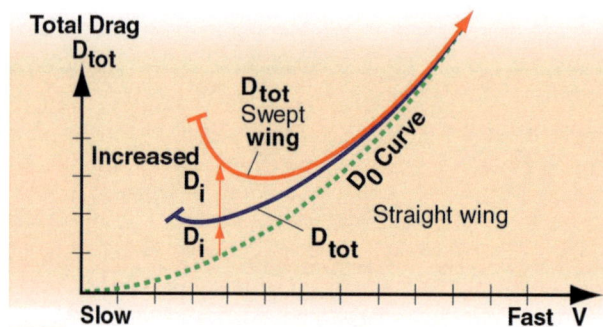

Figure 8.38

As seen in the diagram, it is the induced drag that makes the difference.

Any vortex, controlled vortices included, causes an increase in drag! Consequently, a wing with its leading edge swept back, will allow a high A.of.A before stalling, but at the cost of very high induced drag at these high A.of.A. Therefore swept wings are normally not used to improve low-speed characteristics but, as you will find in the chapter on Aerodynamics of High-Speed Aircraft, to improve high-speed capabilities. The requirement of powerful engines on high-speed aircraft makes it possible, however, to take advantage of the high critical A.of.A of swept wings, despite the increase in drag.

8.3.2 Applications of controlled vortex flow

Many modern jet fighters including the supersonic transport aircraft, Concorde, take advantage of controlled vortices when flying at low speeds or sharp turns. This allows an aircraft like the Concorde to have a sufficiently low speed for take-off and landing on most international airports despite its Mach 2 cruising speed and its lack of other types of high lift devices.

CRANFIELD AVIATION TRAINING SCHOOL LTD. PART-FCL GBR.ATO-0136
CATS CATS INNOVATION CENTRE, LUTON, Bedfordshire LU2 8DL U.K.   www.catsaviation.com

8-16   Principles of Flight

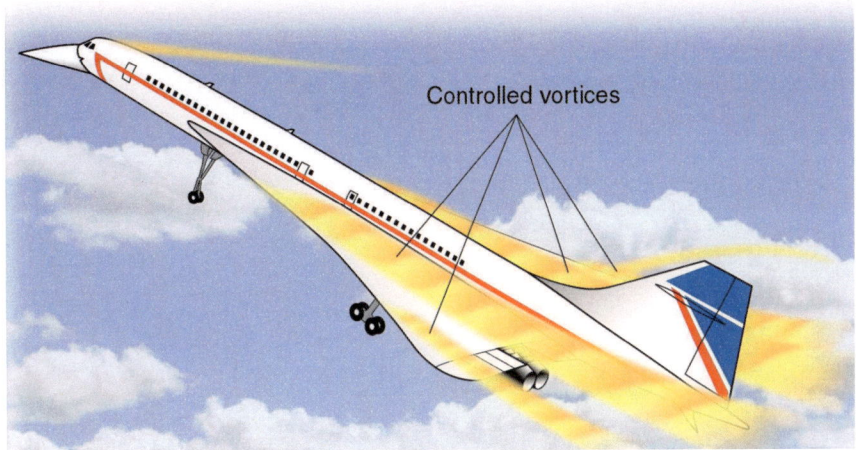

Figure 8.39

The curved double delta wing planform of this aircraft is a combination of both good supersonic and low-speed characteristics. When flying at normal and high speed the airflow behaves much like that of a normal wing, but at low speeds there are several controlled vortices over the wing (shown in the previous picture) which allows very high A.of.A without flow separation.

Today's jetfighters often have a strake in front of the wing root to make the same controlled vortices improve lift at high A.of.A required for high turning rates as well as for good low-speed characteristics.

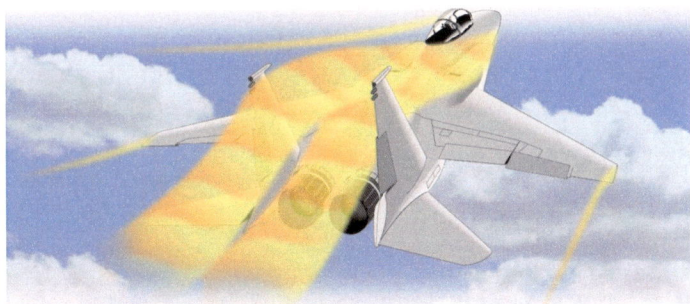

Figure 8.40

Controlled vortices may be used to improve low-speed characteristics and on jet fighters also to improve turning performance. The picture below shows controlled vortices on the wing leading edge extension as well as on the wings.

Photo: FLIGHT International July –97

8.3.3   *Vortex generators*

When the aircraft designers have failed to reach the design goal (for example, the effect of a control surface) they may use so-called vortex generators to improve the aerodynamic characteristics of that surface.

As said before, any vortex generates an increase in drag, increasing the CD_0, therefore we start with a clean surface. However, the improvement achieved by using vortex generators may be so great that the increase in drag is excused.

Vortex generators may be used to improve the performance of an aerodynamic surface at high A.of.A . Vortex generators are very small, often only ~2 cm high metal pieces located in front of the area that needs improved flow characteristics.

They are angled towards the airflow in such way that they induce undisturbed air from above into the low energy turbulent boundary layer in front of the flow separation; they energise it, and consequently a higher A.of.A is allowed before flow separation occurs.

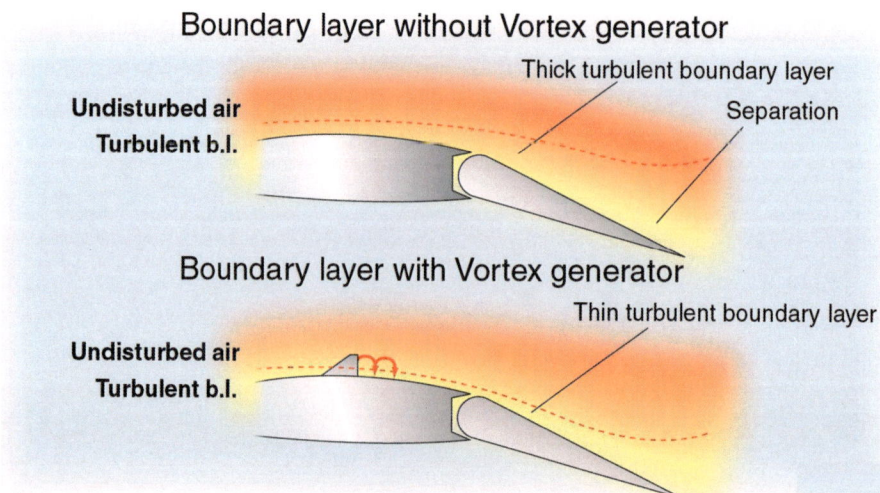

Figure 8.41

Vortex generators take undisturbed air from above the boundary layer into the low energy turbulent boundary layer; they energise it, allowing a higher A.of.A

A common application of vortex generators on the upper surface of the wing in front of the ailerons is shown on the picture below. The generators allow greater aileron deflections at low speed without aileron stall.

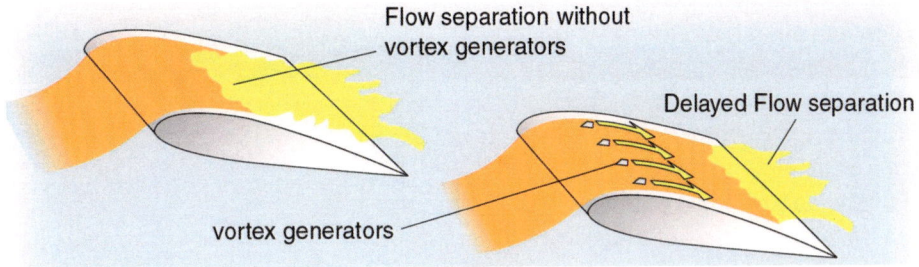

Figure 8.42

Vortex generators may be used for other purposes as well, e.g. to improve high-speed characteristics and reduce drag. This will be further explained in the chapter Aerodynamics for high-speed aircraft.

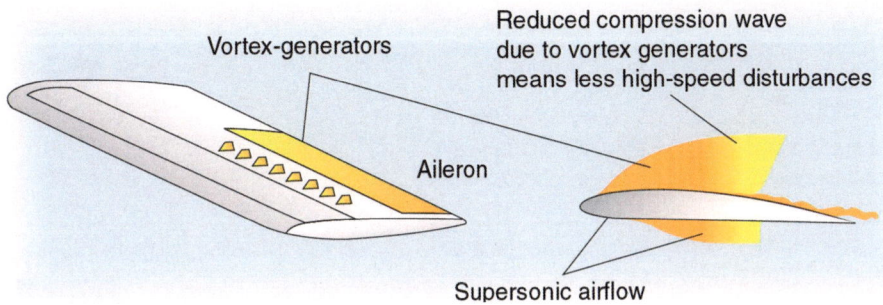

Figure 8.43

A very sophisticated method to extend the laminar boundary layer in order to decrease drag and increase stall A.of.A. is to suck the turbulent boundary layer into the wing through tiny holes on the wing upper surface. However, the difficulty in keeping the holes free from contamination has prevented this kind of boundary layer control system being used on mass produced aircraft, it has seen only limited use.

Self Assessment Test 04

1   Simple trailing edge flaps:
A)   Markedly increase the stalling angle of attack
B)   Markedly decrease the stalling angle of attack
C)   Have no effect on the stalling angle of attack
D)   Decrease the stalling angle of attack slightly

2   A combination of leading and trailing edge slats/flaps:
A)   May increase the stalling angle of attack to 25° or more
B)   Will increase the stalling angle of attack by no more than 5°
C)   Will not increase the stalling angle of attack at all
D)   Will reduce the stalling angle of attack

3   A type of trailing edge flap generally unsuitable for take-off is:
A)   The slotted flap
B)   The Fowler flap
C)   The plain flap
D)   The split flap

4   Use of flap:
A)   Increases the lift/drag ratio
B)   Decreases the lift/drag ratio
C)   Has no effect on lift/drag ratio
D)   Decreases C_L

5   A leading edge slat is a device for:
A)   Increasing the stalling angle of attack of the wing
B)   Decreasing the drag of the wing
C)   Decreasing the stalling angle of attack of the wing
D)   Increasing the stalling speed of the wing

6   The purpose of a drooped leading edge is to:
A)   Increase wing camber for high speed flight
B)   Increase wing camber to prevent separation of the airflow when trailing edge flaps are lowered
C)   Increase the wing area for take-off and landing
D)   Increase lift without altering wing camber

7   The type of flap which increases wing area is:
A)   Split flap
B)   Fowler flap
C)   Plain flap
D)   Krueger flap

8   Lowering a flap to its landing setting will:
A)   Give a large increase in drag and a lower stalling speed
B)   Give a large increase in drag and a higher stalling speed
C)   Give a small increase in drag and a lower stalling speed
D)   Give a small increase in drag and a higher stalling speed

CRANFIELD AVIATION TRAINING SCHOOL LTD. PART-FCL GBR.ATO-0136
CATS   **CATS INNOVATION CENTRE, LUTON, Bedfordshire LU2 8DL U.K.**   www.catsaviation.com

8-20   Principles of Flight

9   If the flaps are lowered but the airspeed is kept constant, to maintain level flight:-
A)   The nose must be pitched down
B)   The nose must be pitched up
C)   The altitude must be held constant
D)   Spoilers must be deployed

10   The type of flap which extends rearward from the trailing edge as it is lowered is:-
A)   A zap flap
B)   A fowler flap
C)   A split flap
D)   A kreuger flap

11   When deploying the flaps the effective angle of attack: -
A)   Decreases
B)   Remains the same
C)   Increases
D)   May increase or decrease depending on the aircraft type

12   The lift coefficient (C_L) of a wing at a given angle of attack:-
A)   Is dependent on the surface area of the wing
B)   Is increased by the use of high lift devices
C)   Is constant and not affected by high lift devices
D)   Is reduced when high lift devices are used

13   C_{LMAX} may be increased by the use of:-
A)   Flaps
B)   Slats
C)   Boundary layer control
D)   A, B and C are correct

14   Slats:-
A)   De-energise the boundary layer, thereby decreasing the stalling angle of attack
B)   Re-energise the boundary layer thereby decreasing the stalling angle of attack
C)   Re-energise the boundary layer thereby increasing the stalling angle of attack
D)   De-energise the boundary layer thereby increasing the stalling angle of attack

15   Slats:-
A)   Increase C_{LMAX}
B)   Decrease the minimum angle of attack
C)   Both A and B
D)   Neither A or B

Self Assessment Test 04 Answers

1	D
2	A
3	D
4	B
5	A
6	B
7	B
8	A
9	A
10	B
11	C
12	B
13	D
14	C
15	A

CRANFIELD AVIATION TRAINING SCHOOL LTD. PART-FCL GBR.ATO-0136
CATS INNOVATION CENTRE, LUTON, Bedfordshire LU2 8DL U.K.

www.catsaviation.com

8-22

Principles of Flight

CHAPTER 9

Ice and Contamination

9.1   *Introduction*

9.1.1   *Effects of wing contamination*

We have just seen that the airflow closest to the surface, the boundary layer, has a very great influence on the creation of both lift and drag. Since modern aircraft have very carefully designed lifting surfaces in order to be as effective as possible, any disturbances in the boundary layer will deteriorate the performance significantly.

As a commercial pilot you will fly in most weather conditions with ice, snow or frost contamination, all of which demand special attention. Frost, snow and ice can vary in appearance and have different effects depending on their location. The most critical areas for frost, snow and ice contamination are the wing and tail surfaces, the engine air intakes, propellers and the pitot-static system.

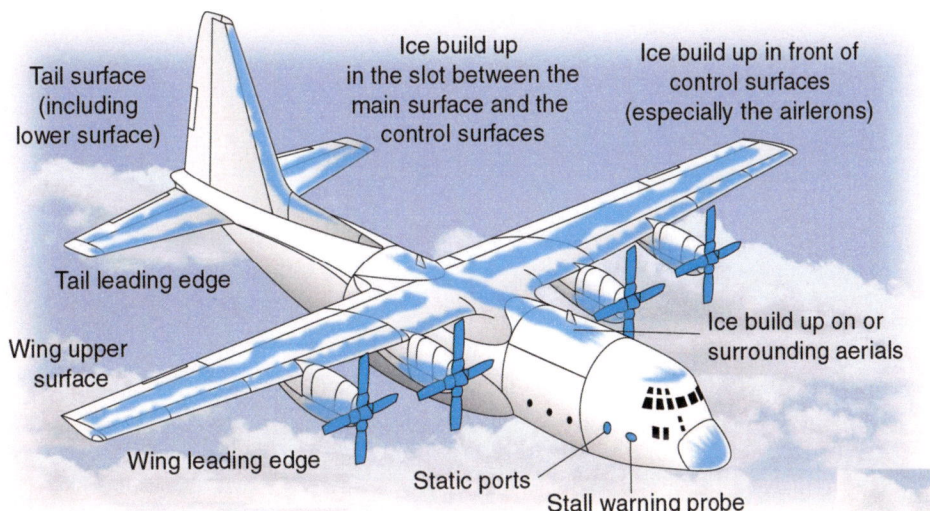

Figure 9.1

The most critical areas for ice contamination are the wing and tail surfaces, the engines and the pitot-static systems

Ice contamination may reduce performance considerably by reducing lift and thrust and by increasing drag and weight. As shown below, each effect tends to decrease the performance of the aircraft and increase the stalling speed.

CRANFIELD AVIATION TRAINING SCHOOL LTD. PART-FCL GBR.ATO-0136
CATS INNOVATION CENTRE, LUTON, Bedfordshire LU2 8DL U.K.   www.catsaviation.com

9-1   Principles of Flight

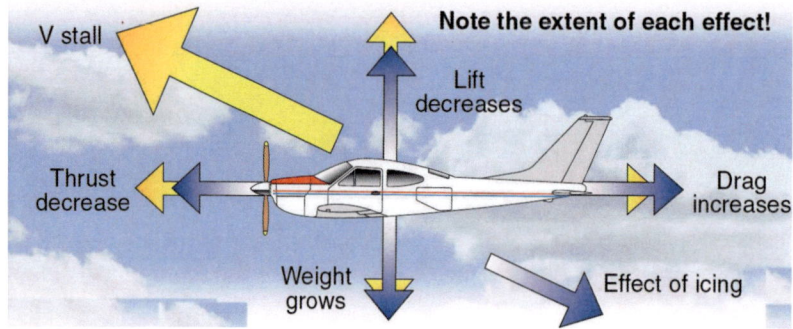

Figure 9.2

Ice, snow or frost contamination can be extremely dangerous if not given adequate consideration, and effective actions taken.

9.1.2   *Increase in drag*

Any deposit that makes the surfaces of the wing rough will increase the thickness of the boundary layer. A thick boundary layer results in a wide wake being formed behind the body. With increasing wake thickness, the forward acting pressure at the trailing edge decreases, and a powerful form drag, in addition to increased friction drag, is created.

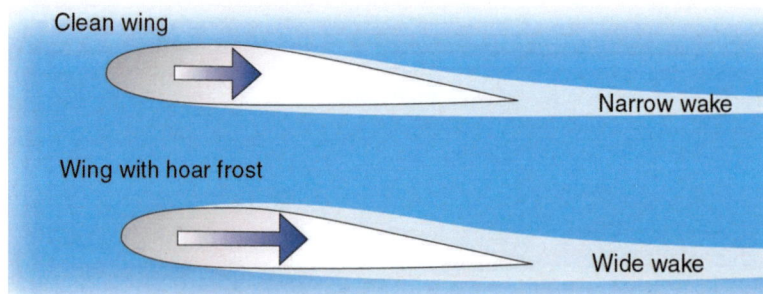

Figure 9.3

The potential increase in drag caused by a thin layer of frost, snow or ice is great because of the very significant effect it can have on wake thickness

A wide wake results in a great suction force not only from the wings but also from all the trailing edges of the tailplane, the fuselage or antennas and of course, from the extended landing gear as well. The contamination will also reduce the maximum lift.

CRANFIELD AVIATION TRAINING SCHOOL LTD. PART-FCL GBR.ATO-0136
CATS INNOVATION CENTRE, LUTON, Bedfordshire LU2 8DL U.K.   www.catsaviation.com

9-2   Principles of Flight

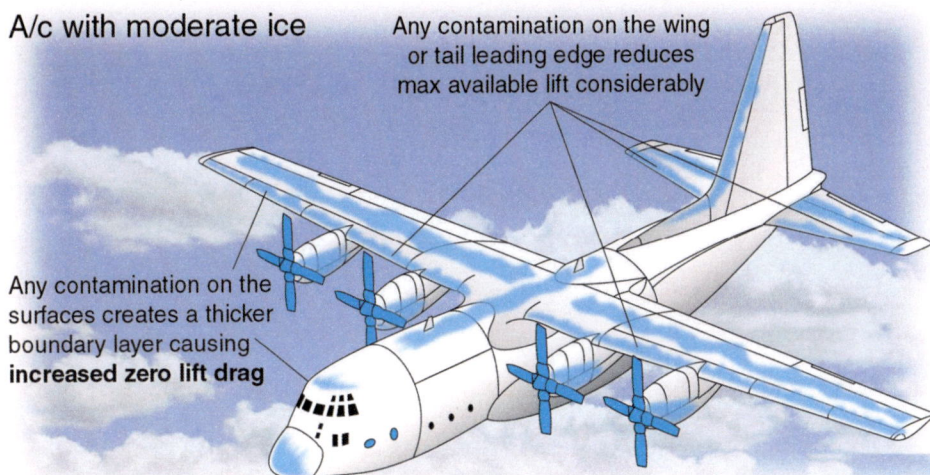

A/c with moderate ice — Any contamination on the wing or tail leading edge reduces max available lift considerably

Any contamination on the surfaces creates a thicker boundary layer causing **increased zero lift drag**

Figure 9.4

A wide wake creates a significant suction force on the trailing surfaces which increases zero lift Drag. The drag may be doubled. Contamination also reduces max available lift.

9.1.3 *Decrease in lift*

The effect of contamination along the profile of the upper surface or at the leading edge will be a sharp reduction in the maximum lift capabilities of an otherwise efficient profile.

This is an especially important factor for modern aircraft with highly efficient aerofoil sections. The tolerance towards any changes in the aerofoil shape is very limited.

Old aircraft had less critical aerodynamics. Even with non-contaminated wings the boundary layer was considerably thick, creating a lot of drag, consequently making them less sensitive to any form of contamination.

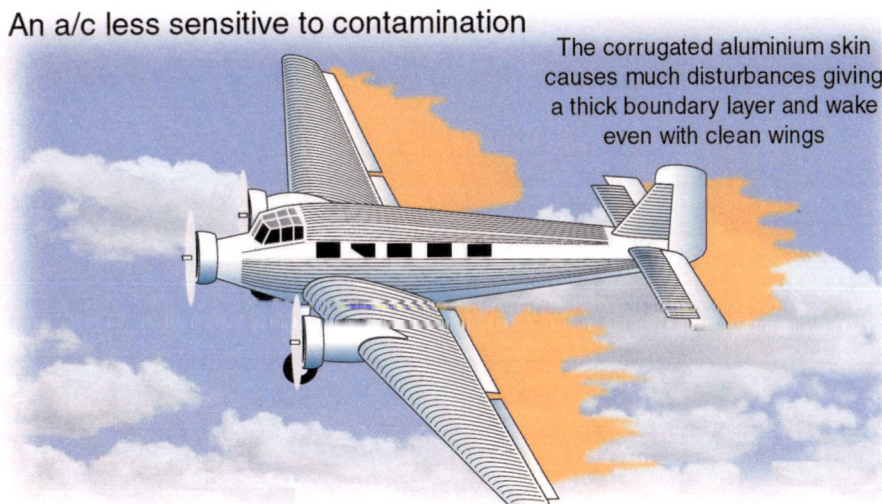

An a/c less sensitive to contamination

The corrugated aluminium skin causes much disturbances giving a thick boundary layer and wake even with clean wings

Figure 9.5

However, small as well as big modern transport aircraft are very sensitive to any contamination. The more refined the aerodynamics, the more sensitive they are to contamination.

CRANFIELD AVIATION TRAINING SCHOOL LTD. PART-FCL GBR.ATO-0136

CATS CATS INNOVATION CENTRE, LUTON, Bedfordshire LU2 8DL U.K.

www.catsaviation.com

9-3

Principles of Flight

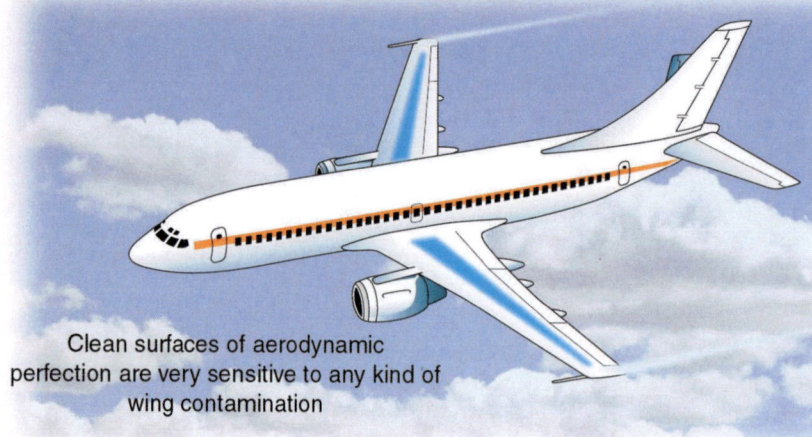

An a/c very sensitive to contamination

Clean surfaces of aerodynamic perfection are very sensitive to any kind of wing contamination

Figure 9.6

With the increase in thickness of the boundary layer caused by contamination, maximum lift may approach the flat plate level. A rough surface can reduce lift by 50%. This in turn increases stalling speed by 30%.

9.1.4   *Total effect*

Summarising the effects of wing contamination on the efficiency of a modern profile and modern high lift devices, we can say: when contamination increases, the drag of a streamlined body comes close to the drag of bodies with separated flow. In addition, the maximum lift of the profile decreases towards that of a flat plate.

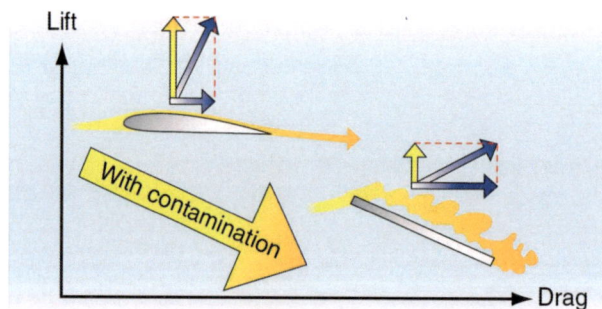

Figure 9.7

The increase in lift due to slotted high lift devices of the leading and trailing edge is reduced to the lift of simple flaps.

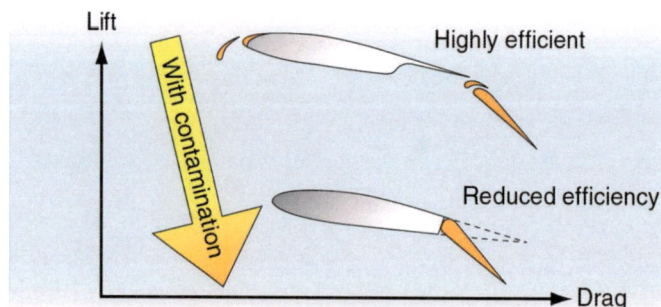

Figure 9.8

The ice contamination on the upper surface of the profile or at the leading edge can reduce lift by 50%. This increases stalling speed by 30%.

9.1.5 *Changed points of separation*

In order to better understand the dangerous consequences of ice contamination, we will take a closer look at the separation point of a wing and the reduction in lift coefficient in the case of ice contamination.

A kind of contamination that is often neglected is hoarfrost. Its rather smooth appearance and very thin layer allow us to be deceived. But, as we already know, the shape of the boundary layer is the determining factor for the creation of lift and drag, and hoarfrost will obviously affect the boundary layer. Hoarfrost will slow down the speed of the boundary layer, creating drag and early separation. The next pictures show the separation point (where the flow separates from the surface) on a clean wing; and one with contamination. There is also a diagram which shows the correlation between the lift coefficient and the angle of attack.

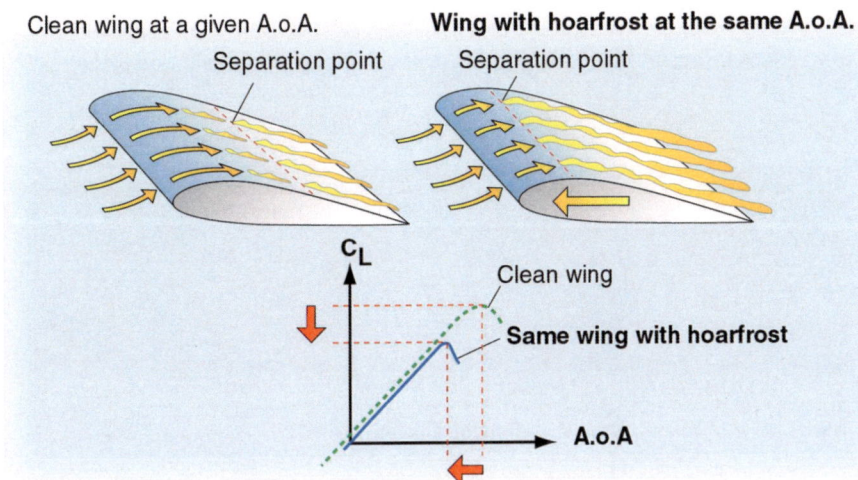

Figure 9.9

Hoarfrost slows down the speed of the boundary layer, it creates drag and early separation. The separation point will be moved forward and the maximum lift coefficient will be reduced

In this case the maximum value of lift coefficient is about 60-65% of a clean wing.

Hoarfrost will form when the aircraft is on the ground and it is obviously dangerous if not removed before take-off. Hoarfrost may also form when the aeroplane descends from high altitude into a moist lower atmosphere. In this case little can be done about the formation except to be aware of its existence.

When flying, however, other kinds of ice contamination can appear.

9.1.6 *Ice at stagnation point and on leading edge*

The worst type of ice contamination is ice on the leading edge caused by super-cooled water droplets in the air. A wing with ice on the leading edge has a separation point close to the leading edge. This results in a large wake. The reason why super-cooled droplets greatly affect severity and location of icing on the leading edge of the wing is that they do not follow the change in direction of the airflow close to the leading edge. The greater the size and mass of the droplets (having more inertia), the straighter the flow direction towards the leading edge of the wing, making the build-up of ice on the leading edge more widespread and dangerous. The next figure shows the different flow pattern of air molecules and of water droplets. Note that 1 micron = 0.001 mm. The greater the mass of the super-cooled droplets, the more widespread and dangerous the creation of ice on the leading edge. A wing with leading edge ice has a separation point close to the leading edge. This results in a large wake.

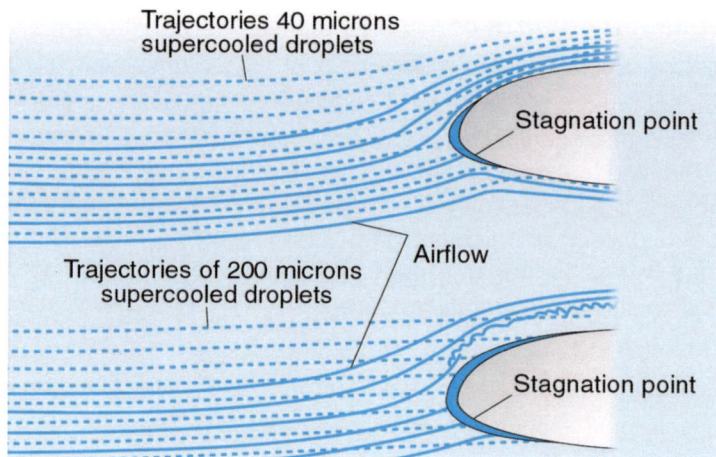

Figure 9.10

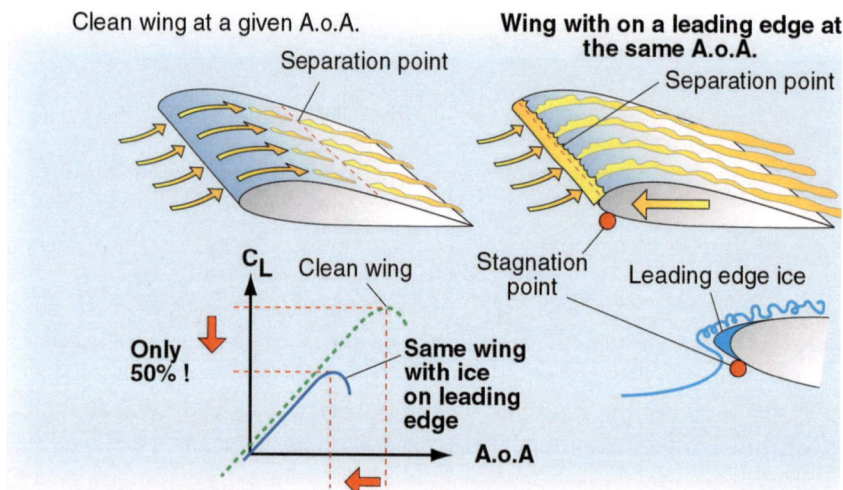

Figure 9.11

In the case of a wing with leading edge ice, the situation may be even more dramatic than a wing with hoarfrost. Never forget that a few millimetres of rough ice on the leading edge profile can reduce the maximum lift coefficient to 50% of that of a clean wing. This maximum lift coefficient is normally required at critical stages of the flight near the ground such as take-off and landing.

9.1.7   *Effects on the control surface moment*

The wings are not the only surfaces affected by contamination. All lift producing surfaces like the control surfaces will be more or less affected. Ice on the horizontal stabiliser may reduce the pitch up moment of the elevator to such a degree that, for example, a flare out during landing is impossible to perform or, if it comes to the worst, the stabiliser may stall causing a rapid pitch down instead. Ice on the vertical tail will reduce the effect of the necessary counteracting directional moment when having asymmetrical power, which increases the minimum control speed VMC considerably.

9.1.8   *Ice in front of aerodynamically balanced control surfaces*

Manually operated control surfaces have some kind of aerodynamic balancing surfaces in front of the hinge line, (see chapter Flight ``controls). If the airflow in front of this is different from what was anticipated because of ice, and/or if the balancing surfaces are contaminated with ice, the control surface might be overbalanced which may lead to a deflection of the control surface. For instance, if one of the ailerons is overbalanced, it may start an undesired roll.

This may be dangerous, especially if the aircraft is flown by means of the autopilot the time during which the ice has been building up, giving no warning that the stickforce in roll is not trimmed to zero. When you disconnect the autopilot, a rapid roll may start immediately and you might enter a steep descent in seconds.

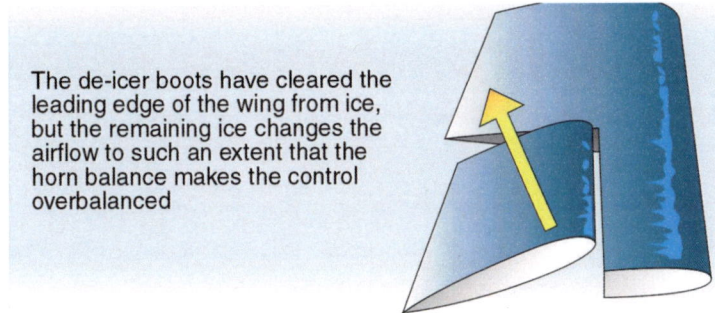

Figure 9.12

Ice build up may overbalance the control surface, which may lead to an undesired angle of the control surface.

9.2 Effects On Flight

9.2.1 Take-off in icing conditions

Snow, frost or ice on the wings is sometimes neglected by transport pilots as well as private pilots. This is because the pilot, and also the ground personnel, believes that the snow will be completely blown away during the ground roll in the take-off phase and that a thin layer of frost or clear ice has no dangerous influence. The fact is that the layer of snow will normally only be completely blown away after the airspeed for lift-off has been passed. The remaining snow or thin layer of frost or clear ice will always increase the drag and may eliminate the margins to the stall. The normal margin to the stall must be maintained during rotation. It is even more important to maintain safety margins in situations when for example, an engine failure occurs or when entering wake turbulence while in the air.

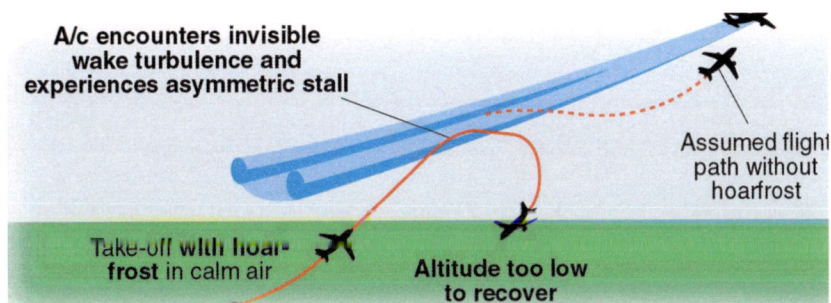

Figure 9.13

Many aircraft accidents are caused by the pilot's negligence to ensure that the aircraft is clean from snow, frost or ice before take-off. A thorough pre-flight inspection in ice conditions must be carried out. All surfaces must be clean, including wings, the tail, the body and the static ports.

9.2.2 Asymmetric contamination

Imagine this scene. An aircraft parked overnight with one wing under a roof and one wing unprotected. The unprotected wing gathers hoarfrost. A sloppy pilot who does not make the mandatory walk around-check of clean wing surfaces. After lift-off, the wings do not create the same amount of lift at the same angle of attack and the aircraft rolls towards the frosty wing, the pilot applies aileron to the opposite side (frosty aileron downwards) and the frosty wing stall.

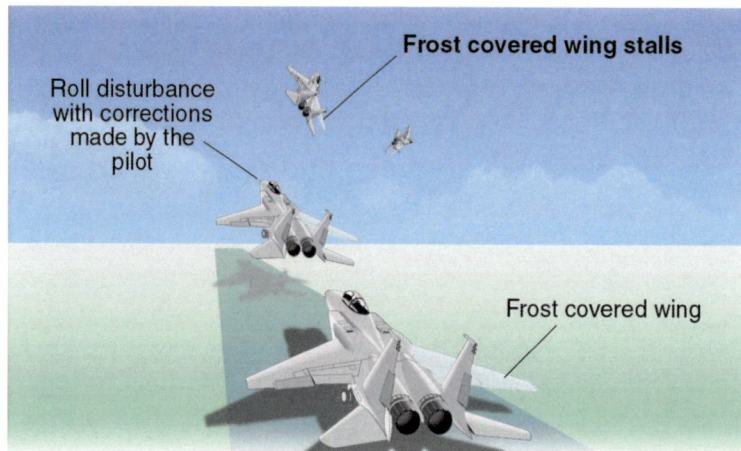

Figure 9.14

The remaining snow or thin layer of frost or clear ice will eliminate the margins to the stall and increase the drag.

9.2.3   *Clear ice*

A very insidious kind of ice contamination is a clear smooth ice layer on the upper surface of the wing. After a long flight at high altitudes, the fuel in the wings will be very cold. On the ground, humid air is sublimated on the wing skin, creating a layer of very clear smooth ice that is hard to detect. During the rotation for lift off, the bending of the wing causes this ice to break away and it may be sucked into the engines, which may be severely damaged and lose vital thrust. This is a problem for aircraft types with engines mounted aft on the body.

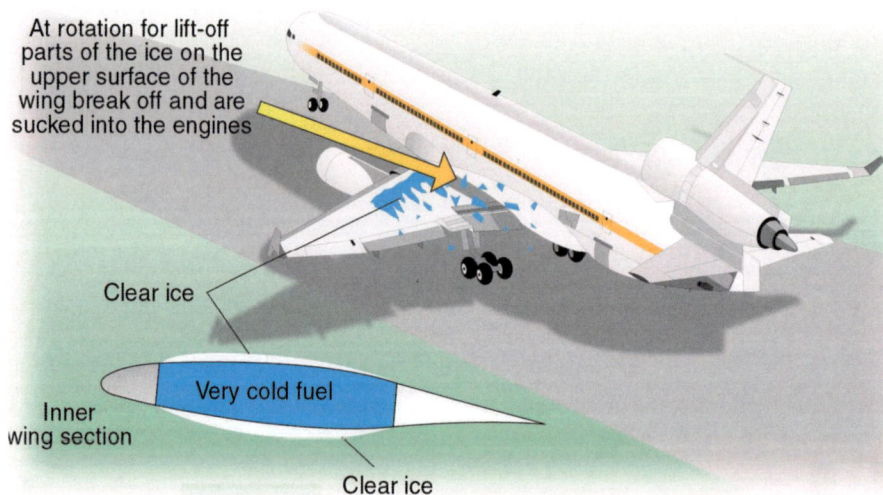

Figure 9.15

Clear smooth ice on the upper surface of the wing can break off and be sucked into the engines during rotation for lift-off. In order to be certain that clear ice has been completely removed, you have to check with your bare hands.

9.2.4   *Frozen controls*

If the wing is not completely clean from snow, when airborne, the remaining snow may move rearwards to the slot between the control surfaces and the fixed surfaces and freeze, causing trouble with controlling the aircraft.

The same may happen if the aircraft is sprayed with anti-ice fluid. All flight controls work satisfactorily when checked on the ground. After lift-off, it may become impossible to move some, or all, controls due to the freezing effect. In this case, de-icing fluid slush has frozen between the controls and the fixed surfaces. This may indeed happen if the surfaces are not completely clean.

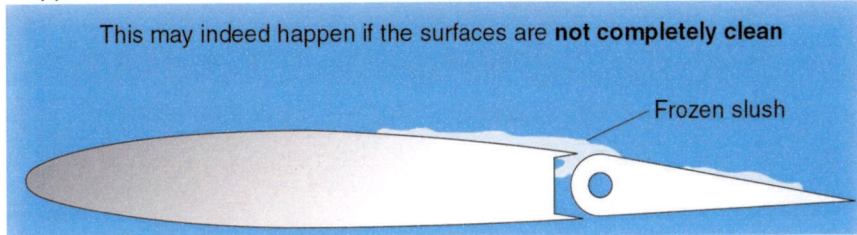

Figure 9.16

Remaining snow or slush may get caught and freeze in the slot between the control surface and the wing or tail, making the aircraft impossible to control.

9.2.5 *Take-off or landing in heavy rain*

Even a very wet wing in heavy rain may have the same problem. The rain hitting the wing surface damages the boundary layer, decreasing the lift and maximum A.of.A, which causes a decrease of the margins to stall. At temperatures near the freezing point at ground level, the water might also freeze on the wings, or block the controls during the take-off roll, due to the cooling effect.

In addition to this, severe turbulence and downdrafts often appear together with heavy rain, requiring maximum aerodynamic performance. This combination makes the situation even worse.

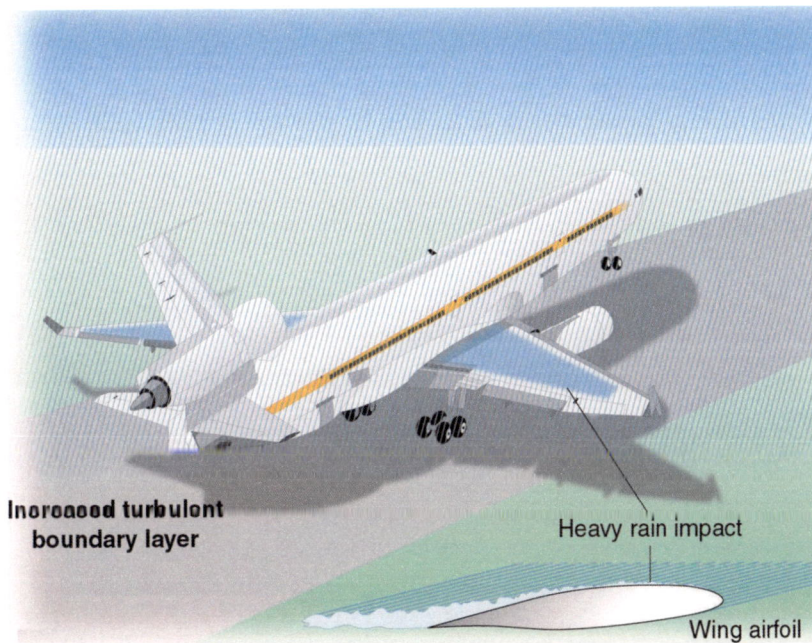

Figure 9.17

Heavy rain hitting the wing surface damages the boundary layer and decreases the margins to the stall

Take-off or landing in a very heavy rain shower can be very dangerous.

9.2.6 *Use of anti- and de-ice fluids*

Many accidents have occurred because pilots attempted to fly their aircraft with snow or frost on the wings. In many cases the aircraft had been de-iced but a great deal of time passed and a lot of snow had fallen in the interim. In some cases, the aircraft actually left the ground, but controlled flight was never attained and they literally fell back to the ground with horrible consequences.

Never compromise between safety and snow and ice contamination. Air safety regulations require the same: you need all the C_L you can get.

In order to ensure clean wings at the actual time for take-off, the de-ice fluid has to have enough "holdover time", abbreviated HOT, which means: the time during which the fluid will be effective.

If we take time to study the tables below, we will see how limited the effective time of the anti-ice fluids is. The most common de-ice fluid to be found on most airports is Type I which has a very short HOT as shown in the table below.

Guide line for holdover times (Hot) that may be expected with
de-ice fluid **Type I** as a function of weather conditions and OAT.
(Note, this table shall not be used for operational purpose).
The freezing point of the fluid must be at least 10° lower than the actual OAT.

OAT:	Approximate, expected Hot during different weather conditions in hours and minutes:				
°C	Hoar-frost	Freezing fog	Snow	Freezing rain	Rain on cold surface
Above 0	0:18-0:45	0:12-0:30	0:06-0:15	0:02-0:05	0:06-0:15
-1 to -7	0:18-0:45	0:06-0:15	0:06-0:15	0:01-0:03	
Below -7	0:12-0:30	0:06-0:15	0:06-0:15	not applic.	

Warning:
Hot is reduced during intense weather conditions, strong winds or jetblast from jet-engines. The deterioration can be considerable during severe weather conditions and/or if the fuel temperature is essentially lower than OAT.

Figure 9.18

As is shown in the next figure, the HOT will be considerably longer when using Type II fluid, and consequently this should always be used as anti-ice fluid when there is precipitation during taxi before take-off.

Guide line for holdover times (Hot) that may be expected with
de-ice fluid **Type II** as a function of weather conditions and OAT.
(Note, this table shall not be used for operational purpose).

OAT:	Rate of concentration fluid/water	Approximate, expected Hot during different weather conditions in hours and minutes:				
°C		Hoar-frost	Freezing fog	Snow	Freezing rain	Rain on cold surface
O and above	100/0	12:00	1:15-3:00	0:25-1:00	0:08-0:20	0:24-1:00
	75/25	6:00	0:50-2:00	0:20-0:45	0:04-0:10	0:18-0:45
	50/50	4:00	0:35-1:30	0:15-0:30	0:02-0:05	0:12-0:30
-1 to -7	100/0	8:00	0:35-1:30	0:20-0:45	0:08-0:20	
	75/25	5:00	0:25-1:00	0:15-0:30	0:04-0:10	
	50/50	3:00	0:20-0:45	0:05-0:15	0:01-0:03	
-8 to -14	100/0	8:00	0:35-1:30	0:20-0:45	Not applicable!	
	75/25	5:00	0:25-1:00	0:15-0:30		
-15 to -25	100/0	8:00	0:35-1:30	0:20-0:45		

Warning:
Hot is reduced during intense weather conditions, strong winds or jetblast from jet-engines. The deterioration can be considerable during severe weather conditions and/or if the fuel temperature is essentially lower than OAT.

Figure 9.19

Preparing a take-off in snow and ice conditions ALWAYS demands maximum attention and must not be performed if the wings cannot be kept clean.

It may not be possible to operate in winter conditions and maintain absolutely clean wings. A safety precaution is to make a visual check of the aircraft at the holding point before take-off.

You must always make a close visual pre-flight check and in snow or icing conditions, MAKE A VISUAL CHECK of the aircraft AT THE HOLDING POINT BEFORE TAKE-OFF.

Good safety requires excellent knowledge of the possible problems and a reasonable increase of the margins to the stall. Always check the Flight Operation Manual for the correct actions to be taken.

9.2.7   *Ice and the jet- or turboprop engines*

Another kind of engine problem for all types of jet engine aircraft in icing conditions, is the risk that the ice that has accumulated at the air intake lip may break loose and be sucked into the engine.

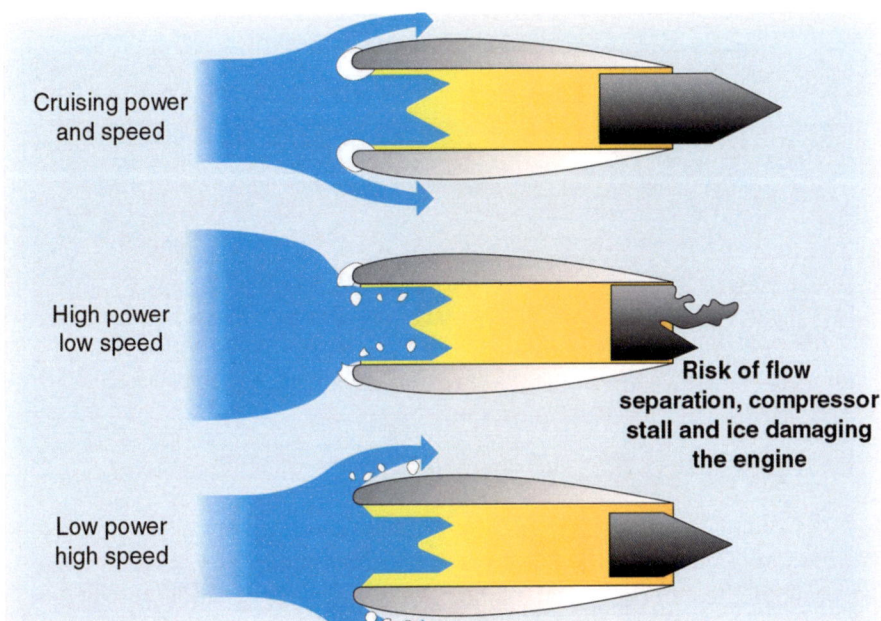

Figure 9.20

As is shown in the picture, ice accumulated during cruise flight may break loose into the engine if power is increased and speed is lowered. But if the speed can be increased despite lower power, most of the airflow will flow outside the engine due to the relative higher pressure in the intake, making the ice pieces flow outside the engine.

Ice in the engine may, at the least, result in a costly engine repair, but it can also cause total loss of power due to compressor blade failure.

The main engine problem in ice conditions is the risk that accumulated ice at the air intake lip may break loose and be sucked into the engine.

To avoid engine damage and a reduced air intake area due to ice, jet engines are equipped with anti-ice devices. These heat engine parts such as air intake surfaces and struts in order to prevent formation of ice on these parts.

In order to heat these engine parts, bleed air from the compressor is used. This will reduce the amount of air entering the combustion chambers and the torque from the turbine, which turns the compressor, will be limited by the maximum temperature of the turbine.

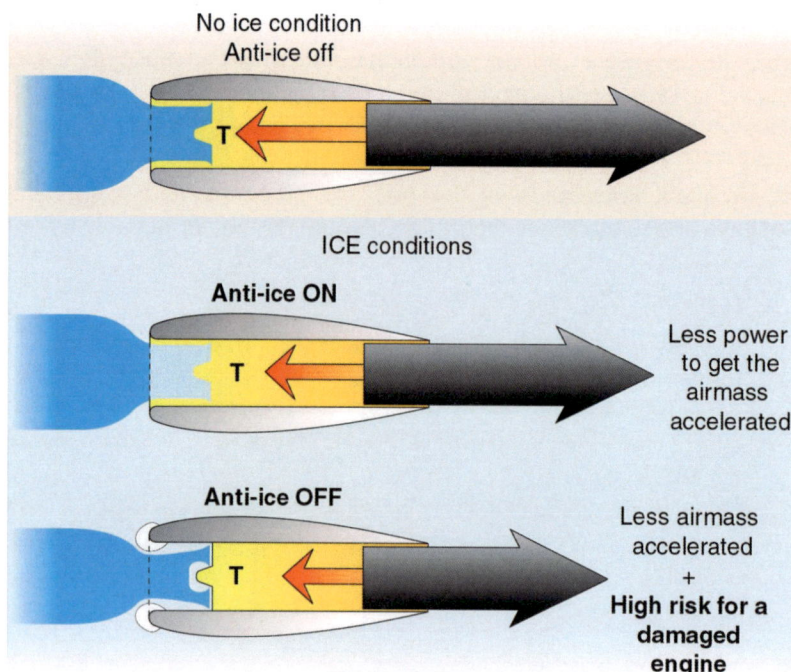

No ice condition
Anti-ice off

ICE conditions

Anti-ice ON

Less power
to get the
airmass
accelerated

Anti-ice OFF

Less airmass
accelerated
+
**High risk for a
damaged
engine**

Figure 9.21

With the anti-ice off, the accumulated ice at the intake will produce a disturbed airflow and allow less air into the engine, which will degrade the performance of the latter. In addition to this, as said before, ice may break loose and damage the engine.

9.2.8 *Ice on the propeller*

During flight in icing conditions the propeller is rapidly affected. In fog conditions at a temperature of minus 3°C a propeller can be contaminated with ice in one single revolution. It will accumulate leading edge ice outside the anti-ice boots on the inner part of the blade and several ice spots on the side of the blade face as well.

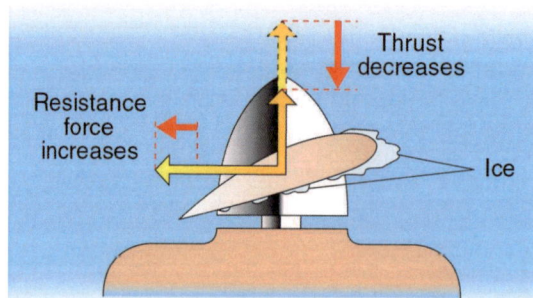

Thrust
decreases

Resistance
force
increases

Ice

Figure 9.22

Ice contamination on the propeller has the same effect as ice on the wings in the way that both reduce the efficiency of the aerofoils. The leading edge ice on the propeller blade will reduce the generated thrust in the same way the lift of the wing is reduced.

In the same way as the drag of an ice contaminated aircraft increases, the resisting force of the propeller will increase for a given blade angle and rotational speed. Ice that separates from propeller blades may also damage the body surface of the aircraft and cause severe vibration.

Ice on the blades reduces the available thrust of the propeller

---

In addition to that, when you are flying in severe icing conditions, you need extra power to compensate for the increased drag, but you may get reduced thrust instead. The combination of increased drag from the whole aircraft and reduced thrust from the engines will make the situation significantly worse when flying in severe icing conditions.

When flying in severe icing conditions the increased total drag may require maximum thrust. In such conditions, however, the AVAILABLE thrust may be reduced.

9.2.9   *Contaminated leading edge*

Among the most common problems when flying in snow and icing conditions are the ice contaminated leading edges of the wing and tail. The anti and de-ice equipment of an aircraft will clean the leading edge from ice more or less efficiently while the surfaces outside of the active area will not be free from ice. Remaining ice will cause drag and lower cruising speed, shorter range etc. Flying in icing conditions with anti or de-ice equipment "ON" will therefore not guarantee ice free wing and tail surfaces: you must still have safety margins.

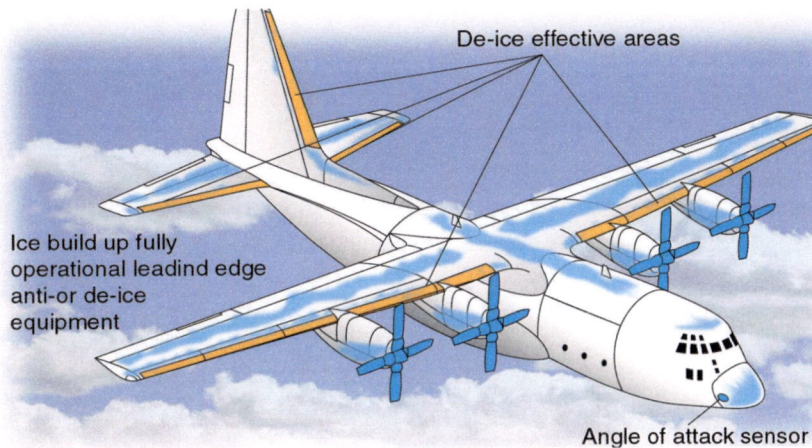

Figure 9.23

The use of anti and de-ice equipment does not guarantee contamination free leading edge and surfaces of wings and tail. Remaining ice causes increased drag and reduced range. The stall warning sensor may also freeze. An area that is sometimes not sufficiently de-iced is the stall flapper switch, which can freeze in a non-active position.

9.2.10   *Insects or dirt on leading edge*

Remember that any wing or tail surface, contaminated by a heavy layer of mosquitoes or other insects, dirt or ice, will change the stalling speed and stall characteristics of the aircraft.

Contamination on the leading edge may cause very different stalling characteristics, especially on aircraft with advanced aerofoil sections or narrow wing chord. An aircraft that, with clean wings, will lower its nose when entering the stall, may instead make a surprising snaproll well above calculated stalling speed.

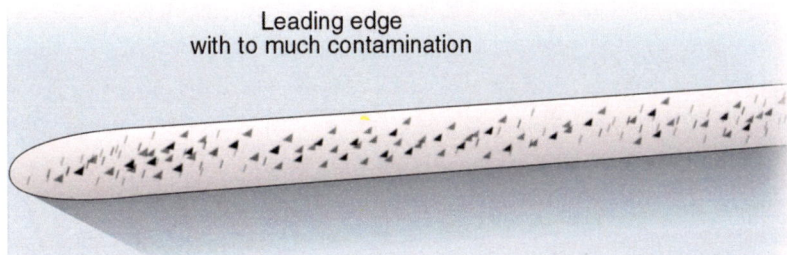

Figure 9.24

When making the walk around inspection, always feel with your hand if there is a heavy layer of insects on the leading edges.

9.2.11 Ice on stabiliser leading edge

We will now deal with the effects of tail ice. For most aircraft, the lift force moves rearwards when the flap is extended. As a result, a large nose-down moment tending to rotate the aircraft into a dive is created.
This nose-down moment has to be balanced by the horizontal tail. So a significant flap deflection will force an increase in the down-acting load on the tail.

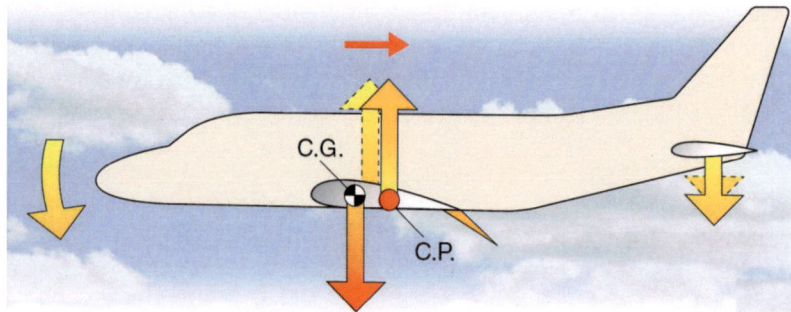

Figure 9.25

When speed increases, the A.o.A of the wing will be lower, causing an even higher negative A.o.A on the stabiliser, which may lead to a reduced tail down force due to flow separation or a complete stabiliser stall.

Increasing speed = increasing negative A.o.A on the tail

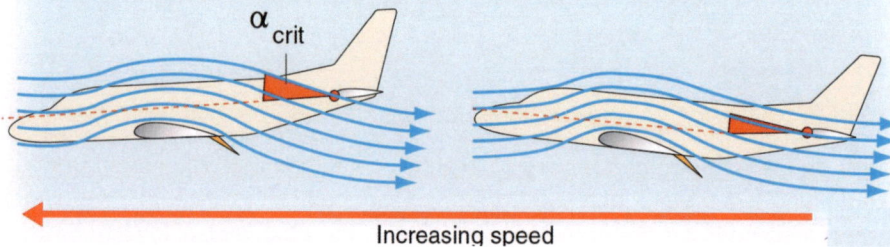

Figure 9.26

The risk of flow separation on the tail increases with increased speed and increased flap deflection.
When there is ice on the horizontal stabiliser, its maximum aerodynamic download will always be reduced. You may notice this reduction of the elevator efficiency by the need for more pitch-up input than usual. The aircraft seems more nose-heavy. The immediate action is to reduce flap deflection.
With ice on the stabiliser and the resultant degraded control force, it can be difficult to pull up during the landing flare or to perform a go-around.

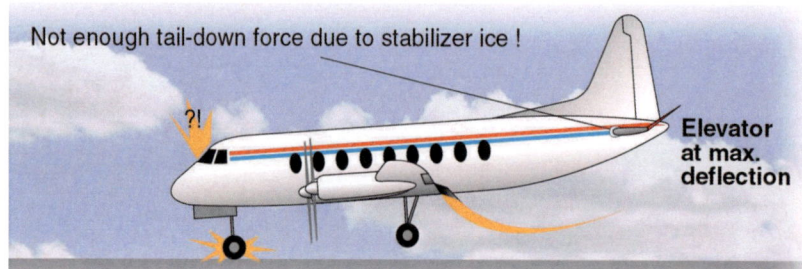

Figure 9.27

You will always get a nose down moment from deflected flaps but the total effect might instead be a nose up! The effect of the flap deflection depends on the aircraft layout. When the flaps are extended, the increased downwash behind the wings may have far too great an influence on the horizontal tail so that the total effect is nose up instead of nose down. The downwash increases the download on the tail surfaces too much.

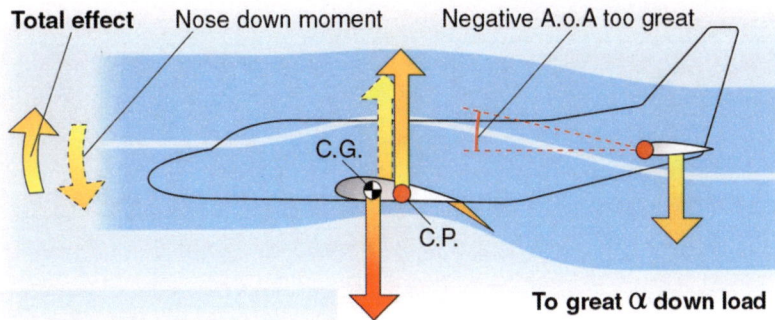

Figure 9.28

The total effect of flap deflection may be a nose up pitch motion instead of the expected nose down.
This effect may lead to the false impression that the tail is not heavily loaded with deflected flaps. But the truth is that this stabiliser is as sensitive to contamination as an aircraft with strong nose down tendency.
If too much ice is allowed to gather on the stabiliser leading edge, the maximum lift capacity of the stabiliser may be reduced by 50% and the tail may then be already stalled at the normal speed of approach.
Stabiliser stall is extremely dangerous. If complete stabiliser stall occurs, the aircraft will be affected by a strong a nose down moment. This can end up in a nearly vertical dive.

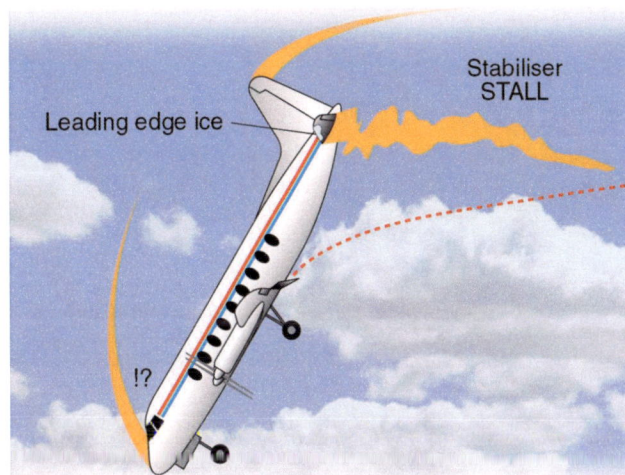

Figure 9.29

When stabiliser stall occurs, the aircraft will flip into a negative tail stall and go into a vertical dive.
There may be another problem with stabiliser ice. When there is ice on the stabiliser leading edge it may become nearly impossible to keep the nose up during approach. If tail ice is expected at this moment and the tail de-icing is switched on, the control effectiveness is regained when the ice blows off the tail and the aircraft may suddenly pitch up.

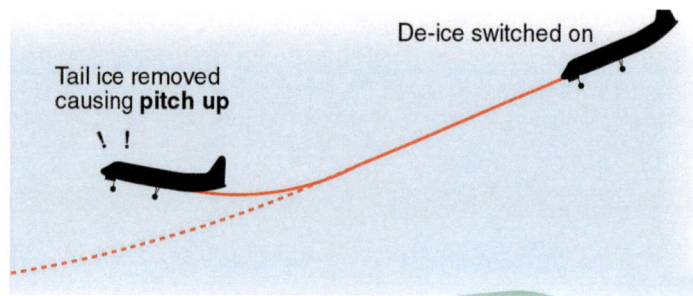

Figure 9.30

When stabiliser ice is present and the flaps are deflected, you may get serious problems with the pitch control.

9.2.12　　　*Effects on landing performance*

As you know, leading edge ice can increase the stalling speed by 20-30%. This requires a higher threshold speed, which always has to be 30% over V_s. This will increase the landing distance by 40-50% provided that the landing speed is increased to maintain safe margins to stall.

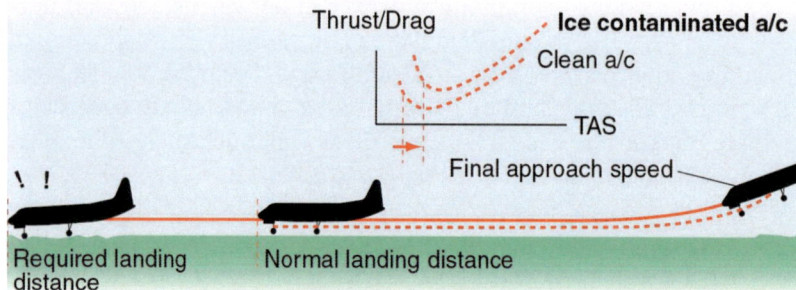

Figure 9.31

Due to leading edge ice the landing distance may increase by 40-50% if the stall/speed margins are kept constant. If the margin to the stall is not increased, the risk of high sink rate due to high drag is great, resulting in uncontrollable loss of altitude close to the ground, especially in wind-shear conditions.

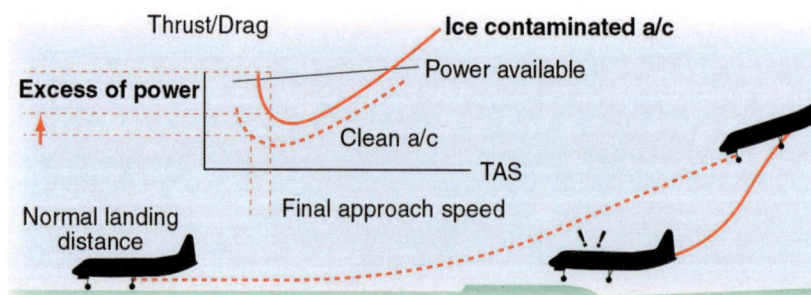

Figure 9.32

If the margin to the stall is not increased, the risk of high sinking rate is great. Many factors in ice conditions degrade aircraft performance so that the ability of the aircraft to climb with large flap angles after an unsuccessful approach may become marginal.

CRANFIELD AVIATION TRAINING SCHOOL LTD. PART-FCL GBR.ATO-0136
CATS INNOVATION CENTRE, LUTON, Bedfordshire LU2 8DL U.K.　　　　　www.catsaviation.com

9-16　　　　　　　　　　　　　　　　　　　　Principles of Flight

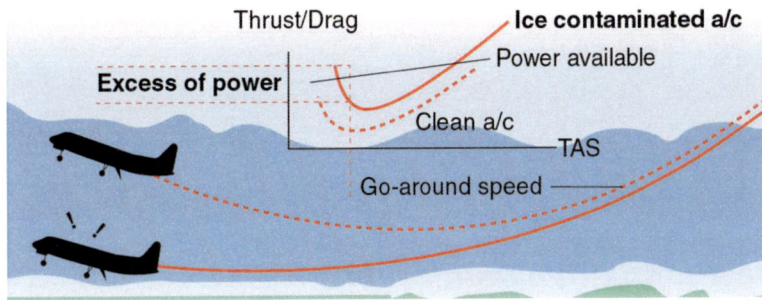

Figure 9.33

Aircraft certified to fly in ice conditions must have functioning anti-ice or de-ice equipment. But this equipment cannot remove all ice. Very often there is remaining ice outside the working anti- or de-ice surfaces, but there are also severe conditions of ice formation, where no aircraft is tested, or certified to maintain flight.

During the pre take-off weather briefing, the meteorologist cannot always guarantee that there are no "severe ice conditions" en-route, so when encountering an area with ice:

Always try to avoid icing conditions by changing flight level or route. When ice is formed on your aircraft, remove it as quickly as possible!

9.2.13   *Deformation and modification of aircraft, ageing aircraft*

Any kind of contamination causes a greater or lesser modification of the aerodynamics of the aircraft surfaces. So does a deformation, e.g. a buckle on the structure. At the buckle, local points of flow separation may originate which change the pressure distribution. This may influence an area much wider than the buckle itself. Thus, a deformation of the leading edge of the wing may have a very large effect on the C_{LMAX} and the critical A.of.A.

An aircraft (new or old) which has been well used may have small but significant deformations of its skin, e.g. hatches that are not perfectly adjusted to the surrounding skin, etc. The smooth surface of a newly built aircraft may have become a rough and rugged surface over a period of time. Such deformations, regardless of where they appear on the aircraft, will undoubtedly increase the zero lift drag and reduce the performance of the aircraft.

A rugged and poorly maintained aircraft has less efficient aerodynamic characteristics, causing reduced performance in all respects.

CRANFIELD AVIATION TRAINING SCHOOL LTD. PART-FCL GBR.ATO-0136
CATS INNOVATION CENTRE, LUTON, Bedfordshire LU2 8DL U.K.   www.catsaviation.com

CATS

9-17   Principles of Flight

CHAPTER 10

STABILITY

10.1   *Static And Dynamic Stability*

10.1.1   *Static stability*

Stability is defined as the capability of a body to return to its original condition after a disturbance. In this section we shall deal with the two aspects of stability: static stability and dynamic stability.

> Stability is the capability of a body to return to its original condition after a disturbance

There are three different cases of static stability. The first is defined as positive static stability. A body has positive static stability when it returns to its previous condition after a disturbance.

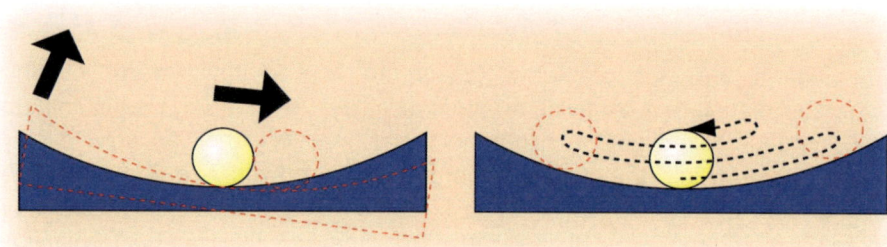

Figure 10.1 Positive static stability

The second case is neutral static stability. A body has neutral or indifferent static stability when it maintains its new position after a disturbance.

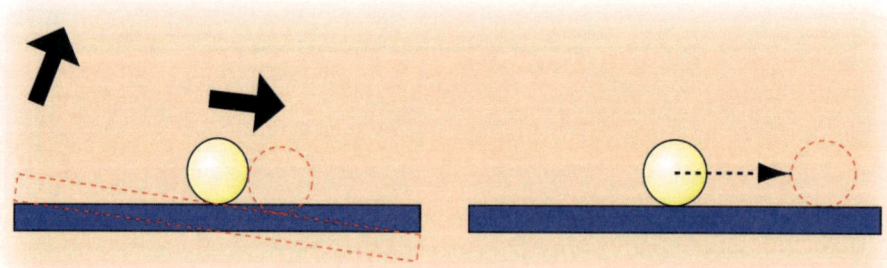

Figure 10.2

The last case is negative static stability. A body has negative static stability when it continues to move away from its previous condition after a disturbance.

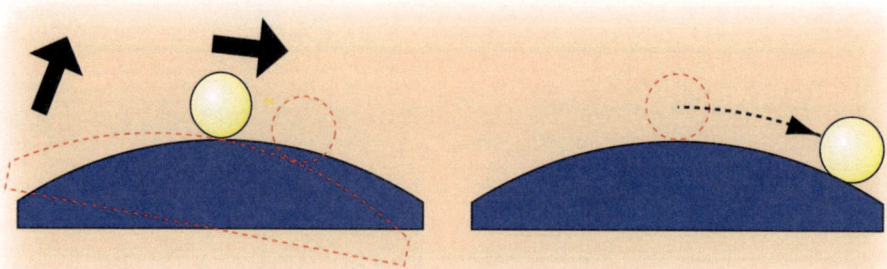

Figure 10.3 Negative static stability

CRANFIELD AVIATION TRAINING SCHOOL LTD. PART-FCL GBR.ATO-0136
CATS INNOVATION CENTRE, LUTON, Bedfordshire LU2 8DL U.K.   www.catsaviation.com

10-1   Principles of Flight

Static stability is:
Positive when a body returns to its original condition after a disturbance
Neutral when it maintains its new position;
Negative when it continues to move away from its previous condition

An aircraft must be designed to have positive static stability. In turbulence, the aircraft must be able to follow its flight path without allowing rough air to provoke any significant change in its flight path. This must happen without any intervention from the pilot and with no variations in the position of the control surfaces.

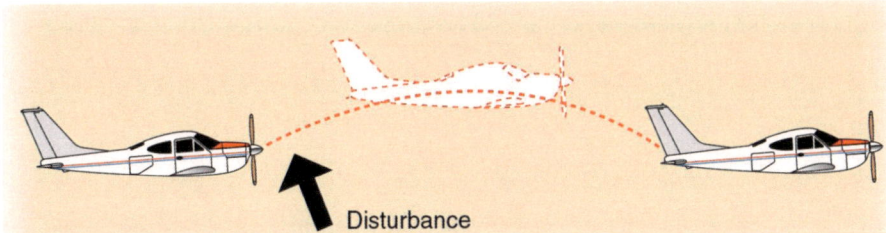

Figure 10.4 Aircraft with positive static stability self-correct for disturbances from their flight path

10.1.2   Dynamic stability

Consider a system that has positive static stability. One possibility is that, having been displaced from equilibrium, the system will, under the action of the forces created, simply subside gently back to its original condition, and remain there, as shown. If so, the system is said to be dynamically stable with aperiodic damping.

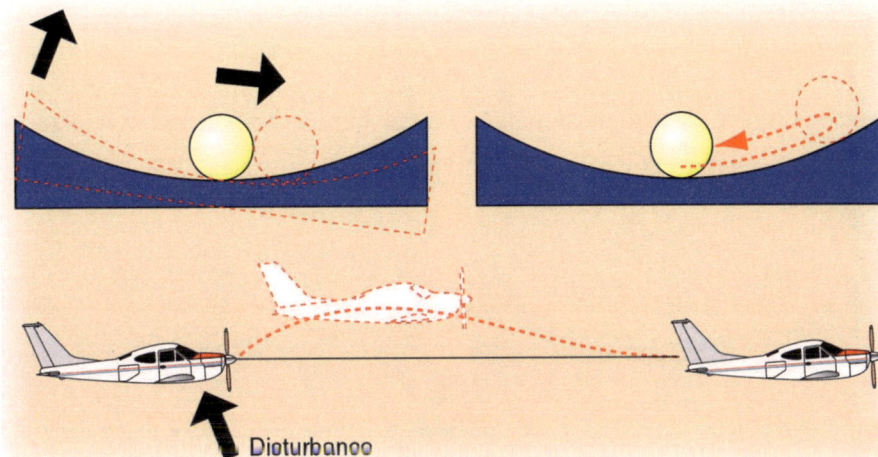

Figure 10.5

However, the system may, when it reaches the equilibrium point, do so with a certain velocity, so that it overshoots. The new forces will now, since it is statically stable, retard the system, so that the ball makes a sequence of oscillations around its previous position, as in fig 10.1, in a periodic motion. This period is defined as the interval of time taken by the body (e.g. the ball) to make a complete oscillation.

If we apply this to a statically stable aircraft and study how it will act after a disturbance, we will see that it will oscillate around its intended flight level.

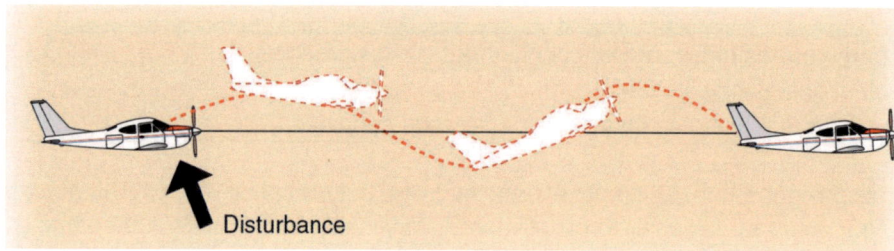

Figure 10.6

Dynamic stability is the study of how and if a body returns to its previous condition after a disturbance

If the period remains the same in length, and the amplitude continues to decrease, the dynamic stability is defined as positive.

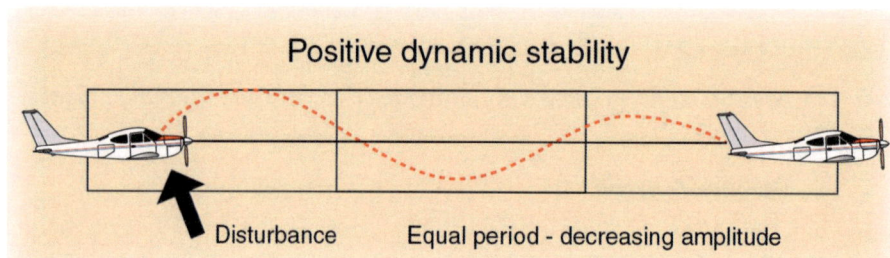

Figure 10.7

A body has positive dynamic stability when it returns to its initial condition through a sequence of periodic (equal time) oscillations of decreasing amplitude.

Let us go back to the system with the ball in the bowl. We know that it has positive static stability. As soon as the body starts moving we start rocking the container so that the oscillations do not decrease.

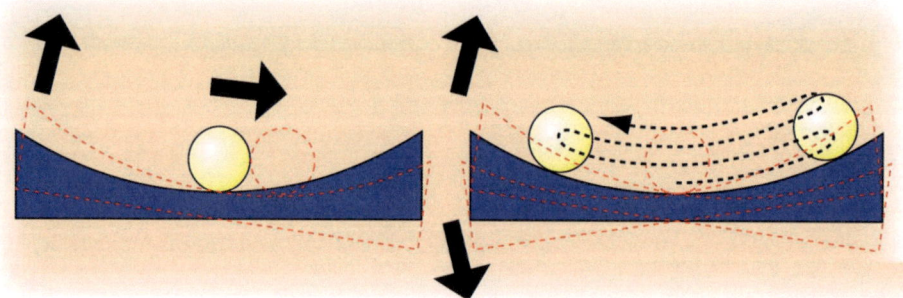

Figure 10.8

Because of the force from the outside, the oscillation of the ball maintains a constant amplitude: the body has neutral dynamic stability. An aircraft that oscillates with constant period and constant amplitude has neutral dynamic stability.

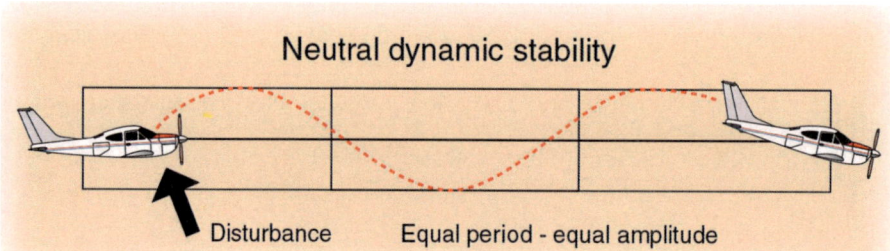

Figure 10.9

CRANFIELD AVIATION TRAINING SCHOOL LTD. PART-FCL GBR.ATO-0136
CATS INNOVATION CENTRE, LUTON, Bedfordshire LU2 8DL U.K.

www.catsaviation.com

10-3

Principles of Flight

A body has neutral dynamic stability when its oscillations continue without any change in amplitude.
Let us go back again to the bowl with the ball and suppose that we rock the container more violently so that the oscillations of the ball continue to increase in amplitude until it flies out of the container: here we have a case of negative dynamic stability.

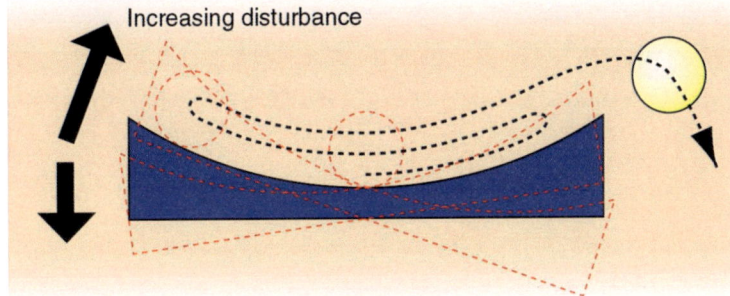

Figure 10.10

An aircraft that oscillates with constant periods but with increasing amplitude after the disturbance, has negative dynamic stability.

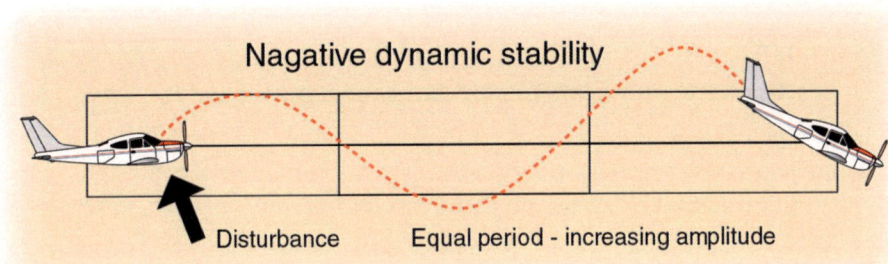

Figure 10.11

An undamped oscillation cannot be acceptable for an aircraft. The normal requirement is: after one oscillation the A.o.A should only be 1/10 of that at the beginning of the disturbance and the oscillations should be completely damped after approximately two oscillations. In other words: a normal aircraft has both positive static stability AND positive dynamic stability. However, there are some modern jetfighters that have neutral aerodynamic static stability and the latest designs even have negative static stability.

10.2 *Different positions of centre lift and weight. The isolated wing and the need for a tailplane*

10.2.1 *Centre of gravity and centre of pressure*

The centre of gravity is defined as the point where the weight vector of a body is positioned. This is the first important aspect of the centre of gravity; the second is that it is the point around which a body rotates if disturbed.

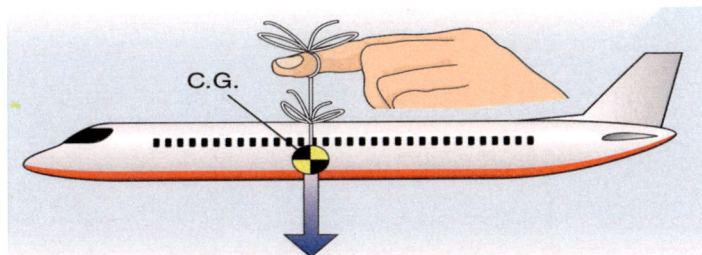

Figure 10.12 The Centre of Gravity

The centre of pressure is the point of application of the aerodynamic force. For the sake of simplicity, let us consider this point as lying on the chordline. The centre of pressure (C.P.) changes its position at different A.o.A and moves towards the leading edge as the angle of attack increases.

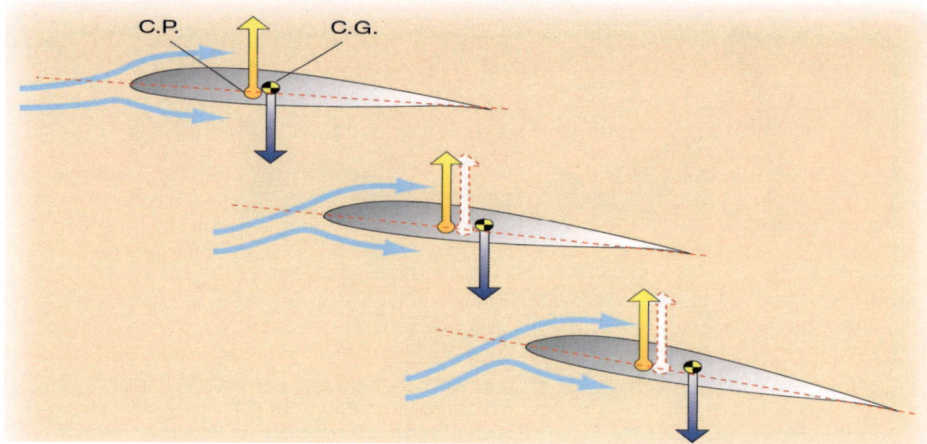

Figure 10.13 The centre of pressure moves forward as the angle of attack increases

10.2.2 *Moment and stability of the isolated wing*

When the C.P. does not coincide with the C.G. a moment is created and the aerofoil tends to rotate around the C.G. making it negatively stable. However, the effect on a three-dimensional wing depends on the wing planform and the spanwise aerofoil section. At every section along the wing span, the C.P. may have different locations.

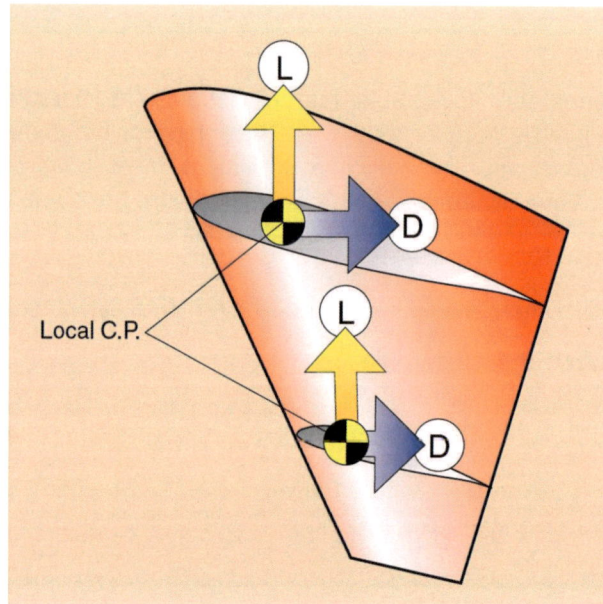

Figure 10.14 The centre of pressure is at different locations on different chord lines of the wing

The effect on the whole wing acts at a place known as the mean Aerodynamic Centre, (A.C.). The turning moment of an isolated wing ($M_{a.c.w}$) is thus dependent on the location of the A.C. in relation to the C.G. of the wing.

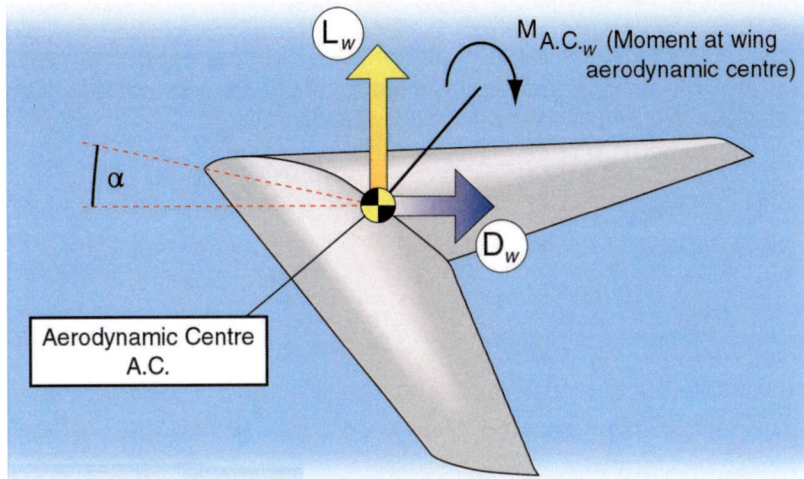

Figure 10.15 The overall mean aerodynamic centre turning moment for the wing

When the A.C. is located in front of C.G. the aerofoil will rotate in an unstable manner. In fact, depending on the shape of the aerofoil section, it may continue to rotate in the same direction.

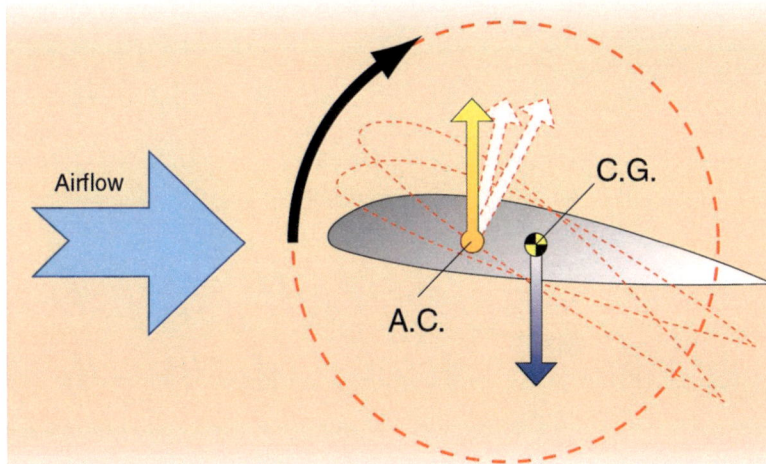

Figure 10.16

The turning moment around the C.G. is the product of the force multiplied by the distance between the C.G. and the A.C. As a formula: Moment = Force x Arm.

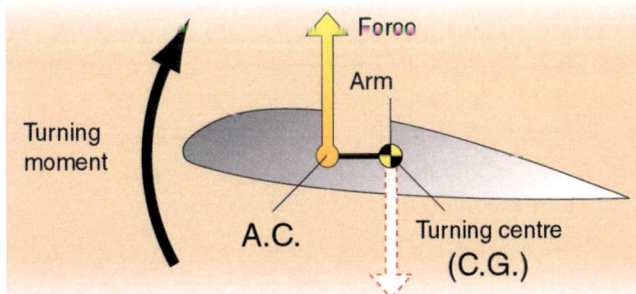

Figure 10.17

In this situation the aerodynamic force produces a moment which will cause the profile to rotate so as to increase the angle of attack. This phenomenon causes an increase in the intensity of lift. This, in turn, causes a further increase in the value of the moment. With an isolated wing we therefore have an unstable situation.

If we change the turning centre so that it lies in front of the A.C. of the wing, we will get a new situation. The wing will act as a vane. If the A.o.A increases, a turning moment is created that forces the wing to resume its earlier A.o.A, which will finally change the wing to a new attitude.

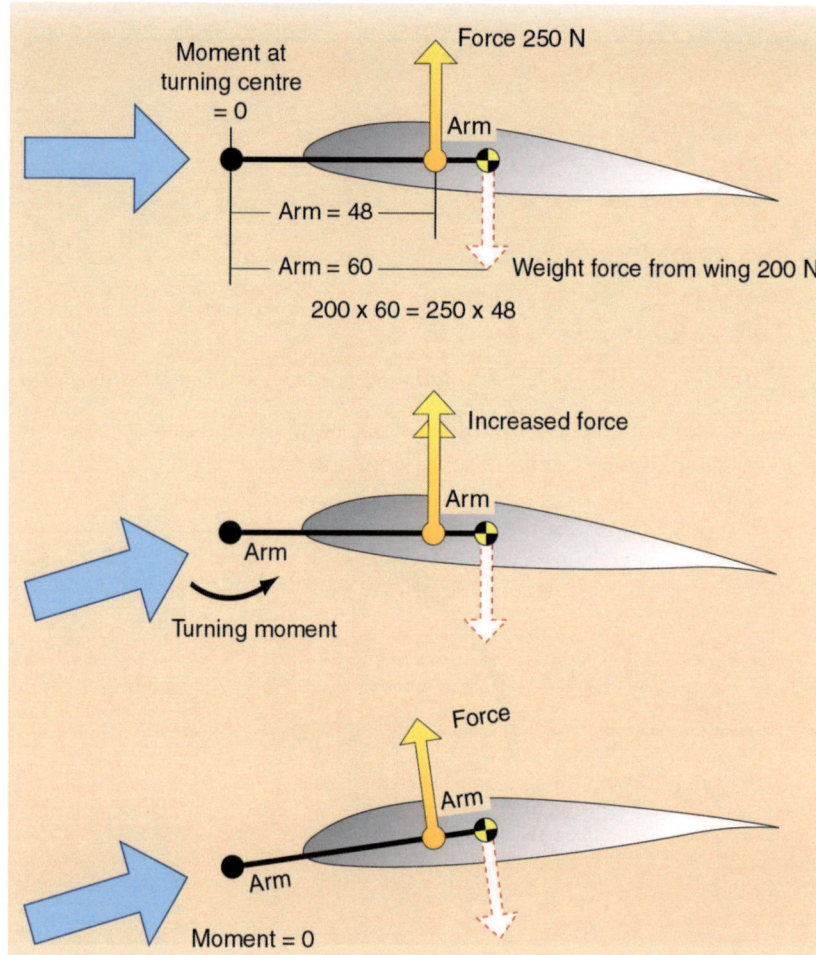

Figure 10.18

With the turning centre in front of the lift force, the wing will be stable

10.2.3   *Moment and stability of the entire aircraft*

The wings are not the only aerodynamic surfaces that create turning moments. The fuselage and tail surfaces also generate a C.P., which varies with different A.o.A., consequently the C.P. of the entire aircraft may be differently located in relation to the C.P. of the wings.

Consequently, when designing a statically stable aircraft, the wing has to be located on the fuselage in such position that the C.G. of the entire aircraft is at the C.P. of the entire aircraft in a steady flight. In this situation the sum of all forces and moments is zero and the aircraft is in trim.

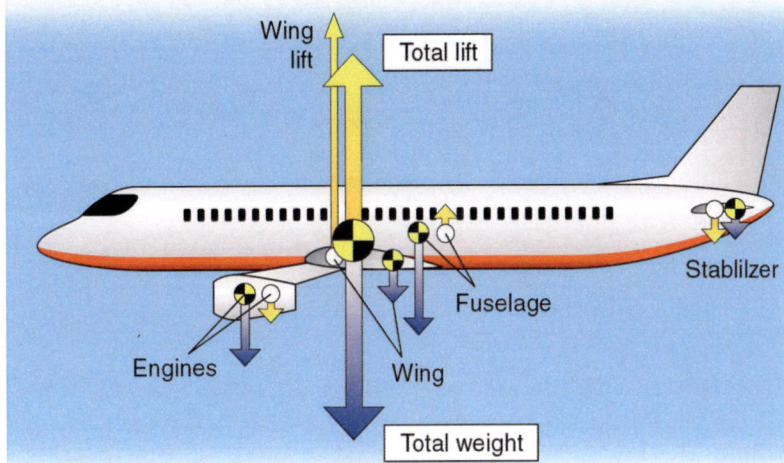

Figure 10.19

Note that the figure is much simplified and not geometrically perfect.

Furthermore, on a statically stable aircraft, the A.C. of the entire aircraft has to be located behind the total C.G. of the aircraft. In this situation where the total C.G. is in front of A.C. an increased A.o.A. will increase the lift which turns the nose down, thus decreasing the A.o A. It will also reduce the lift to what it was before the disturbance. In this situation the aircraft is statically stable.

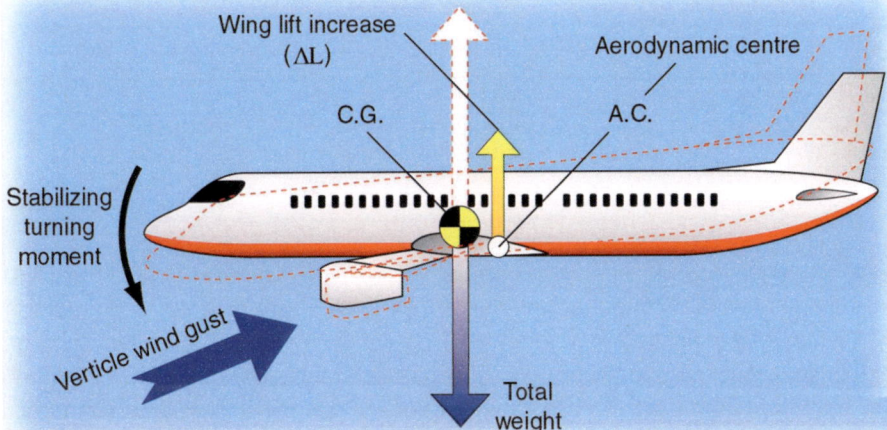

Figure 10.20

The changed lift after a disturbance acts at a point called the aerodynamic centre: A C

> In order to have a stable aircraft, the C.G. of the entire aircraft must be in front of the A.C.

10.2.4 Pitching moments

Before continuing, we should have a look at the moment in the pitching plane around the C.G.

We assume that all pitching down moments are negative and all pitching up moments positive.

> Nose down moments are negative while nose up moments are positive

If we plot a graph of lift and pitching moment for a statically stable aircraft, we will see something that is very important. Let us suppose that we are flying in a trimmed condition. A disturbance caused by a vertical up-wind component causes an increase in the angle of attack, which in turn generates an increase in lift.

This produces a nose down rotation that decreases the angle of attack and, as a consequence, also the lift and the moment.

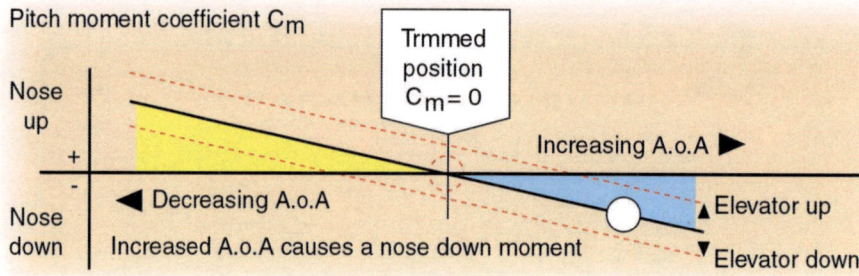

Figure 10.21

The final result is a return to the trimmed position.

Due to the effect of inertia, the angle of attack decreases a little too much, thus decreasing the lift. The aircraft enters the positive moment area, which will result in a nose up moment and an increase in the A.o.A. and, as a consequence, a further increase in lift, thus bringing the aircraft back towards its initial trimmed position.

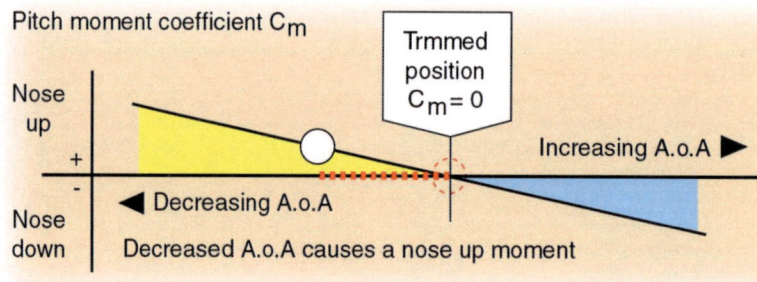

Figure 10.22

It can be stated as a rule that, when aircraft generate this kind of variation in lift, they have positive static stability. The aerodynamic reason for this behaviour is that (in respect of a conventional stable aircraft) the centre of gravity of the entire aircraft is usually in front of the point where the disturbed centre of lift (aerodynamic centre) acts. Aircraft usually have positive static stability by having C.G. of the entire aircraft in front of A.C. From now on, when we are dealing with the C.G. we mean the C.G. of the entire aircraft, and when we are dealing with the impact of a disturbance, it is acting on the A.C.

10.2.5   *Effect of the tailplane*

Even though the change in lift moment acts in a stabilising way, it is normally not enough to give sufficient positive static stability. However, there are some aircraft, the so-called "flying wings", which are solely stabilised by changes in the lift moment of the wings.

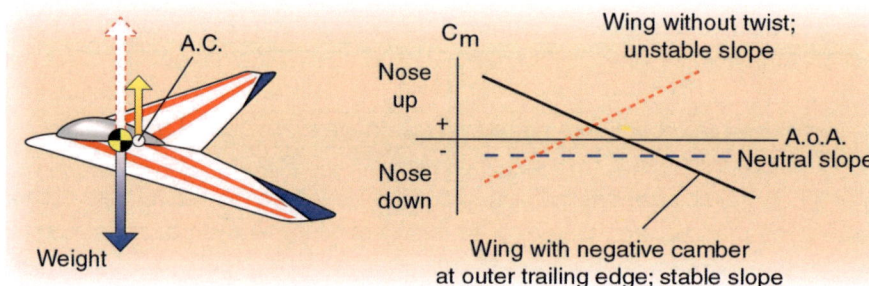

Figure 10.23

The necessary downward force at the outer part of the wing reduces the total effect of the flying wing. One way to increase the stability is to add an aerodynamic surface, called tailplane or horizontal stabiliser, at a relatively long distance from the main wing.

When the distribution of forces from the C.G. and C.P. causes a nose down moment, the tailplane has to provide a downward aerodynamic force to generate an equal nose up moment.

However, the horizontal stabiliser should not only balance the nose down moment, it should also improve the total stability. Consequently, it is another aerofoil that can produce either negative or positive lift. It is either symmetrical, or it has a negative camber.

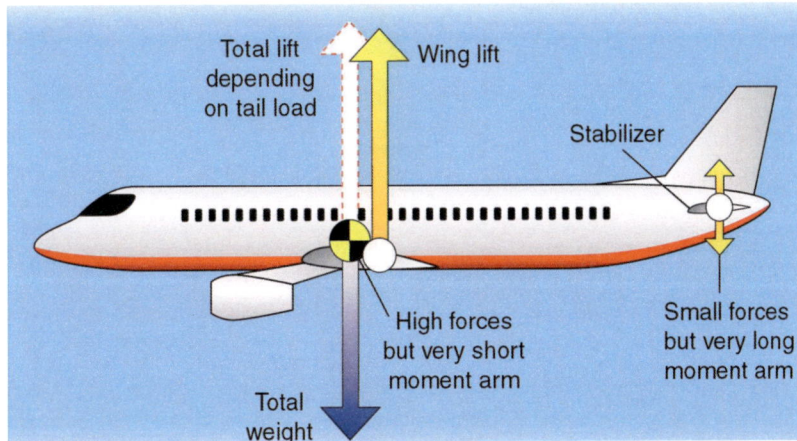

Figure 10.24

The tailplane is a surface that generates negative or positive lift

The force it generates must only be sufficient to generate a pitching effect necessary to balance the aircraft. Due to the long moment arm between the tailplane and the C.G, its surface can be much smaller than that of the mainplane.

10.3   *Aircraft axes and planes of rotation trim condition*

10.3.1   *Definition of the three axes of reference*

We refer the rotating motion of an aircraft to the motion around three axes, each one passing through the centre of gravity and each one perpendicular to the other. The lateral axis runs through the aircraft from one side to the other, passing through the centre of gravity. Movement around the lateral axis is called pitching. Stability around the lateral axis is called longitudinal stability because it is concerned with stability in the longitudinal or pitching plane.

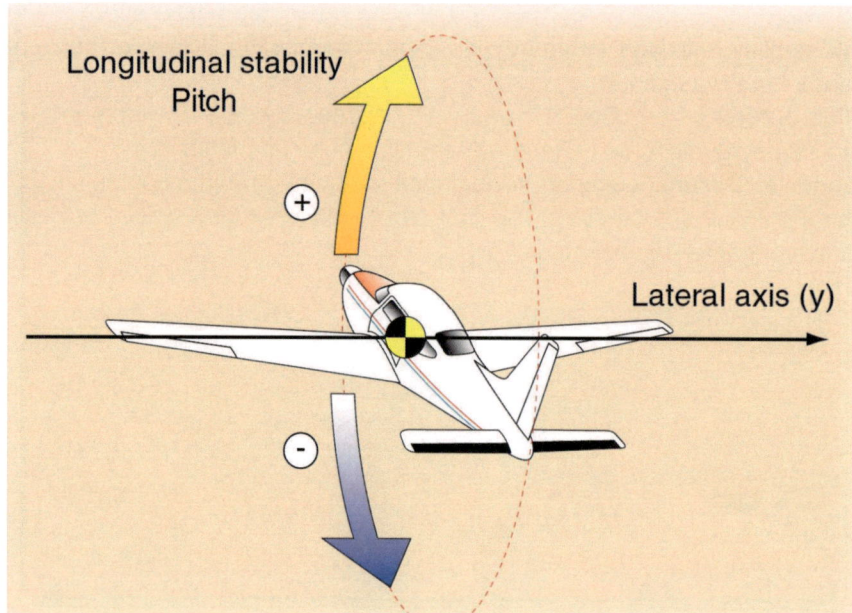

Figure 10.25

Pitching is the movement around the lateral axis. Stability around the lateral axis is called longitudinal stability

The longitudinal axis runs forward and aft, from the tip of the tail to the nose of the aircraft, passing through the centre of gravity. Movement around the longitudinal axis is called rolling. Stability around the longitudinal axis is called lateral stability because it is concerned with movements in the lateral or rolling plane.

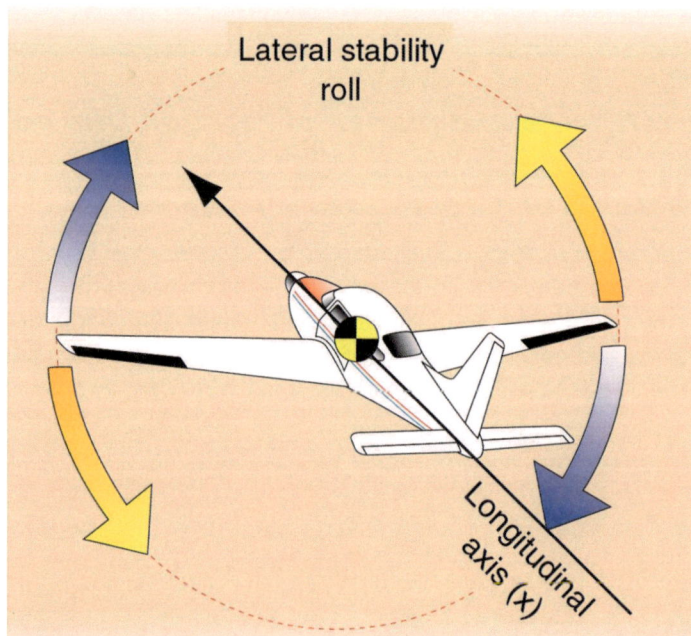

Figure 10.26

Rolling is the movement around the longitudinal axis. Stability around the longitudinal axis is called lateral stability

The directional axis, also called the normal axis, forms a right angle with the plane formed by the intersection of the longitudinal and lateral axes, passing through the centre of gravity. Movement around the directional axis is called yawing. Stability around the directional axis is called directional stability because it is concerned with stability in the directional or yawing plane.

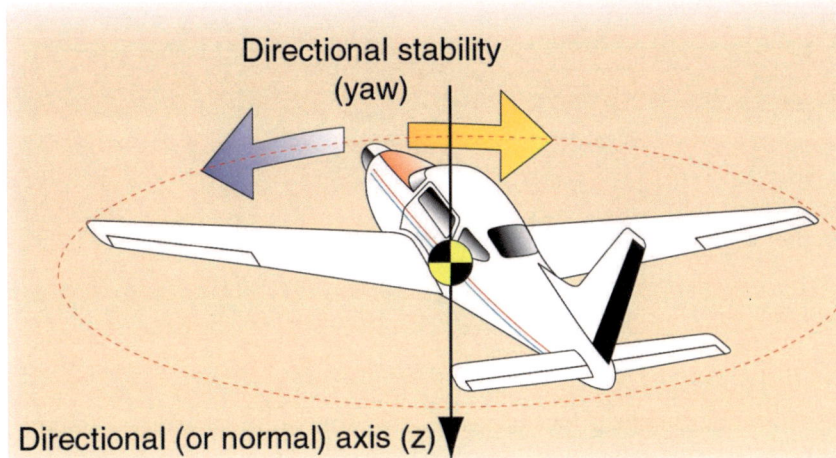

Figure 10.27

Yawing is the movement around the directional axis. Stability around the directional axis is called directional stability

10.3.2 *Trim condition*

Positive pitch stability means that a forward movement of the stick is required to increase the aircraft speed (forward stick lowers the aircraft nose, reduces the A.o.A and trims the aircraft to a higher speed). A backwards movement of the stick decreases the speed. It should be possible to trim the aircraft to all desired flight conditions by use of the control surfaces. The trimmed situation is reached when the sum of all forces and of all moments is zero.

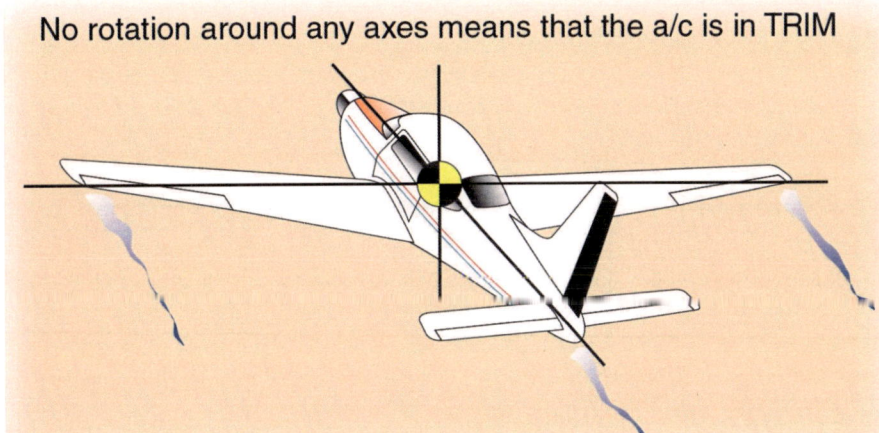

Figure 10.28

An aircraft is trimmed when the sum of all forces and all moments is zero. You trim the aircraft by means of the control surfaces

To ease the workload for the pilot, the aircraft has some kind of trimtabs to change the stick forces round all three axes. As a minimum requirement the stick forces for pitch round the lateral axes should be adjustable during flight. When you adjust the trim or set the trim at a certain position, your intention is to reduce the control forces to zero.

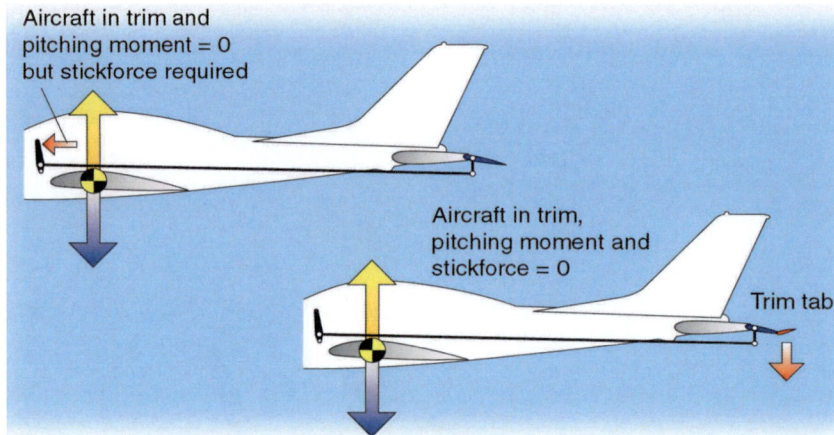

Figure 10.29

Notice the difference between trimming the aircraft and trimming the stickforce. Trimming the moments to zero is done by means of the control surfaces, trimming the stick force to zero is done by means of trim tabs on the control surfaces

When there are changes in the aerodynamic forces on the wing or tailplane due to small or large variations in speed or use of high lift devices, you have to trim the aircraft and the stick forces. Another reason for trimming is when a change in the position of the C.G. occurs, e.g. longitudinal motion of passengers or lateral difference in wing tank fuel. To ease your workload, trim the stick forces to zero as soon as possible. However, do not trim the stick forces to zero in a turn; it should be trimmed for straight flight only.

10.4 Longitudinal Stability

10.4.1 Definition of the tailplane as main stabilising factor

To be longitudinally stable, an aircraft must have the tendency to return to trimmed angle of attack after any disturbance without being influenced by the pilot.
In the case of conventional aircraft the horizontal stabiliser provides the main stabilising force. Depending on where the centre of gravity is positioned with respect to the wing/fuselage centre of pressure, the tail lift for trim can be either upwards or downwards.

On a conventional aircraft the horizontal stabiliser provides the main stabilising force

We shall now look at how the position of the C.G. with respect to the centre of pressure of the wing/fuselage affects the direction and magnitude of this force and the longitudinal stability of the aircraft.
In the next figure you see an aircraft in straight and level flight with the C.G. located well ahead of the wing/fuselage C.P. With respect to the moments around the centre of gravity we see that the wing/fuselage lift produces a nose-down moment of 1680 Nm.

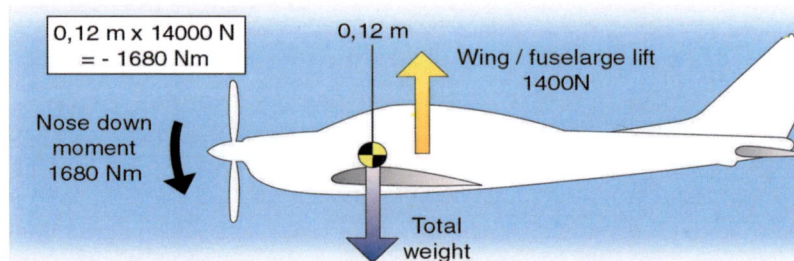

Figure 10.30

To maintain level flight there must be an equal moment in the opposite direction. This is provided by the stabiliser and is of course also 1680 Nm. The distance between the centre of gravity is 3.36 m, so the tail down force must be 500 N.

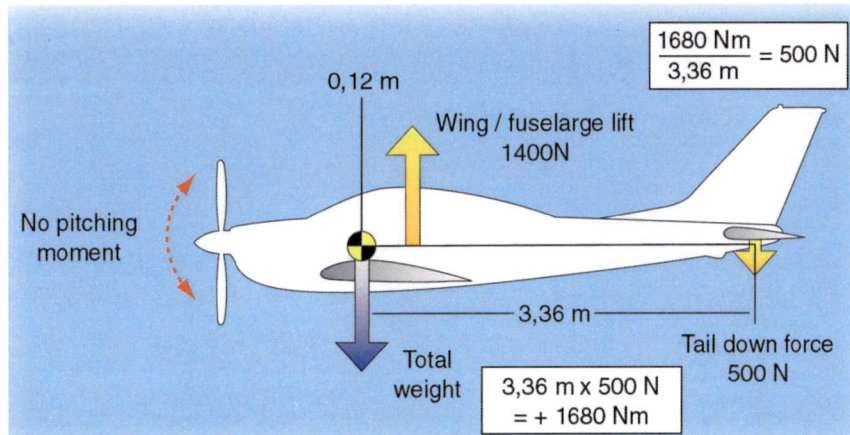

Figure 10.31

The sum of the moments is now zero. The same must be true for the forces acting on the aircraft. We see that the weight of the aircraft of 13500 N and the tail down force of 500 N is balanced by the wing lift of 14000 N.

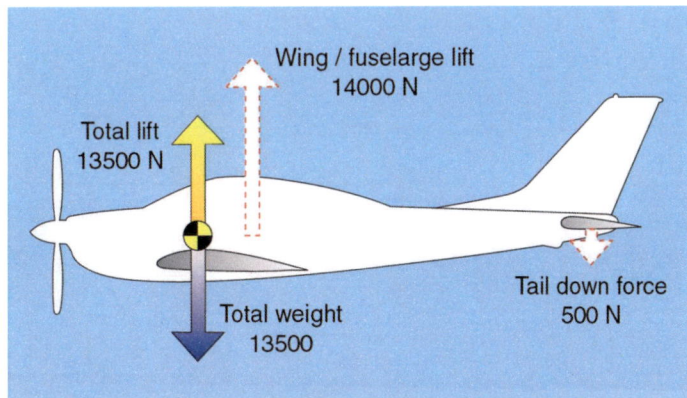

Figure 10.32

Now let us assume that the aircraft is hit by a gust so that the angle of attack for both wings and stabiliser changes. The wing/fuselage lift increases and the force downward of the stabiliser is reduced. The nose down moment of the wing will therefore increase and the stabiliser 'nose up' moment will decrease. The net result for the statically stable aircraft is a nose-down moment because of the change in total lift DL, which acts at the aerodynamic centre A.C. and which brings the aircraft back to its original angle of attack.

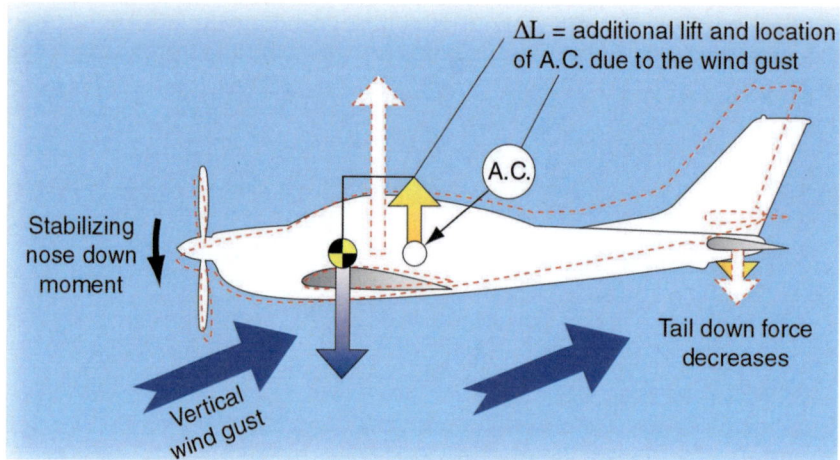

ΔL = additional lift and location of A.C. due to the wind gust

A.C.

Stabilizing nose down moment

Tail down force decreases

Vertical wind gust

Figure 10.33

What happens when the C.G. lies behind the wing/fuselage C.P? In this case the wing lift causes a nose-up moment. In order to balance this, the stabiliser, now having a shorter arm, must produce a relatively higher upward force to produce a nose-down moment, higher than the nose-up moment of the wing. In this case there still is a stabilising moment.

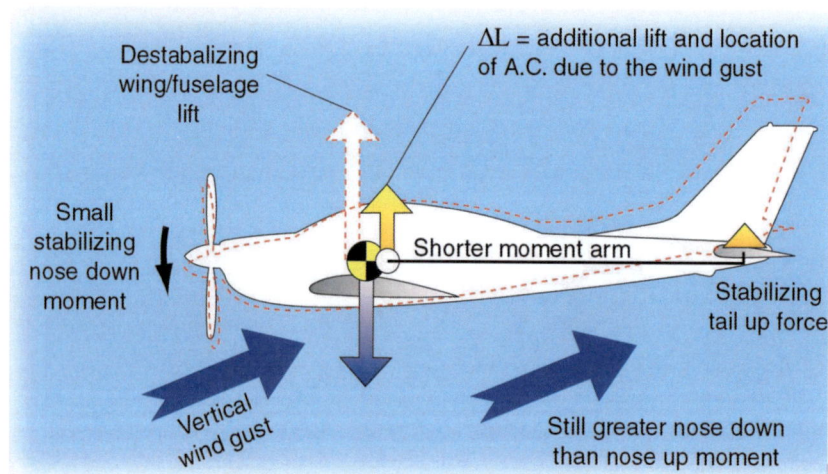

Destabalizing wing/fuselage lift

ΔL = additional lift and location of A.C. due to the wind gust

Small stabilizing nose down moment

Shorter moment arm

Stabilizing tail up force

Vertical wind gust

Still greater nose down than nose up moment

Figure 10.34

Finally we look at the case where the C.G. is located at the same position as the A.C. The tail may very well still give a large upward force, but the change in total lift (ΔL), that acts at the A.C. will not give any turning moment. With respect to the moments around the centre of gravity we see that a disturbance from a wind gust produces no moment since the A.C. has the same location as the C.G.

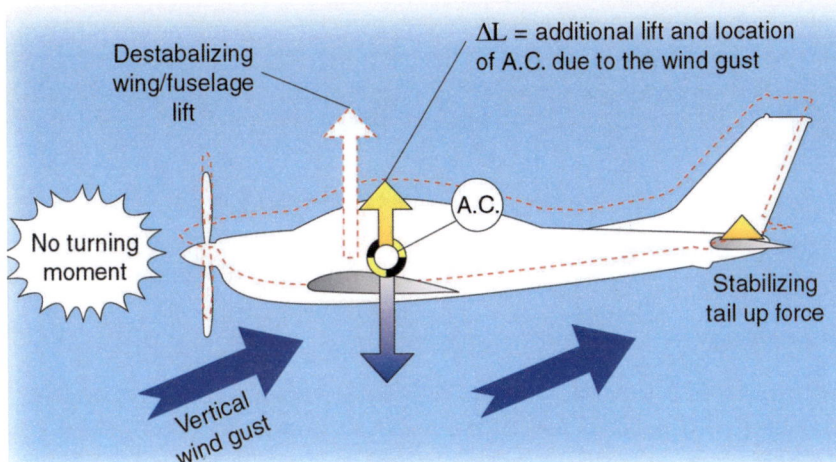

Figure 10.35

If the C.G. has the same vertical position or is aft of the A.C. of the wing, the wing/fuselage lift produces a destabilising moment and the moment arm for the stabiliser is reduced.

10.4.2   *Neutral point*

When the C.G. has a certain position compared to the wing/fuselage C.P. the aircraft will not receive a sufficiently stabilised moment from the tail surface. It will remain in the new attitude instead of turning back to its previous position. Consequently, when the C.G is located far too aft of the C.P. of the wing, i.e. the C.G. and A.C. of the aircraft coincides, the aircraft will be indifferent, or neutral static stable.

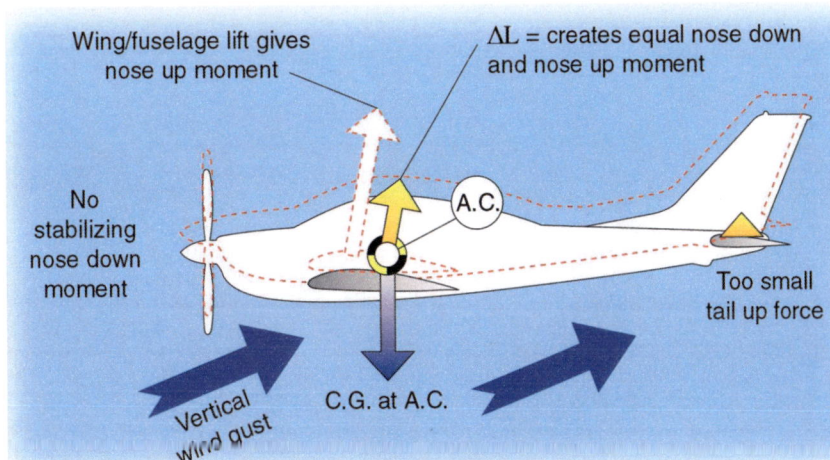

Figure 10.36

Consequently, the point along the longitudinal axis where the position of the C.G. causes neutral or indifferent stability is called the Neutral Point.

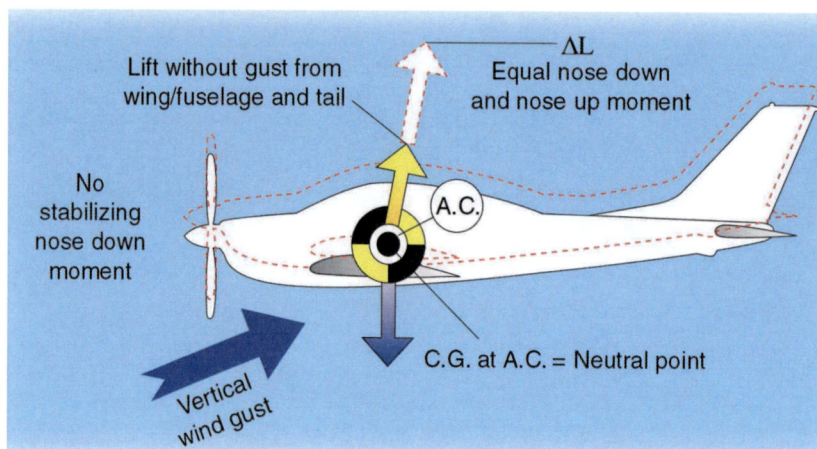

Figure 10.37

When the C.G is positioned aft of the neutral point, the increase in stabiliser lift is not great enough, thus a destabilising moment is created. In this situation the whole aircraft becomes unstable. It will pitch up, causing a higher A.o.A which creates a further increase in lift and a greater nose up moment. Consequently, an unstable aircraft shows a natural tendency to diverge from the trimmed flight attitude.

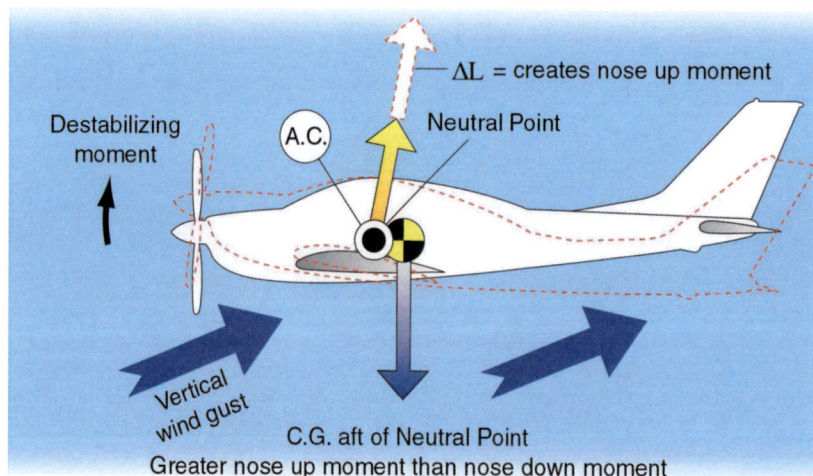

Figure 10.38

If you try to use elevator you may not be able to provide the correct moment at the correct time. The elevator will become too light and sensitive and the aircraft will eventually go out of control.

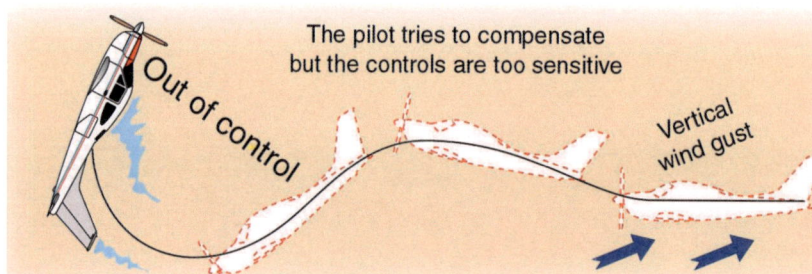

Figure 10.39

Consequently, as the position of the centre of gravity moves aft, the longitudinal stability is reduced and the aircraft may become dangerously unstable.

> If the C.G. is positioned behind the neutral point, the aircraft is statically unstable

10.4.3   *Static Margin and MAC*

To assure good longitudinal stability an aircraft is usually designed to avoid the C.G. being too close to the neutral point. The distance between C.G. and the neutral point, expressed as a fraction of the wing Mean Aerodynamic wing Chord (MAC) in %, is called the static margin. The designer, using a complex formula, defines the Mean Aerodynamic wing Chord (MAC). Its location is approximately wing area/wingspan. In the example below, the MAC is where the wing chord is 1.5m.

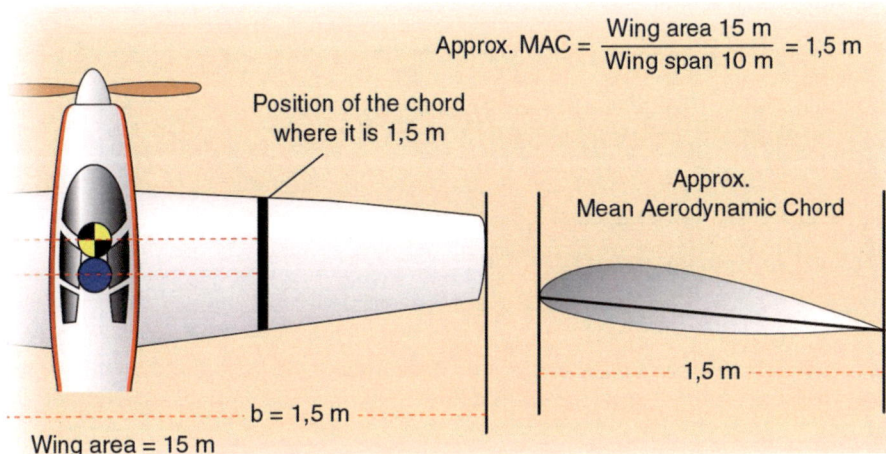

Figure 10.40

The distance between the C.G. and the neutral point is a direct measure of the longitudinal static stability.

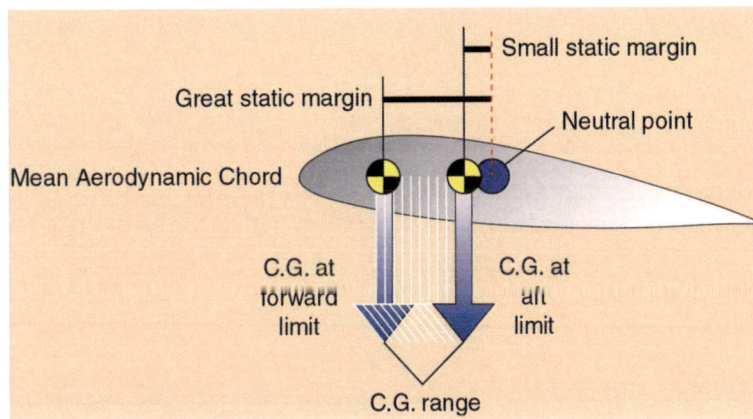

Figure 10.41

> The distance between the C.G. and the neutral point is called the static margin and is expressed as a percentage of MAC. A small static margin gives reduced pitch stability and vice versa

A small static margin reduces the pitch stability of the aircraft (and vice versa) as can be seen on the coefficient graph below of the pitch moment.

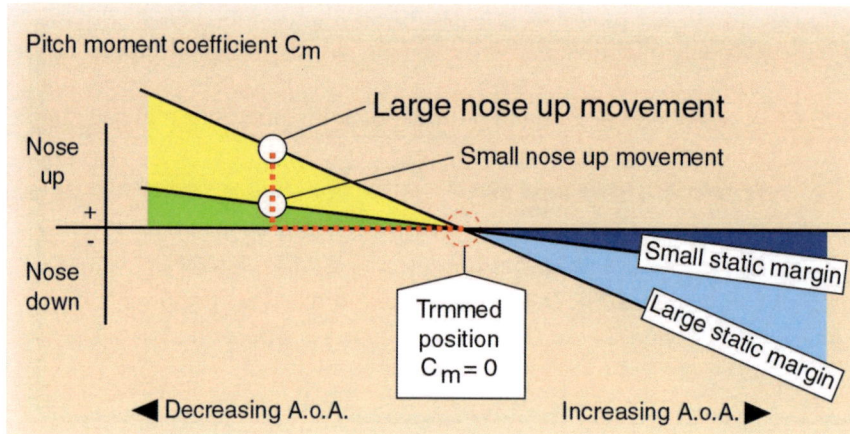

Figure 10.42

10.4.4   *Ballast or weight trim*

If the static margin in a certain loading situation is too small, the aircraft has to be loaded with ballast or be weight trimmed. It has to be located at such a location that the position of the C.G. is within the stated range. It may also be necessary to add ballast in some aircraft when operating without payload.

10.4.5   *Stick force*

Since the elevator changes the lift forces of the whole tail in order to induce pitching motions, the stick deflection and force will change with the static margins. A large static margin gives a large elevator stick force while a small static margin gives a small elevator stick force.

If the stick force is too small, the manoeuvre will easily be too great and it will be nearly impossible to find the trimmed position of the controls. It follows therefore, that the stick force cannot be allowed to be too low. By restricting the aft limit of the C.G. the designer can set the lower limit for the stick force necessary to change the A.o.A.

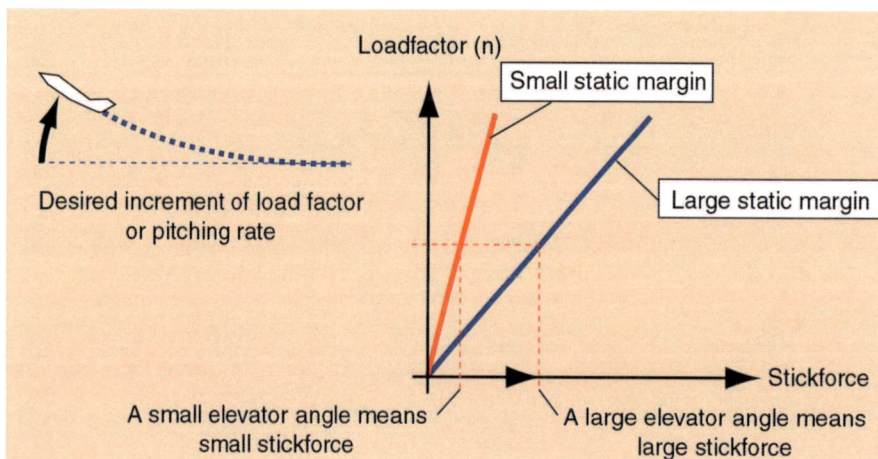

Figure 10.43

Exceeding the aft C.G. limit means too low stability and too low pitch control forces. On the contrary, the forward limit of C.G. is often reached when the pitch rate from the elevator input is at its lower limits.

However, the stability must not be so great that it requires a large control force for manoeuvring. If so, the aircraft has become what we call: dangerously stable. Consequently the range of the static margin is often determined by forward limit: not too low pitching rate or a large control force, aft limit: not too high pitching rate or a small stick force for a given pitching rate.

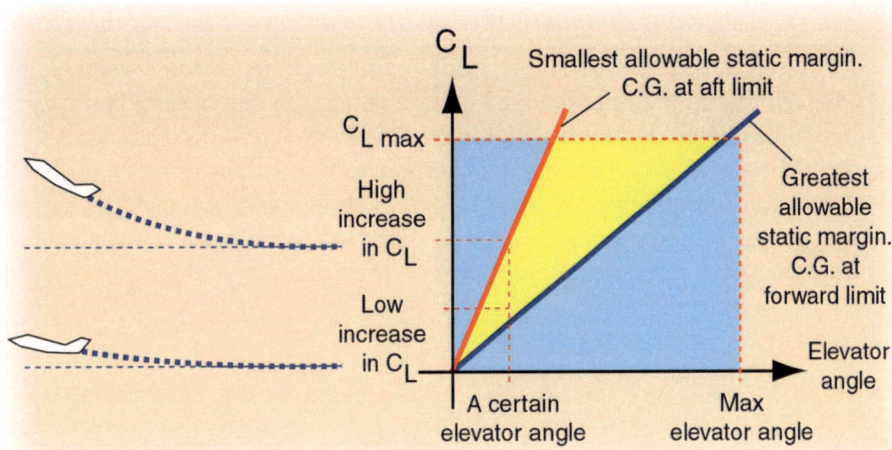

Figure 10.44

> Exceeding a forward C.G. limit means too heavy elevator and low pitching rate

Here we have a design problem; an aircraft with great positive stability, which is desirable, is heavy to manoeuvre. But an aircraft with reduced positive stability is easy to manoeuvre!

> High positive stability makes the aircraft heavy to manoeuvre. Reduced positive stability makes the aircraft easy to manoeuvre

10.4.5.1 Variation in stick force with airspeed

When you have trimmed the stick force to be zero at a given airspeed, the lift coefficient and the A.o.A are fixed by the airspeed and weight, and so is the A.o.A of the tailplane. When the speed is increased without changing the trim setting, the tail down (or up) force will be changed accordingly, making the aircraft untrimmed. The nose tends to rise. In order to maintain longitudinal balance you have to push the stick forward and re-trim the stickforce. This change in stick force with speed is valid for all controls. Consequently, you have to trim the aircraft again when you have changed the airspeed or changed the aircraft configuration, e.g. lowered the flaps.

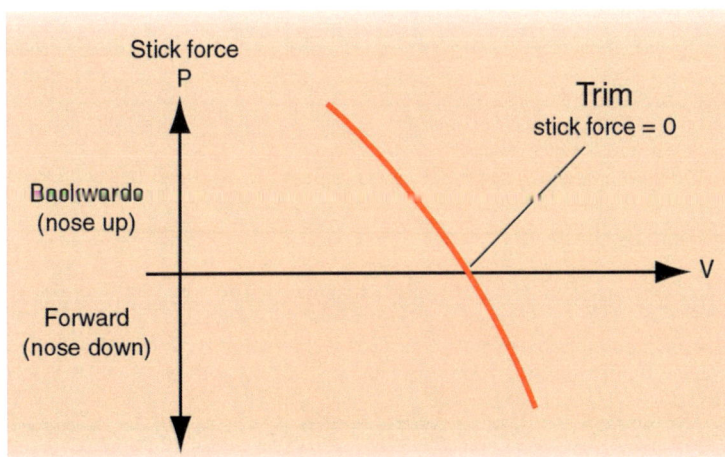

Figure 10.45

A change in airspeed or in aircraft configuration, will change the trim control setting.

10.4.5.2   *The contribution of friction in the system, down-spring, Bob Weight*

Low friction in the control system is desirable. The hinge moment of the control surfaces, due to a change in α or β, should be small. However, the moment caused by the angle of the control surface should be defined so that it can be made to harmonise with the stick force/g. In other words, the stick force should mainly be a result of the movement of the stick. Another way to increase the longitudinal speed stability is to add a spring that tends to pull the elevator downwards. One way to obtain certain stick forces independent of the position of C.G. and flight conditions is to add a Bob Weight to the stick or the control column. The Bob Weight is mounted in front of the stick and it exerts a force forward (on the stick) that increases with increased load factor.

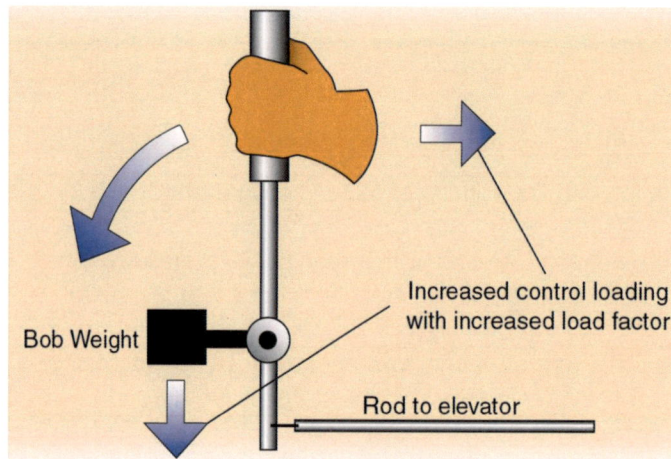

Figure 10.46

10.4.5.3   *Trim drag*

In most flight conditions the aircraft will have more or less downward load on the stabiliser. Trimming an aircraft is done by giving the elevator (or the whole horizontal surface) a certain deflection. The deflection of the elevator causes a total aerodynamic force that has a component of drag called trim drag. Usually the trim drag is 1 - 2% of the total drag.

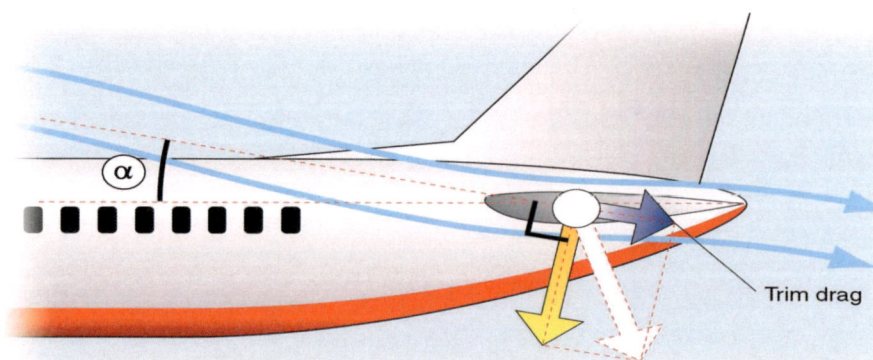

Figure 10.47

> The total aerodynamic force from the tail surface has a component of drag called trim drag

In order to obtain the lowest possible drag, which is especially important at long range cruising speed, the load inside the aircraft should be distributed in such way that the C.G. is rather aft, maybe as aft as possible within the approved limits. This will reduce the trim drag considerably. However, as you know, the stability will be reduced, so you have to be sure that the C.G. really is within the stated limits for the aircraft.

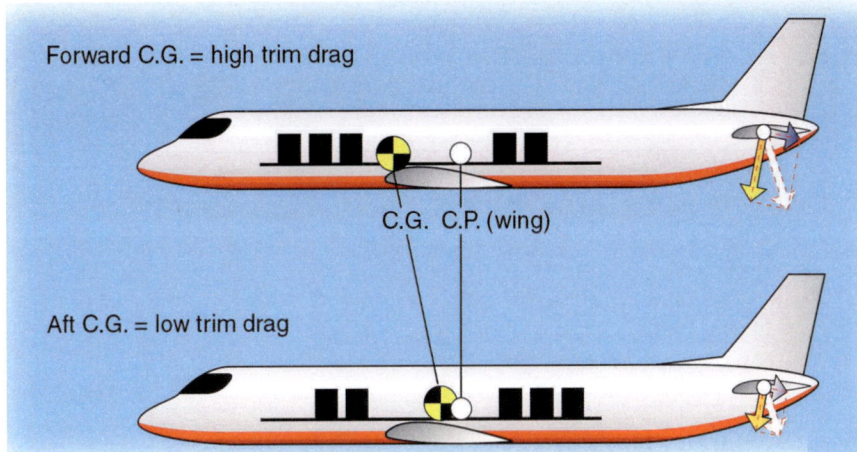

Figure 10.48

From the fuel economy point of view the C.G. has to be near its aft limit in order to produce the smallest possible trim drag

At this point, an important rule must be learnt and remembered, i.e. that of staying within the loading limitations given in the Pilot Operating Handbook or Flight Manual, while also taking into account the changes in the centre of gravity which result from the consumption of fuel. Large transport aircraft with extensive speed and C.G. ranges often use a variable incidence stabiliser, because this allows a wide C.G. range without sacrificing useful elevator deflection in a wide speed envelope.

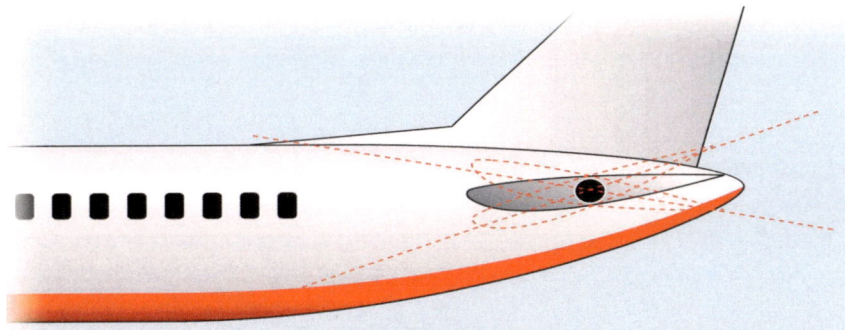

Figure 10.49

A variable incidence stabiliser allows a wide C.G. range at a wide speed envelope and reduces the trim drag

Another way to reduce the trim drag is to use a lifting surface in front of the main wing, a so called canard, instead of a downloaded surface behind the main wing. The download on the aft surface requires an extra lift from the main wing in addition to that required to counteract the aircraft weight. This means higher induced drag than from the canard configuration. However, a canard configuration must be very well designed to assure that the canard reaches stall before the main wing in order to get the required stability within the whole speed- and C.G. range. A common disadvantage of the canard design is that it requires a longer take-off distance than a conventional design.

CRANFIELD AVIATION TRAINING SCHOOL LTD. PART-FCL GBR.ATO-0136
CATS INNOVATION CENTRE, LUTON, Bedfordshire LU2 8DL U.K.   www.catsaviation.com

10-22   Principles of Flight

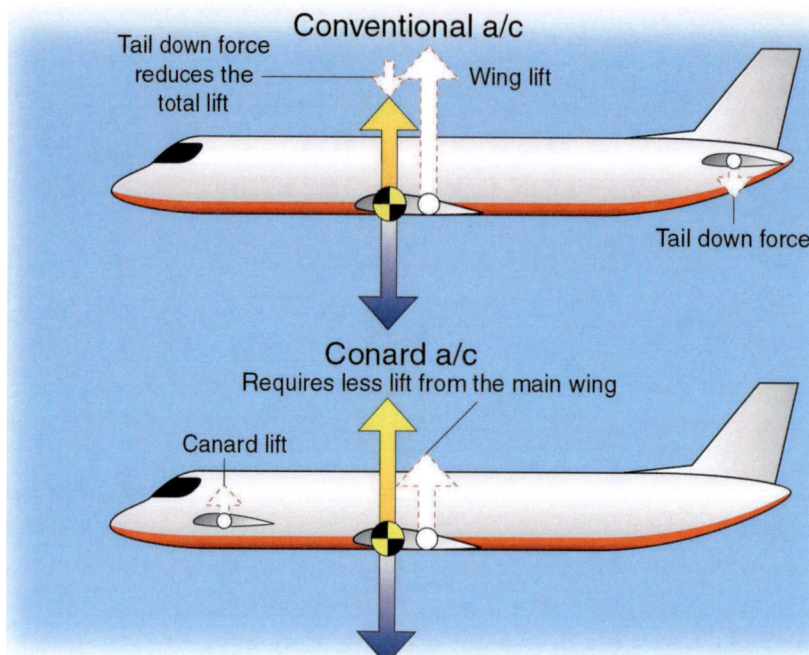

Figure 10.50

It is also important to know how the trim and stability of an aircraft is affected when the high lift devices are extended or retracted. A delta-winged canard aircraft with the canard close to the wing, i.e. close coupled canard configuration, has a high total increase in lift at low speeds and high A.o.A. But a straight-winged canard aircraft will only experience a limited increase in the total lift at low speeds due to the limitation in pitching moment when using trailing edge flaps on the wings. The total effect instead may be an increase in take-off distance.

10.4.6   *Use of high lift devices*

When the flaps are lowered, the total lift will be the same at a lower A.o.A, but the centre of pressure will move more or less aft due to the changed pressure distribution, which increases the nose down moment.

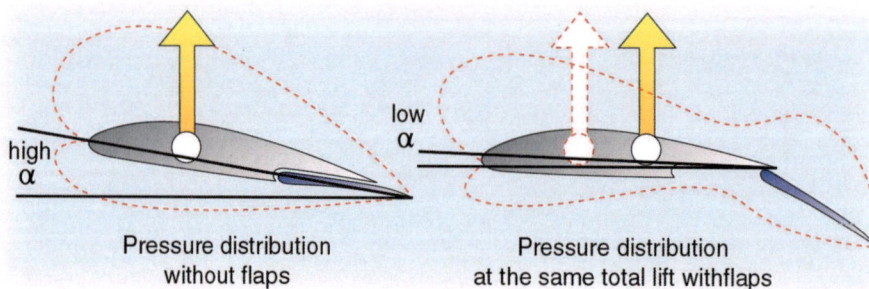

Figure 10.51

The increased nose down moment must be compensated for by an increase in the horizontal tail download.

CRANFIELD AVIATION TRAINING SCHOOL LTD. PART-FCL GBR.ATO-0136
CATS CATS INNOVATION CENTRE, LUTON, Bedfordshire LU2 8DL U.K.   www.catsaviation.com
10-23   Principles of Flight

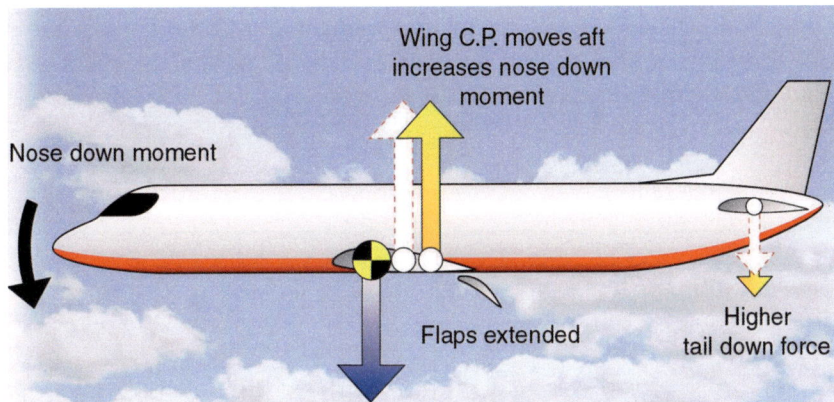

Figure 10.52

Some aircraft pitch up when lowering flaps despite an aft C.P. This is due to the downwash effect behind the wings, which increases when lowering the flaps and results in a more negative stabiliser angle of attack than required. In general, an aircraft with a large horizontal tail will usually get a nose up moment and an aircraft with a small horizontal tail will usually get a nose down moment.

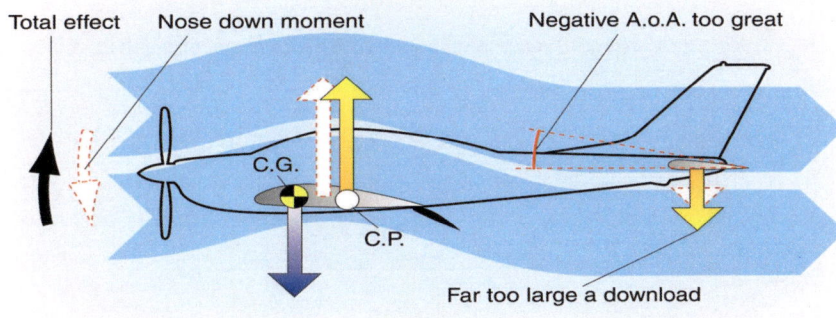

Figure 10.53

Lowered flaps always moves the C.P. rearwards and increases the tail-down force. Depending on the location of the stabiliser and its size, an increase in the downwash effect may lead to a change in trim into a nose up instead of a nose down moment. Lowered flaps will always result in an increase in the downward load on the stabiliser, which in turn will increase the risk of stabiliser stall when the C.G. is too far forward.

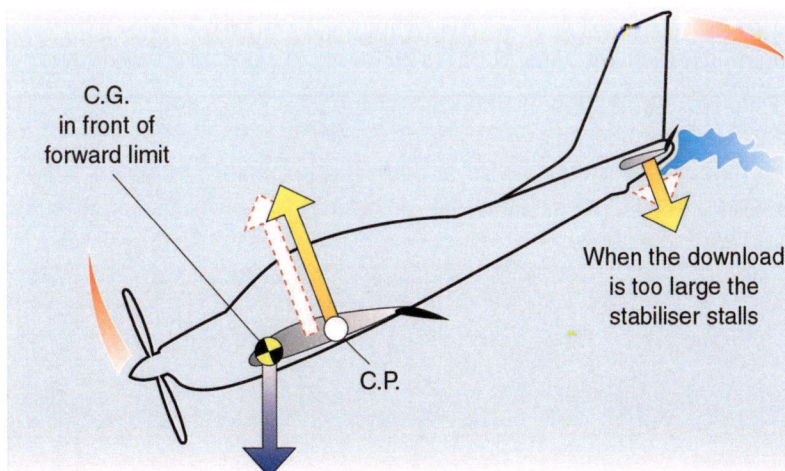

Figure 10.54

Contrary to trailing edge flaps, the C.P. will be moved forward when the slats of the leading edges are deflected. This is due to the increased suction over the leading edge that causes a slightly reduced nose down moment, maybe resulting in a very slight effect on trim.

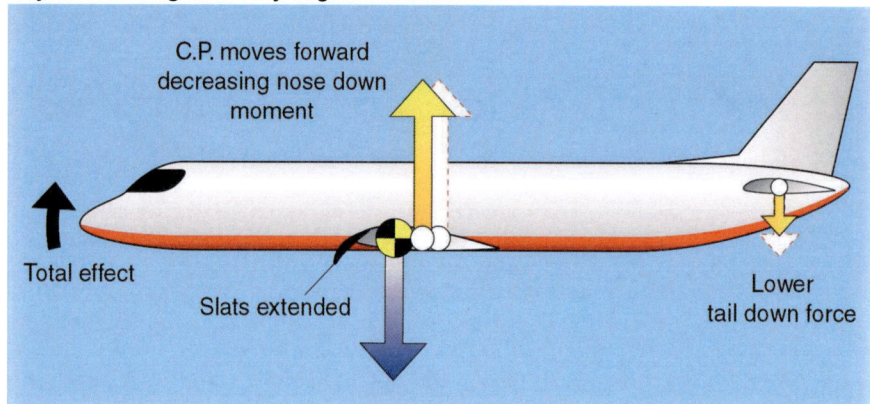

Figure 10.55

However, this motion of the C.P. forward is much smaller than the motion of the C.P. rearwards caused by deflected trailing edge flaps. So when slats are used together with flaps, the total effect may still be a pitch down motion.

10.4.7   *Effect of thrust and drag on longitudinal stability*

Any position of the trim is valid only at the speed at which it was set. As soon as the conditions change, a change in trim is necessary. If the engine's line of thrust is above or below the aircraft's centre of gravity, a change in pitch will occur as soon as the power is changed.

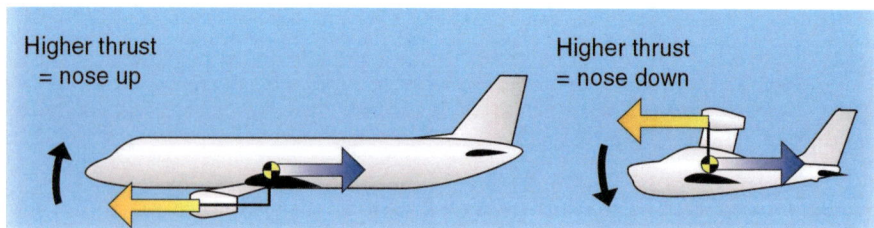

Figure 10.56

Due to the location of the engines, a power change often generates a longitudinal pitching moment

When the thrust line runs through the centre of gravity, a pitching moment can also occur due to the changed downwash effect on the stabiliser. The tail down force is the result of the free stream velocity and downwash from the wing, in other words, the airspeed. When the airspeed is increased the wing downwash effect of the wing also increases and so does the angle of attack of the tail and the tail down force, resulting in a nose up pitching moment. In the case of propeller-driven aircraft, the propeller slipstream affects the airflow around the tail. If the throttle is suddenly closed, the force of the slipstream drops together with an equal drop of tailforce and the aircraft lowers its nose.

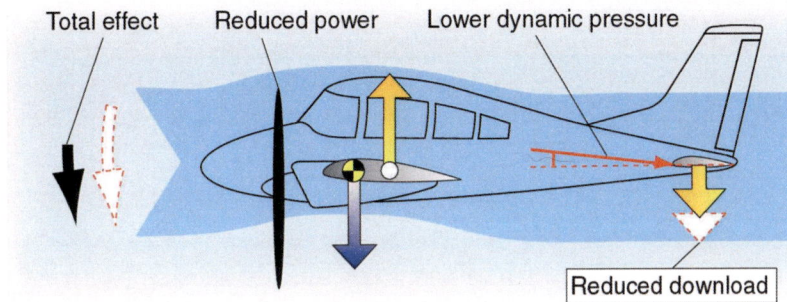

Figure 10.57

A change in power (slipstream) and/or airspeed alters the downwash effect and the tail down force, resulting in a changed pitching moment

Extended landing gears create very high drag. Since the landing gear is located below the C.G, of the aircraft, the drag from it will cause a nose down moment. This increased nose down moment will cause an increase in the tail down force required to maintain constant pitch attitude. The amount of drag, hence also the nose down moment, may vary when extending or raising the landing gear since the landing gear doors operate in various ways simultaneously.

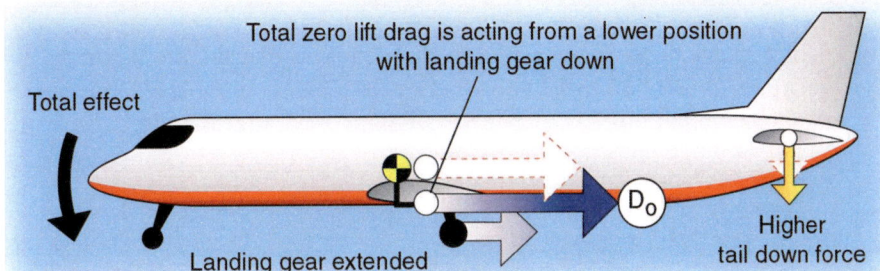

Figure 10.58

The drag from an extended landing gear causes an increased nose down moment making the tail down force higher

10.4.8   *Oscillations due to longitudinal dynamic stability*

The longitudinal stability of an aircraft may be divided into two main aspects: the static stability at a trimmed flight condition (trimmed speed and flight path) and the dynamic stability (the oscillation round the flight path of trimmed condition). An aircraft that has positive static stability may or may not have positive dynamic stability. As we have already learnt in section one, the oscillation of a body round its original path may or may not end with the return to its original path.

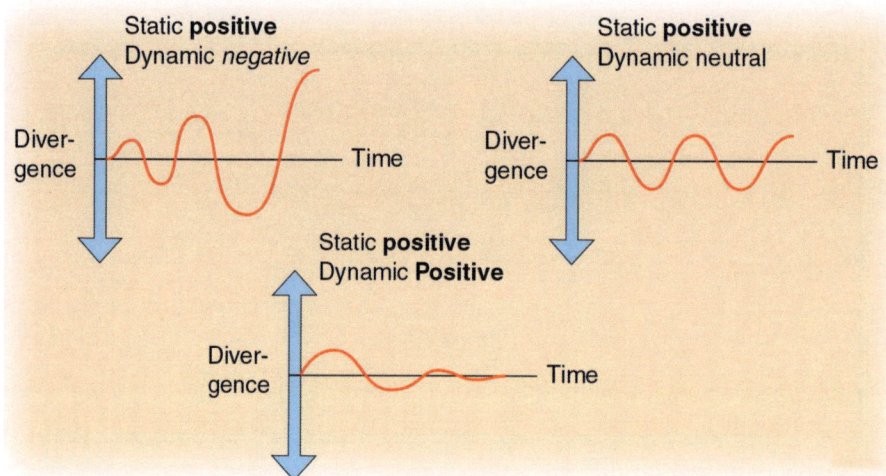

Figure 10.59

Dynamic stability is the oscillation round the trimmed condition.

An aircraft that has positive static stability may or may not have positive dynamic stability

All aircraft have two kinds of pitch oscillations: first a short period oscillation, secondly a long period one called phugoid or long mode oscillation. The short period oscillation must have positive dynamic stability where a change in attitude changes the A.o.A. and vice versa. If an aircraft is forced off its path abruptly, it will return to its original longitudinal position through a series of rapid converging oscillations.

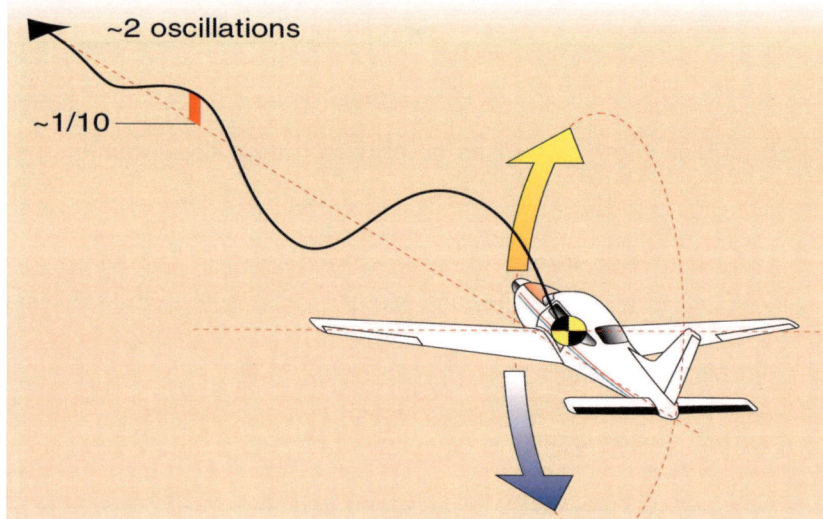

Figure 10.60

For small aircraft, the disturbance is normally damped after one oscillation to 1/10 of the initial amplitude, and completely damped after approximately two oscillations. Large aircraft, especially at high altitudes, are less damped, making it necessary to use the autopilot as an active dynamic damper. Usually, aircraft must have positive damping of the short period, even though they will return to their original longitudinal position through a series of rapid converging oscillations. The damping decreases with altitude. The short mode or rapid oscillations may last a second or less. If the short mode is unstable, the oscillations can increase dangerously before the pilot realises what is happening.

10.4.8.1   *Pilot induced oscillations*

Even if the short periods of oscillations are damped while the pilot is trying to stop them, he may get out of phase and reinforce the oscillations to the point where structural damage can occur. This is called Pilot Induced Oscillation. To stop it: let go of the control stick.

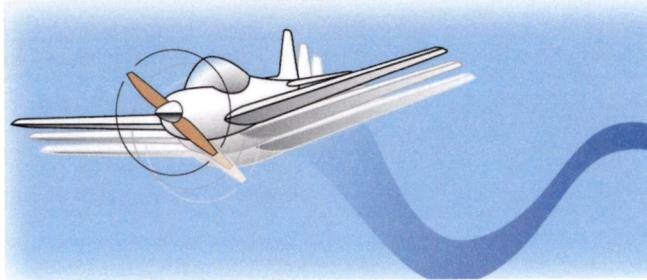

Figure 10.61

Phugoid is a long term constant trim and constant angle of attack oscillation

The oscillation is caused by the combination of a change in altitude and a change in speed. A disturbance will cause a reduction in speed, the reduction in speed will cause a loss of lift and a change in altitude which will cause an increase in speed etc. In other words: altitude is exchanged for speed and vice versa.

An aircraft may have a neutrally or negative phugoid and still be completely safe, notwithstanding it may cause rather great variations in altitude. The periods are tens of seconds or even minutes which, allow you enough time to keep the aircraft at the right attitude and to counteract oscillations. The most common way to counteract the phugoid oscillation is to use an auto-pilot in altitude hold mode.

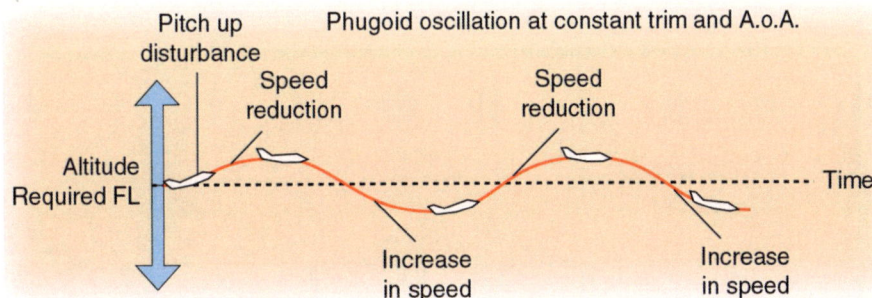

Figure 10.62

10.4.8.2   *Aircraft with static neutral or static negative longitudinal stability*

As you know, increased stability means decreased manoeuvrability. Jet fighters must be extremely manoeuvrable to be able to aim their weapons on another sharp turning enemy jet fighter making evasive actions. The fighter that can make the highest rate of turn may quickly have an advantage over the enemy aircraft, an advantage of highest importance for all fighters since World War One.

CRANFIELD AVIATION TRAINING SCHOOL LTD. PART-FCL GBR.ATO-0136
CATS CATS INNOVATION CENTRE, LUTON, Bedfordshire LU2 8DL U.K.   www.catsaviation.com

10-28   Principles of Flight

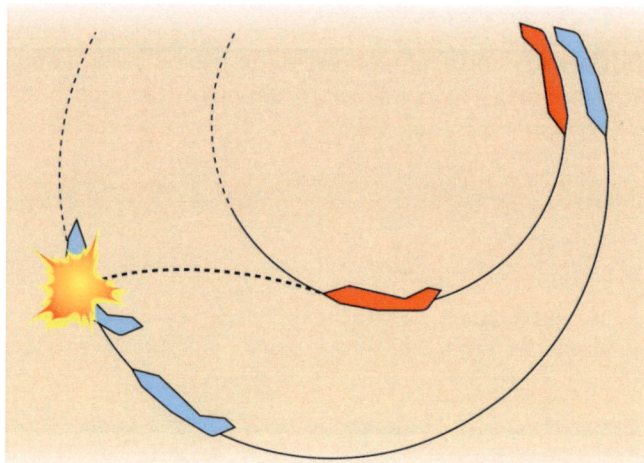

Figure 10.63

Very sharp turns require high manoeuvrability and low static stability. Having increased the manoeuvrability by being able to trim higher lift at lower drag, the aircraft designers have made it possible to reduce the static stability of an aircraft. To compensate for the low or negative static longitudinal stability, they have increased the dynamic stability by means of very rapid computers linked to the control system. In this way disturbances are immediately damped by means of control inputs from computers to the elevator and/or canard wing without the interference of the control stick. In other words: the pilot is not aware of the various stabilising inputs to the elevator, and experiences the aircraft as being stable.

Another advantage with this kind of control system is that it can adapt to changes in load, position of C.G. and the use of high lift devices without any action from the pilot. The pilot may have the same control response regardless of C.G.etc. This makes the aircraft very easy to fly.

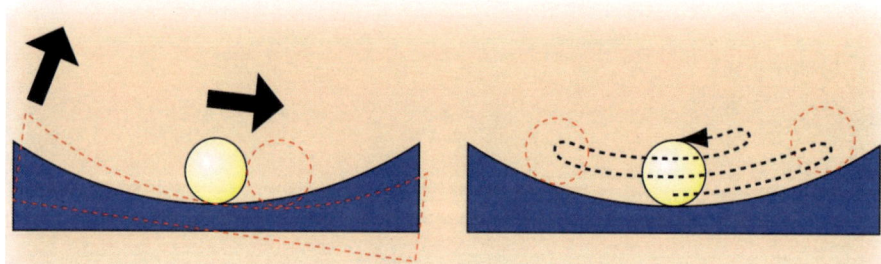

Figure 10.64

This highly manoeuvrable aircraft may be of conventional or canard design. However, a negatively static stable aircraft with a conventional aft stabiliser that has been damaged, may rapidly have an uncontrolled change in pitch leading to extreme load factors and a complete structural failure of the aircraft.

Modern fighters usually have relaxed or negative static longitudinal stability in order to increase the manoeuvrability.

10.4.9   Directional Stability

This section deals with stability in the yawing plane and how the design of the aircraft can affect this type of stability.

10.4.9.1   Definition

Directional stability is the natural ability of an aircraft to recover from a disturbance in the yawing plane

If the aircraft is disturbed from its flight path by a crosswind gust, it will first keep moving in the original direction due to its inertia. The aircraft will then be moving somewhat sideways through the air with its side surface exposed to the airflow. This is known as a sideslip.

All surfaces in front of the C.G. are directionally destabilising. If the aircraft has a greater side area aft of the C.G. than in front of C.G it will straighten up again towards the free stream and be directionally stable. In order to assure directional stability during the whole flight envelope, most aircraft are equipped with a vertical fin. The vertical fin, or vertical tail stabiliser, has a symmetrical aerofoil.

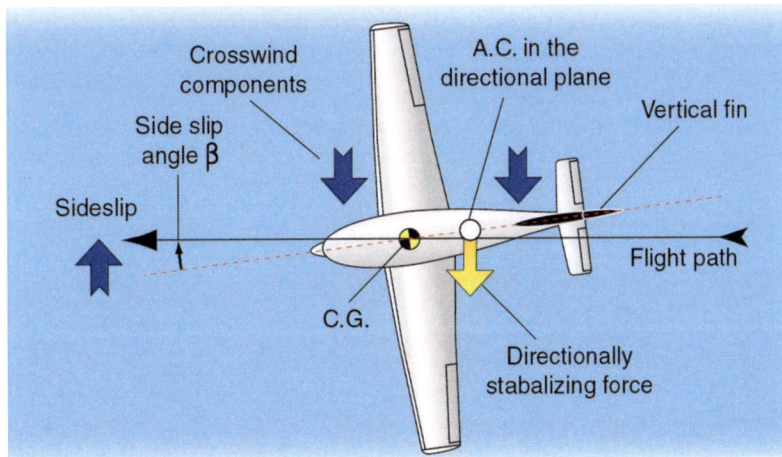

Figure 10.65

In case of a sideslip in any direction, the fin experiences an angle of attack that generates a lift force sideways that tends to reduce the sideslip angle (β) to zero. However, the heading will not be resumed as in the case of the altitude after a disturbance in pitch. The angle of yaw (ψ) is referred to as the angle between the longitudinal axis and a reference on earth.

10.4.10 *Aircraft design features affecting directional static stability*

10.4.10.1 *Side surface area*

Let us consider an example of an aircraft without a fin where the centre of pressure, thus also the aerodynamic centre of the side area, will be in front of the centre of gravity. (Compare with a symmetrical wing section.) In this case a destabilising moment is present. If the aircraft were displaced in yaw by a gust it would not go back to its original position.

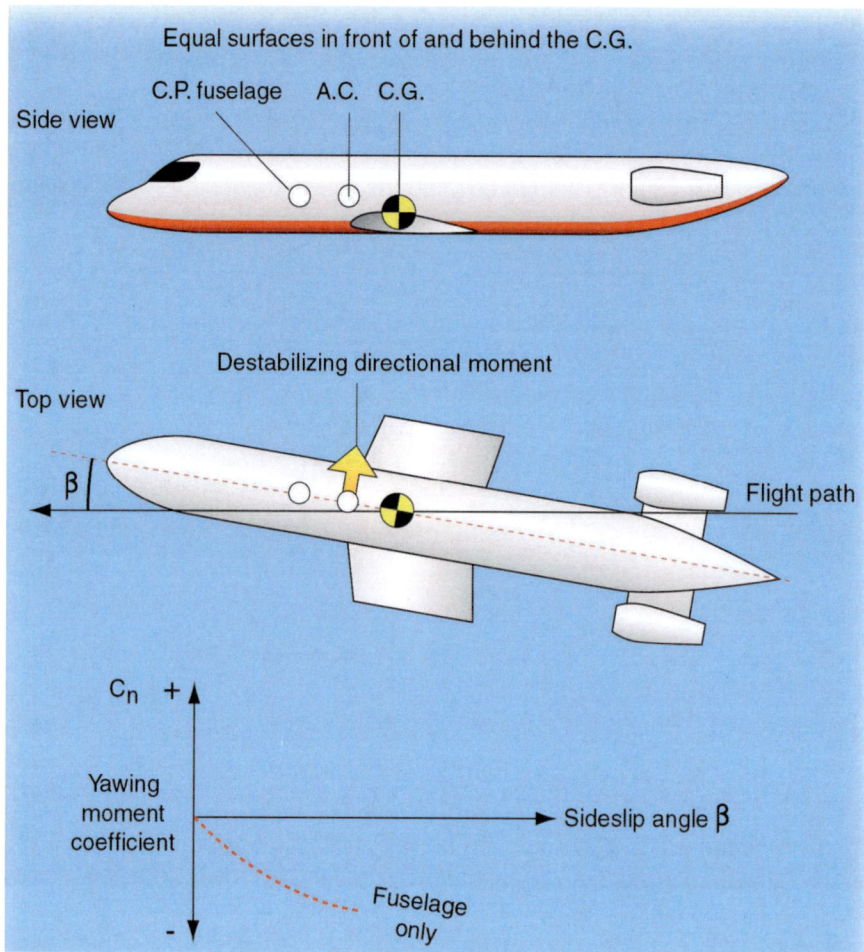

Figure 10.66

The designer must ensure positive directional static stability by positioning the aerodynamic centre, A.C., behind the centre of gravity. Adding a fin does this.

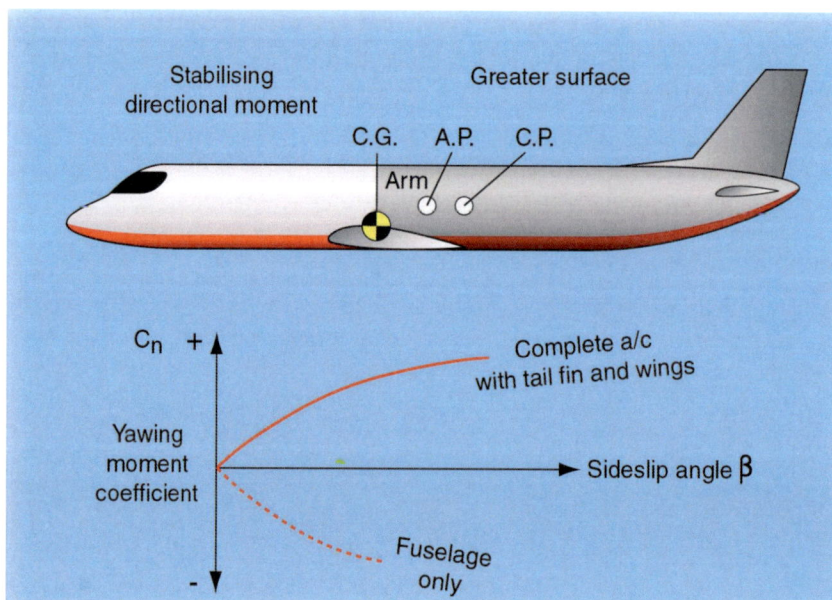

Figure 10.67

CRANFIELD AVIATION TRAINING SCHOOL LTD. PART-FCL GBR.ATO-0136
CATS INNOVATION CENTRE, LUTON, Bedfordshire LU2 8DL U.K.

www.catsaviation.com

10-31

Principles of Flight

The fin ensures positive directional static stability

10.4.10.2 *Position of the centre of gravity*

A forward centre of gravity produces a greater moment arm than an aft one, consequently, the directional static stability increases somewhat as the centre of gravity moves forward.

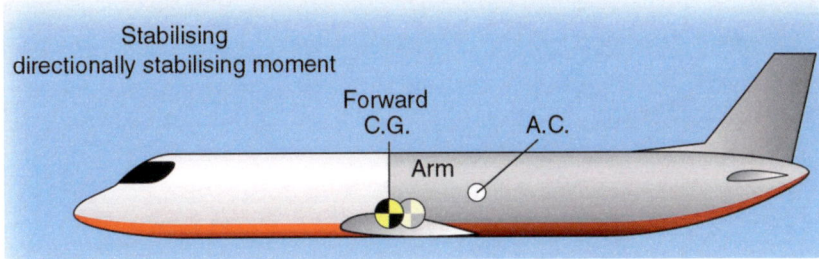

Figure 10.68

Directional static stability increases as the centre of gravity moves forward

10.4.10.3 *Swept fins, additional fin areas and strakes*

One way to increase the moment arm from the fin without making the aft fuselage longer, is to design the fin with an angle of sweep. In this way the C.P. of the fin will be positioned further aft compared to a straight fin. Furthermore a swept fin tolerates higher b without stalling.

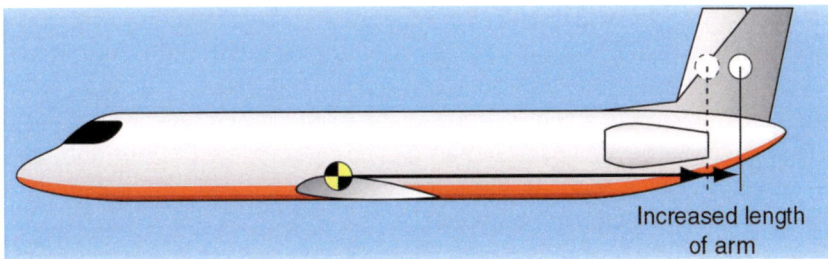

Figure 10.69

One way to increase the directional stability at extreme sideslip conditions, is to add a dorsal fin in front of the main fin or a ventral fin.

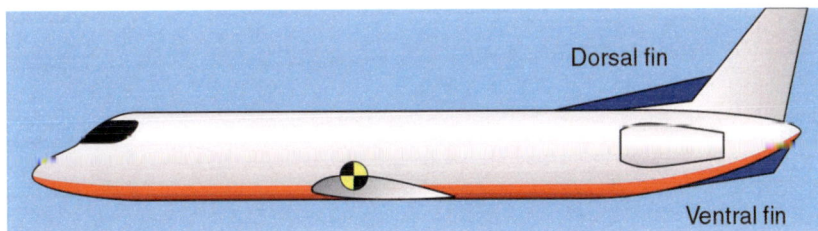

Figure 10.70

These additional fins do not increase the parasite drag significantly during normal straight flight conditions but are effective at large sideslip A.o.A, (of course a high sideslip A.o.A. also causes additional drag).
The ventral fin has its greatest effect when flying at high pitch angles e.g. at low speed where the main fin may have reduced effectiveness. Another advantage of these delta formed fins is their higher critical A.o.A as opposed to the main fin.

Swept fins and especially dorsal fins and ventral fins increase stability at high sideslip angles

Aircraft with long fore bodies may create vortices which cause yawing disturbances due to crossflow. In order to minimise the adverse effects of these vortices, some aircraft are equipped with small vortex strakes. Each of them sheds an intense narrow vortex which causes the main fore-body vortices to be more stable.

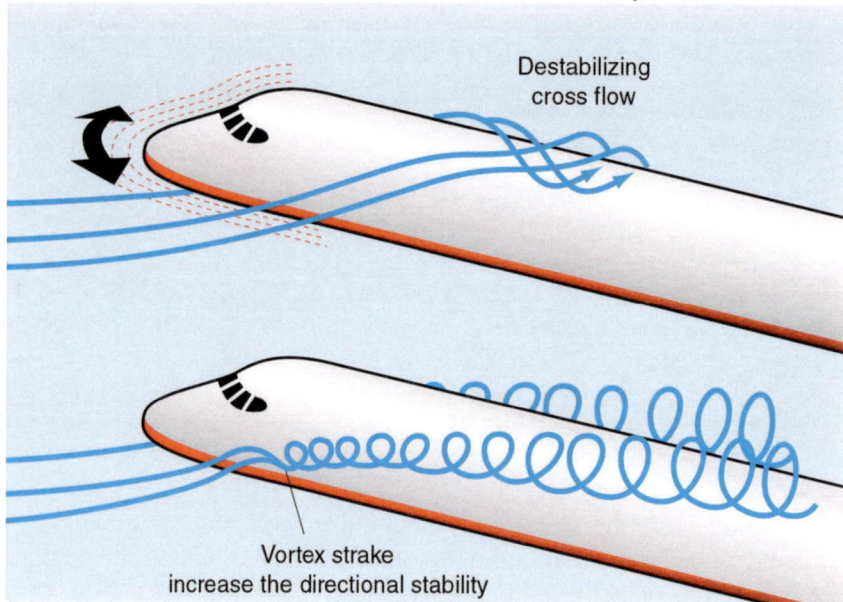

Figure 10.71

Vortex strakes are mounted on the aircraft nose in order to reduce yawing disturbances at high A.o.A.

Aircraft that need to have extremely good directional stability at high A.o.A, i.e. jet fighters, are often equipped with twin fins. A single centrally positioned fin may be affected by the turbulent wake above the upper surface of the fuselage, which reduces the effectiveness. The twin fins, however, are positioned in a free undisturbed airflow. This increases the total effect.

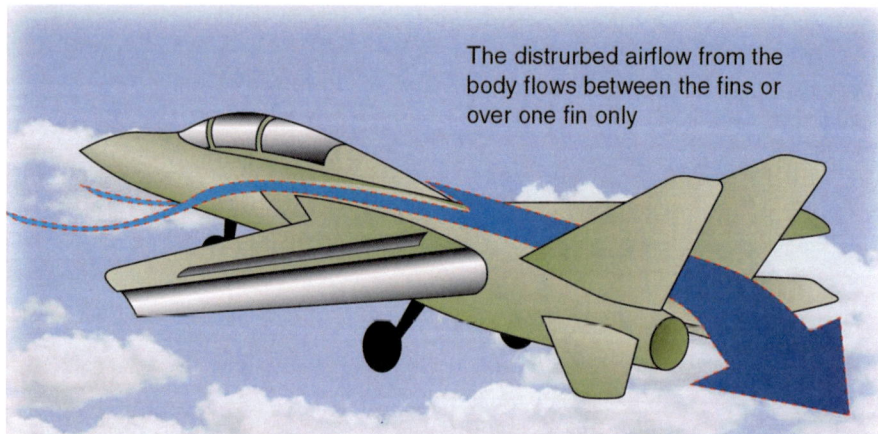

Figure 10.72

Twin fins may also be used to increase directional stability at asymmetrical thrust after an engine failure. A fin positioned inside the propeller slipstream increases its effectiveness considerably when the highest efficiency is needed most to maintain directional control near minimum control speed V_{MC}.

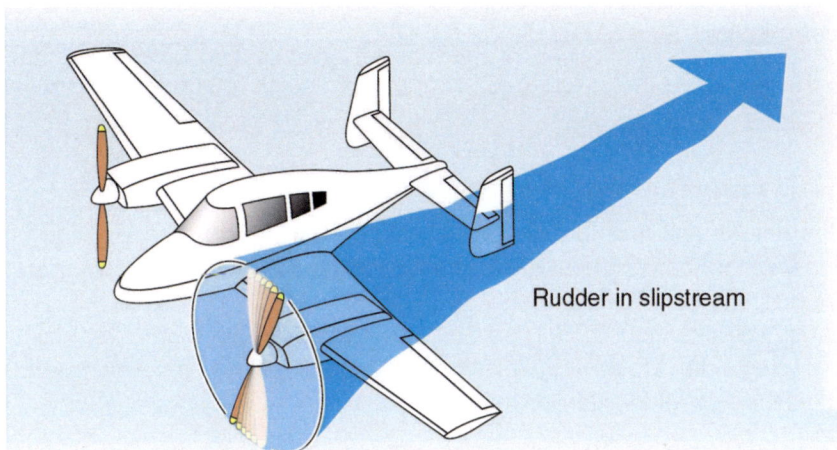

Figure 10.73

10.4.10.4   *Swept wings*

Swept wings contribute to directional stability. As the aircraft sideslips, one wing presents more of its span to the airflow than the other one, giving asymmetrical drag from the wing. This condition generates a turning moment that tends to restore the initial condition of the aircraft.

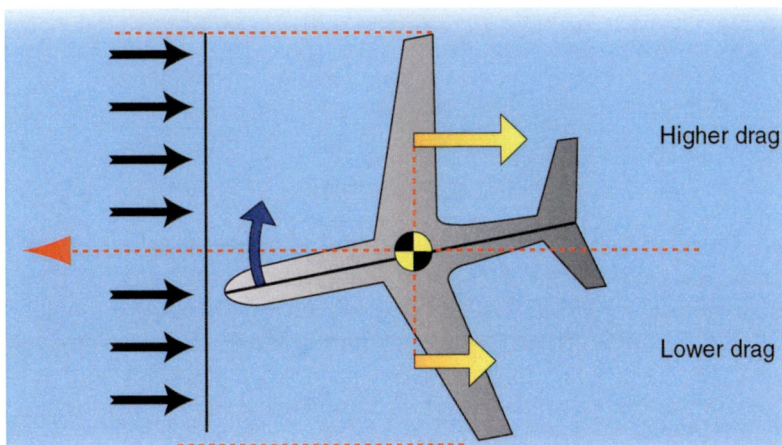

Figure 10.74

Flying wing aircraft mostly do not need any vertical fins, or very small ones, due to the great directional stability effect of the swept wing, and to the lack of destabilising fuselage in front of the wing.

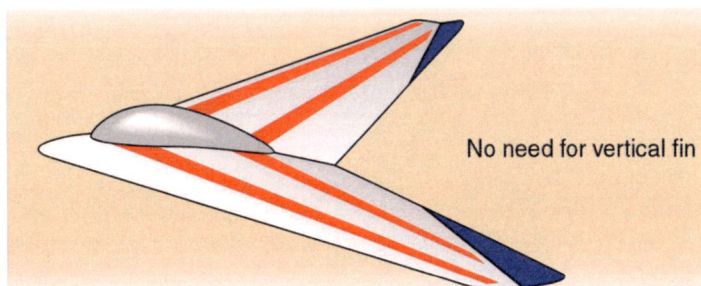

Figure 10.75

CRANFIELD AVIATION TRAINING SCHOOL LTD. PART-FCL GBR.ATO-0136

CATS   CATS INNOVATION CENTRE, LUTON, Bedfordshire LU2 8DL U.K.

www.catsaviation.com

10-34

Principles of Flight

10.5 Lateral Stability

Here we will deal with the stability in the rolling plane and how design features affect the lateral stability of an aircraft.

10.5.1 Lateral static stability, definition

Lateral stability is the natural ability of the aircraft to recover from a disturbance in the lateral plane, nearly recovering from an involuntary bank without any pilot intervention.

When an aircraft banks, the lift vector is inclined and is not directly opposed to the weight. The resultant of these two forces is a force sideways on the aircraft. This force sideways, combined with the forward motion through the air, causes the aircraft to sideslip.

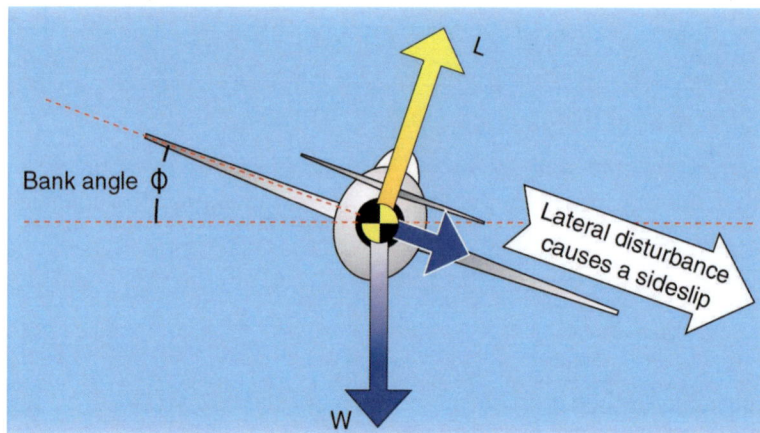

Figure 10.76

When an aircraft banks, the lift vector is inclined and not directly opposed to the weight, causing a sideslip. As a result of this sideslip, the aircraft is subjected to a component sideways of the relative airflow. If the C.P. from this relative airflow coincides with the C.G there will be no restoring moment, and the aircraft will continue to sideslip with a bank angle. There will be no lateral stability.

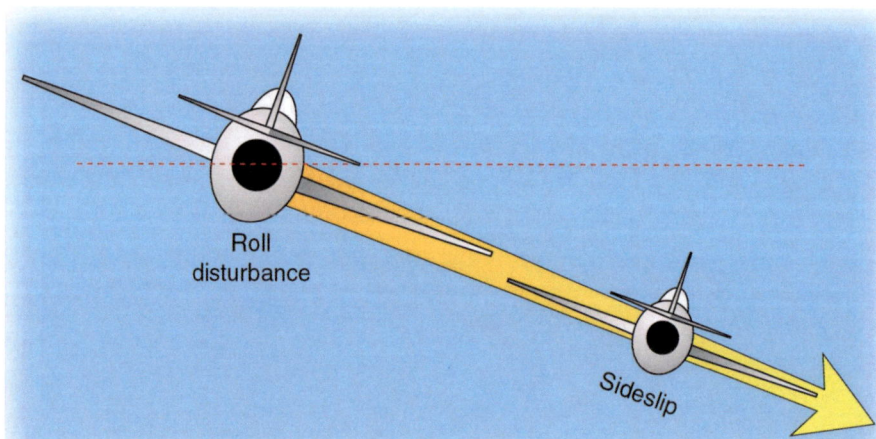

Figure 10.77

10.5.2   *Aircraft design features affecting lateral stability*

10.5.2.1   Dihedral

Several aircraft design features can be used in order to obtain lateral stability. The designer will of course choose the most appropriate solution for the aircraft being designed. The first of these features is the dihedral. Dihedral of the wing is the angle between the 0.25 chord line of the wing and the lateral axis. Dihedral is the most common design feature for ensuring positive static lateral stability. It is an inclination of the wing span where the wing tips are higher than the roots, which is regarded as positive. The effective dihedral of an aeroplane component means the contribution of that component to the static lateral stability.

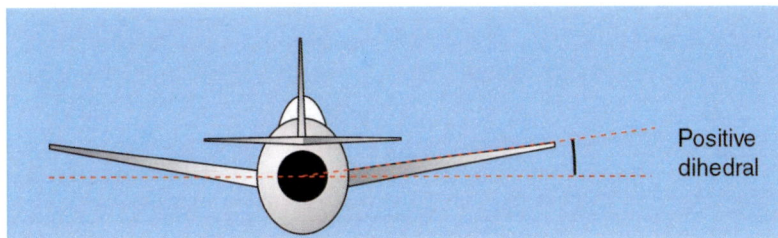

Figure 10.78

The dihedral is the most common design feature for ensuring positive static lateral stability. The positive dihedral has a stabilising effect, because as the aircraft sideslips, the lower wing will meet the relative airflow at a greater angle of attack and will produce increased lift.

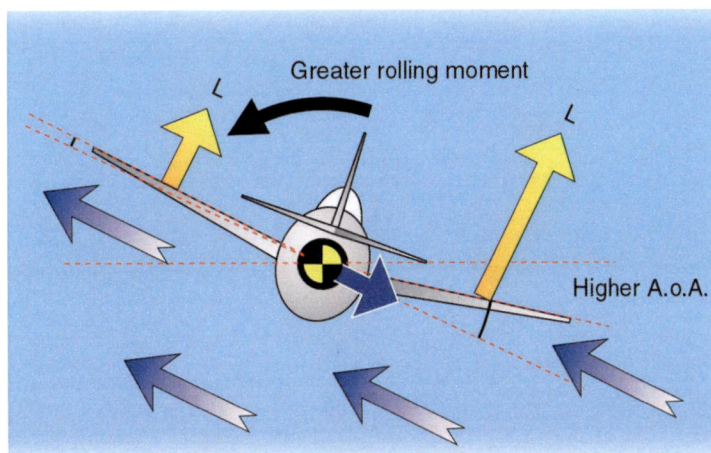

Figure 10.79

The upper wing will meet the relative airflow at a lower angle of attack and will therefore produce less lift. It may also be shielded by the fuselage, causing even lower lift to be generated. The rolling moment produced strongly tends to return the aircraft to its original level wing position.

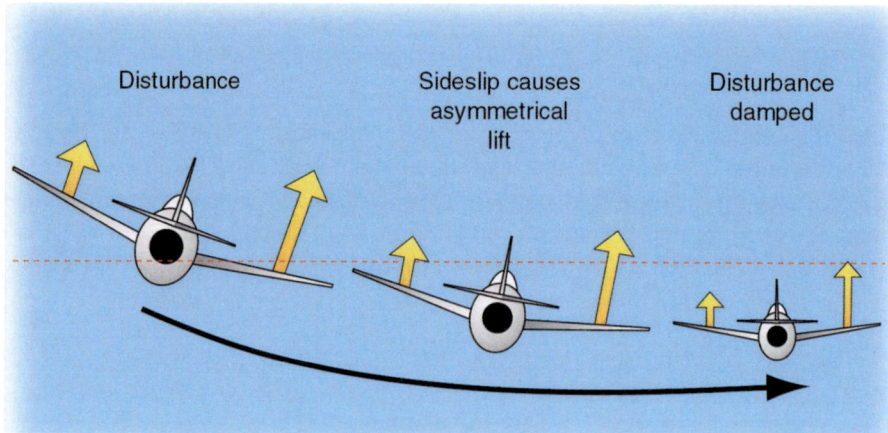

Figure 10.80

Sideslip is the main lateral stabilising factor. A positive dihedral increases the lateral stability

Notice that the sideslip always causes a motion sideways relative to the surrounding air in order to attain lateral stability. This can be noticed when flying close to another aircraft that is flying wings level, while you are giving your aircraft a slight lateral disturbance. In straight flight, a greater angle of bank will cause a greater angle of slip making the stabilising rolling moment higher and vice versa. The rolling moment at a certain angle of slip is also dependent on the A.o.A.

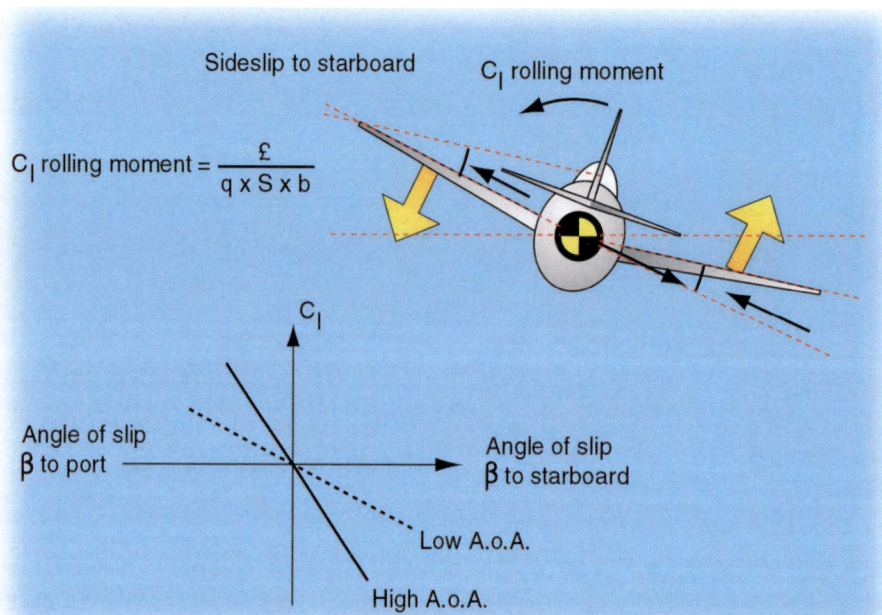

$$C_l \text{ rolling moment} = \frac{£}{q \times S \times b}$$

Figure 10.81

The greater the angle of slip, the greater the stabilising rolling moment

10.5.2.2 Swept wings

Another factor that contributes to lateral stability is the swept wing. When the aircraft sideslips, following a disturbance in roll, the lower wing exposes a greater effective span and wing area towards the relative airflow. Because of this, the lower wing generates more lift and tends to restore the aircraft to a level wing position. Consequently, the yaw-roll coupling increases with increased sweep angle of the wings.

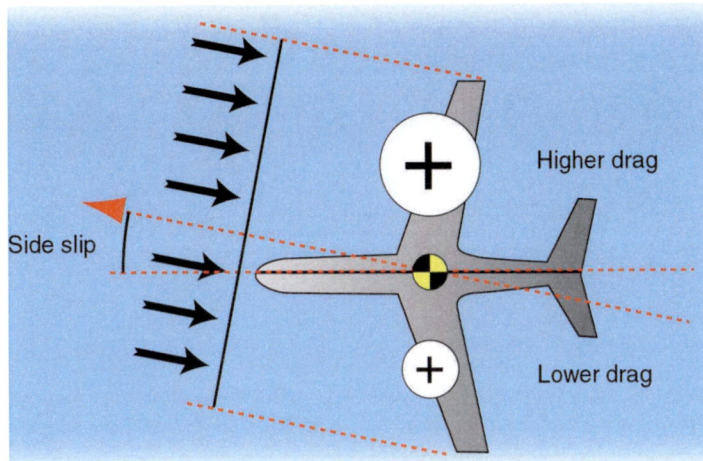

Figure 10.82

Swept wings increase yaw-roll coupling which contribute to static lateral stability

10.5.2.3   *Surfaces above the C.G. and wide wing span*

In the sideslip that follows a roll disturbance, the high drag line sideways caused by surfaces above the C.G, such as high fins or a T-tail stabiliser, and by a low centre of gravity, produces a restoring moment tending to raise the lower wing to the original level wing position.

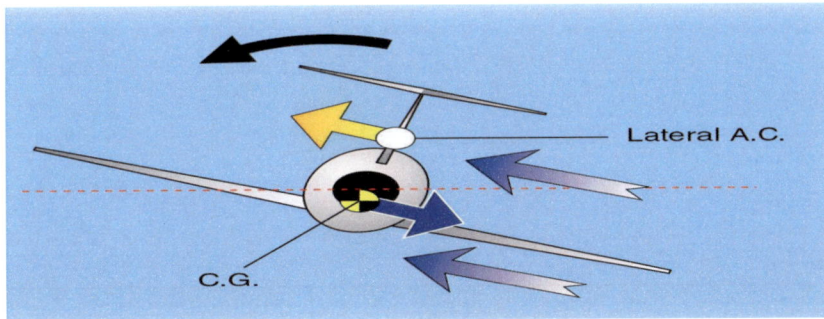

Figure 10.83 Surfaces above the C.G. increase lateral stability

Surfaces above the C.G. increase the lateral stability

A high wing helps to correct involuntary bank. Its effect is comparable to that of surfaces above the C.G. The high wing is a surface positioned above the centre of gravity and it therefore tends to level the wings.

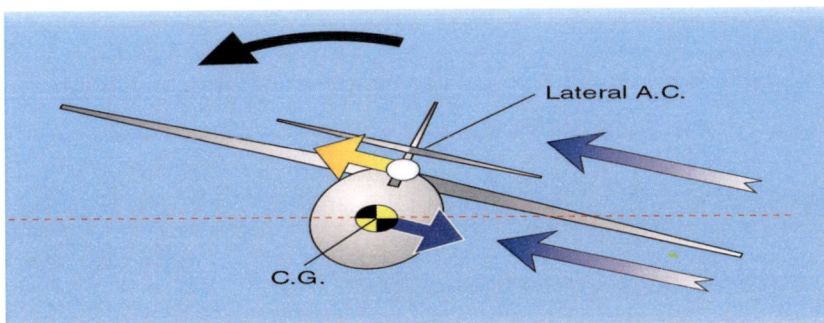

Figure 10.84 High wings provide lateral stability

A high wing increases lateral stability

CRANFIELD AVIATION TRAINING SCHOOL LTD. PART-FCL GBR.ATO-0136
CATS CATS INNOVATION CENTRE, LUTON, Bedfordshire LU2 8DL U.K.

www.catsaviation.com

10-38

Principles of Flight

Small asymmetrical lift factors have greater influence on a wing of large span than on a wing of short span, giving the larger wing span higher lateral stability.

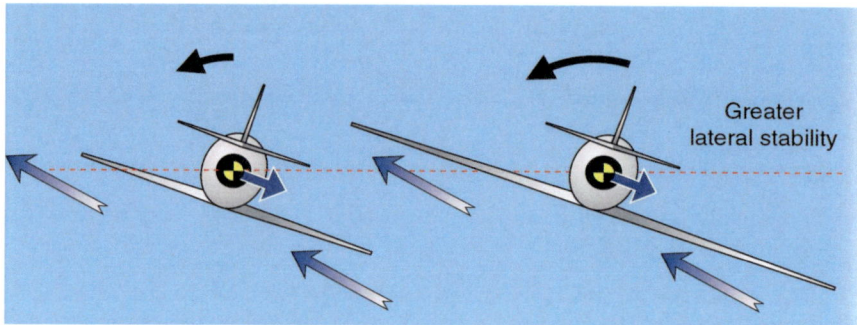

Figure 10.85 Wide wing span increases lateral stability

10.5.2.4   *Negative dihedral (anhedral) and ventral fin*

An aircraft with excessive lateral stability may be difficult to manoeuvre in roll. Aircraft with swept and high wings therefore often have a negative dihedral, sometimes called anhedral, to reduce lateral stability.

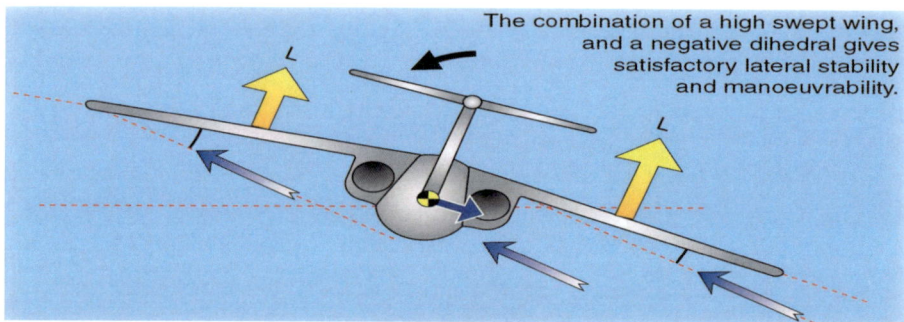

Figure 10.86

> Aircraft with high wings and / or swept wings may have a negative dihedral (anhedral) employed to reduce lateral stability

10.5.3   *Dynamic lateral stability*

The damping of a roll is the rolling moment associated with the angular velocity of the roll. This damping is provided mainly by the wing. If the aircraft meets a disturbance which lowers the right wing, the right wing will have a downward velocity, and as a consequence, the effective A.o.A, and so the lift, of that wing is increased. In the same way, the lift of the left wing will be reduced because of its upward velocity. The difference in lift between the two wings causes a rolling moment in the opposite direction to the rolling velocity. This dampens the roll. The vertical tail fin and the horizontal tail plane make small additional contributions.

> The damping of a roll is associated with the angular velocity of the roll, and is mainly caused by difference in A.o.A of the two wings

10.6   *Lateral and Directional Stability*

10.6.1   *Roll and yaw connection*

The lateral and directional motions of an aircraft cannot be considered independent of each other. If the aircraft is displaced in yaw, it will start to sideslip. This causes the lateral stability features, such as dihedral,

CRANFIELD AVIATION TRAINING SCHOOL LTD. PART-FCL GBR.ATO-0136
CATS INNOVATION CENTRE, LUTON, Bedfordshire LU2 8DL U.K.   www.catsaviation.com
10-39   Principles of Flight

sweepback, or high wing, to increase the lift of the forward wing and decrease the lift in the trailing wing. Since the aircraft is yawing, the outer wing moves faster and produces more lift than the inner wing, increasing the tendency to bank towards the inner wing. These two effects cause a rolling moment in the same direction as the yaw that raise the forward wing further.

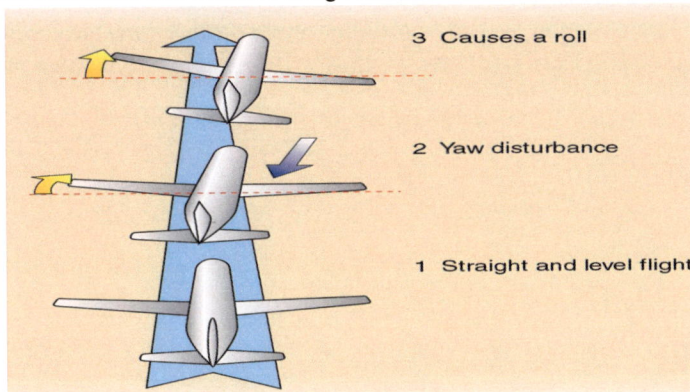

Figure 10.87 Yaw causes roll

Yaw causes a roll the same direction

The sideslip exerts a rolling force on the aircraft which, if the aircraft is directionally stable, causes it to yaw further into the relative airflow. The aircraft turns further off its original heading in the direction of the lower wing.

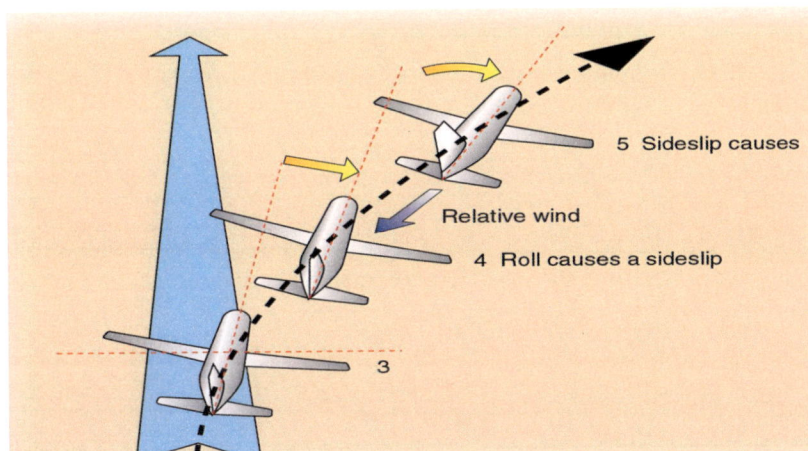

Figure 10.88 The secondary roll causes further yaw in the same direction

A roll disturbance usually generates a yawing moment

The greater the aircraft directional stability during the yawing moment caused by a rolling disturbance, the greater the tendency to turn away from the original heading in the direction of the lower wing. The nose tends to pitch down resulting in a spiral descent. Recovery from this sequence of events is facilitated by lateral stability features of an aircraft which cause the lower wing to produce increased lift and to return the aircraft to the level wing position. However, there is a conflict between these two effects: a very directionally stable aircraft will steepen the turn and pitch the nose down further while a very laterally stable aircraft will level the wings.

10.6.2   *Spiral instability*

If the directional stability is too great compared to the lateral stability, an effect called spiral instability can occur. This may happen to an aircraft with a large fin and insufficient dihedral.

Spiral instability occurs when the directional stability is too great compared to the lateral stability

An aircraft with great directional stability has a rapid initial turn which causes the outside wing to move faster, amplifying the initial roll. The resulting sideslip produces a secondary yaw, which remains until the relative slow roll damping has ended. The flight path spirals downwards and is known as a spiral descent.

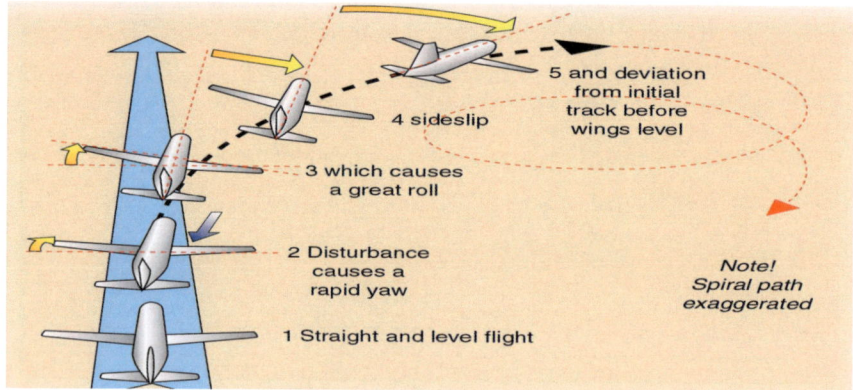

Figure 10.89 Spiral descent

Moderate spiral instability is acceptable for most aircraft because it is easy to level the wings again and it makes the aircraft more manoeuvrable laterally.

10.6.3　　　　　*Lateral instability, Dutch roll*

If lateral stability is too great compared to directional stability, an undesired effect known as Dutch roll occurs.

Dutch roll occurs when lateral stability is too great compared to directional stability

When a roll disturbance occurs to an aircraft with a large degree of sweep back or with a small fin, the aircraft may show no tendency to turn in the direction of the sideslip and may even turn away from it, causing an undesired Dutch roll effect.

CRANFIELD AVIATION TRAINING SCHOOL LTD. PART-FCL GBR.ATO-0136
CATS INNOVATION CENTRE, LUTON, Bedfordshire LU2 8DL U.K.

www.catsaviation.com

10-41

Principles of Flight

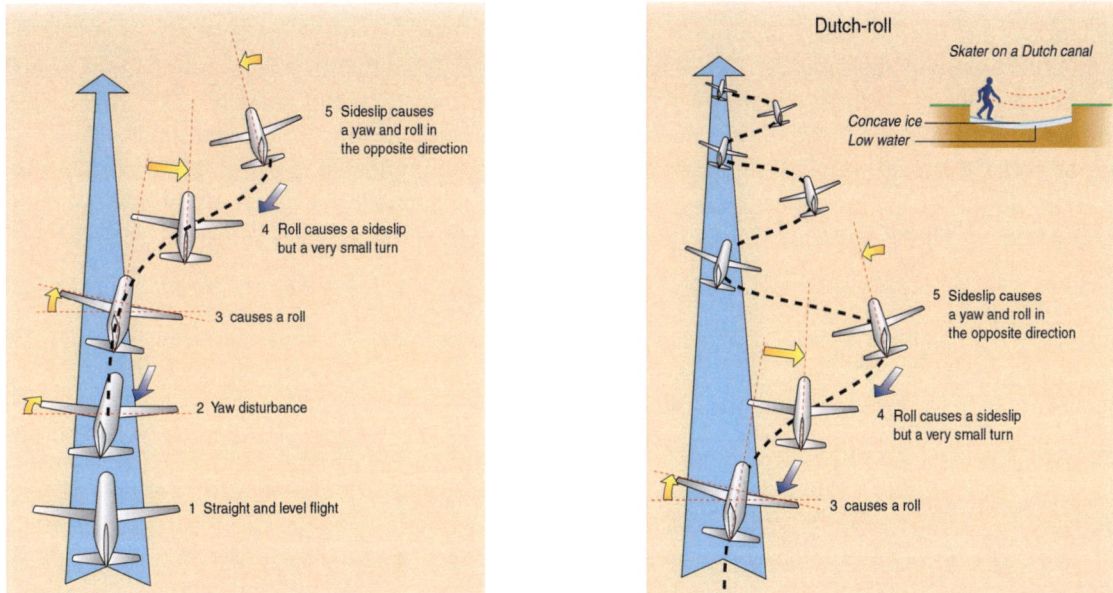

Figure 10.90 Dutch roll

The aircraft may continue to be destabilised making small rolls, alternately to the left and then right. All aircraft have a more or less Dutch roll damping, giving the aircraft a rather weak "snaking" motion after a disturbance. Dutch roll may become so great that it makes flight very difficult and uncomfortable, especially at high altitudes. For this reason many aircraft, from light twins to large commercial jets, have a device called a yaw damper.

10.6.4 Yaw damper

A yaw damper automatically increases the directional damping, hence it follows that the Dutch roll effect is decreased.

> The yaw damper acts through the rudder and the system usually senses information related to a change in yaw rate, sending signals to the rudder deflection system. When a slight right turn is started the yaw damper gives slight left rudder to counteract the yaw

10.6.5 Good stability characteristics

To produce good stability characteristics, an aircraft must have a balance of directional and lateral stability. This limits spiral instability and Dutch roll.

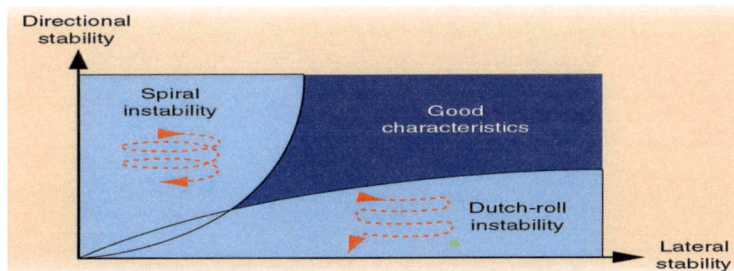

Figure 10.91 A balance between directional and lateral stability

Stability characteristics may differ a lot depending on the type of aircraft. Spiral instability may be accepted to a certain degree, especially for a manoeuvrable fighter, but not for a light transport aircraft without an autopilot.

10.6.6 *Effects of high altitudes on dynamic stability*

High altitudes mean lower density of air than at low altitudes. The dynamic pressure at a given TAS will be lower and consequently also the IAS. The aerodynamic force created by the stabilising surfaces such as the tailplane and the wings, will be lower which reduces all kinds of dynamic stability. The increment of the moment coefficients on their axes with increased incidence will be lower. Consequently, flying at high altitudes at cruising speed may be similar to flying at very low speeds at low altitude due to the reduced aerodynamic damping. When manoeuvring, the required stick force for a given change in load factor is roughly constant regardless of speed, hence also the altitude, but the elevator angle for a given change in load factor varies with altitude.

> When flying at high altitude aircraft have less damping in all three axes, but manoeuvrability is affected less

10.6.7 *Effects of asymmetrical thrust*

Consider a twin engine aircraft with asymmetrical thrust. In this case the right engine is inoperative. In order to have a statically stable system the sum of all forces and of all moments must be zero. Due to the displacement of the engines from the longitudinal axis, the operating engine gives a thrust that also produces a yawing moment. The yawing moment causes a sideslip that in turn causes a roll to the inoperative engine side. This yawing moment must be balanced by the rudder force generated by a certain amount of rudder deflection.

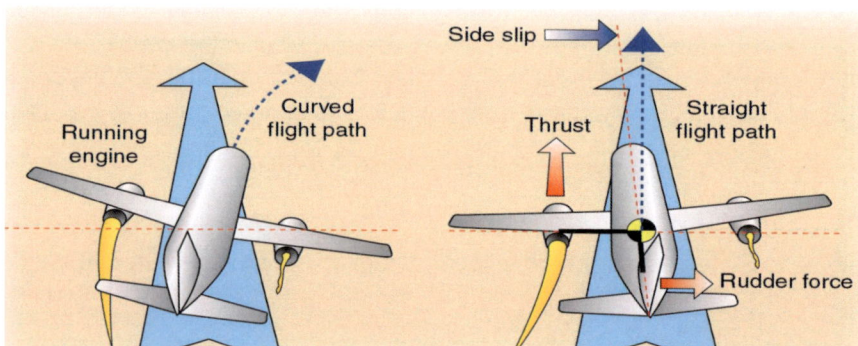

Figure 10.92 Right engine inoperative is balanced with left rudder

Now, momentarily, equilibrium is established, but the rudder force is still unbalanced. In this case the aircraft moves forward with a right sideslip that generates a large amount of drag; this is a very negative condition, especially when flying with reduced available thrust. So when an engine is inoperative at a low speed and in a situation of high power, it is very important to fly in a minimum drag condition. The sideslip in the directional plane can be counteracted with a component of the weight by banking the aircraft slightly to the side of the live engine. But, if we try to balance the asymmetrical thrust with a bank only, not using rudder, the result will instead be a sideslip to the side of the live engine.

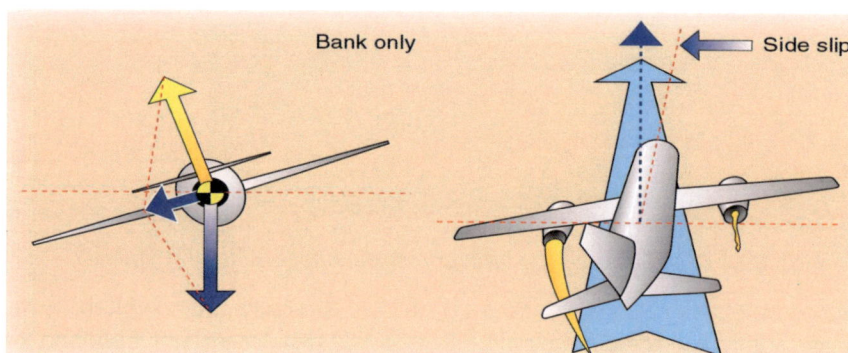

Figure 10.93 Bank to live engine

In order to fly straight forward with a minimum of drag in a high asymmetrical power situation, we must maintain the heading with the rudder, however slightly less than with wings level, and bank slightly to the side of the operative engine to avoid sideslip. This will maintain a straight flight path with minimum drag.

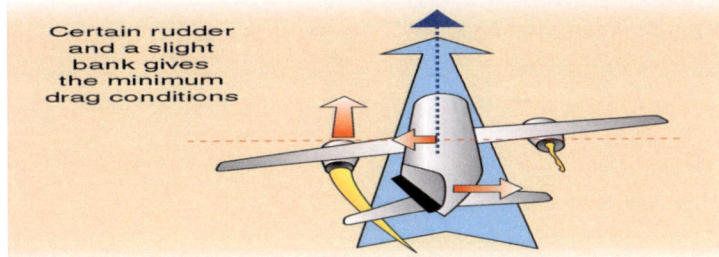

Figure 10.94 Rudder to balance the aircraft yaw and slight bank to live engine

In order to maintain straight flight path with minimum drag in an asymmetrical thrust situation, use rudder and bank slightly (5°) to the live engine side. It is very important not to over bank or bank towards the dead engine. V_{MCA} is the lowest speed at which the aircraft remains controllable in the air after failure of a critical engine. Basically the speed has become so slow that the use of the rudder can no longer control the yaw.

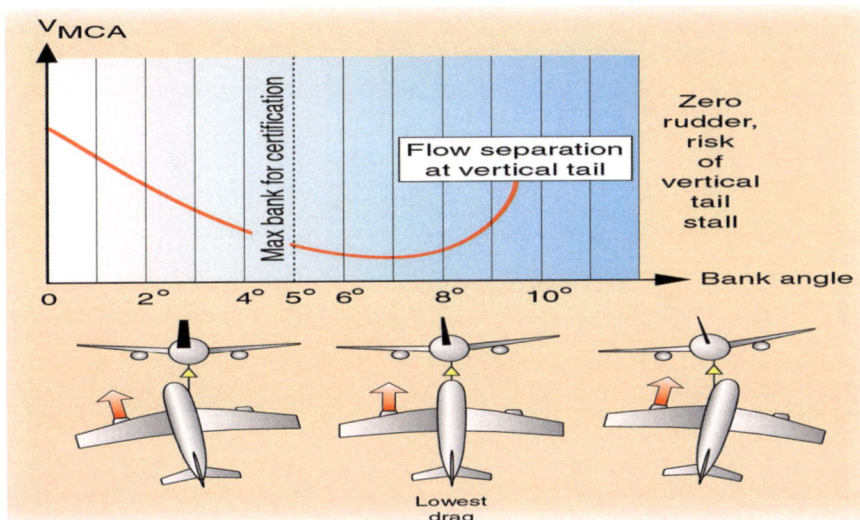

Figure 10.95 Over banking increases V_{MCA} dramatically

Self Assessment Test 10

1   The ailerons of an aircraft give:-
A)   Longitudinal control about the lateral axis
B)   Longitudinal control about the normal axis
C)   Lateral control about the lateral axis
D)   Lateral control about the longitudinal axis

2   The sweepback on a wing will:-
A)   Increase the tendency to tip stall
B)   Cause the stall to occur at lower angles of attack
C)   Reduce the tendency to tip stall
D)   Have no effect on the stall characteristics

3   After a disturbance in pitch, an aircraft continues to oscillate at a constant amplitude. It is exhibiting:-
A)   Longitudinal neutral static stability
B)   Lateral instability
C)   Longitudinal dynamic instability
D)   Longitudinal neutral dynamic stability

4   Dutch roll:-
A)   A type of slow roll
B)   Primarily a pitching instability
C)   A type of static instability
D)   A combined rolling and yawing motion

5   Lateral stability is given by:-
A)   Spoilers
B)   The ailerons
C)   Wing dihedral
D)   The horizontal tailplane

6   Pendulum effect on a high wing aeroplane
A)   Reduces lateral stability
B)   Reduces longitudinal stability
C)   Improves lateral stability
D)   Has no effect on lateral stability

7   Stability on an aircraft means:-
A)   The ability to return to the original trimmed position when disturbed
B)   The ability to continue flight in the disturbed position
C)   The ability to roll around an axis
D)   Divergence from the original trimmed position when disturbed

8   The dihedral angle is:-
A)   The upward inclination of the wing to the lateral axis
B)   The inclination of the wing to the vertical axis
C)   The inclination of the wing to the longitudinal axis
D)   Another term for the "sweepback"

9   Increasing the size of the fin:-
A)   Increases the size of the keel surface giving increased stability
B)   Increases adverse aileron yaw
C)   Improves directional control and longitudinal stability
D)   Reduces lateral stability

10   An aircraft which has neutral static stability after being disturbed:-
A)   Will return to the trimmed position
B)   Will oscillate with a fixed amplitude
C)   Will continue in the disturbed altitude
D)   Will continue to diverge away from its timed path

11   If an aircraft is porpoising, it is:
A)   Pitching
B)   Rolling and yawing
C)   Rolling
D)   Yawing

12   If an aircraft is disturbed and returns to its initial position:
A)   It is neutrally stable
B)   It is neutrally unstable
C)   It is statically stable and may be dynamically stable
D)   It is dynamically unstable

13   If the C of G is aft of the limits:-
A)   Longitudinal stability is unaffected
B)   Longitudinal stability is impaired
C)   Longitudinal stability is improved
D)   Lateral stability is improved

14   Due to the interference effect of the fuselage, when a high wing aeroplane sideslips:-
A)   The lift on the lower wing is reduced causing a destabilizing effect
B)   The lift on the upper wing is reduced causing a destabilizing effect
C)   The lift on the upper wing is reduced causing a stabilizing effect
D)   The lift on the lower wing is educed causing a stabilizing effect

15   The longitudinal stability of an aeroplane is dependent on the size and disposition of:-
A)   Its tailplane
B)   Its fin
C)   Its kreuger flaps
D)   Its mainplanes

16   The wings have anhedral to give:
A)   Longitudinal stability about the lateral axis
B)   Lateral stability about the longitudinal axis
C)   Lateral instability to enhance manoeuvrability
D)   Directional stability about the normal axis

17　The wings have dihedral to give:
A)　Longitudinal stability about the lateral axis
B)　Lateral stability about the longitudinal axis
C)　Lateral instability to enhance agility
D)　Directional stability about the normal axis

18　Longitudinal stability will be greatest:
A)　With the center of gravity on the forward limit
B)　With the center of gravity on the aft limit
C)　With the center of gravity forward of the forward limit
D)　When the center of gravity is coincident with the center of pressure

19　For an aircraft neutrally stable in roll, following a wing drop:
A)　The wing would tend to return to the level position
B)　The wing would continue to drop
C)　The aircraft would develop a dutch roll
D)　The wing would remain in its displaced position

20　In a sideslip:
A)　The dihedral will cause a rolling moment which reduces the sideslip
B)　The anhedral will cause a rolling moment which reduces the sideslip
C)　The fin will cause the rolling moment which increases the sideslip
D)　The dihedral will cause a yawing moment to reduce the sideslip

Self Assessment Test 10 Answers

1	D
2	A
3	D
4	D
5	C
6	C
7	A
8	A
9	A
10	C
11	A
12	C
13	B
14	C
15	A
16	C
17	B
18	C
19	D
20	A

CRANFIELD AVIATION TRAINING SCHOOL LTD. PART-FCL GBR.ATO-0136
CATS INNOVATION CENTRE, LUTON, Bedfordshire LU2 8DL U.K.

www.catsaviation.com

10-48

Principles of Flight

CHAPTER 11

SPIN

11.1 Introduction

11.1.1 Description of a spin

Figure 11.1 Spinning

The spin may be a controlled or uncontrolled manoeuvre. It is a stalled situation, with the nose usually pointed sharply downwards in which the aircraft descends in a helical path with an angle of attack greater than the angle of maximum lift.

A spin normally occurs in the low-speed region. A spin occurs with the wings in a stalled flight condition, and it can develop in any attitude, at any airspeed at / or below manoeuvring speed.

The following descriptions of a spin entry are only valid for a low-speed straightforward condition, which is mostly used during practice with students.

This is not the only way to get into a spin:

- A spin can develop from nearly all attitudes and flight conditions
- To return the aircraft to normal flight from an incipient spin, you must participate actively in the recovery process

11.1.2 Aerodynamic warnings of the approach to spin

To spin, the aircraft must first be in aerodynamic stall. In order to avoid a spin you must therefore first avoid the stalling condition. Aerodynamic warnings of the approach to a spin, depending on the type of aircraft, are: aerodynamic buffet, lateral instability, pitch up and autorotation.

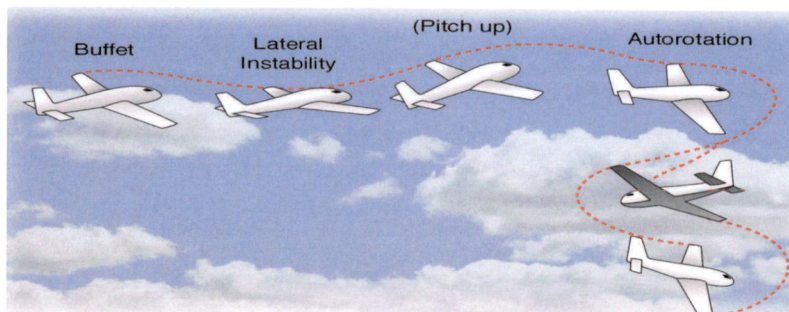

Figure 11.2 Warnings of impending spin

11.1.2.1 *Standard stall recovery technique*

The desirable stall pattern is one which begins at the root section first. In this case the ailerons remain effective at high angles of attack. This is the typical behaviour of low performance straight wing aircraft.

Figure 11.3 Aerodynamic buffet at the stall

To recover from the aerodynamic buffet warning is to decrease the angle of attack by relaxing the back pressure on the control column, easing it forward.

11.1.3 *Lateral instability at the stall*

Aircraft with swept wings, may stall at the wing tips first instead of stalling at the root, because of the spanwise flow. When this happens, it rarely occurs evenly. The contribution of sweepback to lateral and directional stability at lower angles of attack is that it tends to destabilize the aircraft as it approaches stall. This results in a slight wallowing movement similar to the Dutch roll.

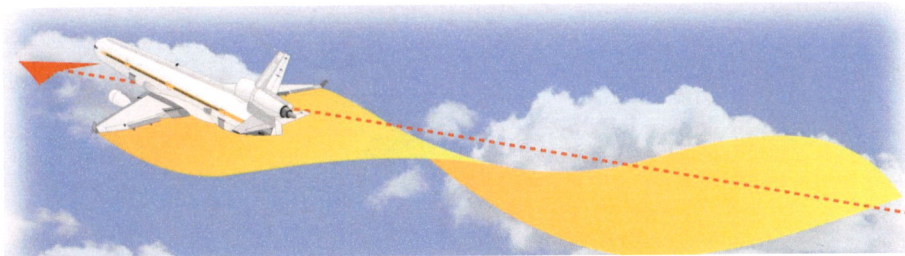

Figure 11.4 Lateral and directional instability at the stall

11.1.3.1 *Lateral instability recovery technique*

The recovery technique is the same as for the aerodynamic buffet: relax the back pressure to decrease the angle of attack, easing the control column forward, and centre the ailerons. A lower wing should not be raised by use of ailerons, since large aileron deflections may increase the local A.o.A which would decrease the lift further and increase the drag, causing it to lower even further. This may generate pro-spin forces. Instead minimize the sideslip and maintain balanced flight. This is done by using the rudder correctly, which becomes extremely important near and above the critical A.o.A. The rudder controls both yaw and roll in the stalled condition.

> The rudder controls both yaw and roll in stalled condition

11.1.4 *Pitch up*

A pitch up tendency near the stall may put the aircraft deeper into the stall. At high angles of attack the horizontal tail may be in the wake from the partly stalled wing, the body and / or the body engines mounted aft, which may cause a pitch up.

Figure 11.5 Pitch up near the stall

In addition, at very high angles of attack, long fuselages can also produce strong cross-flow separation vortices, which increase the local downwash on horizontal tails located above the fuselage.

Figure 11.6 A long fuselage creates vortices which can affect a high T tail

At very high angles of attack, the tail may be put in the wake of the wing, body or engines so that a pitch-up is created

Cross flow separation vortices above a long fuselage may also create yawing disturbances. In order to minimize the adverse effects of these vortices, some aircraft are equipped with small strakes which produce an intense narrow vortex causing the vortices of the main fuselage to be more stable and flow below the horizontal stabilizer.

Vortex strake

Figure 11.7 Vortex strakes direct flow to protect the horizontal stabiliser

11.1.4.1   *Pitch up recovery technique*

To recover, you must decrease the angle of attack by easing the control column forward. But to level the wings near the stall, the aileron should not be used. In order to reduce a pro-spin sideslip, use rudder to reduce the yawing tendency.

The technique of recovery from pitch up is to ease the control column forward, centre the ailerons and use the rudder to avoid sideslip

11.1.5   *Autorotation*

Consider an aircraft that has been subjected to a roll to the left at an angle of attack beyond the angle of maximum coefficient of lift. This rolling motion can be caused by a gust, induced by a sideslip, by pilot input, by unbalanced fuel distribution in the wings or by other factors. The wing moving downwards (in this case the left wing) experiences a higher angle of attack, while the wing moving upwards (the right wing) has a lower A.o.A.

CRANFIELD AVIATION TRAINING SCHOOL LTD. PART-FCL GBR.ATO-0136
CATS INNOVATION CENTRE, LUTON, Bedfordshire LU2 8DL U.K.   www.catsaviation.com

11-3   Principles of Flight

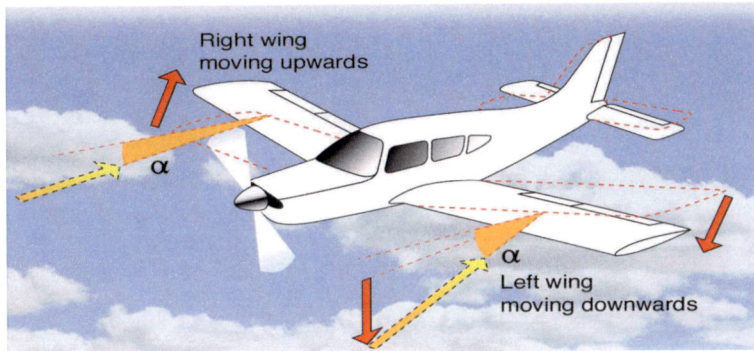

Figure 11.8 The down going wing has a higher angle of attack

The coefficient of lift decreases above CL$_{MAX}$. So at the stall a down going wing will experience a lower coefficient of lift. The wing that moves downwards has greater flow separation than the wing that moves upwards. In addition to this, the left wing has a higher coefficient of drag than the right one since the coefficient of drag continues increasing with the continuing increase in angle of attack.

> The wing that moves downwards experiences a lower coefficient of lift and a greater coefficient of drag

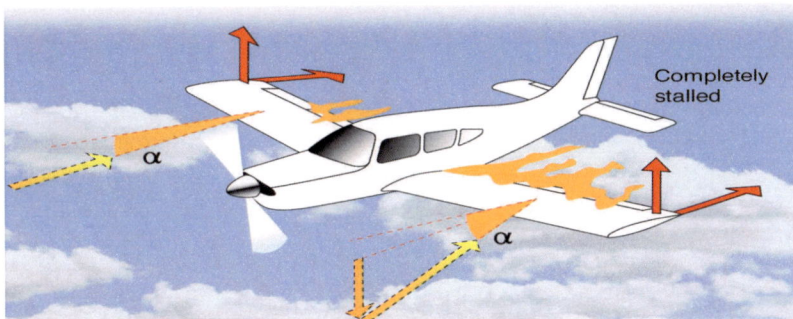

Figure 11.9

The difference in angles of attack resulting in different lift forces between the two wings, keeps the aircraft rolling. The same difference in angles of attack also causes a difference in drag forces, which keeps the aircraft in a yawing condition and the yaw enhances the differences in A.o.A of the wings.

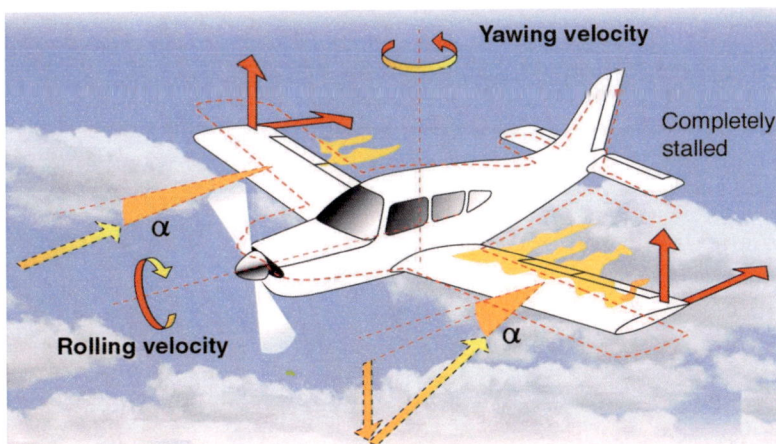

Figure 11.10 Autorotation

> In autorotation, the aircraft continues to roll and yaw due to less lift but higher drag of the down going wing

CRANFIELD AVIATION TRAINING SCHOOL LTD. PART-FCL GBR.ATO-0136
CATS INNOVATION CENTRE, LUTON, Bedfordshire LU2 8DL U.K.

www.catsaviation.com

11-4

Principles of Flight

11.1.6 *Forces of inertia when entering and being in spin*

Spin occurs at angles of attack beyond CL_{MAX}. The autorotates round a point near its centre of gravity while descending usually nose well down. The spin, and the spin entry, are problems of stability with the aerodynamic forces acting on pitching and yawing moments.

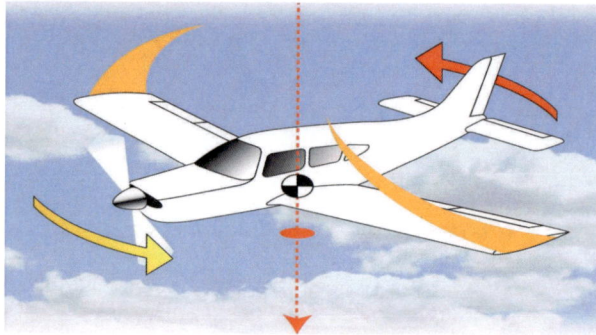

Figure 11.11 The spin

However, the aerodynamic forces are not the only forces acting on a spin. The forces of inertia of the mass of the aircraft moving round the axis of rotation have a significant influence. In a spin, the centre of gravity of the aircraft moves round an essentially vertical axis, called the spin axis.

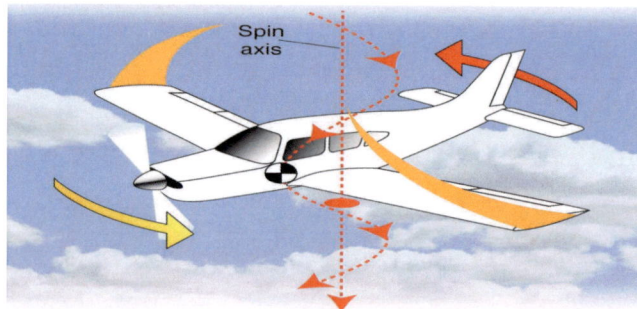

Figure 11.12 The spin axis

The gyroscopic effects of the engine, or the propeller and the fuel load and its distribution have a significant influence on the spin characteristics. No simple analysis of a yawing or rolling moment in the narrow sense can be made to determine the spin characteristics.

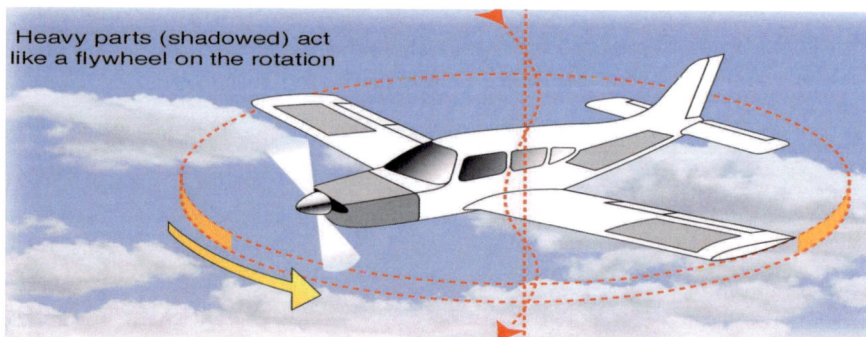

Figure 11.13 Mass affects the spin

The forces of inertia, of the mass of the aircraft moving round the rotation axis, has a major influence on the spin. The gyroscopic effects of the engine, propeller and fuel load and its distribution, influence the spin characteristics. The dynamic nature of spin and the numbers of variables affecting spin make every spin different. However, in general, a forward centre of gravity is more resistant to spin than an aft centre of gravity.

In general, an aft centre of gravity promotes spin

11.1.7   *Spin entry*

The spin is usually a pre-planned manoeuvre, but can also be an unintentional consequence of a lowered wing during stall. Differences in the distribution of lift and drag of the wings are necessary in order to proceed from stall into spin. It may be difficult to enter a spin in some modern aircraft. The negative consequence of this is that the same qualities that make spin entries difficult may make spin recoveries difficult as well, especially from a well developed spin. The spin entry is more difficult to picture than the stabilised spin. In the entry, the angle of attack changes from just above the stall to as much as 70°. At this point, when autorotation is introduced, the rolling and yawing moments have great importance.

A pre-planned spin is obtained by flying close to the stalling speed, a stall is entered by easing the control column backwards and full rudder deflection is applied in the direction of intended spin.

Rudder for yaw
to get asymmetrical
stall

Elevator for pitch
to get stall

Figure 11.14 Pre-planned spinning

In the following case we have a left yaw obtained by applying the left rudder. At this point, the outer right wing speeds up, generating more lift, and rises; the inner left wing slows down, generating less lift, and descends. The aircraft rolls and sideslips to the left and the nose pitches down. The outer wing speeds up, generating more lift, and rises; the inner wing slows down, generating less lift, and descends. The aircraft rolls and sideslips and the nose pitches down.

Normally, an aircraft will not usually go straight from the wing drop after the stall into spin; there is a transition period of unsteady autorotation (usually involving two or three turns) before the aircraft stabilises in a spin. The aircraft will then autorotate (in this case to the left) because the left inner wing generates more drag and less lift, due to its deeper stall than the outer wing. Due to the vertical descent path, the rate of descent in a fully developed spin is very high, it may be 7000 fpm.

The forces of inertia, which were small with aircraft with high wing loading in the normal flight, have become significant. If an aircraft becomes stabilised in a spin, its path will be approximately helical round a nearly vertical axis, and the centre of gravity will maintain a small, nearly constant distance from the axis.

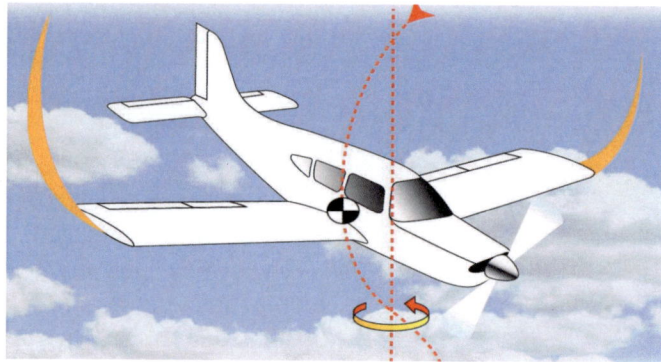

Figure 11.15

However, the stabilised spin is not necessarily always a simple spiralling motion but may involve some coupled unsteady oscillatory motions. Some aircraft never stabilise and their motion may be very erratic.

11.1.7.1 *Aircraft configuration*

The configuration of a conventional aircraft makes a major contribution to the tendency towards autorotation. The spin is characterised primarily by a rolling motion with moderate yawing. The differences in coefficient of lift and drag between the left and right wings generally determine the tendency towards autorotation.

There are significant differences in the influence of lift versus drag between aircraft with straight wings and those with swept wings. For a straight winged aircraft the loss of lift at the inner wing is greater than the increase in drag. For an aircraft with swept wings the condition is the opposite; the increase in drag of the inner wing is greater then the loss of lift.

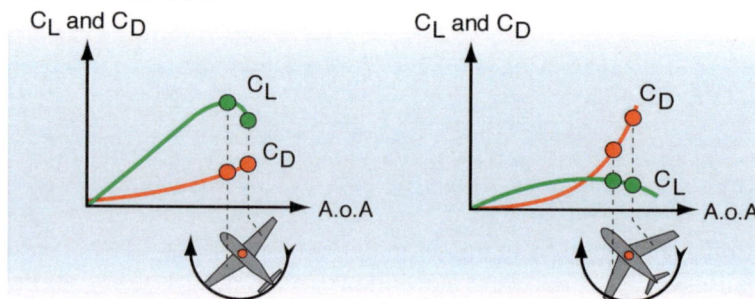

Figure 11.16

The tail design and its location are significant parameters affecting spin and recovery dynamics. On some aircraft the fin and rudder may be "shadowed" by the horizontal tail plane, making them work in a low energy flow wake, which results in a higher rotational speed and less effective rudder to stop the autorotation.

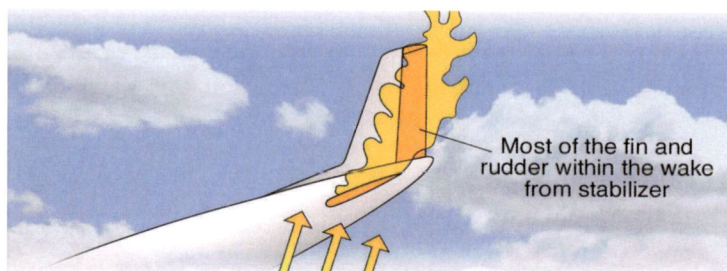

Figure 11.17 The tail plane may shadow the fin and rudder

CRANFIELD AVIATION TRAINING SCHOOL LTD. PART-FCL GBR.ATO-0136
CATS INNOVATION CENTRE, LUTON, Bedfordshire LU2 8DL U.K.   www.catsaviation.com

11-7   Principles of Flight

11.1.7.2   *Mass distribution*

Mass distribution has very great influence on the spin characteristics in both the rolling and the yawing moments. Unbalanced fuel may increase the rolling tendency in one spin direction and contribute to yaw in the other direction.

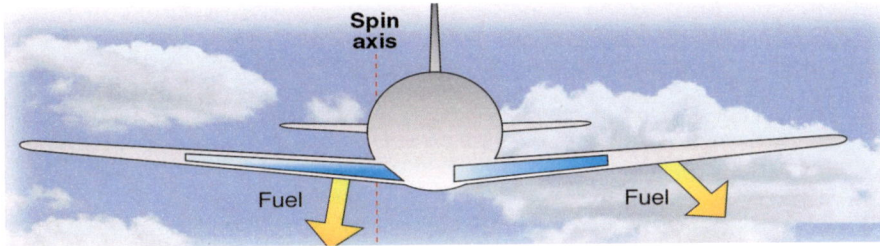

Figure 11.18

Some aircraft may be unrecoverable when having an asymmetrical fuel load during spin in the direction of the light wing. An aircraft that has "good" spin qualities (hard to get into spin, easy to recover from it) and the weight and CG within the limits for practising spin, may have a quite different behaviour when fully loaded or with the CG at its aft limit. Exceeding the aft limit of the CG increases the risk of entering a spin and makes the aircraft which may have been easy to recover from a spin into one which is irrecoverable.

11.1.7.3   *Flat spin*

If the centre of gravity is aft, the distribution of mass in the fuselage can contribute to moments of inertia tending to flatten the spin, which results in extremely high angles of attack. Sink rates associated with this kind of spin may be in excess of 10000 fpm. Due to the higher rotational speed, a flat spin requires more altitude for the recovery.

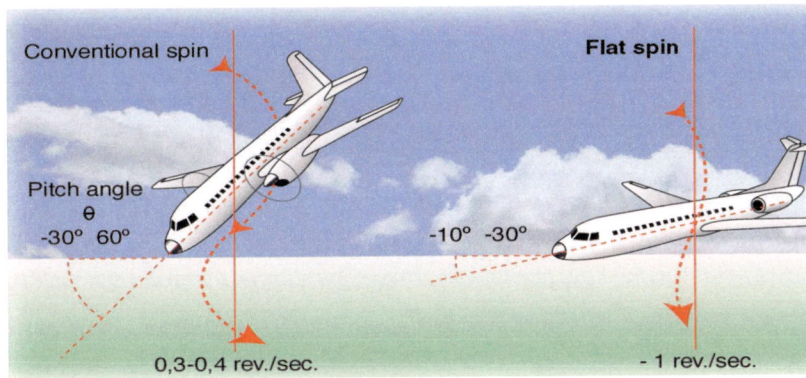

Figure 11.19 Flat spins require more altitude in the recovery

If the centre of gravity is placed aft, the distribution of mass in the fuselage can contribute to moments of inertia tending to flatten the spin. This type of spin is characterised by extremely high angles of attack, high sink rate and a great loss of altitude

An aileron deflection against the spin tends to flatten the spin, increasing the yaw rate, and decreasing the magnitude of roll and pitch oscillations.

11.1.8   *Different spin characteristics*

Each part of the aircraft will contribute to individual pro-spin or anti-spin characteristics. Each type of aircraft spins differently, and even the same aircraft changes its spin characteristics in relation to the momentary configuration and conditions of balance.

CRANFIELD AVIATION TRAINING SCHOOL LTD. PART-FCL GBR.ATO-0136

CATS CATS INNOVATION CENTRE, LUTON, Bedfordshire LU2 8DL U.K.

www.catsaviation.com

11-8

Principles of Flight

11.1.9   *Visual effects of a spin*

Seen from the cockpit point of view the lateral movement is the most significant, in a left spin it looks like it is rolling to the left with a low nose attitude.

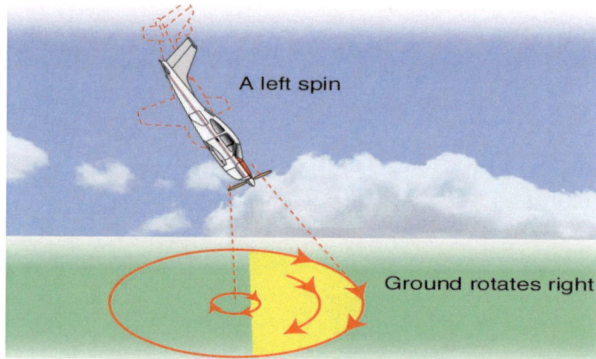

Figure 11.20   Spinning to the left

In an erect spin roll and yaw are in the same direction

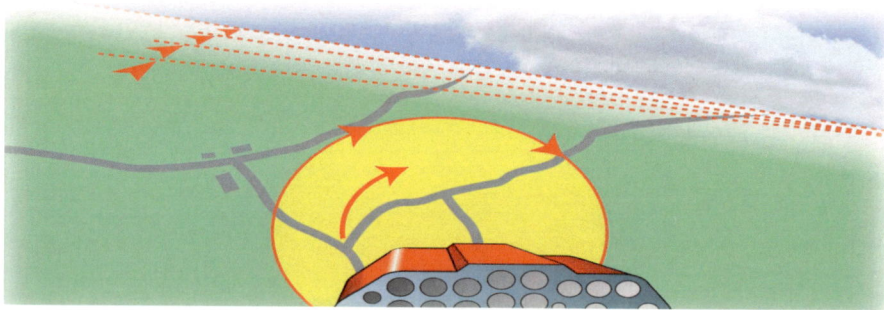

Figure 11.21 Roll and yaw in same direction in erect spin

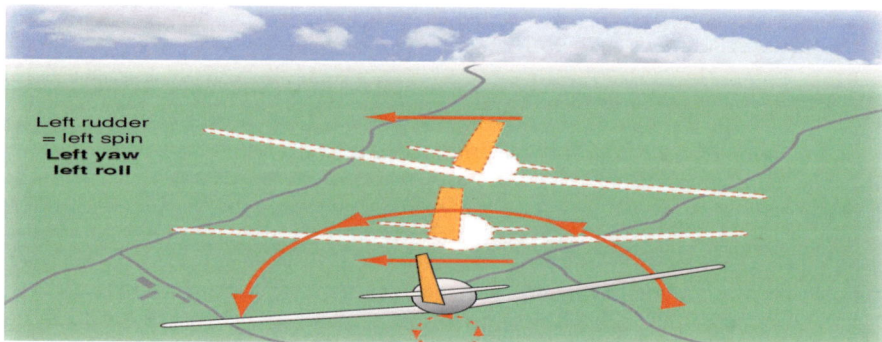

Figure 11.22 Roll and yaw are in the same direction in erect spin

In an inverted spin roll and yaw have opposite directions

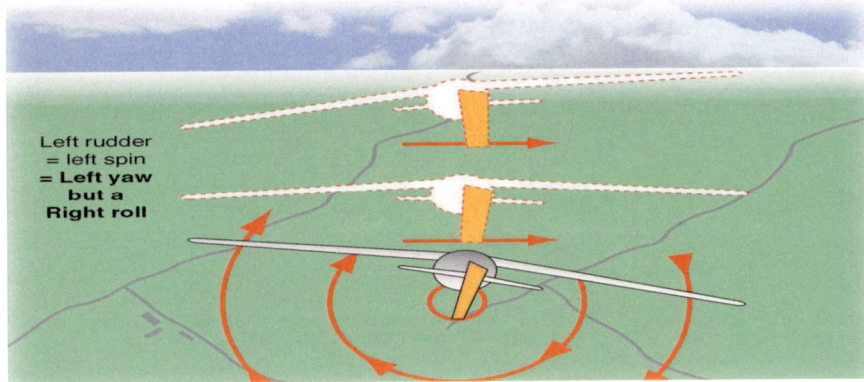

Left rudder
= left spin
= **Left yaw**
but a
Right roll

Figure 11.23 Roll and yaw are in the opposite direction in inverted spin

To stop the rotation, the rudder has to be set in the opposite direction of the yaw.
Do not delay the recovery, check the turn-indicator and apply opposite rudder.

11.1.10 Instrument indications during spin

To be sure that we take the correct actions when recovering from the spin always check the speed and the turn indicator (also called bat and ball indicator). In the following two pictures we see the position of the horizon, the indication of speed and the turn- and bank indicator in normal and in flat spin.
The slip / skid ball is not reliable for spin direction due to its location in the aeroplane and type of spin. It could show in-spin, out-spin or be centred.

The turn indicator always shows the correct yaw direction in an upright or inverted spin

---

On the other hand, a turn co-ordinator is not that reliable when trying to find out the spin direction. Since this instrument shows a combination of roll and yaw, its output may be incorrect.

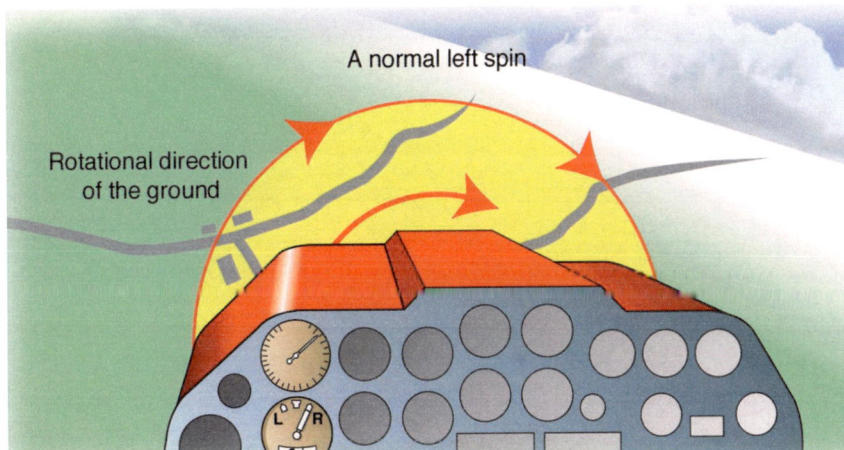

A normal left spin

Rotational direction
of the ground

Figure 11.24   Erect left spin

In a flat spin the nose is higher, the bank angle smaller and the rotational velocity higher.

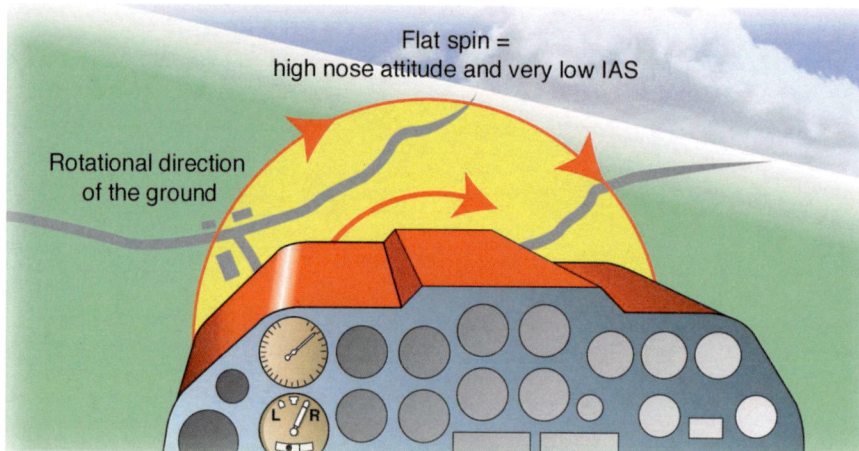

Figure 11.25 Erect flat left spin

11.1.11 *Inverted spin*

In an inverted spin the visual cues are difficult to understand.

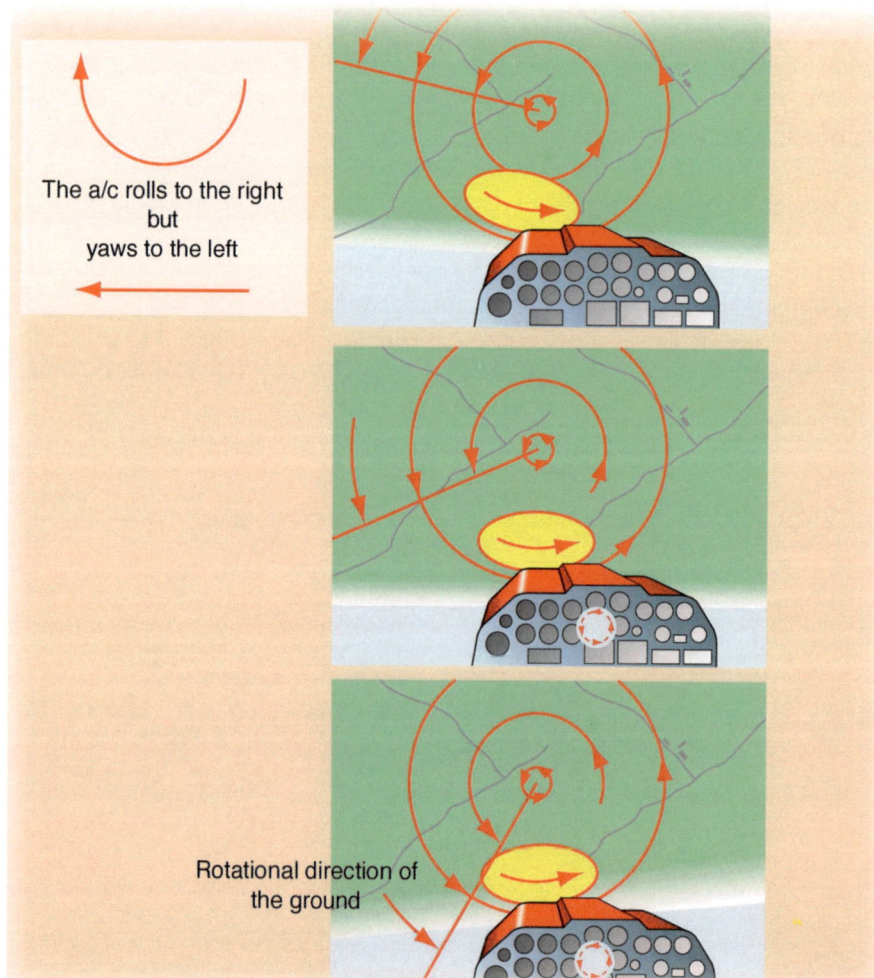

Figure 11.26 Left yaw and right roll in inverted spin

The roll cues may give the impression that this spin is to the right. A look at the area just in front of the aircraft nose may help to see the actual spin direction, but the impression from the roll may make it difficult. Remember: the turn indicator is the only input that gives correct information about the spin direction.

> The turn indicator always indicates the correct yaw, even if the aeroplane is upside-down

So a left indication equals a left spin. Do not rely on the visual cues.

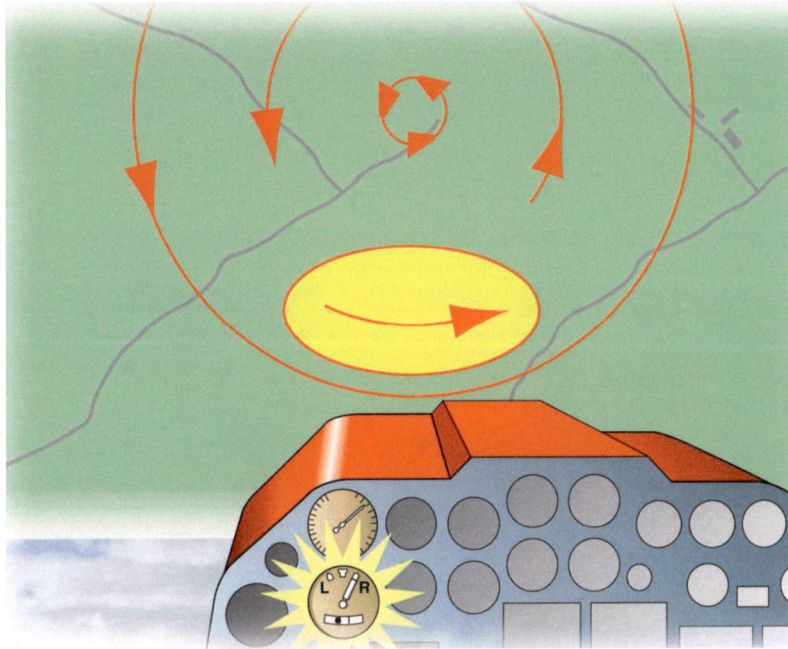

Figure 11.27 Left inverted spin

11.2 *Spin Recovery*

The following procedure is a general recovery technique. Every aircraft spins differently, and the recovery technique also varies with different types and models of aircraft. Most aircraft are not certified for practising spins. You should never intentionally spin an aircraft without being trained or having an experienced instructor on board. Also remember: the longer an inadvertent spin is allowed to develop, the less effective the recovery inputs may be. If a spin is encountered, it is crucial to apply anti-spin inputs quickly and consistently and in correct order.

11.2.1 *Use of power*

The use of power may lengthen the recovery in some cases. The gyroscopic and aerodynamic effects of the propeller can cause increased rates of rotation and flatter spin attitudes. Therefore, you must immediately throttle back.

11.2.2 *Aileron application*

During a spin, the aerodynamic controls that maintain some effectiveness are mainly the rudder and the elevator. The aileron on the inner and lower wing is completely stalled and not effective, but the aileron on the outer wing may at times have some effect.

Figure 11.28 Rudder and elevator have effectiveness in the spin

During a spin, the aerodynamic controls that maintain some effectiveness are the rudder and the elevator. The ailerons are usually not effective since the wings are stalled

The ailerons must normally be in the neutral position during spin recovery. However, there are some aircraft that need some aileron input in the same direction as the spin, i.e. a left roll input in a left spin in the recovery procedure. In many aircraft, if you try to level the aircraft by using opposite aileron (right roll in a left spin), you can cause a very dangerous further wing drop since the angle of attack of the inner wing will increase, and consequently the stall condition gets worse.

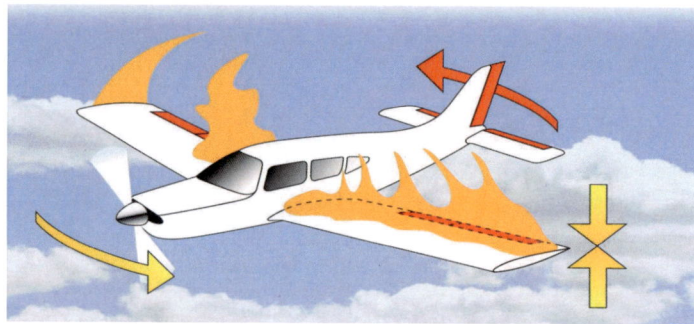

Figure 11.29 Ailerons are ineffective in the spin

During spin recovery the ailerons must normally be in the neutral position

Since the spinning is caused by the asymmetrical distribution of lift and drag caused by the rotation, the most important thing to do is to stop the rotation.

11.2.3 *Rudder application*

Rudder is the most important anti-spin input you can make. To stop the rotation, regardless of the type of spin, rudder must be applied opposite to the direction of rotation. The opposite (anti-spin) rudder usually feels heavier and gives more resistance than the other (pro-spin) rudder. So, if you cannot find out the spin direction in any other way, push the heavy rudder pedal fully forward. In the conventional spin, the rudder is quite effective since the relatively low nose spin allows the free stream to affect the vertical tail surface.

CRANFIELD AVIATION TRAINING SCHOOL LTD. PART-FCL GBR.ATO-0136
CATS INNOVATION CENTRE, LUTON, Bedfordshire LU2 8DL U.K.

www.catsaviation.com

11-13

Principles of Flight

Figure 11.30

In the conventional kind of spin, the rudder is still quite effective. It must always be fully applied opposite to the direction of rotation in order to stop the rotation

It is essential that the rudder is fully applied opposite to the rotational direction. The turn indicator always shows the actual rotational direction.

In a flat spin, the rudder is not very effective because it is often shielded by the elevator. This makes the recovery last longer and uses more altitude.

Figure 11.31

Also in the flat spin, the rudder should be applied opposite to the direction of rotation to stop the rotation

11.2.4   *Elevator application*

During the intentional spin, the stick is normally held in the position furthest backwards in order to maintain stalled wings. During the recovery procedure, the down elevator input should come after the directional rotation has stopped in order to get out of the stall. If the nose is lowered too early, the rotational mass will be more concentrated near the spin axis, causing a higher rotational speed, which will hamper the recovery. (Compare with ballet dancers when they increase spin velocity by pulling the arms tight to the body.) When selecting down elevator input during spin recovery, the elevator must be set to at least the geometrically neutral position in order to reduce the angle of attack of the wing and to avoid the stalled condition. However, remember that the elevator input occurs last, not first.

CRANFIELD AVIATION TRAINING SCHOOL LTD. PART-FCL GBR.ATO-0136
CATS INNOVATION CENTRE, LUTON, Bedfordshire LU2 8DL U.K.   www.catsaviation.com

11-14   Principles of Flight

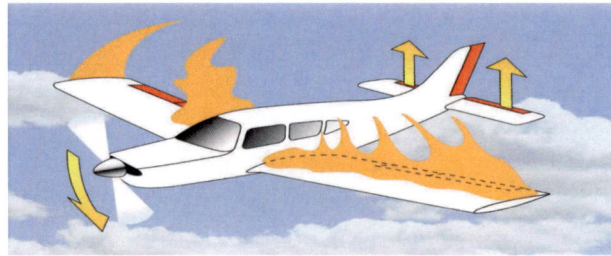

Figure 11.32

The elevator must be pushed through the geometrically neutral position, not to where the stick will put itself (aerodynamic neutral). The airflow from below may raise the elevator surface a bit and this puts the stick slightly backwards.

If the rotation does not stop when pushing the stick to at least the geometrically neutral position while giving full opposite rudder, it may be necessary to push the stick further forward, maybe completely forward, to reduce the angle of attack, especially when the CG is far aft.

During spin recovery the elevator must be set to at least the geometrically neutral position. In some cases the stick must be pushed completely forward

Keep the controls in the recovery position until the rotation stops. It may take several turns to recover from a fully developed spin. When the rotation has stopped, it is very important to neutralise the rudder; otherwise, the aircraft may begin to spin in the opposite direction. If the stick had to be furthest forward to stop the spin, the elevator has to be set to the neutral position when the rotation has stopped, otherwise an inverted spin may be developed.

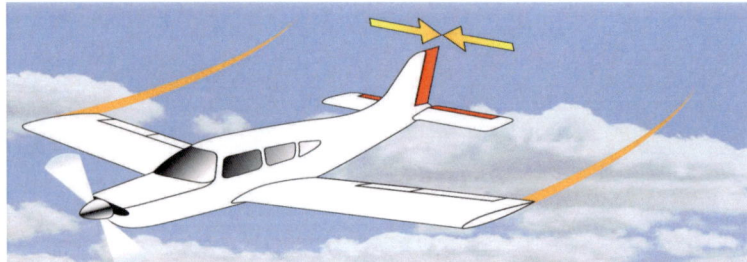

Figure 11.33

As soon as the rotation has stopped, the rudder must be set to the neutral position in order to avoid a new spin in the other direction

The spin is stopped when the rotation has stopped and the speed increases rapidly. The pull up from the low nose situation must be done firmly but gently to avoid high g-loads.

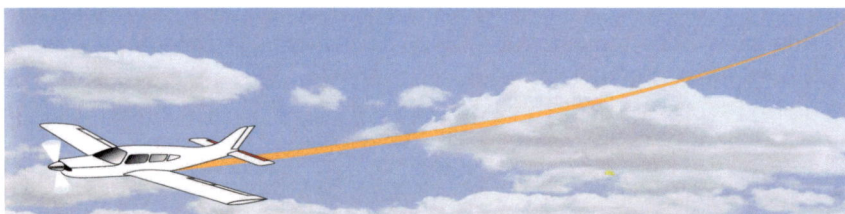

Figure 11.34 Easing out of the ensuing dive

The average loss of altitude from the point where the controls have the correct recovery position to a straight and level flight is 1000'.

11.2.5   *Summary of the recovery technique*

The sooner the anti-spin control inputs are made, the greater the chances are for recovery. Depending on the specific aircraft, the use of power during spin recovery usually does not assist the recovery; instead it may make the recovery slower and more erratic.

- throttle back, check speed indicator and turn- and bank indicators to see what kind of spin you are in
- maintain the ailerons in the neutral position (without pulling the elevator),
- stop the rotation of the aircraft by full opposite rudder application (a left turn and bank indication requires full right rudder application)
- then break the stall by pushing the elevator through the geometrically neutral position
- when the rotation stops, all controls should be neutral. Pull up gently but firmly

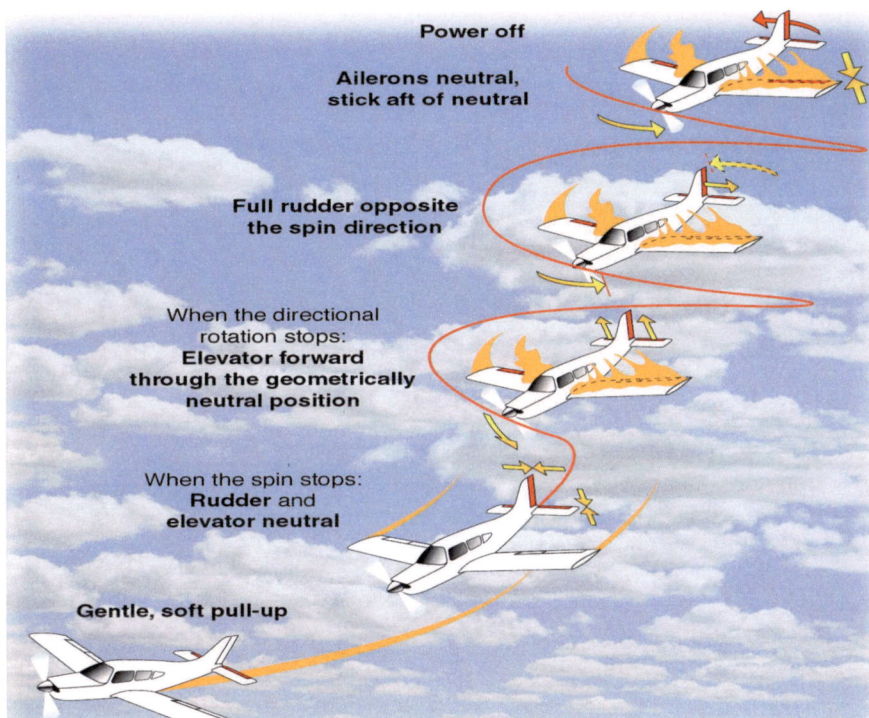

Figure 11.35 Spin recovery

It is essential that the elevator is set in a neutral position. If the aircraft still spins, push the stick further forward Maintain full opposite rudder until the spin stops

Some aircraft may keep rolling after the yaw has stopped. In this case it usually helps to push the stick further forward to stop the lateral rotation.

NEVER try to spin an aircraft which is not certified for such manoeuvres. Neither should you try to spin with an aircraft certified for spin but with the centre of gravity aft of the limit, or with the weight higher than the limit for spin

Self Assessment Test 11

1   Which statement is true concerning the aerodynamic conditions which occur during a spin entry:
A)   After a full stall, the wing that drops continues in a stalled condition while the rising wing regains and continues to produce some lift, causing the rotation
B)   After a partial stall, the wing that drops remains in a stalled condition while the rising wing regains and continues to produce lift, causing rotation
C)   After a full stall, both wings remain in a stalled condition throughout the rotation
D)   After an incipient spin, the wing that drops remain in a stalled condition while the rising wing continues un-stalled, causing the rotation

2   During a spin to the left, which wing(s) is / are stalled:
A)   Neither wing is stalled
B)   Only the left wing is stalled
C)   Both wings are stalled
D)   Only the right wing is stalled

3   During autorotation the:
A)   Outer wing is stalled
B)   Outer wing is more stalled than the inner
C)   Inner wing is more stalled than the outer
D)   Outer wing is not stalled

4   Which of the following statements about the spin is correct?
A)   During spin recovery the ailerons should be kept in the neutral position
B)   In the spin, airspeed continuously increases
C)   An aeroplane is prone to spin when the stall starts at the wing root
D)   Every aeroplane should be designed such that it can never enter a spin

Self Assessment Test 11 Answers

1	C
2	C
3	C
4	A

CRANFIELD AVIATION TRAINING SCHOOL LTD. PART-FCL GBR.ATO-0136
CATS INNOVATION CENTRE, LUTON, Bedfordshire LU2 8DL U.K.   www.catsaviation.com

11-18   Principles of Flight

CHAPTER 12

THRUST

12.1   Introduction to the Propeller

12.1.1   The generation of thrust

Except for gliders, all aircraft need an engine to produce thrust. In level flight the thrust must be equal to the drag, and in order to accelerate the aircraft the thrust must be greater than the drag. When climbing, the engine also has to add energy, which will be transformed into increased potential energy. The thrust may be provided by rocket propulsion, jet propulsion or an engine / propeller combination. All these systems have the common feature that they provide thrust by giving momentum to the air, or other gases. The amount of thrust provided will be equal to the rate at which the air is given momentum. And just as when creating lift, the reaction force from the momentum of air can only act as pressure differences on parts of the engine exhaust or the propeller surfaces. A jet engine (or a rocket) accelerates a relatively small mass of air (or other gases) rearwards at a very high velocity. As a result, the jet engine is pushed forward with a force, the thrust, which is equal to the mass flow times the velocity difference of the exhausted air. A piston or a turboprop engine produces a certain power that is used to rotate a propeller. The propeller is designed to convert the torque effect into thrust. Compared to a jet engine, the propeller accelerates a greater mass of air rearwards but with lower velocity.

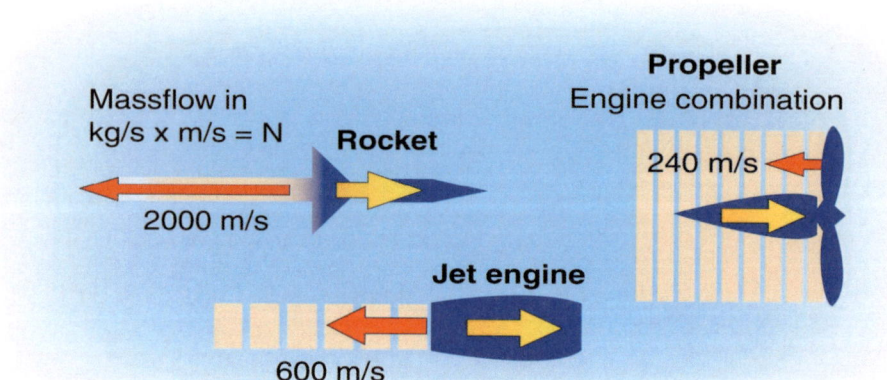

Figure 12.1 Jets accelerate a small mass of air at high velocity and propellers accelerate a greater mass of air at a lower velocity

A jet engine or a rocket expands gas by internal combustion of some kind of fuel and oxygen. In a jet engine, oxygen is taken from the air, while in a rocket; oxygen is included like the fuel.

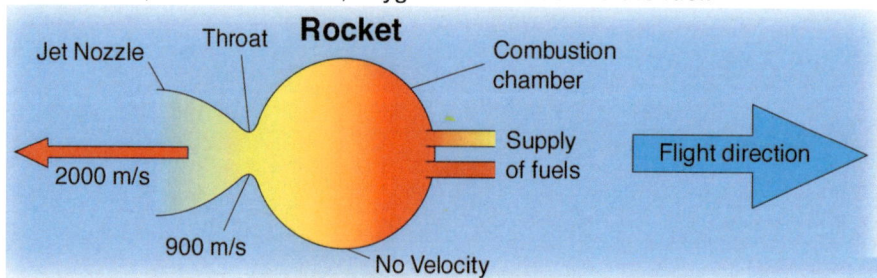

Figure 12.2 Rocket thrust

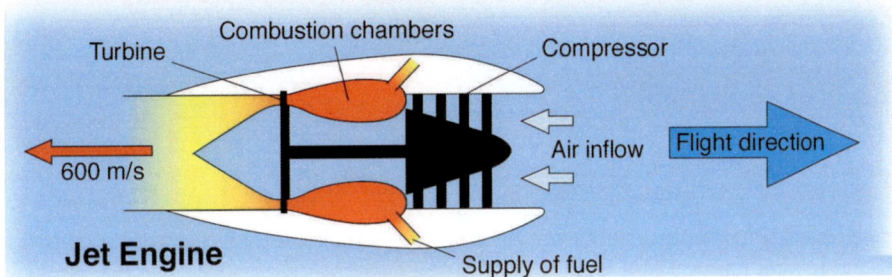

Figure 12.3 Jet thrust

Most modern jet engines have a fan added to the turbine axis in order to accelerate an even greater mass of air. The engine / propeller combination creates power by reciprocating internal combustion or gas turbine engine.

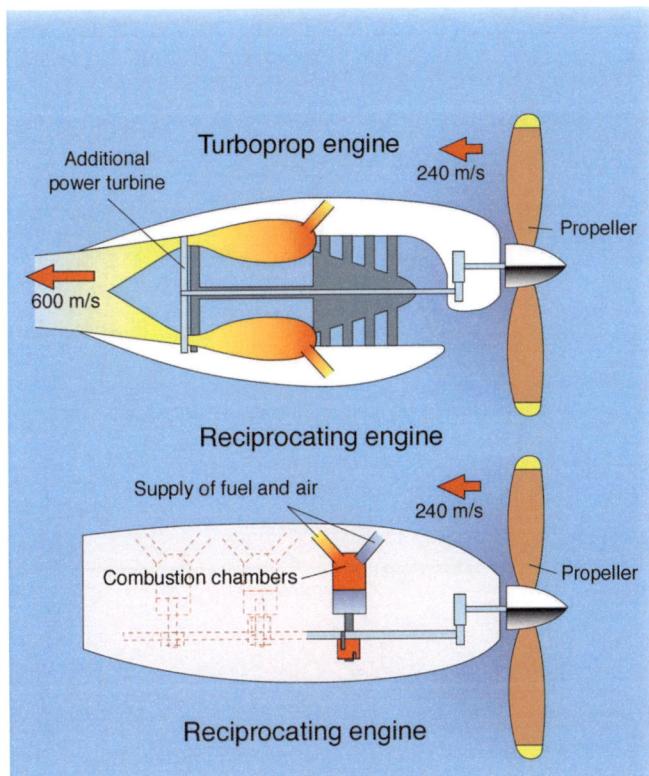

Figure 12.4 Propeller thrust

12.1.2   *Conversion of engine torque to thrust*

A piston or a turboprop engine operates a propeller that converts power into thrust

12.1.3   *Propeller terminology*

Like an airfoil, the propeller blade section has a leading edge and a trailing edge. The propeller blade section is similar to a wing section and has a certain shape and a certain chord. The flatter side of the propeller blade section that strikes the air is called the blade face. The cambered side of the blade section is called the blade back.

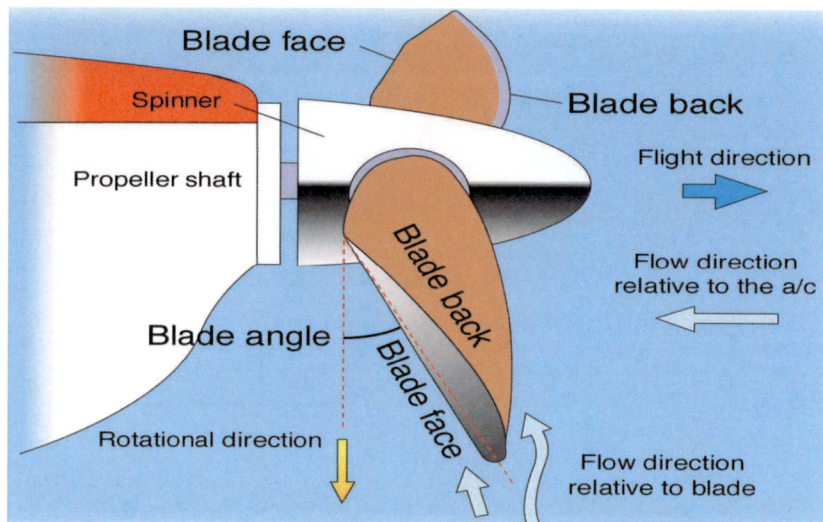

Figure 12.5 Blade terminology

The flatter side of the blade section is called the blade face
The cambered side is called the blade back

The angle between the propeller plane of rotation and the chord of the blade section is called the blade angle.

The direction of the motion of a propeller blade is a helix instead of a straight line, and what makes it more complex, is that every section of the blade travels at a different helix and at a different local speed.

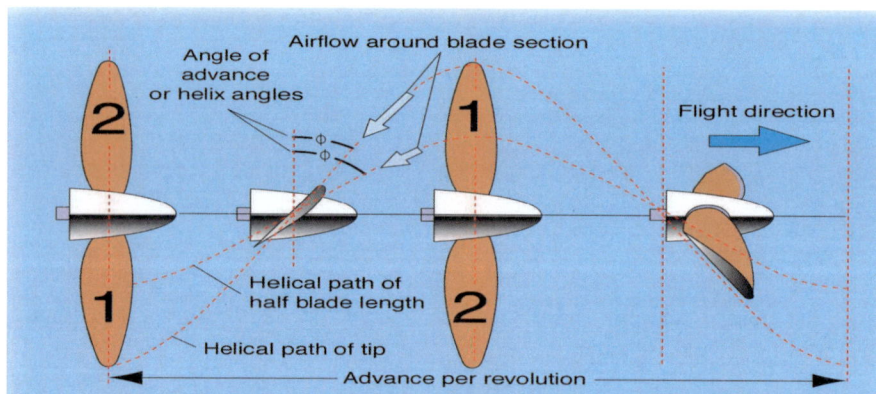

Figure 12.6 Angle of advance (Helix angle)

The angle between the resultant direction of the airflow and the plane of rotation is called the advance angle or the helix angle. It is a different angle for each section of the blade. Sections near the tip move at a helix of much greater diameter, and they also move at much greater velocity than those near the hub.

The angle between the relative airflow and the plane of rotation is called the advance angle or the helix angle

Since all sections must be set at a small extra angle to create the angle of attack that creates lift, the blade angle also has various helix angles from hub to tip.

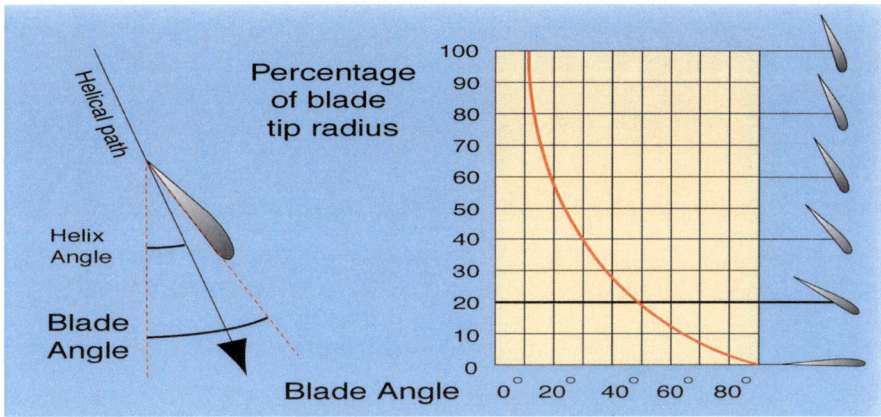

Figure 12.7 Blade angle decreases from hub to tip

Blade angle decreases from hub to tip

If the propeller does not rotate, and the aircraft is moving through the air at a given speed V, the propeller blade section experiences a given relative airflow equal and opposite to the aircraft airspeed V. As the propeller blade rotates, the blade section experiences a different resultant airstream. The increase in air velocity that the propeller creates acts in the same direction as the flow caused by the forward motion with a speed equal to the airspeed of the aircraft. The sum of the two velocities is called the total velocity (sometimes called speed of advance). The increase in air velocity that the propeller creates may be as much as 100%, or even more, at stalling speed and full power. But at cruising speed, it is normally quite small compared to the velocity of the aircraft: approximately 20% higher.

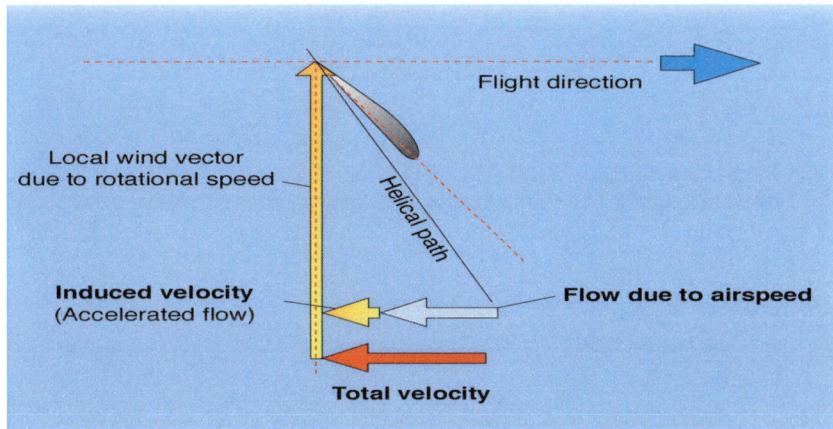

Figure 12.8 Propeller induced increase in air velocity

The sum of the forward speed of the aircraft and the increase in speed through the propeller is called the total velocity or the speed of advance

The rotation of the propeller causes an airflow relative to it that is equal in magnitude but opposite in direction to the helical path. The resultant airflow velocity experienced by the propeller is the vector sum of the airflow velocity caused by the propeller rotation and the advance velocity. The angle of attack is the angle between the section chordline and the relative airflow.

Each propeller blade section experiences a resultant airflow that depends on the total velocity and the section's rotational speed. The advance angle is the angle between the resultant airflow and the plane of rotation.

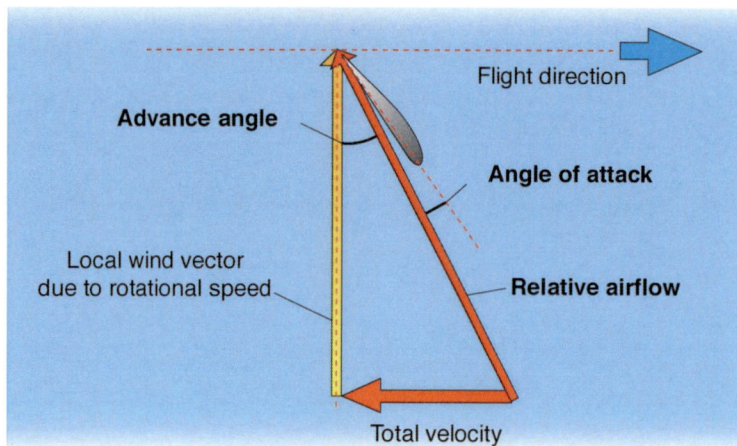

Figure 12.9

> The A.o.A is the angle between the section chord and the relative airflow.
> The advance angle is the angle between the relative airflow (helical path) and the plane of rotation

Like a wing section, the propeller blade section has a chord line and a zero lift line. The angles between these two lines and the relative airflow are called the geometrical angle of attack and the aerodynamic angle of attack respectively.

12.1.4   *Pitch angle*

The distance gained in one revolution (advance per revolution) is not a fixed value. The advance ratio is a non-dimensional measure of the forward speed in relation to the speed of the tip of the propeller blade. The tip speed is proportional to the diameter, (D), of the disc and to the rotational speed of the propeller, (n), the number of revolutions per second. If (V) is the forward speed, then the advance ratio, (J), is defined by J = V / n x D. If an aircraft is flying at 360 kph, i.e. 100 m/s and the fixed propeller with a diameter of 2 m rotates at 1980 rpm, i.e. 33 rps, then J = 100 / 33 x 2 = 1.52. But at a flight speed of 198 kph, i.e. 55 m/s and the same rpm, the advance ratio will be only 0.83.

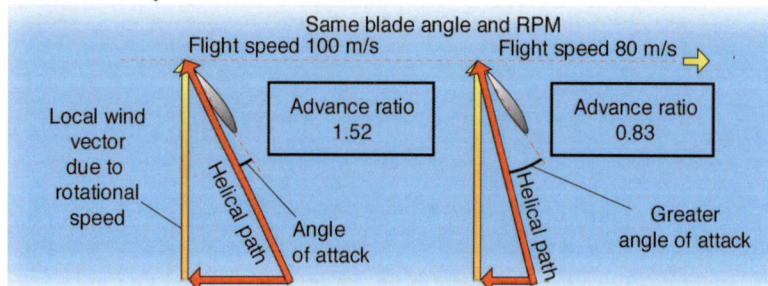

Figure 12.10 Angle of attack decreases with increasing forward TAS

At this combination of low flight speed, RPM and blade angle, the blade sections are working at a large A.o.A. maybe near the stall A.o.A. At large angles of attack the engine is not able to maintain the desired RPM. Since an engine has its highest efficiency at a limited range of RPM, the propeller must be designed to work with its most efficient A.o.A. at a certain speed, hence its pitch angle must be adapted to the speed at which the propeller is supposed to have its highest efficiency. The theoretical geometric distance gained in one propeller revolution is called the geometric pitch. The different sections of the propeller blade will travel the same distance forward but at different rotational and helical path lengths.

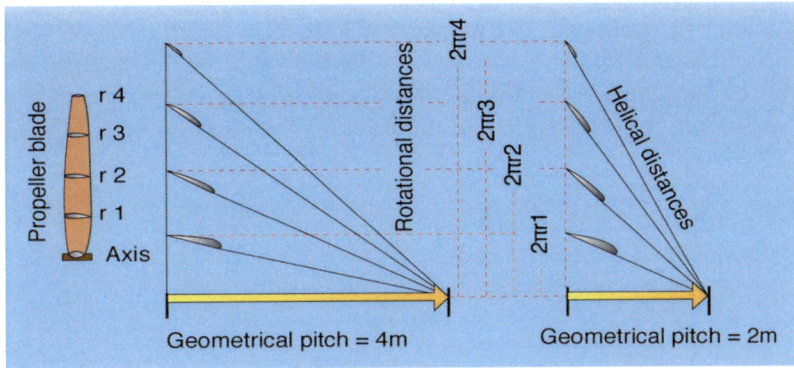

Figure 12.11

The value of the geometric pitch of a fixed-pitch propeller may vary from 1 m for a slow type of aircraft to 5 m or even 6 m for those that were used on racing aircraft in the 1930's. A propeller designed for high speeds should have a high, or coarse, pitch, and a propeller for low speeds should have a low, or fine pitch.

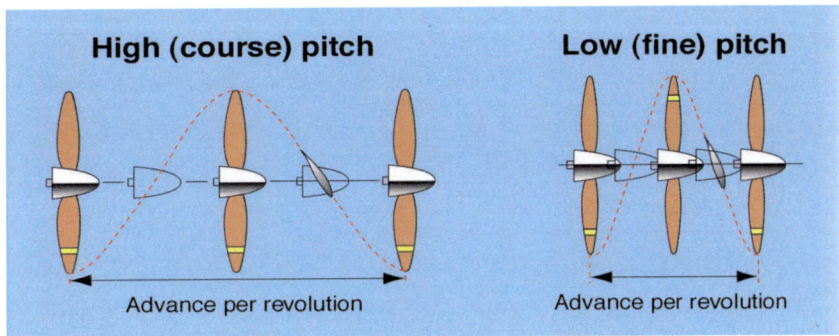

Figure 12.12

12.1.5   *Blade twist*

There is a corresponding decrease in the helix angle at different distances from the propeller axis to get the same pitch for each blade section. Since the A.o.A for each blade section should be optimal, the blade angle has to be adapted to meet the airflow, which is opposite to the helical path, i.e. the blade has to be twisted.

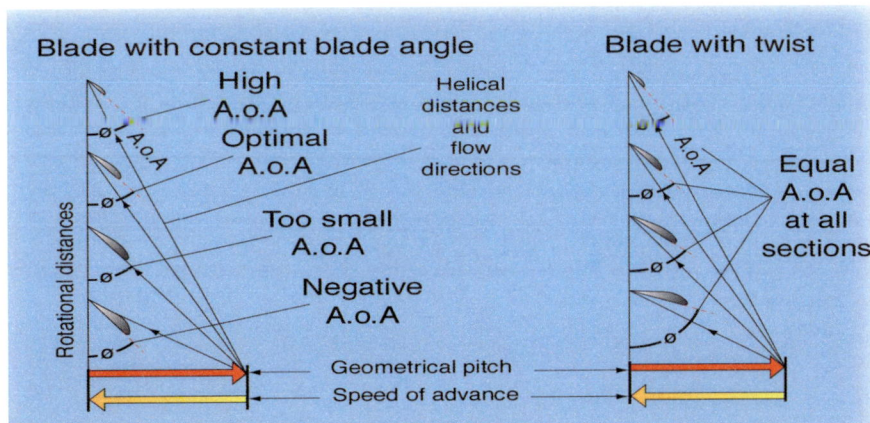

Figure 12.13

By reducing the blade angle from root to tip, an efficient A.o.A. over the whole blade is obtained

However, despite the effort of the designer of the propeller to get the best out of each part of the blade, there will be losses both near the axis and the tip. The sections closest to the axis must be thick to provide strength. The flow of air through these sections is seriously affected by the engine behind or, if a pusher, the engine in front. At the tip there are vortices and induced drag like that of a wing, as well as compressibility effects.

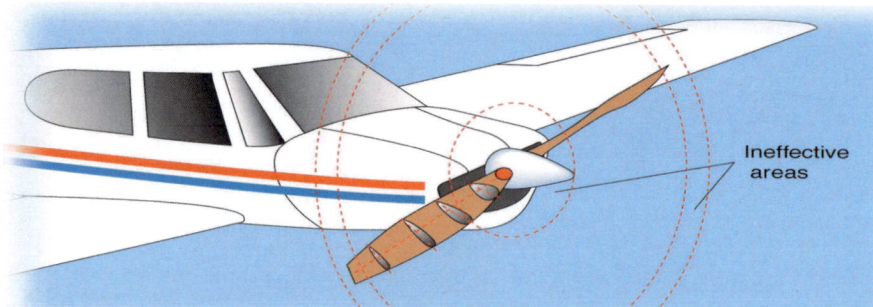

Figure 12.14

The result of all this is that only a small proportion of the propeller blade is really effective. Between 70 - 80% of the radius are the most effective sections. When the aircraft flight manual gives the value of the propeller blade angle, it is referred to as the 75% section for this reason.

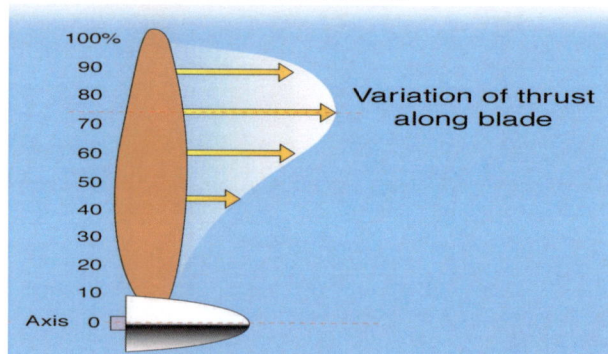

Figure 12.15

12.1.6   *Forces on a propeller blade section*

A propeller blade section creates a total aerodynamic force, like a wings section, which can be divided into two components of which one is perpendicular to the relative airflow, called lift, and the other parallel to the relative airflow called drag. Since the interesting forces are those that produce thrust and the torque, we divide the total aerodynamic force into one component perpendicular to the plane of rotation called thrust and another in the plane of rotation called the propeller resistance force. The resisting force multiplied by its arm gives the torque required by the propeller.

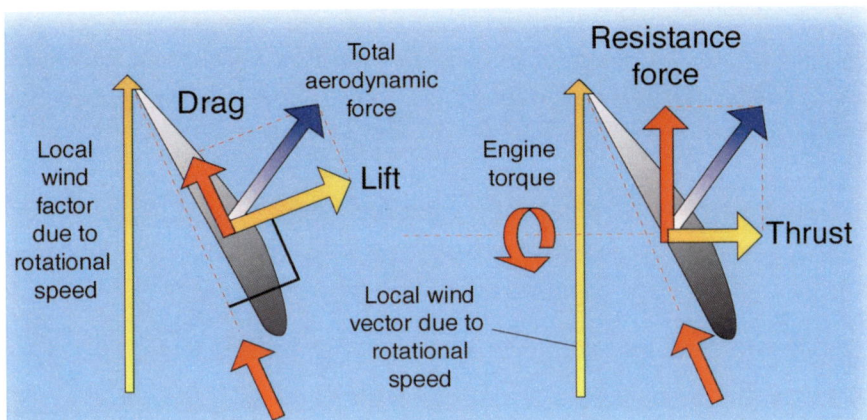

Figure 12.16

The component perpendicular to the plane of rotation is called thrust. The component in the plane of rotation is called the propeller resisting force

Because of the presence of the propeller resisting force, a certain power is required in order to rotate the propeller. This torsional moment is called engine torque. Power = torque x rotational speed.

The useful product of the propeller, i.e. to move the aircraft through the air, is thrust. The engine power is used to counteract the resistance force of the propeller. This torsional moment is called TORQUE.

Torque x rotational speed = power

In general we can assume that the direction perpendicular to the propeller plane of rotation is the same as the direction of flight, and therefore the thrust is also acting in the direction of flight.

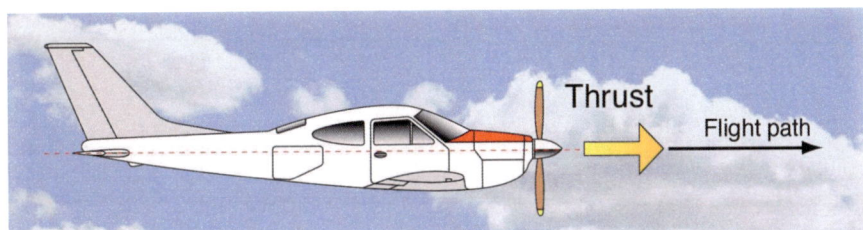

Figure 12.17

12.1.6.1   *Aerodynamic turning moment*

The centre of pressure of a blade section is usually forward of the pitch axis. This provides an aerodynamic twisting moment (ATM) which tends to increase the blade angle to coarse pitch.

12.1.6.2   *Centrifugal turning moment*

The centrifugal force acts outwards on a line from the centre of the propeller shaft. This force can be divided into two components, one parallel to a line radially out from the axis within the blade chord centre, and the other at right angles to this, which also acts in the plane of rotation. The former component causes tension in the blade, the latter causes a centrifugal twisting moment (CTM). which tends to reduce the blade angle, i.e. to turn the blades towards a fine pitch.

Usually, at least on a propeller with a long chord, the aerodynamic turning moment is comparatively small causing the CTM to be the main turning factor.

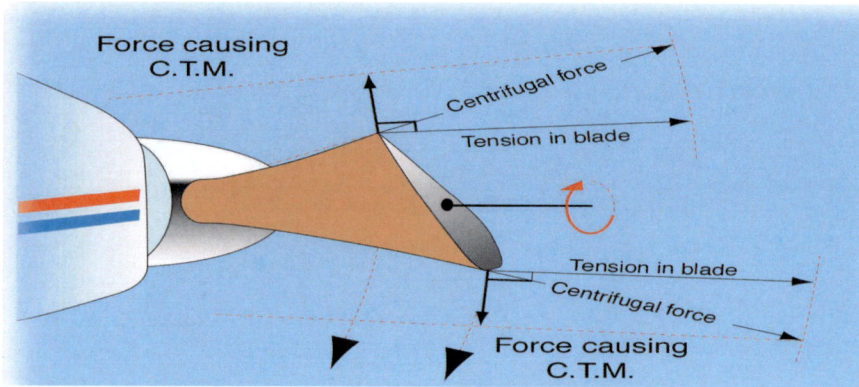

Figure 12.18 CTM is the major turning factor

12.2   *Propeller Efficiency*

The propeller must be able to absorb the power given to it by the engine. Or in other words, it must have a resisting force to balance the engine torque, otherwise the RPM will be too high and both the propeller and the engine will be inefficient. In the same way the propeller and the engine will be inefficient if the resisting force is too high since that would result in far too low RPM.

12.2.1   *Diameter of the propeller*

The propeller designer would like to produce a large propeller diameter having blades of high aspect ratio in order to obtain a high efficiency. But the aircraft designer wants to have a small diameter propeller to allow necessary ground clearance to prevent damage to the propeller tips, and clearance from the fuselage and other problems in multi-engine aircraft. Another problem with a large diameter propeller may be very high tip speeds. In general, a large diameter propeller is preferable at low speeds, giving high static thrust, while at high speeds a small diameter propeller is preferable giving reduced blade tip speed and high efficiency due to the large amount of air flowing through the propeller disc.

12.2.2   *Aspect ratio of blade and number of blades*

One way to increase the propeller efficiency at low speeds, e.g. to increase take-off performance, is to increase the propeller solidity. This means the ratio between that part of the propeller disc which, when viewed from front, is solid and the part which is just air. The ratio is measured by adding up all blades chords at a certain radius and dividing the sum by the circumference at that radius. The greater the solidity, the greater the power that can be absorbed at low speeds.

There are two ways to increase solidity: increase the chord of the blades or increase the number of blades

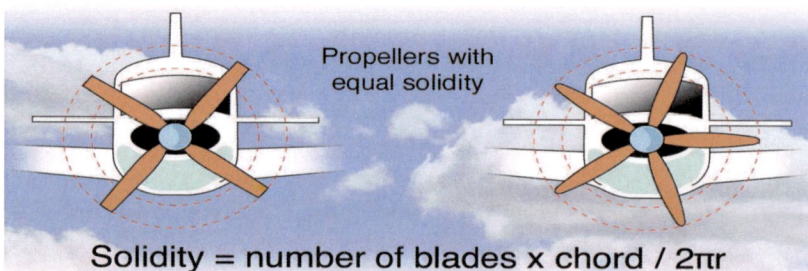

Solidity = number of blades x chord / $2\pi r$

Figure 12.19 Solidity

Hercules 6 blades

CRANFIELD AVIATION TRAINING SCHOOL LTD. PART-FCL GBR.ATO-0136
CATS INNOVATION CENTRE, LUTON, Bedfordshire LU2 8DL U.K.

www.catsaviation.com

12-27

Principles of Flight

Paddle-like blades with wide chords present some difficulties when used. The greater the chord of the blades, the greater the CTM, and the tendency of the blades to turn to a fine pitch angle. This effect may become so powerful that it puts severe stress on the pitch-changing mechanism.

12.2.3　　　　　*Variation in propeller efficiency with rpm and TAS*

A propeller blade section, with a given blade angle, has an angle of attack that depends on that section's rotational speed and on the total velocity. Consider a given propeller blade section turning at given fixed rpm with a given blade angle. If the airspeed is zero, there is a very large angle of attack. When the aircraft accelerates, the total velocity increases. The angle of attack begins to decrease to a more efficient value due to the increasing airspeed of the aircraft. Normally, this causes an increase in thrust.

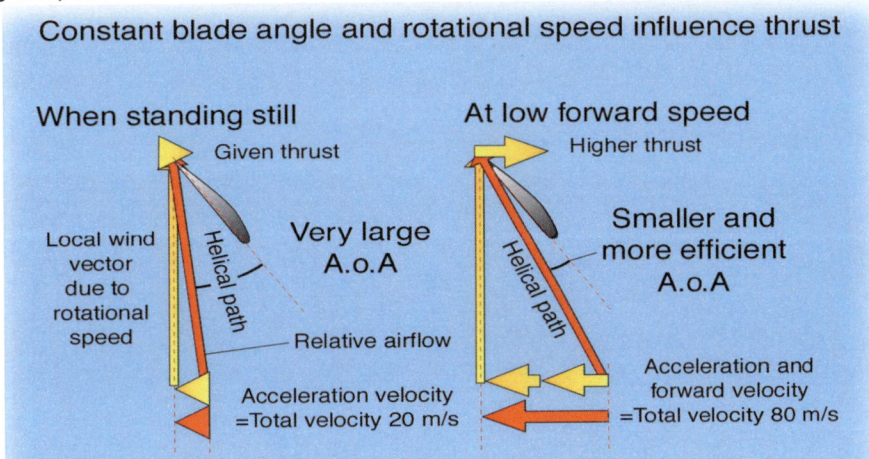

Figure 12.20 Increasing TAS results in reducing thust

As the aircraft accelerates, the forward speed increases, while the angle of attack and the thrust decrease. At a given high airspeed, the angle of attack becomes so small that no thrust is developed.

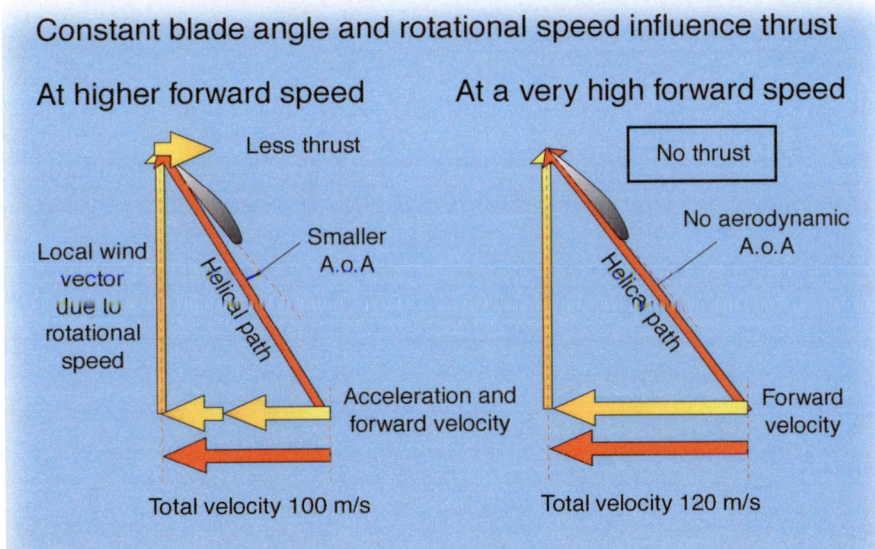

Figure 12.21

At a given rpm and blade angle there is only a narrow band of airspeed in which the propeller will operate close to its most efficient angle of attack

The propeller is not able to convert all of the engine power into power available for propelling the aircraft. The propeller efficiency is a measure of the ability of the propeller to convert the engine power into available power. It is expressed as a percentage. If the propeller efficiency is 70% and the engine produces 100 kW, only 70 kW are available for propelling the aircraft.

So, efficiency = Thrust x V / power on propeller shaft.

> The propeller efficiency is a measure of the ability of the propeller to convert engine power into available power

The propeller efficiency is at its maximum when the A.o.A. over the most important part of the whole propeller blade length is the most efficient one. At a given propeller rpm the propeller efficiency increases rapidly from low airspeed to its maximum and then rapidly decreases. This means that the propeller efficiency is at its maximum at a given airspeed, and that it is lower at any other airspeed.

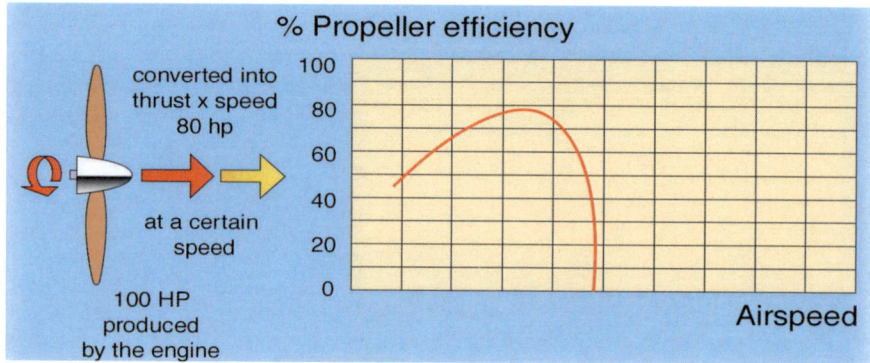

Figure 12.22 Propeller efficiency is optimal only over a narrow speed range

> At a given rpm the propeller efficiency increases rapidly from low airspeed to its maximum and then rapidly decreases

It is necessary to distinguish between available power and thrust. Thrust is a force, while available power is defined as thrust x airspeed. If the airspeed is zero, the available power is zero. The thrust, however, may be near to or at its maximum at zero airspeed depending on the blade angle. At a given rpm and blade angle the thrust decreases but the available power increases as airspeed increases until the propeller reaches the maximum efficiency. At that airspeed, rpm and blade angle, the available power will be at its maximum.

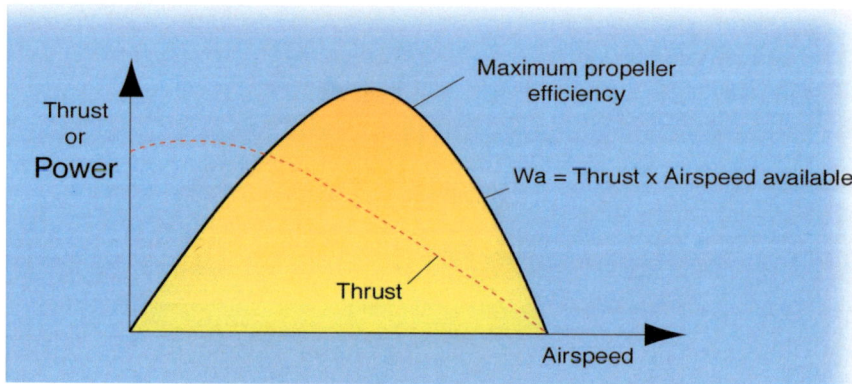

Figure 12.23 Power available depends on TAS

Since the engine has its maximum efficiency at a given rpm, it is of interest to know how the efficiency at different blade angles changes with changes in airspeed while at constant rpm.

CRANFIELD AVIATION TRAINING SCHOOL LTD. PART-FCL GBR.ATO-0136
CATS INNOVATION CENTRE, LUTON, Bedfordshire LU2 8DL U.K.   www.catsaviation.com

12-29   Principles of Flight

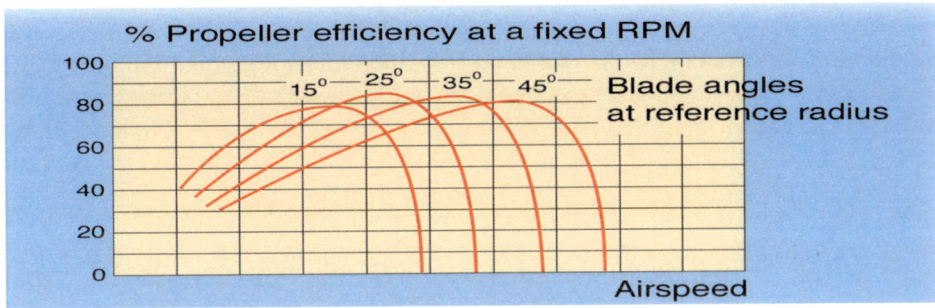

Figure 12.24

A high blade angle is more efficient at high TAS. This has its highest efficiency value at a blade angle of 25°.

12.2.4   *Fixed pitch propeller*

Propellers where the blade angle is fixed are called fixed pitch propellers. The efficiency of a fixed pitch propeller varies greatly with airspeed.

On a fixed pitch propeller, the blade angle cannot be changed and its efficiency varies greatly with airspeed

The designer chooses a fixed pitch propeller with the blade angle that gives the best angle of attack and efficiency at the desired combination of airspeed and rpm, for instance for best climb or best cruise performance. Consider that a propeller rotating at the desired rpm and at cruising speed. The angle of attack is close to optimum for each section of the propeller. The propeller is developing a certain thrust and requires a certain torque to rotate. If the aircraft accelerates, for instance by going into a descent, the airflow through the propeller increases, while the angle of attack of the propeller blades decreases, and less thrust is produced.

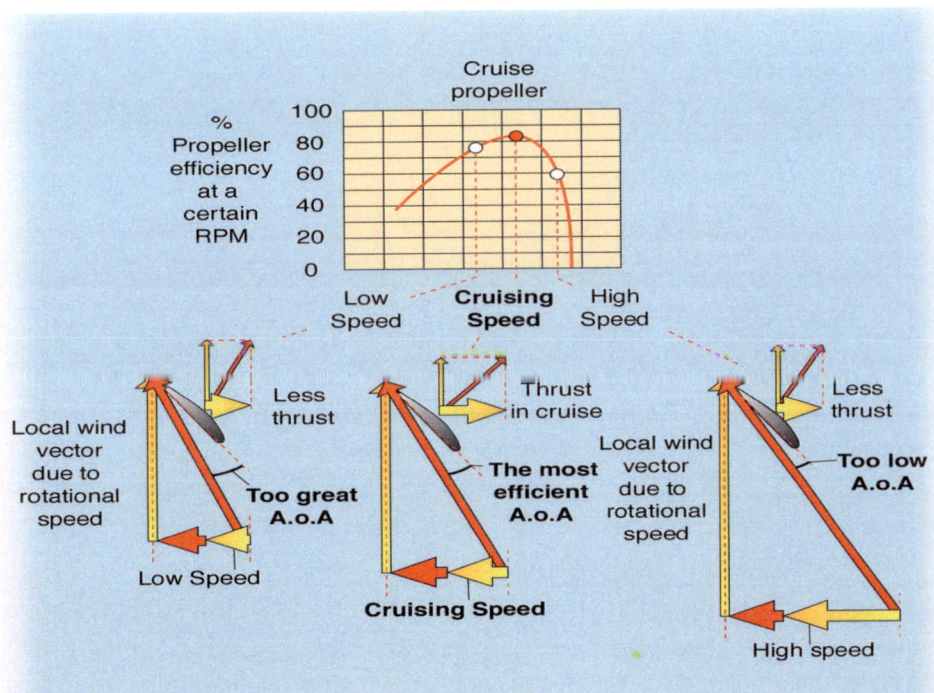

Figure 12.25

As the angle of attack decreases, the torque required to turn the propeller also decreases because the resistance force of the propeller decreases. If power is not reduced, the RPM will increase because engine power is proportional to RPM and torque.

If the aircraft decelerates, for instance by going into a climb, the airflow through the propeller slows down and the angle of attack will increase. As a result, the thrust initially increases but so does the propeller drag. Thus the required torque is increased and, if engine power is not increased, the RPM will decrease, giving a net effect of less thrust. A fixed pitch propeller is generally used only on light general aviation aircraft with low engine power and a limited speed range.

> A fixed pitch propeller has its highest efficiency at the desired combination of airspeed and RPM

12.2.5 Blade stall

A propeller blade may stall, just as a wing may stall. If a propeller with a high pitch angle has a low forward speed, the blade A.o.A may be above the critical one and the blade stalls, loosing most of its thrust. Ice on the propeller increases the resistance force and reduces thrust. This reduces the propeller efficiency and blade stall may occur. When flying in icing conditions ice on the propeller reduces the available thrust considerably.

12.2.6 Variable pitch propeller

A variable pitch propeller has adjustable pitch, the blade angle of which can be varied in order to operate at the most efficient rpm for the engine and at the most efficient A.o.A. for each airspeed. At low airspeeds a small blade angle is preferable; at medium airspeeds a medium blade angle has approximately the same efficiency. And at high airspeeds a large blade angle has nearly the same efficiency. The blades can be rotated at the root by means of an electrical or hydraulic mechanism in order to change the blade angle as the speed of the aircraft changes. A propeller can never be fully optimised for all speeds since the twist of the propeller can only be set for a certain speed.

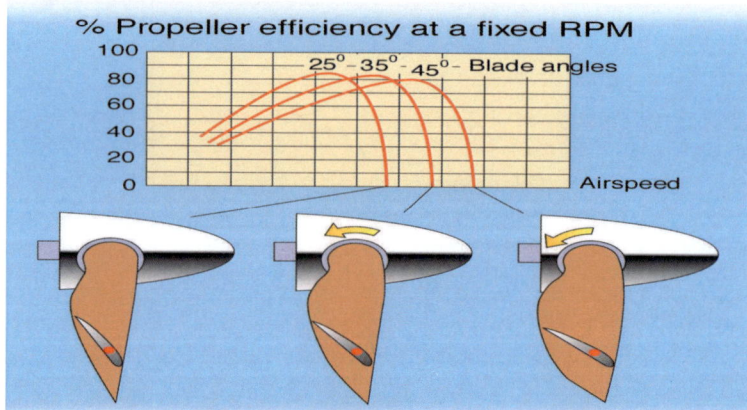

Figure 12.26 Variable pitch propeller

> A variable pitch propeller can change the blade angle to be more optimised for different aircraft speeds, but the highest value of efficiency can only be reached at a certain speed

12.2.7 Constant speed propeller

With a constant speed propeller, you set the desired RPM. The control system of propeller speed senses any change in the desired RPM and automatically adjusts the blade angle to bring the RPM to the desired value. The RPM is therefore automatically kept constant regardless of changes in airspeed or power input, of course within certain limits of speed and power. The constant speed propeller has high efficiency over a wide airspeed range but is more complicated, heavier and more expensive than a fixed pitch propeller. With a constant speed propeller you set the desired RPM. That RPM is automatically kept constant by changing the blade angle.

12.3   *Secondary effects of the propeller*

12.3.1   *Right or left-hand rotation*

When viewed from the cockpit, a propeller rotating clockwise is said to be a right-hand propeller and vice versa.

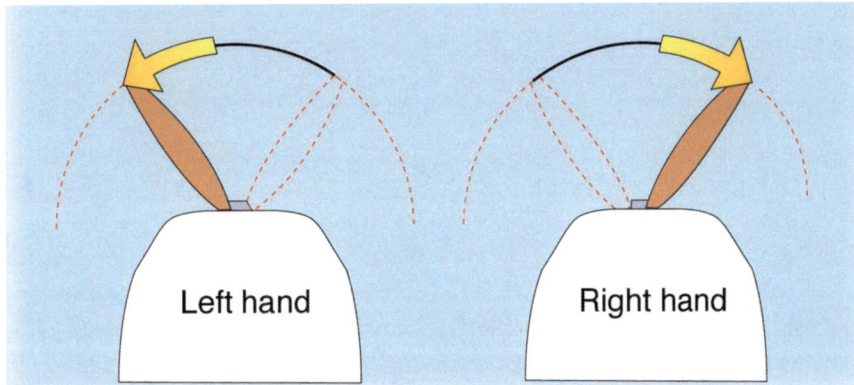

Figure 12.27 Propeller naming – right or left handed

12.3.2   *Torque reaction*

As a propeller is turning with a given rpm, it experiences a given resistance force roughly similar to the drag of an airfoil. This drag causes propeller torque.

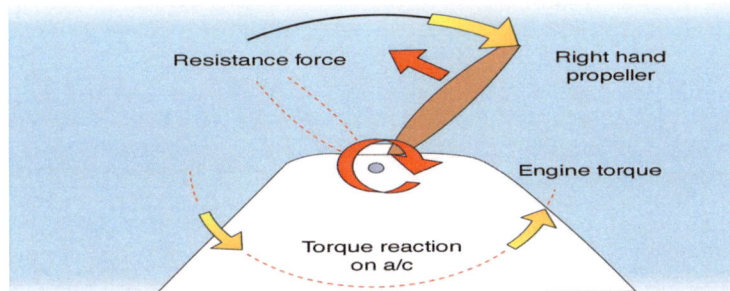

Figure 12.28 Propeller torque

As the propeller rotates clockwise, the torque creates a moment in the opposite direction that tends to rotate the aircraft counter-clockwise. When increasing power with a right-hand propeller, the aircraft will tend to lower its left wing.

In light aircraft the torque reaction is not usually significant, but on single engine high-powered aircraft, the torque reaction is quite noticeable.

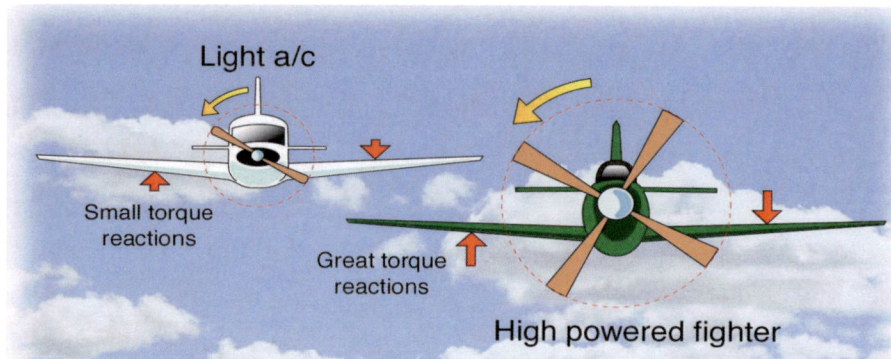

Figure 12.29 Propeller torque reaction

The roll tendency from the torque reaction can be reduced by use of lateral trim.

12.3.3   *Asymmetric slipstream effect*

The propeller produces a slipstream that rotates in the same direction as the propeller. This effect is caused due to the higher velocity and the direction slightly outwards radially of the slipstream. A low-pressure zone is created towards the slipstream centre which creates a force on the airflow elements towards the centre. The path of the flow elements will therefore be curved by that force. The rotational direction of the curved slipstream is determined by the propeller blade rotation due to the downwash behind the propeller blade. As the slipstream corkscrews around the fuselage, it strikes the fin and rudder at a slanted angle. When the propeller rotates clockwise, the slipstream strikes the fin on the left side and pushes the tail to the right. Especially under high power conditions, the slipstream impinges on the left part of the fin, generating a force which pushes the tail to the right and yaws the nose to the left. This effect is called asymmetric slipstream effect.

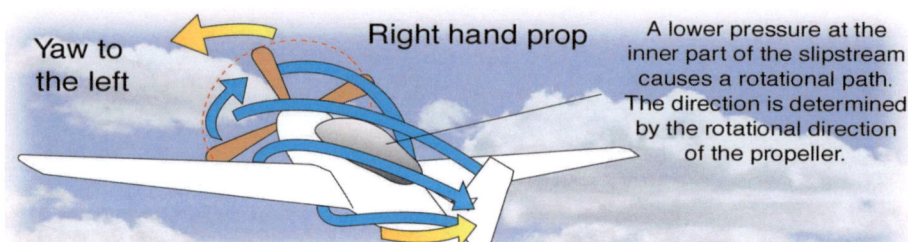

Figure 12.30 Asymmetric slipstream effect

On a single engine aircraft with a right hand propeller, the slipstream effect causes the aircraft nose to yaw to the left

The aircraft designer may offset the fin or the thrust line of the engine. Another method is to twist the fin or rudder to counteract the slipstream effect on a single engine aircraft at cruising airspeed. On a twin-engined aircraft with wing-mounted engines, the slipstream effect is different. When the propeller rotates, the air is accelerated backwards with an airspeed which is higher than the speed of the aircraft. Thus the wing section close to the engines experiences a higher lift.

When both engines are operative, the increase in airflow speed causes an increase in lift on both wings due to the slipstream effect. If one of the two engines is inoperative, the increase in lift due to the slipstream disappears. This causes the wing with the dead engine to experience a lower total lift and the aircraft rolls towards the dead engine.

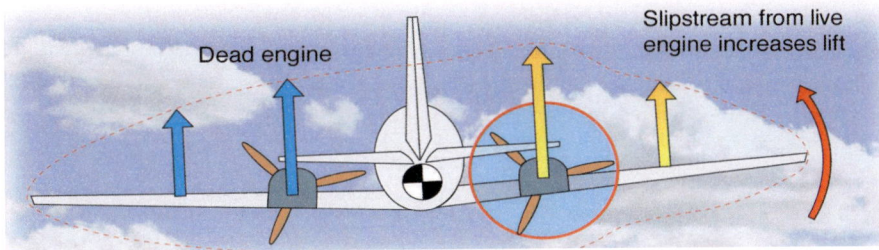

Figure 12.31 Slipstream from love engine increases lift

With one engine inoperative, the aircraft experiences a rolling tendency due to the reduced lift on the dead engine wing

12.3.4 Gyroscopic moments

Since the propeller is a rotating mass, it experiences the effect called gyro moments (gyroscopic precession). The applied force is rotated 90° in the direction of the propeller rotation.

Gyroscopic moments rotates an applied moment 90° in the direction of the propeller rotation

When you want the aircraft to climb, you apply a downward force on the tailplane. This force can be imagined as applied on the low rear part of the rotating propeller disk and as a result of the 90° transfer of the force, the aircraft yaws to the right during the transition from level flight to climbing.

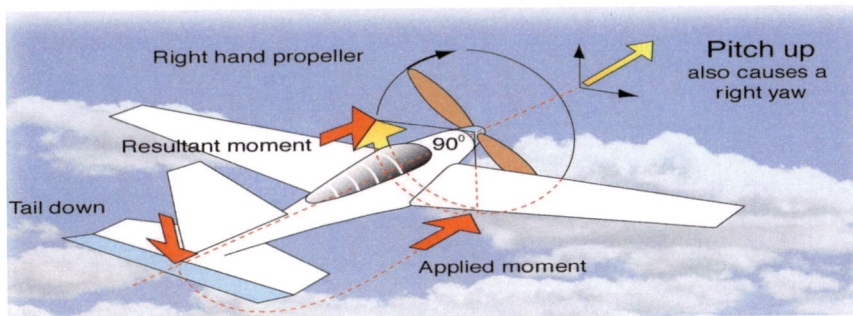

Figure 12.32 Yaw during climb initiation

If the aircraft is pitched down, the moment applied on the tailplane can be imagined as applied to the upper rear part of the rotating propeller disk. As a result of the gyroscopic action, the aircraft will yaw to the left during the transition.

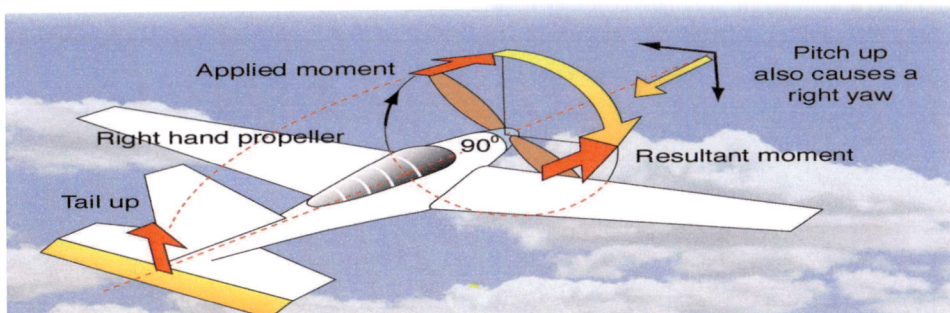

Figure 12.33 Yaw during descent initiation

A pitch UP, with a right-hand propeller, causes the aircraft to yaw to the right
A pitch DOWN, with a right-hand propeller, causes the aircraft to yaw to the left

Torque reaction and slipstream effect are effective when the propeller is rotating at constant speed. Gyro precession is experienced only when the propeller plane of rotation is changed due to a change in pitch or yaw. The greater the speed of this movement or the greater the inertia, the greater the gyroscopic effect.

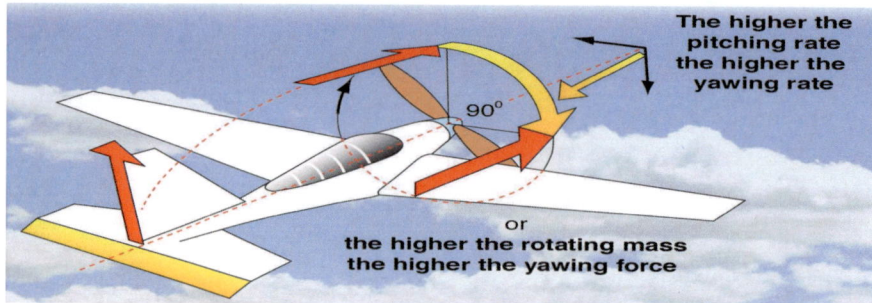

Figure 12.34 Gyro effects depend on change in aircraft pitch

12.3.5 *Asymmetric blade effect*

When flying at a high AoA the propeller shaft is inclined upwards and the plane of rotation of the propeller is not vertical.

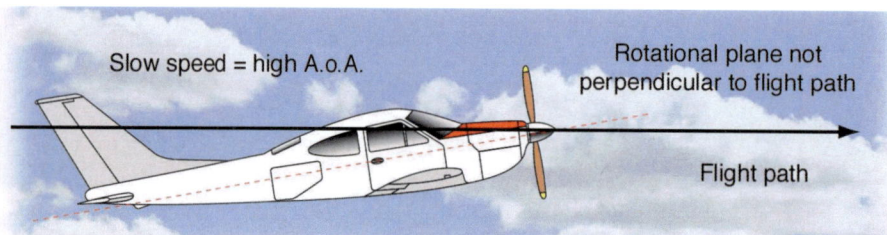

Figure 12.35

The aircraft is travelling horizontally and the down going propeller blade experiences a higher dynamic pressure and have a higher AoA.

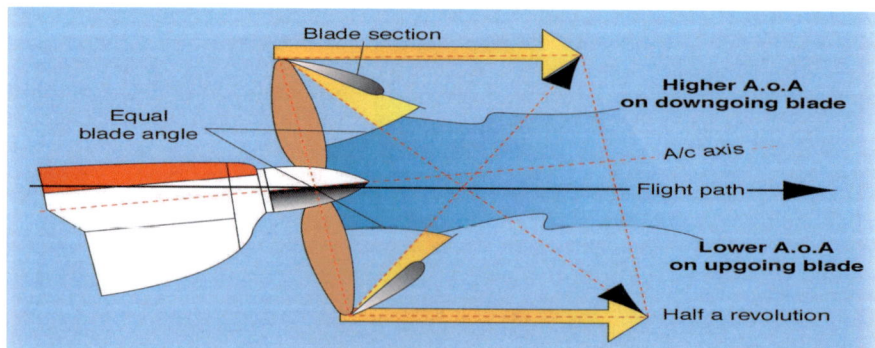

Figure 12.36   P-factor

As a result, the downgoing half of the propeller disk will produce more thrust than the up-going half, causing an aircraft with a right hand propeller to yaw to the left if flying at a high A.o.A. The difference in thrust is called the P-factor. As soon as the tail is raised and the propeller disk is perpendicular to the flight path, the asymmetric propeller blade effect is nil.

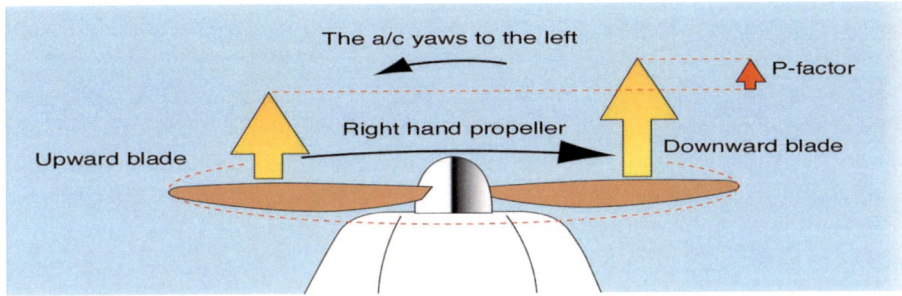

Figure 12.37   P-factor

The asymmetric propeller blade effect, P-factor, occurs when the propeller disk is not perpendicular to the average local flow. In straight and level flight, with a high nose attitude a component of thrust acts perpendicularly to the flight path. The vertical component of thrust is not effective in the direction of flight but helps lift to counteract the weight of the aircraft.

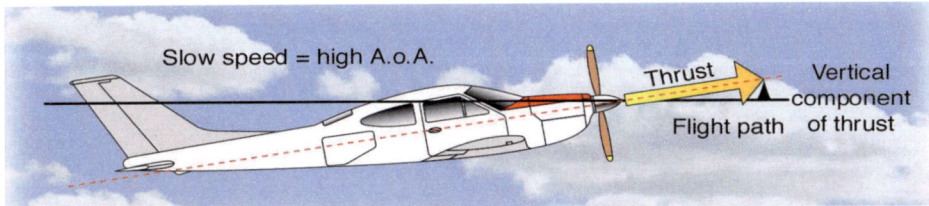

Figure 12.38

Despite being in level flight, there is a vertical component of thrust at low speeds with a high nose attitude

12.3.6   *Take-off swing*

There is often a tendency for an aircraft to swing to one side during the take-off run. If the propeller rotates right-hand or clockwise, the torque reaction will be anti-clockwise, the left-hand main wheel is pressed harder on to the ground than the right-hand one and the extra friction tends to yaw the aircraft to the left. The higher the speed, the higher the compensating lift from the wings.

The slipstream from a right-hand propeller also tends to yaw the aircraft to the left and the gyroscopic effect comes in when the attitude is changed. An aircraft with a tailwheel will first tend to yaw to the left when the tail is raised, then to the right when the nose is raised for lift-off.

12.3.7   *Windmilling drag*

The thrust-producing propeller can also be a very high drag producer. When the engine is not producing any power, the airflow that meets the propeller with a high negative AoA will force it to rotate like a windmill. A dead piston engine increases the required torque to turn the propeller, but even a free turning propeller will create a very high drag. During this impelled rotation, the propeller creates a type of drag called wind-milling drag.

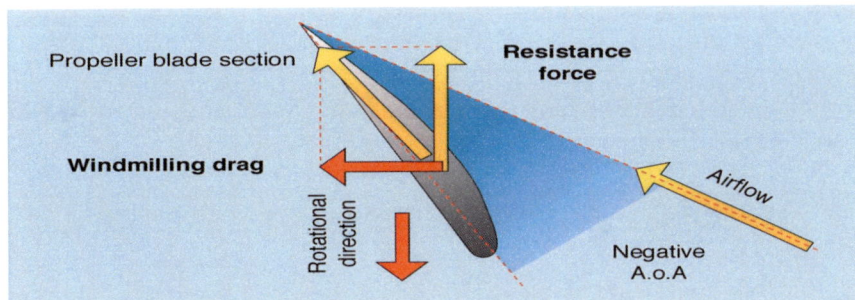

Figure 12.39 Wind-milling drag

> When the engine is inoperative, the airflow forces the propeller to rotate like a windmill causing very high wind-milling drag

An aircraft with twin engines having one wind-milling propeller and the other engine at full power will, especially at low mass, usually have a minimum control speed V_{MC} that is higher than the stalling speed. This fact is very important to remember since flying below V_{MC} may cause a very rapid yaw and roll to the dead engine side with total loss of control until power on the live engine is reduced. At worst an unrecoverable spin may have been entered. Never fly with full asymmetrical power at, or near, V_{MC}.

12.3.8   *Feathering*

In order to reduce the drag from a wind-milling propeller, most multi-engine aircraft are equipped with a system that changes pitch angle of the propeller blades in order to give them an AoA almost equal to zero, meaning less drag. This kind of propeller is called a feathering propeller.

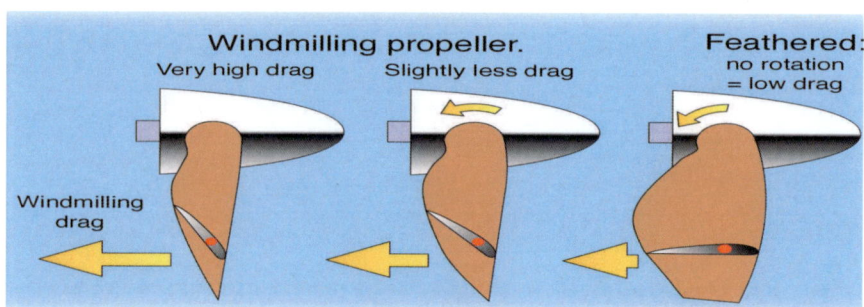

Figure 12.40 Feathering a propeller

> A windmilling propeller creates very high windmilling drag. A feathered propeller creates considerably lower drag

On a multi-engine aircraft never let a dead engine propeller windmill, not even at idle power. In a difficult situation, e.g. a go-around with one engine at high power, aircraft control may be lost.

> On a multi-engine aircraft, leaving the propeller of a dead engine to windmill, even at idle power, will cause the drag and yaw moment to become dangerously high

Additionally, at low RPM the centrifugal latches will lock the propeller in fine pitch.

12.3.9   *Noise abatement*

The noise from the aircraft propulsion system is a rather difficult problem to tackle. The noise from a pure jet engine mainly comes from the thrust producing high-speed jet-flow. A turbo-fan engine has lower speed jet-flow but instead a fan which produces noise. A propeller engine may have a rather loud noise coming from the exhaust gases and, additionally, the propeller may cause a loud noise. A propeller that rotates with relatively high velocity often has tip speed noise. A propeller with a high load, i.e. each propeller blade has to carry a high thrust load, will also produce noise. One solution to reduce propeller noise is to have low tip velocity and many blades. One example of noise reduction is the change of propeller on many glider-towing aircraft. These aircraft have to use high power during long slow climbs. Their originally two-blade propellers are exchanged for a smaller diameter three or four-blade propellers.

> Low tip speed and low blade load reduces the propeller noise

Self Assessment Test 12

1   The blade angle of a fixed pitch propeller remains the same in flight. The angle of attack of the blades:
A)   Increases when airspeed decreases and vice versa
B)   Is always directly proportional to the airspeed
C)   Also remains the same
D)   Decreases when airspeed decreases and vice versa

2   The primary purpose of a conventional propeller is:
A)   To create lift on the aerofoils of the aircraft
B)   To accelerate a small mass of air
C)   To convert engine thrust into horsepower
D)   To convert engine horsepower into thrust

3   The diameter of the propeller blades is necessarily limited by structural limitations, ground clearance and:
A)   The number of blades
B)   Economy of construction
C)   Tip speed
D)   Propeller shaft torque limitations

4   Blade angle is:
A)   The acute angle between the blade chord line and the forward thrust line of the aircraft
B)   The acute angle between the blade back and the forward thrust line of the aircraft
C)   The acute angle between the relative air flow and the plane of propeller rotation
D)   The acute angle between the blade chord line and the plane of propeller rotation

5   A fixed pitch propeller on an aircraft designed for range would achieve an angle of attack between 2° and 4° during:
A)   Take off
B)   Cruise
C)   Flight at speeds close to V_{NE}
D)   Initial climb out

6   The combination of propeller pitch and aircraft speed that will result in the greatest angle of attack of the blade is:
A)   Coarse pitch and low TAS
B)   Coarse pitch and high TAS
C)   Fine pitch and high TAS
D)   Fine pitch and low TAS

7   Increasing the speed of rotation of a fixed pitch propeller will initially:
A)   Decrease the effective angle of attack of the blades
B)   Increase the effective angle of attack of the blades
C)   Increase the blade angle
D)   Increase the angle of advancement of the blades

8 The purpose of twist in a propeller blade is to:
A) Reduce the torque reaction of the propeller by throwing air outwards
B) Reduce the centrifugal effect of the propeller by concentrating the mass towards the root
C) Maintain the thrust vector constant along the entire length of the blade
D) Oppose the aerodynamic twisting force in a rotating propeller

9 With the aircraft cruise at TAS, if flight fine pitch were selected the effect would be:
A) A decrease in aircraft speed
B) An increase in aircraft speed
C) No effect on aircraft speed
D) A decrease in propeller rpm

10 A wind-milling propeller produces:
A) Drag and rotates in the normal direction of rotation
B) Thrust and rotates in the normal direction of rotation
C) Drag and rotates in the opposite direction to normal
D) Thrust and rotates in the opposite direction to normal

11 The geometric pitch of the propeller determines:
A) The distance that the propeller actually advances during one revolution
B) The blade angle when the propeller is at the optimum angle of attack
C) The distance that the propeller would advance during one revolution if there were no slip
D) The difference between root and tip blade angles

12 The centrifugal twisting moment:
A) Tends to rotate the blades towards fine pitch, unless balanced by counterweights
B) Tends to rotate the blades towards coarse pitch, unless balanced by counterweights
C) Tends to rotate the blades towards feather unless prevented by a centrifugal latch
D) Tends to stretch the blades

CRANFIELD AVIATION TRAINING SCHOOL LTD. PART-FCL GBR.ATO-0136
CATS CATS INNOVATION CENTRE, LUTON, Bedfordshire LU2 8DL U.K.   www.catsaviation.com

12-39   Principles of Flight

Self Assessment Test 12 Answers

1	A
2	D
3	C
4	D
5	B
6	A
7	B
8	C
9	A
10	A
11	C
12	A

CHAPTER 13

LIFT / DRAG and

WAKE TURBULENCE

13.1 *Lift / Drag Ratio*

13.1.1 *Review of C_L / α and C_D / α curves*

An aircraft designer not only has to make sure that enough lift is produced by the wings but also at a reasonable amount of power, i.e. without simultaneously producing too much drag. Up until now we have been dealing with lift and drag separately. In order to determine the performance and efficiency of an airfoil at a particular angle of attack (and airspeed), lift and drag must be considered together.

You remember that the lift curve shows a steady increase in the coefficient of lift with an increase in the angle of attack, up to the stall angle of attack. Beyond the stall angle of attack, the coefficient of lift decreases rapidly due to the stall of the airfoil. The coefficient of drag versus angle of attack curve shows that C_D, after a minor initial decline, increases steadily all the way as the angle of attack increases.

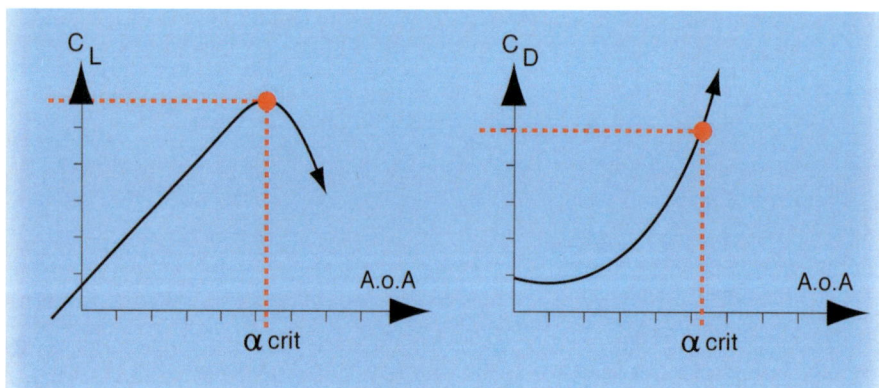

Figure 13.1

C_D has its minimum value at small angles of attack. As the stall angle is approached, the drag increases at a progressively higher rate due to separated flow.

> C_D has its minimum value at small angles of attack. With an increase in the A.o.A., drag increases at a progressively higher rate

In order to evaluate the wing efficiency we must consider more than just the lift produced. In fact, a wing has its greatest lifting ability just prior to the stalling angle of attack. Unfortunately, near the stalling angle, the wing also generates considerable drag.

> An airfoil has its greatest lifting ability (C_{Lmax}) at the stall A.o.A. but also very high induced drag

The minimum drag occurs at a fairly low angle of attack, in this case slightly above zero degrees A.o.A. Unfortunately, the lifting ability is very low at low angles of attack.

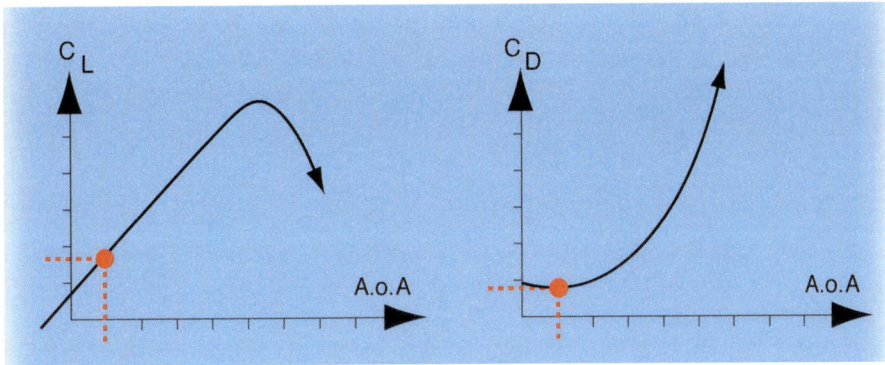

Figure 13.2

At each angle of attack, the lift/drag ratio is the ratio between lift and drag or between the coefficient of lift and the coefficient of drag. It expresses the aircraft efficiency.

13.1.2   *Polar and lift/drag ratio curves*

We can draw a curve that shows the variation of the C_D as a function of the C_L. In other words, for a given aircraft it shows how much drag is produced for a given lift at every angle of attack. This curve is called the polar curve.

The polar curve shows the variation in C_D as a function of C_L

Each point of the polar curve is obtained for a given angle of attack and shows the corresponding values of the coefficients of lift and drag.

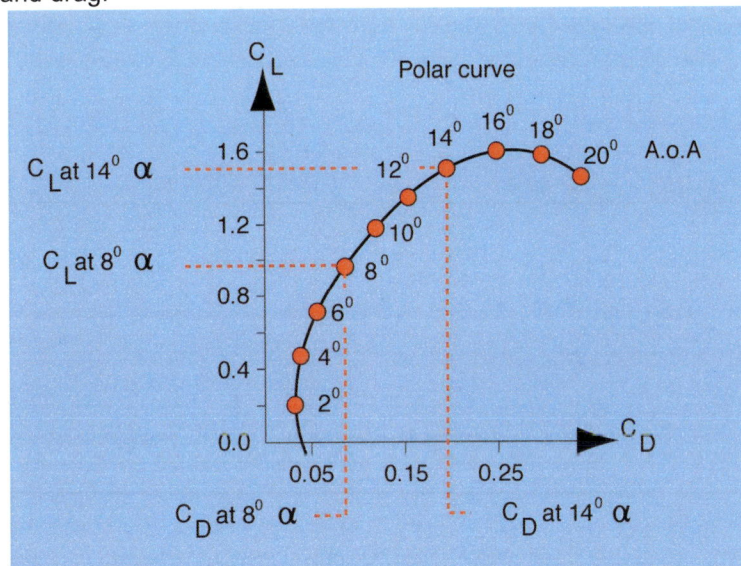

Figure 13.3

For each angle of attack we can calculate the lift/drag ratio by dividing C_L by C_D (or lift by drag). In this way we can draw a curve representing the variation of the L/D ratio as a function of the angle of attack.

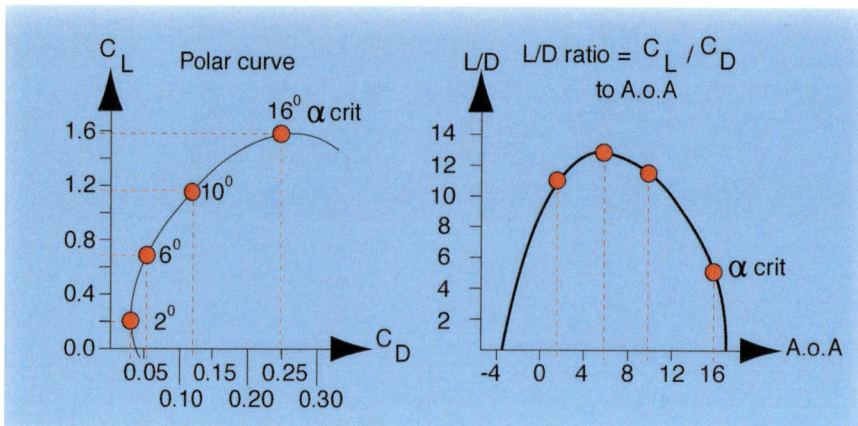

Figure 13.4

13.1.3   *Best lift/drag ratio*

For a light aircraft with a normally cambered wing we can see that, when the angle of attack is increased, the L/D ratio rapidly increases from zero to the maximum value. Then, as the angle of attack is increased further, the L/D ratio decreases until the stalling angle is reached and keeps decreasing even beyond that angle. The reason for this behaviour is that when the angle of attack is increased until the lift/drag ratio reaches its maximum value, both C_L and C_D increase but C_L increases more than C_D.

> When the angle of attack is increased beyond the maximum lift/drag ratio, C_D increases more than C_L

If we draw a straight line inclined at a given angle γ (gamma), starting from the axis origin, we see that the ratio between C_L and C_D (the lift/drag ratio) for point A as well as point B is equal to 5.

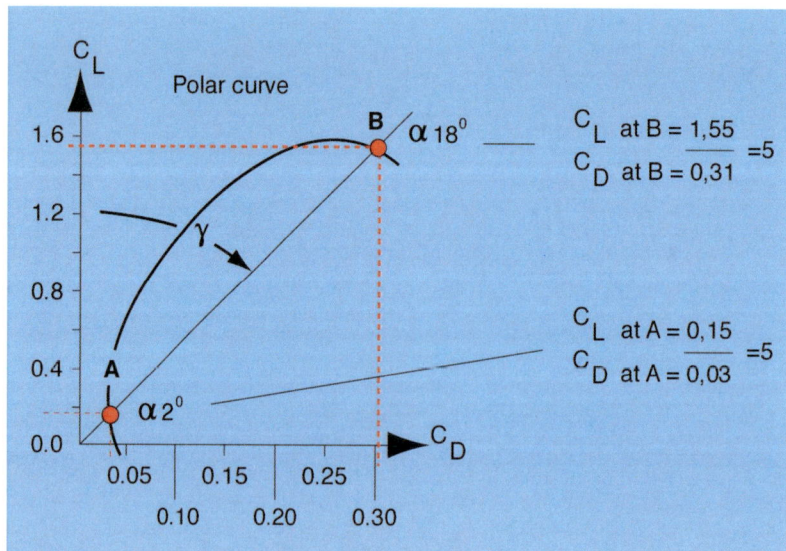

Figure 13.5

A straight line inclined at a given angle, γ, from the axis origin on C_L - C_D plane, represents the LIFT/DRAG RATIO. The smaller the angle between C_L axis and the straight line, the greater the lift/drag ratio. If we draw another straight line from origin of coordinates through point C and D we find the ratio between C_L and the C_D to be equal to 10.

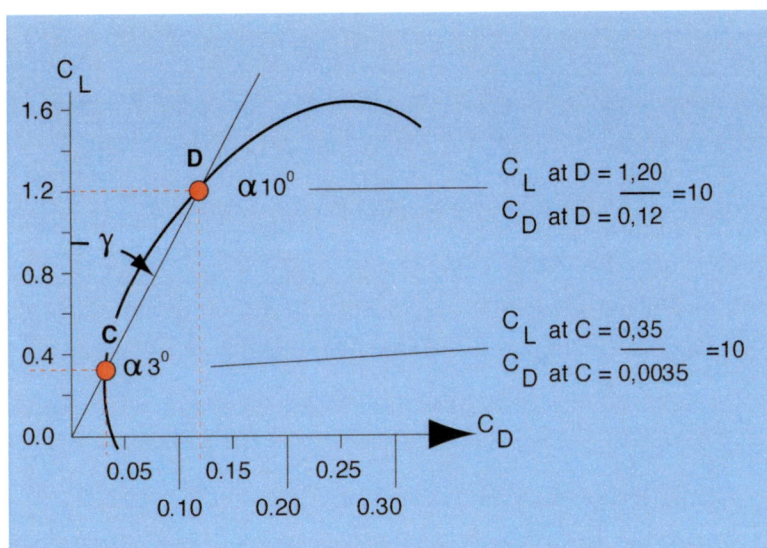

Figure 13.6

We can say that each straight line drawn from the axis origin represents a given lift/drag ratio. This lift/drag ratio is proportional to the straight line inclination which is measured by the angle γ.

The smaller the angle γ, the greater the lift/drag ratio.

We have said that each point on the polar curve represents a given angle of attack. As we can see in figure 13.5, at 2° A.o.A. we have a lift/drag ratio equal to 5. Looking at point B we can say that both the C_L and the C_D are increased but their ratio is still equal to 5. In other words at an A.o.A of both 2° and 18° we have a lift/drag ratio equal to 5! Thus, to create a certain lift at a low A.o.A, the speed needs to be high causing very high zero lift drag D_O, and at a high A.o.A the speed is low causing very high induced drag D_i. The same is true for an A.o.A of 3° and 10° respectively.

The same lift over drag relations exists at low speed as well as high speed. In order to find the Most Efficient Angle of Attack on the polar curve, we must draw the tangent to the curve starting from the axis origin. We can see that the best lift/drag ratio in this example is at 5° A.o.A., which is equal to a lift/drag ratio of 13.

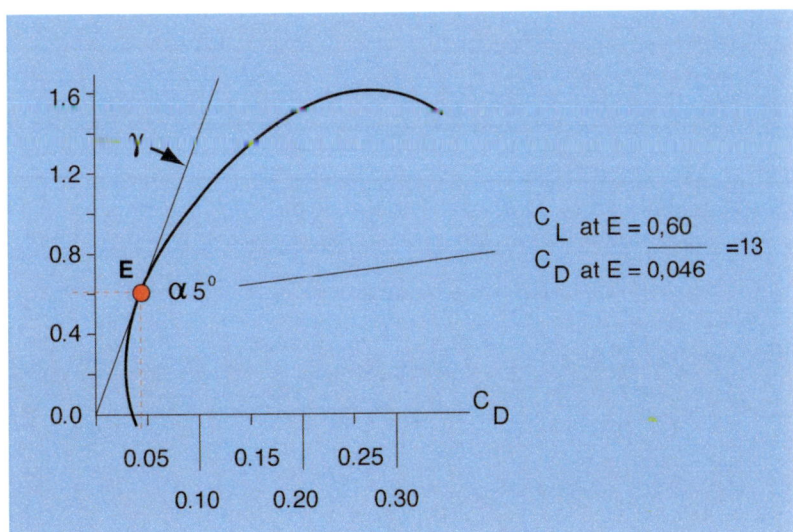

Figure 13.7

CRANFIELD AVIATION TRAINING SCHOOL LTD. PART-FCL GBR.ATO-0136

CATS CATS INNOVATION CENTRE, LUTON, Bedfordshire LU2 8DL U.K.

www.catsaviation.com

13-4

Principles of Flight

The line which is the tangent to the polar curve represents the best lift/drag ratio

In this example the best lift/drag ratio is 13, that is; the lift is 13 x the drag. The best lift/drag ratio for normal light aircraft is typically between 15 and 20 depending on several factors concerning the wings. Consequently; thanks to well-designed wings that create high pressure differences on their lower and upper surfaces despite a low A.o.A, it is possible to fly with relatively low power.

In the case of gliders, the L/D can reach values of 30 to 60, thus the drag is so low that you should be able to pull it in the air with only one finger, despite its weight of 400 to 500 kg, including the pilot! The angle of attack at which we obtain the best lift/drag ratio is called the most efficient angle of attack. For a normal light aircraft the value is approximately a 4-5°.

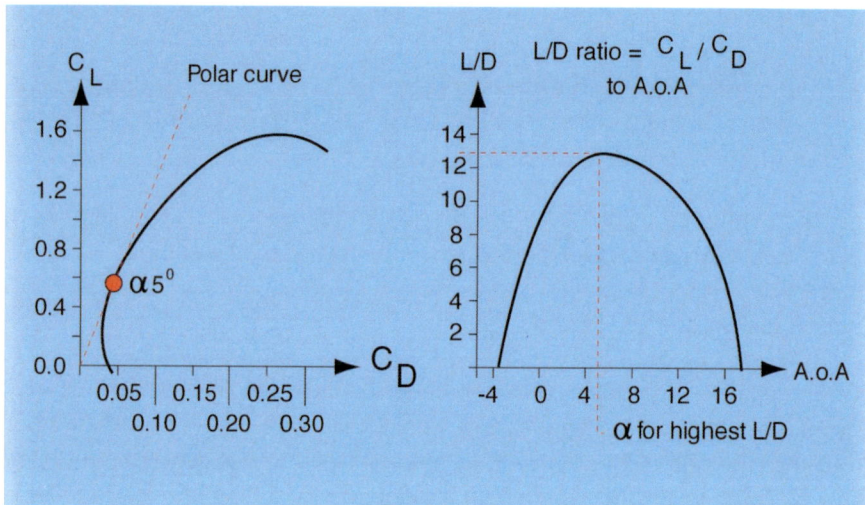

Figure 13.8

The angle of attack at which we obtain the best lift/drag ratio is called the MOST EFFICIENT ANGLE OF ATTACK

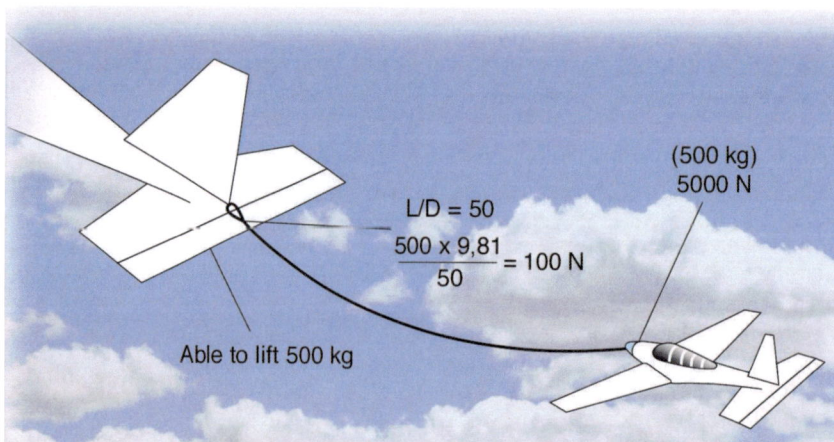

Figure 13.9

CRANFIELD AVIATION TRAINING SCHOOL LTD. PART-FCL GBR.ATO-0136

CATS CATS INNOVATION CENTRE, LUTON, Bedfordshire LU2 8DL U.K.

www.catsaviation.com

13-5

Principles of Flight

13.2   *Factors Affecting The Lift/Drag Ratio*

13.2.1   *Wing section*

One of the most important aircraft characteristics regarding efficiency is the wing thickness. A thin wing will cause less drag than a thick one. However, a thick wing designed to the same strength requirement, can have a lighter structure. Imagine an extremely thin wing and a rather thick one that are able to carry the same given weight. The very thin wing may have to be manufactured by steel, but the thick one requires only light metal or even wood. Another important factor is the maximum lifting capacity of the wing. A moderate thick wing will have a high maximum C_L, but a wing that is too thick will, like a very thin wing, suffer flow separation at a low A.o.A.

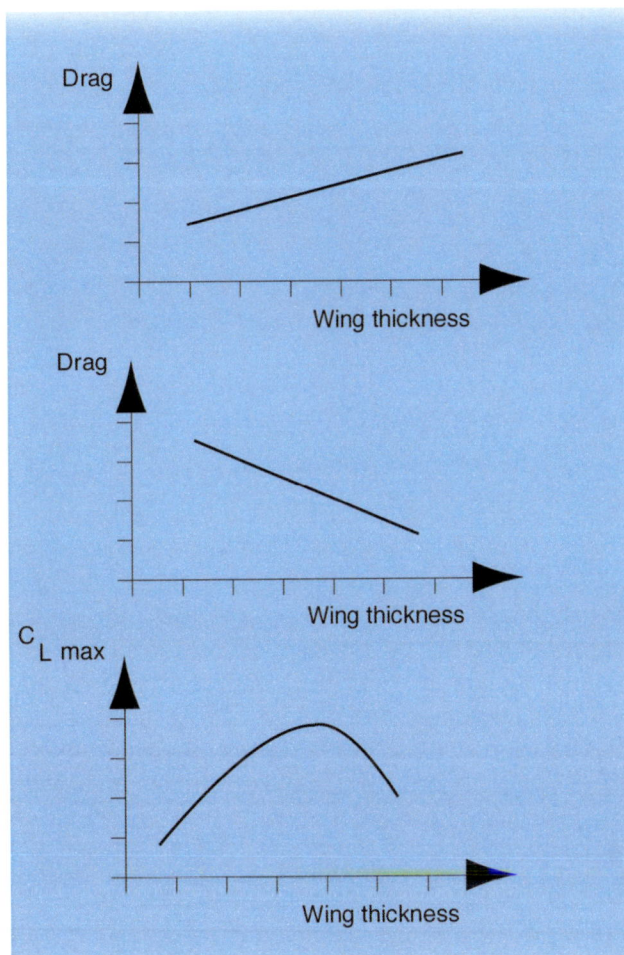

Figure 13.10

Depending on the operational requirements, the wing thickness may vary a lot on different aircraft. Another important factor is the wing airfoil section. A normal airfoil creates minimum drag at an angle of attack that is very close to zero. However, the most efficient A.o.A is that for normal cruising speeds. At the cruising A.o.A. and speed it creates a given drag, thus obtaining a given lift/drag ratio.

If we look at the polar curve of two wings, we can see that at the angle of attack considered, airfoil A produces higher lift and lower drag than airfoil B and is therefore more efficient.

CRANFIELD AVIATION TRAINING SCHOOL LTD. PART-FCL GBR.ATO-0136
CATS INNOVATION CENTRE, LUTON, Bedfordshire LU2 8DL U.K.   www.catsaviation.com
13-6   Principles of Flight

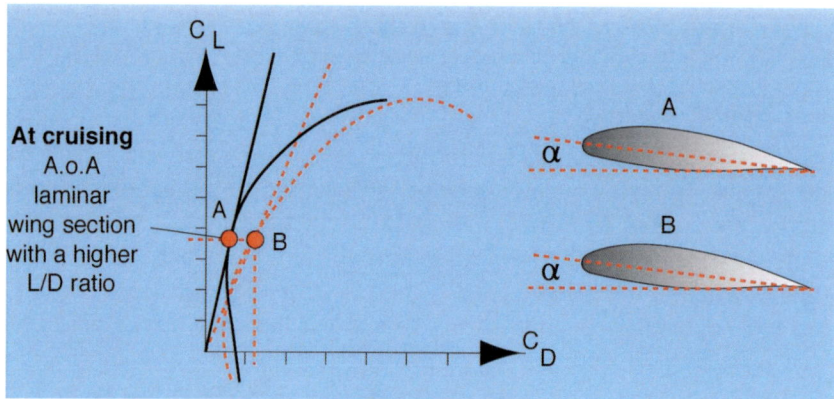

Figure 13.11

At a given A.o.A., different wing sections will create different values of drag and lift.

A particular type of wing section called a laminar wing section is able to create the minimum coefficient of drag at the A.o.A. normally used during cruise giving a higher lift/drag ratio.

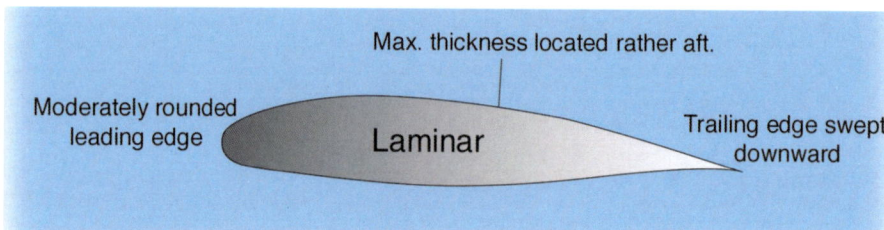

Figure 13.12

As the name implies, a laminar section is able to maintain the laminar boundary layer better than a regular one. However, the major part of the boundary layer is still the turbulent one, except on modern gliders which may have laminar boundary layer up to 60% of the chord. The disadvantage of a laminar wing airfoil section is that it is very sensitive to contamination. When clean, the low drag laminar boundary layer is more extended than that of a regular airfoil section, but the slightest contamination spoils the laminar flow causing the transition to the high drag turbulent flow to begin much earlier. Another disadvantage is that maximum C_L is somewhat reduced on a laminar section compared to a regular section, especially if the wing is being contaminated by dirt, insects, frost, snow or ice. A laminar wing section has it maximum thickness located further aft and has a moderately rounded leading edge. The advantage is low drag, while the disadvantage is the reduced C_{Lmax} and the high sensitivity to contamination.

13.2.2   *Use of flaps*

Deployment of high lift devices will in most cases increase the drag. Only when being near or at speeds for stall for a clean wing can the use of flaps reduce drag somewhat. But during all other flight conditions, high lift devices reduce the lift/drag ratio.

Use of flaps or leading edge devices reduces the lift/drag ratio

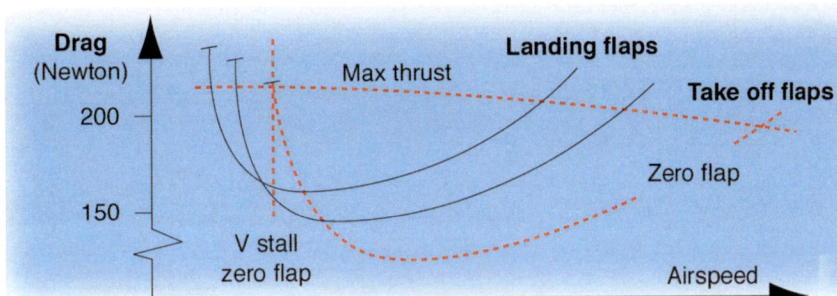

Figure 13.13

13.2.3   *Span loading and aspect ratio*

Another important factor affecting aircraft efficiency is the span loading, sometimes called spanwise load. Two different sets of wings producing the same lift but with different aspect ratios will have two different span loadings. Remember that the lower the span loading, the lower the induced drag.

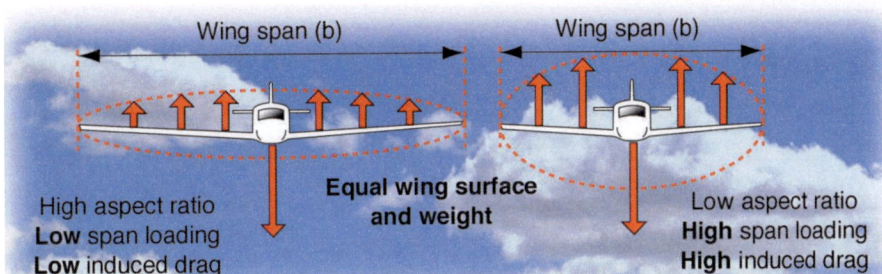

Figure 13.14

You can see that with a lower span loading, the lift/drag ratio for a given angle of attack increases due to the decrease in the coefficient of drag.

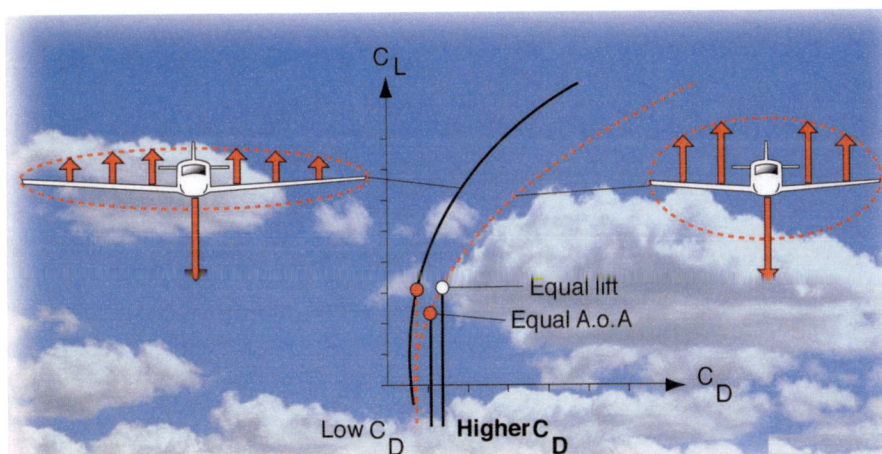

Figure 13.15

A lower span loading gives a higher lift/drag ratio

In fact, all the methods used to reduce induced drag may also be good methods to increase the lift/drag ratio. Winglets, which decrease induced drag, increase the aircraft lift/drag ratio, especially for aircraft cruising for long periods of time at high altitudes where a high C_L is needed.

Figure 13.16

Winglets may be a good method to increase the lift/ drag ratio, especially for cruise at high altitudes

13.2.4   *Aircraft load*

With a heavy load in the aircraft the required lift is higher, the span loading increases, hence also the induced drag increases. In order to maintain the most efficient A.o.A. the speed must be increased correspondingly. If not, the lower speed will shorten the flown distance in comparison with the fuel saved during a certain time.

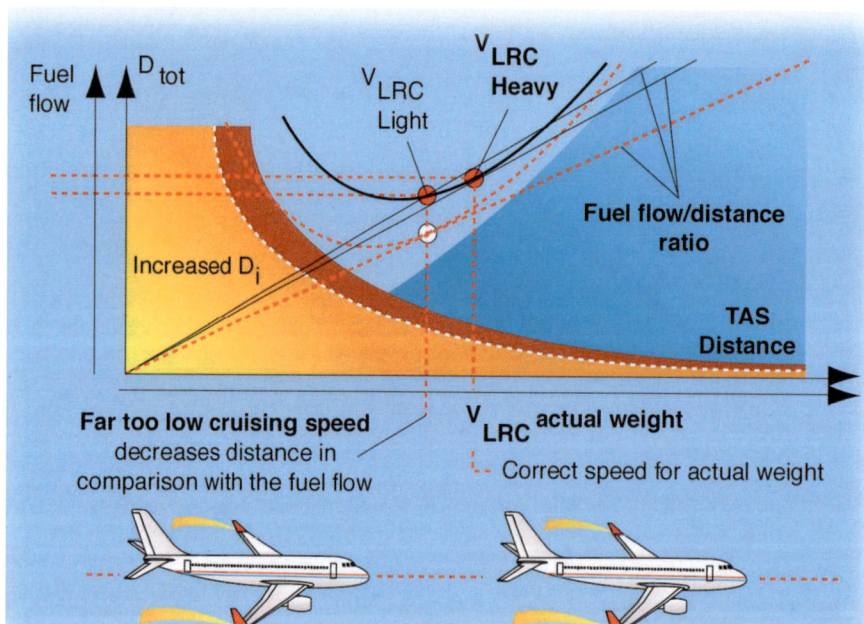

Figure 13.17

With a heavy load to carry, the cruising speed must be increased correspondingly to allow the most efficient A.o.A to be used

13.2.5   *Wing planform, aspect ratio and angle of sweep back*

A tapered wing is characterized by a wing chord that decreases from the wing root to the wing tip. The more tapered the wing, the greater the difference between the length of the chord section at the wingroot, and the length of the chord section at the wing tip.

Near the wing tip of a tapered wing the differences in pressure are smaller, causing smaller wing tip vortices which creates less downwash within the wingspan than a wing with constant chord. Less induced drag is therefore produced, making the wing more efficient, particularly at low speeds.

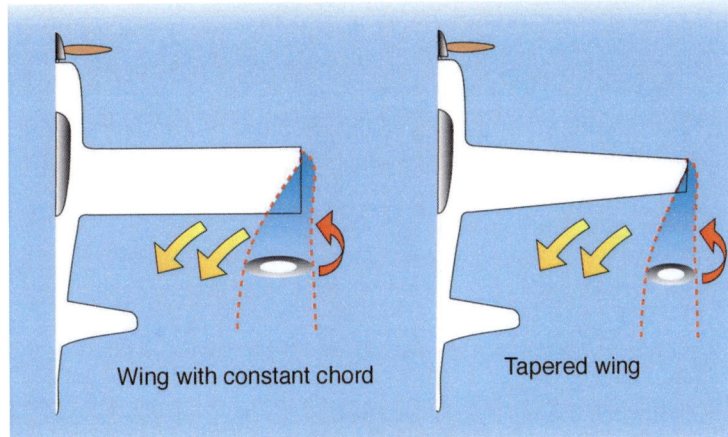

Figure 13.18

A tapered wing produces small wing tip vortices which causes less induced drag. It is therefore more efficient

The angle of sweep back is also a very important factor affecting aircraft efficiency. We usually divide the degree of swept wings into: STRAIGHT WING, SWEPT WING and DELTA WING.

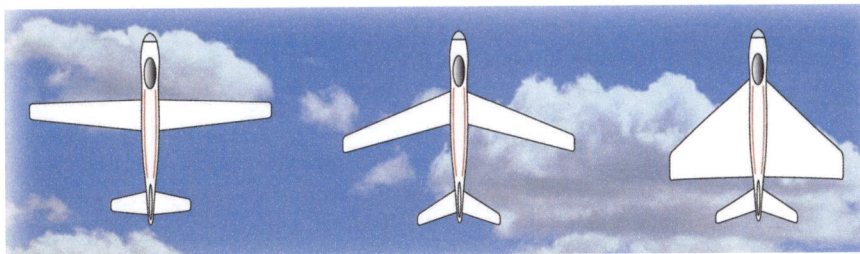

Figure 13.19

Looking at the curve of C_L vs A.o.A. of these three planforms, we can see that in order to create a given amount of lift, the swept wing requires a higher angle of attack than the straight wing. The delta wing requires an even higher A.o.A. This fact obviously affects induced drag. As we can see, at a given angle of attack, the swept wing creates more drag than the straight wing and the delta wing even more.

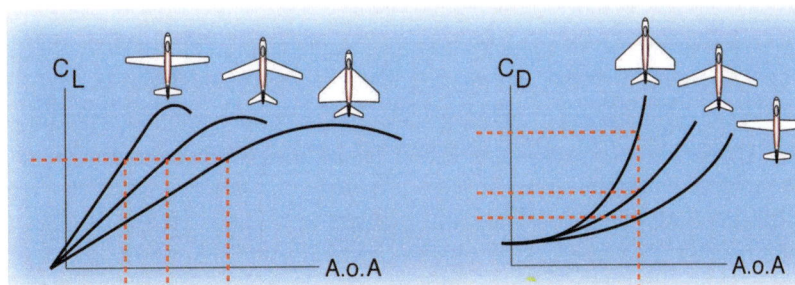

Figure 13.20

At a given angle of attack, the swept wing creates more drag than a straight wing and the delta wing even more. The choice of a particular planform depends mainly on the intended speed characteristics of the aircraft. Straight wings have characteristics that are particularly well suited to low speeds and are therefore generally used for low speed aircraft.

Swept wings provide characteristics suited to speeds near the speed of sound, called transonic speed.
Delta wings are preferred when characteristics suitable for speeds beyond the speed of sound, called supersonic speed are required.
One way to take advantage of the different characteristics of the wing planforms at different airspeeds is, root by means of hydraulic or electrical motors, to make the wings movable at the wing. This allows the planform to be changed, from a straight wing to a swept wing, as the speed of the aircraft increases.
The straight wing is used during take off and landing, the moderate swept wing at normal cruise and at high altitudes, and finally the extremely swept wing at very high speeds and low altitudes.

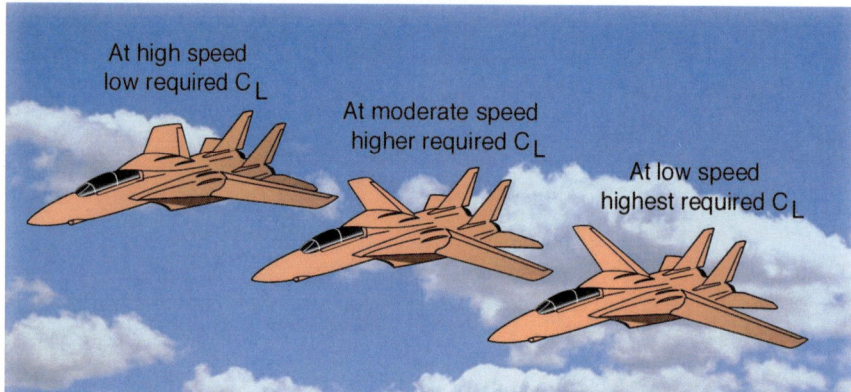

Figure 13.21

13.2.6 *Aircraft speed*

If we reduce the speed from that giving the most efficient A.o.A. when maintaining straight and level flight, we must increase the angle of attack to produce the same lift. In this case the lift/drag ratio decreases due to the increase in induced drag. If we fly with a higher speed than that giving the most efficient A.o.A. the lift/drag ratio also decreases due to the increase in parasite drag. If you do not calculate out the correct cruising speed from the operation manual or adhere to it, the flight may end up short of fuel. The most efficient angle of attack, and airspeed for a given weight, gives the best lift/drag ratio; in other words, it supplies the required lift with the minimum cost in drag. Deviation from the speed required for the most efficient A.o.A reduces the lift/drag ratio.

13.3 *Ground Effect*

13.3.1 *Airflow within ground effect*

When the aircraft is flying near the ground it changes behaviour because the presence of the ground modifies the airflow around the wing. We will now see what the so-called ground effect does to the aircraft. Out of ground effect, the required lift is provided by means of an angle of attack that supplies the wing with a given coefficient of lift. Close to a lifting surface in free air we always have a certain upwash in front of the airfoil and a certain downwash behind it. Due to the wing tip vortices and the downwash, the wing experiences a local mean airflow which is inclined downwards and the total aerodynamic force is inclined slightly further backwards. This increases the induced drag by a given amount.

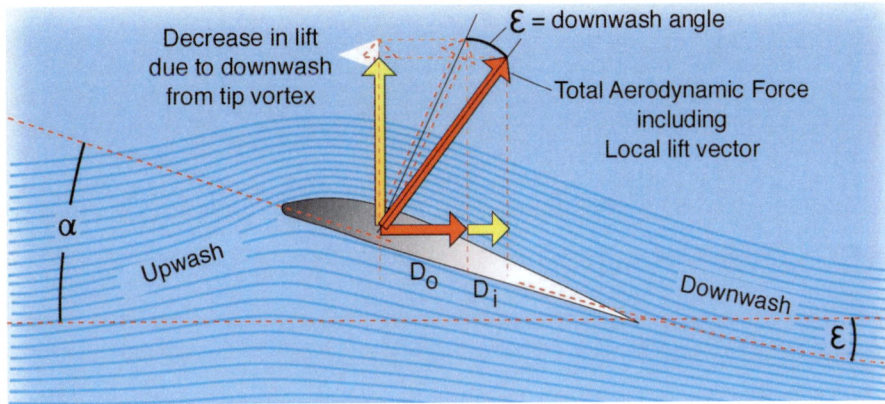

Figure 13.22

When creating lift, the tip vortices and downwash are the direct cause of the creation of induced drag.

13.3.2　　　*Effect on lift and drag*

When the aircraft is very close to the ground at the same A.o.A, the air cannot flow freely under the wings. Below the wing there will be a slightly higher pressure than in the free stream air. In order to avoid this higher pressure, the airflow will increase the upwash in front of the wing, giving an increased circulation. The increased velocity of the flow above the upper surface lowers the static pressure further, thus increasing the lift.

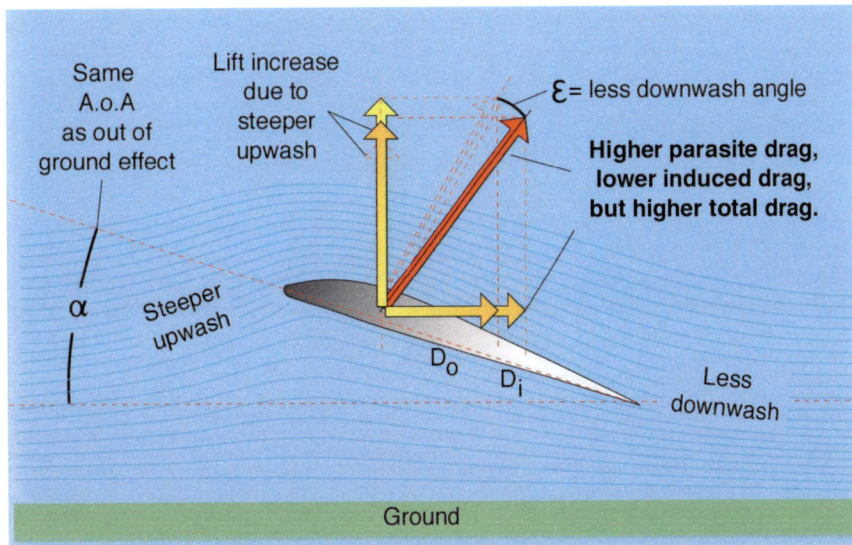

Figure 13.23

Within ground effect with the same A.o.A as out of ground effect, the upwash increases, thus increasing the velocity of the flow above the upper surface. This in turn causes a slightly higher lift. Instead if we look at a rough illustration of the differences in the distribution of pressure, we get pictures like these.

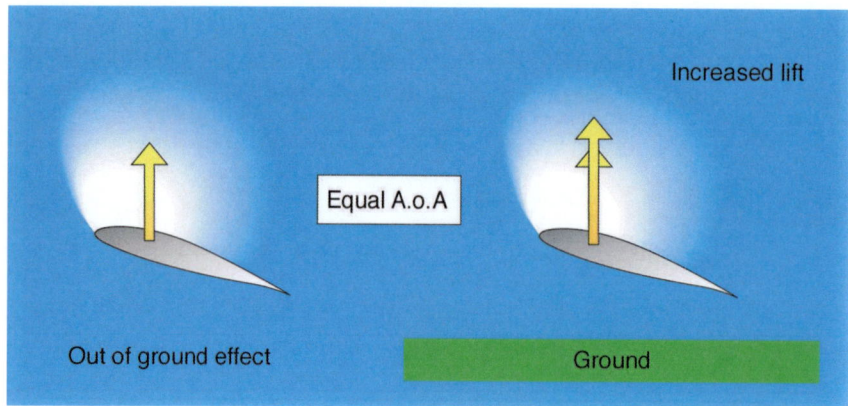

Figure 13.24

Obviously, the increased pressure differences within ground effect cause an increase in lift at the same A.o.A., and an increase in total drag. Thus, while the required lift is the same within ground effect as out of ground effect, we can obtain it at a lower angle of attack when within the ground effect. This means a decrease in tip vortices and consequently also a decrease in the total downwash and the induced drag to such an extent that the total drag will be less.

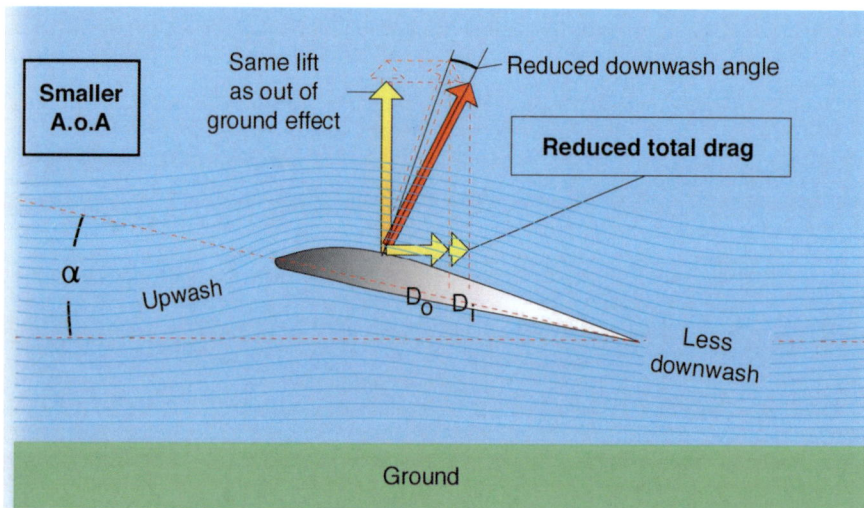

Figure 13.25

Shown as differences in pressure it may roughly look like this out of ground effect and within ground effect respectively:

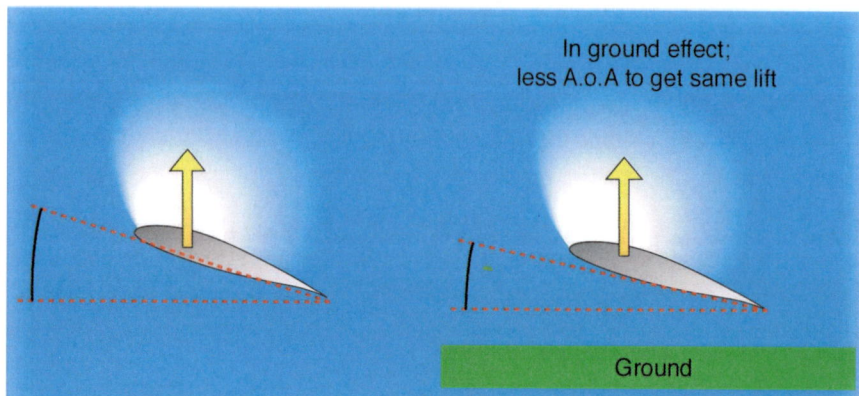

Figure 13.26

> Within ground effect, the same lift can be obtained at a lower A.o.A., thus decreasing total drag

Notice that it is not as much the small increase in pressure below the wing that is the cause for the increase in lift; instead the higher pressure affects the flow in front of the wing causing an increased upwash. This increased upwash in front of the wing causes a lower pressure on the upper surface of the wing which accounts for most of the increased lift. Within ground effect, the lowered pressure on the upper surface of the wing accounts for most of the increased lift.

13.3.3 C_L/α and D/V curves within and out of ground effect

In the next figure you find the difference between the C_L versus A.o.A. curve out of ground effect and the same curve under the influence of ground effect. At a given angle of attack within ground effect, the coefficient of lift is increased, or, for a given amount of lift the A.o.A is decreased. We can also note that the maximum C_L is the same in these two situations but within ground effect we reach it at a lower angle of attack. Looking at the total drag versus airspeed curve we can see that at a given speed within ground effect, the total drag is less than out of ground effect. In general we can affirm that when producing a given amount of lift within ground effect, the aircraft lift/drag ratio increases, because drag decreases.

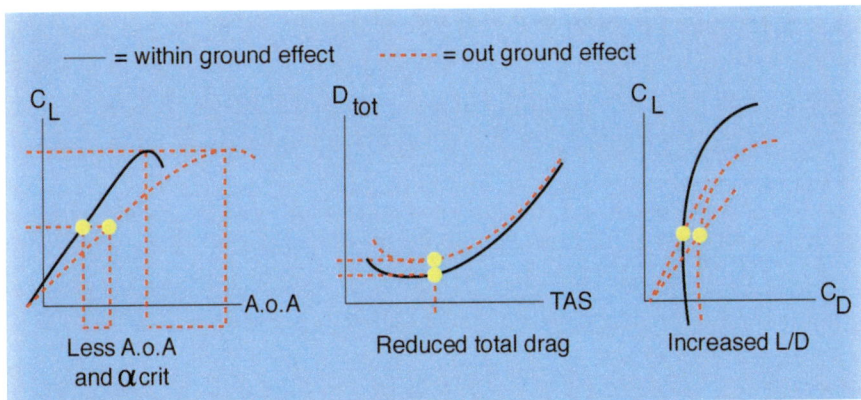

Figure 13.27

> The lift/drag ratio for the aircraft increases when producing a given lift within ground effect

The influence of ground effect depends not only upon the altitude above the ground, but also upon the wingspan of the aircraft. Generally speaking, an aircraft experiences ground effect when it is at or below one wingspan above the ground.

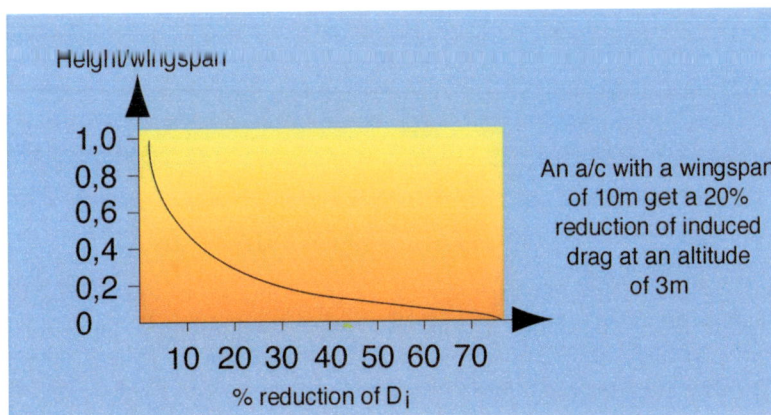

Figure 13.28

The aircraft experiences ground effect when it is at or below one wingspan above the ground.

The intensity of the wing tip vortices varies in different conditions out of or within ground effect. When entering the ground effect at a nose-high attitude the vortices increase, but at a lower nose attitude the intensity decreases.

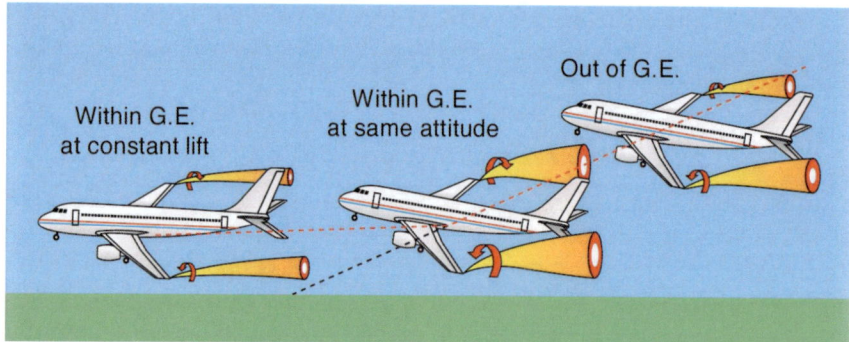

Figure 13.29

13.3.4 *Effects on take-off and landing*

You as a pilot will notice the ground effect during take-offs and landings. When making a take-off in an aircraft with a low power to weight ratio, you will notice that the aircraft is willing to become airborne rather early, but may be more reluctant to climb further out of the ground effect.

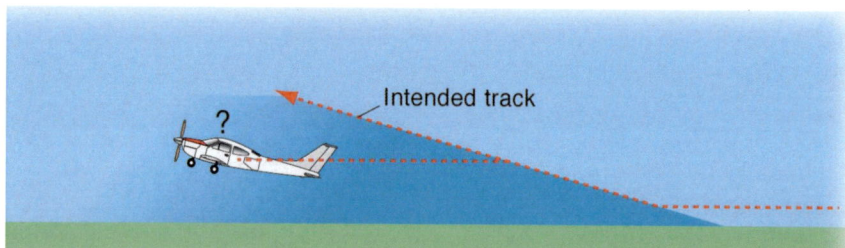

Figure 13.30

When landing at a high nose attitude without making any flare, the ground effect will be felt as a cushion dampening the touch down. When making a normal flare for a soft touch down, the reduced drag within ground effect may make the flare longer that expected.

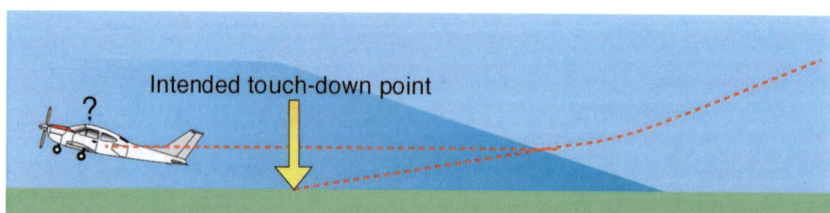

Figure 13.31

During take-off, the ground effect helps the aircraft to be airborne but not to climb. When landing with a normal flare, the ground effect might make the flare longer than desired. When entering or leaving the ground effect, you will also notice a change in trim. Since the downwash is less within than out of ground effect, the horizontal tail will have a different A.o.A, changing the pitching moment. This requires a change in trim in order to maintain the desired attitude. When entering and leaving ground effect, the pitch trim will change.

CRANFIELD AVIATION TRAINING SCHOOL LTD. PART-FCL GBR.ATO-0136
CATS INNOVATION CENTRE, LUTON, Bedfordshire LU2 8DL U.K.   www.catsaviation.com

13-15   Principles of Flight

13.3.5   *Special craft for ground effect only*

Due to the drag reducing effect when being within the ground effect, some Wing In Ground effect craft (W.I.G.) have been produced which are designed to fly only within the ground effect. In this way very heavy loads can be transported at high speeds using relatively low required power. However, the very low flight altitude demands a smooth surface like a sea, big lake or rivers, which limits the use somewhat.

Figure 13.32

The pictures, at figures 13.32 and 13.33, show two different highly efficient Russian W.I.G. research craft, where high speed is one of the important factors, with L/D ratio of 30. The latter weighs approx. 400 tons, is able to keep a speed of 300 KT with a range of 3000 km and a payload 30-40% more than a regular aircraft.

Figure 13.33

13.4   *Wake Turbulence*

13.4.1   *Pressure differences create vortices*

Behind all bodies moving through the air, a turbulent area is created due to the effects of friction and differences in pressure around the body. The normal "pressure and friction wake" and the corresponding turbulent area behind a body is rather short. But, behind a flying aircraft, the wake turbulence has a much greater impact on the environment and has a significant extension. Note, we will here only deal with the turbulence caused by lift, not the turbulence caused by the propeller slipstream or jet blast.

Air always flows from higher to lower pressure. When lift is created by the wings, the acceleration of air downwards and the distribution of pressure around the wings, will cause the surrounding air to avoid the high pressure below the wings and to flow towards the low pressure area above the wings. Thus, in front of the a/c the airflow will already flow somewhat spanwise and a condition has been created where there are great differences in airflow directions near and behind the wing.

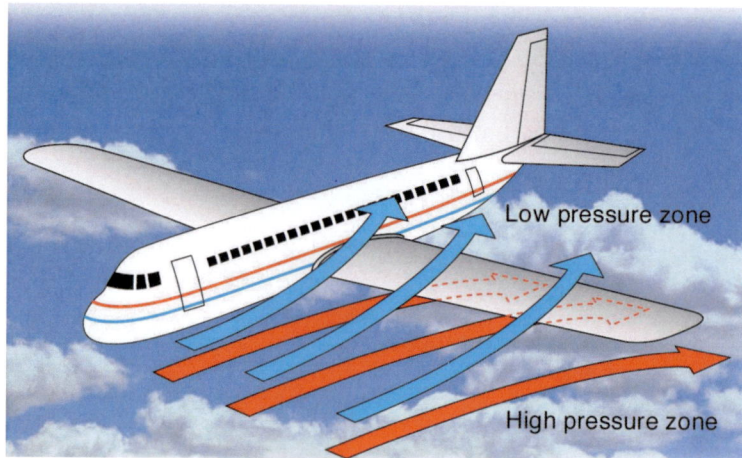

Figure 13.34

When the airflow at the lower outer flow path has reached the wing tip it will change direction again and accelerate in speed in order to fill the low pressure zone above the wing.

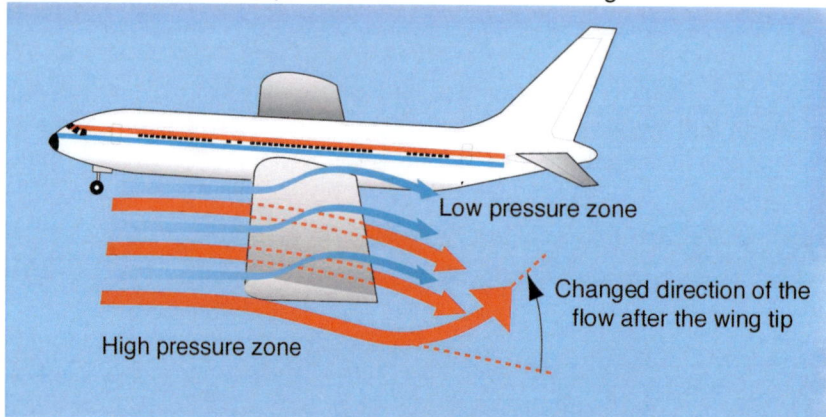

Figure 13.35

The airflow outside the wing tip will also be influenced by the pressure differences from the passing wing by moving away from the high pressure zone below and by moving towards the low pressure zone above the wing.

Figure 13.36

This motion of air will create large vortices behind and slightly within the area of each wingtip.

CRANFIELD AVIATION TRAINING SCHOOL LTD. PART-FCL GBR.ATO-0136
CATS INNOVATION CENTRE, LUTON, Bedfordshire LU2 8DL U.K.

www.catsaviation.com

13-17

Principles of Flight

The circulation in the vortex core can sometimes be so rapid that inside the core the pressure, and thus the temperature, decreases to below the temperature for condensation making the vortex core visible as thin white streaks after each wingtip.

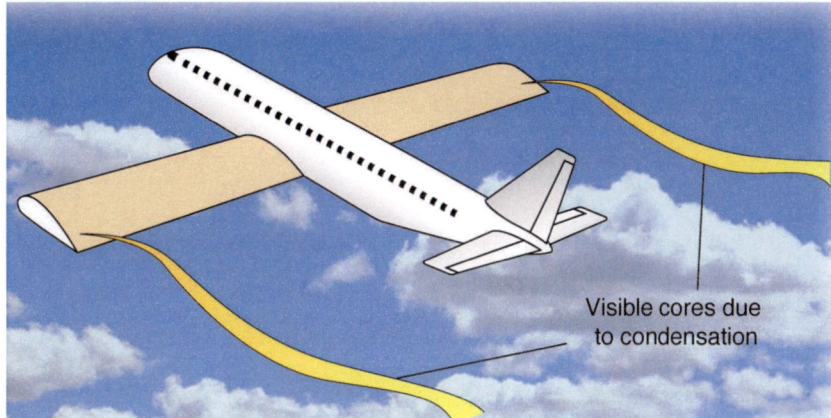

Figure 13.37

However, these streaks reveal only a small fraction of the beginning of a disturbed area reaching a large distance behind the aircraft. It is very important for pilots to know about the extension of and the internal motion in this area.

13.4.2   *Build-up of wing tip vortices*

The downwards accelerated air below the wings will be counteracted by the developed higher pressure, making the air flow out from that area. This outward motion of air below the wings, together with the inward motion of air above the wings, causes a wide circulation to start.

Figure 13.38

At the wing tip, the air in the zone of higher pressure below the wing has the ability to flow upwards around the tip. This narrow tip-flow will follow the overall difference in direction, creating an intense vortex bound to the wing tip; consequently these vortices are called wing tip vortices. This wing tip vortex develops as a core for the whole circulation of air behind the wings.

Figure 13.39

The upward flow outside and the corresponding downward flow inside the span, cause the net direction of flow past the wing to be downwards. Undisturbed air from the area outside and above the space the wing has just left, starts to circulate around these wing tip-cores in order to reduce the pressure difference created by the wing. This filling up with air makes the area influenced by the vortex greater, the farther the distance from the aircraft it is.

Figure 13.40

If the vertical section of air could be visible from the rear, the intense cores and the circulation of the surrounding air would be seen behind the wing tips as shown in the next figure.

Figure 13.41

Note! The vortex is a circulation of air, not a rotation of air.

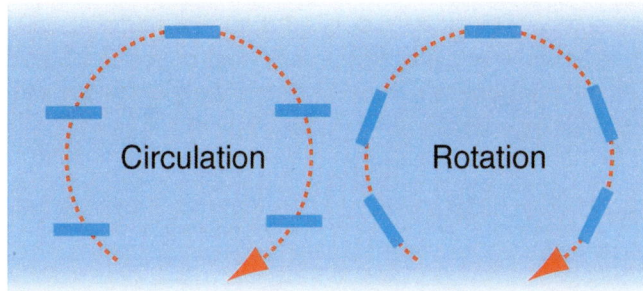

Figure 13.42

13.4.3 *Distribution of wing tip vortices*

Imagine that an aircraft is flying through a number of limited vertical sections of air. The air in these sections will be moved as in the figure below which shows three different sections behind the aircraft.

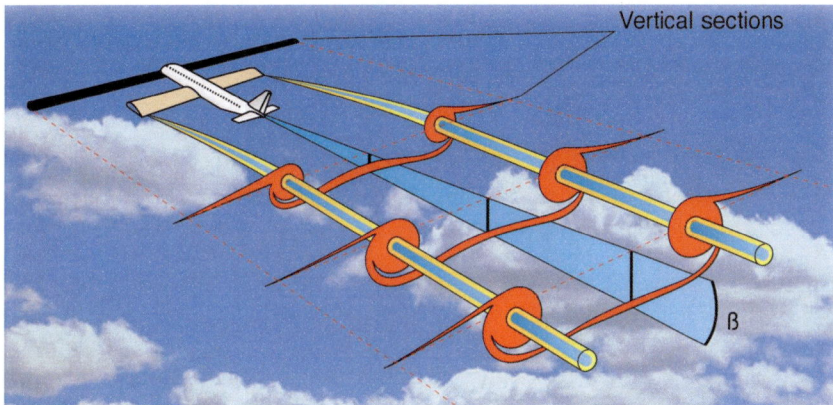

Figure 13.43

As can be seen in the figure, the core of the vortex is only a small part of the wing tip vortex and that the downwash is rather low giving a narrow downwash angle. The distance between the cores are 80 % of the wingspan. The cores are parallel but the total horizontal span is only slightly wider than the wingspan of the generating aircraft.

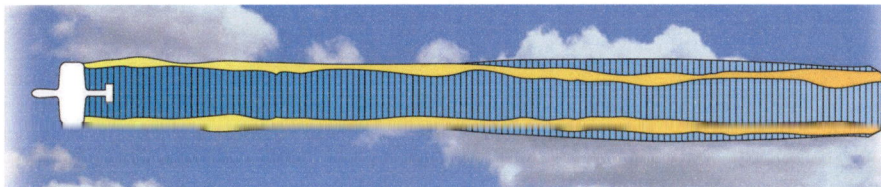

Figure 13.44

The distance between the vortex cores are 80% of the wingspan. The whole area with the wake turbulence moves slowly downwards at 3 m/sec (600 fpm.) and in practice ends at 250 m (800 ft) below the flight path.

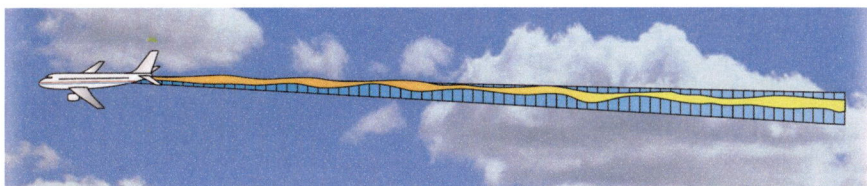

Figure 13.45

The wake turbulence moves downwards at 3 m/sec (600 fpm) and stops at 250 m (800 ft) below the flight path. If you imagine flying horizontally behind the aircraft, from a position outside the left wing tip vortex, through the downdraft and to the right of the right wing tip vortex, you will be influenced by different vertical components depending on the distance behind the aircraft.

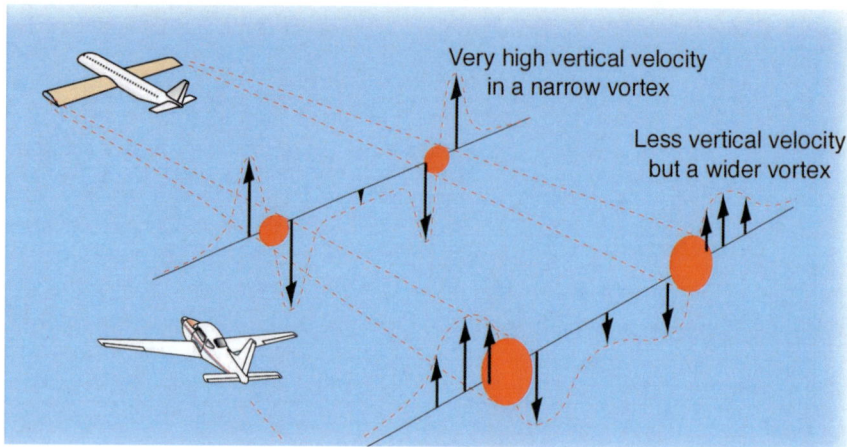

Figure 13.46

The intensity of the vertical component and its horizontal span varies with the distance behind the aircraft.

13.4.4 *Flying through wing tip vortices*

Seen from behind, in the left part of the left vortex you will get a very strong updraft component, but in the right part of the same vortex you will get a very strong downdraft component.

Between the vortices at the same level as the vortex cores, only a small downdraft will influence your flying, but if you go downwards, the turbulence in the thin wake will be felt as vibrations in the aircraft.

When entering the right vortex you will get a strong downdraft component followed by a strong updraft component when leaving the vortex to the right. The circulation in the vortices is so strong that a flight near or within the area for wing tip vortices might be uncontrolled.

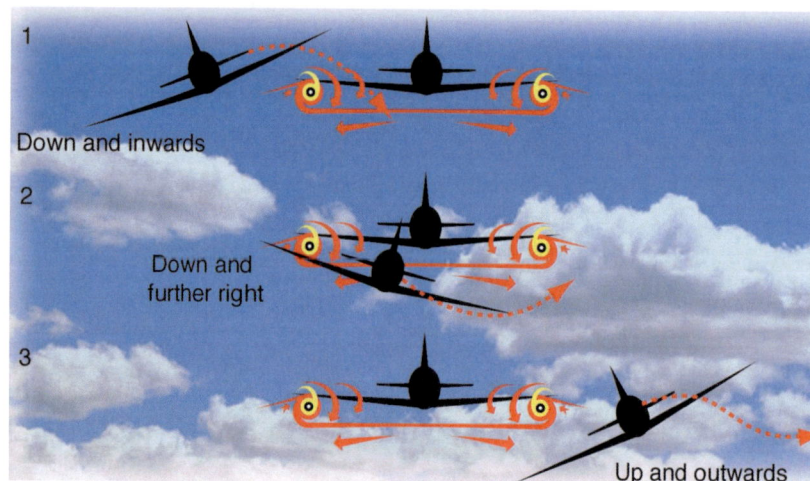

Figure 13.47

In order to fly in formation without being disturbed by the vortices the nearest position should roughly be as the figure illustrates.

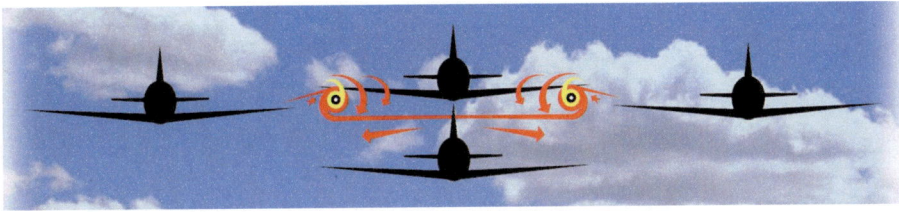

Figure 13.48

Depending on the mass of the aircraft and the distance behind, the effect of the vortices will vary a lot. At a large distance the vortices are less intense but wider and can still make the aircraft uncontrollable for a moment and expose it to far too high a g-load factor.

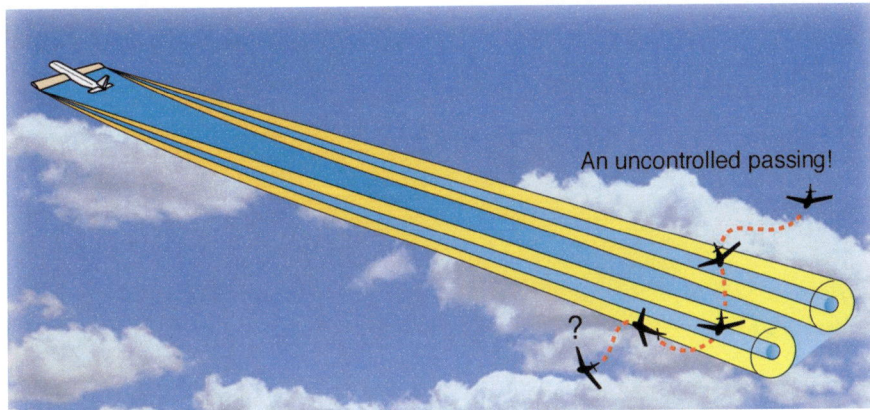

An uncontrolled passing!

Figure 13.49

The degree of influence also depends on the type of aircraft creating the vortices. Note: in all figures the pattern of the wake turbulence is drawn as it trails in a line behind aircraft, but in reality, the pattern can suddenly change direction e.g. dip and rise before it decays.

If you are flying a light aircraft into the vortex from a heavy aircraft you may completely lose control and there is a risk that your aircraft will suffer structural damage.

13.4.5 *Factors influencing the vortex intensity*

The vortex intensity depends on the following factors: it increases with the weight of the aircraft and its load factor (high A.o.A), while it is reduced by high true air speed, low span loading and high air density (low A.o.A).

$$\text{Vortex intensity} = \frac{\text{a/c weight} \times \text{load factor}}{\text{TAS} \times \text{wing span} \times \text{air density}} \times \text{constant}$$

Figure 13.50

Since the vortices are a consequence of the creation of lift, a heavy aircraft and/or high load factors will produce intense vortices. A low TAS requires a high angle of attack, which produces large pressure differences on the wing and a steep downwash, both of which are main factors in developing vortices.

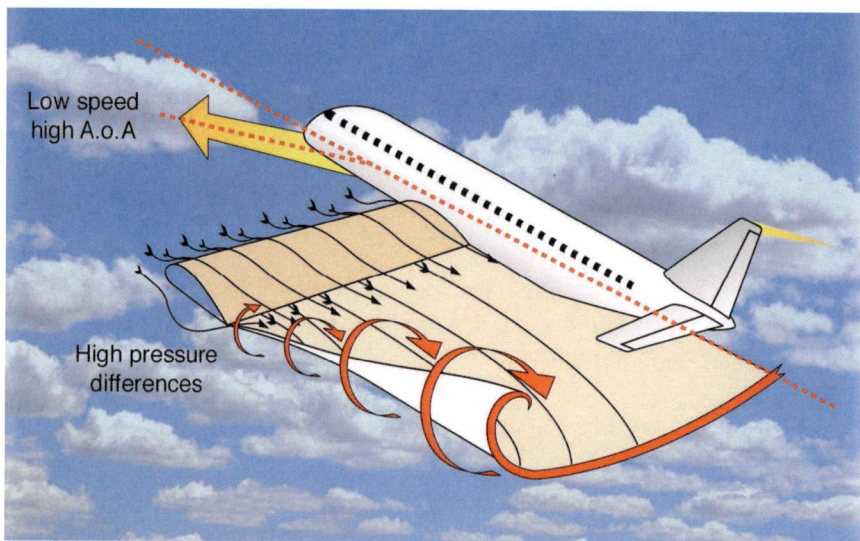

Figure 13.51

Figure 13.52

The wingspan has the following influence. A doubling of the wing span allows 8 times greater weight, causing 4 times stronger vortex intensity. But a heavy aircraft with a short wing span, e.g. the supersonic airliner Concorde, will create the strongest vortices, especially when it makes a turn at a low speed. This is due to the high angle of attack required. But the same aircraft at high speed in straight and level flight will create less intense vortices. Finally, low air density requires a high C_L, in other words, a high angle of attack which creates strong vortices. Remember that the mass, not necessarily the size of the aircraft, determines the intensity of the vortices. A small but heavy jet fighter at low speed or making a tight turn, i.e. at a high angle of attack, will produce tremendously strong vortices.

Figure 13.53

13.4.6 *Break-up of the vortices*

The vortices will decay due to the viscosity and friction of the surrounding air. The distance behind an aircraft where the vortices are harmless depends on the following factors:

$$\text{Vortex length of life} = \frac{(\text{wing span})^2}{\text{vortex intensity}} \times \text{constant}$$

Figure 13.54

This means that:

- An aircraft with a large wingspan creates vortices which last a long time, i.e. a longer distance behind the aircraft.
- For a constant wingspan, vortices that increase in intensity last for a shorter time.

Another factor is the speed of the aircraft. For instance, a jet fighter weighing 13 ton at 300 KT will have vortices lasting for 30 seconds reaching 2700 m behind it. But at 135 KT, the increase in intensity makes the vortices last only 10 - 15 sec. and reach only 550 m behind the position of the aircraft.

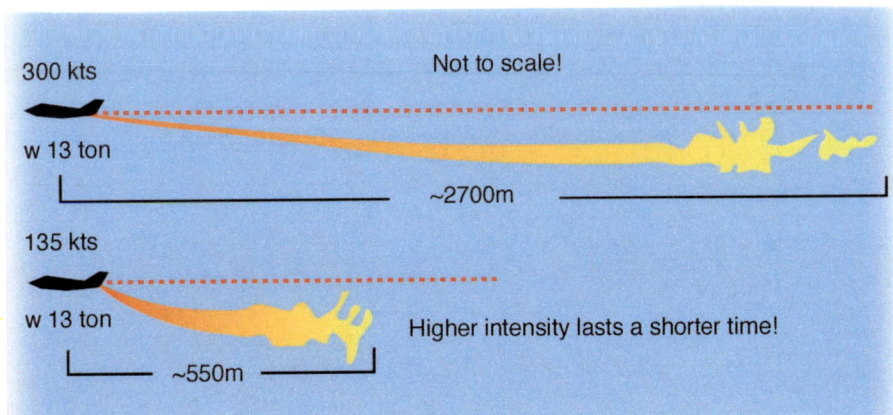

Figure 13.55

Low intensity vortices last longer than high intensity vortices.

The length of life of the vortices from a heavy jet airliner is 2 minutes. The vortex intensity is nearly constant before they suddenly start to break up.

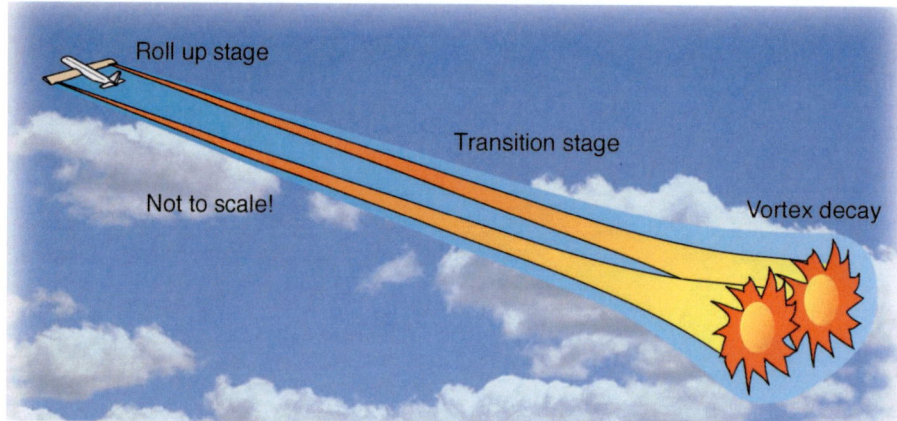

Figure 13.56

13.4.7 *Take-off and landing behind a heavy aircraft*

In order to avoid wing tip vortices when taking off behind a heavy aircraft, the lift-off point must be shorter than the previous one and the climb path needs to be steeper. This is particularly important when there is a strong headwind. Otherwise the wake turbulence will be blown to the position where you lift-off.

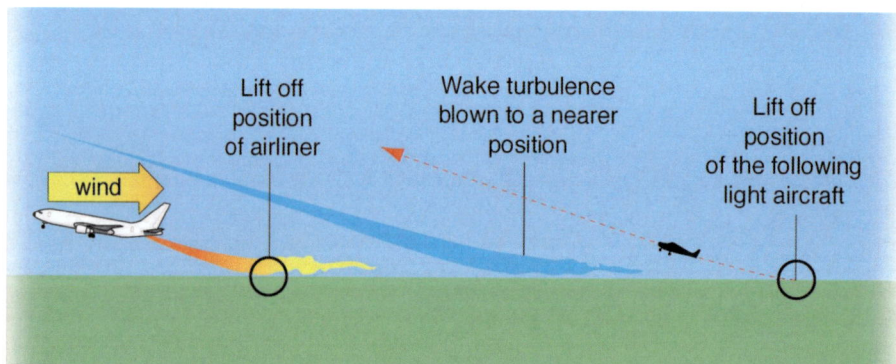

Figure 13.57

> During take-off the lift-off point must be shorter than that of the previous aircraft and the climb path needs to be steeper. When landing, the approach must be above the previous aircraft and the touchdown point further in order to take place in undisturbed air

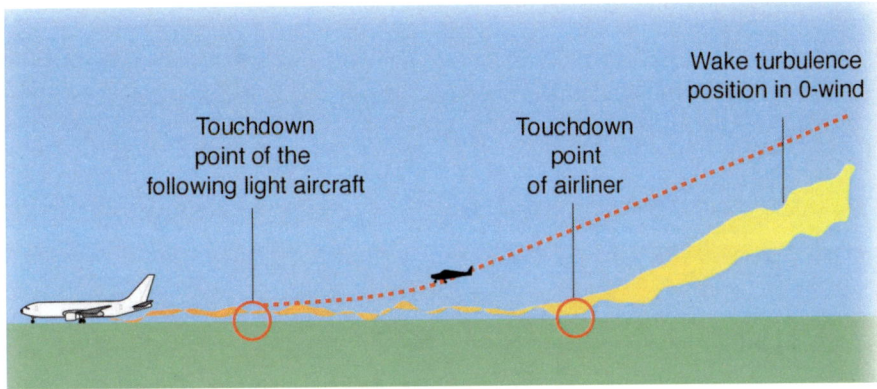

Figure 13.58

Within the ground effect, with wings still producing lift, the wing tip vortices will be intensified since more air from the high pressure area below the wings will be pushed away outwards, then up and inwards to fill the low pressure zone above and behind the wings.

Figure 13.59 Photo: Aviation Week & Space Technology.

13.4.8   *The influences of wind on wake turbulence*

When the wake turbulence with its wing tip vortices reaches the ground, the impact of the air above makes the vortices start to deviate from each other with the same speed as its descent velocity, 3 m/sec.

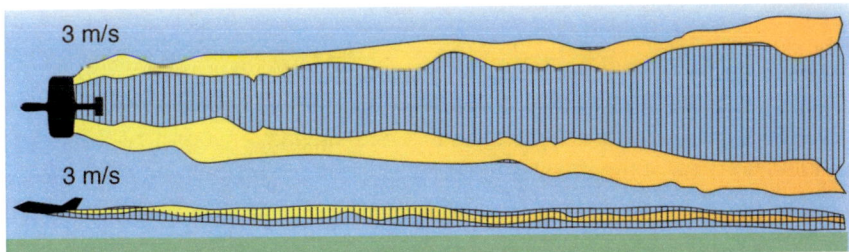

Figure 13.60

This means that if there is a crosswind component of 3 m/sec, the upwind vortex may stay on the runway causing trouble for the following aircraft, while the downwind vortex will disappear with twice the speed. The downwind vortex may cause disturbances on a parallel runway.

CRANFIELD AVIATION TRAINING SCHOOL LTD. PART-FCL GBR.ATO-0136
CATS CATS INNOVATION CENTRE, LUTON, Bedfordshire LU2 8DL U.K.   www.catsaviation.com

13-26   Principles of Flight

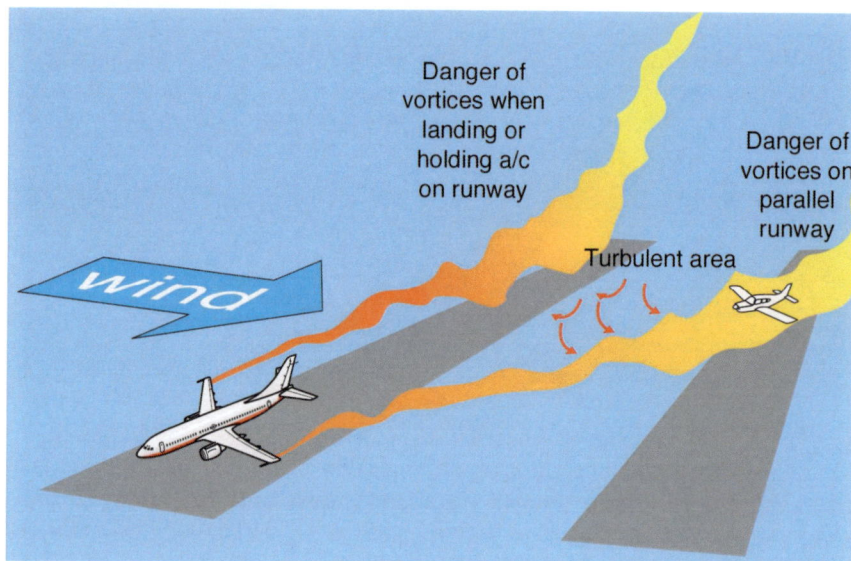

Figure 13.61

When there is a crosswind, the vortices travel sideways with the wind ±3 m/s. When there is a very strong headwind, the vortices from a landing aircraft may reach buildings or a waiting aircraft on the ground near the runway before the intensity has decayed. In such cases the downward descending flight path, together with the headwind, moves the vortices to areas where they, in a normal wind condition, are harmless.

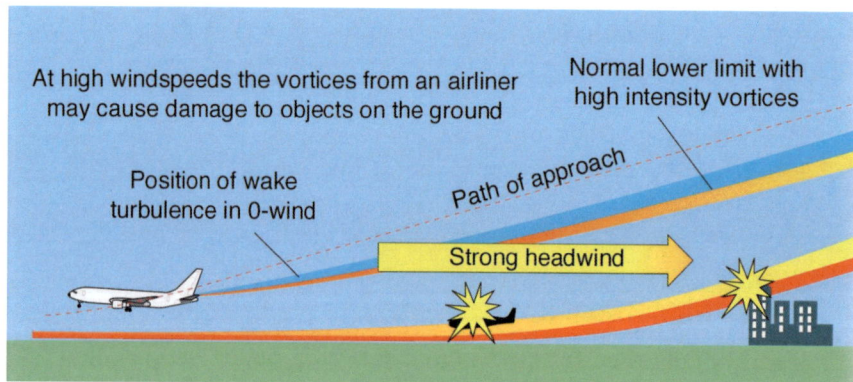

Figure 13.62

- The wake turbulence behind a flying aircraft can cause a following aircraft to be momentarily out of control, despite being a long way behind it.
- When flying in formation near another aircraft, avoid having any part of your own aircraft straight behind the wing tip vortices of the leading aircraft.
- When having to fly behind another aircraft, stay at least slightly lower than its longitudinal axis in order to avoid its downwash and wing tip vortices.
- During take-off and landing behind another aircraft, especially a heavier one than your own, keep your distance. Allow at least 1 to 2 min.
- In strong wind conditions the vortices may move so quickly that they hit objects on the ground before they have lost most of their energy.

Self Assessment Test 07

1   What must a pilot be aware of as a result of ground effect:
A)   Wingtip vortices increase, creating wake turbulence problems for arriving and departing aircraft
B)   Induced drag decreases; therefore, any excess speed at the point of flare may cause considerable floating
C)   A full stall landing will require less up elevator deflection than would a full stall when done free of ground effect
D)   Ground effect is due to the cushion of air generated by a landing aircraft when it is flying very close to the ground

2   Ground effect is most likely to result in which problem:
A)   Settling to the surface during landing
B)   Inability to get airborne even though airspeed is sufficient for normal take-off needs
C)   Becoming airborne before reaching recommended take-off speed
D)   Slow acceleration during the take-off run

3   Floating caused by the phenomenon of ground effect will be most realised during an approach to land when at:
A)   A higher-than-normal angle of attack
B)   Twice the length of the wingspan above the surface
C)   Less than the length of the wingspan above the surface
D)   Target threshold speed

4   What is ground effect:
A)   The result of the disruption of the airflow patterns about the wing of an aeroplane to the point where the wing will no longer support the aeroplane in flight
B)   The result of the interference of the surface of the Earth with the airflow patterns about an aeroplane
C)   The result of an alteration in airflow patterns increasing induced drag about the wing of an aeroplane
D)   The result of an alteration in airflow patterns increasing lift about the wing of an aeroplane

5   The principal cause of hazardous conditions associated with the wake turbulence of large aeroplanes is the:
A)   High speeds at which large aircraft operate
B)   Vortices generated at the wing tips
C)   Propeller of jet "wash"
D)   Laminar flow aerofoil

6   Vortex wake behind large aircraft:
A)   Stays at the same level
B)   Gradually descends to ground level
C)   Gradually descends to a lower level
D)   Gradually ascends to a higher level

7   During a take-off made behind a departing large aircraft, the pilot can minimize the hazard of wake turbulence by:
A)   Extend the take-off roll and not rotating until well beyond the jet's rotation point
B)   Maintaining extra speed on take-off and climb-out
C)   Remaining below the jet's flight path until able to clear of its wake
D)   Being airborne prior to reaching the jet's rotation point and climbing above its flight path

CRANFIELD AVIATION TRAINING SCHOOL LTD. PART-FCL GBR.ATO-0136
CATS INNOVATION CENTRE, LUTON, Bedfordshire LU2 8DL U.K.   www.catsaviation.com
13-28   Principles of Flight

Self Assessment Test 07 Answers

1	B
2	C
3	C
4	B
5	C
6	C
7	D

CHAPTER 14

CLIMBING FLIGHT

14.1   *Forces Acting During The Climb*

14.1.1   *Introduction*

When an aircraft climbs it will gain potential energy that is the energy of its position due to altitude. There are two ways in which an aircraft can do this. First, by zooming, which is transitory and provides a temporary gain in height at the cost of speed. Secondarily, by a steady climb. In the case of zooming the climbing can only be a temporary process, as the velocity cannot be below the minimum speed of flight. Of course, the greater the speed range of the aircraft, the greater the value and capability of zooming. A jetfighter can gain altitude rapidly with a zoom but a glider can only convert the kinetic energy of a dive into potential energy at the top of a zoom.

Figure 14.1

The other way of climbing is by a steady climb where the air speed is maintained at a more or less constant value. In this case the propulsion energy in excess of what is needed for a straight and level flight is used to gain potential energy.

Figure 14.2

The steady climb can only be maintained by using power in excess of what is needed for straight and level flight

14.1.2   *Forces acting during a steady climb*

When we speak of forces acting during a steady climb, we make the assumption that the thrust force acts in the direction of flight directly opposite to the drag force. On the one hand the lift force acts perpendicular to the direction of flight and, on the other, the weight force acts vertically.

When climbing, the weight force can be divided into two components. One component acts in the opposite direction of the lift force and the other one acts in the opposite direction of flight.

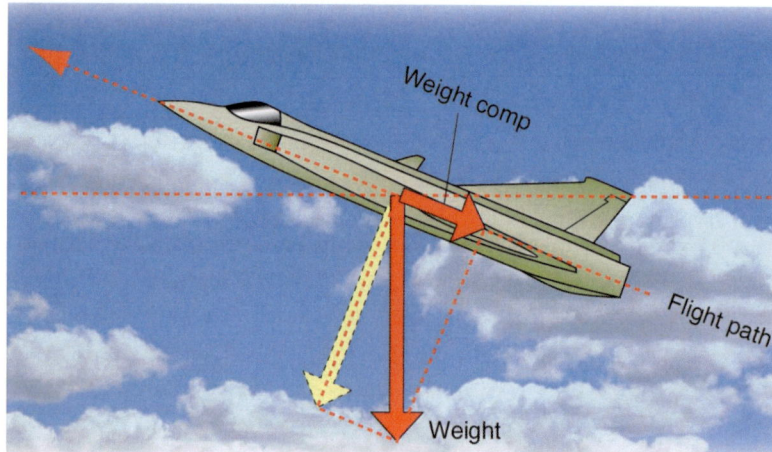

Figure 14.3

If you maintain a steady climb at a constant indicated airspeed IAS the engine or the engine/propeller combination must supply sufficient thrust to overcome both the drag force and to help lift the weight of the aircraft since the lift force from the wings is tilted backwards giving a smaller vertical component.

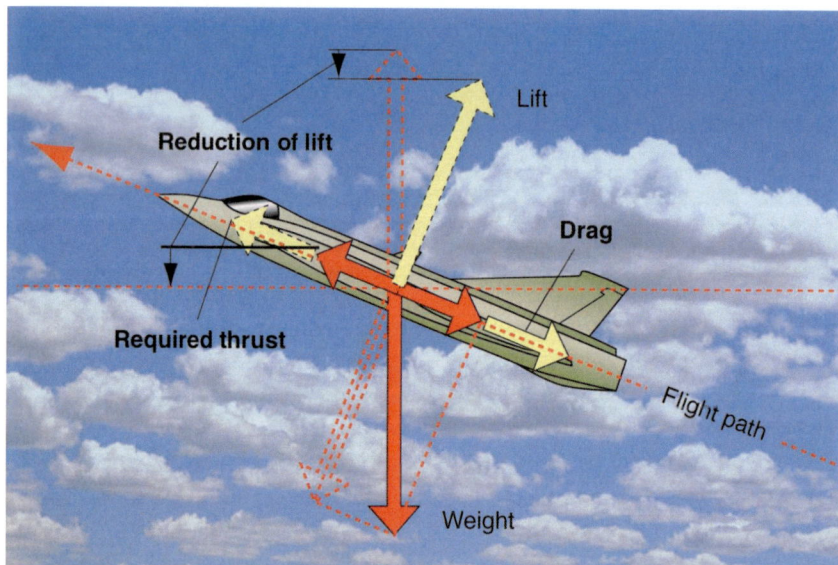

Figure 14.4

The engine must supply sufficient thrust to overcome both the drag force and to help lift part of the weight at vertical speed

In a steady climb at constant TAS there is no acceleration. The system of forces is in equilibrium and consequently the resultant force acting on the aircraft is zero.

The equilibrium of forces in the vertical direction is possible because the vertical component of lift and the vertical component of thrust together are equal to the weight. The equilibrium in the flight direction is possible because the thrust balances the drag and the component of weight. Thus the resultant force acting on the aircraft is zero. It is important to remember that the thrust is greater than the drag while the component of lift is smaller than that of the weight.

> In a steady climb, the thrust is GREATER than the drag and the component of lift is SMALLER than that of the weight

During the climb a vertical speed known as rate of climb is attained.

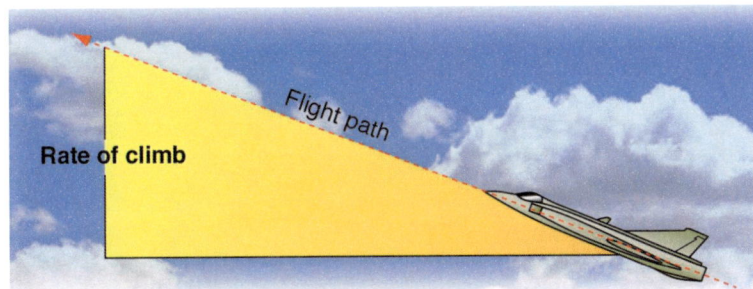

Figure 14.5

The pitch angle θ (theta) in a climb is the sum of the climb angle γ (gamma) and the angle of attack α (alpha).

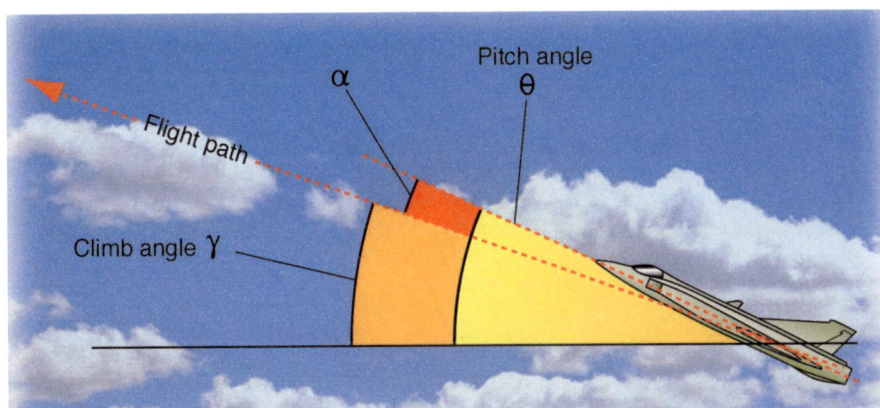

Figure 14.6

14.2   *Angle and Rate Of Climb*

14.2.1   *Rate of climb*

We will now make a definition of the rate of climb. The vertical velocity of an aircraft is known as the rate of climb. It is usually expressed in feet per minute or meters per seconds. The rate of climb is shown in the cockpit on the vertical speed indicator. A rate of climb of 1000 feet per minute means that the aircraft will gain 1000 ft of altitude in one minute regardless of the speed in the flight direction. It can be performed with a slow aircraft at a high angle of climb or with a fast aircraft at a low angle of climb.

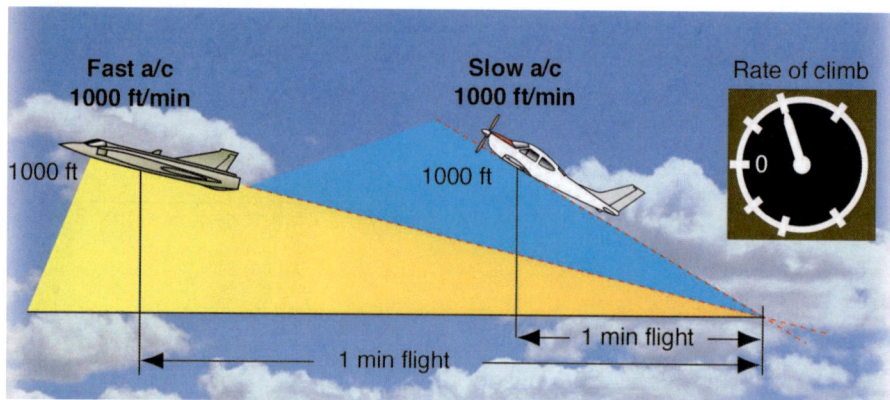

Figure 14.7

14.2.2   *Factors that influence the excess power*

The rate of climb depends directly upon the available power from the engines, versus the power required to counteract the total drag. The difference between these two is the excess of power. When a certain aircraft is heavily loaded it will require more power due to the increased induced drag, which gives less excess of power and the larger weight component. Thus, it will not climb as fast as when it is lighter. For a given aircraft, the higher the weight, the poorer the climb performance. In addition, the speed for the highest rate of climb is increased with increased weight.

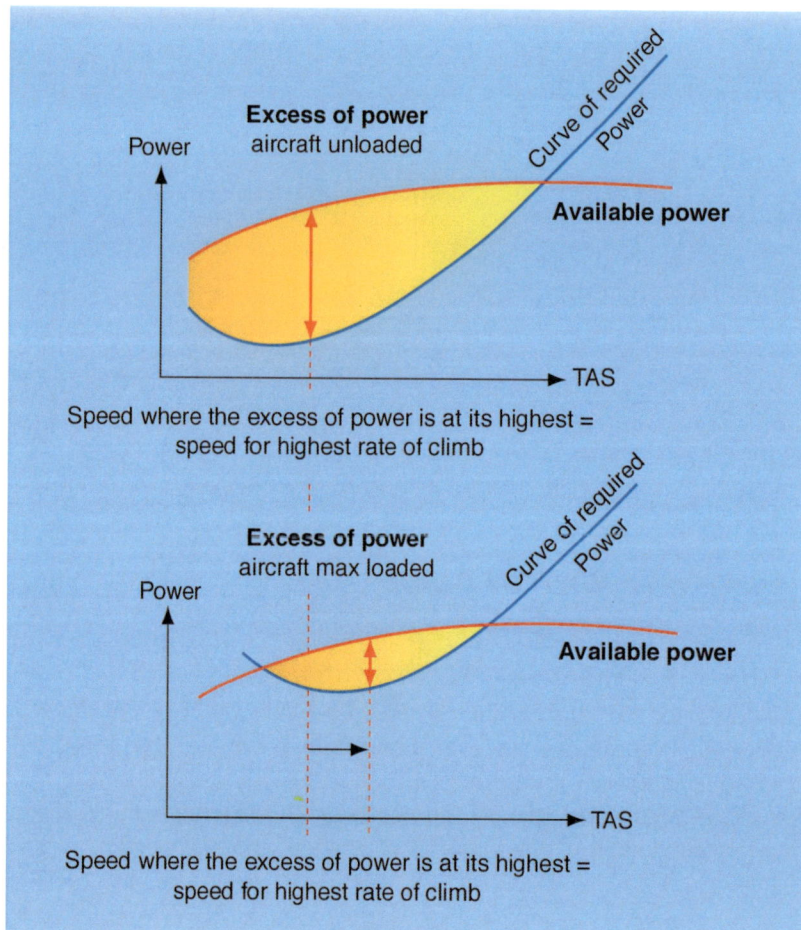

Figure 14.8

CRANFIELD AVIATION TRAINING SCHOOL LTD. PART-FCL GBR.ATO-0136
CATS INNOVATION CENTRE, LUTON, Bedfordshire LU2 8DL U.K.   www.catsaviation.com

14-4   Principles of Flight

For a given aircraft; the HIGHER the WEIGHT the POORER the CLIMB PERFORMANCE. In other words, in order to get the highest climbing performance, the aircraft must be as light as possible.

But the available power differs a lot in different flight conditions. When the flight condition is, for example,. "hot and high", i.e. high temperatures together with high altitudes, the available power is very much reduced.

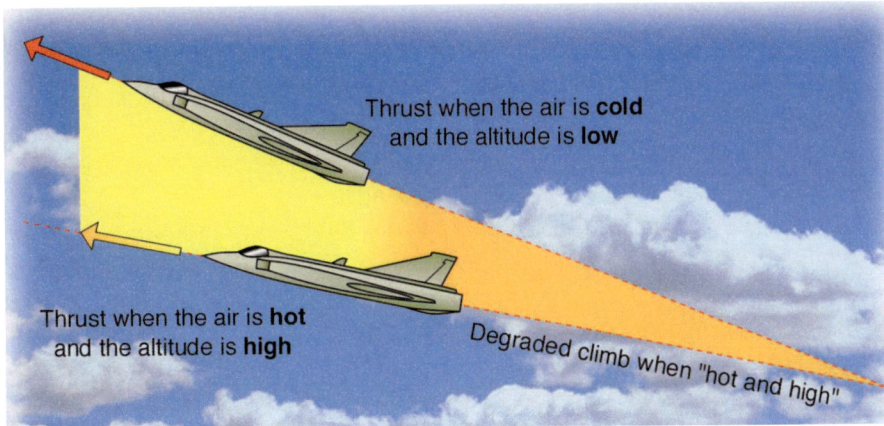

Figure 14.9

Since it is the excess of power that is important, the drag also has a great impact on the climb performance. For good climb gradient capability, the aircraft should generally be kept in a low drag configuration for example with the flaps up.

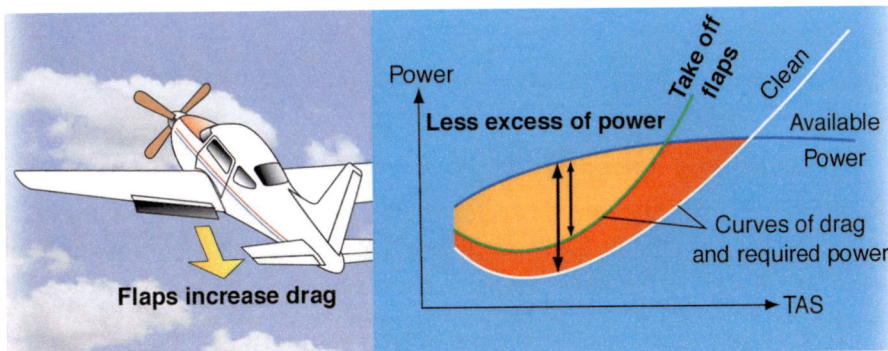

Figure 14.10

Good climb gradient capability requires a LOW drag configuration (gear and flaps UP). Flaps used during take-off, decrease the take-off run prior to lift off, but once flying, the angle of climb will be lower, due to the higher drag.

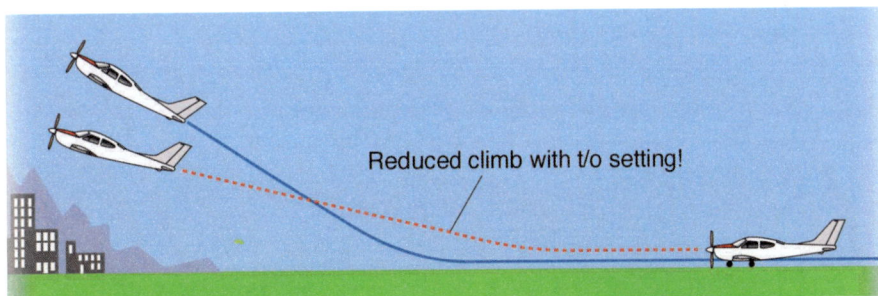

Figure 14.11

The climb gradient will be lower with flaps extended

CRANFIELD AVIATION TRAINING SCHOOL LTD. PART-FCL GBR.ATO-0136
CATS INNOVATION CENTRE, LUTON, Bedfordshire LU2 8DL U.K.   www.catsaviation.com

14-5   Principles of Flight

Since you normally cannot vary the weight significantly in flight, the only way you can improve the angle of climb is to make sure that the aircraft is clean (low drag) and to fly at the speed which gives the maximum excess of thrust force.

> The rate of climb is proportional to the excess of power while the climb angle is proportional to the excess of thrust

To improve the angle of climb, the aircraft must be clean (low drag) and the correct climbing speed be used to give the maximum excess of thrust force.

The climb performance will be degraded with altitude since the required power increases with altitude (increased induced drag), while the available power is reduced.

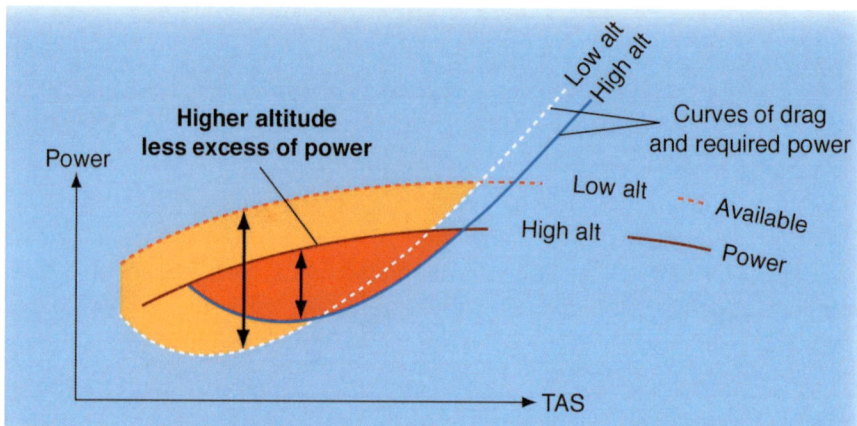

Figure 14.12

14.2.3 *Climbing speed in IAS versus TAS*

As seen in the previous figures, the speed is given as true air speed, TAS. However, the climbing speed that you must keep is of course, the indicated airspeed, IAS. The relationship between IAS and TAS versus altitude is shown in the next figure. At an altitude of 10 km (32800 ft) and an IAS of 250 km/h (135 KT), the TAS is 410 km/h (220 KT).

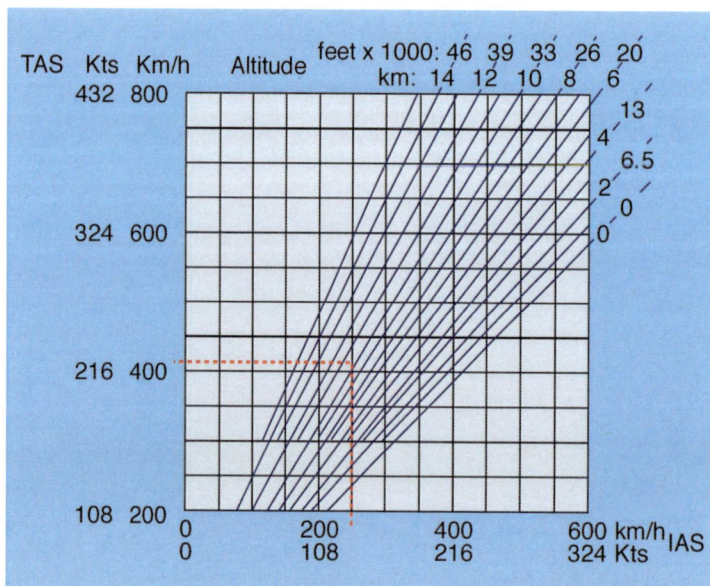

Figure 14.13

Climbing at an angle that gives a constant IAS (lower climb angle with altitude) will cause acceleration in speed with altitude, since the TAS will increase with altitude. This acceleration will degrade the climbing performance

In order to keep the correct IAS for best climbing performance, the aircraft flight manual normally gives a lower IAS climbing speed in relation to the increase in altitude; e.g. the IAS can be reduced by 5 KIAS for each 6000 ft of climbing altitude. A propeller driven aircraft has a lower indicated climbing speed with increasing altitude, while a jet aircraft often has a constant indicated climbing speed until reaching the correct climbing speed in Mach number.

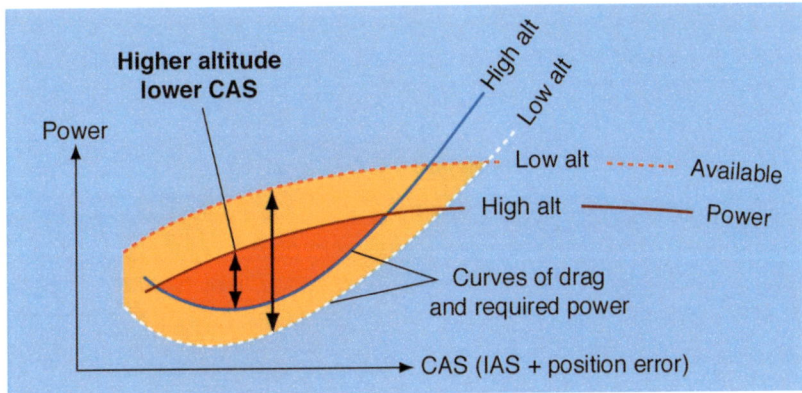

Figure 14.14

For jet aircraft, climbing speed is usually in IAS at the lower range of altitude, but in Mach number* (relative the speed of sound to TAS) at the higher range of altitude. Climbing at a constant Mach number will instead cause a decreasing TAS giving an increasing climbing rate for a given weight.
Constant IAS climbing speed degrades the climb performance with altitude, while constant Mach number climbing speed will increase the climb performance with altitude.

14.2.4   *Different kinds of climbing speeds*

At figure 14.15 you see a diagram showing three different ways of climbing steadily. To the left you see a cruising climb, at the centre a climb with the maximum rate of climb and to the right a climb with the maximum angle of climb.

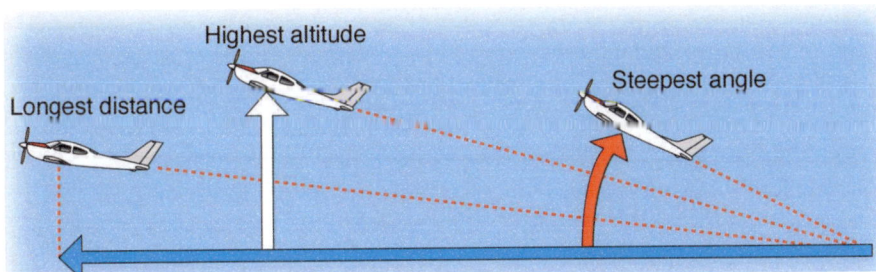

Figure 14.15

14.2.4.1   *Speed for best angle of climb V$_X$*

The maximum angle of climb must be chosen in order to avoid obstacles. It will give you the highest altitude for a given distance. The climb with maximum angle is performed when using the maximum gradient of speed also know as V$_X$. Since the distance flown during the climb should be the shortest possible, it is the lowest of the three climbing speeds.

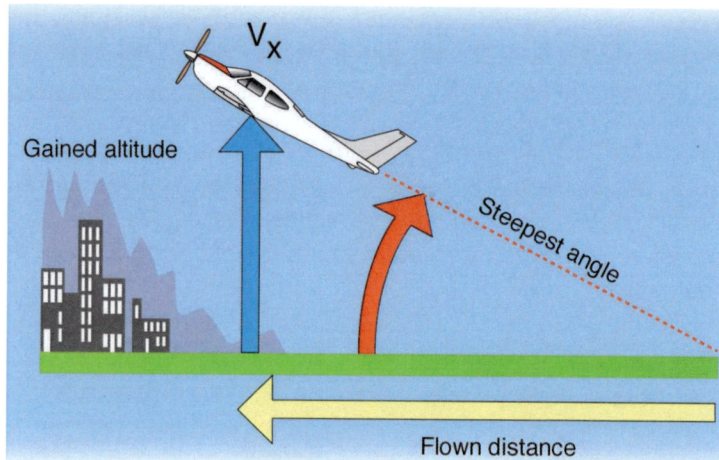

Figure 14.16

In order to reach the max angle of climb, you should fly at the speed where the excessive thrust is greatest. Thus, V_X is determined by the highest ratio between excessive power and true airspeed. The excess power varies with airspeed as is illustrated in next figure. The speed at which the ratio between the excess of power and airspeed is at its maximum, is found by drawing a tangent to the curve from the origin.

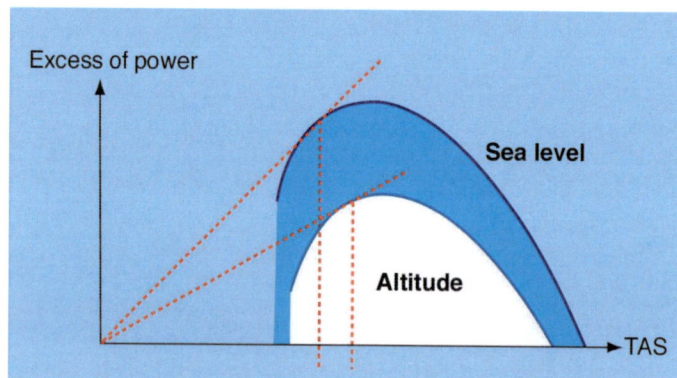

Figure 14.17

As seen in the diagram, the curves of excessive power change with altitude giving a lower max ratio between power and TAS at higher altitude, thus the TAS for max. angle will also increase with higher altitudes. The lowest of the three climbing speeds is the maximum gradient speed or the maximum angle speed (V_X) which is determined by the highest ratio between the excess of power and TAS. It varies with altitude. The climbing speed V_X, of an aircraft with a piston engine, may lie very close to the stalling speed, demanding great attention from you.

14.2.4.2   *Speed for best rate of climb (V_Y)*

The maximum rate of climbing speed V_Y, is chosen to gain altitude in the shortest time e.g. to reach cruising altitude as soon as possible.

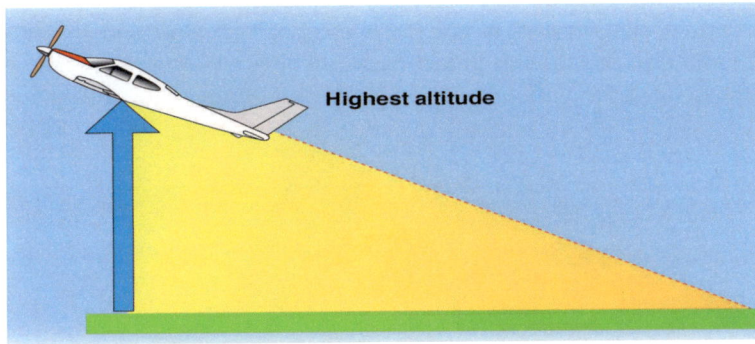

Figure 14.18

You already know that in order to achieve a steady climb, the power has to compensate for the drag and the reduction of the vertical component of lift. To achieve the maximum rate of climb, the speed that gives the highest excessive power to required power, or drag should be used. The speed at which the excess of power is at its maximum, is determined from the curve of excess of power to TAS.

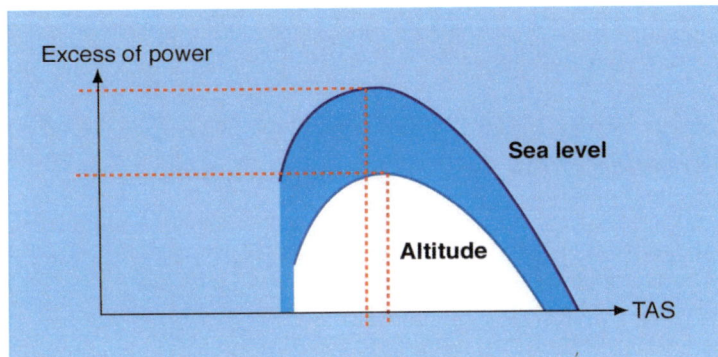

Figure 14.19

This is usually somewhere near the speed for the best lift/drag ratio. The most common for light aircraft is about 10 KT above the maximum gradient of climb. As seen in the next diagram, the excess of power will be lower if the weight is higher, thus the rate of climb decreases with increased weight. You must also note that the maximum excess of power is reached at a higher speed when the aircraft is heavier, thus the speed for maximum rate of climb will also increase with the weight.

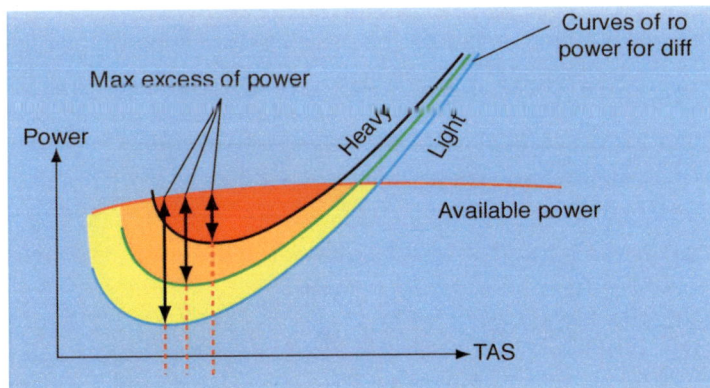

Figure 14.20

The maximum rate of climb decreases if the weight of the aircraft is increased. The maximum rate of climbing speed (V_Y) is determined by the highest excess power in relation to the required power, and is normally near the speed for the best lift/drag ratio. It varies with the actual weight

CRANFIELD AVIATION TRAINING SCHOOL LTD. PART-FCL GBR.ATO-0136

CATS CATS INNOVATION CENTRE, LUTON, Bedfordshire LU2 8DL U.K.

www.catsaviation.com

14-9

Principles of Flight

In order to climb to a certain altitude over a given ground position, you should not circle to maintain the position. The constant turning increases the induced drag which gives less excessive power. Instead, it is much wiser to climb straight ahead to half the altitude (considering the actual wind) and then turn back to the desired position.

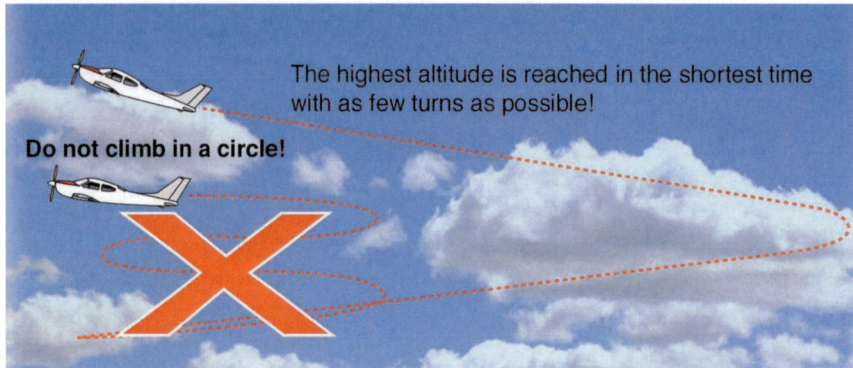

Figure 14.21

A constant turning climb increases the induced drag, which gives less excessive power, and consequently gives poorer climb performance.

14.2.5   *Cruising climb*

A cruising climb is a climb at a constant power setting giving a gain of altitude as a function of fuel consumption and thereby reduced weight. The speed of the cruising climb is determined by the gain of altitude in relation to fuel consumption and weight due to constant IAS (constant A.o.A) and increasing TAS. This speed will be different depending on the actual weight of the aircraft and the air pressure at that altitude, called pressure altitude, and is determined in various ways depending on whether it is a jet or a piston powered aircraft. Always check the flight operation manual for the various climbing speeds for actual weight and pressure altitude. It is very important for climb performance that the correct climbing speed is maintained, i.e. the best angle speed, best rate of climbing speed or cruising climb speed. Flying too fast creates very high parasite drag. Too low a speed during the climb gives greater induced drag. Always fly at the correct climbing speed listed in the flight operation manual for the best performance. Maintain the correct climbing speed for the best performance.

14.2.6   *Effects of temperature and altitude*

The effects of temperature, altitude and speed on the climb performance always have to be considered. In the next figure you see a typical climb performance table. Note that high temperatures and/or high altitudes decrease the climb performance because of the lower air density. You may also notice that the indicated airspeed (KIAS = KT IAS) for the best rate of climb decreases with altitude.

Weight lbs	Pressure altitude ft	Climb speed KIAS	Rate of climb ft/min			
			-20°C	0°C	20°C	40°C
1670	12.000	60	245	190	135	85
	10.000	61	340	285	230	175
	8000	62	440	380	320	265
	6000	63	535	475	415	355
	4000	65	635	570	505	445
	2000	66	735	670	600	535
	Sea level	67	835	765	700	630

Figure 14.22

The rate of climb decreases with higher altitudes and temperatures, and the IAS for the best rate of climb decreases with altitude

14.2.7   *Ceilings*

The altitude at which the climb performance falls close to zero and a steady climb can no longer be maintained is know as the absolute ceiling. When flying at that altitude, the slightest turn or change in speed will start a descent.

The absolute ceiling is the highest attainable altitude in straight flight

However, this altitude has no practical use. Instead the altitude where you still have a certified available climb or ability to perform some manoeuvres is known as the service ceiling. The service ceiling is the altitude at which the steady rate of climb has fallen to a certain value for different aircraft categories.

For aircraft with max t/o weight below 5700 kg; single eng. aircraft, the required climb gradient at the service ceiling is 100 fpm, and for multi engine a/c with one engine out, 50 fpm. For aircraft certified according to the FAR or JAR 25 (above 5700 kg) a positive climb gradient (1.1%) is required if one engine is out.

As can be seen in the next figure, the rate of climb (R.O.C.) decreases linearly with altitude.

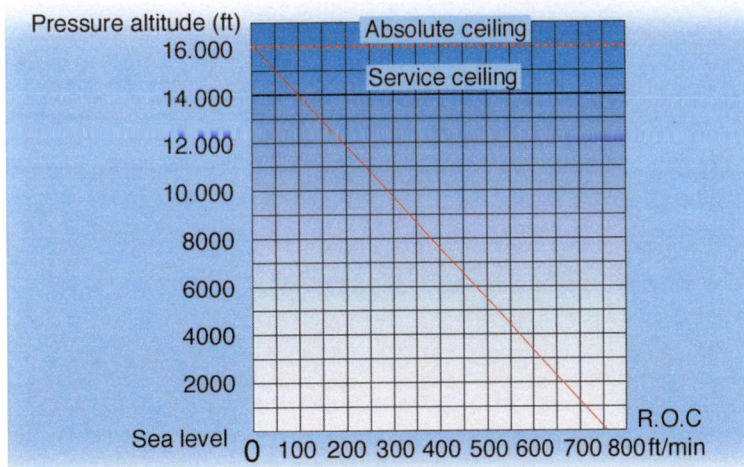

Figure 14.23

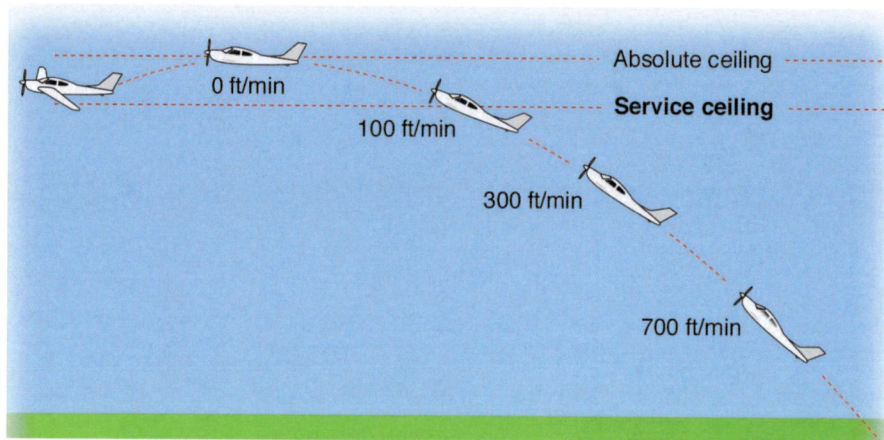

Figure 14.24

The service ceiling is the altitude at which the steady rate of climb has fallen to just 100 feet per minute and you are still able to manoeuvre the aircraft

Remember; the climb performance is only determined by the amount of excess power in relation to drag.

CRANFIELD AVIATION TRAINING SCHOOL LTD. PART-FCL GBR.ATO-0136
CATS INNOVATION CENTRE, LUTON, Bedfordshire LU2 8DL U.K.

www.catsaviation.com

14-12

Principles of Flight

CHAPTER 15

STRAIGHT AND LEVEL FLIGHT

15.1   *Equilibrium of Forces*

15.1.1   *Introduction*

In straight and level flight the aircraft is in equilibrium. This means that the forces acting on it balance themselves, so that the resultant force is equal to zero. It implies that there is no tendency to accelerate or decelerate the aircraft. Acceleration is a change in velocity, which means an increase in speed or change of direction, or both; deceleration is a negative acceleration. In straight and level flight the aircraft is not forced to change either speed or direction. You already know the four forces acting on the aircraft: Lift, Weight, Thrust and Drag. In Sections 2 and 3 we will define the Power (Power is equal to the product of thrust X speed, for propeller driven aircraft) and Thrust (jet driven aircraft). We assume that the thrust acts forward along the flight path: this is not always true, especially at high angles of attack, when the propeller shaft is inclined upward or the exhausted turbine gas is directed downwards in relation to the horizontal direction of flight.

15.1.2   *Review of the equilibrium of forces*

Each of the four forces has its own point of action: the lift and the drag through the centre of pressure, the weight through the centre of gravity and the thrust through points that vary with engine position. The sum of all forces is such that the aircraft is in equilibrium. The thing that must be well kept in mind is that in straight and level flight lift is equal to weight and thrust is equal to drag.

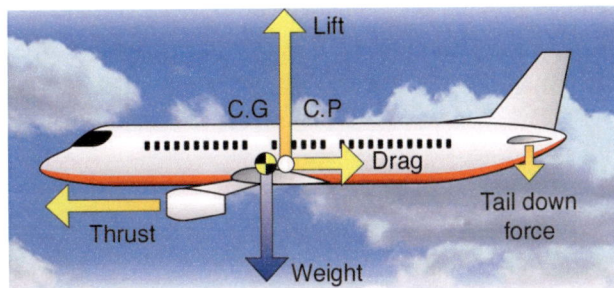

Figure 15 1

The position of the centre of wing lift varies with the angle of attack; and the position of the centre of gravity with cargo and passenger position and with the fuel consumption during the flight. The resultant of the lift-weight forces is normally a nose down tendency because, as shown in the stability chapter, the usual design is to have the centre of pressure of the wing behind the centre of gravity. For that reason the tailplane usually produces negative lift, with a nose up tendency. This allows the resultant lift acting on the wings and on the tailplane to be equal and opposed to the weight. So, in straight and level flight the lift/weight and the thrust/drag couples balance themselves: the equilibrium of forces is achieved when there is no residual pitching moment.

> In straight and level flight the lift/weight and thrust/drag couples balance themselves

To obtain the required lift at low speed, a high angle of attack is required, while at high speed only a low angle of attack is needed. This will also change the location of the centre of pressure, giving a change in

CRANFIELD AVIATION TRAINING SCHOOL LTD. PART-FCL GBR.ATO-0136
CATS INNOVATION CENTRE, LUTON, Bedfordshire LU2 8DL U.K.   www.catsaviation.com
15-1   Principles of Flight

balance with speed. In order to maintain the balance, the tail lift has to be changed if there is a change of speed.

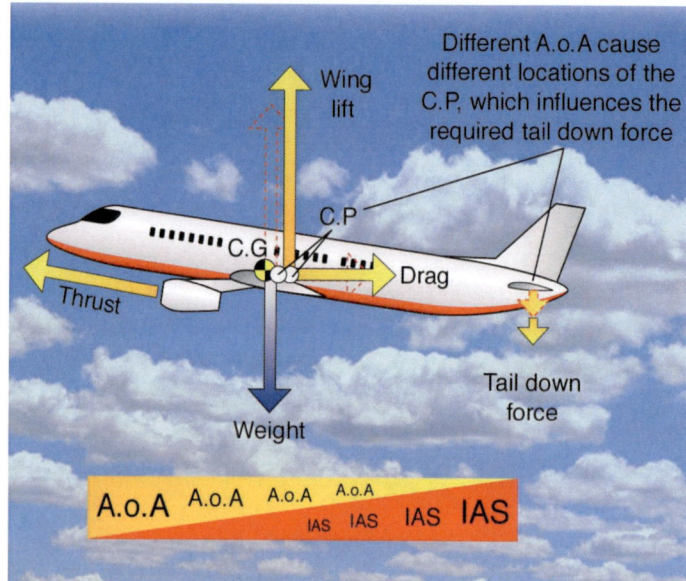

Figure 15.2

15.2   *Propeller Driven Aircraft*

There are two kinds of aircraft driven by propellers: piston engine and turboprop aircraft. On these aircraft, the engine-propeller combination is a power-producing machine. We will now study the curves of performance in order to find the characteristic speed of these aircraft.

15.2.1   *Introduction*

In piston engine and turboprop aircraft, the engine-propeller combination is a power-producing machine, instead of a thrust producer as in the case of jet aircraft. We will therefore refer to a power versus velocity diagram when we analyse the performance of a propeller driven aircraft.

15.2.2   *Required power*

Power is defined as the speed at which the applied force moves a body. Therefore, the power required for flight depends on the product of required thrust and the true air speed TAS. It is easy to transform the curve of required thrust into a curve of required power by simply multiplying the required thrust at every speed by that same speed.

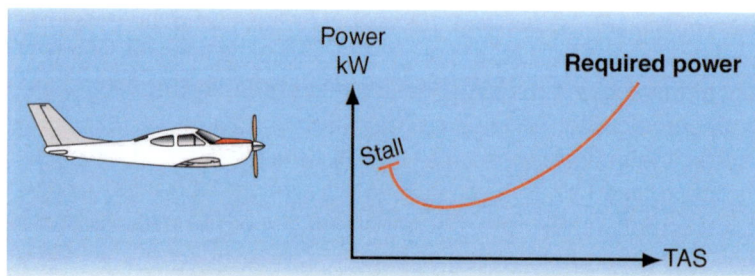

Figure 15.3

POWER required = THRUST required x TAS

The power obtained will balance the drag produced by the aircraft and maintain the speed in straight and level flight. The position of the curve is a function of the weight of the aircraft. The position of the curve is also a function of the pressure of the altitude of the aircraft, called pressure altitude. If not stated, we will assume a constant weight and altitude.

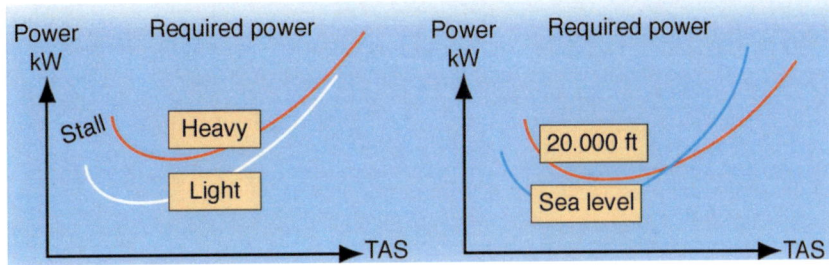

Figure 15.4

The position of the curve of required power is a function of the weight of the aircraft and the actual pressure altitude

On the curve of required power we find four characteristic points, corresponding first to the speed and then to the angle of attack.

1. the minimum speed, or stalling speed;
2. the speed of the minimum required power (also the speed for minimum rate of descent),
3. the minimum drag or maximum efficiency speed (also speed for maximum glide)
4. the maximum speed.
5.

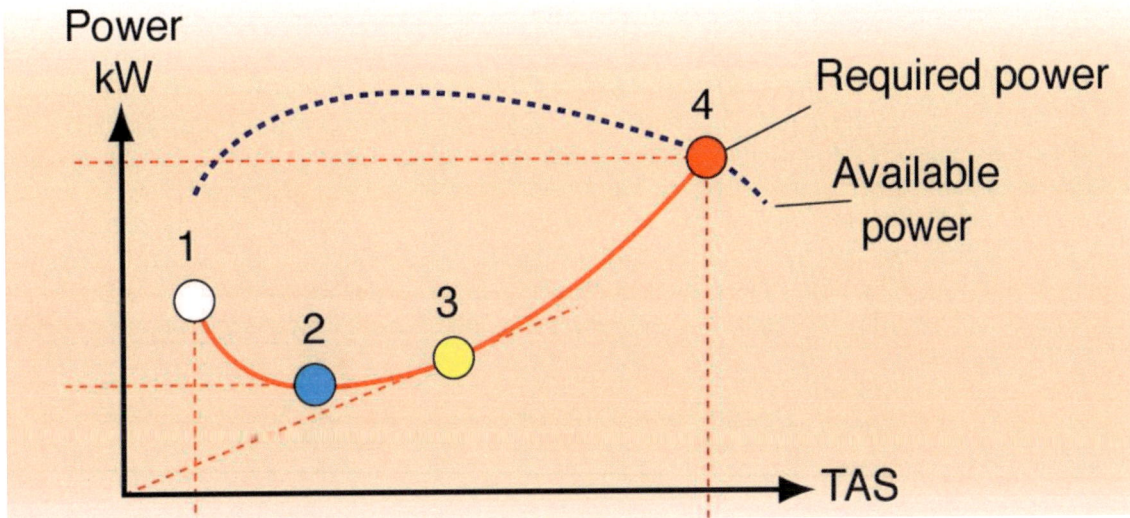

Figure 15.5

15.2.3   *Available power*

The available power is equal to the engine power multiplied by the propeller efficiency. We are here going to consider a variable pitch propeller. Of course the position of the curve is a function of the selected throttle position. The position of the curve is also a function of the pressure altitude of the aircraft, as shown. If not specified, we will consider the selected throttle position and the pressure altitude to be constant.

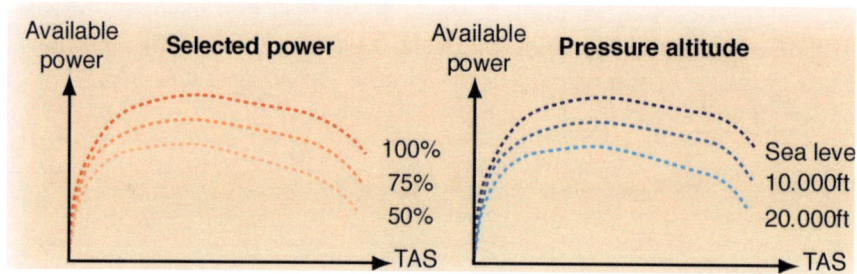

Figure 15.6

> The position of the curve of available power is a function of the selected power and the pressure altitude of the aircraft

15.2.4   *Ranges of speed stability and speed instability*

Let us put the curves of required power and available power together in the same diagram. You can see (in figure 15.7) that there are two points of contact between the two curves at which the values of required and available power are equal.

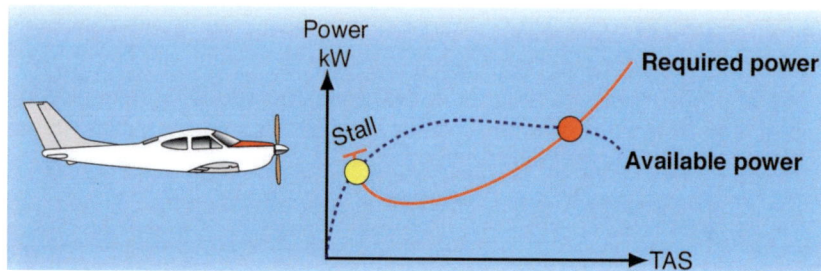

Figure 15.7

These two points represent the condition of equilibrium in straight and level flight. Thus for a given selected throttle position, aircraft weight and flight altitude, an aircraft has two speeds at which it can maintain the condition of straight and level flight: one slower and one faster speed. This unique condition is valid only for flying aircraft, A car or train etc. will only have one point of equilibrium between the required and available power. A flying aircraft has two speeds at which there is equilibrium between the required power and the available power. Let us now divide the curves in two ranges: the instability range of low speeds and the stability range of high speeds. The separation between the ranges is located at the point of maximum excess of power.

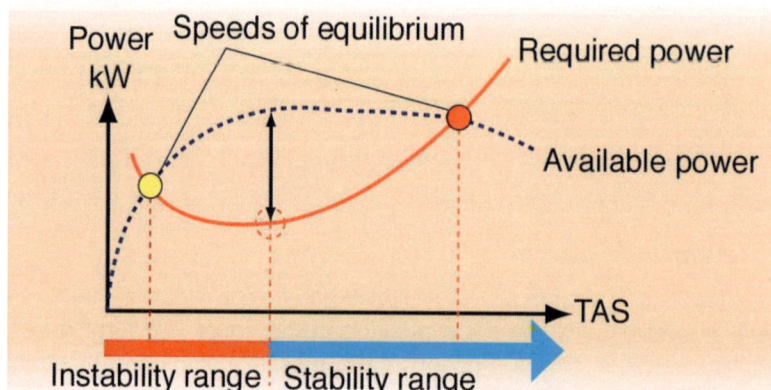

Figure 15.8

Consider an aircraft flying at the speed A: if, for any reason, e.g. due to a short slight dive, the speed increases until the B value, the available power will be more than that required, so there will be an excess of

CRANFIELD AVIATION TRAINING SCHOOL LTD. PART-FCL GBR.ATO-0136

CATS CATS INNOVATION CENTRE, LUTON, Bedfordshire LU2 8DL U.K.

www.catsaviation.com

15-4

Principles of Flight

power. If the throttle is not reduced and the aircraft is re-trimmed, the aircraft will accelerate until the second speed of equilibrium, point C. Consequently, the speed A was in the instability range since the aeroplane did not resume that speed.

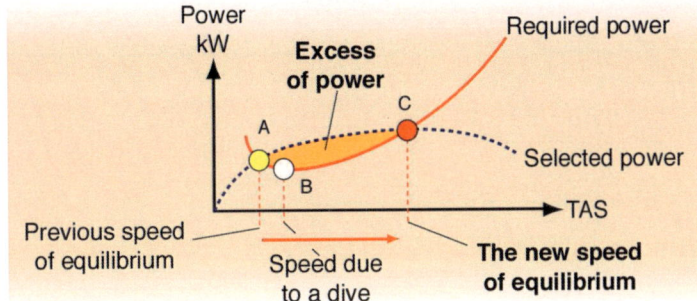

Figure 15.9

If the speed is increased from the lower speed of equilibrium and the altitude and power are kept constant, the aircraft will accelerate until it reaches a new speed of equilibrium if the aircraft is re-trimmed, that is; the original speed is unstable. Again, we will consider an aircraft flying at the speed of equilibrium C. If the speed is reduced (e.g. due to a short slight climb) until the B value, the available thrust will be less than that required. If the throttle is not increased, the aircraft will decelerate until the stalling speed A,. Since the aircraft did not go back to the speed of equilibrium again, the lower speed range is called the speed instability range, or the reversed command region.

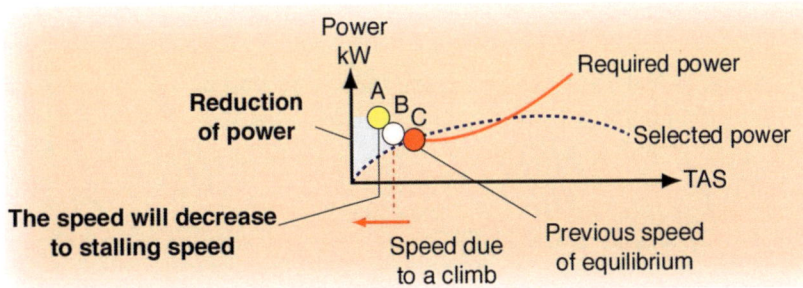

Figure 15.10

If the speed decreases from a lower speed of equilibrium and the altitude and power are kept constant, the aircraft will decelerate if the aircraft is re-trimmed until the stalling speed is reached. Consider now an aircraft flying at the speed A. If the speed increases (e.g. due to a slight dive) until the B value and levels out again, the available power will be less than that required. The aircraft will decelerate until the speed of equilibrium A, where the condition of equilibrium of straight and level flight is. Since the speed goes back to the same value as before the disturbance, this speed range is known as the speed stability range.

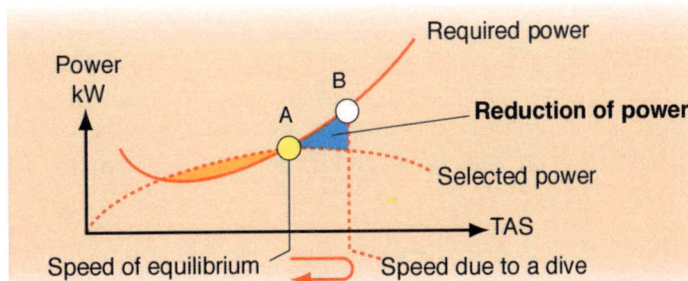

Figure 15.11

Finally, if the speed decreases from the higher speed of equilibrium, e.g. due to a slight climb until the B value, and levels out again, the speed will increase due to the excess of power and the higher speed of equilibrium will be resumed.

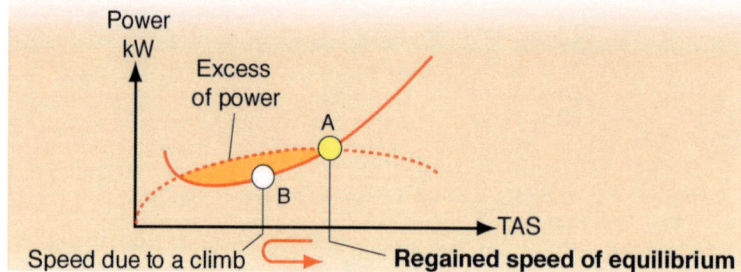

Figure 15.12

the speed is increased or decreased from a higher speed of equilibrium and the altitude and power are kept constant, the aircraft will resume the higher speed of equilibrium.

15.2.5   *Speed for maximum endurance*

The endurance of an aircraft is the measure of the length of time it is able to remain airborne. Of course, there will be a certain speed that makes it possible to fly the longest time, giving the maximum endurance.

To obtain maximum endurance, we must use the least possible fuel in a given time, i.e. we must use minimum power

Power means drag x velocity (TAS). In figure 15.13, the minimum drag speed for this particular aircraft is 160 KT but the minimum power is about 125 KT. Normally, however, the specific fuel consumption (fuel/power) is higher at low power than at higher power, so the speed may be kept slightly higher than the speed for minimum power.

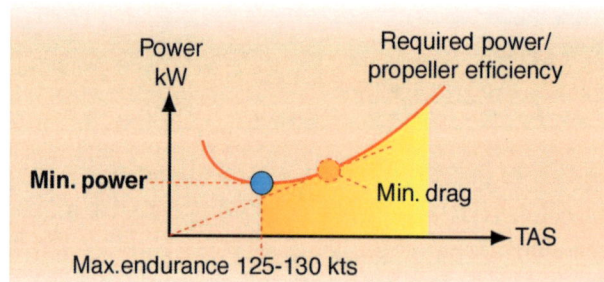

Figure 15.13

15.2.6   *Speed for maximum range*

The maximum range is the maximum distance an aircraft can fly with the available fuel. The maximum range will then correspond to the maximum ratio between nautical miles flown and fuel used. If we divide Nm/fuel and both the numerator and the denominator by time, we will obtain the ratio of KT/fuel flow. The maximum range will then be equal to the maximum ratio between KT/fuel flow, or minimum ratio between fuel flow/KT.

$$\text{Max range} = \frac{\text{Nautical miles}}{\text{Burnt fuel}} = \frac{\dfrac{\text{Nm}}{\text{time}}}{\dfrac{\text{Burnt fuel}}{\text{Time}}} = \frac{\text{Kts}}{\text{Fuel flow}}$$

$$\text{Max } \frac{\text{Kts}}{\text{Fuel flow}} = \text{Min } \frac{\text{Fuel flow}}{\text{Kts}} = \text{Min } \frac{\text{Required power}}{\text{TAS}}$$

Figure 15.14

Then the minimum ratio between fuel flow/velocity is the same as the minimum ratio between required power/velocity, and is reached at the speed for minimum drag. It is represented in the diagram by the tangent point between the half line drawn from the axis origin and the curve of required thrust. Thus the maximum range speed will be higher than the speed for maximum endurance.

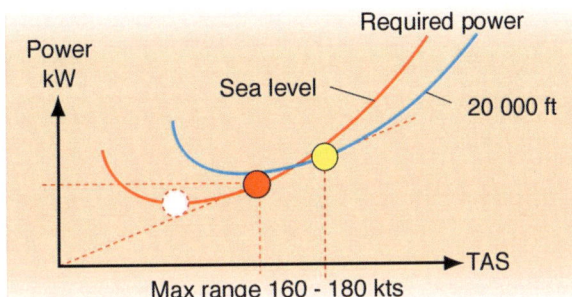

Figure 15.15

Note, in figure 15.15, that the curve of required power for higher altitude and the corresponding tangent point give a higher maximum range speed.

Maximum endurance speed is the speed of minimum required power

Maximum range speed is determined by minimum ratio between required power/velocity, and is always a higher speed than for maximum endurance

15.2.7 Effect of altitude

There is a best altitude to fly at, but that altitude is determined by the engine efficiency and not by the aircraft, which is equally good at all altitudes. Piston and turbine engines are more efficient at high power than at low power due to better fuel burning. More power is required to obtain optimal speed at high altitudes. This fact may have a good influence on range but a bad influence on the max available flight time. The best altitude is usually not very critical for a piston engine aircraft, nor is there generally any great loss in range when flying below that altitude. It may well be that considerations of wind make it advisable to do so. The total time aspect in wind conditions may increase the average true air speed. Check the Pilot Operating Handbook or Flight Manual. When flying a propeller driven aircraft it is very important to select altitude after wind situation and total flight time, taking average TAS into consideration.

15.3 Jet Driven Aircraft

The jet engine is a producer of thrust. It is important to study the thrust curves to find the characteristic speeds of jet aircraft in order to obtain the best performances.

CRANFIELD AVIATION TRAINING SCHOOL LTD. PART-FCL GBR.ATO-0136

CATS CATS INNOVATION CENTRE, LUTON, Bedfordshire LU2 8DL U.K.

www.catsaviation.com

15-7

Principles of Flight

15.3.1 *Required thrust versus speed*

A jet engine produces a thrust force, so in order to analyse the performance of a jet aircraft, we are going to refer to a diagram of thrust versus velocity, instead of one of power versus velocity. As stated earlier, in straight and level flight the value of thrust is equal to the drag, so the thrust required to maintain this phase of flight will be equal to the total drag produced by the aircraft.

In straight and level flight required THRUST = total DRAG.

The required thrust, as well as the drag, has a certain value for every speed and angle of attack. Of course, lower angles of attack correspond to higher speeds. This curve is determined by the aircraft's aerodynamics. Its position is a function of the weight of the aircraft and of the pressure altitude of the aircraft, as shown below. If not specified, we will assume a constant weight and pressure altitude in order to simplify.

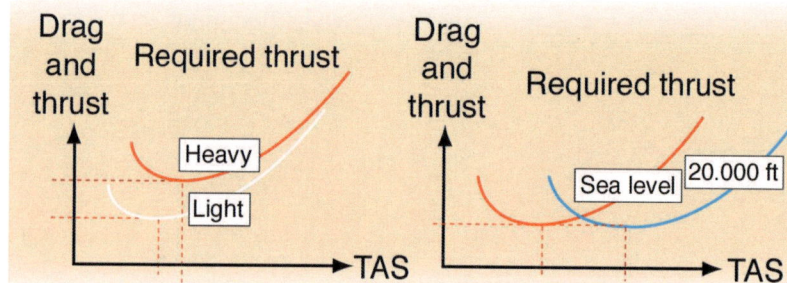

Figure 15.16

The position of the curve of required thrust is a function of the weight of the aircraft and of the pressure altitude. TAS for minimum thrust increases with weight and altitude.
On this curve we also find four characteristic points denoting speeds and the corresponding approximate angles of attack:
1.   the minimum speed (stalling speed);
2.   the speed corresponding to the minimum drag, minimum required thrust and maximum efficiency (note the difference to propeller-driven aircraft),
3.   the speed corresponding to the best ratio between the required thrust and speed, and is represented by the tangent point between the curve and the line drawn from the axis origin,
4.   the maximum speed.

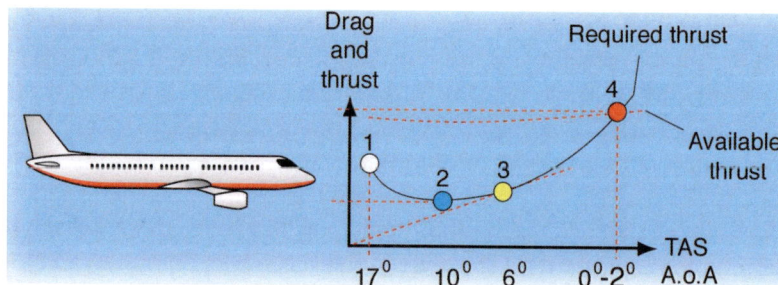

Figure 15.17

15.3.2 *Available thrust*

The available thrust is the thrust given by a jet engine; its value is nearly constant for every speed with a straight jet engine without fan, but resembles a propeller engine when having a big fan. The position of the curve is obviously determined by the selected throttle position. The position of the curve is also a function of the pressure altitude of the aircraft (the thrust decreases when the altitude increases). Even in this case, if not specified, we are going to consider the selected throttle position and the pressure altitude constant in order to simplify.

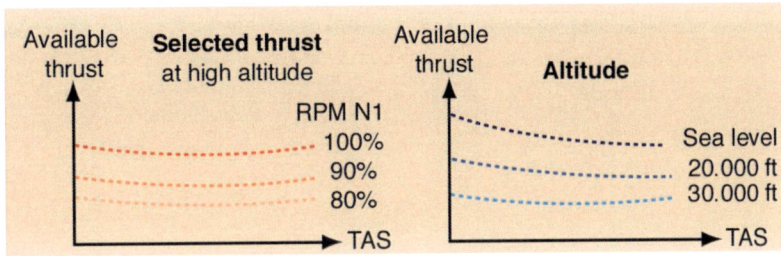

Figure 15.18

The available thrust is nearly constant for every speed of the aircraft for a jet engine without fan, but resembles a propeller engine when having a big fan. The position of the curve is also a function of the pressure altitude of the aircraft.

15.3.3 *Ranges of speed stability and speed instability*

Let us put the curves of required thrust and available thrust together in the same diagram: as for a propeller-driven aircraft, there are two points of contact between the two curves in which the values of the required thrust, or drag, and the available thrust are equal.

But there is a rather large difference between a propeller aircraft and a jet aircraft regarding the range of speed instability. The separation between the ranges is located at the minimum of required thrust, and the characteristics of the two ranges are the same for jet aircraft as for propeller aircraft.

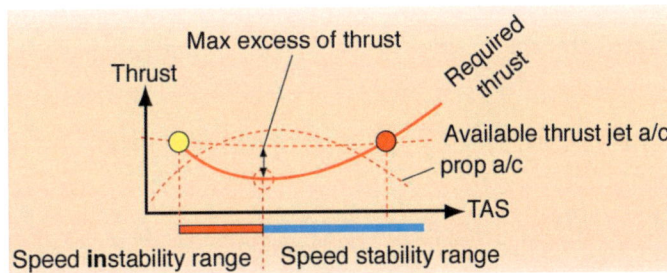

Figure 15.19

It is more difficult to find the correct level of thrust at speeds in low drag flight conditions, and at the same time maintain a certain speed within the speed instability range. The slightest increase in drag (e.g. due to a small pitch-up caused by turbulence) has to be compensated for by a rapid increase in thrust.

When flying within the speed instability range it is more difficult to maintain a given speed

15.3.4 *Effects of flaps on the required thrust*

The use of flaps increases the drag and moves the curve as shown below. It is noticeable that the upper margin of the speed instability range moves to lower speeds with increased flap deflection. (See figure 15.20). If you are flying at a certain speed with the flaps retracted you are in the speed instability range, while with 15° or more flap deflection you will be in the speed stability range. For this reasons the flaps are usually used during low speed approaches for landing to improve handling qualities.

CRANFIELD AVIATION TRAINING SCHOOL LTD. PART-FCL GBR.ATO-0136

CATS CATS INNOVATION CENTRE, LUTON, Bedfordshire LU2 8DL U.K.

www.catsaviation.com

15-9

Principles of Flight

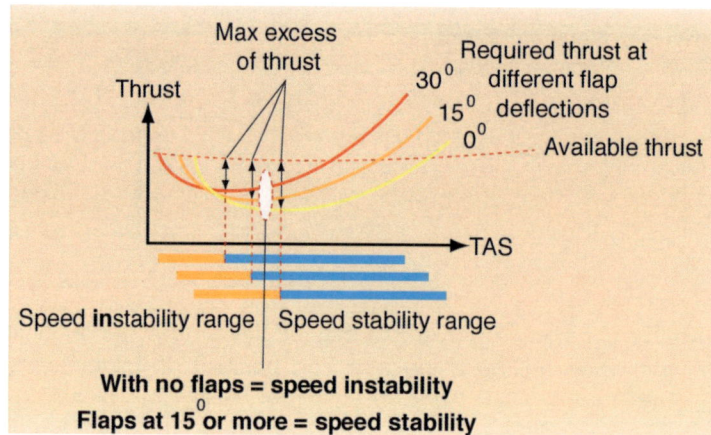

Figure 15.20

15.3.5   *Effects of the altitude on required and available thrust*

You saw that the curves of available thrust decrease and the required thrust moves to increased speeds while climbing. So, there is a certain altitude, at which the available thrust is just enough to maintain flight and consequently the curve of available thrust is tangential to the curve of required thrust at the point of minimum drag. This altitude is the absolute ceiling, which is the maximum altitude for a certain weight at which the engines can make the aircraft fly at the minimum drag speed. Note that the true air speed, for this value, increases with altitude.

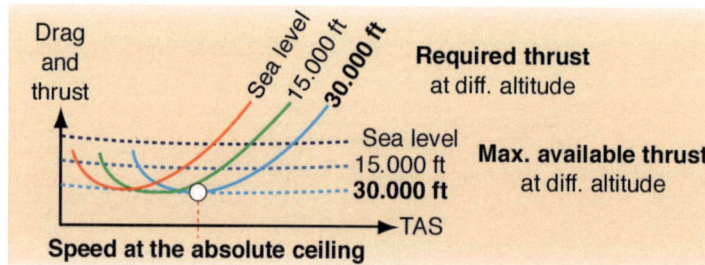

Figure 15.21

The absolute ceiling is the maximum altitude for a certain weight at which the engines can make the aircraft fly at the minimum drag speed. That speed increases with altitude.

15.3.6   *Speed for maximum endurance*

The fuel flow of a jet engine is proportional to the thrust instead of the power (thrust x TAS) which was the case with the propeller aircraft. For this reason, the maximum endurance speed is the same as the minimum drag speed, which is equal to the speed of the minimum required thrust, corresponding to the max L/D, or maximum efficiency. However, since the efficiency of an engine decreases at low power, the determined speed for max endurance is often slightly higher than the speed for max L/D. At that optimal speed, altitude has no significant influence on the max endurance.

CRANFIELD AVIATION TRAINING SCHOOL LTD. PART-FCL GBR.ATO-0136
CATS INNOVATION CENTRE, LUTON, Bedfordshire LU2 8DL U.K.   www.catsaviation.com

15-10

Principles of Flight

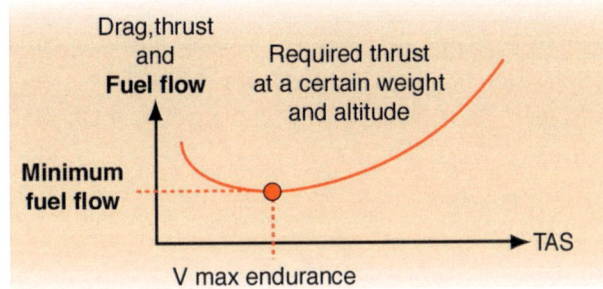

Figure 15.22

The maximum endurance speed is reached at or slightly higher than the point of minimum required thrust, corresponding to the maximum L/D ratio and maximum efficiency.

15.3.7 Speed for maximum range

We said that for propeller-driven aircraft, the fuel flow is proportional to the power. But for jet aircraft the fuel flow is proportional to the thrust, and consequently the ratio between the minimum fuel flow and velocity is the same as the minimum required thrust and velocity (or max L/D x V). This is represented in the diagram by the point where the line drawn from the origin of the axis is tangential to the curve of required thrust. Thus the speed for maximum range will also be for jet aircraft higher than the speed for maximum endurance.

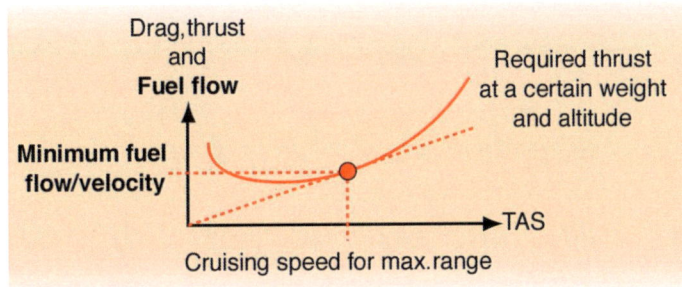

Figure 15.23

The speed for maximum range is found at the minimum ratio between the required thrust/velocity.

15.3.8 Comparison between Power/V and Thrust/V curves

It is interesting to see the differences between the speeds for maximum endurance and maximum range on propeller and jet aircraft respectively. In the next figure we correlate the curve of power versus velocity and the curve of thrust versus velocity for a given aircraft. In the first case the aircraft is equipped with a piston engine and we can determine the Power/V. In the second case it is equipped with a jet engine and we can determine Thrust/V.

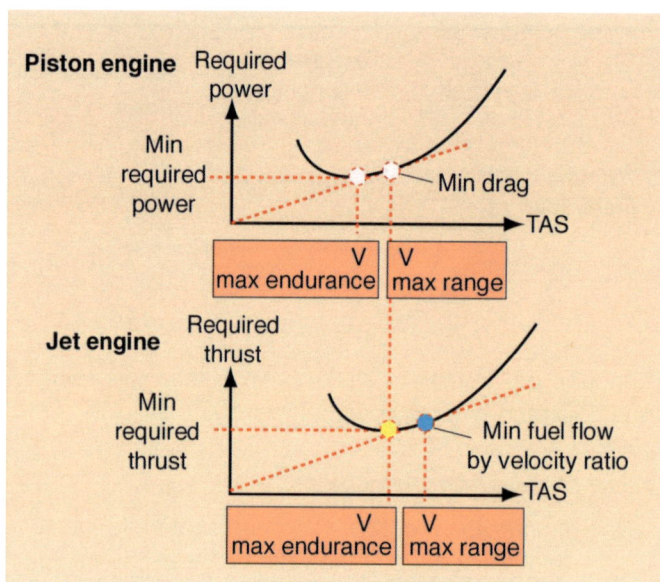

Figure 15.24

As can be seen from the graph; the speed for max endurance is the speed for min required power and min required thrust respectively. The speed for max range corresponds to the minimum ratio between the required power and speed for min drag, and to the minimum ratio between the required thrust and speed for min fuel flow by velocity.

15.3.9   *Effect of wind on speed for max range*

The minimum fuel flow and velocity can be multiplied by time in order to find out the ratio between the fuel used and the distance. As shown in the next diagram, the horizontal line represents the distance flown for a given time and the vertical line the fuel used during the same time. A headwind will result in a shorter distance flown and a tailwind a longer distance. The speed for max range is still represented in the diagram by the tangent point of the line drawn from the axis origin and the curve of the required thrust. In order to obtain the lowest rate of fuel used by distance flown, the TAS has to be corrected for a tailwind or a headwind component. In a headwind situation it is preferable to shorten the time spent in that wind condition and in a tailwind to benefit from it.

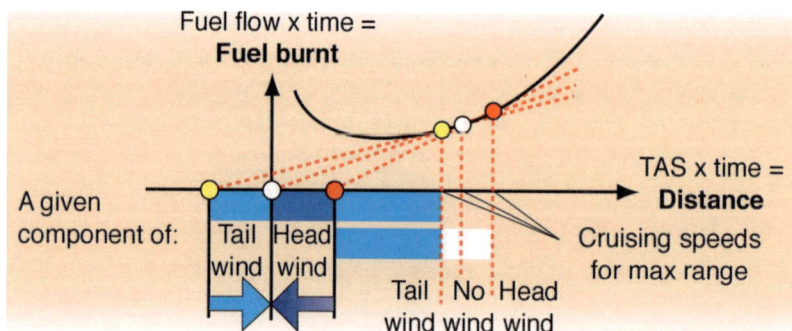

Figure 15.25

The speed for max range is higher in headwind and lower in tailwind than in still air

15.3.10   *Effect of altitude on range*

At the same indicated speed (IAS) but at a higher altitude, the aircraft will have the same pitch attitude, and the same drag and the same thrust, but the true air speed (TAS) will be higher. It is the TAS that determines the propulsive efficiency (a question of momentum). At 40.000 ft (12 200 m) where the TAS is doubled compared to sea level, the efficiency will be doubled, and provided that the fuel consumption remains proportional to thrust, the range will be doubled.

Despite the fact that the available thrust from a jet engine decreases with altitude, the engine specific fuel consumption will decrease with altitude. The next diagram shows how air density, thrust and the specific fuel consumption decreases with altitude compared to at sea level.

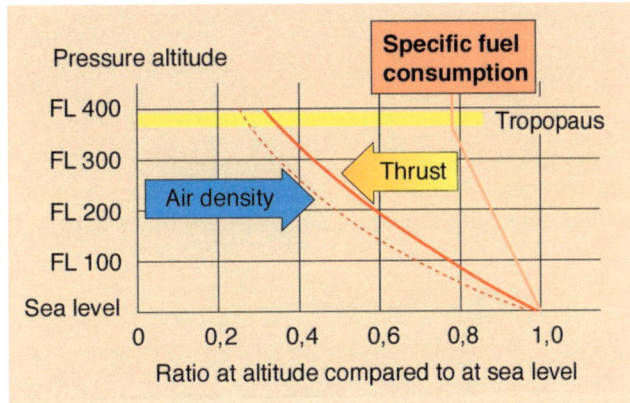

Figure 15.26

At approx. 40.000 ft in zero wind condition, the range will be doubled compared to that at sea level. So, to increase the range of a jet aircraft; fly high.

15.3.11 *Specific air range and speed for long range cruise, V_{LRC}*

The most convenient way to express the range capability of an aircraft is the distance flown versus fuel used. This is called the specific air range, abbreviated SAR. The picture below gives a general view of the specific range versus speed for three different gross weights at a given altitude.

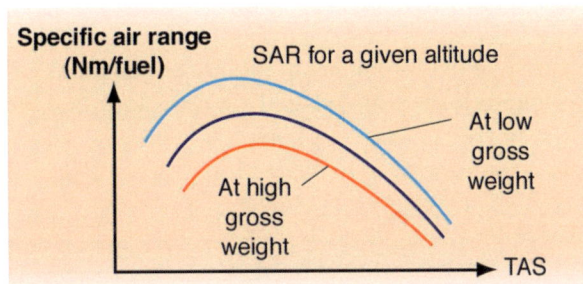

Figure 15.27

Naturally, you will fly more nautical miles for a given amount of fuel with low gross weight than with high gross weight. The optimum speed for Max Range Cruise occurs in the lower part of the speed stability range, and therefore another method called Long Range Cruise, V_{LRC}, has been developed. This speed, V_{LRC}, is slightly higher than speed for Max Range Cruise and is selected to achieve 99% of maximum range. Thus the 1% loss of range is traded for a gain in speed of approximately 5%. Furthermore, V_{LRC} is the same speed as Max Range Cruise but in approximately 100 KT headwind.

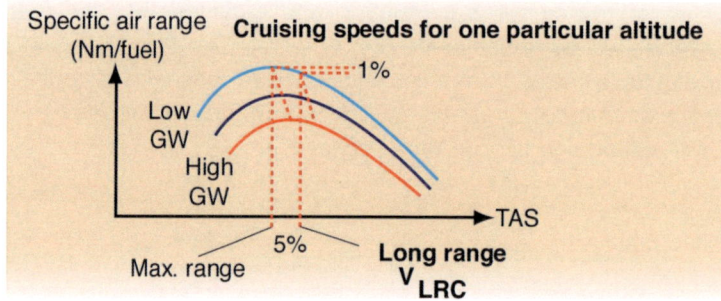

Figure 15.28

Due to the required speed stability, the normal long-range speed, V_{LRC}, is about 5% higher than the speed for Max Range Cruise. The TAS for the speed for Max Range Cruise and V_{LRC} will vary with altitude as shown in the next figure.

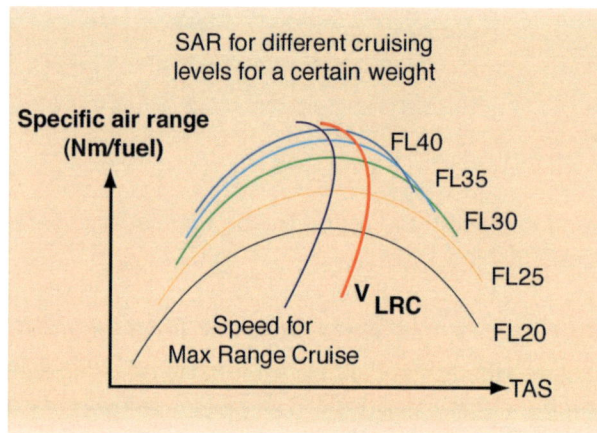

Figure 15.29

There are also other cruising speeds, e.g. normal cruising speed for practical reasons, when the maximum range is not the most important, and speed for minimum direct operating costs. Note that the normal cruising speed is higher than the long range cruising speed and represents a compromise with respect to range, payload and operating costs. The maximum cruising speed is limited by maximum available cruising thrust and the highest approved normal operating Mach number M_{MO}.

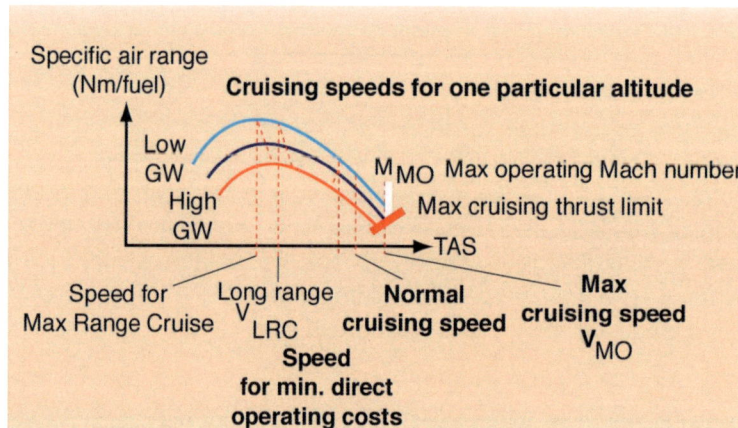

Figure 15.30

CRANFIELD AVIATION TRAINING SCHOOL LTD. PART-FCL GBR.ATO-0136
CATS INNOVATION CENTRE, LUTON, Bedfordshire LU2 8DL U.K.

www.catsaviation.com

15-14

Principles of Flight

15.3.12 *Specific range versus altitude*

For a given cruising procedure, the altitude for best range increases as the weight of the aircraft decreases during flight. The reason for this is very complex and lies in the principles of the jet engine. The optimum range results from a climbing cruise corresponding to the reduction of weight due to used fuel. However, due to ATC restrictions, in normal operations the closest we can get to optimum range is by climbing step-by-step. This is called the step climb concept. Consequently, as the flight time increases and thus the fuel is consumed, a higher and higher altitude is selected in steps.

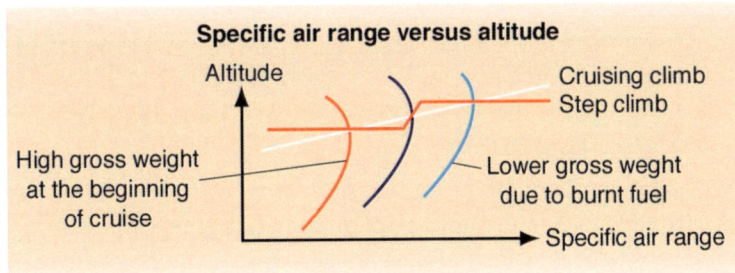

Figure 15.31

The altitude for best range increases as the gross weight decreases

15.3.13 *Summary of differences in speeds between propeller and jet aircraft*

In the next table we summarize the differences between propeller driven aircraft and jet aircraft so far as range and endurance are concerned. However, it is an approximation since only the most important factors have been taken into account.

	Propeller	Jet
Speed for maximum range	Minimum drag	Minimum drag/speed
Altitude for maximum range	Medium to high*	High
Speed for maximum endurance	Minimum power	Minimum drag
Altitude for maximum endurance	Low to medium	Medium

Figure 15.32

FOR MAXIMUM RANGE:
- Propeller aircraft:- fly at min drag speed, altitude medium to high, but wind condition are most important.
- Jet aircraft;- fly according to minimum drag to speed ratio, mostly as high as possible, until very strong headwinds occur on high levels.

FOR MAXIMUM ENDURANCE:
- Propeller aircraft:- fly at the speed of minimum required power, normally at a low to medium level.
- Jet aircraft:- fly at the speed of minimum drag, altitude medium.

CHAPTER 16

LOAD FACTOR

16.1   *Load Factor Formulae*

The load factor (n) is a non-dimensional number obtained from the ratio between the lift produced by the wings, which sustain the acceleration forces of the aircraft, and the weight of the aircraft.

16.1.1   *Acceleration forces*

During flight conditions different from straight and level flight, such as turning, the structure and occupants of the aircraft are subjected to stress due to the horizontal and/or vertical components of the forces acting on it. The resultant component generates an acceleration force different from the weight of the aircraft. (This component is sometimes called apparent weight, abbreviated Wa.)

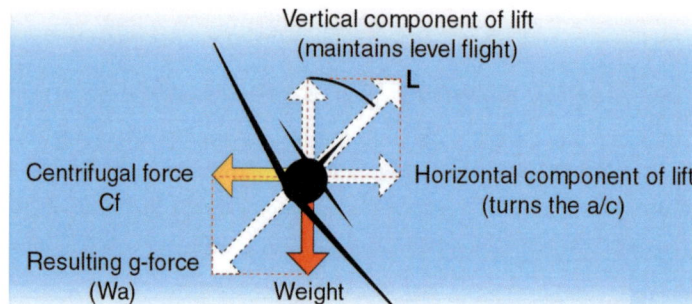

Figure 16.1

Load factor n = ratio between aircraft acceleration and gravity acceleration.

The ratio between the acceleration to which the aircraft is subjected during a manoeuvre and the acceleration of gravity (weight), abbreviated g (equal to 9.81 m/s^2), is a non-dimensional number, n, called the load factor. It has a numerical value of 1 when the aircraft is in straight and level flight. The values are greater or lower respectively, if the g-force is more or less than the weight of the aircraft.

The load factor "n" is determined by the ratio between the acceleration to which the aircraft is subjected and the acceleration of gravity g (9.81 m/s^2). The load factor is considered positive above 0, and negative below 0. On some aircraft, specific instruments called accelerometers or g-meters are used to determine the g-value. The value 0 represents a particular case. It is obtained when the g-force due to a change of angle formed by flight path is equal to and acts opposite to the weight.

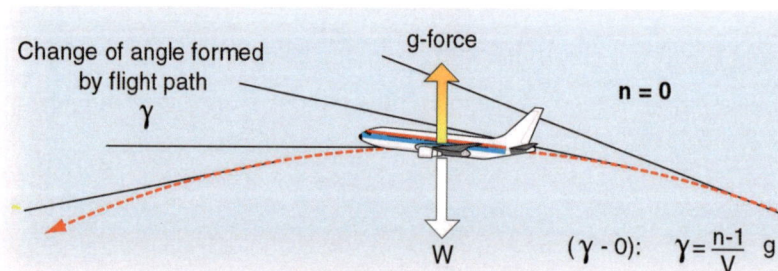

Figure 16.2

The value 0 is obtained when the g-force due to a change of angle formed by flight path is equal to and acts opposite to the weight.

CRANFIELD AVIATION TRAINING SCHOOL LTD. PART-FCL GBR.ATO-0136
CATS CATS INNOVATION CENTRE, LUTON, Bedfordshire LU2 8DL U.K.   www.catsaviation.com

16-1   Principles of Flight

Load factor n = L / W

In addition, as the wings must sustain the increased or reduced g-force, the g-force will be equal to the lift produced by the wings at that instant. For that reason we can also say that the load factor is the ratio between lift and weight of the aircraft.

16.2   *Load Factors and Manoeuvres*

When turning, climbing, descending and pulling out of a dive, the load factor is always different from 1. We are now going to analyse how the load factor acts in these manoeuvres and the effect it has on the stalling speed of the aircraft.

16.2.1   *Load factor and turning*

In a steady coordinated turn during level flight, the vertical component of lift must be equal to the weight of the aircraft so that there will be no acceleration in the vertical direction. Let us consider the angle of bank, ϕ (phi). As we can see from the resulting forces, the resultant acceleration force, and thus the lift, is greater than the weight.

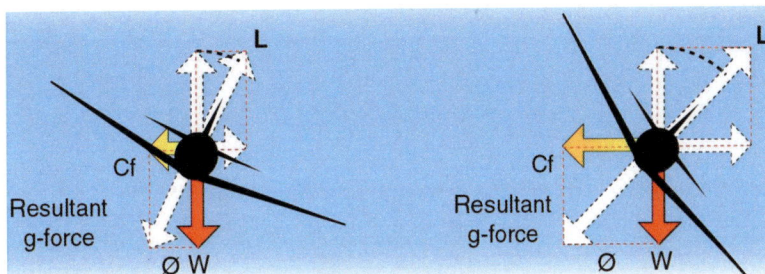

Figure 16.3

In a steady, coordinated turn during level flight, the lift is greater than the weight of the aircraft

The resulting g-force is created by the weight and the centrifugal force. Using trigonometry, we can say that the cosine of ϕ is equal to the ratio between the weight and the resultant g-force, and is also equal to 1 divided by "n". According to this, "n" is equal to 1/cosine of ϕ.

If an aircraft has a mass of 4000 kg, when making a coordinated level turn of constant speed at an angle of bank of 60° the required lift will be 4000 x 1/cos 60° x 9.81 = 78500 N.

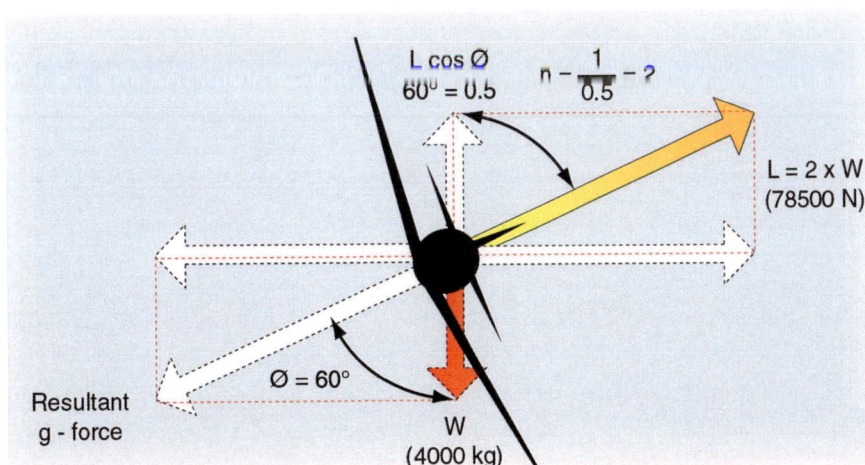

Figure 16.4

The resultant g-force, and thus the load factor, is a function of the angle of bank.

16.2.2   *Load factor versus angle of bank*

From these mathematical considerations we can obtain a diagram of the curve of the load factor versus the angle of bank. We can see that an angle of bank of 60° implies a load factor of 2 g; that an angle of 80° implies nearly 6 g, and that at 90° the curve tends toward the infinite.

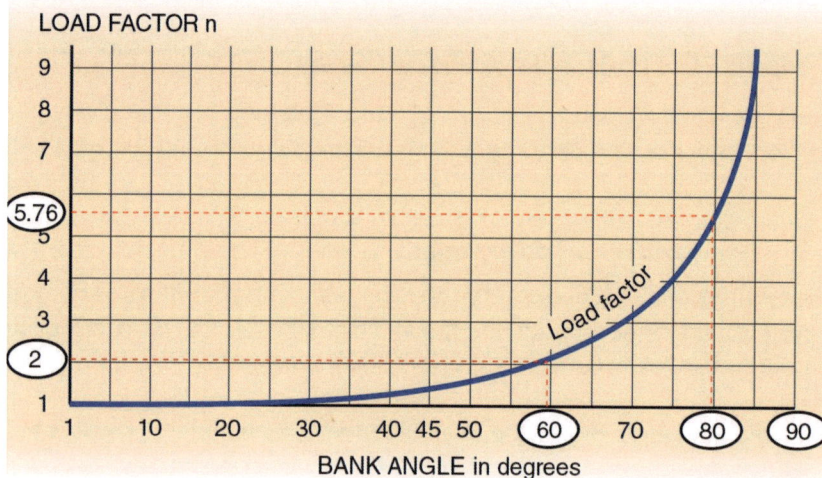

Figure 16.5

16.2.3   *Climbing (or descending) and load factor*

Let us consider the angle of climb or descent γ (gamma) of the flight path. From trigonometry, we know that the cosine of g is equal to the ratio between the resultant g-force and the weight of the aircraft. Therefore, "n" is equal to the cosine of γ, which implies that while climbing or descending the load factor is slightly below 1, requiring less lift from the wings.

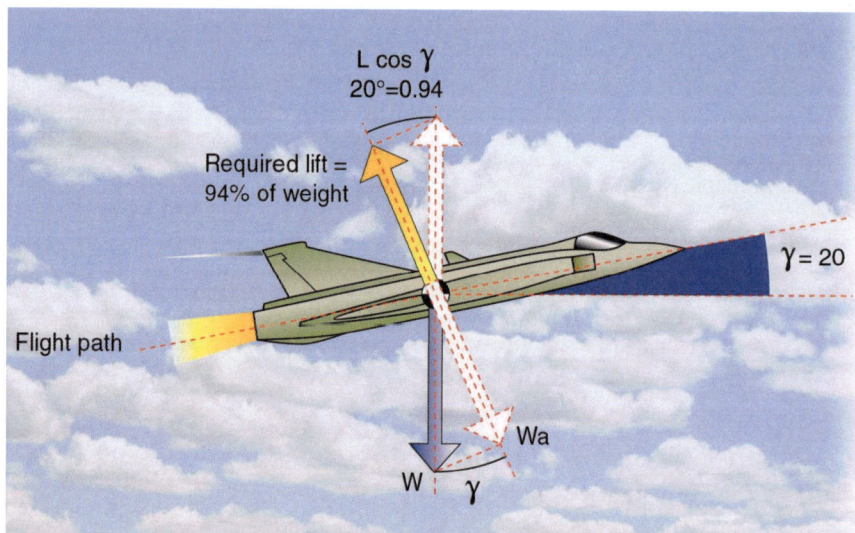

Figure 16.6

The load factor of a climbing or descending aircraft is a function of the angle of the flight path.

16.2.4   *Load factor when pulling out of a dive*

Let us consider an aircraft pulling out of a dive. At the lower point of the flight path, the centrifugal force has the same direction as the weight force, and thus the two forces are combined with each other.

CRANFIELD AVIATION TRAINING SCHOOL LTD. PART-FCL GBR.ATO-0136
CATS INNOVATION CENTRE, LUTON, Bedfordshire LU2 8DL U.K.   www.catsaviation.com
16-3   Principles of Flight

Since the formula for calculating the load factor in this case is rather complicated, we will not study it. But the next figure shows how the weight force will be added to the centrifugal force in order to obtain the resulting g-force.

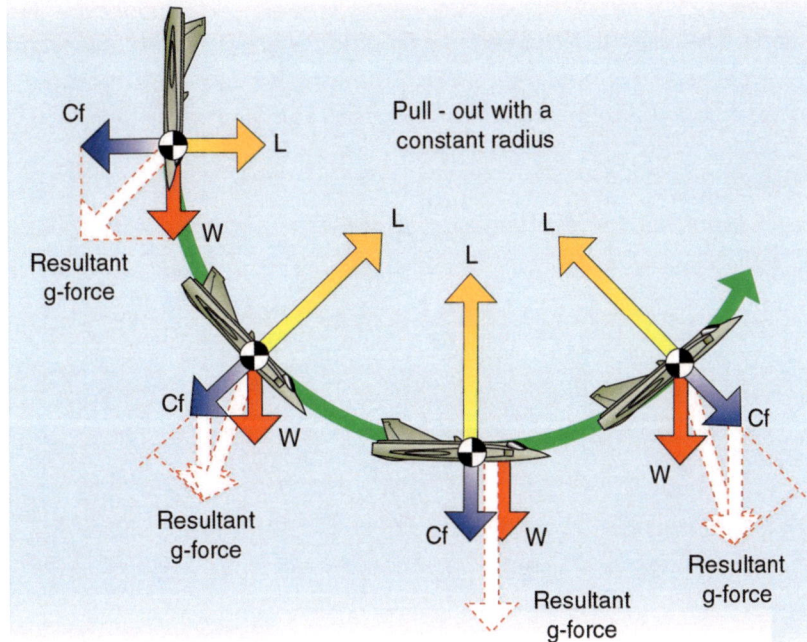

Figure 16.7

You must remember, however, that there is a major increase in the load factor, and that a rapid pull-out can be very dangerous for you or the aircraft, or both.

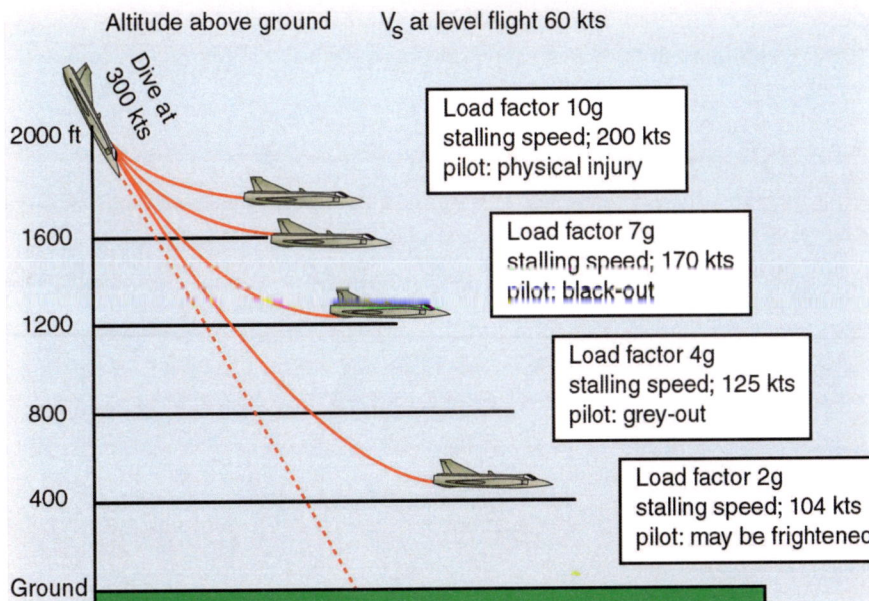

Figure 16.8

If making a circular flight path, e.g. a geometrically perfect loop, at the lower point of the flight path, the centrifugal force and the weight are combined with each other. This means that there is a major increase in the resulting g-force, which causes a very high increase in load factor.

16.2.5   *Load factor and stalling speed*

The stalling speed of a specific aircraft does not have a fixed value for all flight conditions, the stalling speed goes up in proportion to the square root of the load factor. Thus, at a loadfactor of 2 the stalling speed increases by 41% ($\div 2 = 1{,}41$), at 3g, by 73% ($\div 3 = 1{,}73$) etc.

Due to the increase in resultant g-force, a level turn always creates a load factor greater than 1, causing an increase in stalling speed. This can be calculated in a diagram, which is valid for all aircraft.

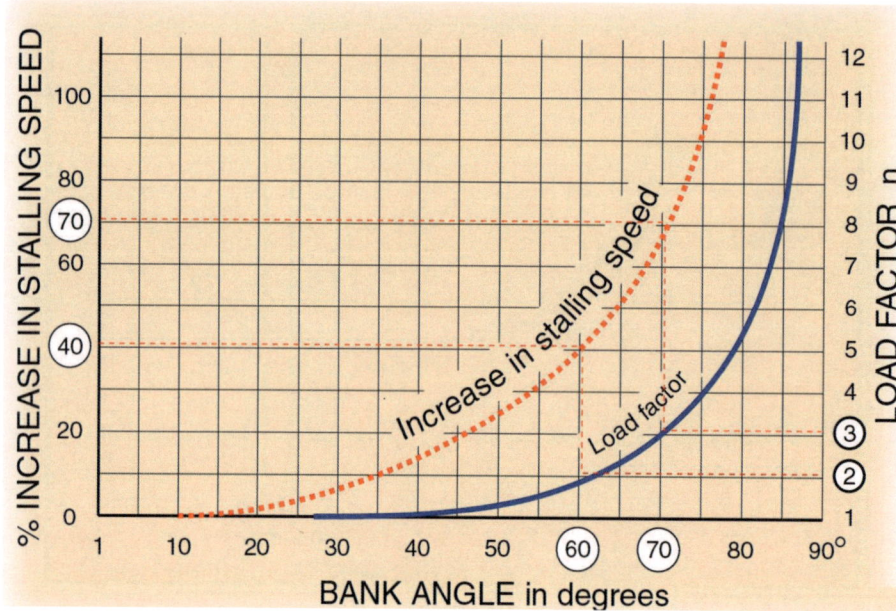

Figure 16.9

The stalling speed increases in proportion to the square root of the load factor which increases with the bank angle in a level turn. At 1,4g (45° bank) +20%, at 2g (60° bank) +40%, at 3g (70° bank) +70%.

The only fixed value regarding the stall of an aircraft is the angle of attack at which it will nearly always stall, regardless of airspeed, weight, air density at the altitude or load factor. This critical angle is usually between 15° and 20°, depending on the aircraft.

16.2.6   *Dynamic stall and load factor*

At a certain speed the aircraft will normally stall at a given load factor. However, the so-called dynamic stall occurs at a higher A.o.A than the normal one. At a speed where a certain load factor would normally cause the aircraft to stall, a very sharp vertical wind gust may rapidly accelerate the aircraft making it produce a momentary load factor that is far too high and which may cause structural damage.

CRANFIELD AVIATION TRAINING SCHOOL LTD. PART-FCL GBR.ATO-0136
CATS INNOVATION CENTRE, LUTON, Bedfordshire LU2 8DL U.K.   www.catsaviation.com

16-5   Principles of Flight

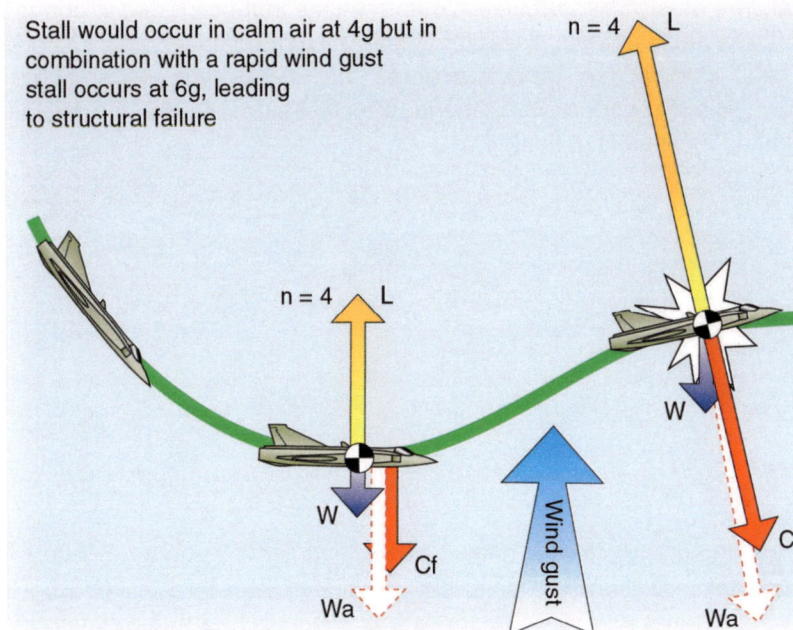

Stall would occur in calm air at 4g but in combination with a rapid wind gust stall occurs at 6g, leading to structural failure

Figure 16.10

On the other hand, stall can also occur at a lower A.o.A than normal, allowing a lower load factor than expected. At very high speeds the compressibility effect of the air causes a so-called shockstall.

16.3   *Structural Considerations*

The structure of every aircraft is designed to be protected against the permanent deformation that can result from structural overstress. For this reason there is always a load factor limit. The limit depends on the type of aircraft. In this section, we explain how to avoid overstress.

16.3.1   *Load factor limits*

As we have seen, there are several opportunities to stress the structure during flight by reaching load factor values different from 1. The structure of the aircraft must withstand elastic deformations that occur due to changed load factor during flight. For this reason there are load factor limits which depend on the aircraft category, as shown.

Load factor limits		
FAR Part 23: Max take-off weight < 12500 lbs (< 5700 kg)		
Catagories		
Normal	Utility	Utility
+ 3.8 g	+ 4.4 g	+ 6 g
- 1.52 g	- 1.76 g	- 3 g
FAR Part 25: Max take-off weight < 12500 lbs (< 5700 kg) + 3.8 to 2.5 g depending on designed weight - 1.0 g		

Figure 16.11

The structure of the aircraft must withstand elastic deformations that occur due to changed load factor during flight. For this reason there are load factor limits for different aircraft categories.

These limits, called limit load factors, must guarantee that if they are reached, the deformation of the structure will be elastic. This means that when the load factor returns to the normal value (1) every point of the airframe must return to its original geometry.

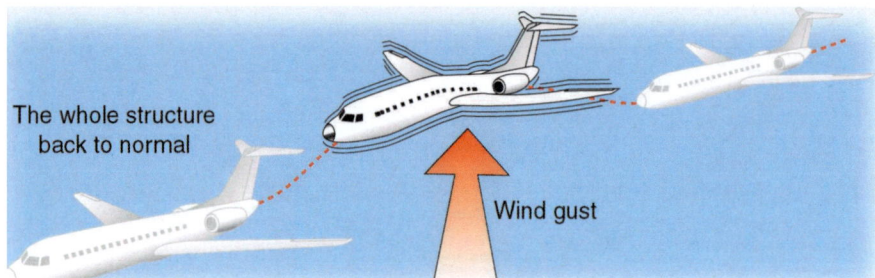

Figure 16.12

The load factor limits must guarantee elastic deformations.

To ensure that the structure will react in a safe way, a safety factor is calculated on behalf of the aircraft design. It is 1.5. This means that if the load factor limit is exceeded up to 1.5 times the designed limit load factor, the deformation will be permanent but no structural or system failure may occur.

The safety factor guarantees that there will be no structural or system failure if the load factor limit is exceeded up to 1.5 times, depending on the aircraft category.

After the safety factor, the ultimate load factor is reached. It represents the load factor value above which the deformation will be permanent and/or may cause structural failure.

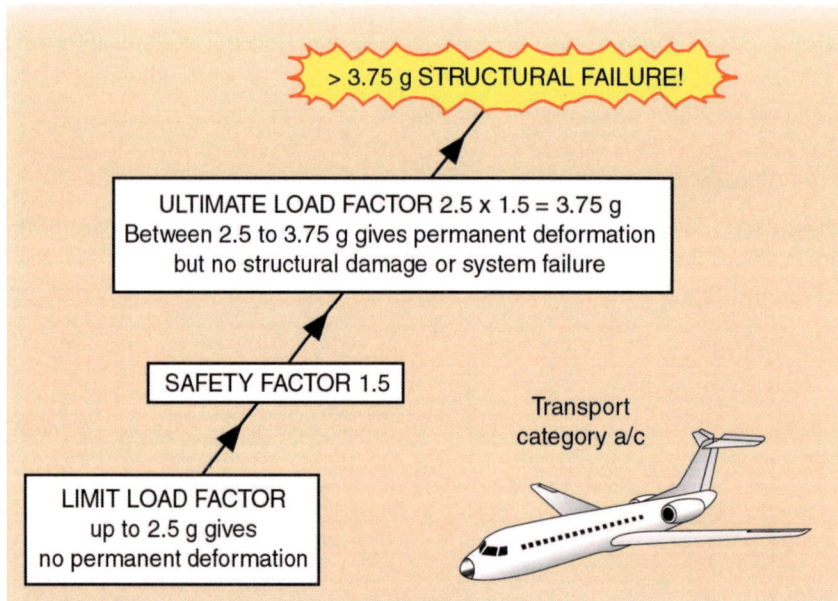

Figure 16.13

The ultimate load factor is the value above which there will be permanent deformation or structural break-up.

16.3.2 *Structural life*

The life of the aircraft depends upon many things, such as cyclic variations of loading, heat, cold, moisture, wear and corrosion. Every part of the aircraft has a designed life which, while representing primarily a compromise between strength and weight, is also determined by economic necessity.

The designed life of an aircraft is based upon a certain kind of life e.g. a certain number of gust-produced oscillations, take-offs and landings etc. within given limits. If an aircraft that has been overstressed e.g. by too hard landings or turns with load factors above the limitations, it can be dangerous to fly when it is getting older, despite careful examination during the normal overhauls. This puts a responsibility on you as a pilot, not to overstress any aircraft. Never overload your aircraft. If it has accidentally been overloaded, you as the pilot, have the responsibility to report that in the aircraft log.

16.3.3   Vn diagram

Every aircraft has a specific diagram that shows its operating limitations. It is called a Vn diagram and gives the airspeed on the horizontal scale and the load factor on the vertical scale. The envelope of this diagram represents the normal flight range of the aircraft, while every point outside it represents a very hazardous or impossible situation.

Every aircraft has a specific Vn diagram. The aircraft must always fly in a condition that lies within the diagram envelope. During the construction of the particular Vn diagram, the designer establishes some specific airspeeds. The ones represented on the airspeed indicator are:

- V_{SO} (stalling speed with flaps fully down),
- V_S (stalling speed with flaps up),
- V_{NO} (normal operating speed)
- V_{NE} (the speed never to be exceeded).

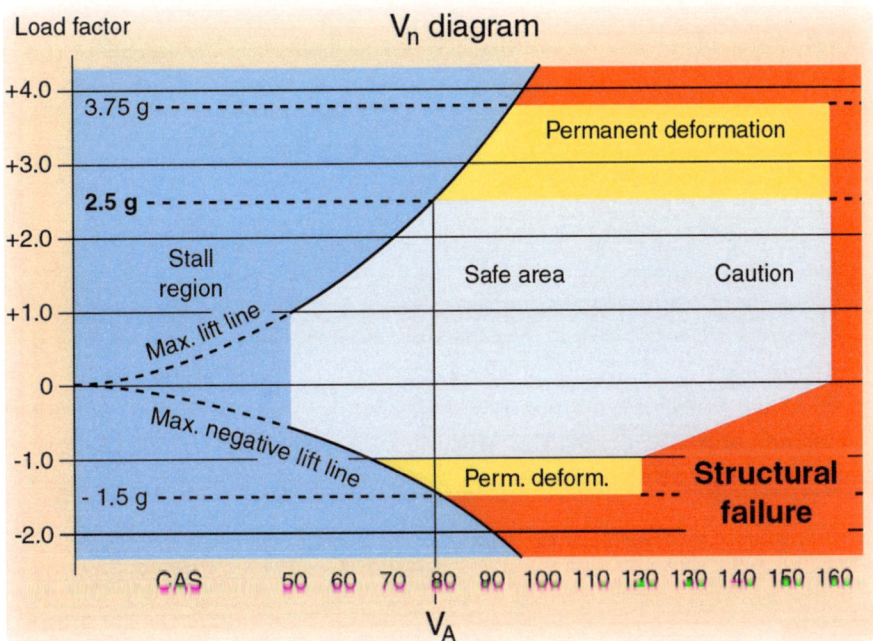

Figure 16.14

There is another characteristic speed not represented on the airspeed indicator: V_A (the designed maximum manoeuvering speed).

V_A speed plays an important role in observing the load factor limit. In fact, it is the maximum speed at which you can abruptly move the control column within the mechanical limits, without exceeding the load factor limit. At lower speeds stall will occur first, as the next Vn diagram shows. When flying at speeds higher than V_A, you can exceed the load factor limit before stall.

This may happen, for example, in a turn with a steep angle of bank, if you raise the aircraft nose by applying further pressure on the control column backwards instead of reducing the angle of bank before raising the aircraft nose.

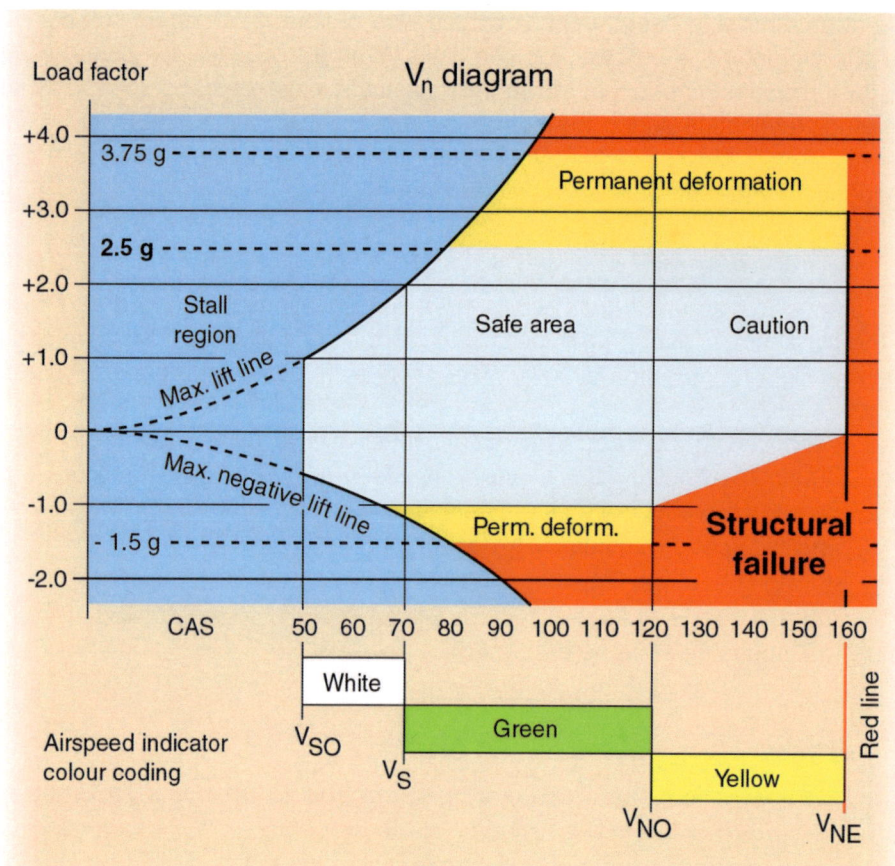

Figure 16.15

At speeds below V_A, you can abruptly move the control column within the mechanical limits without exceeding the load factor limit, since the aircraft will stall instead. When flying at speeds higher than V_A, you can exceed the load factor limit before the stall

There is another speed that plays an important role in remaining within the load factor limits. This speed is V_{NO}. We have already said that it is the normal operating speed, but it is also the maximum speed for flying in moderately turbulent air, in which it is also possible to exceed the load factor limits in straight and level flight. Never fly faster than V_{NO} in turbulent air.

16.3.4   *Load factor and turbulent air*

In turbulent air, the gust has two components: one horizontal and one vertical. The vertical gust is very important in that it causes rapid changes in the relative airflow (and consequently in the angle of attack), while the aircraft's inertia tends to keep it on its flight path. During this short time, the angle of attack increases (or decreases), and the load factor varies along with it.

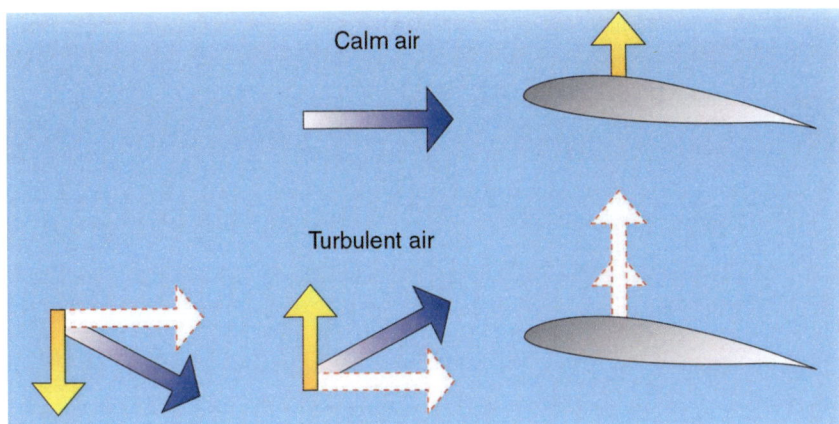

Figure 16.16

The vertical gust component causes rapid changes in the relative airflow and thus in the angle of attack, which in turn causes a rapid change in the load factor.

16.3.5   *Gust diagram*

In severe turbulence, the gusts can reach very high levels. You must use all aids to avoid hazardous situations such as flying into a thunderstorm. But if you have encountered severe turbulence you have to reduce your speed but still be well above stalling speed.

Very violent gusts should be avoided at high speeds. The speed of the gust and the speed of flight together may cause very high loads on the aircraft. For this reason, depending on the actual speed, ICAO has determined three vertical values for the gusts (both ascending and descending) that, for example, a jet transport aircraft must be able to withstand. These are 66 ft/sec, 50ft/sec and 25 ft/sec, up to FL 200 thereafter reducing to 38 ft/sec, 25 ft/sec and 12.5 ft/s respectively at FL500.

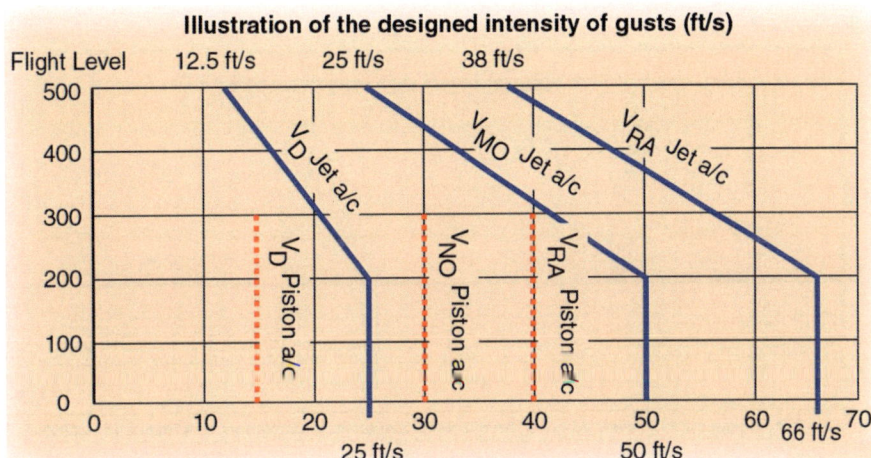

Figure 16.17

There are three vertical gust values that the aircraft must be able to withstand, ascending or descending.
One value of gust intensity will have a greater impact on the aircraft at high speed than at low speed. E.g. a gust load of 66 ft/s encountered at low speed will cause a load factor of only 2g but the same gust intensity encountered at higher speed will cause a load factor of 3g. These values of gust intensity are represented in a Vn diagram in the form of six lines.

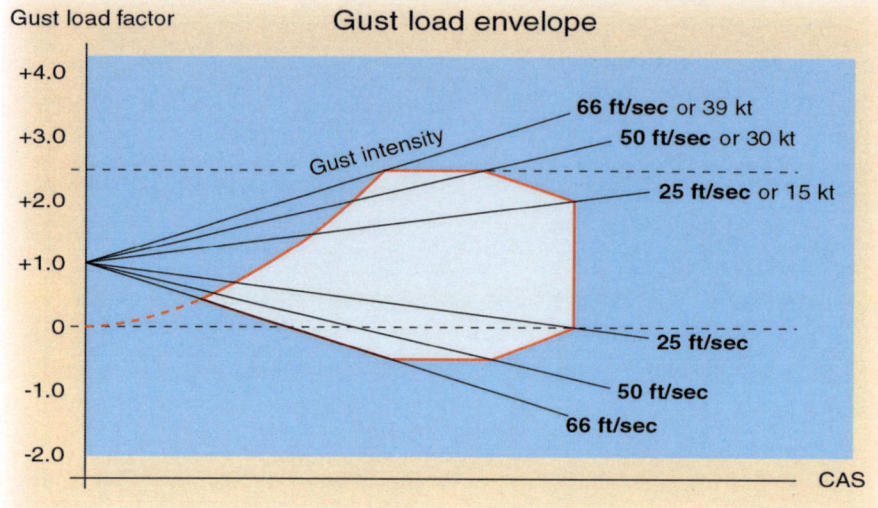

Figure 16.18

The limits of the gust load factor, being calculated from a formula, are a function of aircraft geometry, speed, gust velocity, gross weight and altitude.

In figure 16.19 it can be seen that the structure of the aircraft can withstand higher gust velocities at lower speeds than at higher ones. Obviously, the limits of the gust load factor are lower if the speed is increased.

The intersection points, between the gust lines and the diagram envelope, designate some characteristic speeds at which the aircraft should be maintained between the load factor limits. These are:

V_B min/max speed for severe turbulent air penetration,
V_C maximum designed cruising speed (to determine the V_{MO} and V_{NO})
V_D max speed of dive (called max dive speed).

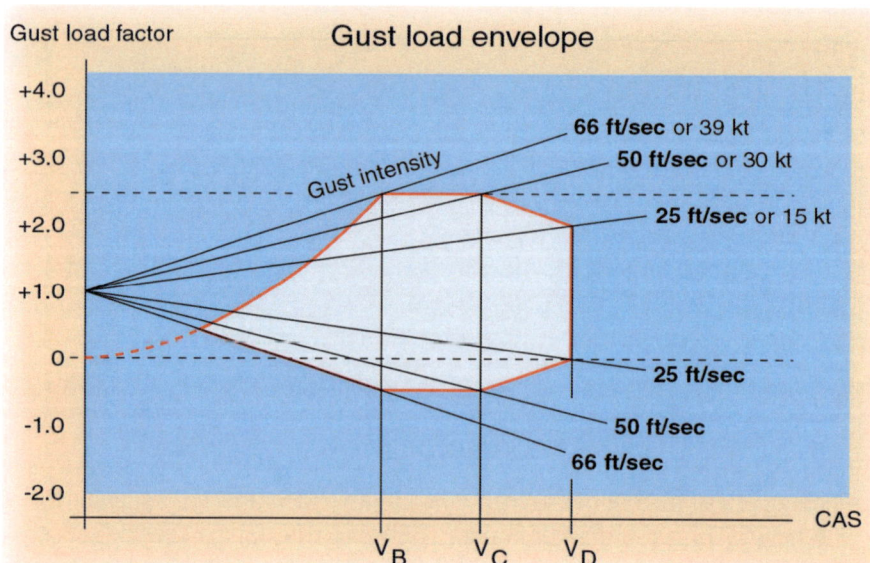

Figure 16.19

Finally, the V_{RA} is a specifically recommended penetration speed for flight in severe turbulent air. This speed, or speed envelope, is usually between the V_A and the V_{NO}, where the load factor limits are higher than at higher speeds. At high speeds, the load factor limits must be lowered along with the increase in speed. Thus it is necessary to reduce the speed during severe turbulence. You may find that, at low speeds, setting the V_{RA} will require you to increase your speed.

CRANFIELD AVIATION TRAINING SCHOOL LTD. PART-FCL GBR.ATO-0136
CATS INNOVATION CENTRE, LUTON, Bedfordshire LU2 8DL U.K.   www.catsaviation.com

16-11   Principles of Flight

16.3.6   *Aeroelasticity*

For weight saving reasons the structure of the aircraft has to be made weak which causes elasticity. Simultaneously the airframe must be able to absorb loads created by momentary elastic deformation occurring due to the changes in load factor during flight. In fact, the structure is subjected to deflections. The airframe is subjected to aerodynamic loads that depend on the external shape of the airframe. The consequence of these loads is to strain the airframe, so that its shape is modified somewhat. The slightly modified shape in turn leads to a modification of the aerodynamic loads. This interaction between the aerodynamic loads and the elastic strain of the airframe is called aeroelasticity. The next figure shows an aircraft wing, bent upwards due to the load it carries. As can be seen, the wing tip has a slightly lower geometrical angle of the chord line than the wing root has.

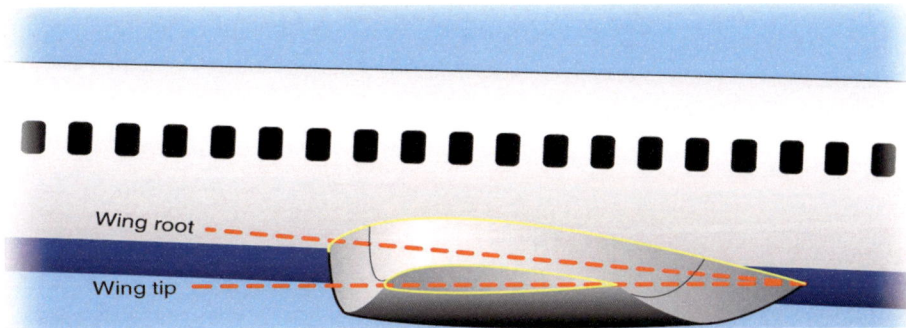

Figure 16.20

At low speeds the effect is negligible, but at high speeds the aerodynamic loads and the elastic strain are correspondingly greater. These aeroelasticity effects may result in three phenomena; wing torsional divergence, control surface flutter and control reversal. The interaction between the aerodynamic loads and the elastic strain of the airframe is called aeroelasticity.

16.3.7   *Wing torsional divergence*

A wing of large span is not only bendable up and down, but also around an axis from root to tip, because the structure is not perfectly rigid. The pressure distribution on a wing has its main loads near the wing leading edge causing the wing to twist in a nose up direction. But the structure of the wing twists about an axis, known as the torsional axis of the wing, which is usually aft of the line of the aerodynamic centre.

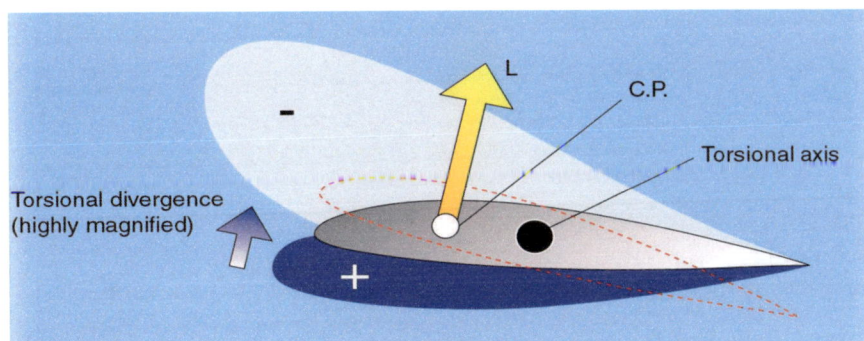

Figure 16.21

If there is an increase in speed, the aerodynamic forces increase in proportion to the V^2, and so does the twisting moment. But the elastic stiffness is not affected by speed, so the amount of twist increases with speed. Eventually, a speed is reached at which the elastic resistance to twist is only just sufficient to counteract the twisting moment. Above this speed, called the wing torsional divergence speed, structural failure occurs - the wing will break apart. At very high speeds, above V_{NE}, the aerodynamic loads will tend to twist the wing off its mounting.

CRANFIELD AVIATION TRAINING SCHOOL LTD. PART-FCL GBR.ATO-0136
CATS INNOVATION CENTRE, LUTON, Bedfordshire LU2 8DL U.K.   www.catsaviation.com
16-12   Principles of Flight

CHAPTER 17

TURNING FLIGHT

17.1   *Forces Involved In Turning Flight*

17.1.1   *Review of Newton's Laws of Motion*

Newton's First Law of Motion states that a moving body tends to continue moving in a straight line at a constant speed.

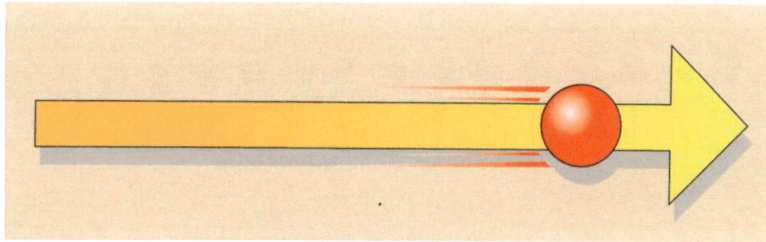

Figure 17.1

Newton's Second Law of Motion states that to change the state of a body moving in a straight line at a constant speed, a force must be exerted on it. For example if you want to change the flight path of a body, you must exert a pushing force on it.

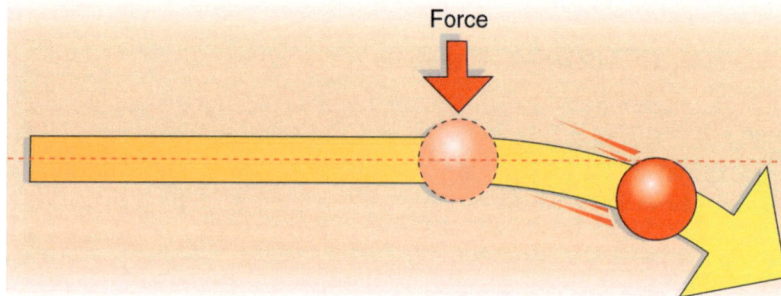

Figure 17.2

17.1.2   *Centripetal force*

If you want to constrain a body to and keep it on a curved path, you must continually exert a force on it toward the centre of the curve. This force is called the centripetal force. The centripetal force counteracts the natural tendency of the body to travel in a straight line and therefore to continue tangentially.

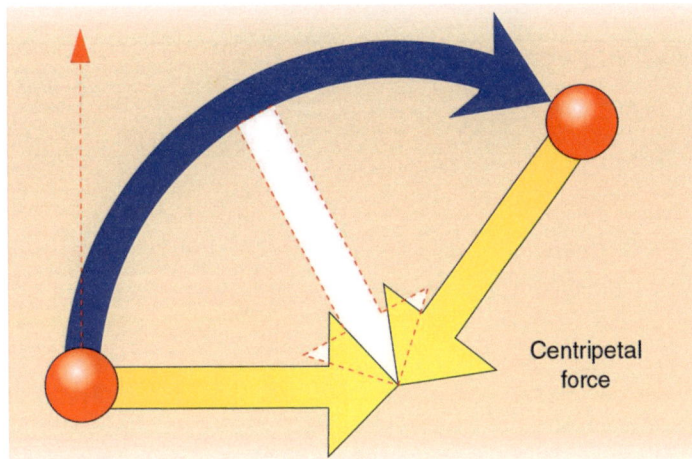

Figure 17.3

The centripetal force maintains a body in a curved path.

Holding a stone tied to a string, your hand supplies a force equal and opposite to the weight of the stone. We can call this force Lift. If you swing the stone in a circle, the lift force supplied by your hand is split into two components: the vertical component balances the weight of the stone while the horizontal component is the centripetal force which keeps the stone turning.

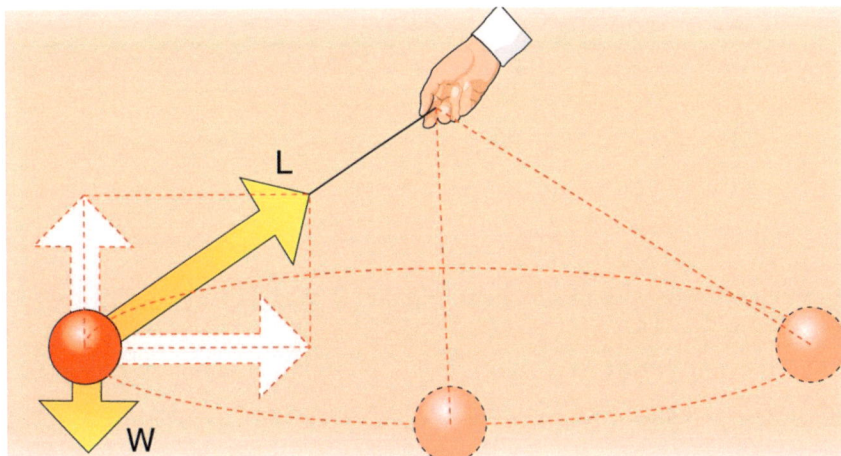

Figure 17.4

17.1.3   *Aircraft in a Turn*

In the same way, the lift force supplied by the wings balances the weight of the aircraft when it is in straight and level flight. To turn the aircraft, a force must be generated towards the centre of the turn. A force can be generated towards the centre of the turn by banking the aircraft. In this way the lift force supplied by the wings is tilted and can be split into two components. The vertical component balances the weight of the aircraft while the horizontal one forces the aircraft to turn.

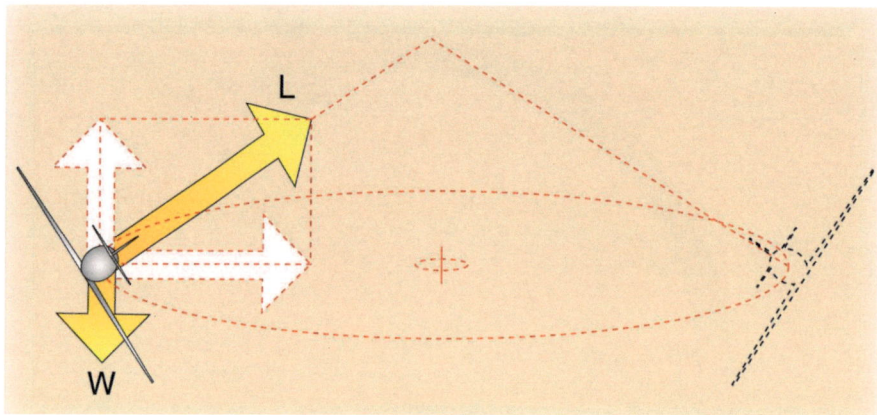

Figure 17.5

When the aircraft is banking, the lift force is split into two components where the horizontal component forces the aircraft to turn. If you want to maintain the aircraft at the same altitude, the lift force from the wings must be increased. To do so without changing the airspeed, the A.o.A. of the wing airfoil must be increased. As a consequence, the lift force required in a steeper turn must be greater in order to maintain altitude.

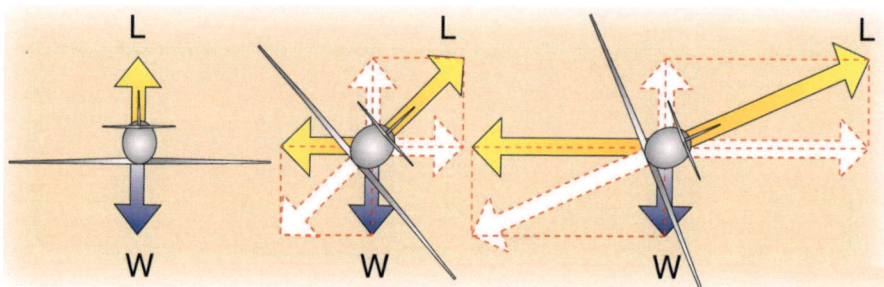

Figure 17.6

The steeper the bank angle, the greater the lift force required to maintain the altitude.

17.1.4 *Extra thrust in a turn*

To increase the lift force without changing the airspeed, it is necessary to increase the angle of attack. But as you know, an increase in the A.o.A. will lead to an increase in induced and zero lift drag. If a constant airspeed is to be maintained in a level turn, an increase in thrust is required to balance the increased drag.

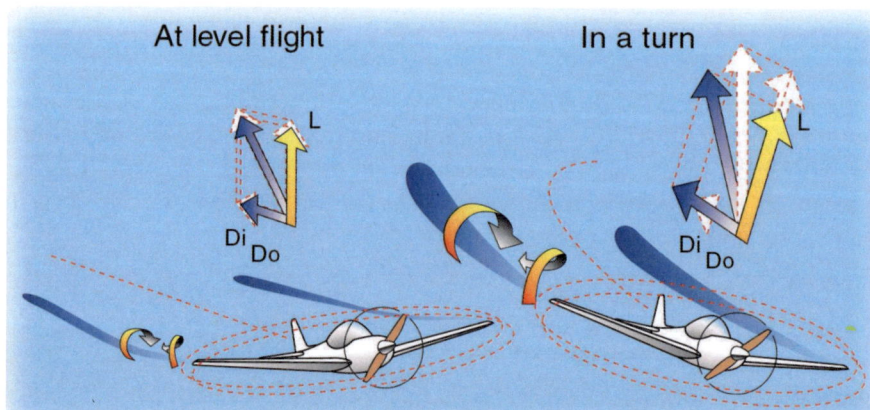

Figure 17.7

Extra thrust is required in order to maintain altitude and airspeed in a continuous turn

CRANFIELD AVIATION TRAINING SCHOOL LTD. PART-FCL GBR.ATO-0136
CATS INNOVATION CENTRE, LUTON, Bedfordshire LU2 8DL U.K.

www.catsaviation.com

17-3

Principles of Flight

17.2   *Load factor in a turn*

17.2.1   *Increase in load factor during a turn*

In straight and level flight the wings produce a lift force equal to the weight. Consequently the load factor is said to be 1. You feel the load factor as a g-force pulling you down in your seat. In straight and level flight this force is equal to your weight. In a banked turn of 60°, the lift force produced by the wings must be twice as high in order to balance the weight, otherwise altitude will be lost. In this condition the load factor is said to be 2. You feel a force from the seat equal to twice your weight. At a bank angle beyond 60°, the lift force generated by the wings must increase considerably so that its vertical component can balance the weight of the aircraft in order to maintain altitude. Consequently the load factor also increases considerably.

17.2.2   *Load factor versus angle of bank*

The relationship between angle of bank and the load factor is shown in the next figure. In a level turn at an angle of bank of 30°, the lift force necessary to maintain the altitude must be 15% more than the lift force in straight and level flight. The load factor also increases and its value is 1.15 g.

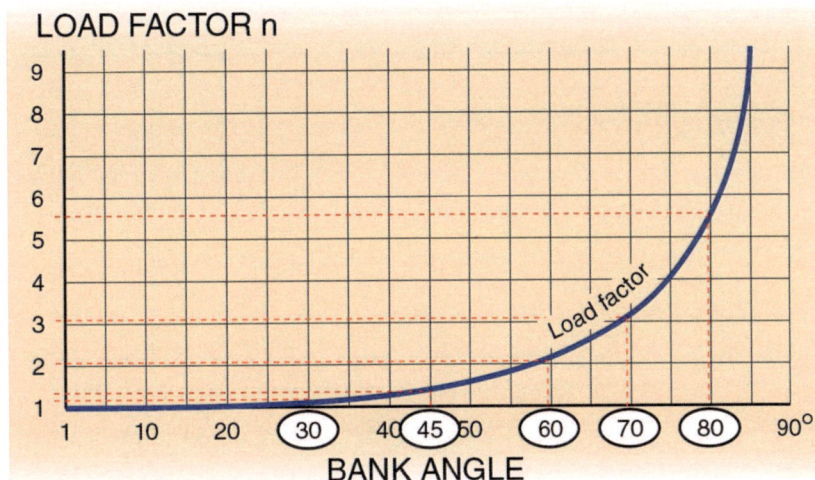

Figure 17.8

17.3   *Stalling speed in a turn*

In an earlier discussion we showed that an aircraft is flying because the wings create sufficient lift to counteract the weight. As you know, lift depends upon: the coefficient of lift C_L), air density (ρ), free stream velocity (V^2) and wing surface area (S), The coefficient of lift covers the variables: wing shape and angle of attack. For a given wing shape the angle of attack is the principal factor that determines the coefficient of lift. In a level turn the angle of attack must be higher than at the same speed in straight and level flight. This means that in a turn, the stalling angle of attack will be reached at a higher speed. In a turn the stalling angle of attack is reached at a higher air speed.

17.3.1   *Percentage of increase in stalling speed versus angle of bank*

In a similar way to that in which the load factor increases with the bank angle in a level turn, the relationship between bank angle and percentage of increase in stalling speed is shown in the graph. In a level turn at 30° angle of bank, the stalling speed increases by 7% over the stalling speed of straight and level flight. For instance, if an aircraft stalls at 50 KT in straight and level flight, in a 30° angle of banked turn it will stall at 53.5 KT.

CRANFIELD AVIATION TRAINING SCHOOL LTD. PART-FCL GBR.ATO-0136
CATS   **CATS INNOVATION CENTRE, LUTON, Bedfordshire LU2 8DL U.K.**   www.catsaviation.com

17-4   Principles of Flight

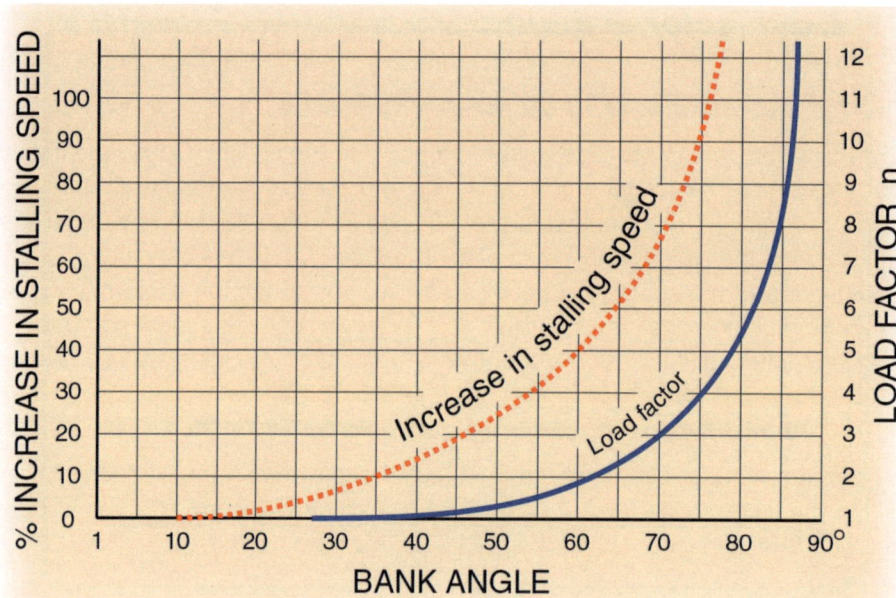

Figure 17.9

17.4 Turning Performance

In this section we will discuss the tendency of the aircraft to underbank or over bank in a turn, i.e. make uncoordinated turns. We will also look at the ways of turning an aircraft according to different standards of turning performance.

17.4.1 Over bank in a level turn

To start a level turn, you bank with the ailerons. Once the aircraft starts turning, it is not necessary to apply the aileron to maintain the bank, since the outer wing travels faster than the inner one and so generates more lift. As the lift generated by the outer wing increases, the bank angle will increase, despite neutral ailerons. To stop any further increase in the bank angle, you must give slight opposite aileron.

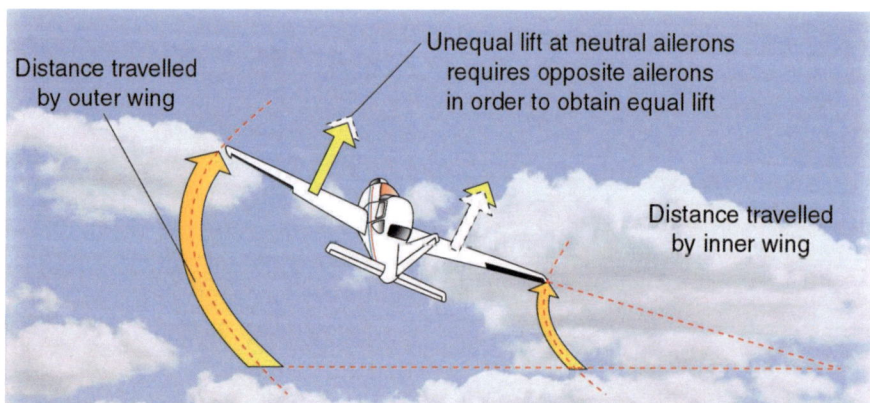

Figure 17.10

17.4.2 Over bank in a climbing turn

In a climbing turn there is also a second effect to consider: since both wings climb at the same altitude the outer wing travels a greater distance than the inner one. The angle of attack of the outer wing is therefore greater than the inner one and the lift produced by the outer wing will therefore be even greater so that there is an additional over bank tendency in a climbing turn. This effect is obvious on slow aircraft making turns of rather small radii even at a low angle of bank.

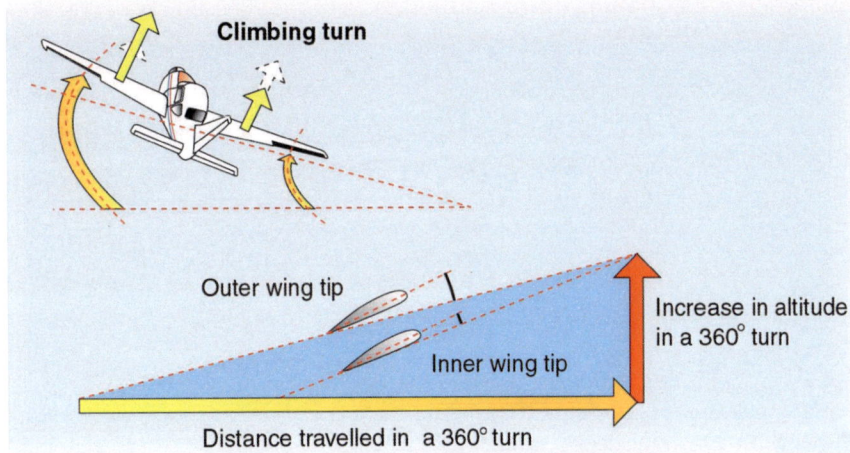

Figure 17.11

17.4.3 *Underbank/overbank in a descending turn*

In a descending turn, like in any turn, the outer wing travels faster and produces more lift than the inner one. Due to the descent, the inner wing travels a smaller horizontal distance to the same altitude loss compared to the outer wing. Consequently, the inner wing has a higher angle of attack and produces more lift, which may compensate for the lift produced by the higher speed of the outer wing.

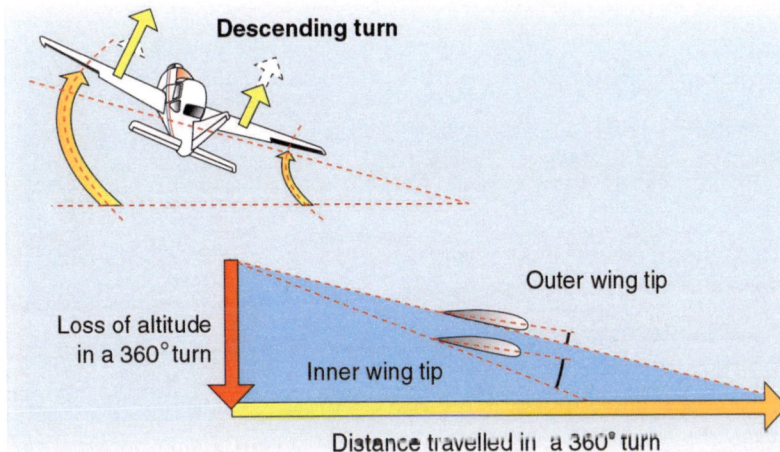

Figure 17.12

The effect of unequal angles of bank in a climbing and a descending turn depends on the speed. It is greatest at low speeds since the travelled distance is shorter, making it more pronounced when flying a light aircraft compared to an airliner. However, the altitude also has an effect since the true airspeed is higher at high altitudes than at low altitudes. The effect of overbanking and underbanking in ascending and descending turns depends on the actual speed, thus also on the small turning radius despite having low angle of bank.

17.4.4 *Adverse yaw*

To make a turn you bank the aircraft using the ailerons. The downward aileron and the increased lift also increase the drag of the outer wing. At the same time, lift and drag are reduced on the inner wing. The changes in lift cause the aircraft to bank as desired. However, the changes in the drag produced by the wings create an unwanted yaw in the direction opposite to the turn called adverse yaw or sometimes aileron drag. This is neither comfortable nor efficient.

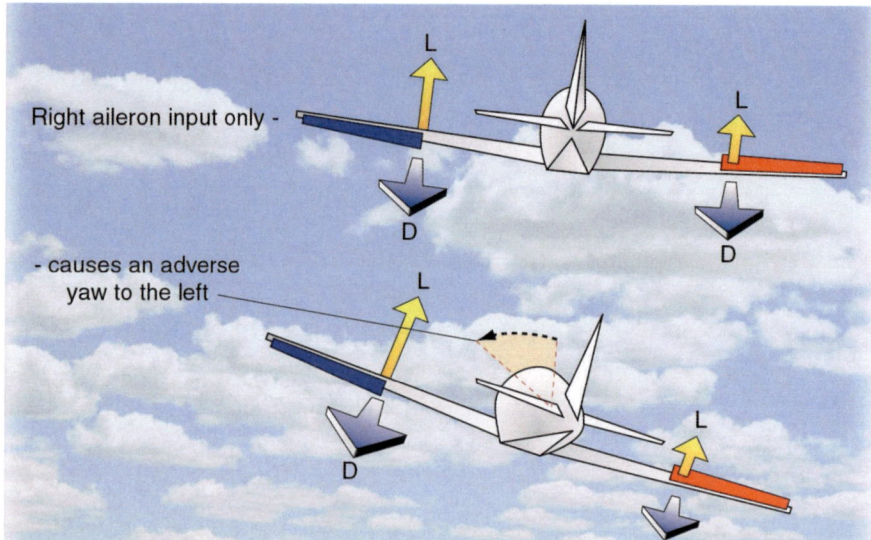

Figure 17.13

> The changes in the drag produced by the wings create a yaw in the direction opposite to the turn

So, when starting a bank to make a turn, you must simultaneously apply a certain amount of rudder in the same direction as the turn in order to compensate for the differences in wing drag and to avoid an adverse yaw.

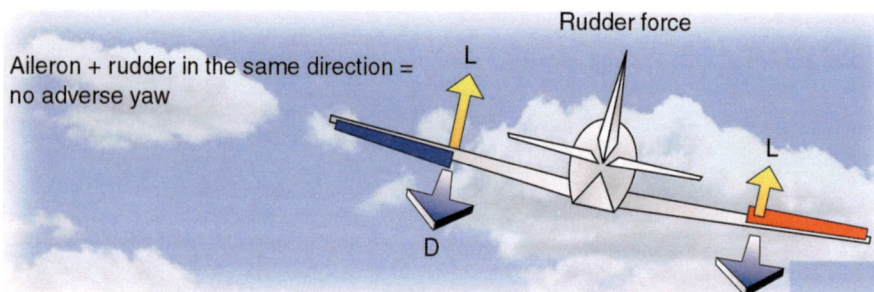

Figure 17.14

When starting a bank, you must apply rudder in the same direction as the turn to avoid an adverse yaw.

17.4.5   *Slipping turn*

If not properly manoeuvred, the aircraft is said to be slipping into the turn, because when the force is not correctly balanced, the aircraft sideslips into the turn. The ball in the slip indicator moves to the inner side of the turn and you feel the effect as if you wanted to slip to the lower side of the aircraft.

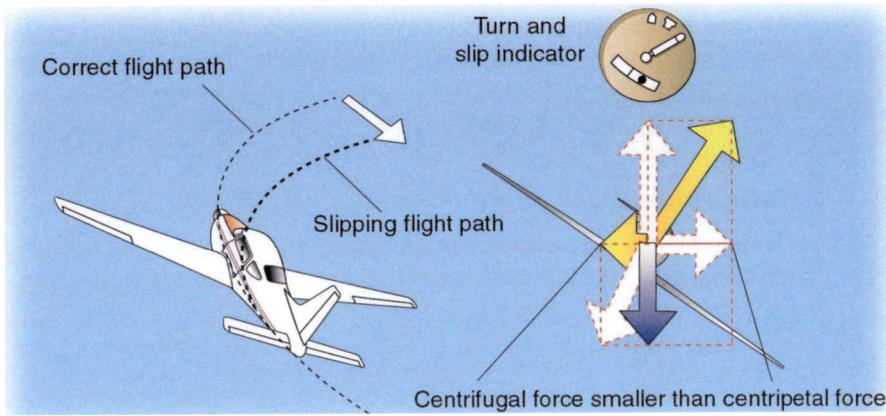

Figure 17.15

To correctly balance the forces you must add rudder input in the same direction as the turn in order to counteract the adverse yaw. Then the aircraft's longitudinal axis becomes tangential to the turn. The ball in the slip indicator moves to the centre and you feel comfortable in the seat. The aircraft is said to be in a balanced turn.

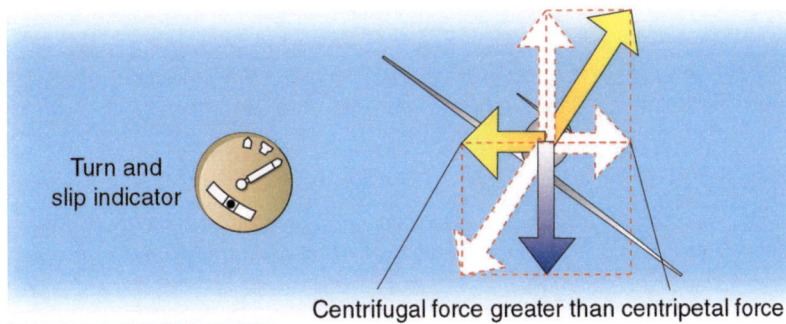

Figure 17.16

To correct a slipping turn, you must add rudder input in the same direction as the turn in order to counteract the opposite adverse yaw.

17.4.6   *Skidding turn*

If the aircraft is not properly manoeuvred and the aircraft tail tends to skid out of the turn, the aircraft is said to be skidding into the turn. The ball in the slip indicator moves to the outside of the turn and you are pushed towards the outside.

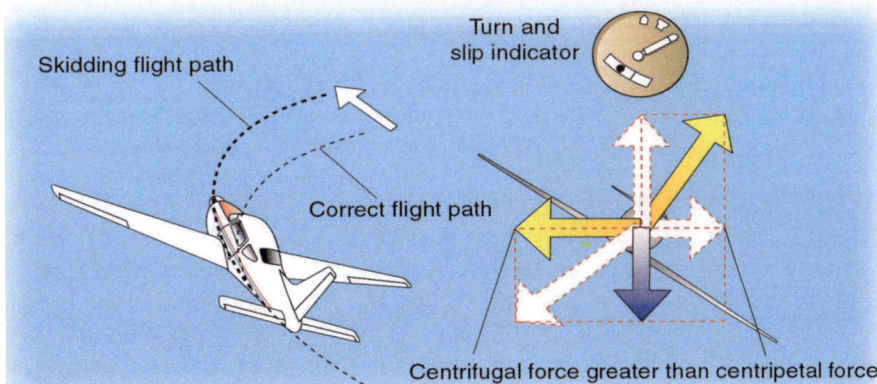

Figure 17.17

To correct a turn you must change rudder input in the direction opposite to the turn, so that the ball in the turn indicator moves to the centre and you feel comfortable in the seat. Again, the aircraft is said to be in a balanced turn. The consequences of slipping or skidding turns are: Higher drag and inducing a snap roll or spin when stalling.

17.4.7   *Turn at constant angle of bank*

An aircraft in a given banked level turn will travel around different circular paths when the airspeed changes because the radius of the turn depends upon the speed of the aircraft. At low speed the turn is tighter than at high speed, thus the rate of turning angle/second will be higher.

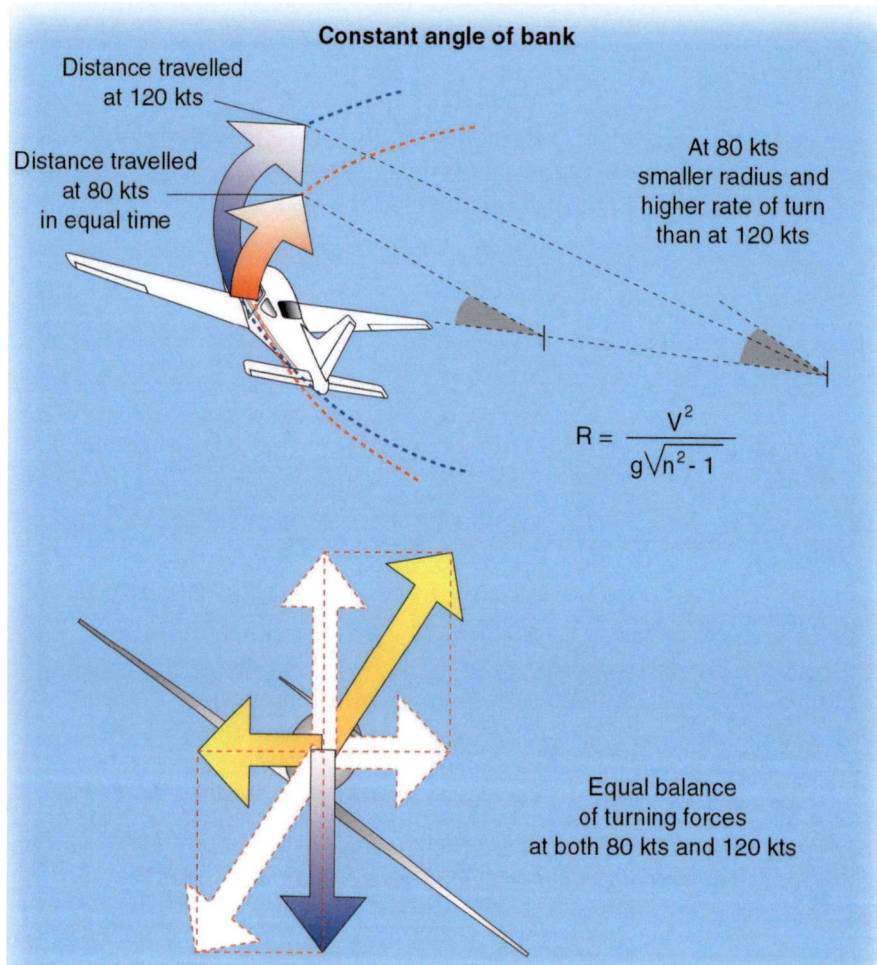

$$R = \frac{V^2}{g\sqrt{n^2 - 1}}$$

Figure 17.18

At a constant angle of bank at low speed the turn is tighter and has a higher rate of turn than at high speed.

17.4.8   *Turn with constant radius*

Different airspeeds require different angles of bank to maintain the same radius of turn. When making a turn of the same radius at a higher speed, the centrifugal force will be greater and a correspondingly higher centripetal force is required to counterbalance this. As you know, the centripetal force is created by a component of lift. Thus, to make a turn of the same radius at a higher speed, a greater angle of bank and a higher A.o.A is required.

CRANFIELD AVIATION TRAINING SCHOOL LTD. PART-FCL GBR.ATO-0136
CATS INNOVATION CENTRE, LUTON, Bedfordshire LU2 8DL U.K.   www.catsaviation.com
17-9   Principles of Flight

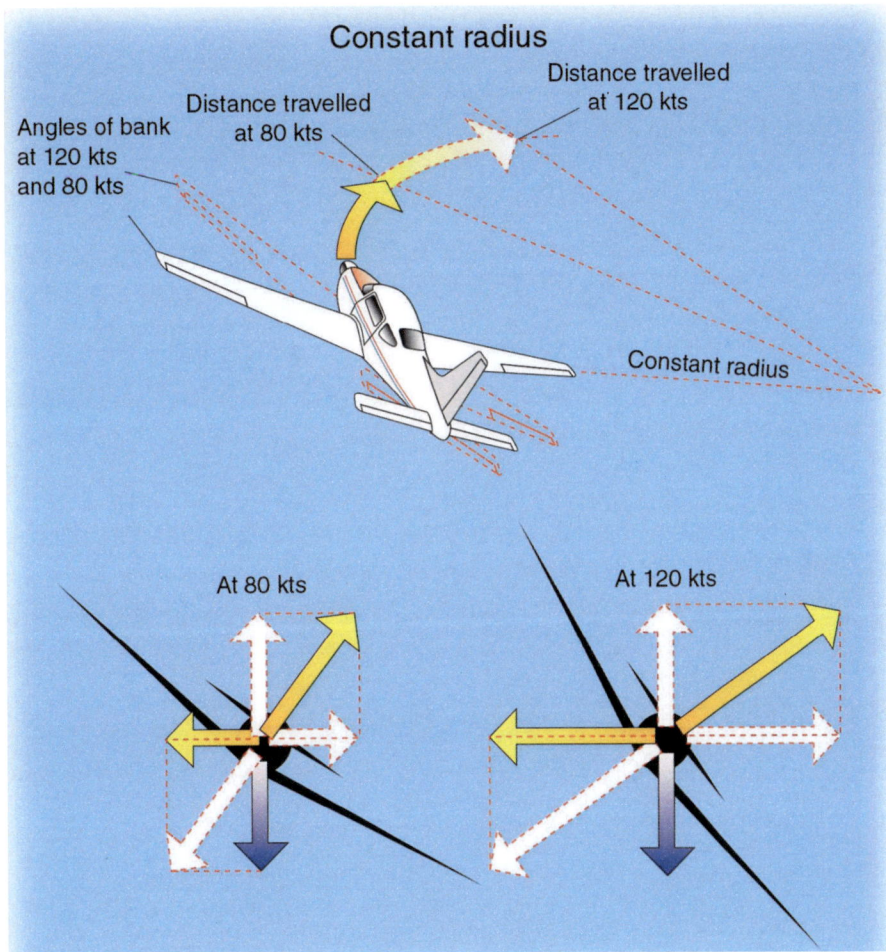

Figure 17.19

Different airspeeds require different angles of bank to maintain the same radius of turn.

17.4.9 *Turn at constant speed*

To make a turn with a smaller radius at a constant airspeed, which also means a higher rate of turn, a greater angle of bank is required to counteract the increased centrifugal force caused by the smaller radius.

CRANFIELD AVIATION TRAINING SCHOOL LTD. PART-FCL GBR.ATO-0136
CATS INNOVATION CENTRE, LUTON, Bedfordshire LU2 8DL U.K.   www.catsaviation.com

17-10   Principles of Flight

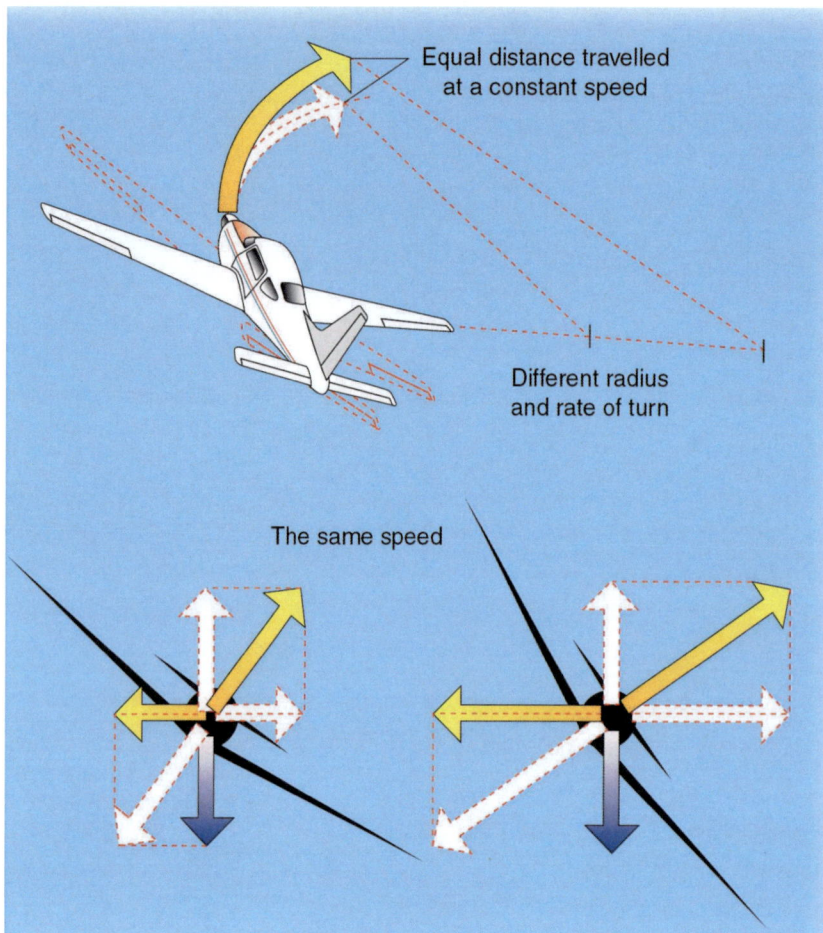

Figure 17.20

In order to make a turn with a smaller radius, i.e. a higher rate of turn at a constant airspeed a greater angle of bank is required. You should be aware of the fact that the speed has a greater impact on the required bank than the radius of the turn.

17.4.10 Turn at constant rate

The rate of turning of an aircraft is expressed in °/second. The instruments which give the rate of turn usually have an indication on a turn of 3°/second. This means that the aircraft flies a 180° turn in one minute (3x60=180). This rate of turning is said to be a rate 1 turn.

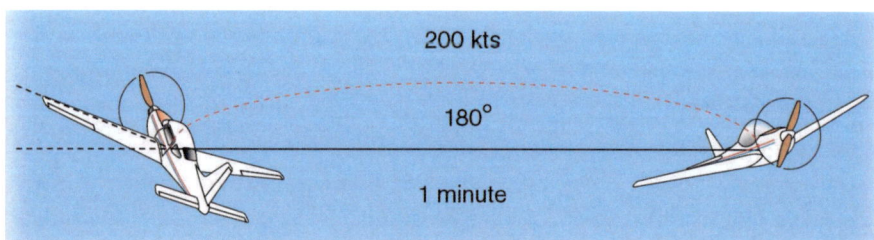

Figure 17.21

Rate 1 turn = 180° in 1 minute.

In order to turn the same number of degrees at a higher speed, a strong centripetal force is required. Therefore a greater angle of bank must be used. The higher speed also creates a greater turning radius.

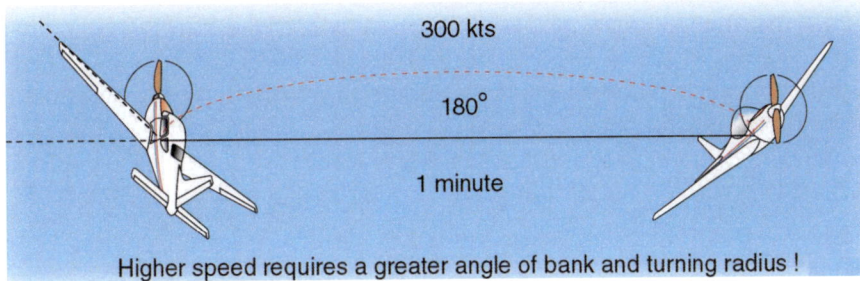

300 kts

180°

1 minute

Higher speed requires a greater angle of bank and turning radius !

Figure 17.22

To fly a rate 1 turn at a higher speed a greater angle of bank and turning radius is required.
At a given speed, the bank angle required for a rate 1 turn can be estimated by using a simple formula: the angle of bank in degrees is equal to 1/10 of the airspeed in KT plus 7°. For example, at 180 KT, for a rate 1 turn the bank angle is 180/10 plus 7, which equals 25°.

The angle of bank in ° of a rate 1 turn approximates to 1/10 of the airspeed in KT plus 7°

17.4.11 *Highest possible rate of turn*

The highest possible rate of turn is limited by the lift created by the wings since the centripetal force, which is a component of lift, increases the higher the speed is and/or the smaller the radius. The factors that influence the centripetal force are mass (m) x V^2 /radius (R). For a given maximum centripetal force and thus maximum lift at a constant mass, a higher speed requires a greater radius.
For you as a pilot it is interesting to know that for a given speed, the angle of bank and thus the load factor must be as high as possible in order to turn as fast as possible without stalling the aircraft.
As the pilot of a commercial airliner carrying passengers, you must also remember that the self loading freight do not like high G forces.

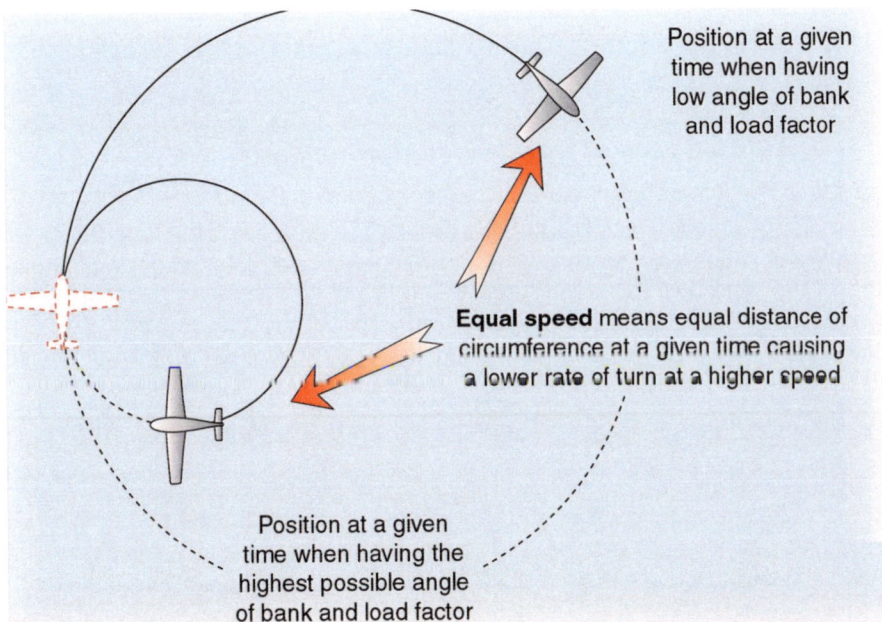

Position at a given time when having low angle of bank and load factor

Equal speed means equal distance of circumference at a given time causing a lower rate of turn at a higher speed

Position at a given time when having the highest possible angle of bank and load factor

Figure 17.23

In order to turn as fast as possible at a given speed, the angle of bank, and thus the load factor, must be as high as possible without stalling.

To make a 360° turn in the shortest possible time for a given aircraft, the speed must be reduced or the load factor increased.

If two different aircraft can reach a certain maximum and equal load factor at different speeds, the slower aircraft will turn faster than the faster one.

This causes some trouble for the high-speed fighters. They need a very high speed to reach a certain high load factor (and lift) without stalling, but a slower fighter may at the same load factor turn at a significantly higher turning rate.

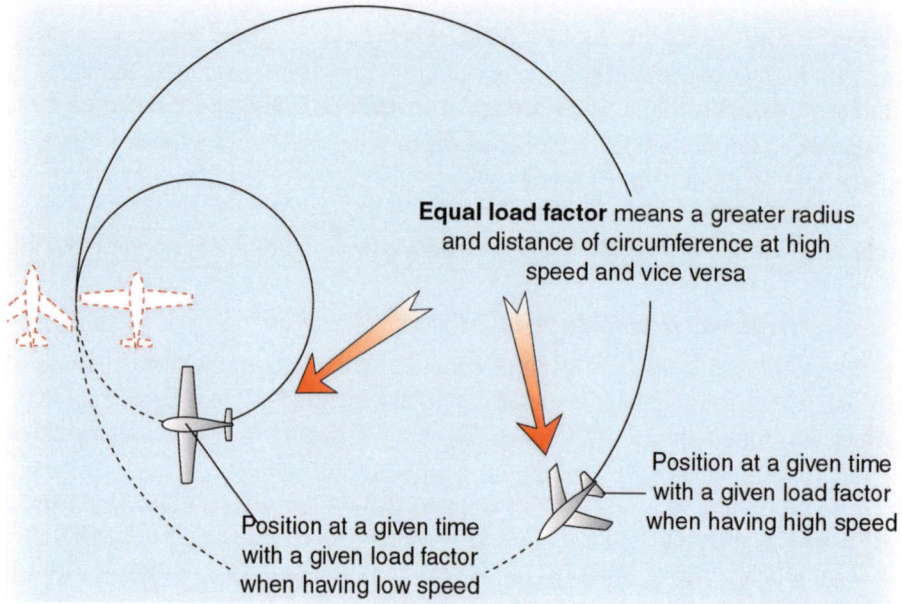

Equal load factor means a greater radius and distance of circumference at high speed and vice versa

Position at a given time with a given load factor when having high speed

Position at a given time with a given load factor when having low speed

Figure 17.24

In order to fly a 360° turn in the shortest possible time at a given max load factor, the speed must be reduced.

17.4.12   *Limited rate of turn at constant speed*

The highest rate of turn for a given aircraft can only be reached in a limited time, since the high induced drag at high load factors reduces speed, which in turn also reduce the max available load factor without stalling.

In order to maintain a very high turning rate, and consequently a small radius, the engine must be very powerful to give a thrust equal to the high total drag in such a turn.

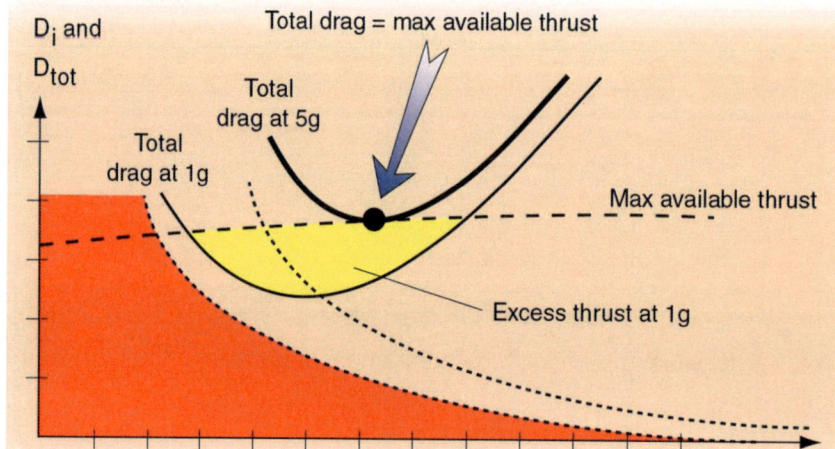

D_i and D_{tot}

Total drag = max available thrust

Total drag at 5g

Total drag at 1g

Max available thrust

Excess thrust at 1g

Figure 17.25

It follows that there are lift limiting and thrust limiting factors which determine the speed for the smallest constant turning radius or max continuous rate of turn.

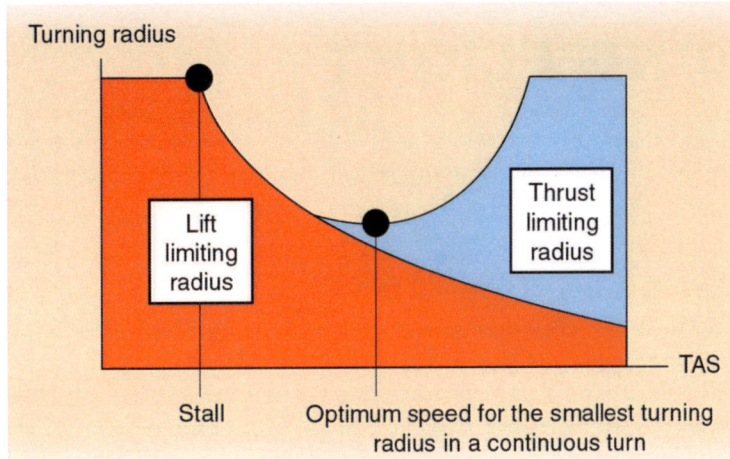

Figure 17.26

The speed for the tightest turn is determined by the turning radius of the lift limit and the turning radius of the thrust limit.

CHAPTER 18

DESCENDING FLIGHT

Aircraft make two different kinds of descent: one is the engine-supported descent, in which there is a reduced thrust from the engine; the other one is made with the total absence of thrust or power. This second type of descent may be either your choice or a consequence of engine failure.

18.1 Engine Supported Descent

In the engine supported descent you can select the rate of descent that seems appropriate to the requirements of the moment. This kind of descent is the normal operating one.

18.1.1 Equilibrium of forces, engine supported descent

Whenever the available thrust is less than the thrust required to maintain a trimmed level flight, the aircraft will start to descend and maintain IAS.

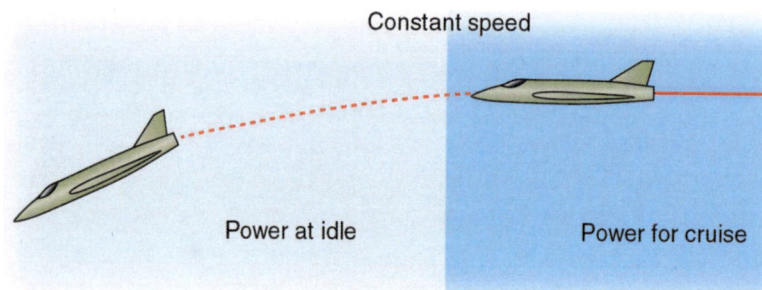

Figure 18.1

If the thrust is less than that required to maintain level flight, the aircraft will start to descend and maintain its trimmed A.o.A and speed, or the aircraft will decelerate if the altitude is kept constant by the use of the elevator. This happens because the forces of thrust and drag acting on the aircraft must be in balance. In a descent, the absent thrust is balanced by a component of the weight that is added to the available thrust so that the total value is equal and opposed to the drag. The value of the component of weight will determine the rate of descent.

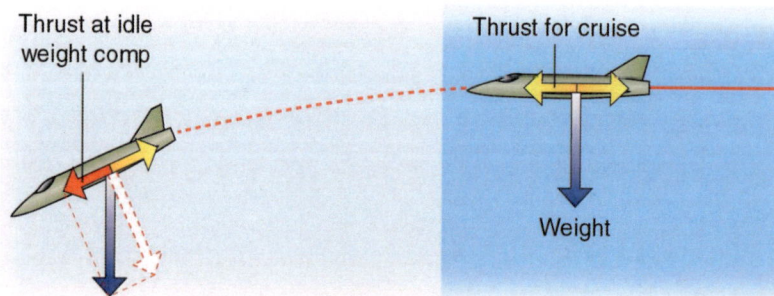

Figure 18.2

The values of the components of thrust and weight determine the rate of descent. Let us analyse the forces acting on the aircraft. As you know, the weight force acts perpendicular to the horizon, the lift force perpendicular to the flight path of the aircraft, the thrust forwards approximately along the flight path and the drag aft along the flight path.

CRANFIELD AVIATION TRAINING SCHOOL LTD. PART-FCL GBR.ATO-0136
CATS INNOVATION CENTRE, LUTON, Bedfordshire LU2 8DL U.K.   www.catsaviation.com

18-1

Principles of Flight

If we divide the weight vector we obtain a vector parallel, equal and opposed to the drag vector and another vector parallel, opposite and equal to the lift vector. The angle between the latter vector and the weight vector is equal to the angle between the horizon and the flight path of the aircraft and is called the descent angle, designated -γ (negative gamma). As seen in the chapter on climb, the required lift will be less than in straight and level flight.

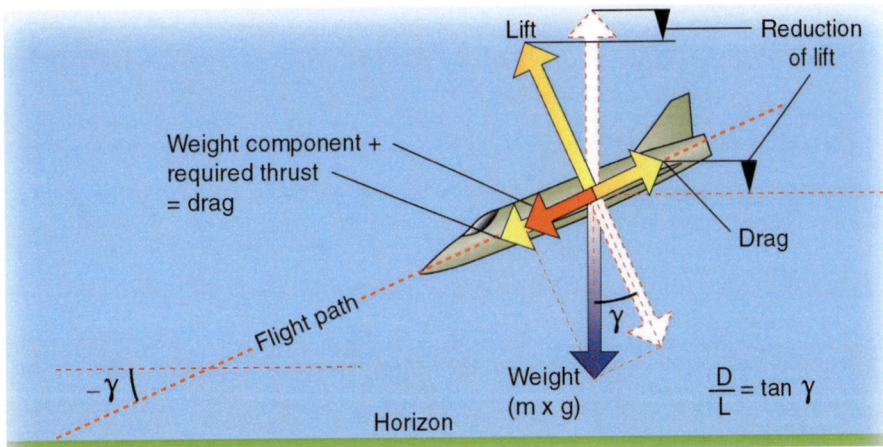

Figure 18.3

The angle between the vector is equal and opposed to the lift vector and the weight vector is equal to the angle between the horizon and the flight path of the aircraft and is called the descent angle, designated -γ (negative gamma). The -γ is then the angle representing the flight path of the descending aircraft. From trigonometry, we can say that lift is equal to the product of the weight force multiplied by the cosine of γ. The component of weight that replaces the absence of thrust is equal to the product of the weight force multiplied by the sine of γ.

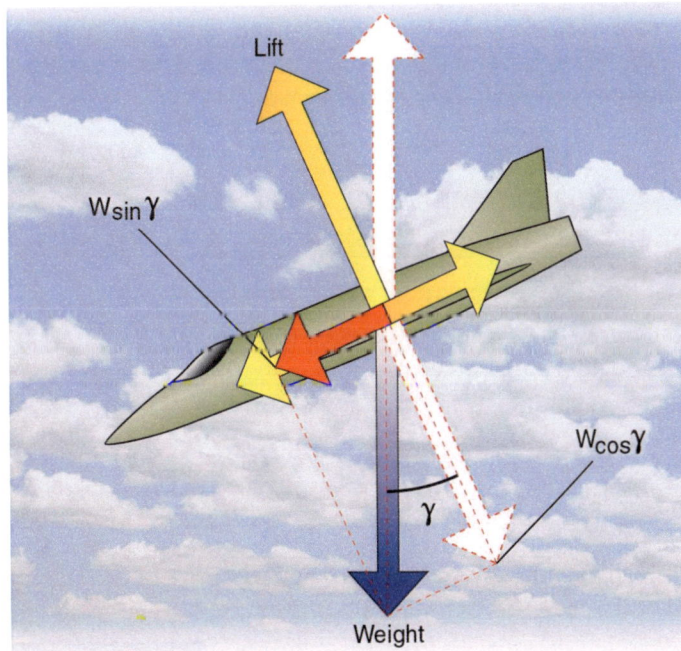

Figure 18.4

CRANFIELD AVIATION TRAINING SCHOOL LTD. PART-FCL GBR.ATO-0136
CATS INNOVATION CENTRE, LUTON, Bedfordshire LU2 8DL U.K.

www.catsaviation.com

18-2

Principles of Flight

18.1.2   *Operating considerations*

The engine supported descent is usually laid down in the aircraft operating handbook, which usually indicates a descent that is a compromise between fuel consumption and flying distance.

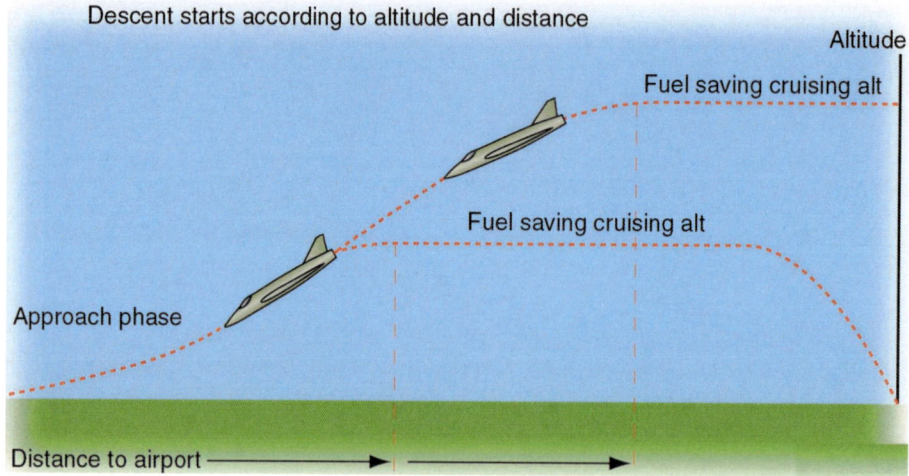

Figure 18.5

The normal engine supported descent is often a compromise between fuel consumption and flying distance. If a very steep descent is required, for instance because of the air traffic situation, and it is a piston-powered aircraft, a descent with the throttle in the idle position is to be avoided because the cylinders will be affected by rapid cooling. This may lead to thermal tensions in the engine and the cylinders may crack. The steep descent can be made at a relatively low speed with flaps and/or landing gear extended if you take care not to exceed the maximum permitted speed. With a jet aircraft, there is no problem with engine cooling but instead of getting a speed that is too high. Consequently, when high rates of descent are required, any kind of speed reducing devices such as fully extended flaps or landing gear or preferably speed brakes, must be used in order to allow a very high rate of descent at a tolerable speed. Just remember your limiting speeds. Very steep descents with low power are to be avoided in piston powered aircraft because the engine cylinders will be cooled too rapidly. With jet-powered aircraft, speed brakes will normally be used to allow a high rate of descent.

18.2   *Gliding Flight*

18.2.1   *Equilibrium of forces during gliding flight*

Gliding flight is a flight with the total absence of thrust; this may be intended or it may be the consequence of engine failure. The study of gliding flight is very important, especially for single-engine aircraft, where engine failure means the total absence of available thrust. In some rare cases, however, this may also happen in the case of multi-engine aircraft.

> Gliding flight is flight in the total absence of thrust

The equilibrium of forces in gliding flight is produced by a component of weight which is the only force that can balance the drag, and which acts forward along the flight path. This component of weight will then be equal to the product of the weight multiplied by the sine of the glide path angle -γ.

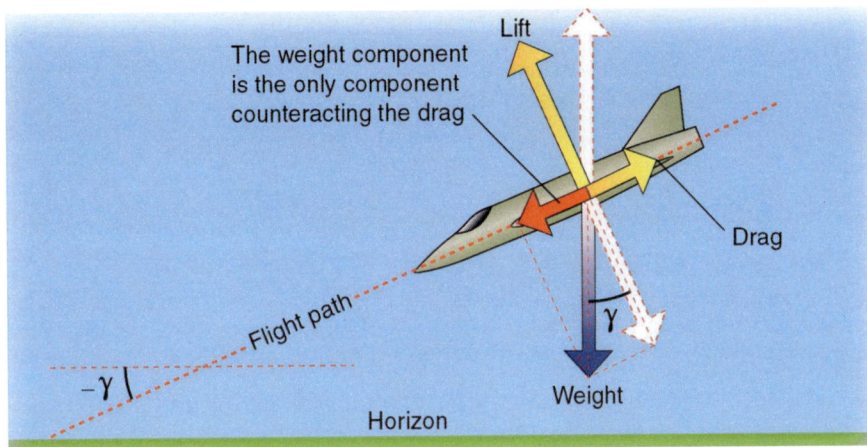

Figure 18.6

If the drag increases, the forward acting force must be correspondingly higher, and since that force is determined by the glide angle γ, the descent must be steeper in order to maintain the speed.

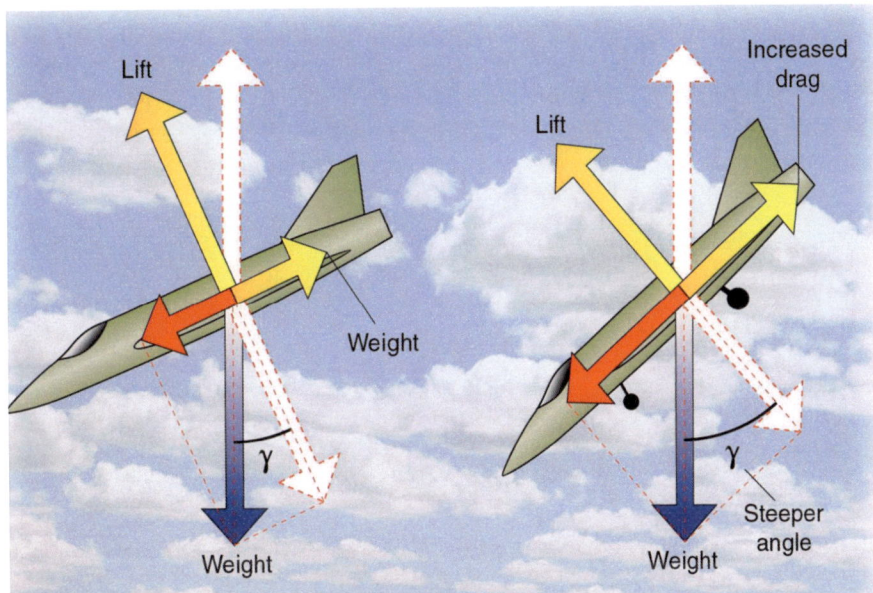

Figure 18.7

In gliding flight, the component of weight acting forward along the flight path is the only force that can balance the drag. Consequently, in order to obtain the smallest gliding angle and thus the longest gliding distance, the drag must be the lowest possible. It is interesting to know which speed should be maintained to glide the longest distance and the speed required to glide the longest time. Since the angle of glide path determines the forward acting force and the angle of attack influences the drag force, there will be certain combinations of these forces that determine the speeds for the lowest angle of glide path and for the longest duration, respectively. There will be different speeds for the lowest angle of glide path and for the longest gliding time respectively.

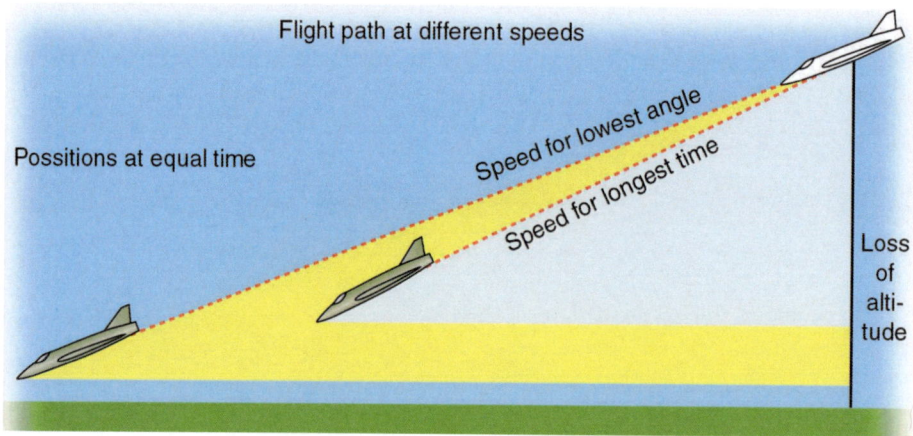

Figure 18.8

18.2.2 Gliding efficiency

Below you see the flight path of a gliding aircraft in relation to the ground. The angle $-\gamma$ is as usual the glide angle; H is the height of the aircraft and R is the range or distance on the ground that the aircraft will fly.

The gliding efficiency is designated e (epsilon) and is the ratio between the gliding range and lost altitude or height. This means that if an aircraft has a gliding efficiency of 12, it will fly a horizontal distance of 12000 feet for every 1000 feet of altitude loss. A rather common value of efficiency usually varies between 15 and 20; for high performance aircraft like gliders it is normally 40 but can reach values as high as 60.

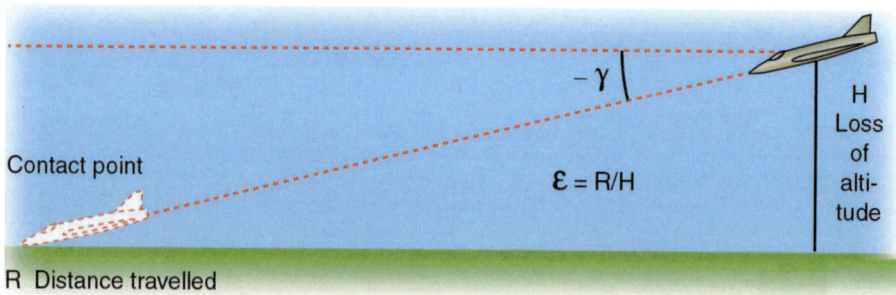

Figure 18.9

The formula of gliding efficiency is: $\varepsilon = R/H$. Normal values are 15 - 20 but can be up to 60 for gliders.

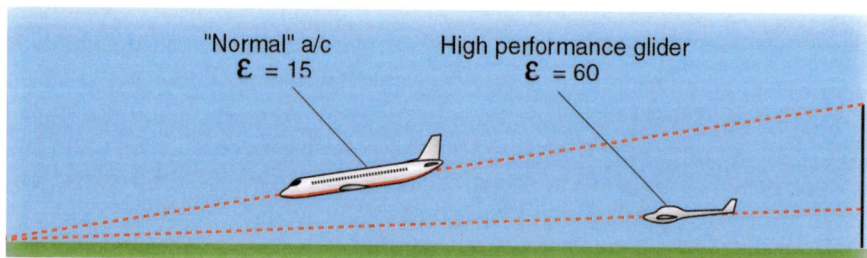

Figure 18.10

The declared gliding efficiency of an aircraft is the maximum efficiency that can be reached for that model of aircraft and is a fixed value. As can be seen in the figure below, the ratio between the distance flown and the loss of altitude R/H which is determined by the angle $-\gamma$, is the same as the ratio between lift and drag, which is determined by the same angle $-\gamma$. Thus, the gliding efficiency is also the ratio between the lift and the drag, and consequently also the ratio between the coefficient of lift and the coefficient of drag C_L/C_D.

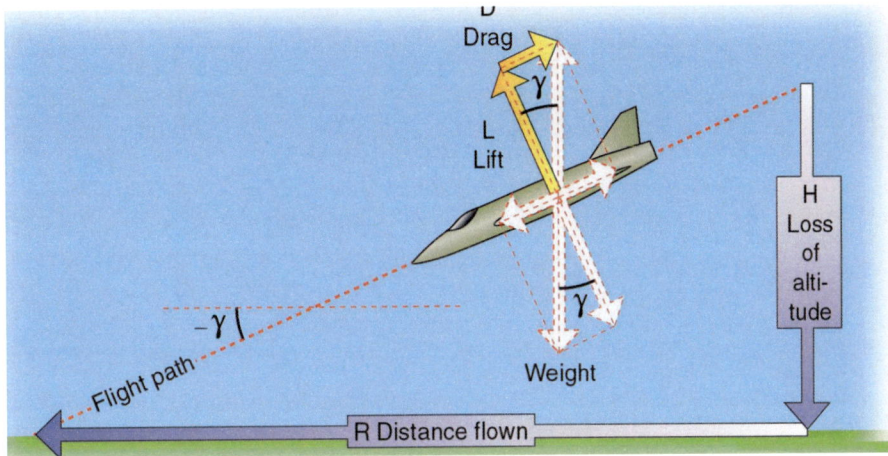

Figure 18.11

The formula of gliding efficiency is:

$\varepsilon = R/H$ which is also; $\varepsilon = L/D$ and thus: $\varepsilon = C_L/C_D$.

18.2.3 *Best gliding speed and speed for minimum rate of descent*

The ratio between the lift and drag varies with the speed. At a very low speed the induced drag is higher for a given lift than at a high speed. At very high speeds the zero lift drag is higher for a given amount of lift than at low speeds. When gliding, the glide angle can be equal for two different speeds in order to counteract an equal total drag, while the smallest glide angle will be reached where the required A.o.A corresponds to the highest L/D.

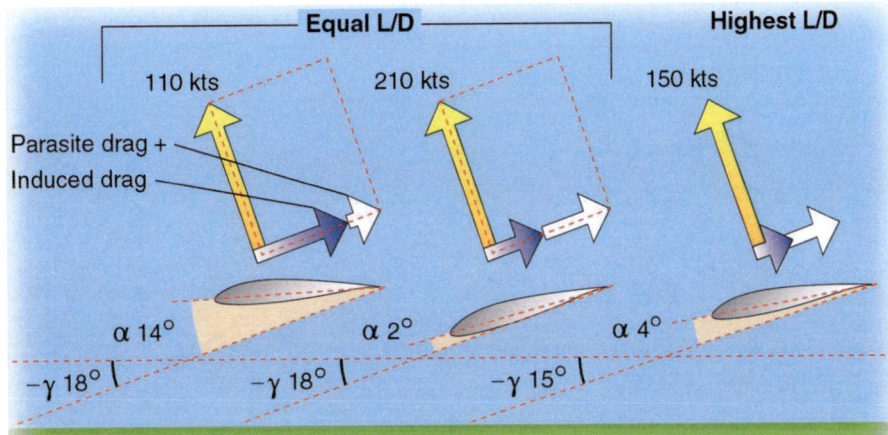

Figure 18.12

To find the speed that corresponds to maximum efficiency, i.e. the best gliding speed, we rotate the polar curve 90°. This allows us to compare the flight path of the aircraft with the glide angle.

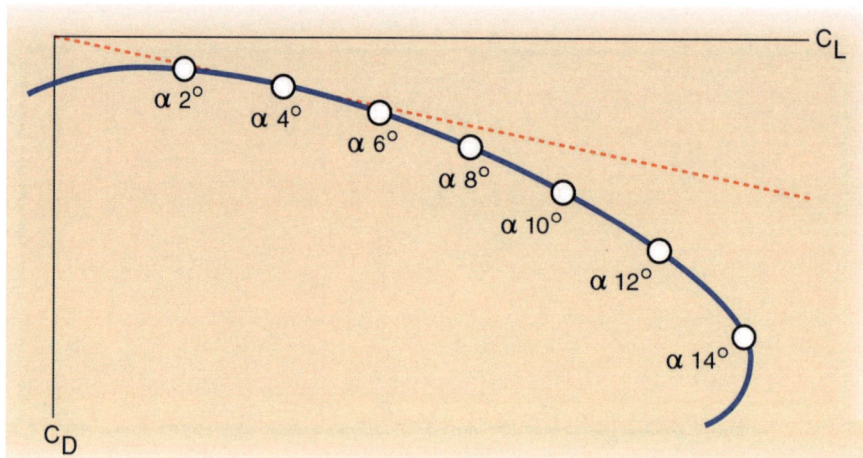

Figure 18.13

As can be seen for this particular aircraft, the tangent is at α 4°. The gliding speed that gives this particular angle of attack will therefore also be the speed where the ratio between the lift and drag is most favourable and consequently, the best gliding speed. This is the only speed that will give you the maximum distance to the ground and the minimum glide angle.

18.2.4   *Highest gliding efficiency = max L/D*

For every angle of attack that represents a certain speed which is different from the best glide A.o.A, the ratio between L/D, and thus the gradient of the flight path, will be greater. Here we see two different A.o.A; the α1.5° representing a higher speed and a lower angle of attack, and α14° representing a lower speed and a higher angle of attack.

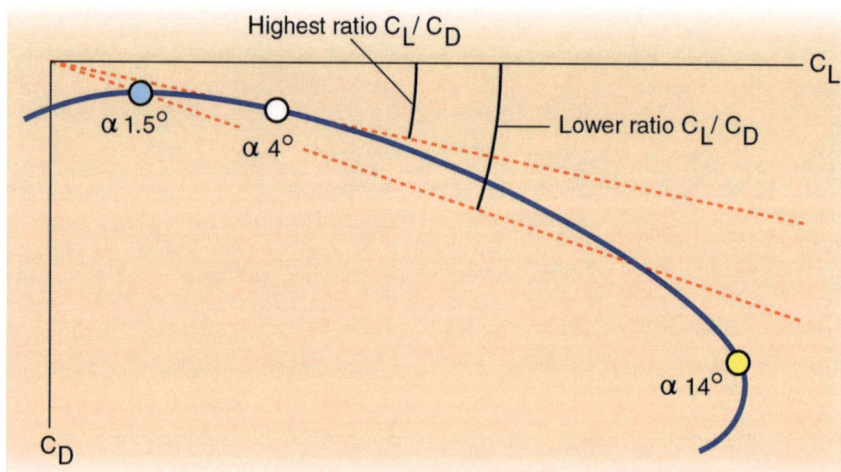

Figure 18.14

Every A.o.A which is different from the best glide A.o.A, implies a lower L/D and thus a steeper flight path.

18.2.5   *Speed polar (or Odograph)*

There is another curve which is very important for gliding flight, called the speed polar or odograph. It is represented in a vertical speed versus horizontal speed diagram. Here we can find the speeds that give best glide and the minimum rate of descent. The horizontal axis represents the ground plane.

The speeds polar, or odograph, is a vertical speed versus horizontal speed curve. The horizontal axis represents the ground plane.

Since the aircraft is not able to maintain level flight in a power off condition, the entire curve is located below the horizontal axis where the vertical speed is negative. The position of the curve is a function of the weight of the aircraft, as shown below. When gliding, the possible vertical speeds are all negative, and the position of the curve is a function of the weight of the aircraft.
The line drawn from the axis origin determines the best gliding speed, located at point G.

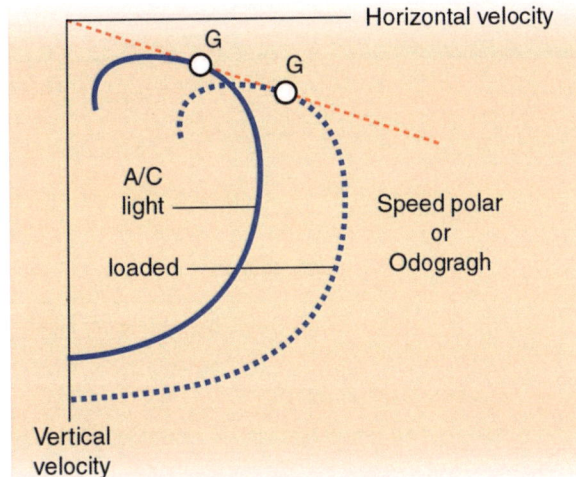

Figure 18.15

The speed for max glide is where the ratio between the horizontal velocity and vertical velocity are at their maximum. The best gliding speed, or speed of maximum efficiency, is found in the aircraft's flight handbook, on the emergency checklist, where one of the first things to do in the case of engine failure is to reach and maintain this speed as soon as possible. You have to reach the speed for max glide as soon as possible in the case of engine failure. You can find it in the EMERGENCY CHECKLIST. For small aircraft the given value corresponds to the maximum take-off weight. The range of weight of such aircraft is relatively limited, and flying at the given speed with less weight will not significantly affect the distance the aircraft can glide. For heavier aircraft, where the weight range is greater, there are different values for max gliding speed in relation to the actual weight. For transport aircraft there are different values for max gliding speed in relation to the actual weight. In the next figure, the speed for minimum rate of descent is at point G1 of the minimum vertical velocity. The glide angle at the speed for minimum rate of descent will, however, be steeper than that for max glide. But if max available time in the air is desirable, e.g. because a safe emergency landing is not possible to perform, you should keep the speed for minimum rate of descent in order to obtain max. available time for restarting the failed engine. The speed for maximum gliding time is always lower than the speed for max glide. Another characteristic point is the point of maximum horizontal velocity here designated G2, which has a greater -γangle and therefore a steeper glide angle. The maximum rate of descent, which will be found in a vertical dive with no horizontal speed component, is represented by the point G3.

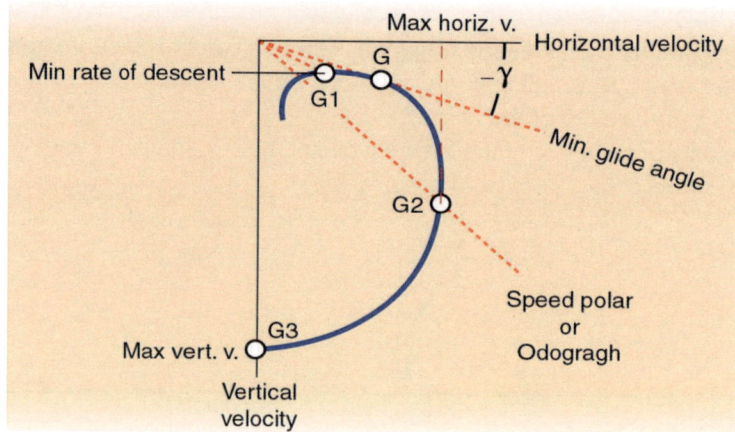

Figure 18.16

| The speed for minimum rate of descent gives a steeper glide path than that of the speed for max glide |

18.3 Effects of External Factors

The use of flaps, the weight of the aircraft and the presence of wind are all factors that influence the flight path of a gliding aircraft.

18.3.1 Effect of flaps on glide performance

As you know, any flap deflection causes a greater increase in the coefficient of drag than in the coefficient of lift. The ratio between C_L and C_D will be less when the flaps are deflected, giving a reduced L/D and thus also reduced R/H. As shown in the picture, the glide angle of an aircraft with deflected flaps must be steeper than that of an aircraft with flaps retracted to compensate for the increased drag from the flaps. The more the flaps are deflected, the steeper the flight path will be.

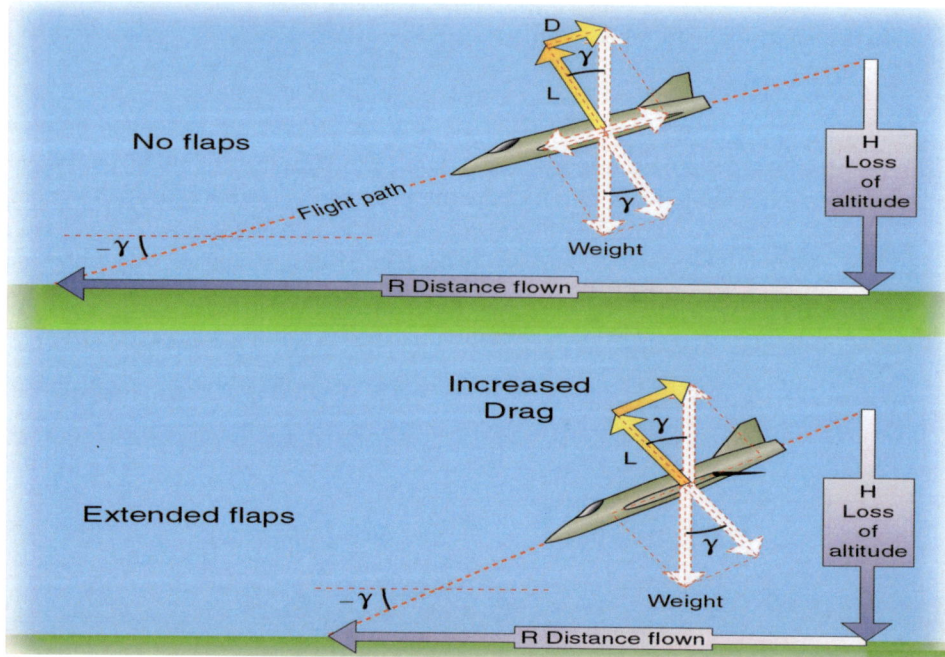

Figure 18.17

| With deflected flaps, the glide angle is steeper and the best gliding speed is slower than with the flaps retracted |

18.3.2   *Effect of weight on glide performance*

An increase in weight does not change the gliding distance since a greater weight will give an equal increase in the forward acting force at the same glide angle. The lift/drag ratio, which determines the distance an aircraft can glide, therefore does not change. The angle of attack is maintained at the value for maximum efficiency specific to the weight of that aircraft.

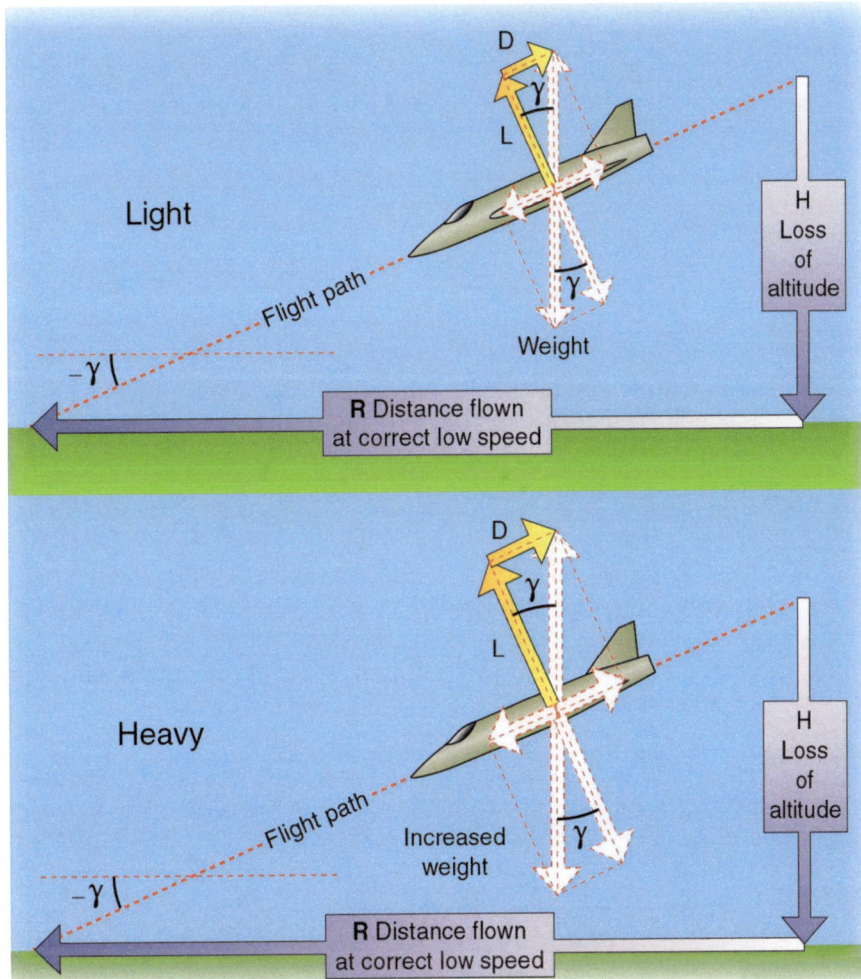

Figure 18.18

Greater weight does not change the L/D ratio at a given glide angle

The only effect the weight has is to vary the speed at which the aircraft will fly the longest distance. But the glide angle, and consequently the flight path, will be the same regardless of the weight of the aircraft.

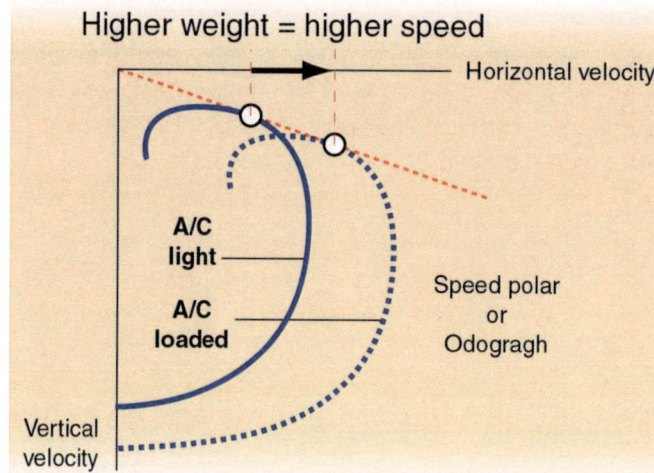

Figure 18.19

The heavier load the aircraft has, the higher the speed for max glide. The aircraft will reach the ground sooner, but the point of contact with the ground will be the same. In practical terms, a 10% increase in weight implies a 5% increase in the best gliding speed in order to maintain the same glide path.

18.3.3 *Effect of wind on glide performance*

Remember that gliding must be considered to be relative to the air. To an observer on the ground an aircraft gliding on the wind may appear to remain still or, in some cases, even to climb. In such instances there must be a wind blowing which has both horizontal and upward velocity. However, to an observer travelling on this wind in a balloon, the aircraft would appear to be travelling forwards and descending.

When viewed from the ground, an aircraft gliding with a fixed value of rate of descent against the wind will appear to glide more steeply, and will in fact, glide more steeply relative to the ground than when gliding with the wind.

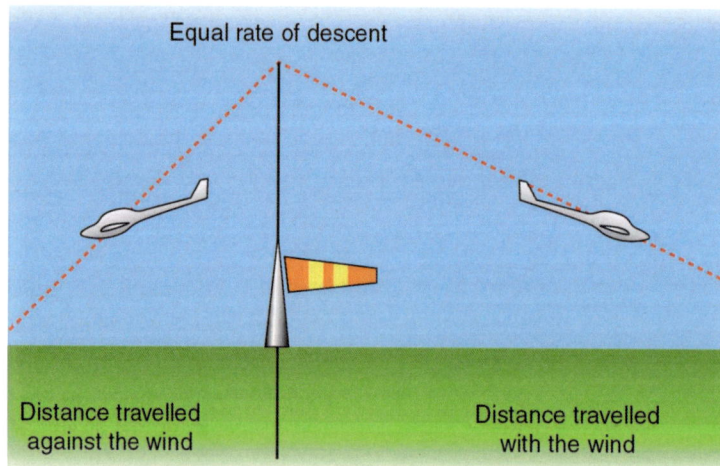

Figure 18.20

The aircraft will glide with a different angle to the ground than the real angle measured relative to the air, or the angle as it would appear to an observer in a balloon. The gliding efficiency, R/H, will change and be higher in tailwind than in headwind. The best gliding speed at which the longest gliding distance is attained will change accordingly.

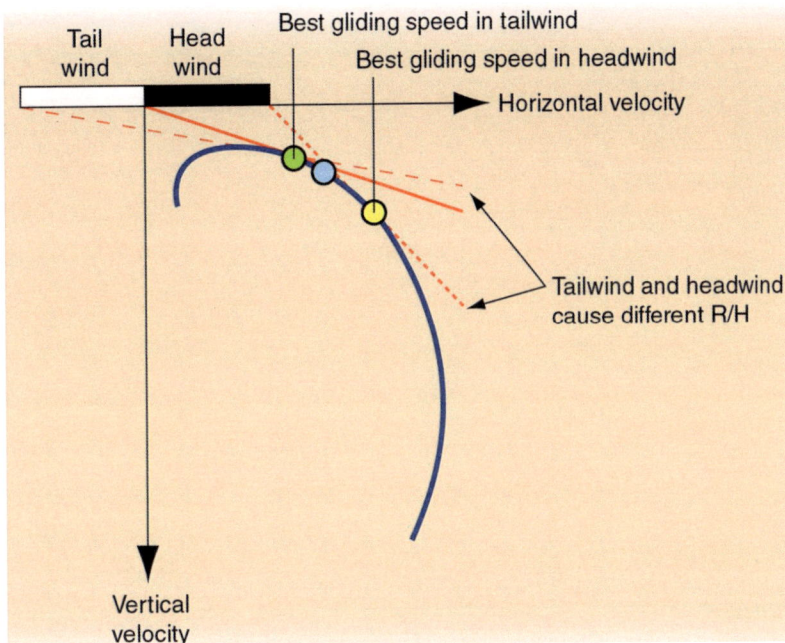

Figure 18.21

In figure 18.22 you see the flight path in headwind and tailwind relative to the air and ground respectively.

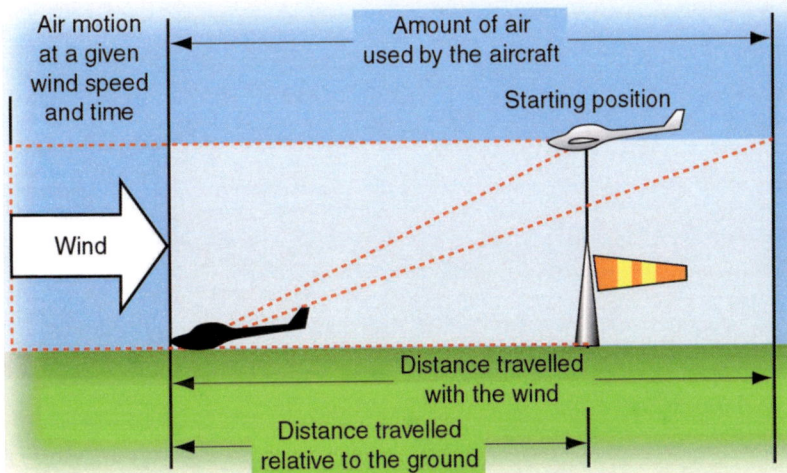

Figure 18.22

The effect of the wind is such that the distance flown relative to the ground will be shorter in headwind and longer in tailwind than in the absence of wind.

CRANFIELD AVIATION TRAINING SCHOOL LTD. PART-FCL GBR.ATO-0136
CATS INNOVATION CENTRE, LUTON, Bedfordshire LU2 8DL U.K.
www.catsaviation.com

18-12

Principles of Flight

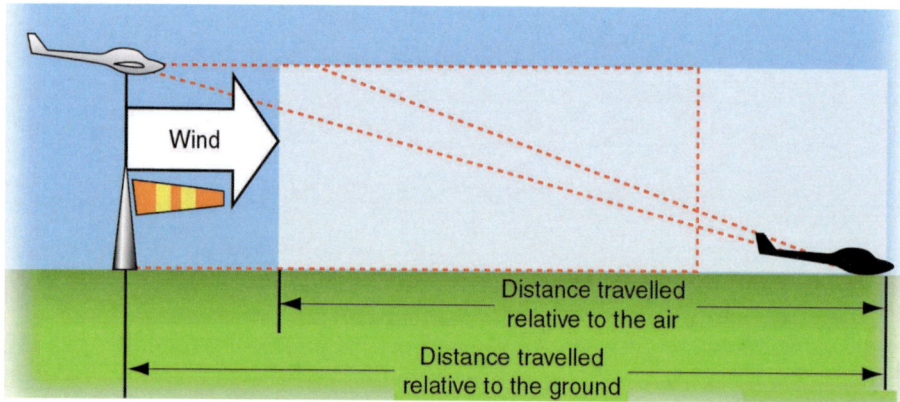

Figure 18.23

To obtain the best performance in the presence of the effect of wind, we need to analyse the effect it has on the flight path together with the effect of weight. This becomes important when gliding from high altitudes and/or with relatively strong winds.

18.3.4 *The gross effect of wind and weight on glide performance*

Let us consider two aircraft of the same model: one has a high load and is flying with maximum total weight, and the other one is flying without any load and has a lighter total weight. As we have already said, if both aircraft are flying at the best gliding speed relative to their weights, the flight path of the two will be the same relative to the air, but the heavier aircraft will reach the ground sooner.

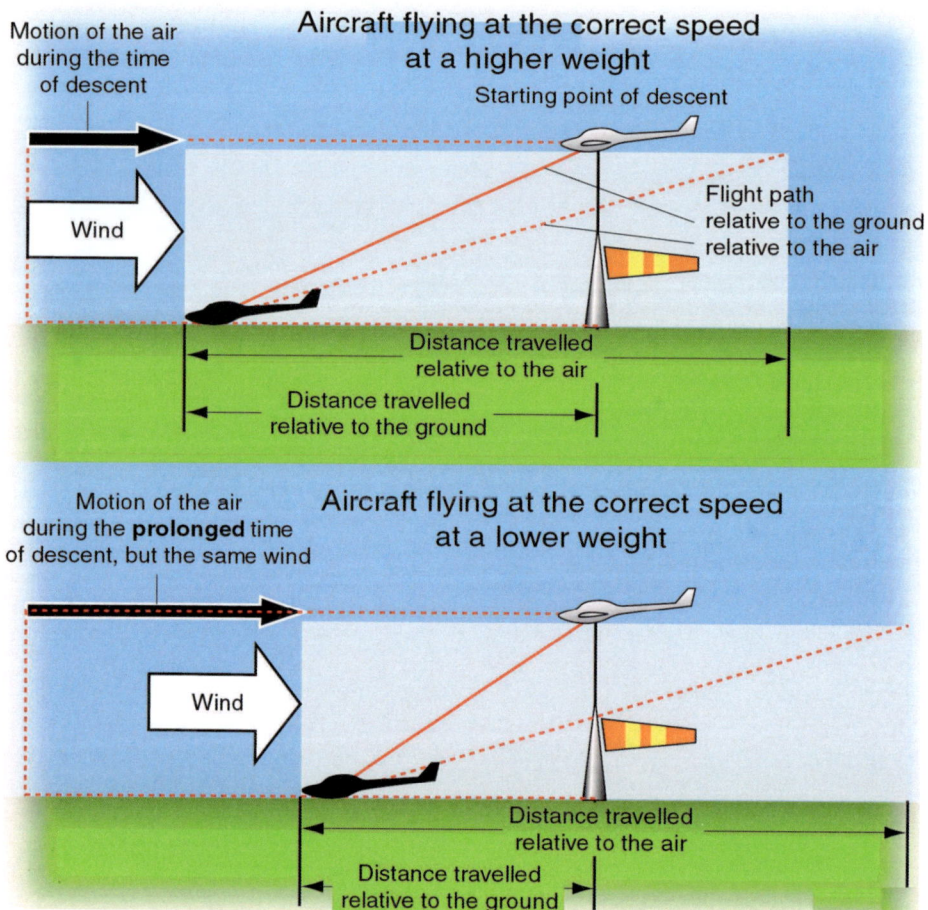

Figure 18.24

CRANFIELD AVIATION TRAINING SCHOOL LTD. PART-FCL GBR.ATO-0136
CATS INNOVATION CENTRE, LUTON, Bedfordshire LU2 8DL U.K.

www.catsaviation.com

18-13

Principles of Flight

In a strong headwind the heavier and faster aircraft will descend in a shorter time and will also be subjected to the headwind for a shorter time; it will therefore fly a distance relative to the ground which is longer than that of the lighter aircraft. On the contrary, in a tailwind, the lighter aircraft, which is flying at a lower speed for a longer time, will be subjected to the component of tailwind for a longer time and will glide a distance relative to the ground which is longer than that of the heavier aircraft.

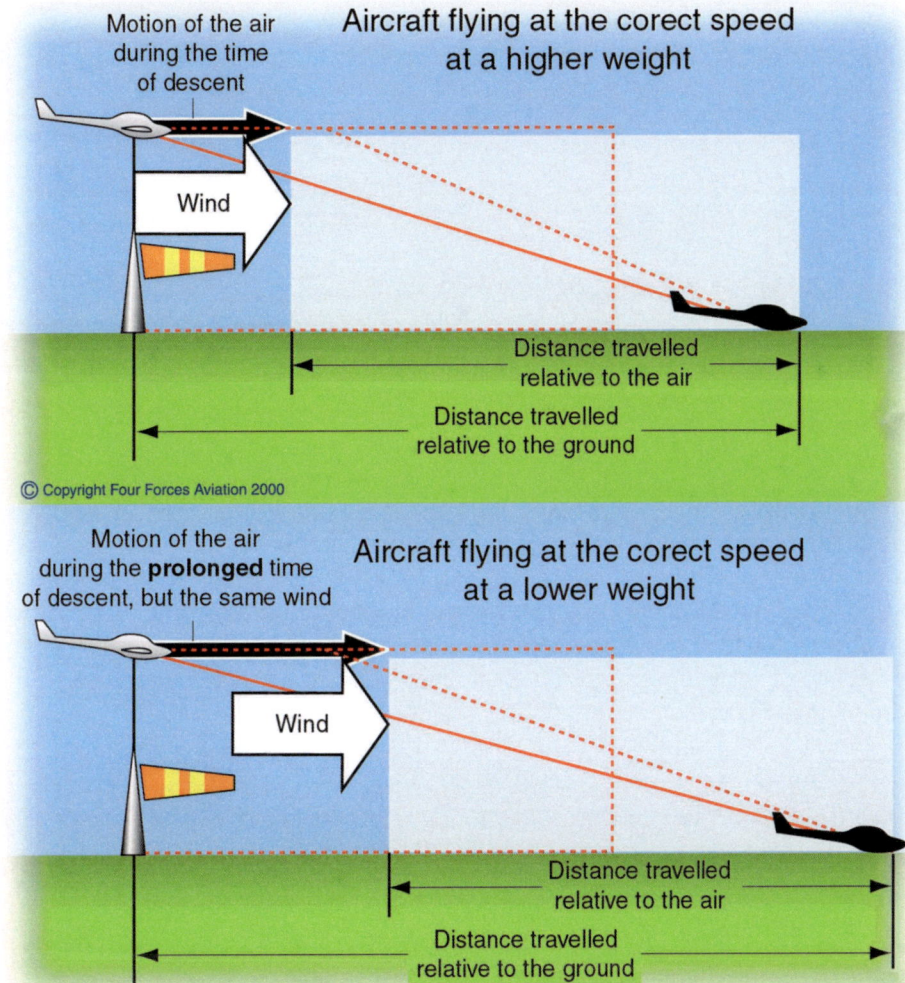

Figure 18.25

The effect of weight and speed on gliding efficiency in different wind conditions can also be shown in an odograph.

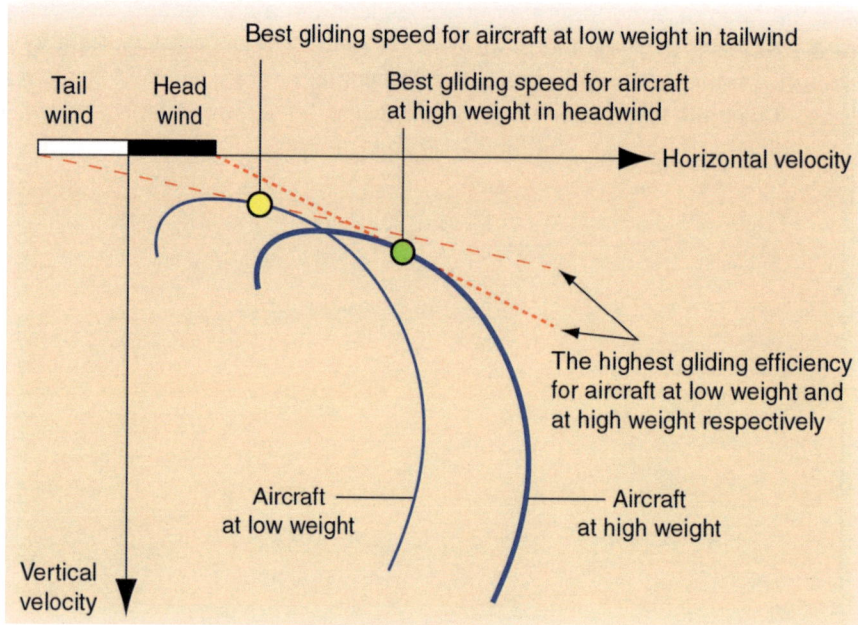

Figure 18.26

In the case of strong headwinds, the heavier and thus faster aircraft will descend in a shorter time and will also be subjected to the component of headwind for a shorter time; it will therefore glide a longer distance relative to the ground than that of the lighter aircraft. In a tailwind, the lighter and thus slower aircraft will be subjected to the component of tailwind for a longer time and will therefore glide a longer distance relative to the ground. Again, if in the case of a strong tailwind you need to fly the longest distance possible, it may be better to fly at the speed of minimum rate of descent since you are, in this case, going to be airborne and therefore subjected to the positive component of tailwind for a longer time.

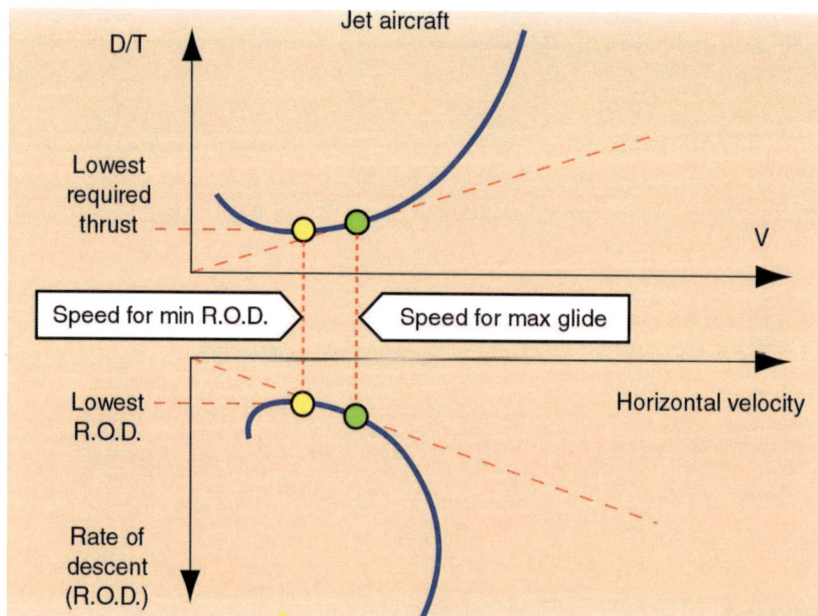

Figure 18.27

To fly the longest distance possible in a tailwind, it may be better to fly at the speed for minimum rate of descent in order to be subjected to the positive component of wind as long as possible.

Summary:
For light aircraft it is very important to maintain the correct speed in a strong wind situation; increased speed in headwind, and if necessary, decreased speed in tailwind.

18.3.5 Emergency descent

For several reasons it may be necessary to descend to a lower altitude in the shortest possible time. As mentioned earlier, a high-speed descent at reduced power may cause problems with a piston engine, but there are also other reasons why an emergency descent should be properly performed. A jet aircraft may reach speeds where the controllability and/or stability is severely reduced; this is explained in the next chapter. For all kinds of aircraft there is another problem; when reaching low altitudes at high speed, gusty wind conditions or windshear at low levels may overstress the structure of the aircraft.

In order to obtain the highest rate of descent without reaching too high a speed, as many air-braking devices as possible should be used, such as deflected air brake/spoilers, landing gear and flaps. However, when using landing gear and flaps, it is very important not to exceed the maximum allowed IAS for these.

Contrary to a descent with max glide, an emergency descent should be performed with the lowest ratio between lift and drag. In the polar curve below, we find a low and equal ratio between C_L/C_D at A.o.A 1°, corresponding to high speeds, as well as at A.o.A 14° corresponding to low speeds.

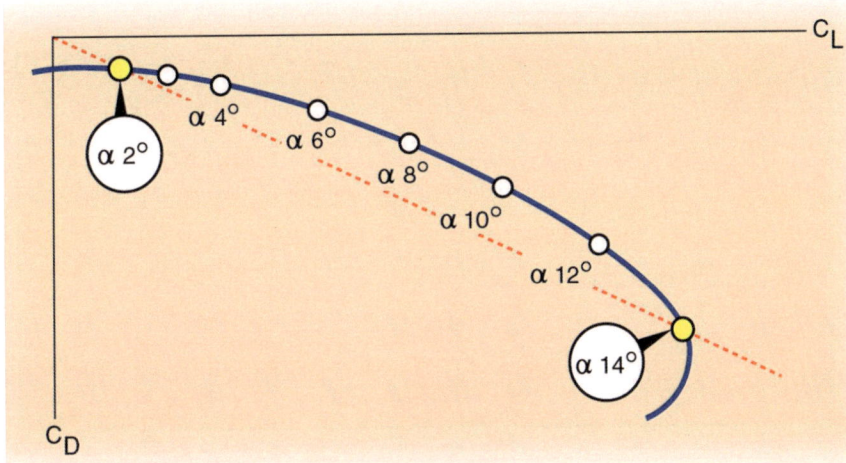

Figure 18.28

You must always be aware of the recommended speed and configuration for an emergency descent of the actual aircraft.

Self Assessment Test 08

1   Speed stability of an aircraft:
A)   Is stable below V_{MD} because total drag decrease as speed decreases
B)   Is unstable above V_{MD} because thrust decreases as speed increases
C)   Is unstable below V_{MD} because total drag decreases as speed decreases
D)   Is stable above V_{MD} because total drag increases as speed increases

2   An aircraft is said to have speed stability if:
A)   It recovers from displacements about any of the three axes at all speeds
B)   It can be trimmed to fly at any speed between stalling speed and V_{NE}
C)   When the speed is disturbed from it's trimmed value, it tends to return to the original speed
D)   It can fly a 3° glide slope without the need to adjust the thrust setting

3   For an aircraft flying at a speed above V_{MD}:
A)   A speed increase causes a drag increase which will cause a deceleration
B)   A speed increase causes a drag decrease causing further acceleration
C)   A speed increase causes a drag increase causing an acceleration
D)   A speed decrease causes a drag increase causing a deceleration

4   If the 'clean' 1g stall speed for an aircraft is 151kt, V_s during a 45° bank turn will be:
A)   151kt
B)   122kt
C)   214kt
D)   180kt

5   What action is necessary to make an aircraft turn:
A)   Change the direction of lift
B)   Change the direction of thrust
C)   Yaw the aircraft
D)   Roll the aircraft

6   When an aircraft is climbing the requirements to maintain equilibrium are:
A)   Thrust equals the sum of the drag and the weight component along the flight path, and lift equals the weight component perpendicular to the flight path
B)   Thrust equals the weight component along the flight path, and lift equals the sum of the drag and weight component perpendicular to the flight path
C)   Thrust equals the weigh component perpendicular to the flight path, and lift equals the weight component along the flight path
D)   Lift equals weight, and thrust equals the sum of the drag and the weight component along the flight path

7   The best speed for obstacle clearance is:
A)   Best angle of climb speed (V_X) with optimum flap setting for runway length, take-off weight and atmospheric conditions
B)   Best angle of climb speed (V_X) with no high devices selected
C)   Best rate of climb speed (V_Y) with no flaps
D)   Best rate of climb speed (V_X) with optimum flap setting for runway length, take-off weight and atmospheric conditions

8   When climbing into a headwind, compared to still air, the climb gradient relative to the ground will be:
A)   Steeper, and the rate of climb increased
B)   Steeper, and the rate of climb unchanged
C)   Less steep but the rate of climb increased
D)   The same, and the rate of climb unchanged

9   A glider has a Lift : Drag ratio of 25 : 1 For every 1,000ft of height lost it would cover a distance in still air of:
A)   4 NM
B)   2.5 NM
C)   25 NM
D)   40 NM

10   In a glide the line of action of the total reaction will be:
A)   Behind that of lift and ahead that of weight
B)   Ahead that of lift and directly opposite that of weight
C)   Behind that of lift and directly opposite that of weight
D)   Ahead that of lift and weight

11   Which statement is correct with respect to rate and radius of turn for an aeroplane flown in a co-ordinated turn at a constant altitude:
A)   For any specific angle of bank and airspeed, the lighter the aeroplane the faster the rate and the smaller the radius of turn
B)   For a specific angle of bank and airspeed the rate and radius of turn will not vary
C)   The faster the true airspeed, the faster the rate and larger the radius of turn regardless of the angle of bank
D)   To maintain a steady rate of turn, the angle of bank must be increased as the airspeed is decreased

12   If an aircraft maintains a constant radius of turn but the speed is increased:
A)   The bank angle must be increased
B)   The bank angle must decreased
C)   The bank angle will remain constant and the 'g' load will be constant
D)   The bank angle will remain constant but the 'g' load will increase

13   In co-ordinated flight for any specific bank, the faster the speed of the aircraft the:
A)   Smaller the radius and the slower the rate of turn
B)   Greater the radius and the faster the rate of turn
C)   Smaller the radius and the faster the rate of turn
D)   Greater the radius and the slower the rate of turn

14   While holding the angle of bank constant, if the rate of turn is varied the load factor would:
A)   Vary depending upon the resultant lift vector
B)   Remain constant regardless of air density and the resultant lift vector
C)   Vary depending upon speed and air density provided the resultant lift vector varies proportionally
D)   Increase at an increasing rate

15 For an aircraft to make a rate 1 turn:
A) There is only one correct speed, and one corresponding bank angle
B) It may be done at any speed but there is only one correct bank angle
C) There is only one correct speed, but any bank angle may be chosen
D) It may be done at any speed, but the higher the speed the greater the bank angle

16 When gliding, the speed which will give the minimum rate of decent is:
A) As close to the stalling speed as possible
B) The same as the speed for maximum glide range
C) Less than the speed for maximum glide range
D) Higher than the speed for maximum glide range

17 In a climb the weight component along with the flight path is balanced by:
A) Thrust
B) Lift
C) Drag
D) Neither of these

CRANFIELD AVIATION TRAINING SCHOOL LTD. PART-FCL GBR.ATO-0136
CATS INNOVATION CENTRE, LUTON, Bedfordshire LU2 8DL U.K.

www.catsaviation.com

18-19

Principles of Flight

Self Assessment Test 08 Answers

1	D
2	C
3	A
4	D
5	A
6	A
7	B
8	B
9	A
10	C
11	B
12	A
13	D
14	B
15	D
16	C
17	A

CHAPTER 19

AERODYNAMICS OF HIGH-SPEED AIRCRAFT

19.1 Introduction

When flying at very high speeds, above approximately 350-500 KTAS, undesirable effects may occur, such as vibrations in the airframe, stiff controls or oscillations in all aircraft axes and a rapid increase in drag. These are all results of the fact that the surrounding airflow starts to behave differently at higher speed.

The airflow near a body varies in speed due to the pressure pattern along the body and to the law of continuity. At certain places along the body the velocity of the surrounding airflow can be higher or lower than the actual true airspeed of the body itself.

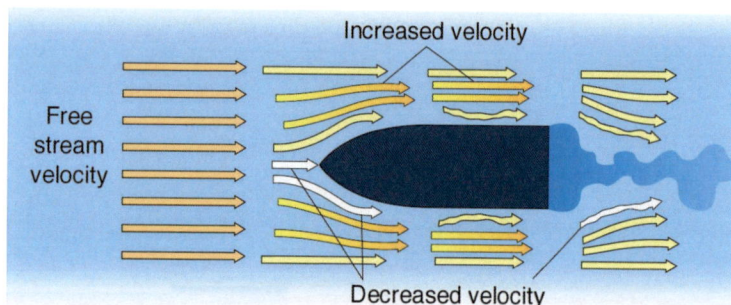

Figure 19.1 Variation of airflow speed around a body

When the speed of the body is so high that the surrounding airflow reaches a local velocity equal to the speed of sound, the air becomes compressible and its density increases. Air molecules at leading edges have difficulty in moving away fast enough and become compressed.

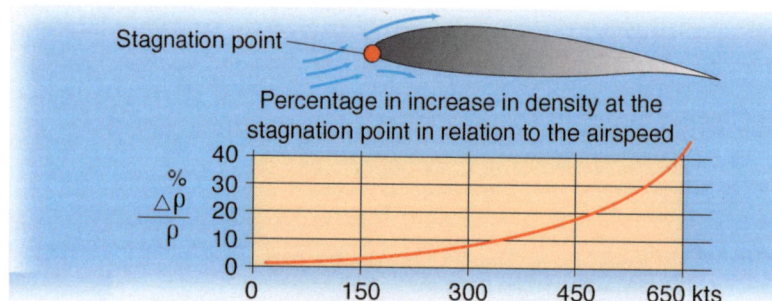

Figure 19.2 Density increases with airspeed

At a speed of 20% of the speed of sound the dynamic pressure will increase by 1.5%, and by 15% at 75% of the speed of sound. The local airspeed around a body will not only experience an increase in speed but in some areas also a decrease in speed due to the law of continuity. Consequently, not until the speed of a body is well above the speed of sound, will the whole surrounding airflow reach supersonic speed. Then the flow pattern will be quite different. Referring to the following diagram, if airflow around a wing section has a pure subsonic speed, which means that all the air has a constant density, a change in flow pattern occurs due to the pressure distribution further back. The new flow pattern can be explained in the way that in front of the wing, the molecules of air detect what is going on further back above and below the wing, and adapt their flow accordingly. The flow avoids areas with higher pressure and tries to fill areas with lower pressure. The length of the arrows represents the local flow velocity.

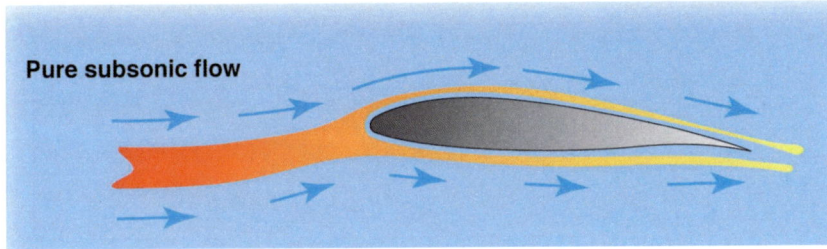

Figure 19.3 Subsonic flow

When a wing reaches a supersonic speed, which causes pure supersonic airflow around its surfaces, the molecules of air in front of it are no longer able to detect the pressure distribution rearwards. The reason for this is that the speed of the information of the pressure distribution has the speed of sound. Consequently, the air is not able to adapt its flow pattern, so in some areas the air is compressed. The combination of these two factors causes the airflow to behave quite differently in subsonic and supersonic velocities.

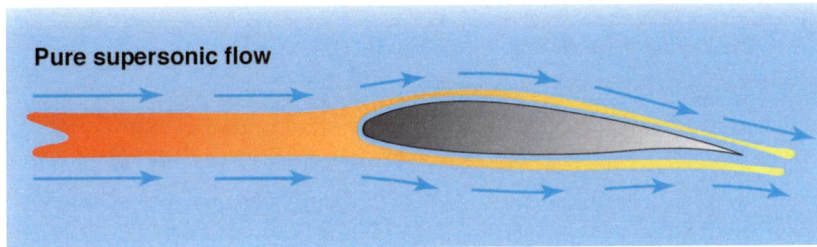

Figure 19.4 Supersonic flow

Supersonic airflow cannot adapt its flow pattern to the pressure distribution around the wing in the same way as at subsonic speed.

19.1.1 Relationship between the speed of sound and temperature.

All air molecules have equal distribution in an undisturbed airmass and have internal motions that depend on the absolute temperature. Their internal motion gives them enough energy to strike their neighbours if a disturbance occurs. When the temperature is high, the internal motion is more violent and the molecules have more energy and greater ability to hit many of their neighbours in a shorter time. At low temperatures, the molecules have less energy and their internal motion is slowed down. It takes longer time for them to strike the same number of neighbours. All air molecules have an internal motion that depends on the absolute temperature of the air.

If there is a very rapid disturbance in the airmass, the closest molecules will change their relative positions in the fluid, hitting the neighbours in their way, and return again to their original position. A pressure wave is created. The molecules that have been struck will in their turn hit the nearest molecules in their way and so on in order to adapt to the new environment.

CRANFIELD AVIATION TRAINING SCHOOL LTD. PART-FCL GBR.ATO-0136
CATS CATS INNOVATION CENTRE, LUTON, Bedfordshire LU2 8DL U.K.   www.catsaviation.com

19-2   Principles of Flight

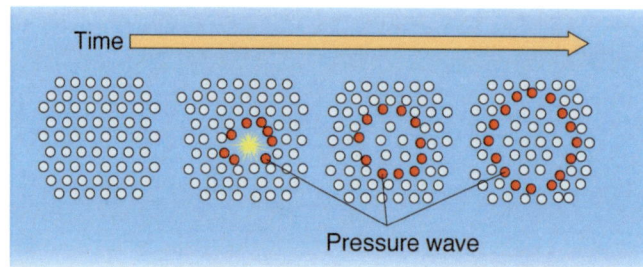

Figure 19.5 Pressure wave formation

Sound is a pressure disturbance of a certain frequency of the airmass. The disturbance forces the air molecules to move circularly from the source of the disturbance like the rings on water after a stone strikes it. The speed of the distribution of this disturbance in the airmass depends on how often and with what force the air molecules strike each other. In other words, the speed of sound in the air depends on the actual absolute temperature. It is proportional to the square root of the absolute temperature, and is determined by temperature alone. At a temperature of +15°C, the speed of sound is approximately 340 m/s, or approx. 1220 kph, or 661 KT. At low temperatures, for instance -60° C, the speed of sound is decreased to only approx. 290 m/s, or 1050 kph, or 570 KT.

19.1.2   Definition of Mach number

An Austrian, Ernst Mach, around the turn of the century studied the behaviour of a body moving in a fluid at high speeds. The relationship between air speed and the speed of sound is expressed as a Mach number.
A body moving in an airmass with a TAS which is half, or 50%, of the speed of sound in that particular airmass is said to have a speed of Mach 0.5. If the same body moves at a TAS equal to the speed of sound, or 100% of the speed of sound, it is said to have a speed of Mach 1. If the same body has a TAS of 150% of the speed of sound, it is said to have a speed of Mach 1.5.

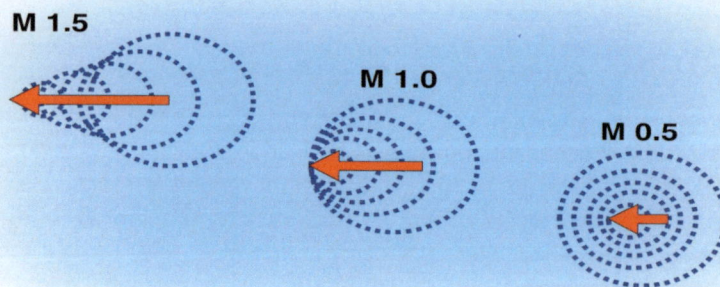

Figure 19.6

It is important to know that the speed of sound in a given fluid is influenced only by the temperature. Consequently an aircraft flying at Mach 1 at low altitude with an air temperature of +15° C, has a higher true airspeed than an aircraft flying at 30000', where the temperature on a standard day is -43° C.

> The speed of sound in a given fluid is influenced only by the actual absolute temperature

In a different fluid such as water the speed of sound is different. Molecules of water are in closer proximity to each other than air molecules are to each other and therefore hit each other in a shorter time than air molecules at a given temperature. The speed of sound in water is therefore much higher, in fact four and a quarter times the speed of sound in the air.

19.1.3   *Compression waves*

Compression of air does not only occur at pure supersonic speeds. It begins when the aircraft is still at speeds that are below supersonic. When the local flow velocity is equal to or faster than the speed of sound, compressed pressure waves, called compression waves, occur perpendicular to some surfaces as well as in front of the structure. The airfoil below has a flight Mach number, or a free stream Mach number, of M0.72. But the local speed of the flow at the upper surface of the wing is higher. The pressure waves, shown here only from a single point on the surface, cannot proceed forward or beyond a point where the local flow velocity towards the pressure waves has reached the speed of distribution; Mach 1. This is because the speed of the pressure waves is the same, Mach 1.

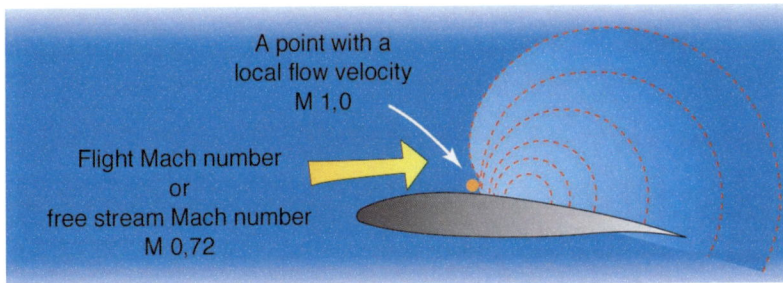

Figure 19.7 Compression waves

When Mach number is increased, an area above the wing develops with a local flow velocity of Mach 1 and faster. This area of supersonic velocities has a forward limit along a line with sonic speed, called the sonic line. The aft limit is where the pressure waves developed behind this area settle in a very thin region between the supersonic and subsonic flow velocities. That thin region has higher density and is called a shock wave.

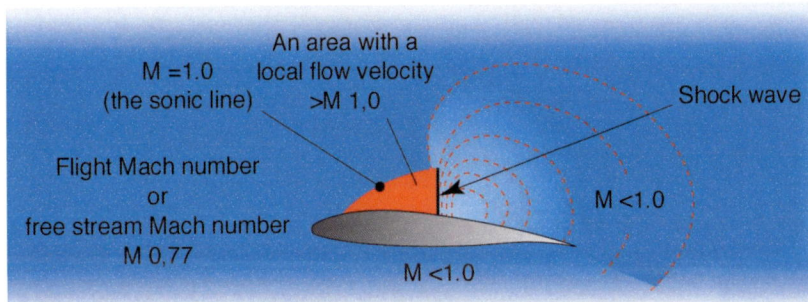

Figure 19.8 Sonic line and shock wave

When Mach number increases, the area with supersonic velocity is enlarged, the shockwave is higher and it moves rearwards.

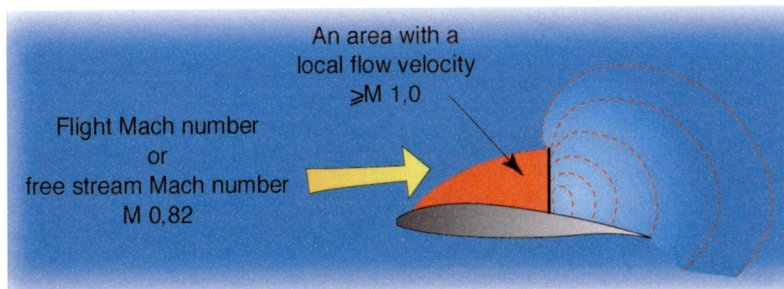

Figure 19.9 Increasing Mach number increases the shockwave and it moves aft

Shockwaves can sometimes be seen on wings at transonic speed. They look like a very thin transparent film perpendicular to the wing surface. The flow velocity over the upper surface of the wing increases chordwise up to the point where the shockwave is positioned. Flow velocity at the shockwave decreases suddenly subsonic velocity.

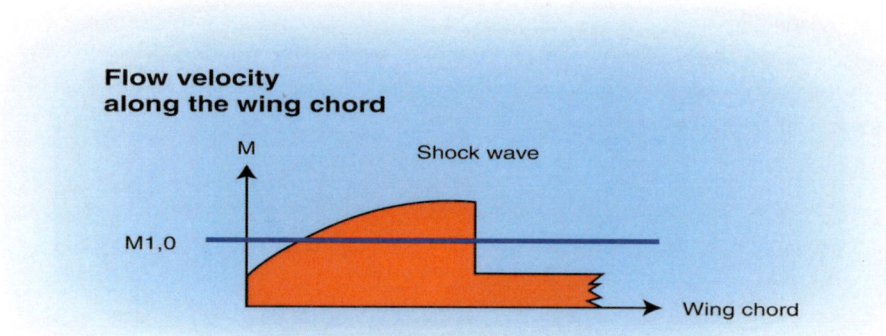

Figure 19.10 Flow velocity decreases suddenly at the shockwave

The shockwave consumes energy when the airflow changes rapidly from supersonic velocity, at which point it is compressed and its velocity is reduced to subsonic. This sudden drop in flow velocity causes disturbances in flow, sometimes causing flow separation after the shockwave.

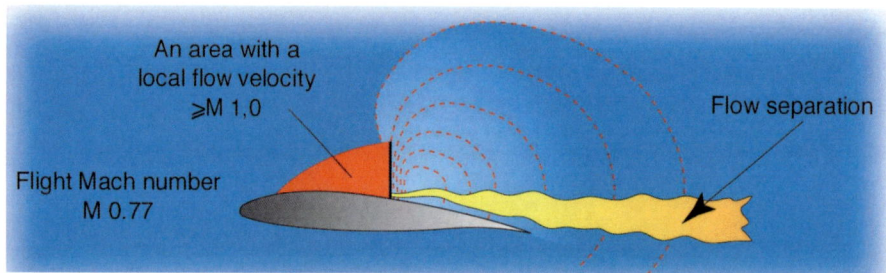

Figure 19.11 Flow separation

The shockwave will provoke a disturbance in the flow, which sometimes causes flow separation after the shockwave

Compressibility effects may begin to appear at a flight speed of approximately Mach 0.7. For aircraft not designed for high speed, for instance aircraft with a thick wing airfoil section, the compressibility effects may even start at M 0.6 or lower. At these speeds, where some compressibility effects occur, the airflow around the aircraft is a mix of subsonic and supersonic airflow. The speed at which the air compressibility affects the aircraft is different for different aircraft, and the effect on the aircraft varies a lot.

19.1.4   *Division of speeds*

Aircraft behave differently at different Mach numbers. Therefore, expressed as a Mach number, the airflow velocity is divided into four stages: subsonic, transonic, supersonic and hypersonic velocity.

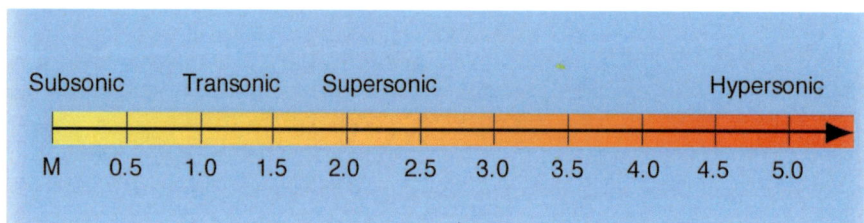

Figure 19.12 Subsonic to Hypersonic Mach Numbers

Subsonic flow velocity means a free stream velocity where all surfaces are surrounded by subsonic local flow velocities only, normally between Mach 0 and Mach 0.8.

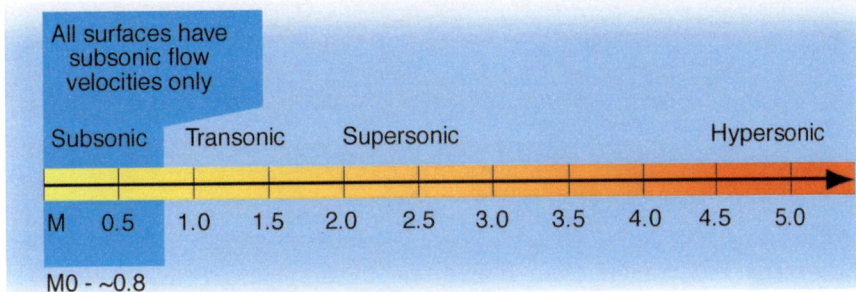

Figure 19.13 Subsonic flow

The flight speed envelope that changes from pure subsonic flow velocities to pure supersonic flow velocities around the aircraft is called transonic. This means: a free stream velocity where the surfaces are surrounded by a mix of subsonic and supersonic local flow velocities, normally between Mach 0.8 and Mach 1.1-1.2.

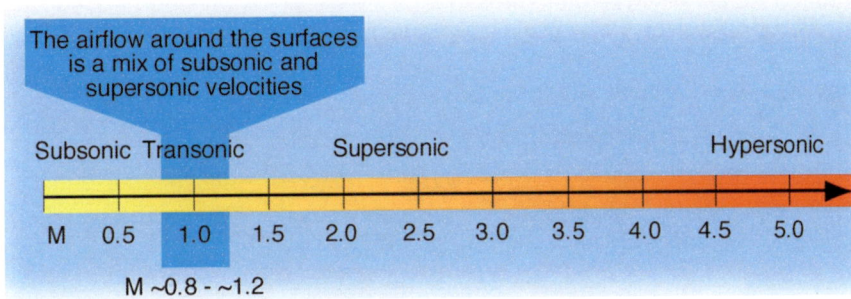

Figure 19.14 Transonic flow

An aircraft flying in the transonic speed range with a true speed near Mach 0.8 may have local airflow varying from M 0.3 in the engine air intake to M 1.2 at the upper surface of its wing. Supersonic flow means a free stream velocity where all surfaces are surrounded by supersonic local flow velocities only, which is normally between Mach 1.2 and Mach 5.

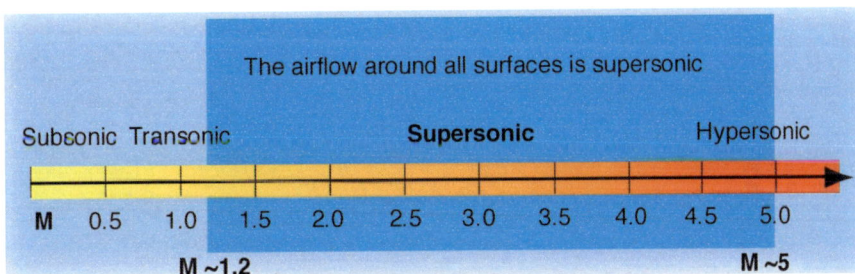

Figure 19.15 Supersonic Flow

Hypersonic flow means a free stream velocity where, due to the very high friction temperature, the air becomes ionized. It normally ranges from Mach 5 and up.

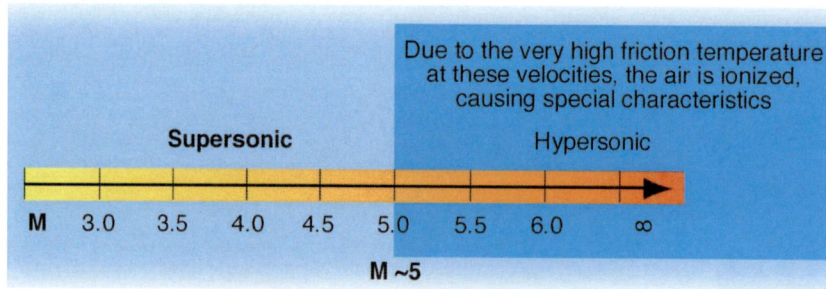

Figure 19.16 Hypersonic Flow

Spacecraft descend through the atmosphere of the earth at hypersonic velocity.

19.2 *Effect of Fluid Compressibility*

Relationship between dynamic, static and total pressure in supersonic flow.

The velocity of the airflow flowing into a convergent tube at subsonic velocity increases due to the equation of the continuity effect.

According to Bernoulli's equation, the total pressure is constant in undisturbed subsonic flow, and the density will remain almost constant since the static pressure decreases with increased dynamic pressure $(P_{tot} = p + q)$.

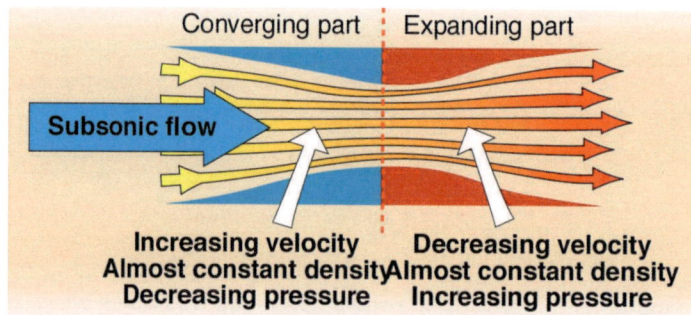

Figure 19.17 Velocity and pressure in subsonic flow

When the incoming subsonic flow speed is so high that the increase in speed at the contraction reaches Mach 1, a shock wave is formed at the throat just as it is on the position for the maximum speed on an airfoil. So instead of a gradual increase in pressure and reduction in speed beyond the throat, there will be a sudden increase in pressure, a sudden reduction in speed, and the flow behind the shock wave is turbulent.

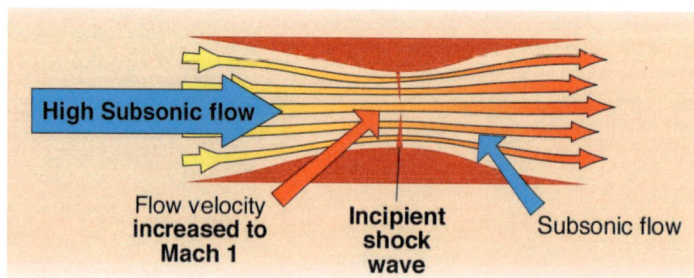

Figure 19.18 Mach 1

However, if the incoming flow velocity is supersonic, the converging and the expanding parts cause disturbances that create Mach waves. In the contraction part, these Mach waves, so-called compression waves or shocks, will increase the density of the air as well as the static pressure.

CRANFIELD AVIATION TRAINING SCHOOL LTD. PART-FCL GBR.ATO-0136
CATS INNOVATION CENTRE, LUTON, Bedfordshire LU2 8DL U.K.   www.catsaviation.com

19-7   Principles of Flight

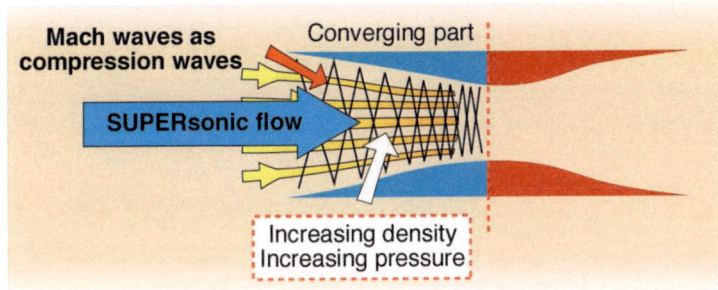

Figure 19.19 Supersonic

The increase in density and static pressure opposes the incoming airflow, causing the flow velocity to decrease towards the contraction. The decrease in the velocity is gradual after each compression wave and reaches M 1 at the minimum section.

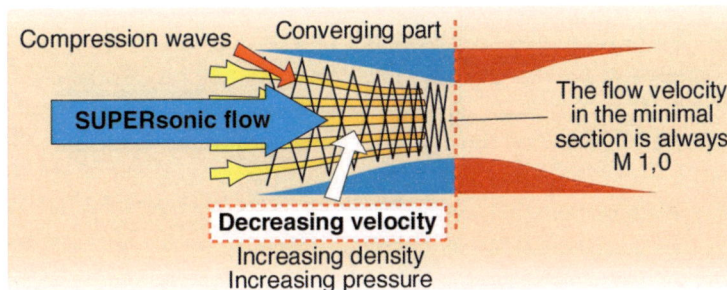

Figure 19.20 Supersonic flow

In the expanding part of the venturi, the opposite effect takes place. The density decreases, creating expansion waves and pressure decreases.

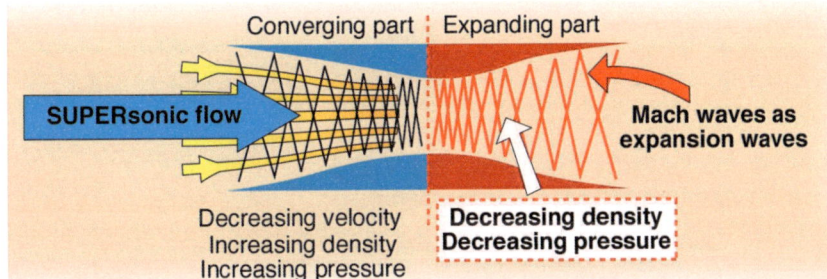

Figure 19.21 Expanding part

This decreasing density and pressure cause an increasing velocity.

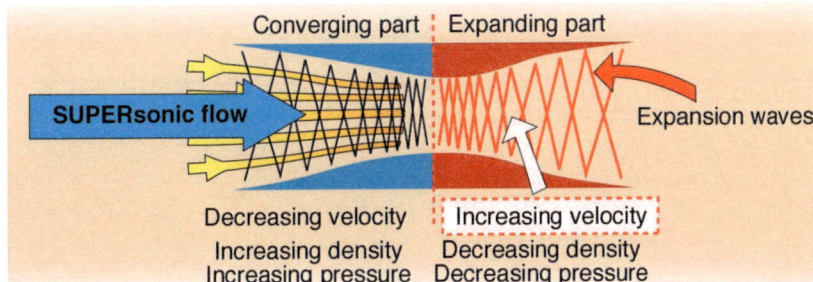

Figure 19.22 Expanding part

Supersonic airflow entering an expansion, experiences decreasing density and static pressure which causes increasing velocity contrary to subsonic flow

A good example of how an expanding nozzle can be used, is on a rocket. The rocket nozzle must be designed to permit very high supersonic flow velocities and must therefore be of expanding design, a so-called De Laval nozzle. In some conditions of flight, expansion waves can be seen in the exhaust flames.

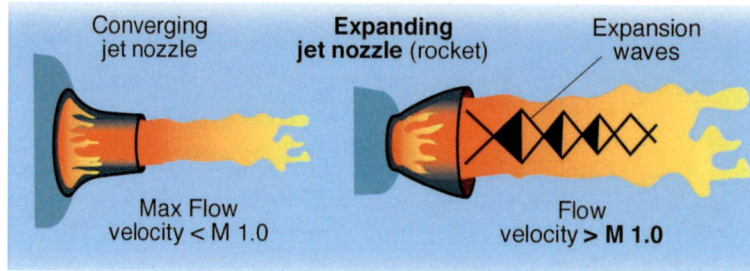

Figure 19.23 Expansion waves

Only an expanding nozzle permits supersonic flow velocity.

The compression and expansion waves do not only occur in a tube. An aircraft flying at transonic or supersonic speed will create Mach waves as compression waves (shocks) and expansion waves (expansion fan). The Mach waves will change the local density, the pressure and the velocity in their vicinity.

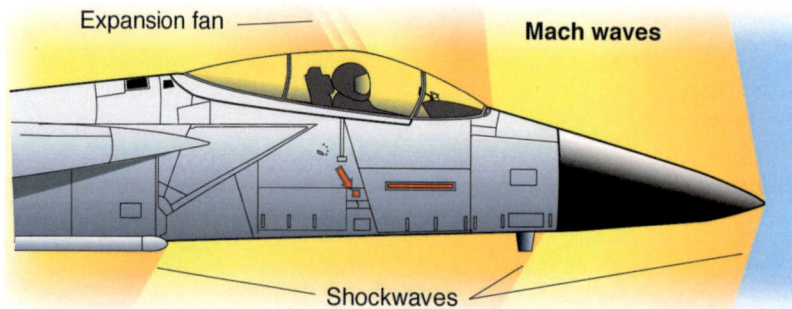

Figure 19.24 Mach waves, shockwaves and expansion fan

At the speed of sound the shockwaves will be perpendicular to the flight path, but if the speed is increased the shockwaves will be swept more and more rearwards.

When these shockwaves from an aircraft reach the ground, regardless of the supersonic speed being low or high, you will hear them as a bang after the aircraft has passed above you.

If an aircraft is flying at a speed 40% higher than the speed of sound M 1.4., the sound and the shockwaves can only reach the velocity of M 1.0, thus the engine sound of the aircraft can only be heard well after the aircraft has passed.

> The shock wave moves across the Earth surface at the same speed as the ground speed of the aircraft

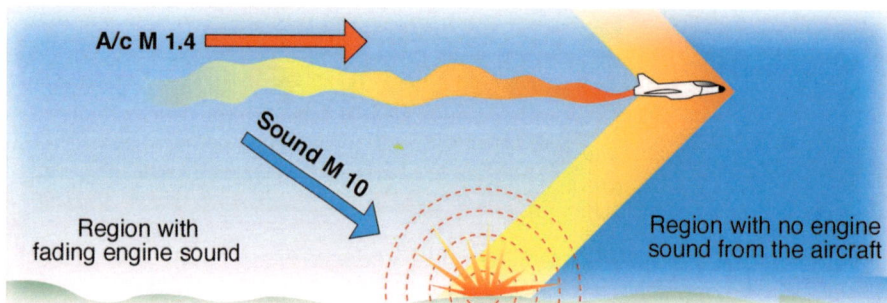

Figure 19.25

CRANFIELD AVIATION TRAINING SCHOOL LTD. PART-FCL GBR.ATO-0136
CATS INNOVATION CENTRE, LUTON, Bedfordshire LU2 8DL U.K.   www.catsaviation.com

19-9   Principles of Flight

19.2.1 *Behaviour of airflow and pressure distribution when increasing the Mach number*

When flying at a speed well below the speed of sound, the local flow velocities around the aircraft, and especially around the wings, will also be below the speed of sound so practically no compression will occur.

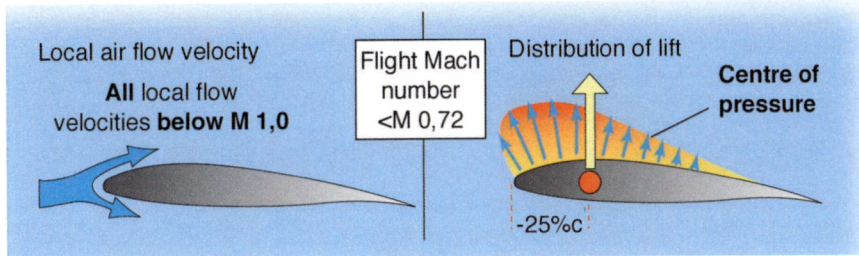

Figure 19.26

When the flight speed is increased, in this case to M 0.77, an area on the upper wing surface will have the local velocity of M 1.0 and higher. A shockwave perpendicular to the flow will first develop on the upper surface. The shockwave constitutes a very high adverse pressure gradient and thus produces at least a thickening of the boundary layer and often flow separation. These changes of the local air velocities and the increased turbulent area will change the pressure distribution around the wing. Below you see that the pressure distribution will be different and the centre of pressure will therefore be moved a little bit forward.

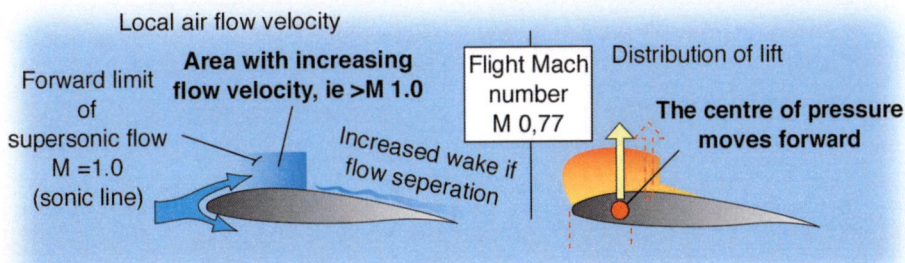

Figure 19.27

The shockwave produces a thickening of the boundary layer and often cause flow separation. When the airspeed is further increased, in this case to M 0.82, the area of supersonic speed is enlarged, especially rearwards, and the lower surface also has an area with supersonic velocity. The difference in and distribution of pressure will change accordingly and the centre of pressure moves rearwards to the position it had at subsonic velocities only.

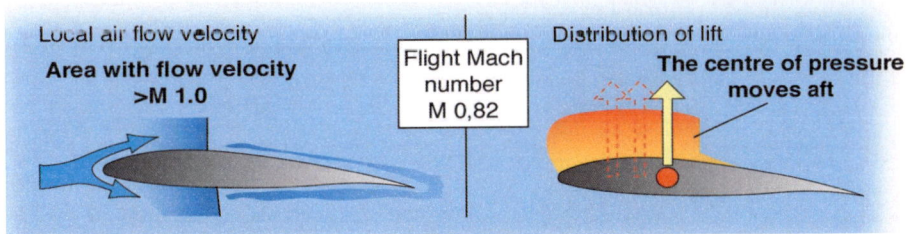

Figure 19.28

At an airspeed of M 0.95, the supersonic area and the shockwaves have reached a position near the trailing edge, and the area of low pressure is almost symmetrical. Consequently the centre of pressure has moved further aft.

> At increased transonic speed the C.P. moves aft

19.2.2   Tuckunder (or Mach Tuck)

The changed position of the centre of pressure will increase the longitudinal stability and change the trim of the aircraft so that it becomes more nose-heavy.

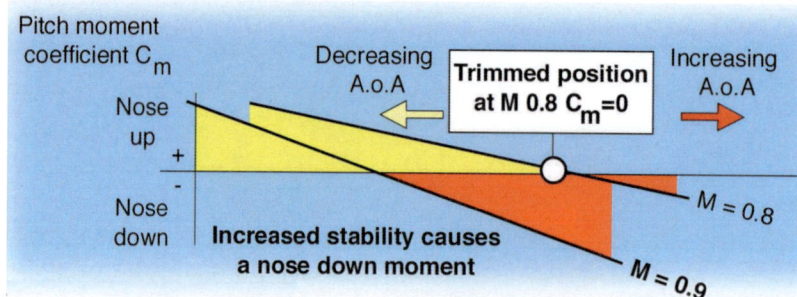

Figure 19.29 Mach tuck

With increased Mach number, the aircraft will slowly enter into a dive. This undesired phenomenon of the aircraft is called "tuck-under" or Mach Tuck.

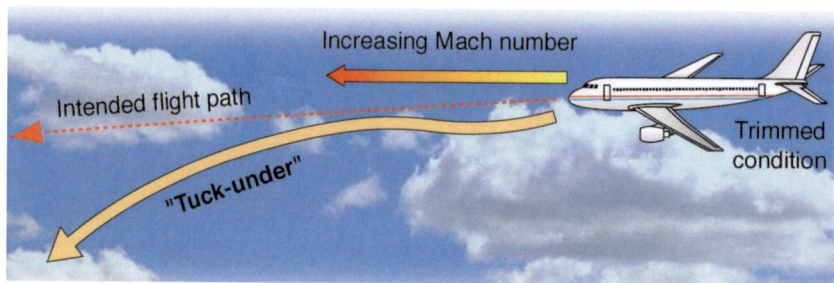

Figure 19.30

The phenomenon of the aircraft becoming more nose-heavy in transonic flight is called tuck under

The effect of this movement of the centre of pressure varies a great deal according to the type of aircraft. Aircraft not designed for supersonic speeds normally undergo very obvious changes of trim in pitch while some may experience uncontrolled behaviour. However, supersonic aircraft with e.g. delta-wings, and aircraft with an all-flying-tail (having no separate elevator surface) may have no obvious problems when flying at transonic airspeeds.

19.2.3   Transonic buffeting

The increased and separated boundary layer behind the shockwave will hammer on the wing skin and may be felt in the aircraft as a buffeting, called high-speed buffeting or Mach buffeting. The thick and separated boundary layer causes the lift coefficient to fall and the drag to rise rapidly.

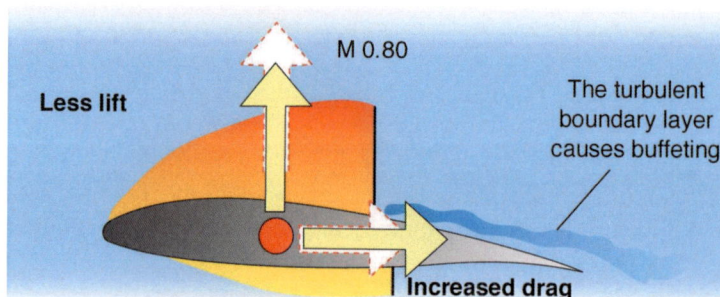

Figure 19.31 High speed buffet

CRANFIELD AVIATION TRAINING SCHOOL LTD. PART-FCL GBR.ATO-0136
CATS INNOVATION CENTRE, LUTON, Bedfordshire LU2 8DL U.K.
www.catsaviation.com

19-11

Principles of Flight

When the speed is further increased the aircraft may stall. This phenomenon is known as shock stall. It differs from the conventional low-speed stall in that it may occur at a low A.o.A. It feels like the low-speed buffeting but is often of a higher frequency.

High speed buffeting and shock stall are caused by shockwaves causing flow separations

The flow separation over the wing will often be asymmetrical. It will have a slightly wider area or, due to small differences in the shape of the airfoil section of the wing, start earlier on one wing than on the other. This will cause one of the wings to drop suddenly or will provoke rolling disturbances. The boundary layer may also affect the control surfaces making them vibrate or lose efficiency. The different positions of the upper and lower shockwaves may also cause undesirable deflections of manual control surfaces.

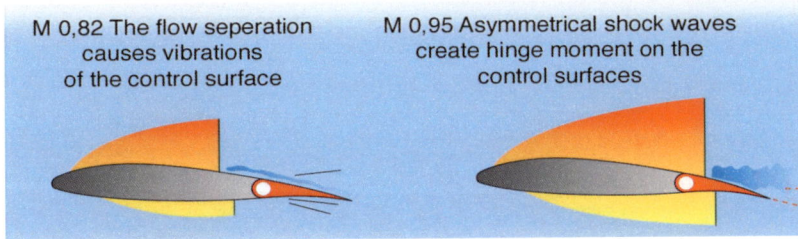

M 0,82 The flow seperation causes vibrations of the control surface

M 0,95 Asymmetrical shock waves create hinge moment on the control surfaces

Figure 19.32

19.2.4   *Critical Mach number*

These disturbances, the movement of the centre of pressure and the high-speed buffeting and stall, may be critical to flight safety. Thus by definition, the free stream Mach number at which sonic flow is first achieved above the surface of the airfoil is called the critical Mach number, abbreviated M_{crit} or M_{cr}. The body of the aircraft may have one critical Mach number and the wings another. Shock-induced flow separation on the tail section may have a great impact on the directional stability. The critical Mach number of the whole aircraft is the speed at which any disturbance may affect the stability, controllability, lift or drag of the aircraft. The critical Mach number of the whole aircraft is the speed at which any disturbance may affect the stability, controllability, lift or drag of the aircraft. The critical Mach number varies with aircraft type. It is rather low for aircraft not designed for high speeds and high for modern high- speed aircraft. Supersonic jetfighters have a very high critical Mach number and there is no significant disturbance of stability or control.

19.2.5   *Effect on lift*

At a constant angle of attack of the wings, the lift coefficient is almost constant up to transonic velocities, where it will vary with the Mach number. At low transonic speed, the increase in the pressure differences of the upper and lower surfaces of the wing will cause the C_L to increase. At low speeds, the disturbances due to the wing are transmitted ahead of the wing with the speed of sound, which is much higher than the speed of the wing consequently the streamline pattern is affected far ahead. At higher Mach numbers the streamlines are affected only a short distance ahead, which means that they approach the wing at a steeper angle. This causes an increased suction, especially near the leading edge, giving a higher C_L. At a higher speed if shock stall appears, the flow separation after the shockwave will reduce the C_L and finally, when the shockwave of the lower surface has reached the trailing edge, C_L will increase again.

CRANFIELD AVIATION TRAINING SCHOOL LTD. PART-FCL GBR.ATO-0136
CATS INNOVATION CENTRE, LUTON, Bedfordshire LU2 8DL U.K.   www.catsaviation.com
19-12   Principles of Flight

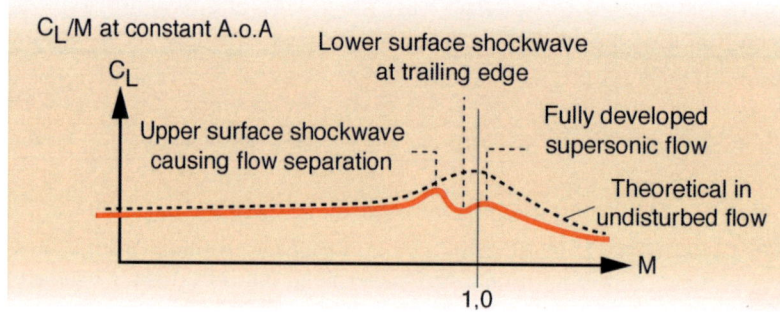

Figure 19.33

The maximum lift, or max C_L, will also be affected. The shockwave will cause flow separation over the wing, which decreases the maximum angle of attack. It will also produce a lower maximum lift coefficient.

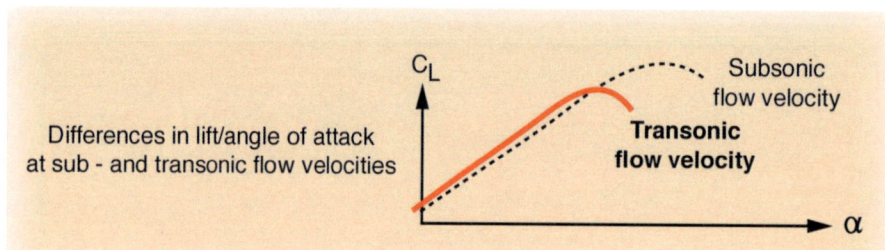

Figure 19.34

At transonic flow velocities, C_L changes with the Mach number and the maximum C_L is reduced

When there is an increase in the lift coefficient, or in other words, an increase in the wing load, the higher angle of attack required then will increase the local velocity over the wings. This means that supersonic flow velocities will be reached over the wing surface at a lower flight speed, reducing the critical Mach number.

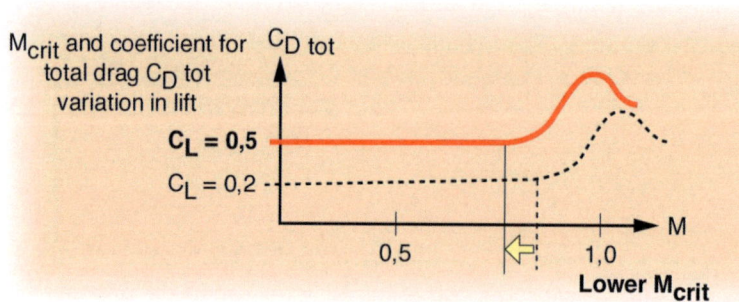

Figure 19.35

An example of this is when making a pull-up from a dive. The increased lift required will lead to supersonic flow velocity over the wings at a lower flight speed than in a straight flight. The critical Mach number will therefore be lower with increased wing load, and the drag will be higher.

CRANFIELD AVIATION TRAINING SCHOOL LTD. PART-FCL GBR.ATO-0136
CATS INNOVATION CENTRE, LUTON, Bedfordshire LU2 8DL U.K.

www.catsaviation.com

19-13

Principles of Flight

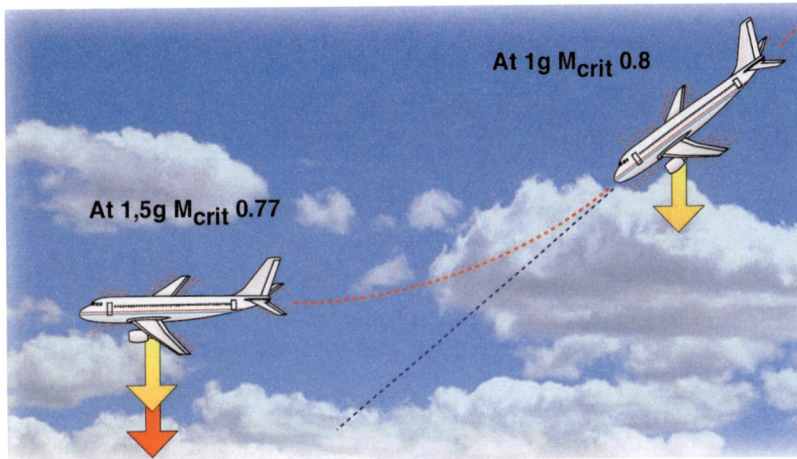

Figure 19.36

Critical Mach number decreases with an increased A.o.A i.e. C_L

19.2.6 The production of wave drag

The compressibility effect consumes energy when the flow velocity changes from supersonic to subsonic over a very short distance and heating is created by the compression. The increase in drag starts as soon as supersonic flow is reached over some part of the body at transonic speeds. This additional zero lift drag at transonic speed is called wave drag, D_M. With increased volume of the body the wave drag will increase. As a result there is a sharp increase in drag in the transonic region until the shock waves have reached the trailing edge of the body. The wave drag may be combined with the increase in drag due to shock induced boundary layer separation. After the supersonic flow becomes fully developed, the increase in the zero lift drag becomes proportional to the dynamic pressure, as it is at subsonic speed.

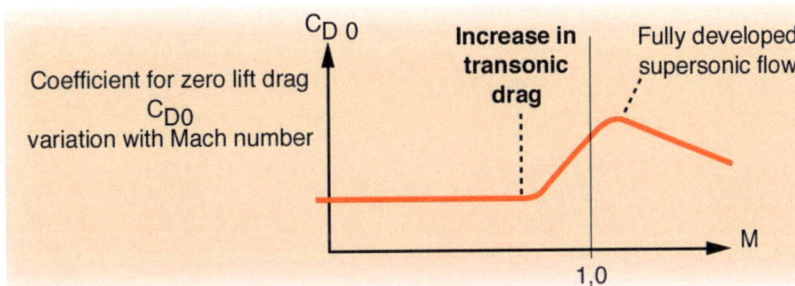

Figure 19.37

But also the induced drag will increase at M>1. Total drag increases rapidly at transonic speeds and higher.

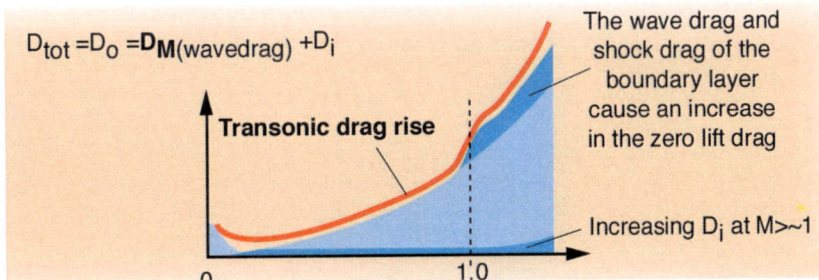

Figure 19.38

The compressibility effect creates a wave drag, D_M, causing the total drag to rapidly increase when the aircraft reaches transonic speed

Before the increase in transonic drag was fully understood in the late forties, it was called "the sound barrier", because even the fastest aircraft could not reach any higher speed despite having enormous power and despite flying in a nearly vertical dive.

19.2.7 Maximum Operating Speeds: Mach number M_{MO} and V_{MO}

In general the maximum speeds are limited by two requirements.

Firstly; the aircraft must be able to withstand certain gust intensities and gust load factors without permanent deformation. These speed limitations are denoted as for example V_{MO} and represent maximum indicated air speed at the lower altitude range. At these altitudes the max. speeds are normally constant or increase slightly with altitude. Secondly the aircraft must not show any irregularities with regard to control forces, control effectiveness and stability. This can be expected when the aircraft approaches higher Mach numbers. These speed limitations are given as Mach numbers, for example, M_{MO}. The requirement limits the speeds of the upper altitude range. At these altitudes the max. speeds are given as constant or slightly varying Mach numbers. The corresponding IAS will decrease with increasing altitude.

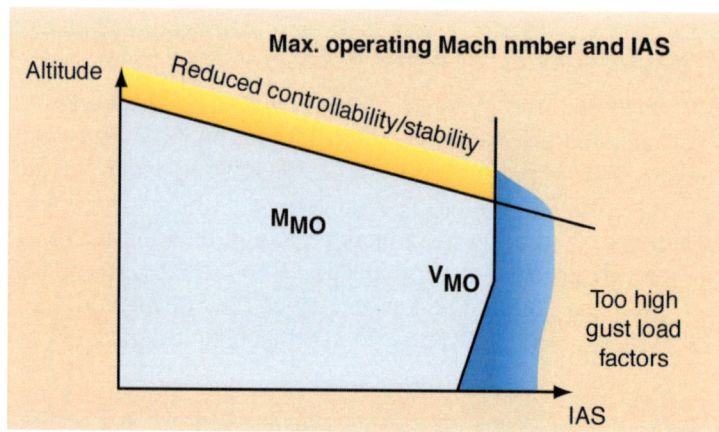

Figure 19.39

19.3 How to increase the critical Mach number

The critical Mach number can be increased by altering the wing section, by using swept wings or devices such as vortex generators.

19.3.1 Wing section

In the transonic speed range there is a large increase in drag associated with the formation of shockwaves.

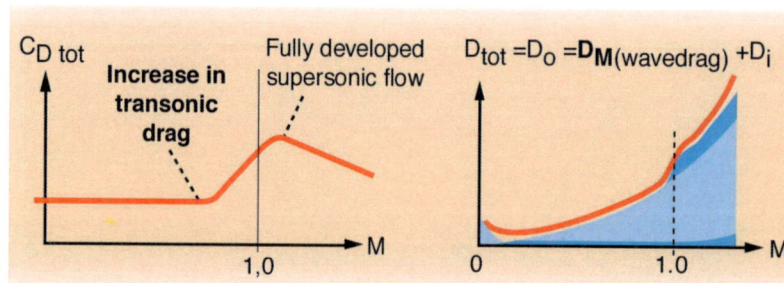

Figure 19.40

CRANFIELD AVIATION TRAINING SCHOOL LTD. PART-FCL GBR.ATO-0136
CATS INNOVATION CENTRE, LUTON, Bedfordshire LU2 8DL U.K.
www.catsaviation.com

19-15

Principles of Flight

Various design features can be used to overcome or reduce these effects by working in two possible ways. They may increase the value of the critical Mach number or, without delaying the onset of transonic flow, they may minimize its effects. Some design features work in both ways.

One of the problems is that the increase in transonic drag is caused by the same source that creates the main part of the lift, the difference in local flow velocity between the upper and lower wing surfaces. Consequently, in order to delay the development of shockwaves, a smaller increase in the local flow velocity over the wings is required. A traditional wing section may have supersonic flow velocity above the upper surface at a rather low flight Mach number.

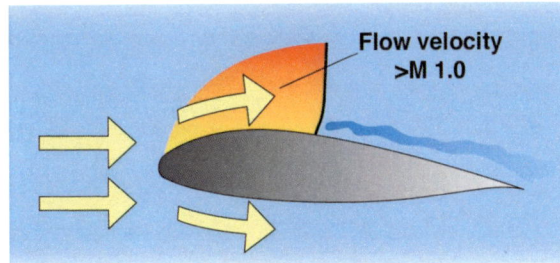

Figure 19.41

The local high flow velocity over the wing, which creates suction for lift, also causes drag increasing shockwaves and lift reducing flow separation. To minimize this effect, a wing with a very low thickness to chord ratio, or in other words, a very thin wing section, may be used.

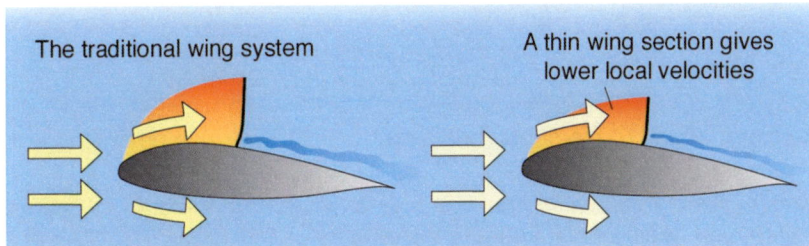

Figure 19.42

But the camber and the rounded leading edge also increase the local velocity. Thus a thin wing section with a small camber and a sharp leading edge is desirable, at least at low angles of attack.

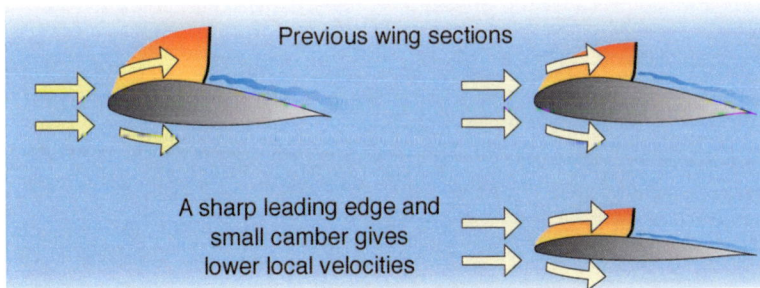

Figure 19.43

One way to increase M_{CRIT} is to have a wing airfoil section with a low thickness to chord ratio, or almost symmetrical airfoil section with a sharp leading edge

Another way to delay the development of shockwaves is to have an airfoil section with the point of maximum thickness well aft, at about half the chord, which gives a flat top pressure distribution with no high suction peak and no high velocities, which delays the development of shockwaves.

Today's modern aircraft have so-called supercritical wing sections, which allow a rather high critical Mach number together with a moderately swept wing optimized for cruising speed performance. This type of wing has a relatively large thickness, allowing a light structure and a large fuel volume, and a rather flat upper surface, flatter than a laminar section, a rounded leading edge, a cambered lower surface and a trailing edge pointing downwards.

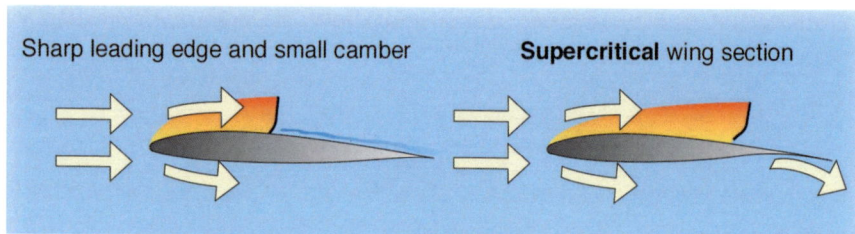

Sharp leading edge and small camber   **Supercritical** wing section

Figure 19.44

There is a difference in the ratio between C_L and C_D of a supercritical and a traditional wing section.

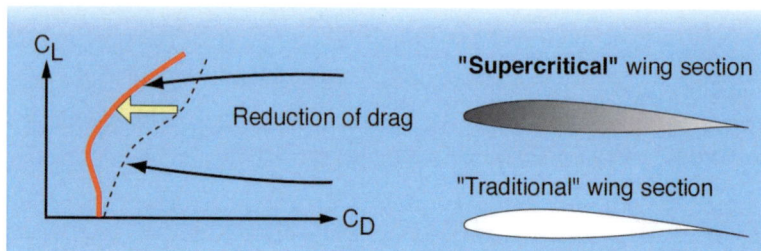

C_L

Reduction of drag

C_D

"**Supercritical**" wing section

"Traditional" wing section

Figure 19.45

However, the max angle of attack of the supercritical wing section will also be limited without having leading edge flaps or slats.

The supercritical wing section allows a rather high critical Mach number and is optimised for high speed cruising performance, despite having relative large thickness and low angle of sweep. It has a reduced max angle of attack.

19.3.2   *High-speed wings at high speed and low speed flight*

At high speeds at a given lift, the lift coefficient, which is determined by the airfoil shape and the angle of attack, may be rather low since the dynamic pressure is very high. This allows a thin and almost symmetrical wing section to be used.

$L = C_L \times \tfrac{1}{2}\rho\, V^2 \times S$
Low   High

Figure 19.46

At low speeds, however, the low C_L and restricted max angle of attack of this type of airfoil section requires a large wing area or effective high lift devices for reasonably low take-off and landing speeds.

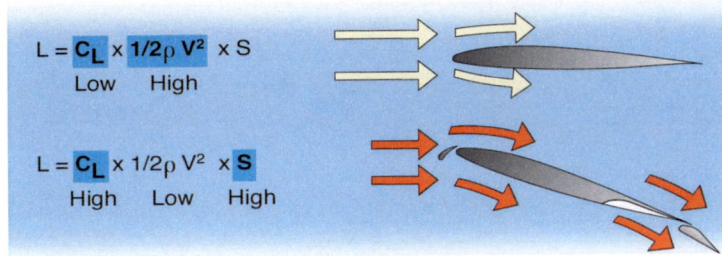

$$L = C_L \times \tfrac{1}{2}\rho \, V^2 \times S$$

Low   High

$$L = C_L \times \tfrac{1}{2}\rho \, V^2 \times S$$

High   Low   High

Figure 19.47

The wing with a wing section optimised for very high speeds normally needs advanced high lift devices for low speed.

19.3.3   *Swept wings*

The wing needs to have a certain thickness to be strong enough, especially at the wing root. One way to reduce the local flow velocity near the wing due to its thickness is to sweep it backwards.

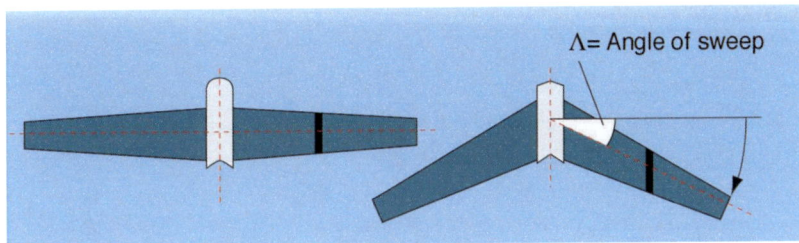

Λ = Angle of sweep

Figure 19.48

By sweeping it, the wing section will have a lower thickness/chord ratio in the direction of the airflow, and give a light structural weight to fuel volume.

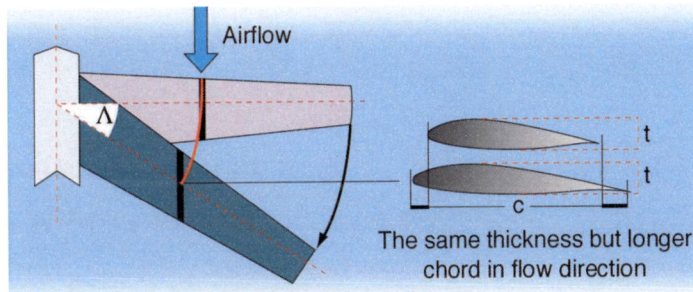

Airflow

The same thickness but longer chord in flow direction

Figure 19.49

The free stream velocity vector can be divided into components perpendicular and parallel to the leading edge. The component of the flow parallel to the leading edge does not affect the aerodynamic properties of the wing, and the pressure distribution will only depend on the velocity perpendicular to the wing section. The local flow velocity perpendicular to the wing section will then be lower than the local flow velocity parallel to the free flow. This reduces the critical Mach number.

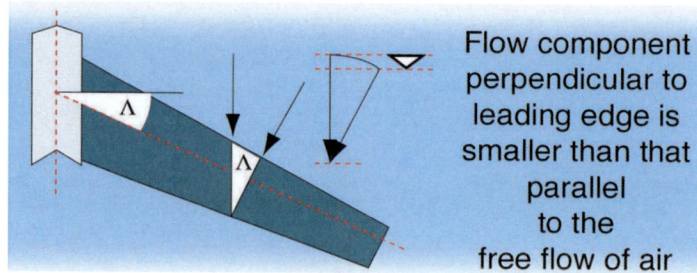

Figure 19.50

Around a swept wing, the local flow velocity perpendicular to the wing section will be lower than the local velocity parallel to the free flow. This reduces the M_{CRIT}

The flow velocity normal to the wing section will decrease with an increase in the angle of sweep of the wing, which increases the critical Mach number.

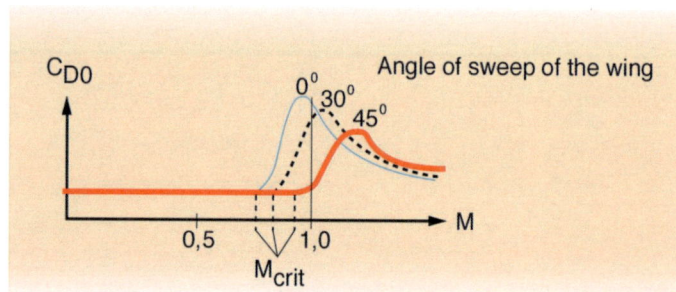

Figure 19.51

A wing with high angle of sweep needs a higher A.o.A for a given lift, which causes great induced drag at low speeds. But a given A.o.A also causes higher drag on a highly swept wing than on a moderately swept or a straight wing with the same aspect ratio.

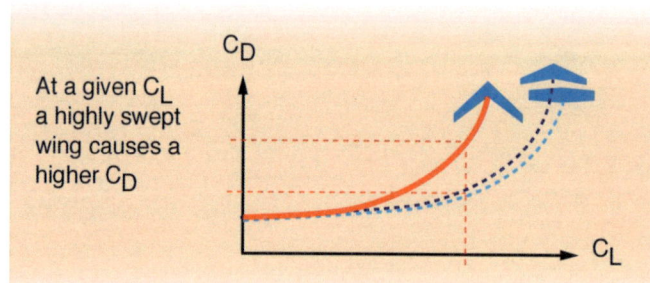

Figure 19.52

Thus, a swept wing should not be used when improved high-speed characteristics are not needed. A wing with a great angle of sweep has the advantage of a high critical Mach number.

19.3.4 Aspect Ratio

At all speeds, a high aspect ratio is required in order to keep the induced drag low. But at high speeds, the additional wave drag causes the designer to make the wing airfoil section as thin as possible. This requires a heavy structure to withstand the bending forces of wings with high aspect ratio. Therefore, in order to reduce the weight, the aspect ratio of the wings must be limited on aircraft designed for high transonic or supersonic speeds.

Figure 19.53

Due to the requirement of saving weight, wings with low aspect ratio are common on aircraft that are designed for high transonic and supersonic speeds.

An example of a wing with a very low aspect ratio is the delta wing. This planform with a very high angle of sweep at the leading edge gives a low thickness/chord ratio despite a rather thick wing root. It creates relatively low wave drag and has very positive characteristics at transonic and supersonic speeds.

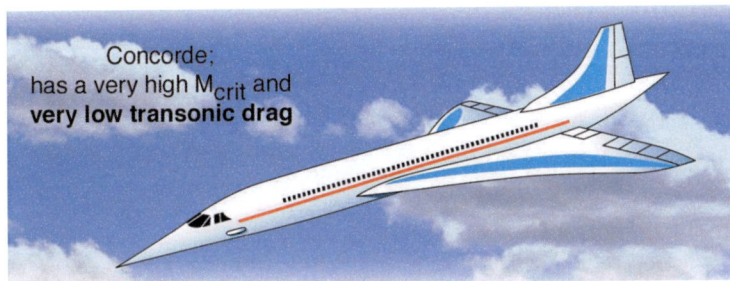

Figure 19.54

However, at low subsonic speed it requires a greater angle of attack than a swept wing for a given lift, creating very high-induced drag. The delta wing has low transonic drag and good characteristics at transonic and supersonic speeds, but it has very high induced drag at low speeds.

19.3.5   *Vortex generators*

Vortex generators may be used at all speeds but for different reasons. If the design features such as thin, or supercritical wing sections are not sufficient to allow the aircraft to reach the desired critical Mach number, the designer may add so-called vortex generators in some critical areas such as in front of the ailerons.

The vortex generators energise the boundary layer by pulling fresh air from the region above the boundary layer down to the slower flowing boundary layer. In this way the vortex generators distribute the development of shockwaves to a longer chord, reducing the effect of the boundary layer separation.

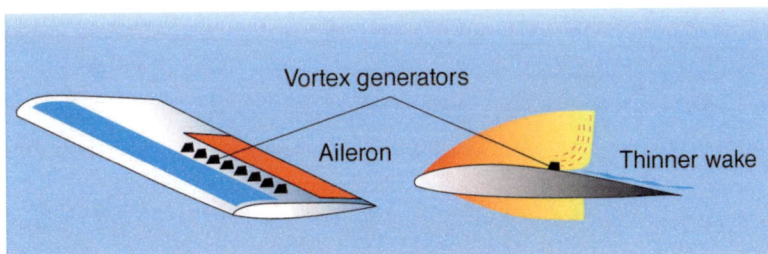

Figure 19.55

Vortex generators will of course increase the drag at subsonic speeds, but at transonic speed the transonic adverse effects might be reduced considerably.

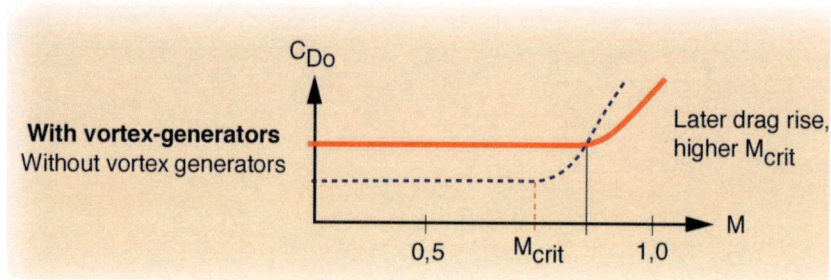

Figure 19.56

The vortex generators distribute the development of the shockwaves to a longer chord, reducing the effect on the boundary layer separation. They increase drag at subsonic speeds, but reduce drag at transonic speeds.

19.3.6 *Summary of design features to increase M_{CRIT}*

In order to increase the critical Mach number or to minimise its adverse effects, the following design features or a combination of them may be used:

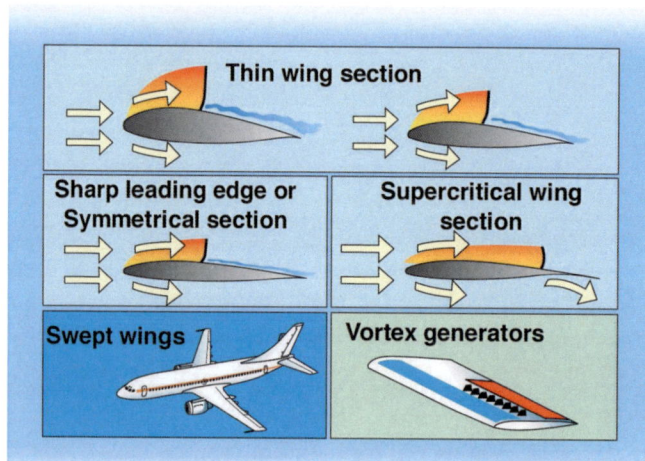

Figure 19.57 Features increasing M_{CRIT}

19.3.7 *The tailplane*

The tailplane behaves in a manner very similar to the wing. The shock drag must be kept low by using thin tails, fairly sharp leading edges and sweepback.

Figure 19.58 Tailplane

It is important from the control point of view to avoid formation of shocks waves on the tail since they result in loss of elevator effectiveness. The tail is therefore designed to have a higher critical Mach number than the wing.

19.3.8 *Wave drag and area rule*

In any aircraft configuration, in general, there is an extra amount of drag due to the fact that the shockwave from one component of the aircraft can cause flow separation on another. This wave drag can be minimised at transonic speeds by ensuring that the distribution of its total cross-sectional area follows a smooth path along the length of the axis of the aircraft. This optimised cross-sectional distribution is called the transonic area rule.

Next figure shows the cross-section area distribution of a traditional aircraft design, to the left, and of an aircraft according to the area-rule, to the right. The total reaction force to distribute the air along the aircraft will be weaker for an area-rule shaped aircraft.

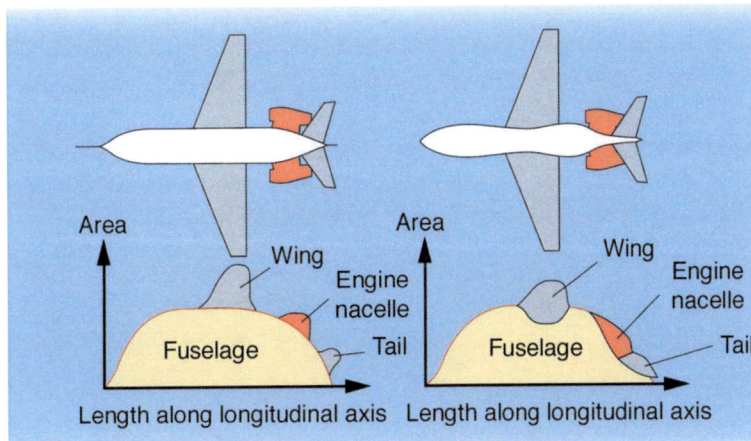

Figure 19.59

The area rule minimises wave drag at transonic and super-sonic speeds by ensuring that the total cross-sectional area of the aircraft follows a smooth path.

19.3.9 *Transonic area rule bulb.*

Figure 19.60

19.4 *Shock Stall*

19.4.1 *Aircraft behaviour during shock stall*

A stable aircraft returns to its trimmed speed after a disturbance, but this is usually not the case when reaching transonic speeds. Due to the changed position of the aerodynamic centre A.C. when the local supersonic flow over the wing increases, the ΔL forces will cause a change in pitch trim. To begin with there is a slight nose-up moment and after that a nose-down moment with increasing Mach number.

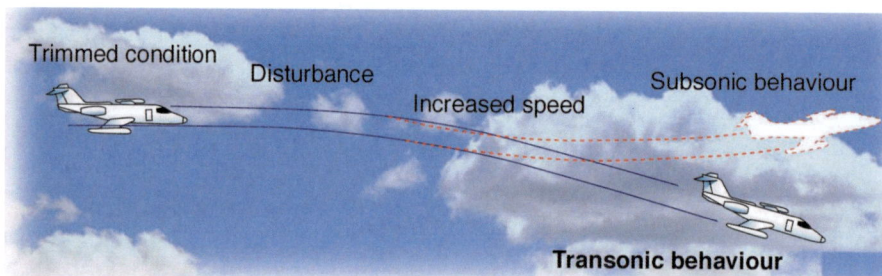

Figure 19.61

In a subsonic jet aircraft flying near its high speed limit, a slowly increasing dive may easily lead to over-speed. When reaching the speed of the critical Mach number, buffet is encountered. Since the most common reaction to (low-speed) buffet is to lower the nose and increase the speed, a high-speed buffet can lead to a dangerous situation if you are not aware of its causes.

A pull-out from a trimmed transonic dive may be very difficult to perform for aircraft designed for subsonic speeds: Firstly: an increase in stick force is caused by the increased stability due to the different pressure distribution over the wing and elevator surfaces than at pure subsonic velocity.

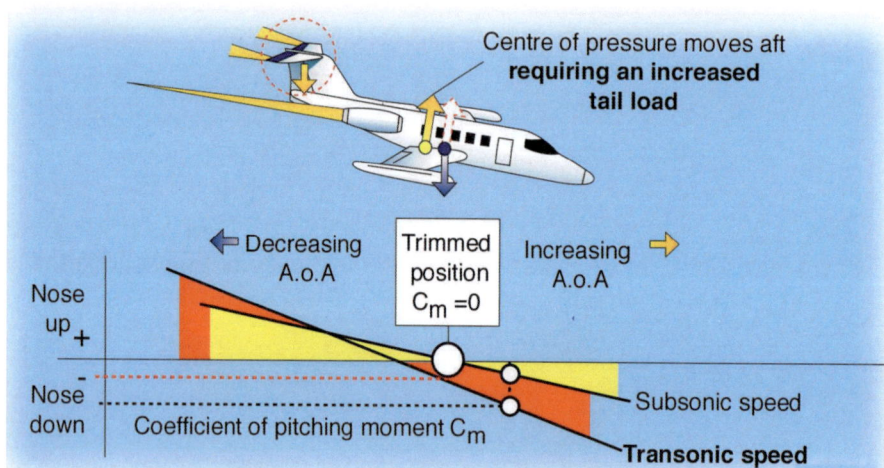

Figure 19.62

The downwash over the tail will also be reduced so that the nose down moment may become so large that the elevator angle for trim will be too small. The aircraft will slowly go into an increasing dive.

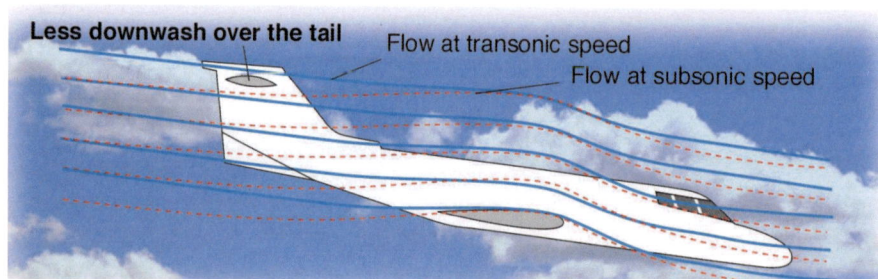

Figure 19.63

Secondly: shock induced flow separation at the tail may result in a significant reduction of elevator effectiveness.

19.4.2   *Reduced elevator effectiveness*

At subsonic velocity over the tail, the deflection of the elevator changes the pressure distribution and so the lift of the whole unit, also in front of the elevator.

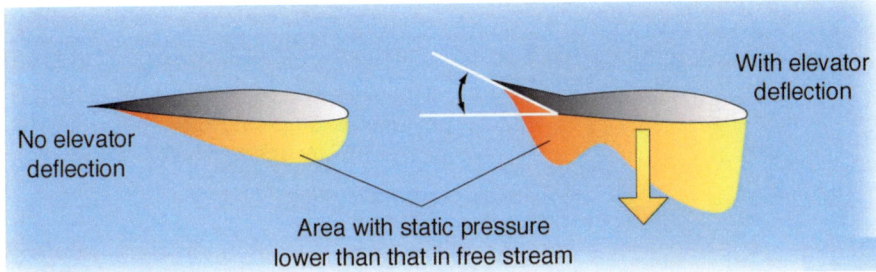

Figure 19.64

However, when flying at high transonic or supersonic speeds, the flow in front of the elevator does not "feel" the changes in pressure caused by the elevator deflection. The pressure distribution in front of the elevator is therefore not changed so the total effect of an elevator deflection is much smaller at supersonic than at subsonic velocities.

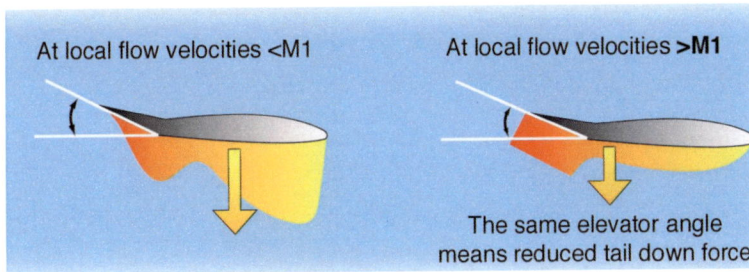

Figure 19.65

The reduced effectiveness of the control surface requires a large increase in the angle of the control surface to obtain the increased trim force.

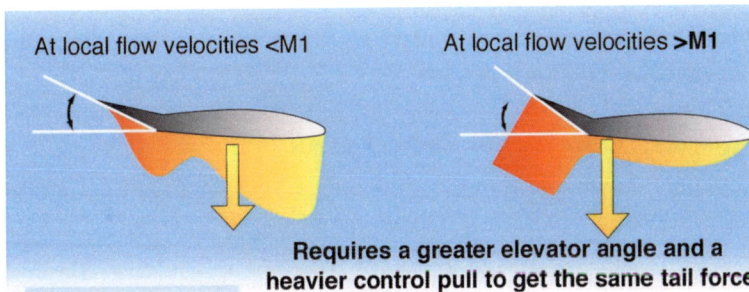

Figure 19.66

Another effect of supersonic flow around the control surfaces is that the centre of pressure of the control surface moves aft due to the change from approximately triangular to rectangular pressure distribution. The centre of pressure is moved to half the chord of the surface in supersonic flow.

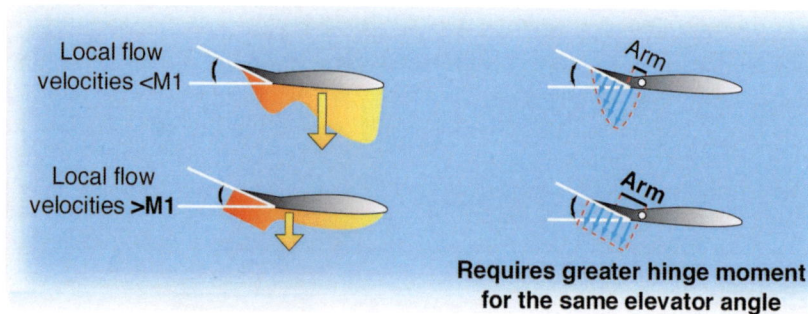

Figure 19.67

Thus there is a difficult combination of a control force heavier than normal which simultaneously needs a deflection much greater than normal. In transonic flow the control force is heavier than normal but also needs a deflection much greater than normal. When flying into high transonic speed, shock induced flow separation on the horizontal tail surfaces reduces the available tail down force a lot, which in the most severe cases may lead to an uncontrolled dive! However, this should not happen until above M_{MO}.

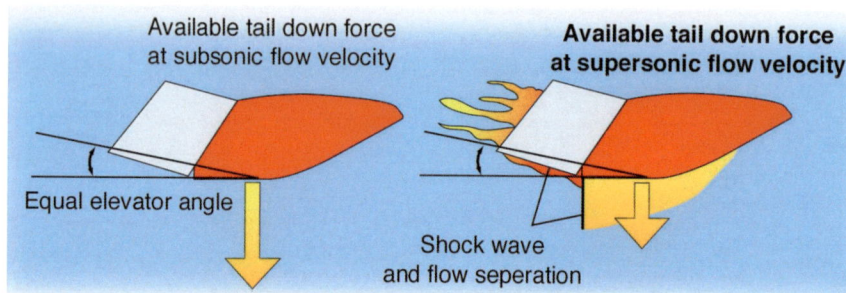

Figure 19.68

The effect of an elevator deflection is much smaller at supersonic than subsonic velocities. Reduced effectiveness of the control surfaces requires a large increase in the control surface angle. When there is supersonic flow over a surface, the centre of pressure is moved near half the chord of that surface. The aft moment of the resultant force on the control surface increases the required moment and the stick force needed to deflect the surface to a certain angle. The stick force required to trim or manoeuvre an aircraft at high transonic or supersonic speeds may be excessive. A pull-out from a transonic dive may be very difficult to perform for aircraft designed for subsonic speeds only.

19.4.3 *Use of variable incidence stabiliser*

One way of improving the pitch control is to make a pull-out with the help of the trim if this rotates the whole stabiliser. The force downward will be greater at a lower angle.

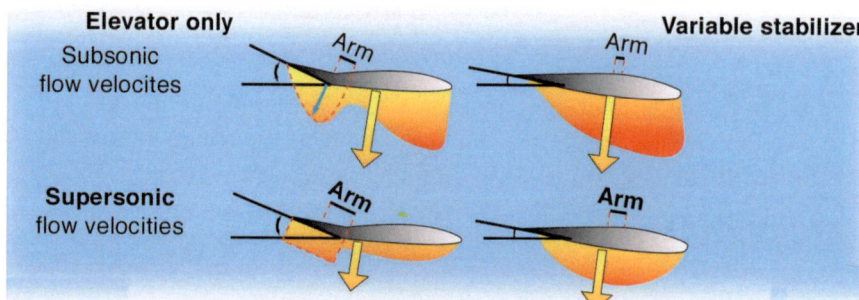

Figure 19.69

Pull as hard as you can and use the elevator trim to reach the maximum load factor. However, as soon as you feel you have regained control, complete the manoeuvre on the elevator alone. Do not use the stabiliser

CRANFIELD AVIATION TRAINING SCHOOL LTD. PART-FCL GBR.ATO-0136
CATS INNOVATION CENTRE, LUTON, Bedfordshire LU2 8DL U.K.   www.catsaviation.com

19-25

Principles of Flight

more than necessary, otherwise the aircraft might pitch hard nose up as the Mach number decreases and the elevator response increases.

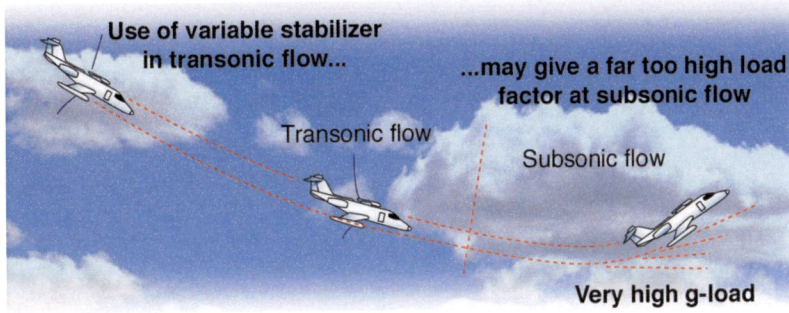

Figure 19.70

A moving tail improves the pitch control at transonic and supersonic velocities.

19.4.4   *Pull-up in a transonic dive*

The shock stall also affects the control in yaw and roll, making the total manoeuvrability difficult. Notice that if, for example, left rudder is used to pick up a lowered right wing, it will only increase the local velocity over the right wing causing shock stall, and consequently it may have the opposite effect. Therefore, the ailerons alone should be used even though they will be very heavy. During this pull-out, the loss of altitude will be much greater than expected.

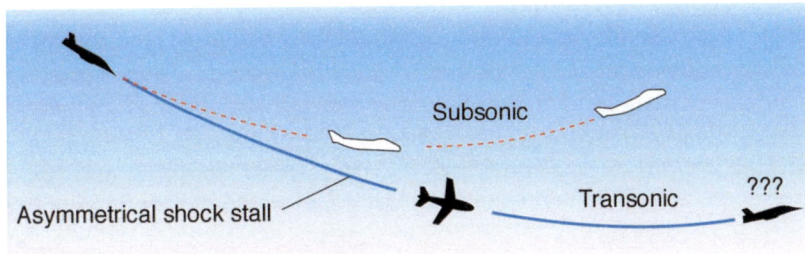

Figure 19.71

There also is a risk in pulling out too rapidly. The speed at which the high-speed buffet occurs is decreased as the load factor is increased and the shockwaves will be stronger. If a dive near the critical Mach number is not correctly recovered from, a rapid pull-out may increase the load factor too much and the aircraft will be above the actual critical Mach number for straight and level flight. In that high load factor situation, shock stall may occur, making the aircraft uncontrollable for a moment.

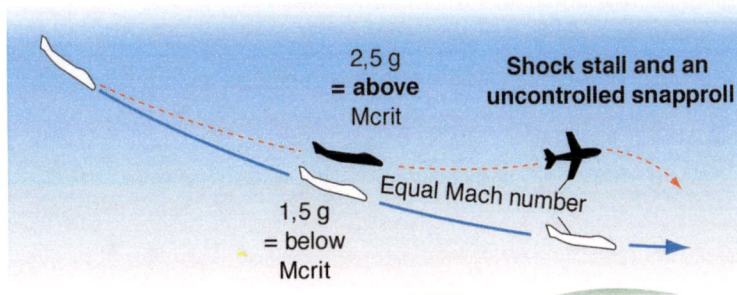

Figure 19.72

The movement rearwards of the centre of pressure lowers the nose further, making the situation worse by causing an additional increase in speed. The speed may now be well above the speed of the critical Mach number at 1 g load factor.

Figure 19.73

In the worst of situations, the aircraft may be completely out of control at a steep angle of dive, or will lose too much altitude before a complete recovery.

An attempt at too rapid a pull-out may increase the load factor too much causing the speed of the aircraft to be above the critical Mach number for straight flight and resulting in a shock stall.

A shock stall may make the aircraft uncontrollable for a moment. This lowers the nose, and the simultaneous rearward movement of the C.P. will lower the nose further, and cause an uncontrolled increase in speed.

If the aircraft is not recovered properly from a slight dive when flying at a speed higher than the allowed upper limit, it may get into an uncontrolled dive.

19.4.5 *Shock stall recovery procedure*

When in shock stall, the aircraft may lose its stability, especially its lateral stability, due to the asymmetrical development of the shock stall over the wings. That effect may lead to a steep dive with a further increase in speed - a very dangerous situation. Consequently, when approaching a shock stall it is very important to pull out of it without going into it again. It is best to decrease speed to well below the critical Mach number. Thus, immediately decrease the engine thrust as much as possible. However, when reducing power to idle, the hydraulic pressure needed to change the angle of the elevator may be too low. This varies with aircraft type, so only reduce to the recommended lowest power setting, i.e. flight idle.

Normally, aircraft capable of flying at transonic speeds have some kind of speed brakes. These are very efficient at high speeds, but spoilers on the wings in speed brake mode may cause roll disturbance.

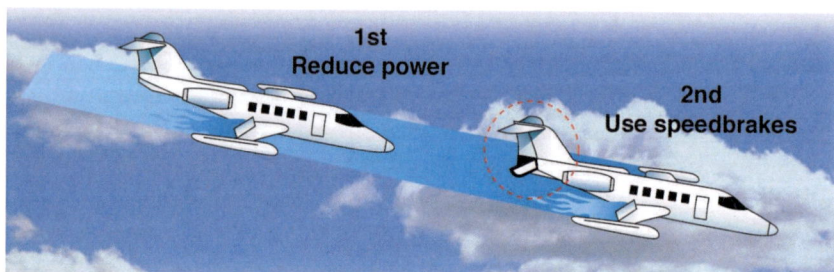

Figure 19.74

The next step is to pull up, but, that pull-up must be very smooth, say 1.5 g, because a pull-up requires more lift from the wing. More lift is created by a higher angle of attack and this will also increase the speed of the local airflow over the wings. This increase in speed over the wings may lead to another shock stall at a lower indicated Mach number than in unaccelerated flight.

19.5   *High altitude limitations*

19.5.1   *Stalling speed and buffet onset diagram*

The speed envelope, within which the aircraft can operate, is limited at the lower end by the stalling speed. At the upper end, the limit is set by the speed at which it structurally can withstand only a small vertical gust, or at which it starts to have problems with regard to controllability due to Mach effects.

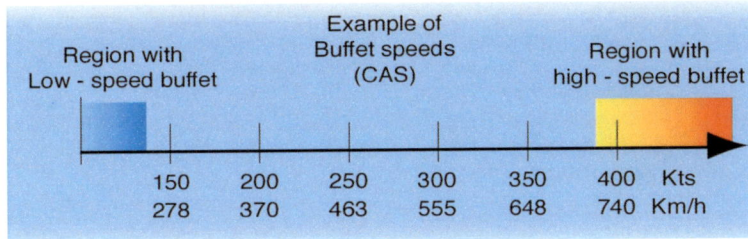

Figure 19.75

The indicated stalling speed for general aviation aircraft is constant with altitude. But, because of the Mach effects, this is not the case for an aircraft at high altitudes. Mach effects reduce CL max and also cause compressibility error of the airspeed indicator. These two effects cause the indicated stalling speed to increase with altitude.

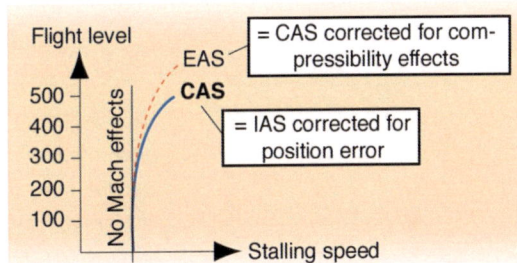

Figure 19.76 V_S increases with altitude for high speed aircraft

The calibrated stalling speed, V_S CAS, increases with altitude

The main factor affecting the buffet speeds is the weight, and/or the load factor, which has a great influence on these speeds. In the figure below there is an example of calibrated stalling speed in relation to weight. Higher weight gives a higher buffet speed.

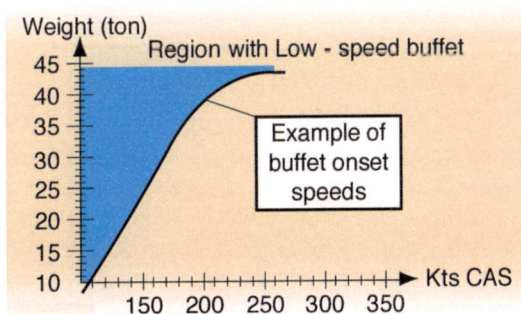

Figure 19.77

The limit of the high-speed buffet will instead decrease with increased weight. This is so because the greater amount of lift causes higher local velocities over the wing and shockwaves at a lower speed.

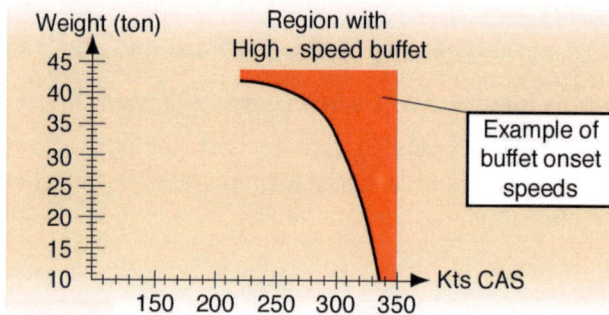

Figure 19.78 The limit of the high-speed buffet decreases with increased weight.

Since both the lower and the upper buffet speeds are influenced by the actual weight and the available power, we get a weight and speed envelope for a given altitude like this example.

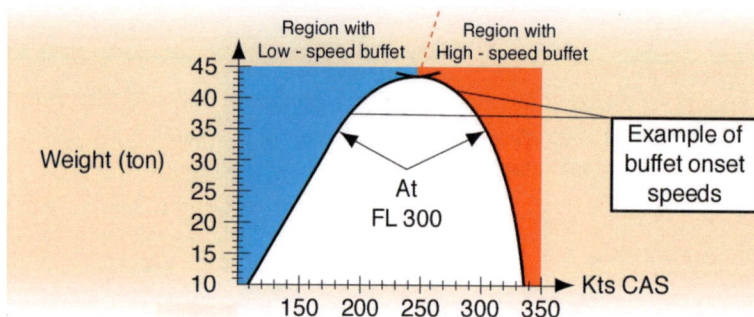

Figure 19.79

A gross weight of 30 tons at the standard altitude of 30000', based on 1013 hPa and designated FL 300, can only be maintained at a speed between 170 and 315 KT calibrated airspeed. At speeds below or above these the aircraft will experience buffeting and may stall. Notice the max weight for flight due to lift limitations of approx. 43 tonnes.

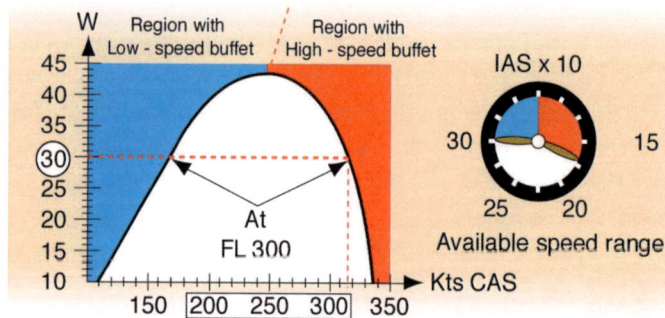

Figure 19.80

At a higher altitude, for instance at FL 350, we will have a narrower speed envelope at 30 tonnes, and it is no longer possible to fly at a gross weight of above 37 tonnes.

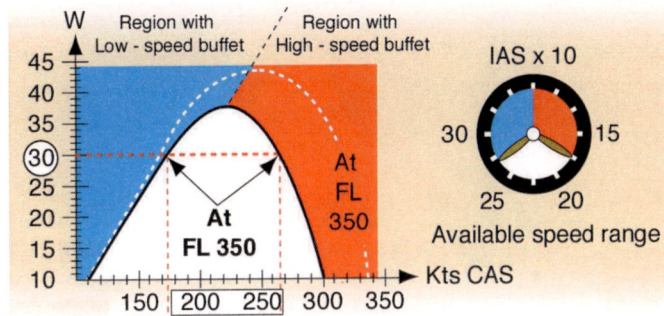

Figure 19.81

At an even higher altitude, of 40000', the speed envelope is very narrow. With a gross weight of 26 tonnes, a small decrease in speed will put you into a low-speed buffet and a small increase in speed will put you into a high-speed buffet.

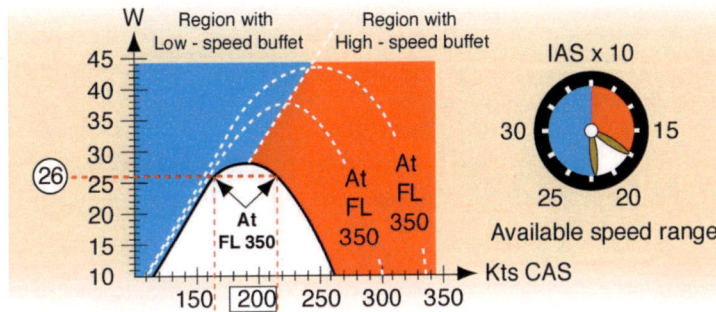

Figure 19.82

At very high altitudes a small decrease in speed will put you into a low-speed buffet and a small increase in speed will put you into a high-speed buffet.

19.5.2   *Coffin corner*

In these conditions, an increase in load factor caused by a vertical gust or by making a turn will put you, so to speak, to a point of no return.

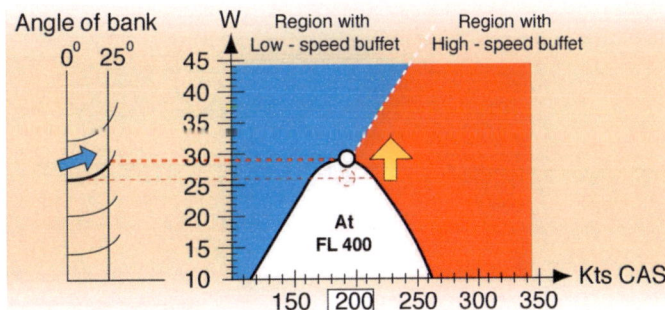

Figure 19.83

With this combination of altitude, weight and available power, you will have low and high speed simultaneously and you will lose control of the aircraft. The point on the graph where speed is too low and too high at the same time is called: coffin corner.

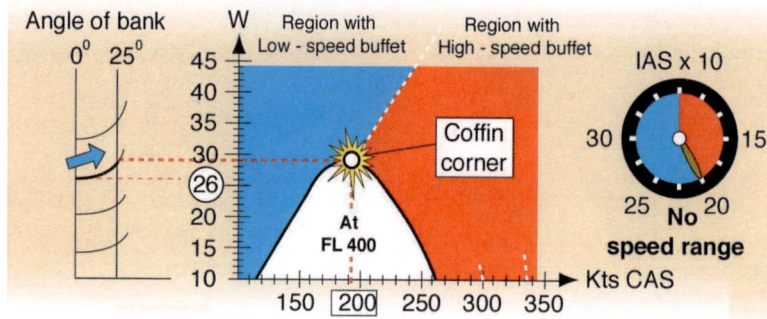

Figure 19.84

When flying in a very narrow speed envelope, it is easy to enter an uncontrolled situation. The point in the speed envelope for a certain altitude where your speed is too low and too high at the same time is called the coffin corner. Since all aircraft are able to fly only due to the speed relative to the air and since there is a lower and an upper speed limit, there will be a limited speed and altitude envelope where level flight at a constant speed can be maintained.

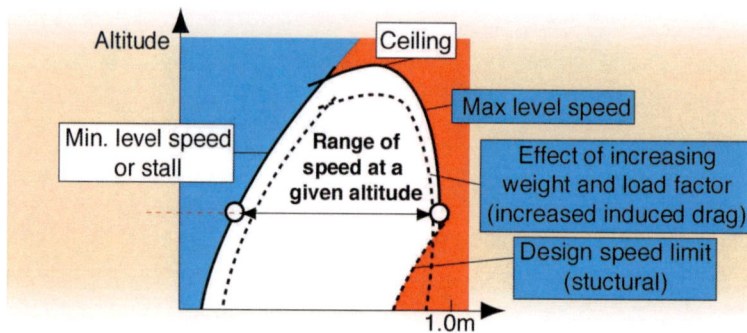

Figure 19.85

Both the lower and the upper speeds are limited by the actual weight and the available power, giving a speed envelope for a given altitude. If a very high altitude is desirable for a subsonic aircraft with moderate engine power, the stalling speed must be very low as well as the induced drag. If a higher altitude is desirable without the trouble of flying with a very limited speed range, the aircraft must be able to fly supersonic.

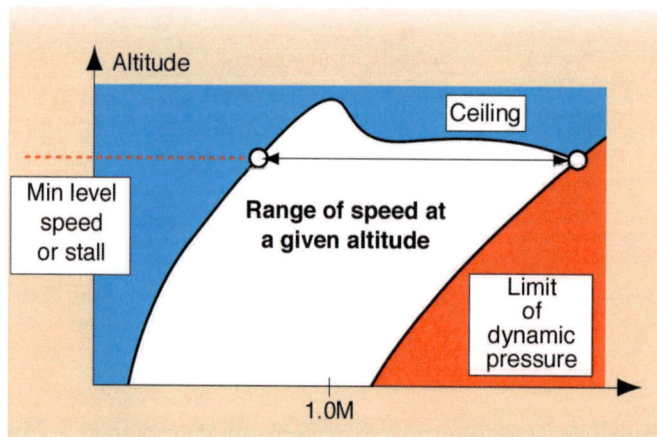

Figure 19.86

Thus, in order to fly at very high altitudes, the aircraft has to be able to fly at very low calibrated airspeeds such as the famous large span U-2 reconnaissance aeroplane, or it has to be a supersonic aircraft like the Concorde.

CRANFIELD AVIATION TRAINING SCHOOL LTD. PART-FCL GBR.ATO-0136
CATS INNOVATION CENTRE, LUTON, Bedfordshire LU2 8DL U.K.

www.catsaviation.com

19-31

Principles of Flight

Figure 19.87

19.5.3   *Diagram of the onset speed of buffet and stall*

The low-speed and high-speed limits for a given jet aircraft can be found in the stall and buffet onset diagram as shown in figure 19.109. The upper curved lines represent altitude or flight level. Where these curves are pointed up to the left they represent high-speed buffeting, while where the curve points to the lower left they represent the low-speed buffeting. In this diagram, only the stalling speeds for zero flap at sea level is shown. At the lower part of the diagram the actual gross weight and angle of bank are noted. From this graph the stalling speed, the speed limit for low-speed buffet and the speed where the high-speed buffeting starts for a given weight and bank angle, can be found. The procedure is: follow the guidelines downward from the actual gross weight, (17.5 tonnes) to the horizontal line through the angle of bank of 40°. From this intersection, straight up to the actual flight level curve 350 (35000'). That gives the following speeds; stalling speed (zero flap) 135 KIAS, low-speed buffet at 148 KIAS and high-speed buffet at 283 KIAS.

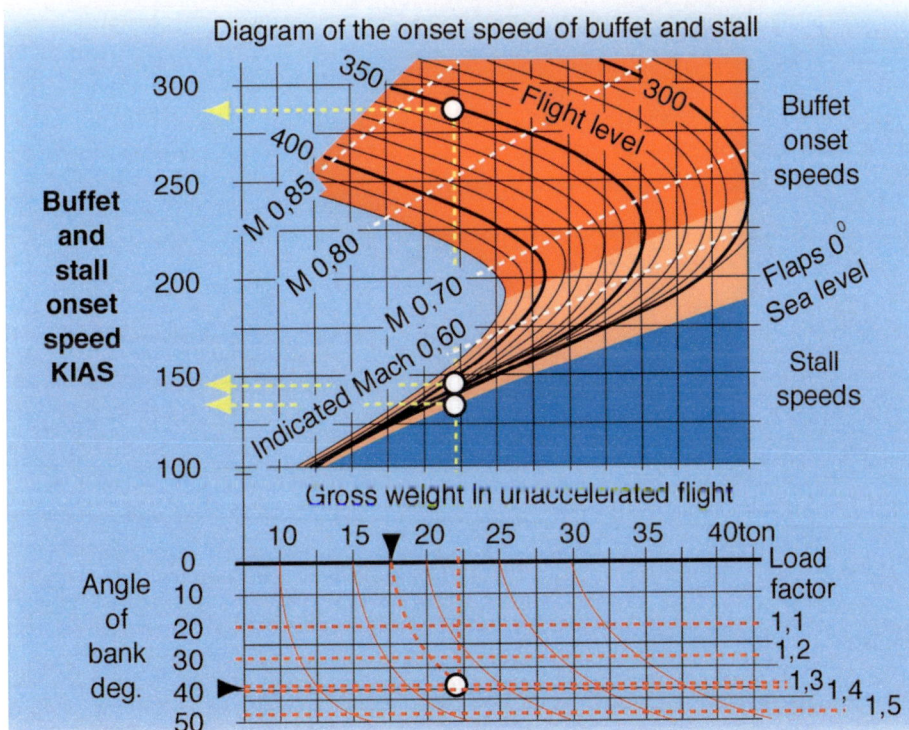

Figure 19.88

You may also find out that with the same gross weight but with an angle of bank of 48° the "coffin corner" will be reach at flight level 420. In a stall and buffet onset diagram you find the flyable speed range for different gross weight, angles of bank and altitudes.

CRANFIELD AVIATION TRAINING SCHOOL LTD. PART-FCL GBR.ATO-0136
CATS INNOVATION CENTRE, LUTON, Bedfordshire LU2 8DL U.K.

www.catsaviation.com

19-32

Principles of Flight

19.5.4   *Mach trim*

Trim changes with Mach number in transonic flight. This will also change the stick force. Below you see a graph of the elevator stick force required to maintain a number of Mach numbers over the critical Mach range from an initially trimmed condition. As shown by the solid line, the stick must first be pushed forward and then pulled backwards to maintain the pitch angle. This change in stick force due to increased Mach number can be corrected or compensated for artificially, by a device called the Mach trim. This is a device that receives an input of the Mach number and is programmed to feed into the elevator, or variable stabiliser, a signal proportional to the Mach number. The result is a stick force that is higher than the force required to increase speed.

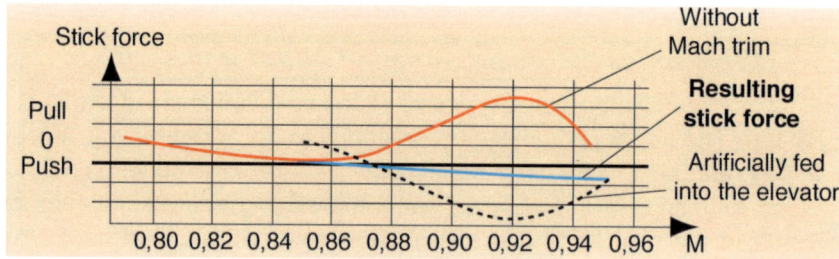

Figure 19.89

The Mach trim is a device which compensates for the elevator stick force in order to make it easier to maintain a range of Mach numbers over the critical Mach range from an initially trimmed condition.

19.6   *Superstall*

19.6.1   *Disadvantages of swept wings. Lift/drag.*

Designing aircraft is always a matter of compromise. Design features that are good for low-speeds are usually not as good for high speeds and vice versa. For instance a swept wing will have good high speed qualities at relatively high critical Mach numbers, while it will have some disadvantages at low speeds.

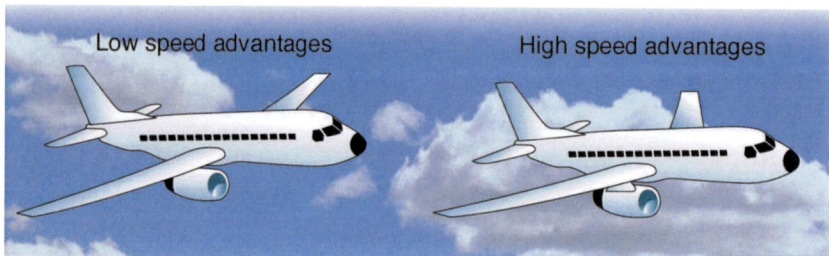

Figure 19.90

A swept wing creates less lift and more drag at a given angle of attack than a straight wing. When the wing is swept, a slightly higher angle of attack is needed to create the same lift coefficient. These factors cause greater induced drag.

CRANFIELD AVIATION TRAINING SCHOOL LTD. PART-FCL GBR.ATO-0136
CATS INNOVATION CENTRE, LUTON, Bedfordshire LU2 8DL U.K.   www.catsaviation.com
19-33   Principles of Flight

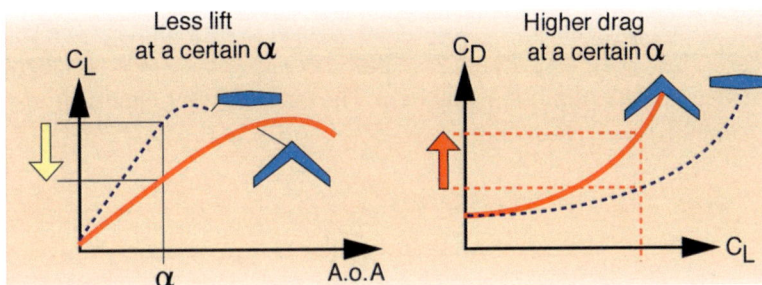

Figure 19.91

19.6.2   *Wing tip stall*

Another disadvantage of highly swept wings is the possibility of going into deep stall or a locked-in situation. A contributing factor to deep stall is the wing tip stall of the main wing.

Figure 19.92

With swept wings at high angles of attack, the air will flow towards the lower pressure area further back and out near the wing tips. This will make the boundary layer very long with low energy flow near the wing tips. This low energy flow will separate earlier at a lower angle of attack than the flow closer to the wing root, which is located further forward. The centre of pressure will thus move forward, causing a pitch-up.

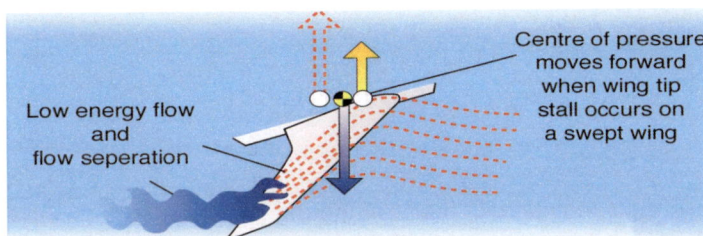

Figure 19.93

The centre of pressure moves forward due to the low energy flow near the wing lips, which separates at a lower angle of attack than the flow nearer the wing root. As the angle of sweep of a wing increases, the pitch-up becomes an important factor in stall development. The initial flow separation may start at the wing tips, well before the actual stall has been reached, and the aircraft may pitch up so rapidly that it may be impossible to stop the rotation before a deep stall has been reached.

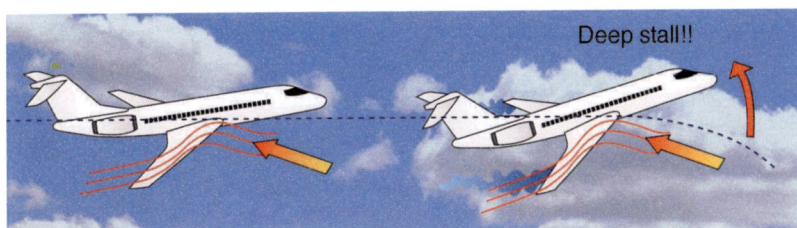

Figure 19.94

CRANFIELD AVIATION TRAINING SCHOOL LTD. PART-FCL GBR.ATO-0136
CATS INNOVATION CENTRE, LUTON, Bedfordshire LU2 8DL U.K.

www.catsaviation.com

19-34

Principles of Flight

However, this behaviour is not acceptable for a certified aircraft. In such cases, an artificial device such as stick shaker or stick pusher has to be installed to limit the max allowable A.o.A. A swept wing may have wing tip stall well before the actual stall has been reached. The aircraft may pitch up so rapidly that it may be impossible to stop the rotation.

19.6.3 *Side slip characteristics*

Another disadvantage of a highly swept wing is its sideslip characteristics. A straight wing can side slip considerably without getting out of control. A swept wing, however, due to the strong yaw-roll coupling, may rapidly roll to the lee side of the side slip. When side slipping, the difference in lift between the forward pointing wing (on the windward side) and the aft pointing wing (lee wing) is caused by the difference in the actual span facing the relative free stream flow.

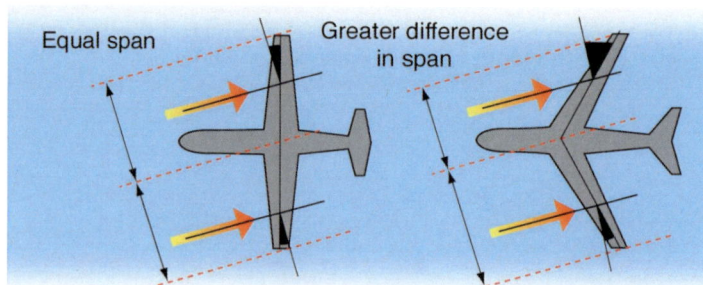

Figure 19.95

A rolling moment towards the lee wing is thus created.

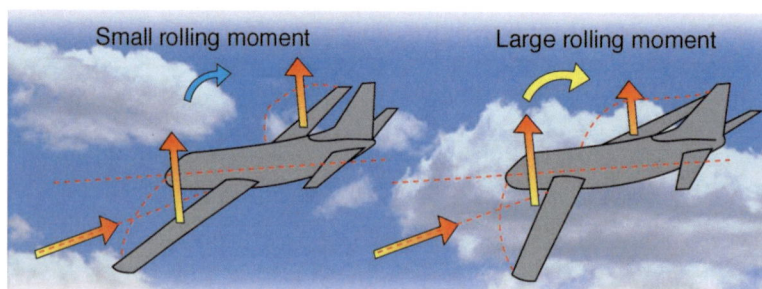

Figure 19.96

When the sideslip is deliberately maintained, the rolling moment upwards is compensated for by the use of the ailerons on the other wing. But there is a risk. The longer boundary layer over the lee wing creates a low energy flow over the aileron.

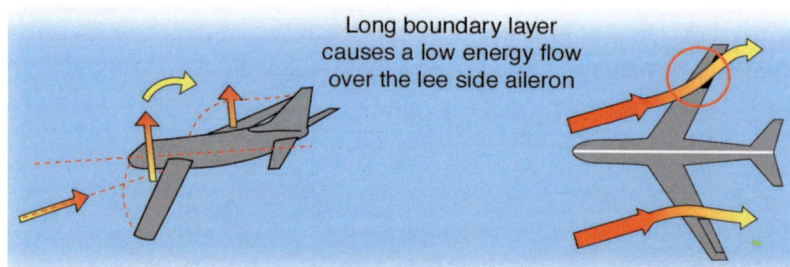

Figure 19.97

The low energy boundary layer over the downgoing aileron causes that wing to stall much earlier than the windward wing. This asymmetrical stall may cause an uncontrolled snaproll.

CRANFIELD AVIATION TRAINING SCHOOL LTD. PART-FCL GBR.ATO-0136
CATS INNOVATION CENTRE, LUTON, Bedfordshire LU2 8DL U.K.

www.catsaviation.com

19-35

Principles of Flight

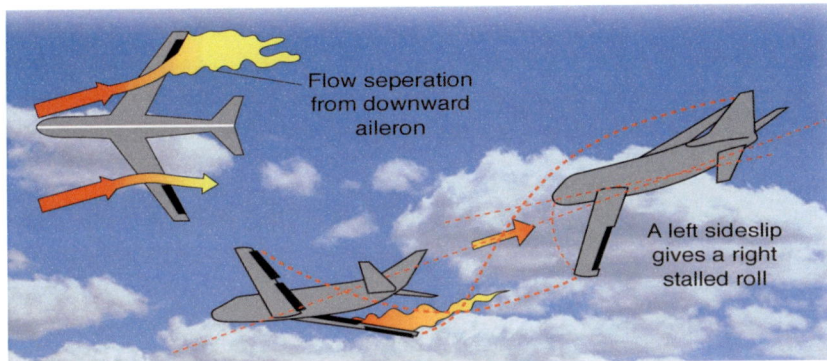

Figure 19.98

A swept wing, when side slipping, will have a greater asymmetric lift over the wing span. The upper lee wing will meet the airflow with a lower span, losing more lift. A rolling moment towards the lee wing is thus created, making the yaw-roll coupling very obvious. To deliberately maintain a sideslip of a swept wing aircraft, e.g. to the left, against the yaw produced roll, to the right, may lead to an uncontrolled snaproll. One way to reduce the loss of lift from the aft pointed wing is to design the aircraft with a negative dihedral, also known as anhedral. With a negative dihedral the lee wing will have a slightly higher A.o.A. than the windward wing, making the difference in lift less prominent.

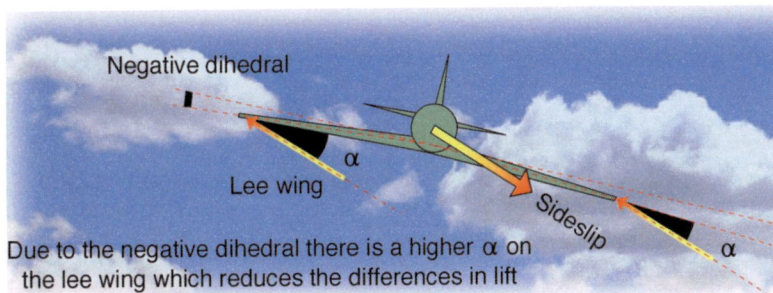

Figure 19.99

19.6.4 Disadvantages of T-tail

When properly balanced, an aircraft with straight wings and a low tail (compared to the wing plane) is stable and will lower its nose and recover from the stall without any problems. When in the stalled condition, the wing wake passes more or less straight aft and flows above the low tail.

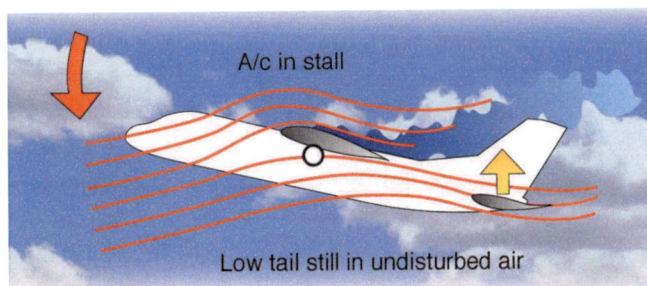

Figure 19.100

This leaves the tail working in high energy air where it experiences a sharp increase in positive incidence, causing upward lift. This lift then assists the nose down pitch of the whole aircraft and a deep stall condition is avoided.

The moment graph in the next figure shows a more or less stable aircraft at all angles of attack. An increase in the angle of attack will give a greater or lesser increase in the nose down moment, also in a stalled condition. The nose down moment will tend to reduce the angle of attack, making the aircraft stable.
The following moment curves are not actual ones but have been drawn in order to better illustrate the effect.

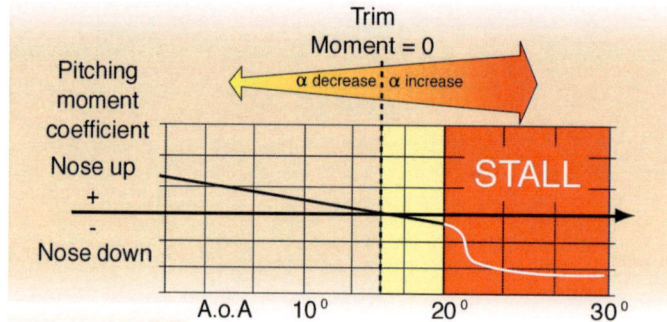

Figure 19.101

A stable aircraft will experience a greater or lesser increase in the nose down moment also in a stalled condition. However, aircraft with mid tail or high tail may be unstable in certain conditions at high angles of attack, for instance when the centre of gravity is too far aft. This will make the moment curve flatter, and the loss of lift at the trailing edge near and in the stall, together with the downwash over the tail, causes a pitch-up instead of a pitch down.

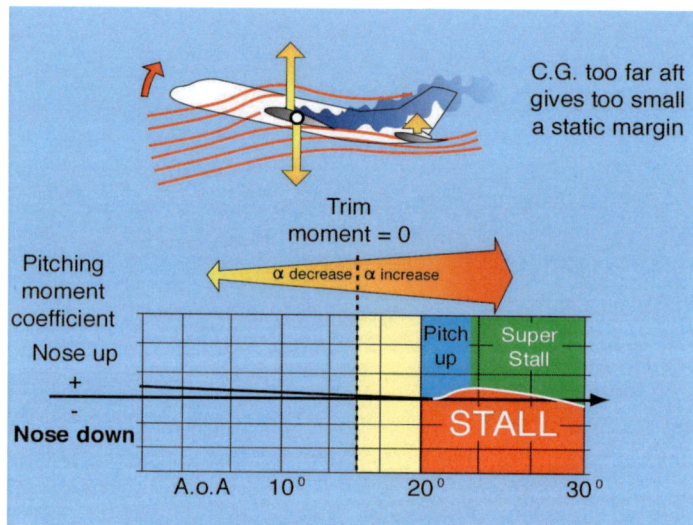

Figure 19.102

The aircraft may go into a locked situation called deep stall or a superstall. However, an aircraft with T-tail may go into a deep stall or locked situation despite having a normal centre of gravity. It is possible that the tail will be in the wing and fuselage wake during the stall and consequently lose the pitch down capacity necessary for recovery.

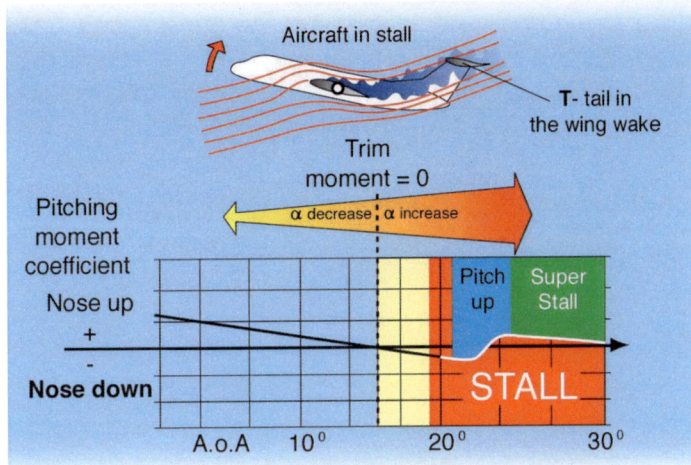

Figure 19.103

In addition, a T-tailed aircraft with a long slim fuselage can make the condition worse. At high A.o.A the forebody itself may cause a pitch- up before the stall and flatten the moment curve when in the stall.

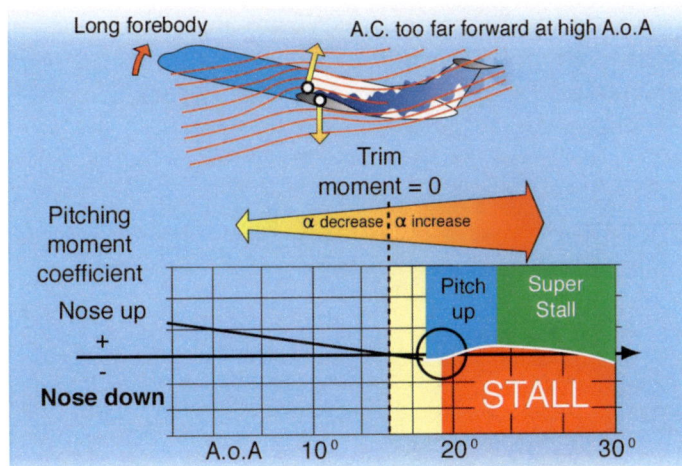

Figure 19.104

A long slim fuselage at a high A.o.A changes the surrounding airflow like a wing with an extremely high angle of sweep. When the fuselage reaches a certain angle of attack, the flow separates into vortices above the body which may reach the horizontal tail. These vortices may push the tail downwards, rapidly increasing the angle of attack into a deep stall, but also causing directional disturbances. Going into a deep stall may be the result of a combination of wing tip stall, long forebody and aft mounted engines. If the downwash becomes great enough, the downward force on the stabiliser cannot be counteracted by full downward elevator deflection. The aircraft then becomes locked at a high angle of attack that rapidly leads to a deep stall condition.

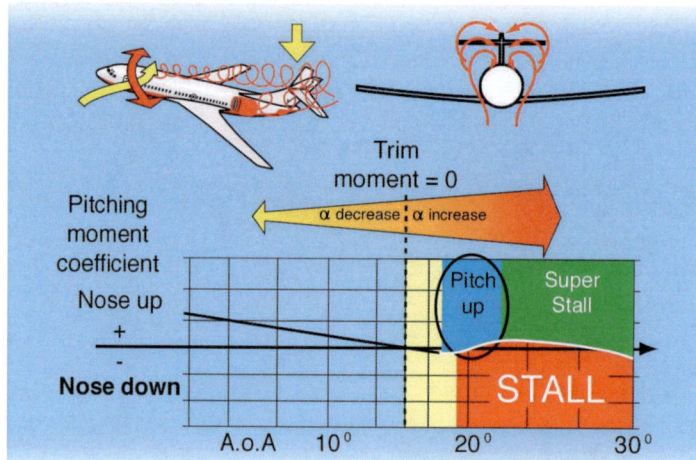

Figure 19.105

A T-tailed aircraft may go into a deep stall or a locked condition in spite of its normal centre of gravity.
A long slim forebody at high A.o.A may cause a pitch-up, especially if body vortices hit the horizontal tail, thus making it difficult to avoid the stall or to recover from the stall.

19.6.5   *Superstall*

When being locked into a high A.o.A. an increase in the angle of attack causes the drag to increase faster than the lift, and the aircraft decelerates rapidly and sinks.

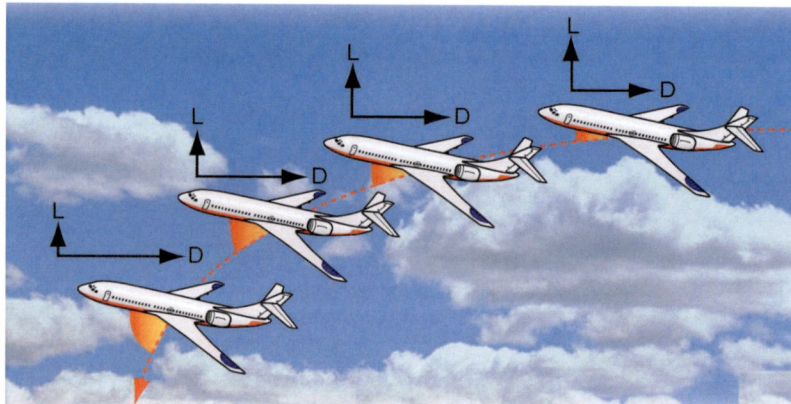

Figure 19.106

The increasing tendency to sink at almost constant pitch attitude results in a rapid increase in the angle of attack as the flight path becomes deflected downwards. Once the stall has developed and most of the lift has been lost, the aircraft will start to sink rapidly; this is accompanied by a further rapid increase in the angle of attack. In superstall, the flight controls are completely useless when trying to control the aircraft.
A closer look at the moment curve of the area for superstall shows that the aircraft will be in a stable situation. An increase in the angle of attack will cause a nose down moment, reducing the angle of attack again. When the A.o.A has been reduced, it will cause a nose up moment which increases the stall again. In such condition the aircraft will fall like a leaf changing slightly in pitch.

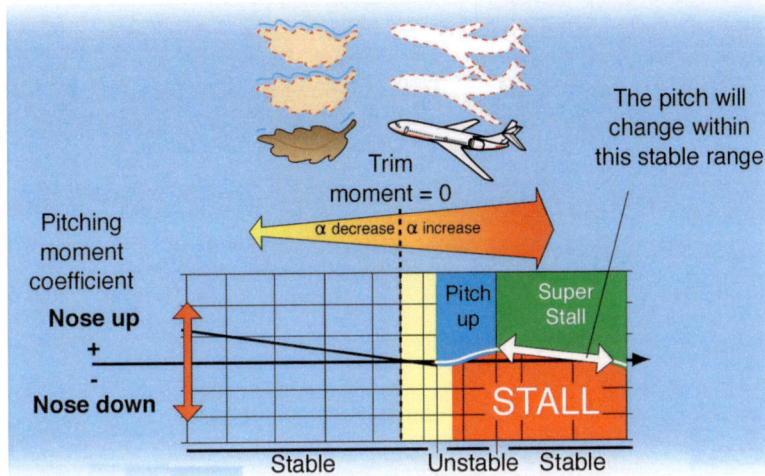

Figure 19.107

Due to this stable stalled condition it is very difficult to lower the nose in order to gain speed. In addition, the drag in a complete stalled situation is very high, making it impossible to gain speed by use of engine power only. In other words, it may be very difficult to recover from.

19.6.6 How to avoid superstall

Since wing tip stall on an aircraft with swept wings may put the aircraft into a deep stall, it is necessary to avoid it. Therefore, aircraft with highly swept wings may have devices to minimise the flow separation near the wing tips. These devices are: boundary layer fences on the upper surface of the wing, and on the leading edge of the wing vortilons and saw-teeth.

19.6.7 Stick pushers

When an aircraft has failed to meet the stalling requirements by normal aerodynamic means such as use of vortilons, that is; the natural stall is quite unacceptable, it may be equipped with a stick-pusher. This device pushes the stick or the control column forward in order to avoid stall by reducing the angle of attack before a pitch-up or deep stall is reached.

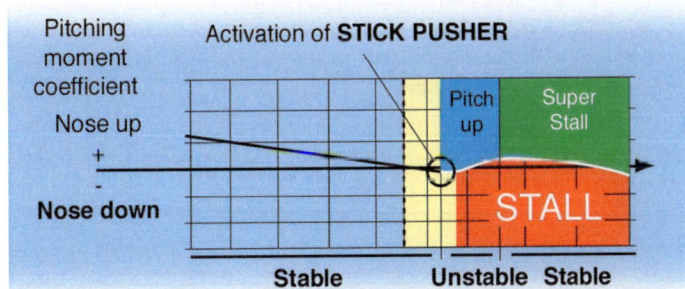

Figure 19.108

The sharpness of the push is necessary for identifying the stall instantly because a slow push might make the pilot pull too far into the deeper area. The impetus and duration of the push is tailored to give a good positive recovery manoeuvre in all configurations, all positions of the CG and from varying rates of entering stall. Because the curves of lift of some second generation jets are typically rather flat topped, the stick pusher is set to operate just after C_{Lmax} and operates at the earliest edge of its tolerance. In a slow straight stall approach, the pusher will therefore never operate before the wing has developed its maximum lift.

CRANFIELD AVIATION TRAINING SCHOOL LTD. PART-FCL GBR.ATO-0136
CATS INNOVATION CENTRE, LUTON, Bedfordshire LU2 8DL U.K.   www.catsaviation.com
19-40   Principles of Flight

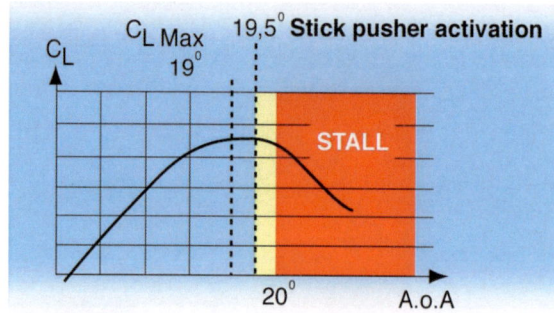

Figure 19.109

A stick pusher reduces the maximum angle of attack which otherwise may lead to a deep stall. The stick pusher is set to operate around C_{Lmax} .

19.6.8   *Spin characteristics*

Transport aircraft are not required to be able to recover from a spin, hence it follows that they are not tested to do so. However if a spin is unintentionally started because of loss of control, e.g. due to coming below the minimum control speed, V_{MC}, the spin may have different characteristics than the spin of, for example, a light aircraft with straight wings.

The spin of a jet transport aircraft may theoretically achieve a nearly horizontal nose attitude, called a flat spin, and a rather high speed of rotation.

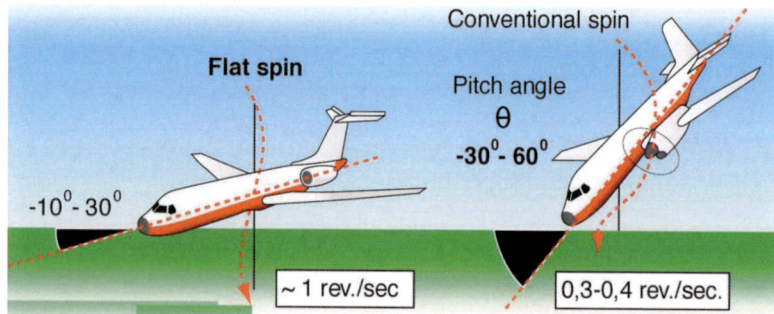

Figure 19.110

One of the contributing factors regarding aircraft with straight or swept wings is the difference in the lift and drag of the inner and outer wings. For aircraft with swept wings the difference in the drag of the outer and the inner wing is more obvious than that of a straight winged aircraft, where the difference in lift has a greater effect on the spin characteristics.

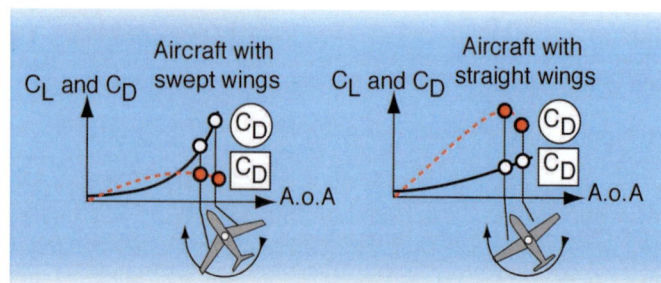

Figure 19.111

However, the most important factor when determining the spin characteristics is the distribution of mass. Heavy parts of the aircraft located far from the centre of gravity, like the tanks in the wings with fuel and the engines far aft or out on the wings, make the aircraft rotate like a flywheel. All these factors may give a spin that is very difficult to recover from.

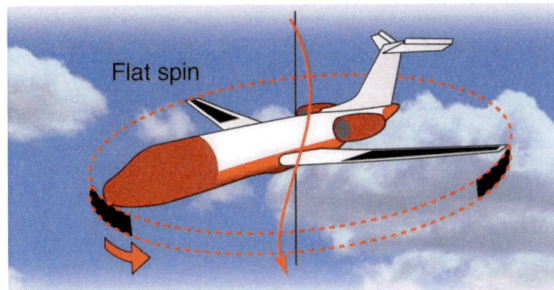

Figure 19.112

An aircraft with swept wings has a tendency to flat spin because of the great difference in drag between the outer and inner wing. The spin characteristics of an aircraft with straight wings are more affected by the difference in lift. The most important factor for spin characteristics is distribution of mass. The flat spin is characterised by a near horizontal nose attitude and a high speed of rotation.

19.7   *Supersonic Flight*

19.7.1   *Basic differences between subsonic and supersonic flow*

The main difference between subsonic and supersonic flow is large changes occur in air density at supersonic flow, which in subsonic flow is nearly constant.

Subsonic flow has the following characteristics:

- It anticipates a corner or whatever it may be, so that the flow pattern changes before reaching the corner
- The change of flow speed takes place gradually on curved parts
- In a contracting (convergent) duct, flow speeds up and pressure falls
- In an expanding (divergent) duct flow slows down and the pressure rises

Supersonic flow differs from subsonic flow in the following ways:

- It cannot anticipate a corner or anything else that lies ahead, because there is no means by which it can know that it is there
- The change in flow speed takes place instantly (after each Mach line)
- In a contracting (convergent) duct, flow slows down and pressure rises
- In an expanding (divergent) duct flow speeds up and pressure falls

19.7.2   *Mach lines and waves*

Imagine a body moving at a velocity that is greater than the speed of sound, in the direction A to D in the next figure.

A pressure wave sent out at point A will travel outwards in all directions at the speed of sound. When the body has reached point D, the pressure waves developed at point B, C and D have reached the positions shown in the next figure.

A line between point D and E represents the limit which all these pressure waves will have reached when the body reaches point D. This tangent line is called the Mach line.

CRANFIELD AVIATION TRAINING SCHOOL LTD. PART-FCL GBR.ATO-0136
CATS CATS INNOVATION CENTRE, LUTON, Bedfordshire LU2 8DL U.K.

www.catsaviation.com

19-42

Principles of Flight

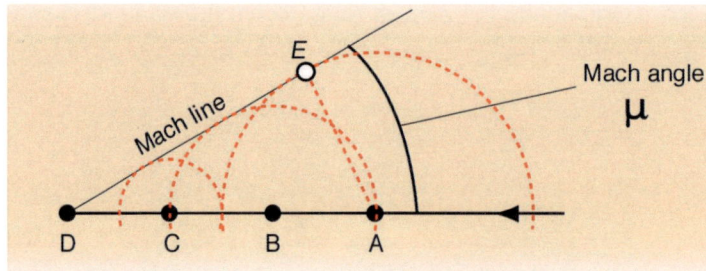

Figure 19.113

The angle between the flight path and the Mach line is called the Mach angle. The greater the Mach number the lower the Mach angle. Sin μ= 1/M, e.g. if M = 1, then μ= 90°, if m = 45° then M = 1.41.

Imagine supersonic flow over a flat plate. This surface can never be perfectly smooth, and may be considered to consist of a very large number of small bumps. All surfaces have a certain shape that causes a change that will result in the formation of a Mach line. Its angle to the surface depends on the speed of the flow. If the speed remains constant over the surface, the Mach lines will be parallel. If the speed is increasing, the Mach lines will diverge as the Mach angle becomes lower with increasing speed. But if the flow speed is decelerating, the Mach lines will converge, being brought together, and form a more intensive disturbance of greater amplitude; an oblique Mach wave or shock wave is formed.

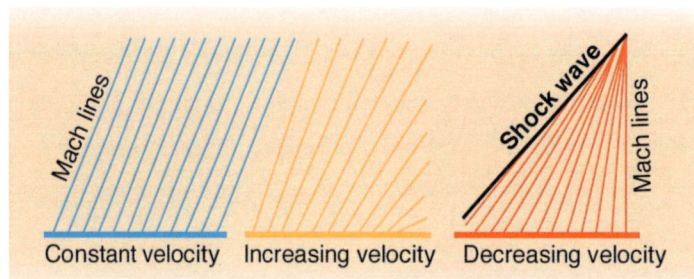

Figure 19.114 The greater the Mach number the lower the Mach angle

When the velocity of a body is equal to the speed of sound, all pressure disturbances from the body settle in front of the body in a common tangent. The disturbance at this point tends to build up into a much stronger disturbance than the one being created by the source; another Mach wave is created. Since this wave will be normal to the flight path, it is called a normal Mach wave or a bow shock wave.

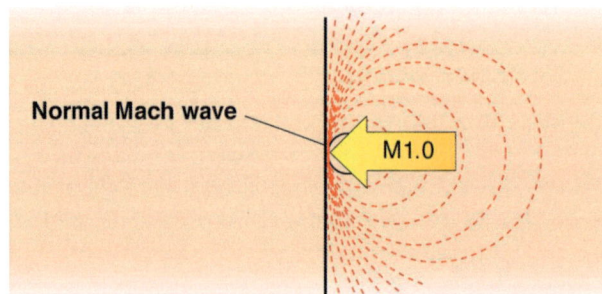

Figure 19.115

The tangent line represents the angle at which small wavelets are formed, and divides the region that is affected by the disturbance from the one that is not. Consequently, the Mach wave represents the front along which the disturbances are propagated. If the velocity of a body is greater than the speed of sound, the source that causes pressure disturbances of the air moves faster than the disturbance it creates. As the source moves, the front travels normal to itself with the speed of sound. The bow shock wave or the front Mach wave will be oblique.

CRANFIELD AVIATION TRAINING SCHOOL LTD. PART-FCL GBR.ATO-0136

CATS CATS INNOVATION CENTRE, LUTON, Bedfordshire LU2 8DL U.K.

www.catsaviation.com

19-43

Principles of Flight

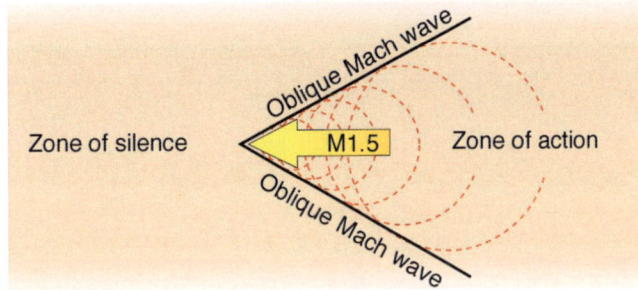

Figure 19.116

Only the region behind these fronts will be affected by disturbances and is consequently sometimes called the zone of action. The region ahead, which is unaffected by the disturbances, is called the zone of silence. In three dimensions, the disturbances emanating from the moving body expands outwards as spheres, not circles. When the speed of flight is above Mach 1, these spheres are enclosed within a cone, called the Mach cone.

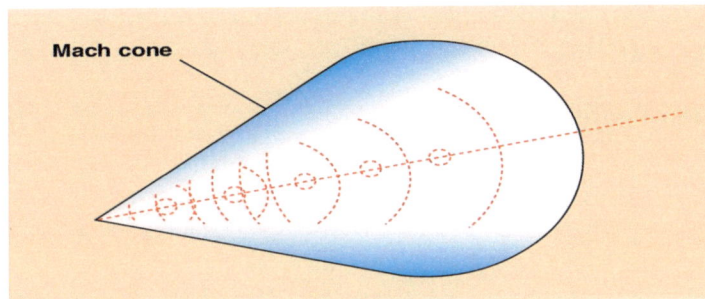

Figure 19.117

If the source of the disturbance is a wing, the Mach lines generate two oblique plane waves like a wedge.

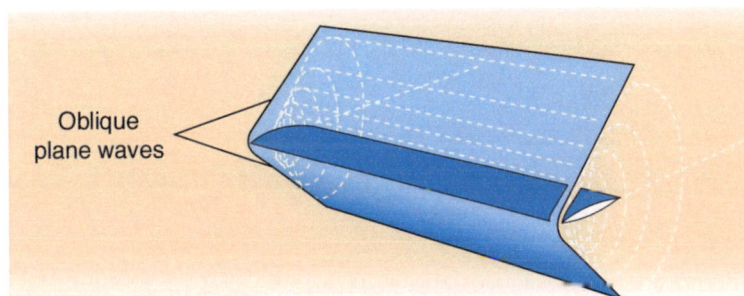

Figure 19.118

Mach lines that are brought together form a Mach wave, also called a shock wave.

19.7.3   *Compressive Flow*

Air flowing into a converging part of a tube increases its density and pressure, causing the flow velocity to decrease. The decrease in velocity is gradual after each compression wave caused by pressure disturbances propagated out from the walls. A body moving at supersonic speed through the air without any limiting walls surrounding it will cause a similar situation. Any kind of contraction of the airflow, e.g. when it hits a body, will cause a compression. The increased density and pressure where the compression occurs will slow down the velocity. When the flow is supersonic, the compression does not occur gradually, but as a shock wave. A shock wave is not only created at a leading edge, but at any surface which increases the compression and slows down the speed such as a surface with a steeper angle towards the flow than the previous.

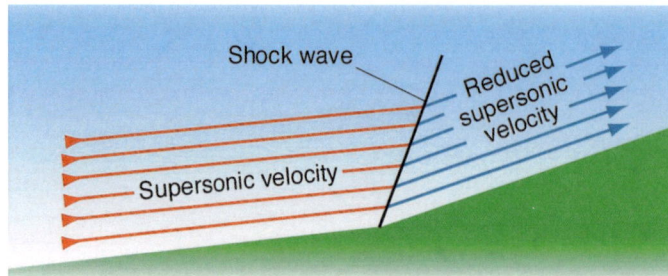

Figure 19.119

Supersonic airflow meeting a steeper surface will, contrary to subsonic flow, experience increasing density, static pressure and temperature, which gives decreasing velocity.

When the flow is supersonic, the shock wave formed at this corner will not be at right angles to the flow, which on the contrary the incipient shock wave formed on top of a wing at transonic speeds was. It will be inclined or oblique. A shock wave at right angles to the flow causes a sudden reduction in flow velocity, but an oblique shock wave causes both a reduction in velocity and a change of direction.

19.7.4   *Expanding flow*

Supersonic flow meeting a region of greater volume, an expansion region, is free to expand, i.e. the density is decreased. This will cause the pressure to decrease as well, as the temperature, and consequently the velocity will increase. Decreasing density and static pressure causes increasing velocity.

In the next figure the first Mach line is caused by the velocity before the corner, the others after the corner. The new ones will have a smaller angle to the surface since the velocity has increased. Between the Mach lines, the flow velocity is changed making the increase in velocity gradual, not suddenly as at a shock wave.

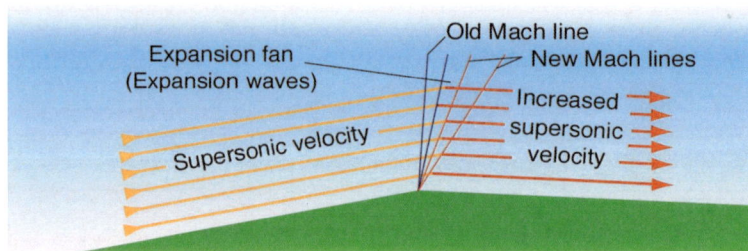

Figure 19.120

Notice that the expansion occurs gradually, even in the case of supersonic flow round a sharp corner. The fan-shaped region of Mach lines is nothing like shock waves. They are small weak waves that may appear anywhere along the surface, not just at corners. This type of flow is called expansion flow and the Mach lines are called expansion fan or expansion waves. Wherever compression or expansion is created, energy is consumed causing an increase in drag, i.e. wave drag.

19.7.5   *Lift creating surfaces designed for supersonic flow*

As shown above, the source to create pressure differences in order to obtain lift, is quite different in supersonic flow than in subsonic flow. The influence of the shape of a body on the distribution of pressure and hence the flow velocity, is completely different. All changes in flow take place suddenly at the leading or trailing edges of the body or at places where the body changes curvature.

Consider a very thin flat plate in pure supersonic flow. At zero A.o.A there is no flow deviation, and hence no change in the flow properties. There is no lift or wave drag. At a low positive A.o.A, where the flow approaching the lower surface is compressed at the leading edge, the flow deviation is equal to the A.o.A.

and as a consequence a shock wave is generated. The flow approaching the upper surface expands through the same angle, forming an "expansion fan" out from the leading edge.

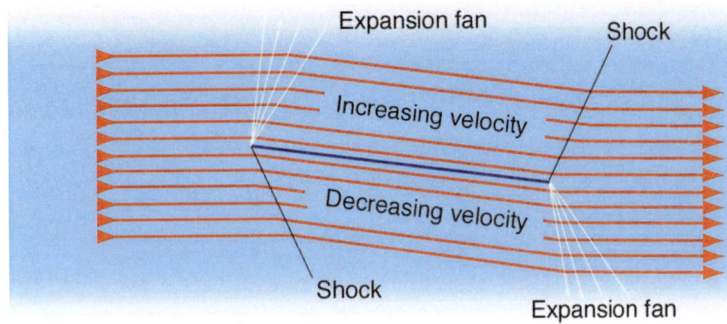

Figure 19.121

At the trailing edge this flow is re-compressed through another shock wave, while the lower surface flow expands through another expansion fan. All flow changes take place suddenly at the leading or trailing edges or at places where the body changes curvature. The pressure coefficient depends only on the net angle through which the flow has turned from the free stream direction, giving a pressure distribution like that shown below.

Figure 19.122

As seen, the low-pressure zone on the upper surface and the high pressure zone on the lower surface is equally distributed along the chord. There is an instant change in velocity at the leading edge, then the velocity is constant along the chord, and at the trailing edge there is another instant change in velocity. In theory, actually, the most optimum wing section for supersonic flow is a simple infinitely thin flat plate.

However, from the structural point of view, some thickness is essential to get the required strength. But in supersonic flow, contrary to subsonic flow, a positive camber reduces the lift and increases the drag.

On a cambered airfoil section at zero A.o.A, the positive pressure increase on the front upper surface is greater in magnitude relative to the free stream value, than the pressure decrease on the rear upper surface. Since there is no pressure increment anywhere on the lower surface, the net effect will be a downward force on the airfoil.

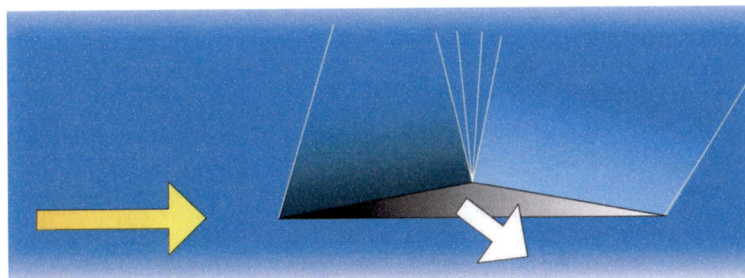

Figure 19.123

For a given thickness/chord ratio, the minimum wave drag is achieved by using the double-symmetric double wedge section shown below. At a small A.o.A, e.g. where the forward upper surface is parallel to the free stream direction, the pressure distribution will be like this:

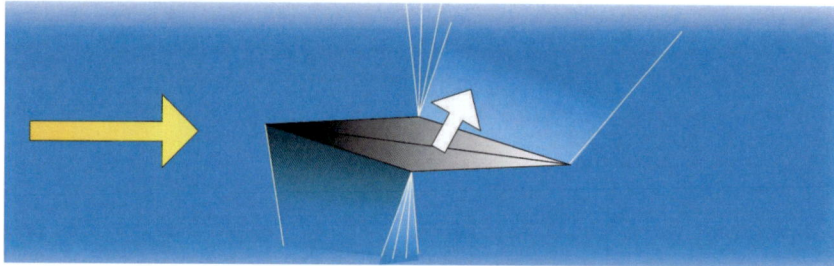

Figure 19.124

If there is an increase in A.o.A there will be an additional decrease in pressure on the front upper surface as well as an additional increase in pressure on the aft lower surface, hence a greater amount of lift is produced.

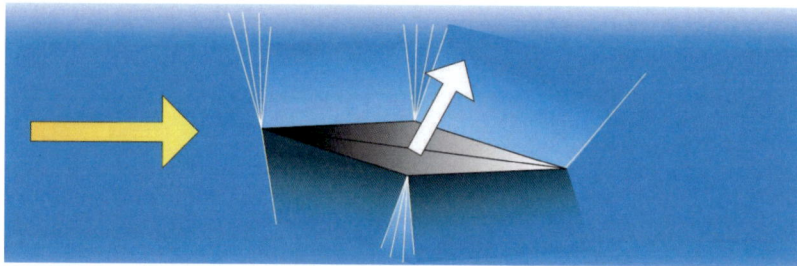

Figure 19.125

A double wedge section does not have good low-speed performance. This makes them suitable for rockets, missiles etc. designed for high speed only.

A more suitable airfoil section for an aircraft, which is also structurally better and has a greater volume, e.g. for fuel, is a biconvex airfoil section. Such a section does, however, give more wave drag than a double wedge section of the same thickness/chord ratio.

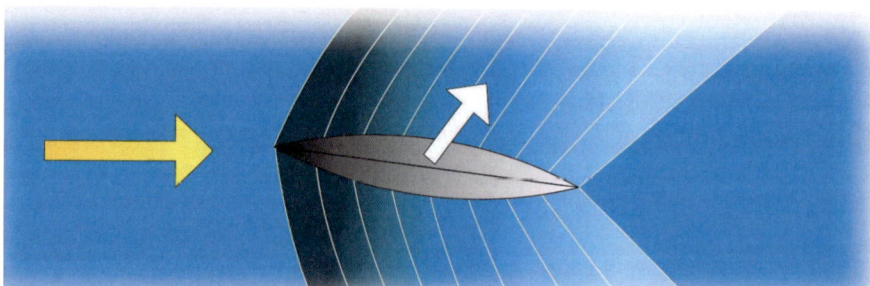

Figure 19.126

The optimum supersonic airfoil section is a thin flat plate, but other suitable ones are double wedge and biconvex airfoils. An ordinary subsonic airfoil cambered, non-symmetrical with the maximum camber at the forward half of chord and a rounded leading edge, may also be used at supersonic flight speeds. However, this airfoil section will produce a lot of wave drag and have inferior transonic characteristics.

19.7.6 The attributes of Mach waves

Different kinds of Mach wave, i.e. normal shock, oblique shock and expansion fan are developed and have the following characteristics:

	Normal shock or Bow shock 	Oblique shock 	Expansion fan 
Develops:	At leading edges at a mix of super-sonic and subsonic flow	Where decreasing supersonic flow such as a change in curvature exists	Where increasing supersonic flow due to a change in curvature exists
Velocity after the shock:	Decreases to subsonic	Decreases bit is still supersonic	Increases to a higher supersonic velocity
Pressure:	High increase	Increase	Decrease
Energy or total pressure:	Great loss of energy	Decrease	No effect

Figure 19.127

19.7.7 Supersonic airfoil sections

A wing section suitable for supersonic speeds should have the following properties:

It should be thin. If the airfoil is thick, the flow deviations, and hence also the shock waves, will be large, causing high wave drag. To minimise this, the wing should be as thin as possible.

The leading edge should be sharp. Consider supersonic flow approaching the leading edge of a subsonic, round-nosed airfoil. In order to flow round the nose, the air has to turn through a right angle. At supersonic speeds, this is impossible since the fluid elements cannot feel any changes of pressure further aft, thus they are not able to adapt their flow pattern. Therefore a normal shock wave is created ahead of the nose. Behind this shock wave, the flow is subsonic, and can therefore flow round the nose. Within a short distance the flow again accelerates to supersonic speed.

CRANFIELD AVIATION TRAINING SCHOOL LTD. PART-FCL GBR.ATO-0136
CATS INNOVATION CENTRE, LUTON, Bedfordshire LU2 8DL U.K.   www.catsaviation.com

19-48   Principles of Flight

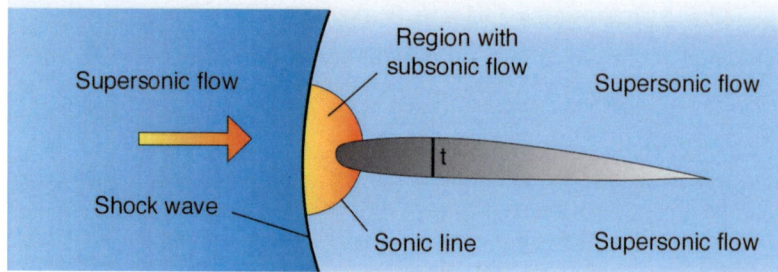

Figure 19.128

As the speed increases further, the bow shock wave moves closer to the nose, and the size of the subsonic region is reduced. But it can never disappear altogether, not even if the leading edge is very sharp.

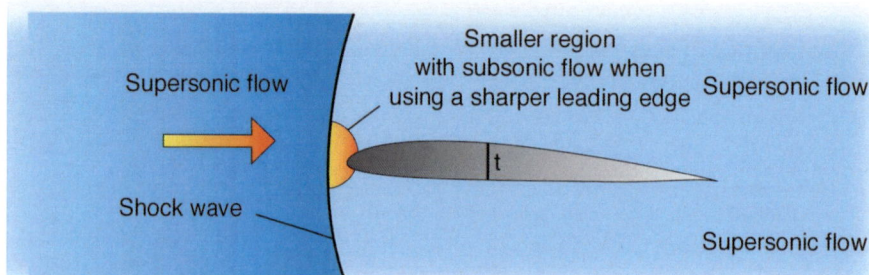

Figure 19.129

The greater the zone of compressed subsonic flow, the greater the wave drag.

The wing should have its maximum thickness at half chord. This gives the most favourable ratio between expansion, at the aft part, and compression, at the front part, for lift versus drag. Another important property is symmetry. As earlier shown, positive camber in supersonic flow results in a positive A.o.A which produces zero lift. Thus, at any given A.o.A the lift is reduced by camber, as shown in next figure.

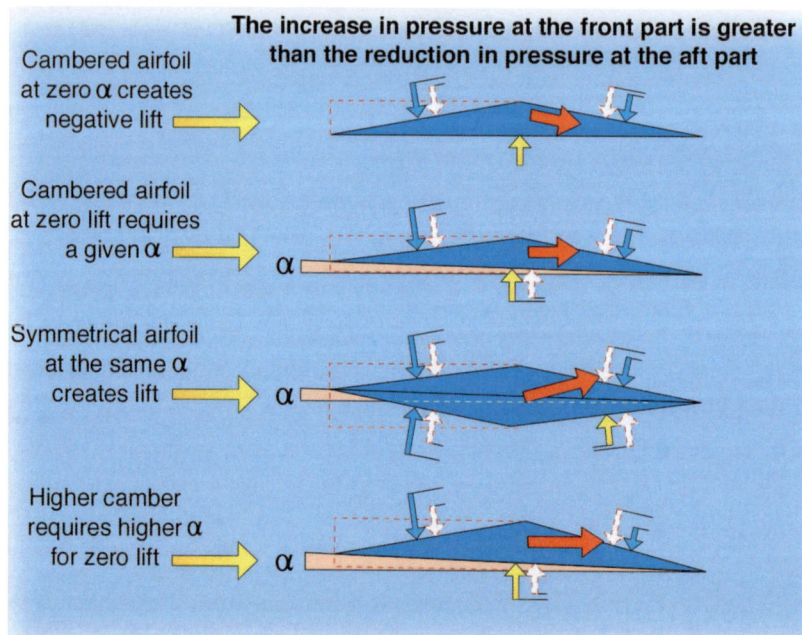

Figure 19.130

A wing suitable for both subsonic, transonic and supersonic flight speeds may have an airfoil section with variable camber and a very sharp leading edge.

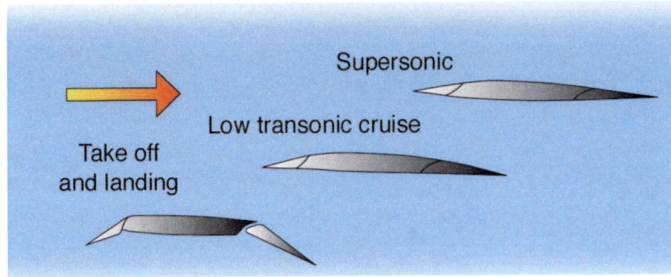

Figure 19.131

A wing section for supersonic speeds should preferably be:
- Thin,
- Have a sharp leading edge,
- Have its max camber at half chord
- Symmetrical

19.7.8   *Influences of aft C.P. caused by supersonic flight*

As seen in the previous figures, the pressure distribution along the chord is such that the centre of pressure will be located at half the chord. This has a very large influence on the aircraft performance, especially on the turning performance. The C.P. will be moved further aft at supersonic speed compared to the position at subsonic speeds. The static margin will be large, requiring a very high tailforce acting downward to trim the aircraft, which increases the total wing load. Even if there are very large, powered elevators to overcome the high hinge moments of the control surface, the turning performance at supersonic speeds will be deteriorated. In addition, the turning radius increases with increased speed.

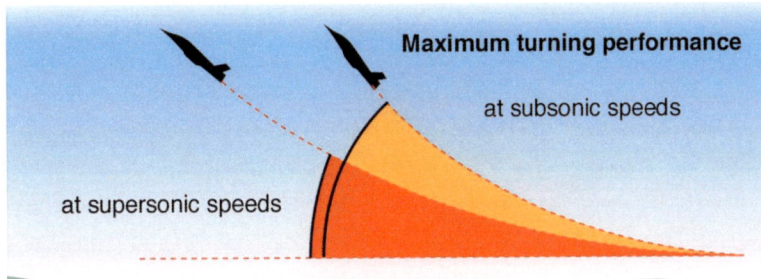

Figure 19.132

If the CG were positioned to achieve the desirable static margin for supersonic speeds only, it would be too small or negative at subsonic speeds. However, most modern jetfighters are able to be stable, despite the lack of static stability.

Also in straight flight, the increased trim drag from the aft positioned C.P. reduces the performance. Supersonic aircraft may have a delta wing planform which is optimised for transonic and supersonic flight speeds, but it also has the facility to transfer fuel from the forward regions to the aft and vice versa. This device makes it possible to achieve a suitable static margin that does not cause higher trim drag at supersonic cruising speed.

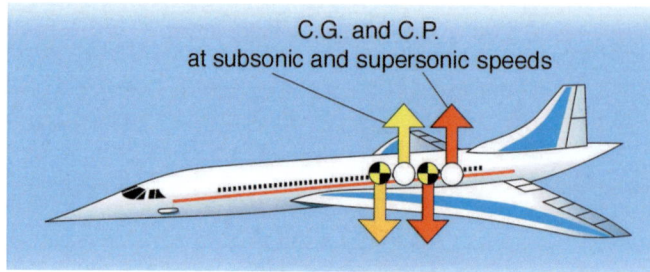

Figure 19.133

The large static margin at supersonic speeds causes a reduced performance and higher trim drag.

19.7.9 *Wing planform*

A swept wing may be used in order to achieve a sufficiently high critical Mach number in transonic flight. In supersonic speeds, the swept wing is only desirable as long as the leading edge of the wings is within the Mach cone.

Consider a swept wing that generates a shock wave at the centre section (at aircraft longitudinal axes) of its leading edge and that the angle of sweep is such that the leading edge lies within the Mach cone.

Further shock waves are generated by other points on the leading edge and this causes a reduction in flow Mach number. These shock waves slow down the flow speed progressively further back and out. Round certain sections and outwards, there will be subsonic flow.

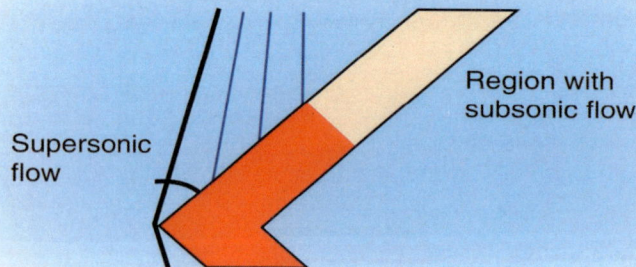

Figure 19.134

The shape of these outward sections should be subsonic, and the shape of the inner sections should be supersonic.

Thus, if the leading edge of the wing is swept back within the Mach cone, the outboard sections are surrounded by subsonic flow only, with a consequent improvement of performance. A long pointed fuselage nose reduces further the Mach number of the flow that approaches the wing. A wing of this type may have a so-called subsonic (rounded) leading edge.

At very high speeds, a very highly swept wing, e.g. a very slender delta wing, is preferable. But at a given Mach number the flow around the leading edge will be supersonic and in this situation a subsonic leading edge causes higher wave drag than a sharp-nosed leading edge of a straight wing.

In the figure below, the coefficient of wavedrag relative to the Mach number is shown. As long as the aircraft with a 45° swept wing has a speed below M 1.41 (which gives a Mach cone with the same angle), the drag is relatively low. The wing is within the shock cone. But at higher speeds, the straight wing is preferable.

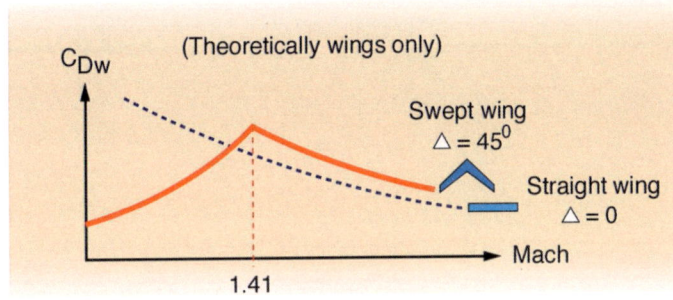

Figure 19.135

A good combination of both low-speed and high-speed qualities is achieved with variable swept wings. The wings may have high angles of sweep for high-speed flight, and have a low or zero angle of sweep for low-speed operating, thus avoiding the high drag and tip stall tendency of wings with high angles of sweep at low speeds.

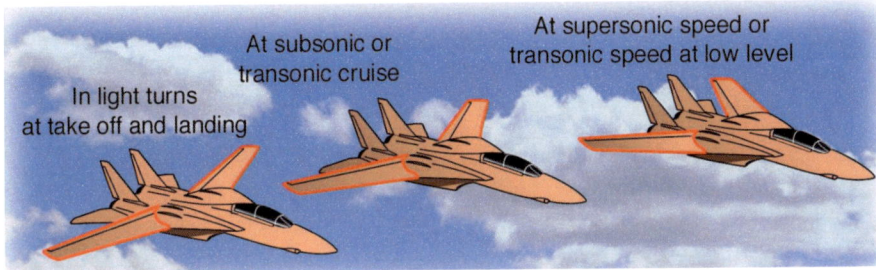

Figure 19.136

The delta wing has the advantage of having a very high angle of sweep at the leading edge, a low thickness/chord ratio at the root, despite the considerable thickness of the root. The aspect ratio is low which raises the M_{CRIT}, and the stable vortices developed over the wings at high A.o.A prevent wing tip stall.

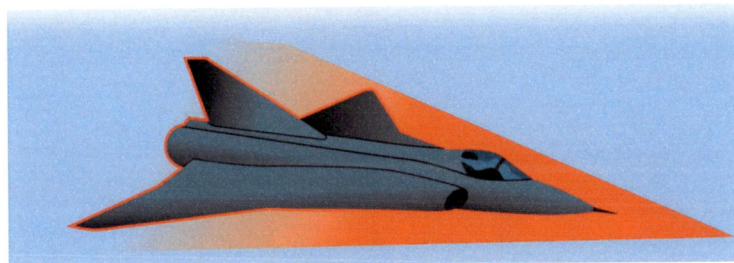

Figure 19.137

The disadvantage of a delta wing is the very high drag at low speeds and the tendency to superstall. From the drag point of view, wings with highly swept leading edges are preferable up to rather high supersonic speeds, but at very high supersonic speeds, straight wings with sharp leading edges are superior, as shown in the next figure.

CRANFIELD AVIATION TRAINING SCHOOL LTD. PART-FCL GBR.ATO-0136
CATS INNOVATION CENTRE, LUTON, Bedfordshire LU2 8DL U.K.

www.catsaviation.com

19-52

Principles of Flight

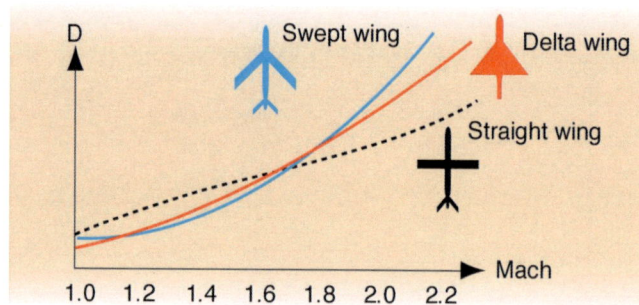

Figure 19.138

Highly swept leading edges may be preferable up to M 2, but at higher speeds straight wings with sharp leading edges may be superior.

19.7.10   *Influence of aircraft weight*

The strength of the shock waves is affected by the dimension of the aircraft and increases with weight and volume. A heavy aircraft produces shock waves of higher intensity than a small aircraft like a fighter.

19.7.11   *Aerodynamic heating*

Unlike the sound barrier, which can be passed, we will only go deeper and deeper into the heat barrier if the speed is increased. Friction creates heat, and skin friction in a flow of air is no exception. But it is not only the friction that causes heat. The compression heat of air at the stagnation point and in the shock waves is transferred to the surfaces of the aircraft. At low speeds it is not serious, but at supersonic and hypersonic speeds the heated skin will lose its strength long before it has reached its melting point.

For long distance supersonic flights, the surface heating is a greater problem than for a jetfighter zooming to high supersonic speeds for a short period of time only. In order to maintain structural strength at supersonic speeds, light alloys are suitable for Mach numbers up to 2, or even higher for short periods. Between M 2 and M 4 titanium alloy is often used, but above M 3 or M 3.5 stainless steel may need to be used. The picture below shows a wing section at high transonic speed in a wind tunnel. The shock waves are visible due to special optics.

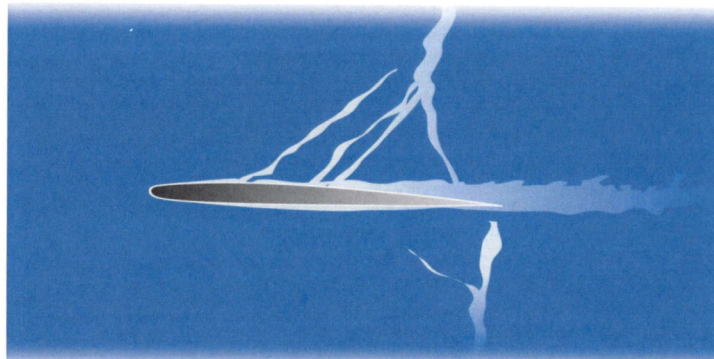

Figure 19.139

Self Assessment Test 18

1   Compressibility effects are usually insignificant below about:
A)   Mach 1
B)   661 KT (at sea level)
C)   350 KT
D)   None of the above. They are always significant

2   Local speed of sound is:-
A)   The speed of sound in the airflow past the aeroplane, taking into account variations in temperature and pressure etc. caused by the aeroplane's passage
B)   The speed of sound in the air displaced far enough away from the aeroplane such that it is unaffected by its passage
C)   The "critical speed" at which air flow at some point on the aeroplane's structure begins to flow supersonically
D)   Dependant (although not exclusively) on the absolute temperature

3   The speed of sound varies with height because:
A)   Temperature varies with height
B)   Pressure varies with height
C)   Both A and B
D)   Neither A or B

4   Critical Mach Number (M_{CRIT}) is:-
A)   The Mach number at which shockwaves are formed at the leading edge of the aerofoil
B)   The mach number at which compressibility effects first appear
C)   The lowest limits of the transonic range
D)   The mach number at which shockwaves impinge upon the control surfaces leading to "aileron reversal"

5   M_{CRIT} will be decreased by:-
A)   Sweepback
B)   Sweep forward
C)   Reduced thickness/chord ratio
D)   None of the above

6   Free stream mach number (M_{FS}) equals:-
A)   IAS divided by local speed of sound
B)   TAS divided by local speed of sound
C)   Local speed of sound
D)   None of the above

7   When the presence of a shock wave causes airflow to separate this is known as:-
A)   Transonic effect
B)   Shock stall
C)   Stall
D)   Mach stall

8   The purpose of designing the aeroplane by area ruling is to:-
A)   Decrease M_{CRIT}
B)   Increase M_{FS}
C)   Minimize wave drag
D)   Decrease longitudinal stability in the transonic range

9   Below M_{CRIT}:-
A)   Oblique shockwave (only) may be present
B)   Normal shockwaves (only) may be present
C)   Both normal and oblique shockwaves may be present as mach one could well be exceeded at some point on the aeroplane even though the aeroplane as a whole is still subsonic
D)   No shockwaves will be present

10   A shock stall consists of:-
A)   An increase in C_D
B)   A decrease in C_L
C)   Erratic pitching moments
D)   All of the above

CRANFIELD AVIATION TRAINING SCHOOL LTD. PART-FCL GBR.ATO-0136
CATS INNOVATION CENTRE, LUTON, Bedfordshire LU2 8DL U.K.
www.catsaviation.com
CATS
19-55
Principles of Flight

Self Assessment Test 18 Answers

1	C
2	B
3	A
4	C
5	D
6	B
7	B
8	C
9	D
10	D

CRANFIELD AVIATION TRAINING SCHOOL LTD. PART-FCL GBR.ATO-0136
CATS INNOVATION CENTRE, LUTON, Bedfordshire LU2 8DL U.K.

www.catsaviation.com

19-56

Principles of Flight

List of formulae

Bernouilli's theorem: $p + q = P_{tot}$.
$\quad\quad$ p = static pressure,
$\quad\quad$ q = dynamic pressure,
$\quad\quad$ ptot = total pressure.

D_O : $\quad$ Zero lift drag (parasite drag)
$\quad\quad$ $= C_{DO} \times \rho \times S$
$\quad\quad$ C_{DO} = Coefficient, ρ = density,
$\quad\quad$ S = reference area

Di $\quad\quad = (1/\pi \times e \times A) \times C_L^2 \times S \times q$

D_{tot}: $\quad$ Total drag $= D_O + D_i$

D_{tot}: $\quad$ Total drag $= \rho \times S \times (D_{tot} + C_{Di})$

Dynamic pressure: $q = 1/2 \times \rho \times V^2 = 0.7 \times p \times M^2$

Equation of continuity: $\quad A \times \rho \times V$ = constant
A = area, ρ = density, V = true air speed

Equation of state: $\quad\quad p = \rho \times R \times T$
$\quad\quad\quad\quad\quad\quad\quad\quad$ ρ = density, R = constant, T = temp K

F: $\quad\quad$ Force $= m \times a$
$\quad\quad\quad$ m = mass, a = acceleration

ft: $\quad\quad$ Feet, 1 ft = 12 inches = 0,3048 m

hp: $\quad\quad$ Horse power 1 hp = 745,7 W

km/h: $\quad$ 1 km/h = 1/3,6 m/s = 0,2778 m/s

kt: $\quad\quad$ Speed in nautical miles/hour (NM/h)
$\quad\quad\quad$ 1kt = 1,852 km/h = 0,51444 m/s

Lift $\quad\quad$ = Dynamic pressure x Coefficient of Lift x Wing Surface.
$\quad\quad\quad$ $L = q \times C_L \times S$.

M: $\quad\quad$ Mach number = V /a (TAS/speed of sound)

Mass: 1 kg = 2,205 lbs, 1 lb = 0,4536 kg

mph: $\quad$ Speed in static miles/hour
$\quad\quad\quad$ = 1,6093 km/h = 0,4470 m/s

p: $\quad\quad$ Static pressure = R x r x T
$\quad\quad\quad$ R = constant (air 29,28 x 9,81 = 287)

ρ = density (kg/m3)
T = absolute temperature (-273,15°C)

Pa: Pressure Pascall, 1 bar = 10^5 Pa

P_{tot}:   Total pressure = p + q

Power available = Engine power x propeller efficiency.

Power required = Drag x TAS

Power: Force x Distance /Time = Force x Velocity.

q: Dynamic pressure = ρ x V^2/2

T: Absolute temperature (Kelvin) (0 K = -273,15°C)
Thrust = Force (N)

Thrust = Power available/TAS

V: True air speed = d/t

Weight (N) = mass (kg or lbs) x g
        g = gravity acceleration 9,81 m/s^2

Work   = force x distance (Nm).

This information is not required in the JAR-FCL but may be of interest:

Wing section designations.
A given wing section can be described in different ways. The designation of a certain wing section describes the parameters in a code, and the characteristics of this is listed, as the example below. The numbers in the code and their significance varies. One common kind of designation is made by NACA in U.S.A. Below there is an example of a four digit airfoil code:

NACA airfoil section (e.g. NACA 2415).
4 digit section:
1:st digit   = Max camber in % of the chord.
2:nd digit   = Position of max camber in tenth of chord,
measured from leading edge.
3 and 4:th digit   = Max thickness in % of chord.

Example:
Section NACA 2415 means:
        max camber 0,02c
        position of max camber, 0,4c, from leading edge
        max thickness 0,15c.
NACA 2415 aerodynamic characteristics:

C_{Lmax}	Zero lift in °	Moment around a.c.		
	Incr.Cl/°α	C_d	a.c. in %	M_{CRIT}
		$C_l = 0$	$C_l = 0,4$	$C_l = 0,8$

1.65   -2,0   0,106   0,0064 0,0064 0,0077 -0,045 0,246 0,677

Influence of the shape variables of the
airfoil on section characteristics:

Parameter	Affected characteristics	Degree of influence.
Thickness	min C_d	Moderate
	max C_l	Low
	M_{CRIT}	High
Thickness distribution	Point of minimum pressure, hence possible extent of laminar flow,	High
	from this; min C_d	Moderate
	max C_d	Moderate
	M_{CRIT}	High
	abruptness of stall	High
Camber	C_l for min C_d	Very high
	C_m a.c.	High
	max C_l	Very high
	M_{CRIT}	High
Camber distribution	C_l for min C_d	Low
	C_m a.c.	High
	max C_l	Very high
	M_{CRIT}	Moderate
	abruptness of stall	High

When selecting an airfoil for the lifting surfaces of an aircraft, i.e. the wing, the tail or the canard, it is important to consider:
the drag, and the behaviour during increasing drag. The drag should be minimum in order to obtain the highest possible cruising speed and good general performance.
L/D. The relationship between C_L and C_D is important to consider when aiming for good aircraft performance during engine failure, a climb or cruising speed;
the thickness, in order to obtain the lowest possible structural weight;
the thickness distribution, in order to obtain favorable span loading and/or high fuel volume;
the stall characteristics, in order to obtain gentle stall characteristics.

Axes of Reference
and Notation:

Axes of Reference and Notation

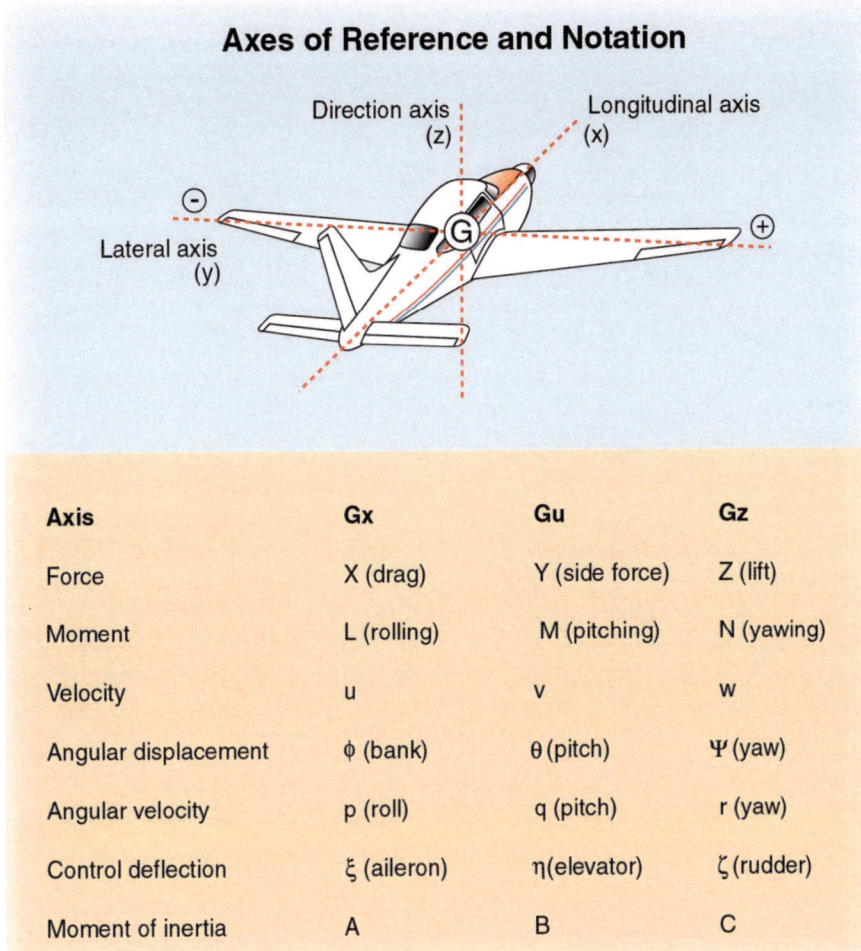

Axis	Gx	Gu	Gz
Force	X (drag)	Y (side force)	Z (lift)
Moment	L (rolling)	M (pitching)	N (yawing)
Velocity	u	v	w
Angular displacement	φ (bank)	θ (pitch)	Ψ (yaw)
Angular velocity	p (roll)	q (pitch)	r (yaw)
Control deflection	ξ (aileron)	η(elevator)	ζ (rudder)
Moment of inertia	A	B	C

Figure 19.140

Axis:	Gx	Gy	Gz
Force	X (drag)	Y (side force)	Z (lift)
Moment	L (rolling)	M (pitching)	N (yawing)
Volocity	u	v	w
Angular displacement	φ(bank)	θ(pitch)	ψ(yaw)
Angular velocity	p(roll)	q (pitch)	r (yaw)
Control deflection	ξ(aileron)	η(elevator)	ζ(rudder)
Moment of inertia	A B	C	

CRANFIELD AVIATION TRAINING SCHOOL LTD. PART-FCL GBR.ATO-0136
CATS INNOVATION CENTRE, LUTON, Bedfordshire LU2 8DL U.K.

www.catsaviation.com

19-60

Principles of Flight

The Greek alphabet:

A	α	alpha
B	β	beta
G	γ	gamma
D	δ	delta
E	ε	epsilon
Z	ζ	zeta
H	η	etha
Q	θ	theta
I	ι	iota
K	κ	kappa
L	λ	lambda
M	μ	mu
N	ν	nu
X	ξ	xi
O	o	omicron
P	π	pi
R	ρ	rho
S	σ	sigma
T	τ	tau
U	υ	epsilon
F	ϕ	phi
C	χ	chi
Y	ψ	psi
W	ω	omega

List of symbols:

A   area; aspect ratio

A, B, C, moments of inertia

a   speed of sound = $\sqrt{K \times R \times T}$ (m/s)
         K = constant (air 1,4),
         R = constant (air 29,28 x 9,81 = 287)
         T = absolute temperature
         (-273,15°C)
         At +15°C a = 340 m/s

a   acceleration (m/s^2)

a   lift-curve slope; inflow factor (propeller)

a/c   aircraft, aeroplane

A.C.   aerodynamic centre

AR   aspect ratio

b   span

C   Centigrade

c   chord length

c   mean chord of the wing

CAS   calibrated air speed

C_D drag coefficient

C_f overall skin friction coefficient

C.G, c.g. centre of gravity

C_L lift coefficient

C_l	lift coefficient of airfoil section
C_m	pitching moment coefficient
C_n	yawing moment coefficient
C_p	pressure coefficient
C.P.	centre of pressure
CQ	propeller torque coefficient
C_T	propeller thrust coefficient
C_L / C_D L/D	lift/drag ratio
c_f	local skin friction coefficient
D	total drag; diameter
D_O	zero lift drag; parasite drag, profile drag
D_i	induced drag
d	distance; diameter
d/c	camber
E	internal energy
e	efficiency factor (of a wing) specific internal energy
F	force; jet thrust
F_{CF}	centrifugal force
G	centre of gravity; braking force
Gxyz	aircraft axes of reference
g	acceleration due to gravity
H	height; altitude; shape parameter (boundary layer); total head; hinge moment
h	height; altitude; position of C.G.
H_n, H'_n	C.G. margin, static margin
h_f	forward C.G. limit position
h_n, h'_n	neutral point position
IAS	indicated air speed
K	Kelvin (0 K = -273,15°C); induced drag factor; kinetic energy
L	lift; length (dimension);
l	rolling moment
L/D	lift/drag
L_T	tail lift
L_W	wing lift
M	Mach number; mass (dimension); pitching moment
m	mass; moment; strength of source; stick gearing
m	massflow (kg/s)
MAC	mean aerodynamic chord
M_{MO}	maximum operating Mach number
N	engine speed of rotation; acceleration factor; yawing moment
n	load factor
P	power; period of oscillation; stick force
p, P, P_s	static pressure; angular velocity in roll
P_{av}	available power
P_{rec}	required power
P_{tot}	total pressure
Q	torque; heat; rate of fuel consumption; rate of volume flow
q	dynamic pressure;

	velocity; speed; angular velocity in pitch
R	range; radius; gas constant; (Reynolds number)
Re	Reynolds number
r	radius; angular velocity in yaw
R.O.C	Rate of climb
R.O.D	Rate of descent
S	area; wing area; representative area; entropy
s	arc length; semi-span; specific entropy
SAR	specific air range
S_T, S_η	Tail; elevator area
T	temperature; time (dimension); thrust; period of oscillation; endurance
t	time; thickness
T_c	propeller thrust coefficient
TAS	true air speed
t/c	thickness /chord ratio
U, V	speed of flow, free stream velocity
u, v, w	velocity components; perturbation velocities
u	friction velocity (boundary layer)
u_r, u_θ	radial and tangential components of velocity
V	velocity of flow; airspeed (true); volume
V_A	designed max. manoeuvring speed
V_c	rate of climb
V_e, V_i,	equivalent, indicated airspeed
V_R	rectified airspeed; rotational (for lift-off) speed
V_{LCR}	speed for long range cruise
V_{MC}	minimum control speed (FAR 23)
V_{MCA}	minimum control speed airborne (FAR 25)
V_{MCG}	minimum control speed on ground (FAR 25)
V_{MCL}	minimum control speed during landing approach (FAR 25)
V_S	slipstream velocity
V_s	stalling speed 1g; sinking speed (rate of descent)
V_{S1}	stalling speed at 1g with engine failure or in other specific condition.
V_{SO}	stalling speed at 1g with landing flaps and gear down
V_X	speed for best angle of climb
V_{XSE}	speed for best angle of climb single engine
V_Y	speed for best rate of climb
V_{YSE}	speed for best rate of climb single engine
W	work; weight
w	downwash velocity, wing loading; complex potential
W_f	weight of fuel
X, Y, Z	force components
x, y, z	a/c axis; distance, space coordinates
z	complex variable
α	angle of attack, incidence
α_f, α_t	effective fin, tail incidence
β	sideslip angle; tab angle; Prandtl-Glaurt factor
ε	range/height
Γ	circulation; vortex strength
g	angle of climb or descent; whirling motion strength of vortex sheet; adiabatic index

CRANFIELD AVIATION TRAINING SCHOOL LTD. PART-FCL GBR.ATO-0136
CATS INNOVATION CENTRE, LUTON, Bedfordshire LU2 8DL U.K.   www.catsaviation.com

δ	boundary layer thickness; flow direction parameter; flow deviation; semi leading edge angle
δD	changed condition
ϵ	downwash angle; shock inclination; surface slope
φ	angle of bank
ζ	complex variable
η	efficiency
θ	angle of pitch; propeller blade angle; angle (polar coordinates); relative temperature; momentum thickness
Λ	angle of sweep
λ	taper ratio; lapse rate
μ	coefficient of viscosity; Mach angle; coefficient of rolling friction; aircraft relative density
ν	flow angle (Prandtl-Meyer) kinematic viscosity
ϵ, h, ζ	aileron, elevator, rudder angles; components of vorticity
ϖ	relative pressure
ρ	density
σ	relative density; source strength; solidity (of propeller disc)
τ	viscous stress; non-dimensional time
ϕ	angle of bank; angle of advance (propeller); velocity potential
φ	angle of yaw; stream function
Ω	vorticity (vector)
ω	angular velocity

Suffixes:

md	minimum drag
mp	minimum power
n	normal component
o	sea level values; stagnation (total) values
s	stalling value; component along given arc
t	tangential component
u, l	upper, lower surface
W	wave (drag)
w	at the wall (boundary layer)